MW01200118

The Life of Laura Barney

The Life of Laura Barney

by

Mona Khademi

George Ronald
Oxford

The Life of Laura Barney

by
Mona Khademi

George Ronald
Oxford

George Ronald, Publisher
Oxford
www.grbooks.com

© Mona Khademi 2022

All Rights Reserved

*A catalogue record for this book is available
from the British Library*

ISBN 978-0-85398-652-2

Quotes from pp. 15, 16, 27, 33, 35, 39, 46, 47, 48, 55, 61, 63, 109, 141, 150, 171, 172, 173, 174, 182, 207, 208, 209, 210, 211, 235, 236, 246, 247, 248, 291, 334, 356, 357 from *Wild Heart: A Life* by Suzanne Rodriguez. ©2002 by Suzanne Rodriguez. Used by permission of HarperCollins Publishers.

Every effort has been made to locate the copyright holders of *Alice Pike Barney: Her Life and Art* by the late Jean L. Kling, whose details when found will be included in subsequent editions of this book.

Cover design Steiner Graphics

CONTENTS

To all the brave women who have or who will dedicate their lives to the betterment of the world

ACKNOWLEDGMENTS

The completion of this book could not have happened were it not for the contributions of many people and the access to the various archives that I was granted. I wish to acknowledge those who have assisted me in different ways over the years. They are numerous.

First and foremost, my immense gratitude to Laura Clifford Dreyfus-Barney, who sent me on this journey. Her life fascinated me and gave me a passion to research it for over two decades. I am eternally grateful for the long, unexpected journey on which Laura Barney has taken me. Through the life of this remarkable woman, I learned a lot throughout these years – about the history of the Bahá'í Faith in the 20th century as well as world history for almost a century. I explored her life of service and her many accomplishments that resulted from her life-long devotion to the Bahá'í Faith that she accepted at a young age. Her exemplary character was teamed with her spiritual devotion. I learned about the lives of interesting people with whom she associated and the fascinating places to which she traveled. I learned from her determination and perseverance in reaching her goals. I followed her example and did not give up in the face of the many obstacles and challenges I encountered in publishing her biography.

I would like to thank all the scholars, historians and researchers whose published works provided the background information, in particular Jean Kling for the biography of Alice Pike Barney and Suzanne Rodriguez for the biography of Natalie Clifford Barney.

I give deep-felt thanks to the following archives and their staff who assisted me with my research: to the Smithsonian Institution Archives, which I visited several times; to the Bibliothèque littéraire Jacques Doucet in Paris, which holds the Natalie Barney collection; to Roger Dahl, Lewis Walker and others at the United States National Bahá'í Archives who helped with numerous requests for information and materials over many years; to the National Bahá'í Archives of France and in particular Parivash Ardeï Amini, the archivist who was most helpful when I visited and when I requested further information via email; to the Research Department at the Bahá'í World Centre for assisting me over the years and making available to me summaries of some of Laura Barney's private correspondence with 'Abdu'l-Bahá and the Tablets He sent to her.

My gratitude also to the archivists at the United Kingdom National Bahá'í Archives and at the archives of the Bahá'ís of Washington, D.C.; to Jacques Oberson, the archivist at the United Nations in Geneva who copied the documents for me; and to the archivist at the London School of Economics where the records of the International Council of Women are held, with special thanks to Caroline Vollans for her help in copying the needed documents. Thanks also to Heidi Stover, the archivist at the Smithsonian Institution Archives, who went beyond the call of duty and provided high-resolution digital pictures right before the publication of the biography; to Monica Varner, the intern at the Archives of the National Museum of Women in the Arts, who copied and sent to me the documents I requested; and to the staff at the Smithsonian Museum of American Arts Archives.

The materials I collected were in Persian, English and French. Fortunately, I had the assistance of two selfless expert translators, Sheryl Mellor for translations from French into English and Riaz Masrour for translations from Persian into English. I appreciate their assistance.

Eileen Maddocks has been of immense help in editing and proofreading the book. She saved me when I thought there was no one to help! I am indebted to her. I am extremely grateful to her editorial work and wise comments about my manuscript, and for her assistance with bringing the manuscript to a much better place.

I wish to thank many people for the information they provided and for their assistance and support. Anita Ioas Chapman gave unwavering support and encouragement throughout the early part of my research and constantly reminded me that I must stop researching and start writing. She never stopped helping me move forward, especially when problems discouraged me from doing so. I am sorry she did not live long enough to see my book published. Amín Egea shared with me the newspaper clippings related to my subject early in my research. Nooshin Mohajerin checked the National Iranian Library Archives,

Rochan Mavvadat helped me whenever he could, and Layli Maria Miron shared some of Laura Barney's talks and letters with me. Moojan Momen answered my questions via email. Farzaneh Milani, my good friend and role model, continued her support for many years during this project. I am grateful to Shapour Rassekh and Iraj Ayman for their continued support and valuable insights throughout the years of my research. My brother Monib Khademi supported me throughout this project with his wise suggestions, especially when I faced problems. My sister Minou Khamsi-Khademi gave me moral support and kept me connected to family.

One disadvantage of having a research project that continues over many years is that some of the persons who helped me did not live to share in the satisfaction of publication, and this I deeply regret. However, the advantage is that many people who knew about my research interest forwarded me information that they discovered. The list is long, and I cannot name them all but I am grateful to each one of them. I am thankful to all those who had met Laura Barney and shared their experiences with me. I am indebted to everyone who answered my questions when I contacted them. My gratitude extends to all my friends who patiently listened to my never-ending stories of Laura and were updated about my progress from the day I started my research in 2000 and when I started writing.

Finally, I express gratitude to the staff of George Ronald Publisher and to Wendi Momen, my editor, who worked with me diligently with her vast knowledge, intelligent comments, and years of experience, to bring the manuscript to the publisher's high standard. My appreciation also goes to the gifted artist René Steiner for the cover.

While writing the book I have been fortunate to draw upon many primary and published sources and have tried not to assume anything. However, if there are any inaccuracies in what I have written, they are my own.

PREFACE

What happens to a story that is never told? It's like the story never happened.
A story needs to be told for it to live on and continue . . .
And the stories that definitely should be told are the ones that
have an impact on our life and others' lives.
Anonymous

I first became interested in Laura Barney in 2000 when I learned that Studio House, her home in Washington, D.C., which had been donated to the Smithsonian Institution in 1960, was being sold and its contents auctioned owing to the expense of maintaining it. At that time, all I knew was that she was a Bahá'í, that her mother, Alice Pike Barney, may also have been one, and that Laura Barney had compiled an important book for the Bahá'í Faith. This book, entitled *Some Answered Questions,* was a compilation of oral commentaries made by 'Abdu'l-Bahá, the son of the prophet-founder of the Bahá'í Faith. Therefore, I decided to visit Studio House to see the furniture and objects that belonged to the Barney family. I later learned that 'Abdu'l-Bahá had visited that house at least three times in 1912 during His tour of the United States and Canada.

Studio House was commissioned and built by Laura's mother, Alice Pike Barney, in 1902. Laura and her sister, Natalie Barney, inherited it in 1931 upon the death of their mother. In 1960 they donated Studio House and its contents to the Smithsonian Institution, a group of museums and research centers, to be used as a cultural center. The house had unusual but exciting architectural features and was designated in 1995 a historical site by the city of Washington, D.C., thus preserving it from destruction. Prominent people, including artists, authors, musicians and diplomats, and even two presidents of the United States, William H. Taft and Theodore Roosevelt, had frequented the opulent rooms of Studio House.

That year I became deeply interested in learning about the life of Laura Barney and began my research. I started by checking the many boxes of documents that had been removed from Studio House and were being kept in the Smithsonian Institution Archives to see if there were any important materials. I found interesting documents, newspaper clippings and letters exchanged with her mother and others, etc. In time, however, I found to my amazement that only limited information about her life had been published.

My life found a new goal exactly one century after Laura found a new religion, the Bahá'í Faith, in 1900. As had Laura one hundred years before, I discovered something new to guide and engage me. The research about her life became my passion and daily thoughts. I found it more interesting as I moved forward. There were many questions to be answered. My interest in Laura, which had started with her Bahá'í activities, expanded to her other achievements in the arenas of women's rights, peace building and humanitarian efforts. Her family life was also fascinating. During the years that I researched and wrote about her life and achievements for articles, papers and this biography, I lived in two different eras – one was the time in which she lived and the other was my own.

Her story was awe-inspiring and every new discovery about it was captivating. Our paths may even have crossed since she was still alive and living in Paris when I was studying there in 1973 and 1974. My place of residence was not far from hers. Did I ever see this distinguished lady at gatherings at the Bahá'í Center in Paris? If so, I would not have known at that time that she would become the focus of my research for over two decades. Had I known about this incredible woman then when she was approaching the end of her life, I would have visited and asked her many questions. Instead, to write her biography, I had to suffice with her correspondence, references in history books, archival materials, and transcribed interviews with individuals who had met her.

By some strange twist of fate, Laura, who had rendered enormous service and whose memory needed to be cherished in history, received little in the way of acknowledgment, whereas her sister Natalie appeared in many memoirs and was the subject of several full-length biographies. Proper recognition has eluded Laura both within her faith group as well as in the outside world. One reason may be the unfortunate fact that her diaries and important documents were stolen during World War

II. Another factor may be that she stood in the shadows of her mother, the mistress of the arts, an accomplished artist and philanthropist Alice Pike Barney; her prominent, brilliant and accomplished spouse, Hippolyte Dreyfus; and Natalie, her famous poet, writer, and literary salon hostess sister. Yet another cause could be that she divided most of her long life between two countries, the United States and France. She considered both countries home and traveled constantly between them. Perhaps she was considered American, in spite of her many years living in France, but to some American Bahá'í historians she was not considered an American since she lived in Paris most of her life. To the French Bahá'ís, she was the American wife of the first Frenchman who became a Bahá'í, Hippolyte Dreyfus. It may have been for these reasons that her heroism in service to humanity and to her faith was mostly forgotten in unexamined archives.

She has been well known to Bahá'ís as the person who compiled the book *Some Answered Questions* but little has been known about the details of her life. Even the humanitarian organizations for which she worked, such as the League of Nations, the United Nations and the International Council of Women, acknowledged only a very few of her many contributions. That is why I decided to bring to light her accomplishments and give her the appreciation that she truly deserves.

The primary unused source information for this book, besides the Archives of the Smithsonian Institution, came from several archives in the United States, France, Switzerland, Israel and England, as well as from references to Laura in published articles, newspaper accounts, journals, interviews and books. There was also her voluminous correspondence with family and friends and the biographies of her mother and sister. My knowledge of the three languages that Laura spoke – English, Persian and French – was helpful in my research.

It has not been easy to put all the pieces of Laura's life together. Unfortunately, Laura's personal notes and diaries, in particular those of her early years and visits to 'Akká, were stolen during the Nazi occupation of Paris between 1940 and 1944. I have not been able to find her diaries despite my many efforts in searching the National Archives in Germany, the archives of the Holocaust Museums of Los Angeles and Washington, D.C., and asking for help from the German Embassy in Washington, D.C.

I am, however, grateful that Laura saved everything that she did – all the letters that she received, copies of letters that she sent, invitations, and even the envelopes. One advantage for me was that since she lived long and was in good clear mind, she managed to distribute her letters and documents for historical preservation to appropriate archives. For example, the Bahá'í documents and important letters were sent to the Bahá'í World Centre; the reports, minutes and letters from the International Council of Women were sent to its archives; and the family correspondence was merged with her sister's papers at Bibliothèque littéraire Jacques Doucet. By this act of sorting out her important letters and materials and sending them to appropriate archives, she selected what she wanted to be preserved. The result is that her biography includes much of what she wished to be remembered for. It also means that I have automatically respected her wishes – except that her letters to her sister Natalie were preserved by her sister.

Most fortunately, Laura dated all her letters, and when writing from hotels she used hotel stationery as it was customary at the time for hotels to have stationery printed with the emblem of the hotel and its location. This enabled me to trace her whereabouts throughout her life. Although Laura's letters were useful in reconstructing some parts of her life, caution was required when using them to analyze her life. Like most correspondence, Laura's written communications often lacked information about the persons who were close to her and her daily encounters. While some people may correspond primarily with individuals who are not near, with loved ones who are away or for work-related matters, and therefore not much information can be gleaned about the writer's close relationships, fortunately, there was an advantage in Laura's case. Since she traveled a lot, she wrote many letters even to those family members who were close to her, such as her mother and her sister. Also, her references in these letters to her friends and family give glimpses into her character.

This biography is not about the details of the organizations Laura worked for or of the teachings of the faith she had embraced but only about her involvement and activities in those organizations and groups. Also, I have chosen not to discuss the life of her illustrious friend and later husband, Hippolyte Dreyfus, and his incredible contributions to the Bahá'í Faith at its early stages. Much has already been written about this Frenchman and his biography published. References to him are made only when he and Laura collaborated on projects or when accounts of their life together shed more light on Laura's inner light and drive.

Nor had I planned to discuss the life of Laura's sister Natalie unless their lives crossed paths. However, since Natalie, whom she loved and admired, was the most important person in Laura's life, I tell her story when it impacts Laura's. Laura was born in 1879, three years after Natalie, and died in 1974, two years after her sister's death. Neither had children and they both lived long lives. The Barney sisters, as they were known in those days, lived in Paris most of their adult lives. Natalie was a major presence in Laura's life, even though they chose different paths and were very different in character and lifestyle. Despite the different directions they took in life, their connection to each other, especially from Laura to Natalie, never diminished. Furthermore, as I progressed in my research, I realized more fully how important Natalie was in Laura's life. She had no other family member living in Paris. Even Laura's burial place is not with her husband but with her sister Natalie. It is for these reasons that I have decided to include Laura's relationship with her sister.

Despite years of research and the study of hundreds of letters and documents that I found in various archives, I still feel I could have investigated further. I know there is still more information about Laura in archives not yet searched. However, at some point research must transition to writing! Undoubtedly in the future other researchers and writers will add to Laura's story.

In the introduction to a drama Laura published, she wrote: 'Introductions should often be divided into two unequal parts: one for the reader of little patience; the other for the heroic investigator.' In that spirit, this book is both for the reader of little patience who can select the parts that she or he likes and for the heroic investigator who wants to know everything about Laura's life.

This is my account of Laura Clifford Dreyfus-Barney's life. In writing about her I have chosen to title the book with the simple name of Laura Barney instead of the longer names – Laura Clifford Barney, Laura Dreyfus-Barney and Laura Clifford Dreyfus-Barney – by which she was known.

When I started my research in 2000, no one had undertaken extensive research about her. I consider myself a pioneer in this area. It is a privilege to bring her story to life, to present her achievements, contributions and spiritual qualities in an effort to give her the honor that she deserves. This is my contribution to the history of all those women who were courageous enough to follow new paths in life and of the western women who embraced a faith from the East at the turn of the 20th century.

Mona Khademi
Washington, D.C., 2022

PART I

FAMILY AND CHILDHOOD

1879 – 1899

A Remarkable Woman

It is in Cairo, Egypt, end of winter 1935. An elegantly-dressed American woman is waiting in the lobby of a luxury hotel with charming and convincing simplicity. During this stay her hotel room so overflowed with flowers that she could not move easily about in it. Three dozen Easter lilies had also been sent to her room. This is Shepheard's Hotel in downtown Cairo, a historic hotel, the playground of the international aristocracy.[1] The hotel's guestbook is a Who's Who of dignitaries. It is steeped in history. Every person of social standing wants to have tea here, to see and to be seen in the lobby. Kings and queens, crown princes and presidents have stayed here. Among the famous people who have stayed here is the celebrated explorer Henry Morton Stanley, who was in love with this woman's mother when she was a teenager.

This elegant woman has just arrived from Alexandria. Even though she is in the sixth decade of her life, her youthful face glows with intelligence and kindness. This fascinating woman speaks French in a refined voice without an accent that would otherwise betray her American origin. She has put her roots down in France to serve a greater homeland, that of men of goodwill who pursue selfless and impressive 'adventures of the spirit'. This adventurous woman is transplanted to France but she never had to choose between her two homelands. She believes that one is never without roots when one can serve the greater homeland. On both sides of the ocean, she surrounds herself with spiritual people, artists and intellectuals.

This elite woman has an astonishing personality and lucid intelligence. She knows 'how to think globally' at a time when so much hatred and so many minds make brothers into enemies, once again threatening the return of war. She has already seen a world war and its victims. For her vital, selfless service to the refugees and injured of the greatest conflict the world had yet seen, she was awarded the title of Chevalier of the French Legion of Honor.

This extraordinary woman is a never-tiring traveler who has visited distant lands extensively to bring understanding between peoples and had used her feminist ideals for peace. She is a wonderful liaison between nations as she travels to work with others to establish social justice, to promote women's rights, and to unite the world to bring about peace and harmony. Her life is devoted to bringing together people of different cultures and races. Eradication of racial prejudices through mutual understanding is one of her goals.[2]

This remarkable woman has already seen and lived with people of faraway lands and studied their living conditions and daily problems. She has already embarked on many noble causes. She has already presided over an important world congress in Rome. She has already traveled triumphantly across Canada and given talks at universities, private clubs, and women's organizations about disarmament and world peace, receiving testimonies of appreciation.

This international woman met a spiritual leader from the East and accepted his teachings, the Bahá'í Faith. She gave those beliefs a central role in her life. She traveled to the native land of the Prophet-Founder of her Faith, Iran, and was the first western Bahá'í woman to do so. She compiled a book that was of inestimable value and service to her Faith.

She has been to Egypt many times and loves being in that country. Her first trip was at the turn of the century when she was not yet 21 years old! She likes the Egyptians very much and finds them very kind. But this time she is nostalgic. She misses her husband, who has passed away. They had stayed at Shepheard's Hotel some years ago though there was unrest and violent rioting in Egypt at the time. This time she is on her own; however, she is carrying his suitcase, which is a reminder of him. She has also spent time in this city with her beloved mother some years earlier. She is missing her sister, especially after meeting some people who knew her and had read her books, and she is proud of her.

Not even separation from her loved ones and her loneliness will stop her from continuing forward on her mission of serving humanity and bringing peace to mankind. She will soon leave for other cities on her journey to continue a series of lectures on peace and disarmament, in Alexandria, Haifa, Beirut, Damascus, Ankara and Athens, before returning home to Paris. But who is this woman?

Who is this woman who at the turn of the 20th century had an 'undaunted zeal for the objective of the brotherhood of man' and remained vibrant and immersed in life to her very last day on earth? Who is this woman who met 'Abdu'l-Bahá, Gandhi, Mussolini, Ezra Pound, Whistler and Eleanor Roosevelt? Who is this notable woman who held many positions with the International Council of Women and served as the Vice President of its Disarmament Committee? Who is this woman who was the only female member of the Committee of Experts of the League of Nations? Who is this woman who compiled a book that took its place with the sacred writings of the Bahá'í Faith? Who is this amazing woman who learned fluent Persian? Who is this accomplished woman whose death was reported in the major newspapers of the time on both sides of the Atlantic? Who is this woman who shares a burial site with Natalie Barney?

This woman is Madame Dreyfus-Barney, born Laura Clifford Barney. Some people may know her by her greatest achievement, which was compiling the book *Some Answered Questions,* which was to hold invaluable significance for the followers of a new religion, the Bahá'í Faith. Many will not know her. Yet, in addition to the book she compiled in her twenties, she accomplished much more during her long life.

Laura lived in two different worlds: one of her wealthy family and the other of her spiritual family. Her privileged family mingled with the elite social, political and artistic circles of Washington, D.C.; New York; Bar Harbor, Maine; and later Paris. She had another world of her own, that of significant people in 'Akká, Palestine (today's Israel), who in the early years of the 20th century spoke Persian and wore oriental garb and turbans. Later in life she mingled with those who believed in the unity of mankind and worked towards peace, equality and women's rights. Her family members spoke English and were fluent in French but she spoke an additional language, Persian, well enough to be able to ask questions of a spiritual leader from the East.

Laura Alice Clifford Barney was born on November 30, 1879 to Alice Pike Barney, artist and philanthropist, and Albert Clifford Barney, a wealthy industrialist, in Mount Auburn near Cincinnati, Ohio. To understand Laura's story, one must begin by learning about her parents and their lineage.

The Lineage of Laura's Mother, Alice Pike

Alice Pike was descended from an aristocratic French family that included her great-great-grandfather Ennemond Meuillion, a trained doctor who arrived in Louisiana around 1770.[3] Her great-grandmother, Ursula, born in 1784, was Meuillion's second child by a second marriage. Though petite, she was a determined young woman and refused to learn English so that anyone in her company had to speak French.[4]

In 1802 Ursula married William Miller, Laura's great-grandfather, a prominent and successful trader from Rapids County, Louisiana. Several years later in 1815, the young family moved north and settled in Cincinnati, Ohio, where Miller prospered in real estate. Ursula passed away five years later of yellow fever. Miller followed his wife in death after five years, from cholera, but lived to see the marriage of his youngest daughter Ellen to Samuel Napthali Pike.[5]

Samuel Pike, Laura's maternal grandfather, was the first child born to a poor German-Jewish father and a Dutch-Christian mother in Heidelberg, Germany, in 1822. The family immigrated to America when he was five years old. The only items that Samuel's parents had brought from Europe were two Dutch Renaissance paintings and a few pieces of silver. One day while on a stopover in Cincinnati in July 1844, Sam walked through an upscale neighborhood whose streets were lined with fine houses. A young woman named Ellen Miller appeared on the balcony of one of them. While he was gazing intently up at her, he fell into a hole in the street and the young woman came to his rescue. They subsequently fell in love and were married the following year. Ellen had a sister called Louise, whose great grandson David Bruce became a dear friend of Laura and of her only close family members several decades later in Europe.

The young couple had grown up in wildly different circumstances. Sam Pike had known poverty all his life; he was determined to make a fortune and was willing to work hard to obtain it. Ellen had been raised in luxury and did not worry about money. And there were other major differences. He was intelligent, clever, attentive and cordial and developed interests in poetry and painting, while she was private and introverted and spent much of her time reading. She was a practicing Catholic but he professed no faith. Rather than follow one of the family religions – Catholicism, Judaism and Protestantism – they took a middle road and joined the Episcopal Church. Despite their differences, the marriage was considered to be a happy one.

Sam Pike made his initial money in the distilling and bottling of whiskey for which there was a big market but then diversified, investing in property from hotels to office buildings and land and even a trolley system. In time he became a multimillionaire entrepreneur and distiller with wide-ranging interests that included collecting paintings and rare books, playing the flute and writing poetry.

His interest in the arts took him in a surprising direction. While hearing the famed Swedish opera singer Jenny Lind in Cincinnati during her American tour, Sam Pike noticed the inadequacies of the theater in which she was singing. Soon after, he decided to build a true opera house. He modeled the new opera house on the Teatro alla Scala of Milan, with five stories and seating for 3,000 people. Located on 4th Street between Walnut and Vine Streets, his opera house was completed in 1859 and became the first home of the Cincinnati Symphony Orchestra. It transformed the city of Cincinnati by attracting leading artists and performers. This was Sam Pike's gift to Cincinnati and is how his name became connected with the arts. On the occasion of the visit of the Prince of Wales to Cincinnati in 1860, Pike's usually reclusive wife was on the Prince's arm as they walked to the grand ballroom inside Pike's Opera House. Unfortunately, after several successful years and many programs, the opera house burned down in March 1866 as a result of an accident and nothing could be salvaged. It was rebuilt and reopened in 1868 but burned down again in 1903 and was not rebuilt.

In 1866 Sam Pike and his family moved to New York City where he built another five-story opera house located at 8th Avenue and 23rd Street that opened in 1868. However, he had to sell it two years later because the public felt that its location in lower Manhattan was too far from the center of activity. Sam Pike passed away of a heart attack on December 7, 1872.

The last and fourth child of the Pike marriage was Laura's mother, Alice Pike, who was born in 1857 in Cincinnati. Governesses educated Alice at home during most of her childhood, although when she was six years old she was sent to a convent school for a year where she excelled in the arts. At the age of 13, after her family moved to New York, Alice was sent to a strict convent school. A few years later she attended the Cooper Female Academy in Dayton. Coincidentally, the first headmaster of that school had been E.E. Barney, the father of her future husband.

Alice was surrounded by art from early childhood.[6] She was the student who was always called upon to perform when there were visitors to the school. Alice preferred performing to studying. She was the only one from among her siblings who loved the arts as much as her father did and she accompanied him to many cultural events. Her family's wealth allowed her to learn to speak French, to play the piano, and to dance and sing. Since her mother did not like socializing, it was Alice who from a young age served as hostess to many famous performers who came to dinner, and she was soon able to imitate them.

Alice was about 16 years old when her father passed away. The loss was especially difficult for Alice, who had shared many interests with him. Difficult times followed for the family. Alice's mother became more reclusive during the months following her husband's death and rarely left the house. The four daughters arranged a European tour to help their mother emerge from the grieving process and in March 1874 they all sailed to Paris.

This was a providential trip for Alice. Now she was exposed to the creative energy in Europe and the art masterpieces, visiting various art galleries and museums such as the Louvre. Her passion for the arts increased and Parisian artists fascinated her. She was captivated by the artists of the Left Bank, perhaps because of their lifestyles and fashion statements, and began to sketch herself, discovering that she had some talent.[7]

Paris at that time was becoming a dynamic, innovative environment for artists, 'creating striking contrasts between the old and the new'.[8] After the American Civil War, thousands of American artists and art lovers went to view the art exhibitions, to exhibit their own work, and to attend the many salons held in Paris. The city was in the process of becoming the center of the art world.[9]

The next stop after Rome on this European tour was London. Alice, with her blond hair and blue eyes, her social grace and personal charm – not to mention her family's wealth – attracted many suitors throughout this trip. The most important of them was Henry Morton Stanley, the 'most celebrated man in England' and 17 years her senior.[10] Stanley was a journalist and explorer who had made many expeditions to Africa and is perhaps best known for his successful search in central Africa for the missionary-explorer David Livingstone. Stanley would be elected to Parliament in 1895 and knighted in 1899.[11]

Stanley immediately fell in love with the charming and elegant Alice Pike and considered marriage a few days later. Though he was a handsome man and one of the most eligible bachelors in London, Alice's mother rejected the proposal because of the age difference. But Stanley did not give up and traveled to New York when Alice returned home. Since he would soon be embarking on another expedition, he asked

Alice to wait for him and she agreed. However, she had an active social life and rarely wrote to him, nor did she read his letters while he was away.[12]

After their return home, Alice's mother worried that her youngest daughter would marry Stanley or some playboy from New York, so she sent Alice to visit her sister, Jeanette Schenck, in Dayton, Ohio. On Alice's arrival at the station in spring 1875, among the family and friends welcoming her was a well-dressed young man, Albert Clifford Barney. Alice sensed right away that this had been pre-arranged so that the two would meet.

The Lineage of Laura's Father, Albert Barney

Albert Clifford Barney, Laura's father, could trace his lineage in America back to the 1630s when his ancestors left Buckingham, England for the New World. His ancestors were generations of American pioneers who 'hewed a rough existence from the wilderness'.[13] However, the more recent generations had managed to acquire wealth. Benjamin Barney, Albert's grandfather, moved from Vermont to New York in 1806. He and his wife had 11 children who were raised in an educated family in a home full of books. Their first child, Eliam Eliakim, or E.E., Laura's grandfather, was born in 1807.

After graduating from college and a two-year stint as principal at Lowville Academy in the Adirondack region of upstate New York, E.E. moved to Ohio to improve his financial circumstances and was hired as the principal of Dayton Academy in 1831. His marriage to Julia Smith of Saratoga, New York, took place in 1834. They had five children: Eugene, Edward, Agnes, Albert and Mary. The Barneys were all members of the First Baptist Church and E.E., a devout Baptist and active churchgoer, remained modest and unassuming with his newly earned wealth.

Mr Barney changed career paths several times as he strove to combine his love for learning with the need to make money. He became the principal of a new school for girls, the Cooper Female Academy, a prestigious school that attracted the daughters of the wealthy from all over Ohio. In 1849 he went into business with Ebenezer Thresher. Industry had not been an important part of Dayton's economic growth until the advent of the railroads, in particular the railroad line that was built

9

in the late 1840s to connect Dayton with the port cities of Lake Erie. E.E. and Thresher established the first manufacturing plant in Dayton, the Dayton Car Works, which started by building cars for horse-drawn street railways and then 'rapidly became a leading manufacturer of rail-road cars for the Midwest'.[14]

E.E. also changed business partners several times over the years and continued to prosper. The partner's interest in the company was eventually acquired by a gentleman called Preserved Smith. The company, renamed Barney & Smith Car Works, was for a time the largest builder of railroad cars in the nation. By 1890 the company had over a thousand employees and was the largest industry in Dayton. The Barneys became rich as more and more customers rode the train and larger quantities of freight were hauled by rail. E.E. passed away in 1880.

Albert Clifford Barney was born to E.E. and Julia Barney on May 28, 1849. He was educated at Phillips Exeter Academy, an exclusive prep school in New Hampshire, and then entered Brown University at the age of 16. Following the example of the other rich young men there, he became increasingly dissolute.[15] E.E. sent his son on a year-long trip to Europe after graduation. Albert visited Paris, where he improved his French, and then went to London where he developed a liking for private clubs.

Upon Albert's return, E.E. wanted him and his other son Eugene to take over the family business. Eugene was the dutiful son and had learned his father's business from the bottom up and eventually rose to vice president and superintendent and became president but he disliked it intensely. He considered himself a gentleman who was above working when his father passed away. Albert also followed his father's wishes by working for the company in the car company. He was now an eligible bachelor and a dream for the Dayton families with unmarried daughters. He started courting the petite Alice Pike as soon he met her at the Union Station in Dayton in 1875.[16]

Albert found his match when he met Alice. She had all the qualities he needed for a wife of his social station. He fell in love right away but she did not immediately reciprocate because she did not care for 'all the customary sentimental rubbish'.[17] It took her a while to get used to Albert and then to like him, but even when she accepted his proposal for marriage, she was not sure that she loved him. Right after agreeing to marry him Alice began to ponder what she had done. Although she

Albert Clifford Barney, likely 1891

Laura, Alice and Natalie at Bar Harbor in 1889

Laura and Natalie in 1881

Laura in 1892

*The Barney Family in
Bar Harbor, Maine
(picture is damaged)*

*Young Laura
in a carriage
at Bar Harbor
Maine, 1888*

*Ban-y-Bryn
house, in 1891,
the summer
house built by
Albert Barney
in Bar Harbor*

May Bolles (Maxwell), in 1900

Natalie and Laura, in 1900

Group of western Bahá'ís of Paris, 1901 or 1902. Standing, left to right: *Elsa Bignardi, Herbert W. Hopper, Florence Robinson, Hippolyte Dreyfus, Berthalin Lexow, Charles Mason Remey, unknown, Marie-Louise MacKay, Margarite Bignardi, Stephanie Hanvais, Sydney Sprague;* seated, left to right: *Edith MacKay, Miss Holzbecker, Edith Sanderson, Sigurd Russell, Thomas Breakwell, May Ellis Bolles, Mrs Hanet, Marie Watson*

Hippolyte Dreyfus

Ellen Goin and Laura Barney, in 1902. The cousins traveled together to 'Akká in October 1900 to meet 'Abdu'l-Bahá

Shoghi Effendi, in 1900. Laura met the four-year-old Shoghi Effendi on her second pilgrimage to 'Akká in early 1901

William Jennings Bryan
American politician who met with 'Abdu'l-Bahá
in 'Akká in 1904 to discuss universal peace

Ethel Jenner Rosenberg

Dr Youness Afroukhteh
in 1906

Mírzá Abu'l-Faḍl and Ali-Kuli Khan in
Washington, D.C., in 1901

A group of pilgrims from Europe and America, photograph taken in the Haifa/'Akká area in 1901. Back row, left to right: *Charles Mason Remey, Sigurd Russell, Edward Getsinger, Laura Clifford Barney.* Front row, left to right: *Ethel Rosenberg, Edith Tewksbury Jackson, Harriet Thornburgh holding Shoghi Effendi, Lua Getsinger, Helen Ellis Cole*

*The House of 'Abdu'lláh Pá<u>sh</u>á, in 'Akká, where 'Abdu'l-Bahá lived
at the time of Laura's visits between 1904 and 1906*

The reception room in the House of 'Abdu'lláh Pá<u>sh</u>á, where 'Abdu'l-Bahá received pilgrims

The House of 'Abdu'l-Bahá at 7 Haparsim Street, Haifa, which He and His family moved into in August 1910 (photograph taken in 1920)

doubted her decision as soon as Albert proposed, she accepted and her family members gathered to congratulate her. She did not love Albert Barney but she was fond of him. She thought that he was attractive and rich, and he was good company.[18] So, she theorized, she might as well marry him as anybody because she did not believe that she would ever fall in love with anyone. If she had to marry someone, Albert might as well be the one.[19] She had forgotten about Stanley.

Alice was married to Albert Clifford Barney at her family's 5th Avenue home in New York on January 11, 1876 when she was almost 19 years old. They took up residence in Dayton. It was one day during that first year of their marriage that Albert found the unopened letters from Stanley to Alice that were wrapped with a ribbon and saved in a trunk. Some of them had very recent dates. Alice was five months pregnant with Natalie.

Albert asked her about the letters and did not accept her explanation that she had not opened them and that the relationship had been over for her. He forced her to burn them.[20] It was at that moment that Alice realized she had made a mistake. She was more of a free spirit, had an indiscriminate openness to others and loved to sketch.

Their first child, Natalie, was born on October 31, 1876 in Dayton. Albert quit the car company and became an agent for the Pike estate in Cincinnati. He moved immediately to Cincinnati and his family joined him a year later. Albert welcomed this move since he disliked his job in Dayton and Cincinnati was much bigger and more cosmopolitan.

Laura's Early Years

Laura Alice was born to Alice and Albert in Cincinnati on November 30, 1879 and slept in a satin-lined, flower-bedecked baby carriage. As with other wealthy women of the time, Alice did not see her children very often and did not involve herself in their day-to-day care. Rather, she gave instructions to the nurses who took care of the two sisters and to the French governesses and private tutors who educated them during their early years. As the girls grew up, their wealthy, spacious subur-ban home included many pets including a goat, a Mexican parakeet, a parrot, alligators, a Shetland pony and two dogs.[21]

Alice was not a physically expressive mother but she did love her daughters. Thanks to her laissez-faire attitude about discipline and rules,

Natalie and Laura had far more freedom and latitude in their lives than was usual for girls of their social class. They were raised with little discipline and were allowed an unusual degree of independence. Years later, Natalie remarked, 'She never punished us . . . We were not spanked, and the stick was spared in order, preferably, to spoil the child.'[22] Maybe this explains why they both became independent-minded at an early age.

When the family first moved to Cincinnati they lived in a suite in Burnet House, a luxurious hotel owned by the Pike family, where Abraham Lincoln, the Prince of Wales and Jenny Lind had stayed and Laura was born. When Laura's grandfather, E.E. Barney, died the year after her birth, his wife and children, including Albert, inherited large sums of money and a share of the profits of the factory. The family's fortunes having increased, they moved into an even more exclusive neighborhood when Albert bought a mansion in an elite hillside suburb of Cincinnati.

Their new home became 'the center of most delightful hospitality', as the Barneys entertained often.[23] Seven years later, in 1887, Albert's mother died and left what she had inherited from E.E. to her children, making Albert even wealthier. After her estate was settled, Albert's worth was about five million dollars. The Barney & Smith Manufacturing Company was also sold in 1892 for 3.4 million dollars and Albert must have received a large sum again.[24]

Albert, now living on inherited money, did not have to work and could live the good life. He also became more critical of Alice and was drinking heavily. He resented her continued interest in the arts. The marriage ended in all but name, but Albert 'wished to preserve the facade of marriage' as long as he could be unfaithful to her while Alice 'remained true to him'.[25] Albert became a very demanding and domineering husband. Natalie would not forgive the harm he caused her mother as his uncontrolled temper was vented on 'a good and surely kindly woman'.[26] His behavior must have affected Laura as well. Albert's treatment of his wife must have shaped both daughters' views about a woman's role and their need for independence. Despite the luxurious life that Natalie and Laura had during childhood, they suffered the effects of their father's alcoholism and their parents' unhappy marriage.

At the age of three Laura went with her family on her first trip to Europe. Her father wanted to show his daughters Europe, the home of their ancestors, the girls' 'Anglo-Saxon forbearers, the professors, businessmen, industrial magnates who had built what an American multimillionaire, Florence Jay-Gould, called "the fabulous fortune of the Barneys"'.[27] While in Paris her parents searched for a suitable boarding school for their girls and they found the prestigious school Les Ruches in Fontainebleau. During this trip, their mother also spent a lot of time visiting museums while her daughters wanted to spend time at the zoo.[28] The family also traveled to Belgium. It was there that they saw a woman and a dog pulling a cart that was packed with heavy milk tins while the man was walking alongside smoking. Even though Laura was too young to understand feminism, Natalie later said that she and Laura 'considered themselves feminists from that day on', that 'the sight of that woman harnessed to the dogcart began to shape, and would forever color, their views on the role of women in the world'.[29]

The Early Formation of Laura's Personality

Laura's personality emerged at a young age and was the opposite of Natalie's. By middle childhood Natalie was a beautiful blond, humorous, confident, good-natured and fearless, who made friends easily. Laura was also a beautiful girl with brunette hair but she was shy and thoughtful. Natalie was rebellious, charismatic and outgoing, whereas Laura tended to be obedient and quiet. Natalie once said that she played the devil to Laura's angel in childhood. Natalie played tennis, rowed, fenced and swam. Laura was not at all athletic. She studied hard and learned more slowly, and she thought of Natalie as 'the intelligent sister'.[30] But signs of Laura's true intelligence and curious nature became apparent later. Unlike the other members of her family, she was serious-minded and insightful.[31] She was a dutiful child from a young age who studied diligently at school, always tried to do better and apologized when she felt her work had fallen short.

Laura never caused any problems for her parents while growing up. She had a highly developed sense of duty. Her mother would look at her somber dark-haired daughter with wonder.[32] Though Laura was three years younger than her sister, their roles were reversed in their youth. Natalie sought out her 'practical younger sister' to 'take care of mundane matters'.[33]

For the most part, the sisters maintained their love and respect for each other throughout their childhood, adulthood and into their elder years, although Laura's feelings were stronger than Natalie's. One anecdote illuminates this. At the age of three, Laura, whom Natalie referred to as the 'saint', hit her over the head with a shovel and for a long time Natalie bore a scar and not a little rancor towards her sister.[34] According to a biographer of Natalie, perhaps Laura's absolute devotion to Natalie was in vain as she tried to make up for that incident.[35] Whether it was that incident or not, she did try throughout her life to be close to Natalie.

The Sisters at Les Ruches Boarding School

The Barney family returned to Paris in the summer of 1887 where the girls were to start school at Les Ruches ('The Beehives') in Fontainebleau. This was a suburb of Paris famous for its scenic forest and its historic château.

However, having arrived at Les Ruches, the girls were both traumatized at the idea of being left at the school, as this was the first time the two sisters would be separated from their parents, so the whole family returned to Paris. It was not until January or February 1888 that the girls started school. Natalie was eleven and Laura eight years old. The girls adjusted to their new environment within a few months. In a letter to her father in August 1888, Laura wrote that she was very happy at the school, asked him if she could stay there the next year and that she did not mind if she did.[36]

Les Ruches Boarding School had been founded by a feminist, Marie Souvestre. She would go on to establish a second school in England, where she became a mentor to the future First Lady of the United States, Eleanor Roosevelt. Eleanor was sent to this boarding school, which was near London, in 1899. It was under Souvestre, the headmistress, that Eleanor gained confidence, poise and maturity while being encouraged to develop her keen intellect. Eleanor believed that it was the headmistress of this school who had had the greatest influence on her after her father during that period of her life.

Souvestre's goal with Les Ruches was 'to nurture and develop independent women with sharp, analytical minds and strong characters'. She believed that women must learn to think for themselves.[37] This philosophy may have stayed with Laura throughout her life and influenced her path, and one can only believe that it reinforced Natalie's path.

The school's curriculum was traditional, teaching history, poetry, literature and languages. The girls were only allowed to speak in French and were expected to write to their parents regularly. The students were encouraged to create theatrical entertainment as well. Laura wrote to her parents frequently and many times talked about her daily activities including horseback riding, practicing piano, visiting neighboring towns, attending concerts, reading the Bible and going to church.[38] The sisters sometimes visited French families and went to social events.

Laura's letters to her parents during those years at Les Ruches, some of which have been preserved, have misspelled words and smudges. In one letter she wrote, 'Natalie refuses to help me. If she only would, I could be so much better.'[39] In another letter, written when she was nine years old, she shared her excitement at the arrival of a new little boy, writing how much she liked him.[40] In a letter to her father containing many grammatical errors and written in a childish hand she wrote that she was very happy and that she had just finished her Bible lesson.[41]

While languages came easily to Natalie, Laura struggled until she mastered them. Natalie sailed through examinations and received high marks with little study. Laura, who truly cared about her grades, spent hours in preparation for exams.

Laura missed her parents and looked forward to seeing them. She also missed her cousin Bertha and, wishing to see her, asked her parents to bring her with them.[42] Her letters almost always ended on the same note: 'I must say goodbye. Love to all. From your loving daughter, Alice [Laura] Barney.'[43]

In 1889 Laura received an autograph book from her mother as a Christmas present, a common gift in those days that was meant to impart inspiration from messages written by family and friends. The first entry in the book was by Natalie dated January 3, 1890. Her advice was: 'Give every man thine ear, but few thy voice: Take each man's censure, but reserve thy judgment.' Her mother wrote: 'Nothing is sweeter than love, nothing more courageous . . . nothing finer nor better in heaven and earth. Love one another.'[44]

Artistic Life of Paris and Laura's Mother

Back in Cincinnati, Alice started taking china painting classes and met some interesting people including Elizabeth Nourse (1859–1938), a professional artist. Alice commissioned two paintings from her, one of them an oil painting of her daughters in 1884. It was during those sittings that she became close to Elizabeth and established a life-long friendship. Elizabeth encouraged Alice to go to Paris to study arts after she noticed Alice's natural talent. Elizabeth herself moved to Paris in 1887.[45]

Alice had supported the idea of enrolling her daughters at the boarding school because her marriage to Albert was not happy. By moving to Paris, Alice could be near her daughters and also pursue her own interests such as taking painting lessons, of which Albert approved. Paris was a fast-growing city that had doubled in size within one decade. It was also the heart of the European art world and attracted artists and tourists from all over the planet. Every ten years Paris hosted the *Exposition Universelle* (Universal Exhibition) that brought even more global recognition to the city. The exhibition was a meeting point for many world cultures and their art, industry and other accomplishments.[46] The growing importance of Paris as a center for the study of art was enhanced by innumerable salon exhibitions and the great art collections at the Louvre.[47] Travel had become easier, and many adventurous American artists, writers, doctors, politicians, architects and others of high aspiration set off for Paris in the years between 1830 and 1900.[48] Thus Alice was among the over one thousand Americans who flocked to Paris in 1888. Many of these, perhaps a third, were women.[49] The city of light was both vibrant and modern artistically and intellectually, while the beauty of its traditions was reflected in the architecture of its old buildings. Its bustling street life, elegance and seediness, grand boulevards and squalor, created an urban personality that held great attraction for these Americans.[50] Paris was the world capital of culture in these years.

Laura's mother was now an active artist who was socializing with male and female artists. However, men and women were not treated equally in the arts. At L'École des Beaux-Arts, the foremost art school of the time, women received less instruction in their classes than men and were charged double the fees that men paid. Despite this inequality, many women, such as Mary Cassatt, succeeded.[51]

Alice, of course, shared her love of art with her daughters. Jean Chalon, a friend of Natalie and later her biographer, believed that Natalie was the one who followed her mother's artistic pursuits, not Laura.[52]

However, later in life Laura did make some sculptures, wrote and published a drama, wrote several manuscripts that remained unpublished, and supported and sponsored the arts. Alice was noted as saying that she took pride in directing her children 'in the fullest expression of their individual inclinations'.[53]

Alice was thrilled to be in Paris and she took classes with the famed French painter Charles E. A. Carolus-Duran (1837–1917), the teacher of John Singer Sargent. Alice commissioned Carolus-Duran to paint Laura and Natalie. Laura, who was seven years old at the time, was depicted wearing a hat and Natalie wore the costume of an Oscar Wilde character, Happy Prince.[54] Alice painted a picture of a peasant woman while visiting Brittany that summer with her daughters, and the work was accepted in a Paris salon in 1889. While Alice stayed in Paris to be near her daughters, Albert retreated to London. He seemed to begrudge Alice's interest in painting. Even as his own conduct deteriorated, perhaps partly under the increasing and pernicious influence of alcohol, he made an unfounded accusation against her of the same kind of infidelity he indulged in excessively himself. Not happy with the situation and before Alice could pursue her career more fully, Albert decided to relocate the family to Washington, D.C.

The Family's Move to Washington, D.C.

The family moved to Washington, D.C. in 1889. Albert had selected Washington over New York since he thought that he would be accepted more easily by Washington's high society than New York City's. Washington society was a more transient mix of politicians and military men as well as old and new money, and he wanted to be in the top social echelon and show off his wealth. At that time, the family's net worth was about five million dollars (over 140 million dollars today).[55] The Barneys took up temporary residence at 1439 K Street, N.W., while their new house was being built just off the fashionable Scott Circle at 1626 Rhode Island Avenue, N.W.[56]

Soon after the move to Washington Alice met another resident of K Street, Juliet Thompson, a young American who was studying art at the Corcoran School. Juliet was 14 years younger than Alice but they became close friends. Alice encouraged Juliet in her art and they often painted together, sometimes on the same painting, as their styles were similar. They both exhibited their work at the Philadelphia Art Club in 1895, where Juliet's artwork was given the highest honor and Alice's was said to be the 'discovery of the exhibition'.[57] Juliet, who later became a friend of Laura as well, became a well-known portrait artist and traveled with Alice to Europe in 1899.

By 1880 there were 30 hotels in Bar Harbor, Maine, and the rich and famous, such as the Vanderbilts and the Pulitzers, frequented the town. Known as Eden until it was renamed in 1910, Bar Harbor with its sumptuous cottages became a resort for the wealthy elite during the Gilded Age, rivaling Newport, Rhode Island.

In the early 1890s Albert and Alice visited the town, which had become the place to be for members of high society. The socially ambitious Albert built a 26-room summer 'cottage' in Bar Harbor that he named Ban-y-Bryn after a Welsh castle. This mansion had a gorgeous view of the ocean and the social events held there quickly matched those held in Newport in the caliber of its guests.[58]

The Barneys' summers at Bar Harbor were busy with teas, balls, formal dances, coming out parties, elaborate dinners and sports activities. There were special activities for children in which the Barney girls participated. The family, with its wealth and good looks, fit in well with Bar Harbor society.

Laura's Return to the US

Laura was 13 years old when she returned to America and entered Visitation, a Catholic convent school in Georgetown, Washington, D.C.[59] After their return home, the girls were cared for first by a German governess who had worked at Les Ruches; she was later replaced with an Austrian. Laura, who had become absorbed in philosophical subjects at that early age, began to develop 'unique spiritual and political philosophies that would eventually bring her into conflict with her father'.[60] While at Visitation, she disclosed that she wished to devote her life to 'noble causes'.[61]

A tragedy befell Laura in 1892 during the family's summer vacation in Bar Harbor: she seriously injured her leg when a pony cart overturned. Her parents took her to a medical specialist in New York City. She was put into traction and had to stay in bed for months. She tried to be stoic as she endured much pain and tedium. Although she stayed in the hospital until nearly the next spring, this injury never completely healed and she limped and felt various degrees of discomfort in the leg for the rest of her life. Her treatment included an operation on her leg in 1896 in Paris to improve the limp and she later visited and stayed at several thermal baths in France for treatment and therapy.

Natalie was enrolled in an exclusive boarding school in New York City, Miss Ely's School for Girls, so that she could be near Laura during her initial recovery period.[62] Even though the sisters were quite different in character and personality and had frequent arguments while growing up, they had a strong bond that had been forged between them from their childhood years. Whenever Natalie was in trouble, she would ask Laura for help. A biographer of Natalie believed they 'held a respect for each other and a strong underlying sense of kinship'.[63]

Natalie maintained that their attraction was based on the telepathy that had developed between them in childhood. For example, it is said that when they played games, Laura had to leave the room and Natalie and their friends would select a book and a page number. When Laura returned to the room, many times she would go straight to the book they had selected and open it to the correct page. They also played this game while Laura was in traction. Her neurologist noticed the telepathy between the girls and wrote an article about it that was later published in a medical journal. The family asked him not to mention the names of their daughters. Natalie later wrote, 'We were nevertheless proud to learn that we figured in an article as the case of L. and N. [Laura and Natalie].'[64]

During her recovery Laura, who was in constant pain, spent long hours reading books. Already different from the rest of her family because of her serious nature and deep thoughts, she became even more contemplative after the accident.

During the presidency of Benjamin Harris, the Barney family was invited to the White House for lunch at Christmas 1892.[65] Most probably Laura was able to join her family. But that Christmas holiday was generally a sad one as she was still pale and had lost weight. The winter was difficult for young Laura, who was still recuperating from her accident. However, things started to improve in the spring. The summer found the Barneys again at Bar Harbor. Laura and her sister took roles in the plays written and presented by their mother: Natalie appeared in a pantomime and Laura recited an enthusiastic composition about social injustice.

Natalie had started having unconventional attitudes from an early age and now she became more defiant, was increasingly insolent and was even less submissive to her father. She was argumentative and always ready with an impudent reply.

At first Alice only tacitly supported Natalie's rebellious behavior but later on did so openly. Laura had become unconventional too, although in her case it was not rebellion but her developing ideas and views that her father disliked. Alice always defended her daughters when Albert complained about their behavior.

Alice Finds Herself while Albert's Health Declines

Alice had become a powerful patron for the arts in Washington with her wealth and social connections. Her name became synonymous with an unwavering commitment to fostering creativity in both Washington and Paris. Her friends in London and Paris included Anna Pavlova, Sarah Bernhardt and Ruth St Denis. Easygoing and charming, she was variously described as 'willful', 'eclectic' and 'eccentric', terms used to 'explain her lack of conformity to so many conventions and mores'.[66]

Alice continued with her art and received a commission to paint the official portrait of John C. Calhoun, a former Secretary of State, which was exhibited at the 1893 Chicago World's Columbian Exposition. Laura and Natalie were frequently used as her models for other paintings. The girls' approach to posing reflected their different personalities. Laura was quiet and patient while Natalie was restless and irritated. However, both girls learned the value of determination and perseverance from their mother. Laura later applied these qualities selflessly to her public services and spiritual activities and developed an attitude of tolerance towards others, while Natalie learned 'not to be dissuaded from a goal by another's objections', possessed an unusual open-minded tolerance for many things and would not judge people.[67]

Laura's mother continued being patient with her husband while he spent much of his idle time in clubs. Albert founded the Chevy Chase Club and was a member of the Metropolitan, the Washington Golf, and the Alibi Clubs. He had several affairs and his excessive drinking continued. Despite his own marital infidelities, Albert often accused his wife of unfaithfulness although there is no evidence that she ever had an extramarital affair.

Albert's drinking became an increasing problem for the family. On one occasion, he got angry and took the girls on a train to Dayton. He continued drinking on the train and suggested to Natalie that they should jump beneath the train's wheels. Laura, who was ten years old, was sleeping when this scene started. Natalie was shocked and threatened to pull the emergency cord and stop the train. While he wavered, Laura woke up and the girls started weeping together. After this incident Albert promised Natalie that he would never drink again in her presence. Natalie did not believe him and, as is often true with alcoholics, it is unlikely he kept his word.

Laura's Treatments in Europe

In the 1890s Laura spent weeks at the thermal baths in France, most of them at Aix-les-Bains in the eastern part of France, as part of the therapy for her damaged leg. Despite this treatment, this health issue never left her for the rest of her life, though she never complained about it or even spoke of it.

Laura stayed in touch with her parents regularly. Regardless of the family's dysfunction owing to Albert's alcoholism and the broken marriage, Laura's letters in her early teens from France show that she maintained a loving relationship with her father and used endearing terms to show her affection towards him. Once while she was in Aix-les-Bains she explained to him that during her six weeks of vacation she was going to get treatment to improve her health, even though she was missing her studies, as she felt she needed a vacation to do so.[68]

When she was 19 Laura gave her father an update on her health. Her knee and leg were better and she felt she could not complain.[69] In another, letter written to both parents, she told them that she was settled in a hotel in Aix-les-Bains. She could not yet walk entirely without her canes but she had learned a lot and was enjoying what she was learning. 'And I am delighted at the thought of being able to continue my interesting work till the middle of July,' she wrote, 'and how I hope to do same next winter. I have learnt so much these few weeks, and I would hate to be forced to come to a standstill by stopping my present life.'[70] In a letter to her mother, which may have been written around the time that Alice was leaving her and sailing back to the United States, Laura expressed how much she already missed her.[71]

Alice traveled back and forth between Paris and the United States and by the summer of 1899 she and the girls were back in Paris. That summer they also visited Rome, since a close friend of Natalie was there and had invited them. Natalie was able to convince her mother to go as well, as Alice was a close friend of the wife of the United States Ambassador to Italy. The Barney women stayed at the American Embassy in Rome. Both Laura and Natalie loved the Roman countryside.[72] They both visited Rome many times later in life, Laura mostly for work and Natalie for pleasure.

Laura's Spiritual and Humanitarian Development

Laura and Natalie were baptized at St John's Episcopal Church, one of wealthiest parishes of the Dioceses of Washington. Laura reminded her sister a few decades later, 'opposite this place stands St John's where we were confirmed'.[73] From a young age Laura showed a lively interest in spirituality and raised questions about faith. But she always had questions about church theology and sermons. At the age of 12 she wrote to her father saying she had gone to the church and that 'the sermen [sermon] was good but I don't think Mr Dudelses' sermens [sermons] are as good as usual'.[74] Alice and her daughters attended church faithfully. But Albert, who was a member of the initial building committee of the Washington Cathedral, seemed to have had little interest in religion.

When Laura was 19 she discussed with her father matters that were important for her future spiritual development. She informed him that she was reading the New Testament and had gone to her 'favorite church – the only one that truly elevates me above my pety [petty] self and actions'.[75] She later complained of the more limited view of other parishioners and asserted her own universal beliefs:

And it is hard for people to believe in the soul of the body! Why do they not see the sky constantly over the earth, can they not compare it to the soul, does not the life come from above in the form of the sun, moon, rain, etc. Is not the earth (or body) a simple after life of the former, a movement of the superior action? And we need Christ's martyrdom to prove to us the Palpably! Before Christ, immortality was understood; but not universal love; so to me, every day means

as much as Easter. Every moment of every day, he lived and suffered
to prove and spread his new doctrine. As usual I suppose I have had
false ideas, but I have them as firmly as a conviction.[76]

Laura had shown interest in humanitarian activities from a young age.
She was back in Paris pursuing her studies, perhaps dramatic arts and
sculpture, and getting physical therapy when the United States declared
war against Spain on April 25, 1898. Laura begged her father for permission to go to Key West, Florida, to help the wounded soldiers of
the war, if it continued, because she felt it was her duty to do so. She
believed that 'all intelligent people will understand you allowing your
daughter to do a good thing – and the stupid & silly ones do not need
to be thought of at all. I do not see a logical reason to stop me from
doing what I feel is my duty.' She asked him to say 'yes' to her request.
'I am sure,' she wrote her father, 'that you will come to my conclusion
that it is good and best to do every good action that can possibly cross
one's path on this short life.'[77] She ended her letter by saying that she
was sure that her mother would agree with her that it was Laura's social
and religious obligation, which was why she did not ask her mother for
permission.[78] Needless to say, Laura's father did not give his permission.
This was the first time that Laura had asked for something unconventional and at odds with her usual exemplary behavior. However, her
mother did help the sick and wounded of the Spanish-American War
by organizing a theatrical program presented at the original Corcoran
Gallery (currently the Smithsonian Renwick Gallery) that raised funds
for their relief.[79]

The Barney family sailed to Europe in July 1898. Natalie's fiancé Will,
as Natalie called him, joined them later. His full name was Robert Kelso
Cassatt, the son of a wealthy family from Pittsburg and the nephew
of Mary Cassatt, the American artist. They had met in Bar Harbor
during their summer vacations and become unofficially engaged. The
Barneys and Will spent the summer at Étretat, a fashionable seaside
resort in Normandy. Then it was back to Paris where Alice and her two
daughters settled into the Villa des Dames (House of Women), a boarding house for women artists. Albert left for London and then went to
Washington in September. While staying at Villa des Dames, Laura's
mother took classes with the American painter James McNeill Whistler
at Académie Carmen.

The Dreyfus Affair and the Barneys in Paris

The Dreyfus Affair was a political scandal in France, which indirectly came to haunt Laura many years later. A young French officer of Jewish descent named Alfred Dreyfus was convicted of treason in 1894 without evidence and sentenced to life imprisonment on the infamous Devil's Island, where he spent about five years. The fraudulent evidence made Dreyfus a national figure and put the government in jeopardy. Daily newspaper headlines showed both sides and questioned his innocence or guilt about giving military secrets to Germany. French society was divided between those who supported Dreyfus and those who condemned him. Pressure mounted as hundreds of scholars and writers throughout Europe and America publicly supported the Dreyfusards, who believed Dreyfus to be innocent. Among those supporting Dreyfus was the great French writer Émile Zola, who was convicted of libel following the publication in 1898 of his pro-Dreyfus letter 'J'Accuse' that put pressure on the government to reopen the case.

Alice and Albert had opposite opinions about the matter. Alice supported the Dreyfusards in opposition to her husband. She avidly read the lists of people who supported Dreyfus, grateful that few artists were mentioned. She told Albert that during her studies 'she would not be surrounded by Dreyfusards' and that he could safely leave her in Paris without worrying she might take part.[80] The Dreyfus Affair increased Albert's dislike of Paris and he left after a month in late summer 1898.

Dreyfus was acquitted in 1899, rearrested on other false charges, found guilty, sentenced to ten years' imprisonment, and pardoned and released in 1906. Coincidentally, Laura met a Jewish man named Hippolyte Dreyfus in 1900 who became a significant person in her life but he was not related to Alfred Dreyfus.

Albert asked Alice to rent a house suitable for entertaining on the Right Bank of Paris. In May 1899 she rented a four-storied house at 53 Ave Victor Hugo, an elegant neighborhood. He came to visit them that summer and was happy not to hear unpleasant stories about Alice, Natalie or Laura. He was looking sick and pale and had lost weight. He was also relieved that the Dreyfus Affair was no longer an issue, heartened that the French government had, in his opinion, prevailed over the anarchists and socialists of whom he disapproved.

Laura's mother was not happy in her new digs. She decided to turn one room of their house in Paris into a studio and began painting there. She also surrounded herself with creative and intelligent guests by inviting them to her salons. Laura and Natalie often participated in the intellectual discussions among the influential writers and artists who attended. Laura always had serious questions and made insightful remarks. Natalie made sharp and intelligent comments and with her wit 'enlivened conversations'.[81] The guests were from many countries and could discuss art intelligently and creatively. Among the guests on one occasion was Alice's friend Phoebe Hearst from California, who also had homes in Washington, D.C. and Paris. She was the wife of George Hearst (1829–91), a rich miner, businessman and, later, a senator; and mother of the newspaper magnate William Randolph Hearst. One of the early western Bahá'ís, Mrs Hearst had just returned from 'Akká, Palestine.

In the meantime, Laura had started studying dramatic arts and sculpture in Paris. She was much intrigued with theater like her mother, which was surprising given her naturally quiet nature. Among the three Barney women, it was Laura who felt responsible for the other two. Someone close to them commented that it was Laura who adopted 'the role of mother'.[82] She was only 20 years old at the time.

PART 2

FAITH FROM THE EAST AND
LIFE-CHANGING EFFECTS

1900 – 1910

Turn of the Century and Laura

The year 1900 was not only the turn of a new century for Parisians, it was also the year of the *Exposition Universelle*. Opening in the middle of April, it was the largest world's fair of the time and had a split location on both sides of River Seine spread over 600 acres. People in Paris were excited and buzzing over the opening of the legendary Exposition. Preparations had taken nearly ten years, and it is said that it attracted more than 40 million people. At night the city was ablaze with electric light. There were pavilions and other structures built in the Beaux-Arts style, a form of neoclassical architecture drawing on Gothic and Renaissance elements and exemplified by buildings from the Exposition that are still standing today: the Grand Palais, the Petit Palais, and the Musée d'Orsay (originally the Gare d'Orsay).

However, for Laura Barney, who was in Paris at the time, the beginning of 1900 marked not only the turn of a new century, the many happenings with her sister and family, and the Universal Exhibition, it was a turning point in her spiritual life. This defining moment came when she heard about a movement from the East, the Bahá'í Faith, and its spiritual leader, 'Abbás Effendi, who was known as 'Abdu'l-Bahá. 'Abdu'l-Bahá, which means Servant of Bahá (Bahá is Arabic for 'glory'), a title He chose for Himself, was the head of the Bahá'í Faith at the time. He was the son of Bahá'u'lláh (1817–92), the Prophet-Founder of the Faith, who had been exiled to and confined in the prison-city of 'Akká in Ottoman Palestine.[1]

At this time the two sisters were still dependent on their parents for their financial support. Laura was studying dramatic arts – perhaps under some of the best teachers of the Théâtre Français[2] – sculpture and philosophy, while continuing therapy for her leg.[3] The sisters had been born into a society that 'shielded daughters from the world's realities, a custom that tended to keep them naive and dewy'. Despite her family's travels, Laura 'knew little about life's rigors'.[4]

By 1900 Laura had been seeking spiritual enlightenment for a decade and in her letters had written of such deep subjects as the soul and martyrdom, as well as universal love and her desire to serve humanity.[5] She was looking for something to touch her soul and had always been curious about religion. Even though Laura had attended church regularly while growing up, she was becoming skeptical about Episcopalian

Christian teachings and felt that she was in darkness and sought spiritual enlightenment. It is important to remember how young Laura was at the time: she had just turned 21.

Hearing of an Eastern Faith

How did Laura hear about the Bahá'í Faith? Phoebe Hearst had learned of the Bahá'í movement and was on her way to 'Akká, Palestine, to meet its spiritual leader from the East when she stopped in Paris in September 1898. In her party were Lua and Edward Getsinger, two of the first American Bahá'ís. An American woman, Mary Martin Bolles, was house-sitting Phoebe's apartment in Paris[6] with her daughter, Mary Ellis Bolles, nicknamed 'May', and her son Randolph. May, who was Phoebe's god-daughter, was very ill and Lua was asked to speak to her. Lua told May, 'There is a Prisoner in 'Akká who holds the key to peace.' As soon as she heard this, May exclaimed, 'I believe, I believe.'[7] Over the next weeks Lua taught May everything she knew about the Bahá'í Faith, confirming her as the first American Bahá'í on the European continent.[8] May longed to meet 'Abdu'l-Bahá. Her health improved and Phoebe, learning of May's interest, invited her to join the group, which included the Getsingers and Ibrahim Kheiralla, one of the first teachers of the Faith in the West, on their pilgrimage to 'Akká at the end of 1898.[9] On her return from pilgrimage, May Bolles established the first Bahá'í group on the European continent in Paris. Her enthusiasm for her new religious faith caused many people to flock to her new home at 100 rue du Bac to hear about the Faith.[10]

May Bolles's intense love for 'Abdu'l-Bahá was infectious and drew people to her. Even though the early Bahá'ís had only a slight knowledge of the teachings of the religion 'their faith was pure and their unity was strong'.[11] Laura became seriously interested in the Faith of Bahá'u'lláh after hearing of it through May Bolles. Obviously seeing something to wrap her soul around, she accepted the Bahá'í movement, the teachings of which included the equality of women and men, the absence of formal creed and clergy, the oneness of humanity, and the singleness of God.

Laura may have also heard about this new faith from others. Phoebe Hearst had converted to the Bahá'í Faith in 1898 and was a friend of Alice Barney and frequented her salons. Laura may have also met

'Abdu'l-Karím Ṭihrání, a Persian Bahá'í teacher, in April 1900 in Paris. He was on his way to New York to teach the Bahá'ís there the history and tenets of their new religion.[12] But Laura regarded May Bolles as her spiritual mother and felt indebted to her throughout her life for teaching her the Faith.

Laura Meets 'Abdu'l-Bahá

In those early years of the Faith there was no formal way of joining or registering in this new religion so new converts would send a letter of supplication to 'Abdu'l-Bahá. Laura sent a letter to 'Abdu'l-Bahá dated May 31, 1900, stating that she wanted to meet Him before accepting the teachings of the Faith,[13] and made her first pilgrimage to Haifa in October of that year to learn more. Her soul was longing for spiritual and religious truths and she wanted to discover them for herself. She left everything behind and went to the prison-city of 'Akká, where 'Abdu'l-Bahá and His family lived under conditions of Ottoman imprisonment.

Though her home was in Paris at that time, Laura was visiting the United States and sailed from New York with her maternal cousin Ellen Goin. They were joined by their chaperon, Mme Emma Trouvé, in Paris. Mme Trouvé was a fervent Catholic and knew nothing about the new religion, so Laura taught her on the way.[14] Traveling to Haifa was not easy in those days. The primary modes of travel were steamers and trains. The small party sailed to the continent, then traveled by train from Paris to Constantinople (Istanbul), then by steamer to Haifa after stopping at several ports. Upon their arrival in Haifa, Palestine, they stayed at a hotel in the German Colony.[15]

German adventists, who called themselves Templers, had emigrated from Germany to the Holy Land and founded several settlements. The first was the German Colony, built in 1868 at the foot of Mount Carmel.[16] The motivation for the Templers' move to the Holy Land was their belief that living in the Holy Land would hasten the second coming of Jesus, which they believed would occur there. The main street of the German Colony in Haifa ran directly from the seafront to the foot of Mount Carmel. The stone houses on this avenue had sacred scriptural verses about the coming of the Lord chiseled on lintels above their front doors.

The conditions of 'Abdu'l-Bahá's confinement in 'Akká had by then had been greatly relaxed and He was allowed to travel between 'Akká and His home on the seafront in Haifa as needed. He was extremely busy with work and His duties in Haifa required much of His time. Overseeing the excavation of the foundation for the tomb of the Báb on a slope of Mount Carmel was especially pressing. The Báb was the forerunner of the Bahá'í Faith who was martyred in 1850, and His remains were to be interred on Mount Carmel.

Among His followers 'Abdu'l-Bahá was called the Master (*Áqá*). He had rented a house in Haifa and either His sister, Bahíyyih Khánum, or one of His daughters and a son-in-law, would go there to look after Him.[17] Bahíyyih Khánum, who was two years younger than 'Abdu'l-Bahá, was known as the Greatest Holy Leaf.

One of the first people Laura met upon arrival in Haifa was the Persian Ali-Kuli Khan (1879–1966), who was serving in 'Abdu'l-Bahá's household as a translator and secretary. Khan was also one of several secretaries who helped the Master with His correspondence with persons from all over the world. His daughter Marzieh Gail described the arrival of Laura and her cousin as seen by Khan:

> One morning in Haifa, 'Abdu'l-Bahá sent for Khan to meet Him at the little house on the German Colony street where He had passed the night, attended either by His sister or one of His daughters.
>
> He told Khan that two American ladies had arrived from Paris and were staying at the German hotel near the sea, and Khan was to call on them and escort them to the house. They were cousins, Elsa [Laura] Barney and Ellen Goin (pronounced Goween), the first from Washington DC and the other from New York.
>
> Khan walked over to say that 'Abdu'l-Bahá had sent him to fetch them.
>
> They were two beauties, dressed in the latest Paris fashions, and Khan already abnormally shy, nearly sank into the ground. He had never before seen such strikingly beautiful American girls – or many lovely girls of any kind in those veiled Middle Eastern societies.[18]

Years later, Laura recalled her first meeting with Khan and she would tell him: 'Khan, you were so shy that all the time we were talking to you, you were looking at your shoes. You must have had a brand new pair that day, and were more interested in them than us.'[19]

As to the details of Laura's first visit to the Holy Land and meeting 'Abdu'l-Bahá, nothing is more powerful than her own words. The year after her first visit, she gave a talk and made the following remarks about her meeting with the Master. Since Laura's memoirs were stolen, this is valuable information and is one of the earliest and rarest existing documents that describes in her own words that first meeting and how she felt meeting 'Abdu'l-Bahá:

I knew very little about this great belief when I first went. In fact, I knew hardly anything beyond the fact that a wonderful forerunner had appeared on this earth, whose name was the Bab; that, after the Bab, an extraordinary and marvelous Being, named Baha'u'llah, had also declared Himself; that He was exiled from His country and imprisoned in Acca ['Akká], and from there His teachings went out that are now beginning to engulf the whole world; and when Baha'u'llah passed away, He left all His great teachings to be taught by His wonderful Son Abbas Effendi ['Abdu'l-Bahá], the Center of the Covenant. So, it was to go to see this wonderful Being that I left America (a year ago). I was in the company of my cousin and a friend, a lady who knew nothing about this Religion; was a Catholic; and so I taught her on the way.

I arrived at Haifa and sent this message to the Master: 'That I believed that He must be the Christ Spirit of the day, that the whole world was waiting for Him, but that I could not feel it; but that if He was the Christ Spirit of the day, He, of course, could prove it to me by making me yearn to follow the only path of true self-sacrifice and virtue.' I sent this message because I always believe that everything should be based on sincerity, and I do not want to go in an attitude which I did not absolutely feel was mine.

So, I went with my cousin the next morning. We arrived at the humble house of Abbas Effendi and were sitting with a number of the believers, when the Master came in. Before He had really entered the room, I was so surprised and overwhelmed by a wonderful atmosphere that I had never felt before – an atmosphere of perfect, complete humility and majesty at the same time. The Master swept into the room and, bidding us to be seated, began to speak. Of course, I could not understand the tongue in which He spoke (very unfortunately), but the Spirit was so strong that went forth that one could follow the words that came to us through the clear translation of Mr X [Ali-Kuli Khan]. My eyes that had until then been blinded, gradually opened. First, we remained perfectly still. After a while – (I do not know what my cousin did, because I was too much occupied) – I felt the tears coming to my eyes and running down my cheeks. They were not tears of sadness; they were tears of absolute gratitude; tears that one might shed if one had been locked up in a dark prison for years. It seemed that I had often tried to get out of this darkness that surrounded me – but in vain. So, as I heard the Master's words and felt that He was the Christ Spirit of the day, my tears continued to flow and my heart to beat with absolute love, absolute hope and happiness.

When I returned, I told my friend that I had had a very great joy and that before night I would tell it to her, but that I was too upset to begin then. That afternoon we drove up Mt. Carmel and when we went there we entered a picturesque monastery and there the Madam prayed, with all the fervor of the heart, and we came down.[20]

Then Laura continued that her friend had dreamed of the figure of Christ on the cross. When she met the Master for the first time, she said that indeed it was the same face and the same form that she had seen in her dream and that He had come to answer her prayers.[21] Years later, Ellen, who had also accompanied her, wrote that even though her memory was not fresh, she did remember the first day, October 19, 1900, when they saw their 'Beloved 'Abdu'l-Bahá' in that little simple straw mat room.'[22]

The house of 'Abdu'l-Bahá was located about a block from the Haifa Beach and the embarcadero, or landing place, where Laura's ship must have landed. It had been built for the arrival of Kaiser Wilhelm II in 1898. The house was not isolated as there were other houses around it on a street that ran roughly parallel with the sea and extended to the German Colony. 'Abdu'l-Bahá's home in Haifa was described by Marzieh Gail:

A flight of brick steps led up from the street to an open courtyard surrounded on three sides by rooms; and a door giving directly on the street was the one to the Master's reception room. Here there was an iron bedstead where He sometimes rested in the daytime . . . Besides several chairs, the room's other furniture consisted of a large table at one side, on which 'Abdu'l-Bahá kept writing materials, papers, some flowers, rose-water and a plate heaped with rock candy.[23]

There was a room at the back of the house where travelers could stay for a short time before leaving for 'Akká, and next to His room was another.[24]

Khan described the details of the Master's clothing:

The Master's usual clothing . . . was a long, straight coat (qabá) with narrow sleeves. Over this came His long robe with sleeves (labbádih) of heavy woolen material which folded over the front like a wrapper, and over His 'abá, heavy in winter, light in summer . . . His garments worn beneath the qabá – materials varying with the season – were a thin linen shirt, a woolen undershirt, and woolen drawers, over which came the outer shalvár (trousers). The colors He wore often were light gray and beige.[25]

During Laura's stay, 'Abdu'l-Bahá addressed and discussed many subjects, such as the strength of spirituality, the immortal soul, gratefulness for having knowledge of God, divine power and detachment from the material world.[26]

Laura and her two companions stayed for at least six days in 'Akká and then they had to leave, which greatly saddened her. The Master told Laura that He would never leave her, but still she felt distraught at the parting. The Master comforted her by saying, 'You must not be sad; you will return again, so rejoice!' She longed to be near Him, but He consoled her by saying, 'To be near me, you must be far from here.'[27]

For many of the early visitors who traveled to Palestine to meet 'Abdu'l-Bahá, it was His pure spirituality that immediately impressed upon them the truth of the Bahá'í Faith and motivated them to spread the teachings of Bahá'u'lláh. Laura was quoted as saying some years later:

I think the impression one has of 'Abdu'l-Bahá is in that it grows gradually and suddenly at the same time. I know when I first had the honor of going to Haifa, I think a little over eight years ago, at once I was impressed by His sanctity, by His wisdom, His majesty, His humility, by the manifestation of all the great qualities in such a simple, natural way.[28]

A Bahá'í biographer of an early Bahá'í wrote:

> . . . many of them believed that in 'Abdu'l-Bahá they saw the spirit of Jesus Christ in the world, placing the Master's station far above that which Bahá'u'lláh had assigned to Him. However, 'Abdu'l-Bahá swiftly and forcefully dismissed such pronouncements, stressing His humility and nothingness, His selfless devotion to the Cause of the Manifestation, Bahá'u'lláh, and His desire to be nothing else but a servant to the entire human race.[29]

Laura may have initially responded in the same way to 'Abdu'l-Bahá. However, since she was schooled in both the Old and New Testaments, the teachings of the Faith must have also had an extra and immediate appeal for her. The emphasis of the teachings on the eradication of prejudice, the unity of the races, the rights of women, the brotherhood of all mankind, and universal peace must have appealed strongly to her.

Many years later, a close friend of Laura wrote that her belief in the teachings of Bahá'u'lláh and acceptance of His faith proved to be 'the spark that ignited a fire never to be quenched. Her ideals and aspirations found fulfilment in her activities in the service of the Bahá'í Faith . . .'[30] Laura thus became one of the early Bahá'ís from the West.

Second Trip to 'Akká

As soon as her parents left for New York in early 1901, Laura traveled from Paris back to 'Akká, this time via Egypt. On this second visit, she was accompanied by Edith Tewksbury Jackson, an American Bahá'í who lived in Paris, and Sigurd Russell.[31] Sigurd was a 15-year-old boy whom Edith Jackson had accepted as a foster child.[32] They traveled by train with a small group of Bahá'í pilgrims to Constantinople and then took a steamer to Port Said, Egypt. There they met up with Helen Ellis Cole, Emogene Hoagg and Monsieur Henri, who had just become a Bahá'í.[33] All except Monsieur Henri were American. Helen Cole was an outstanding pianist and vocalist. Emogene Hoagg was the first to become a Baháʼí in California and would later travel extensively to teach the Faith throughout the Americas and Europe. For some reason, the group could not continue its trip directly to Haifa, so Laura remained in Port Said with Emogene while Edith Jackson went to Cairo.[34]

In Port Said Laura met Mírzá Abuʼl-Faḍl Gulpaygani (1844–1914), who was one of the most erudite and greatest of the early Baháʼí scholars and teachers. He had been born in Iran and had studied Arabic and Islamic jurisprudence, had knowledge of mystical philosophy and had become an authority in those fields. He converted to the Baháʼí Faith from Islam in 1876, afterwards dedicating his life to teaching and serving the Faith. His teaching travels took him to Turkmenistan, Egypt and France and later to the United States. In 1900 he was living in Port Said and was finishing one of his books.[35] This outstanding scholar had deep knowledge of the Baháʼí Revelation, of the Bible, European theology, and deep scientific questions. He called himself Abuʼl-Faḍl (progenitor of virtue), but ʻAbduʼl-Bahá called him Abuʼl-Faḍáʼil, progenitor of virtues.[36] He also gave Abuʼl-Faḍl the honor of conducting the marriage ceremony of His youngest daughter.

Laura took full advantage of this incredible opportunity to slake her spiritual thirst. She deepened her knowledge of the Baháʼí teachings from this wise scholar and may have asked questions of Abuʼl-Faḍl about the Bible and the fulfillment of biblical prophecy. He was well-known for his ʻprofound learning, especially in philosophy and religious history, his exceptional mastery of the Persian language, his skill in debate, the simplicity of his life, and his great personal humility'.[37] Laura established a respectful relationship with Abuʼl-Faḍl from the start, later addressing him as her ʻrevered teacher and dearly loved friend'.[38] She, Edith and others spent their many evenings with him and learned a great deal from this distinguished gentleman.[39] She wrote: ʻThe evenings were spent near him and we learnt a great deal from this wise scholar.'[40] It was during this time that Laura became interested in learning Persian in order to better understand the teaching of this new movement, and this visit must have given her a good opportunity to start.

None of the pilgrims spoke Persian and Abuʼl-Faḍl did not speak English. It is possible that the translator for his talks was Mírzá Aḥmad Yazdí, who was able to translate from French and English into Persian and vice versa.[41] Aḥmad Yazdí's French was superb and many of the American visitors spoke French.[42] He had left Iran when his life was imperiled because he was a Bahá'í and moved to Egypt, residing in Port Said. He and his two brothers actively served the Bahá'í Faith while supporting themselves as merchants. He also served as Honorary Consul for Persia to Egypt. He married Munavvar <u>Kh</u>ánum, the youngest daughter of 'Abdu'l-Bahá. Many of the letters sent to 'Abdu'l-Bahá from the West passed through him for onward transmission, and Tablets of 'Abdu'l-Bahá to the West were also sent through him. He received and entertained American and European Bahá'í pilgrims en route to Palestine.[43]

Another American Bahá'í from Paris who was in Port Said at the time was Mason Remey.[44]

Laura had first met Remey in Paris at May Bolles's home. He was the son of Rear-Admiral George Collier Remey of Washington, D.C., and was studying architecture at L'École des Beaux-Arts in Paris. Remey had met Randolph Bolles, another student at the school who was residing in Phoebe Hearst's large apartment. May Bolles, Randolph's sister, had met Remey and taught him the Faith in 1899. He accepted it immediately and became the third Bahá'í in Paris.[45]

Remey recalled that Edward and Lua Getsinger joined the group, as did Anton Haddad, a Lebanese from a Christian family who had become a Bahá'í, and several Persian Bahá'ís. Last to arrive was Edith Jackson, who was returning to Port Said from Cairo along with Sigurd Russell.[46] Every afternoon in Port Said, the visitors gathered at the place where Abu'l-Faḍl was staying and assembled around him. They had tea and sweet meats and chanted prayers. Then Abu'l-Faḍl would give them religious lessons, frequently from the Bible.[47]

After about a month in Port Said, the pilgrims went to the Holy Land, where they met other western Bahá'ís, including Ethel Jenner Rosenberg, the first Englishwoman to become a Bahá'í in her native country.[48] They arrived on March 1. Laura described her second visit in this way:

> We arrived in Haifa-Acca early in the morning. I was told that I was not to see the Master until evening. My impatience was great. In the afternoon, as I was dreaming of the heavenly joy in store for me (for heavenly is the only word which can express the feeling

that comes to one in the Master's presence), yet the joy of anticipation was mingled with apprehension, for I feared that since my
former meeting, my imagination and love had idealized Him, and
that perhaps a great disillusion might be awaiting me. The Master
entered suddenly. I instantly realized that this ideal was an absolute
reality and far beyond my anticipation. I then comprehended that
we can only see in Him that which we are capable of seeing, for what
we seek we find. I beheld the absolute mirror of the Divine Spirit!
When we ascend a mountain the horizon stretches ever further and
further and so it is with the soul the higher the spiritual state, the
greater the power of comprehension, there is no limit to perfection.[49]

Laura's visit lasted ten or twelve days. She wrote of this second visit:

After my second visit, the real delight of this religion opened before
me. Formerly I had looked at it as an extraordinary Truth, but I had
not realized its stupendous proportions. At first, I had thought that
one could go into it full of past habits and many ambitions, but now
I know that all worldliness must be cast aside at the very Threshold,
the moment we accept the name Behaist, we must live the life of one.
Religions have taught what is right and wrong to all nations, but this
great Revelation has brought one special truth and command to all
men, it has come to teach all absorbing universe and harmony and if
we do not follow this command this great command, we are casting
aside the foundation and how can we seek to build on nothingness!
Let the lives of every believer be built on the Rock of Truth and
Union and not on the shifting sands of fancy and imagination![50]

In 1901 'Abdu'l-Bahá was restricted to the city limits of 'Akká by the
Ottoman rulers. The pilgrims from East and West gathered in a large
room of the house of 'Abdu'lláh Páshá and visited each other every evening.[51] This large mansion had been rented by 'Abdu'l-Bahá when it
became clear that the house of 'Abbúd, where He and His family had
lived previously and which was nearby, was too small.[52] During those
days, whenever 'Abdu'l-Bahá came to the room to meet them at tea
time, it was Laura who rushed to the terrace to greet Him.[53]

News about Laura was reported in the newspapers. A long article in
the United States reported her visits to the Holy Land, remarking:

Miss Barney's contribution is interesting as showing the attitude of a woman follower of the head of this faith . . . She is a firm believer in Abbas Effendi ['Abdu'l-Bahá], who she calls 'a perfect being'.[54]

It listed a series of questions asked by Laura and the answers of 'Abdu'l-Bahá. It is not clear how the reporter learned about these questions, although the article states that Laura had written these accounts to her cousin Ellen Goin, who had accompanied her on her first pilgrimage.[55]

It was during this visit that Laura met Shoghi Effendi for the first time, on the last morning of her stay. Shoghi Effendi had been born in 'Akká in 1897, the first son of Ḍiyá'íyyih Khánum, the eldest daughter of 'Abdu'l-Bahá, and Mírzá Hádí, an Afnán, which means a descendant of the Báb's family. He was the first grandson of 'Abdu'l-Bahá and later succeeded Him as head of the Faith, known in that capacity as the Guardian.[56] Laura later remembered her first encounter with Shoghi Effendi when he was a little boy:

> Shoghi Effendi! How well I remember the first time I saw him in the Holy Land. He was then a little boy of five or six years of age, clothed in a brown Persian garment, chanting a prayer in 'Abdu'l-Bahá's presence; his earnest eyes, his firm mouth looked predestined.[57]

She found him 'rather small for his age, but very keen and attentive'.[58] She remembered that extraordinary child vividly.[59] Laura later wrote to a friend,

> Did I ever tell you that on my second trip to the Holy Land, when seated with the Holy Family at the break of dawn, the Master turned to a lovely little boy of four (who later became your husband) and said, 'Sing the Morning Prayer.'[60]

At the end of her second visit, 'Abdu'l-Bahá asked Laura and Ethel Rosenberg to accompany Abu'l-Faḍl to Europe and then to 'the United States to give the Believers further knowledge of the Cause'.[61] It may have been Laura's wish to have Abu'l-Faḍl go to the United States.[62] Khan had heard that she had especially requested that Abu'l-Faḍl be sent to 'America to unfold the true teachings of Bahá'u'lláh and to interpret the prophecies of the Holy Scriptures'.[63] Laura herself wrote that 'Abdu'l-Bahá had called her to say that He would like her to take Abu'l-Faḍl to the United States to 'give the believers fuller knowledge of the Cause'.[64]

Laura, Ethel Rosenberg and Anton Haddad boarded a ship to Marseilles which had a stop in Port Said. Haddad had been asked to accompany them to help with translation.[65] In Port Said, Aḥmad Yazdí accompanied Abu'l-Faḍl to the ship and stayed until the departure time.[66]

It took about five to six days to arrive at the port city of Marseilles. Upon arrival, the travelers took a night train to Paris. Ethel left for London immediately to begin preparations for Abu'l-Faḍl's trip to the United States, while the three others continued to Paris.

No. 7 Haparsim (Persian) Street

It was during her second visit to the Holy Land, when Laura was accompanied by Edith Tewksbury Jackson, that she realized that 'Abdu'l-Bahá's rented house in Haifa by the sea was only modest in size and not suitable for Him and His expanding family. She and Edith helped to build a new one.[67] Laura 'helped in the project of purchasing the land and of constructing a suitable home for 'Abdu'l-Bahá and His family at No. 7 Haparsim (Persian) Street, Haifa'.[68] She later said,

> For some time, therefore, and meeting with many obstacles, I was occupied with purchasing the land, having a design for the house made – of course with the approval of the Master – and seeing that its construction was carried out efficiently and promptly. All this kept me occupied for some time.[69]

The plan for the house was laid out by 'Abdu'l-Bahá Himself[70] and several members of His family moved into it once it was completed.[71] The new home became known as the House of 'Abdu'l-Bahá. He passed away there in November 1921. The Greatest Holy Leaf, Shoghi Effendi and, years later, his wife Rúḥíyyih Khánum also lived there.

Laura with the Persian Scholar in Paris

Upon arrival in Paris, Laura took Abu'l-Faḍl and Anton Haddad to her home. Two or three weeks later Laura helped them to settle in a part of Paris near Mason Remey's home where meetings could be held more comfortably for Abu'l-Faḍl.[72]

Paris had at this time the most important Bahá'í community in Europe and many persons who embraced the Bahá'í Faith there would later become famous for their stalwart service to the Faith. Most of the Bahá'ís of Paris in those early years were expatriate Americans.[73] During Abu'l-Faḍl's visit, about 30 people became Bahá'ís through him.[74] He hosted classes for some time, which Laura also attended. His stay gave Laura ample opportunity to discuss philosophical and religious matters.[75] She was with him most of the time and accompanied him and his translator to meetings.[76]

Ali-Kuli Khan had also arrived in Paris at the end of May 1901 and together with Anton Haddad helped with translations for Abu'l-Faḍl. He had traveled to Paris at the request of 'Abdu'l-Bahá.[77] The Master had put him in touch with the Bahá'ís of Paris, including Laura and her cousin Ellen, whom Khan had met in 'Akká.[78] The spirit in Paris in those days was described by Agnes Alexander: 'An atmosphere of pure light pervaded the Paris meetings, so much so that one was transported, as it were, from the world of man to that of God.'[79] Another American Bahá'í, Juliet Thompson, wrote about her experiences with the Paris Bahá'ís:

> That Paris group was so deeply united in love and faith; May, Lua, Laura and Khán, these four especially so inspired, so carried away, so intoxicated with love for the Master: our great teacher, Mírzá Abu'l-Faḍl, so heavenly wise – that those days were the days of miracle, of all but incredible confirmations.[80]

Abu'l-Faḍl's stay in Paris lasted three months. He left towards the end of July 1901 for America.[81]

Natalie and Ali-Kuli Khan in Paris

An interesting incident happened during that time that involved Laura, Natalie and Khan. Laura was hoping that her sister would be drawn to the Faith, despite her lack of interest or inclination towards religion, so Laura introduced Natalie to Khan. But Natalie, who was uninterested in spiritual matters, was attracted to Khan only because of his attraction and yearnings for 'Abdu'l-Bahá and the long months he had spent in 'Akká. One day, Laura asked Khan to accept an invitation to attend Natalie's dinner party, which he accepted out of respect for Laura's wishes. He wanted to introduce Natalie to Bahá'í principles.

Arriving at the party, Khan felt shy and overwhelmed. He was not accustomed to these types of parties with beautiful young women. Laura and Ellen tried to break the ice by joining him as he entered the house. He tried to control his feelings during the evening and not say much, but then at the dinner table tears poured down his cheeks as he shared his experiences of 'Abdu'l-Bahá. Even this display of emotion had no effect on Natalie, and during the whole evening she did not show any reaction. The only comments she made later were about Khan's teeth and dark brown hair. She later wrote a long poem to Khan that she had composed herself.[82]

With Abu'l-Faḍl in the United States

Laura returned to the United States at the end of the summer of 1901. Abu'l-Faḍl arrived in the United States around that time as well and was greeted with much excitement. As an academic of high repute in Islamic scholarship in Cairo, he attracted great attention from the press and others, as well as from the Bahá'í community.[83] He spent a few days in New York and then, accompanied by Laura and Ethel Rosenberg, who had also traveled to the United States, they went to Chicago.[84] Laura and Ethel helped him settle there. Haddad translated for him and when he had to return to Syria it was Khan who acted as his translator.[85] Khan, who was in New York with them, joined Abu'l-Faḍl in Chicago at the request of the Master.[86]

Bahá'ís from Chicago and nearby cities came to Abu'l-Faḍl's classes, where he worked from notes to answer questions that had been sent by mail or were asked during class. He also spoke at weekly meetings in downtown Chicago, at which he never referred to notes.

The early 1900s were the formative years for the Bahá'í community in the United States. The first converts to the Faith were mostly former Protestants, and the majority were middle and upper-middle class professionals.[87] The number of Bahá'ís in the United States in 1899 was about 1,400, and half of them lived in Chicago.[88] The Bahá'í Faith was first introduced into the country in 1893 at the World's Parliament of

Religions in Chicago when it was mentioned in an address made by Rev Henry H. Jessup.[89] In 1894 Dr Ibrahim Kheiralla (1849–1929), a physician in Lebanon who had originally been a Maronite Christian from a mountain village of Ottoman Lebanon, was the first to systematically hold classes on the Bahá'í Faith. He met the Faith in Egypt through Ḥájí 'Abdu'l-Karím Ṭihrání in 1889, became a Bahá'í in Cairo in 1890, came to the United States in 1892 and went to 'Akká with the first group of pilgrims in 1898, which is when he met 'Abdu'l-Bahá.[90] However, Kheiralla represented the Faith in his own way, which was often inaccurate. He questioned the authority of 'Abdu'l-Bahá and later separated from the Bahá'í Faith. Besides Kheiralla, there were other Eastern Bahá'ís in the United States, such as Mírzá Asadu'lláh Iṣfahání, who had come as a personal emissary of 'Abdu'l-Bahá.[91]

While in Chicago, Laura gave a talk about her experiences visiting 'Akká and meeting 'Abdu'l-Bahá. Then Laura and Ethel managed to travel to California to visit Phoebe Hearst.[92] While on the west coast Laura constantly checked to make sure that all was well with Abu'l-Faḍl.[93]

Laura Back in Washington with Abu'l-Faḍl

After some time in Chicago, Abu'l-Faḍl was to travel to Washington, D.C. Laura sent a telegram to Abu'l-Faḍl and Khan to inform them that she had found quarters for them in Washington on De Sales (also spelt DeSales or Desales) Street, which was only one block long.[94]

It was Laura and her mother who financed Abu'l-Faḍl's trip. They hosted him in Washington, where he took up residence with Khan at a boarding house in a fashionable section of the city as the guest of the Barney family.[95] Their rooms were on the fourth floor of an apartment house. Since Abu'l-Faḍl could not tolerate noise, he changed his residence several times during his stay in Washington.[96]

It seems that Laura's mother had already met Khan, perhaps in New York. While she was still in Europe, Laura asked her mother to meet him.

> Mother Dear,
>
> I am more than happy to be able to ask Ali Kuli Khan to meet you. I admire him immensely for he has such a fine intel[l]igence – large heart and rock like faith.

I am sure that you will both have the greatest pleasure in knowing one another. And I only wish that I could be there too . . . I am in wild haste – I cannot speak too kindly about Ali Kuli Khan – but you will see for yourself.[97]

In Washington, Abu'l-Faḍl gave public talks and after a few months he started having study classes, which took place twice a week in the afternoon. A few people were invited to attend, among them Laura.[98] According to one of the attendees, Abu'l-Faḍl

explained with the greatest care & exactness the Prophecies of our Bible – explaining the use of the different symbols which are current in the orient, & of which we in the Occident are unfamiliar & have little or no knowledge of, & gave us a college course as he termed it.[99]

Abu'l-Faḍl also gave a series of talks every evening in the library of the Barney's home.[100] The Barneys were living at 1626 Rhode Island Avenue N.W., an elegant neighborhood of Washington. Many society women came to his talks for instruction.[101] 'His Eastern garb of flowing white robes and turban around his long white hair were an exotic sight for Washingtonians at the turn of the century.' It was reported that 'eyebrows were raised' by his presentations of Bahá'u'lláh's teachings, especially that 'there is one God, or first cause, for all mankind and that God's divine teachings are revealed through many prophets. These beliefs were a far cry from traditional religion of the time and, to the dismay of many prominent clergy, Fazl [Abu'l-Faḍl] was attracting some of Washington's most prominent and wealthy churchgoers.'[102] He also gave a lecture at the Fete Day of 'Abdu'l-Bahá – now known as the Day of the Covenant, a Bahá'í holy day recognizing the appointment of 'Abdu'l-Bahá as the Center of Bahá'u'lláh's Covenant – celebrated for the first time on November 26 at Laura's home.[103]

Laura was actively involved with the local Bahá'ís as well as was being in touch with 'Abdu'l-Bahá. She was aware of the growing strength of the Bahá'í community in Washington and wrote to 'Abdu'l-Bahá about establishing a board of consultation. She received a Tablet from Him in response:

As for thy question regarding the formation of a 'consultative assembly': instead of this, gather thou together a radiant, spiritual group of souls, whose single aim shall be to spread abroad the divine sweet savours, and give to this assemblage the title of 'Spiritual Assembly'. In this manner the need for appointing members is avoided, and they that are first in service are first in favour before the Lord.[104]

In addition to classes and talks, Abu'l-Faḍl with the help of Laura took responsibility for the most important task of writing about the Faith for western readers. Abu'l-Faḍl spent much of that year writing the book *The Baháí Proofs* for the American audience in accordance with instructions from the Master.[105] He 'wrote in Arabic, in a style and depth which he alone could command'.[106] Khan translated everything he wrote. Laura was instrumental in getting this book published, the first English edition being published in New York by J. W. Pratt, in April 1902.[107]

Abu'l-Faḍl had asked Khan to make sure that his gratitude to Laura Barney was recorded in the introduction to his book. Khan was asked to write in the 1902 English edition, in which he referred to Laura as Miss B. in his Translator's Preface:

> . . . yet, were it not for the untiring efforts of the brilliant Pearl, the verdant Leaf, the revered Miss B. (May God increase her honor and excellence!), not one of the pages of my compositions would have been written during this arduous journey. For it is an evident fact to the learned, and notably to those who are writers, that a man of advanced age, and weak constitution, who, in less than one year has traveled from Egypt to Syria, thence to Europe and America, hurrying from city to city, moving from place to place, addressing meetings two or three times a week, continually speaking to people of different tastes, both ignorant and learned, prejudiced and unprejudiced, would not be able to produce over two thousand pages upon philosophical subjects, – containing explanations of the most intricate and abstruse points, proofs, arguments, and interpretations of Scriptural verses, – were it not for the kind efforts and thoughtfulness of such an excellent soul. She has taken much trouble and labor for the writer, in order that his works may be published.[108]

Years later Laura wrote: 'Yes, I had the privilege also of having *The Baháʼí Proofs* printed in the United States and had the good fortune to secure M. Howard McNutt to supervise the publication.' She described her respect and admiration for this scholar, Abuʼl-Faḍl, and how her explanations would give 'an idea of how and why an outstanding oriental teacher and a young American girl became appreciative friends through the Cause they both loved'.[109] Concerning *The Baháʼí Proofs*, one American Baháʼí scholar wrote:

> When it was published in 1902, Americans acquired their first thorough and accurate account of the Baháʼí Faith. The first part, which had been written as a separate work, provided biographies of the Báb, Baháʼuʼlláh, and ʻAbduʼl-Bahá and an excellent summary of Baháʼí history to 1900, information that hitherto had been available to Westerners only in fragmented, incomplete and inaccurate form. Abuʼl-Faḍl included detailed comparative information on Islam and Christianity. The missionaries of the Syrian Protestant College had translated into Arabic a good scholarly history of Christianity and Mírzá Abuʼl-Faḍl had given it a thorough and rigorous reading.[110]

Khan began to worry about Abuʼl-Faḍl's health that year in Washington, as the scholar was living on only tea, tobacco and a few crackers a day. Since it was Laura who had asked ʻAbduʼl-Bahá to send Abuʼl-Faḍl to the United States as her guest, Khan decided to ask her and her mother, whom he much respected, for advice. He knew that Abuʼl-Faḍl also held Mrs Barney in high regard and would listen to her suggestions. Therefore, Khan went to Laura first and told her how difficult it was to manage him for his own welfare.[111]

One day Abuʼl-Faḍl fell unconscious on the floor. Obviously, he needed to eat. However, Khan had promised Abuʼl-Faḍl that he would not discuss his diet or recommend he take time off to rest. Laura urged great caution in the matter, otherwise Abuʼl-Faḍl would say that Khan had broken his promise. They decided to consult with her mother. The next day Mrs Barney's cook prepared a chicken for Abuʼl-Faḍl. Alice took it to him and, not wanting to go against her wishes, he ate some of it.[112]

Abuʼl-Faḍl spent almost three years in Washington and also traveled to New York City and to Eliot, Maine.[113] He was old, delicate and suffering from the climate, which is why 'Abdu'l-Bahá asked him to return to the Middle East.[114] His departure from America was mid-December of 1904.[115]

Laura's Mother and Her Activities

Alice Barney may first have learned about the Bahá'í Faith from her daughter Laura. Or, it is also possible that she had heard about it earlier from her friend Phoebe Hearst, who had homes in Washington, D.C. and Paris. Alice was in Paris when Phoebe arrived there on her way to 'Akká in the fall of 1898 and on her stopover after that trip in the spring of the following year.

Alice opened her home to Bahá'í gatherings soon after Laura and she returned to Washington, D.C. in 1901. She paid Abu'l-Faḍl's travel expenses and those of his stay in Washington. Alice was particularly attracted to the Faith's progressive social teachings and spiritual principles. Her appreciation for the Bahá'í Cause grew 'because of its broad teachings of tolerance, its humanitarianism, its love of beautiful and fruitful action'.[116]

Some early Bahá'ís did not see any conflict in being a Bahá'í and a Christian at the same time. One author wrote: 'Many still considered themselves to be Christians who, while under no compulsion to eschew their connections with their previous forms of worship or religious activities, had accommodated a broader, more modern interpretation of doctrine.'[117] This attitude was fairly common among early Bahá'ís, both in the East and the West, and it changed only with gentle counsel from Shoghi Effendi, who emphasized the independent identity of the Faith. Recognition of this fact, and a gradually increasing understanding of Bahá'í history and the writings of Bahá'u'lláh, resulted in Bahá'ís withdrawing from other religious bodies. Thus it may have been that Alice, like so many others of the time, may not have fully understood the Faith.[118] Her religious identity was Episcopalian. But, according to her biographer, Kling, 'Of the two, the Bahai faith with its emphasis upon women's equality was appealing to her. Moreover, the faith's Persian roots appealed to her sense of the exotic.'[119]

Later in life Alice undertook many initiatives based on the principles of the Faith, such as advocating for peace, taking care of the poor, the equality of men and women and supporting women's movements. She let the National American Women's Suffrage Association use her house in Washington as its headquarters.[120] She opened her home to meetings that included people of different races including African-Americans with absolute equality.[121] She also depicted characters from Bahá'í history in various art forms, such as her play *The Woman*, a series of tableaux based on famous women from history, including Sappho, Esther, Joan of Arc, Jane Austen and Ṭáhirih (Qurratu'l-'Ayn, c. 1814–52).[122] Ṭáhirih was a Persian disciple of the Báb, a preeminent Islamic scholar, a poet, an advocate of social reform and a women's rights martyr.

In early 1902 Alice was the vice president and a member of the executive committee of the Society of Washington Artists. The works of new and established artists were displayed together at the annual exhibitions organized by this society. For that year's exhibition she submitted a pastel painting on canvas called *Medusa*. She had based it on a photograph of Laura, who was one of her mother's favorite models, in costume, taken at Bar Harbor. Alice's biographer found the painting to be the most jarring entry in the exhibition. The 'compelling head study of the mythological monster' in vivid shades of blue and gray highlighted by strokes of red chalk, was 'disturbing because it was as much a realistic portrait as it was a treatment of an often seen Symbolist theme', made the more powerful and immediate by her use of her daughter as the model.[123]

The critics were divided over whether 'Medusa' was even art. One wrote that the portrait was beautiful and realistic but, hearing no sound, the viewer was horror-struck. Another critic found the painting to be 'weird', 'too horrible and too well done to be other than an outrage of the highest principles or aims of true art'. Indeed, this critic found it to have violated not only the aims of true art but also the genius of the painter.[124] Regardless of the painting's merits, 'Alice had confounded Washington's little arts world with her entry'.[125]

Laura, Her Conversion and May Bolles

Unlike some Bahá'ís, such as Kheiralla, who later turned away from the Faith, Laura stayed firm. A Bahá'í in Washington wrote to May Bolles, Laura's spiritual mother: 'Dear lovely Elsa [Laura] is very firm in the love of the Master – and she and I are trying to unite and work for the Cause . . .'[126] An American woman who became a Bahá'í through May

Bolles in Paris and met Laura in the United States mentioned Laura in a letter to May: 'Elsa [Laura] Barney spent an afternoon with us . . . she was lovely – she made my family love her as well as the believers.'[127]

Laura was grateful to May Bolles for having introduced her to the Faith. During those early years, Laura told May how much she felt that a new light had been reflected into her life. In a letter written while she was returning to the United States from a trip, Laura acknowledged how much she owed May for teaching her the Faith:

> It is your sweet illuminated being that led me to that lofty resting place, and through eternity my voice will ring forth my thanks. When I look at the immense ocean, the thought that it is but as a drop of water to the Creator, makes me dimly realize His endless Being.[128]

Laura found the only way to repay May was by teaching others in turn. In a letter to May, she said she felt there was a great deal of work for her to do, and she was happy to be giving a talk over the weekend.[129] Laura was grateful to May for her 'lovely spirit' too.[130] She wrote to May, 'You are ever shining in the heaven of my thoughts. You are ever growing & living in the garden of my heart.'[131]

While Laura was in Washington in 1901 she corresponded with May, whom she addressed as 'Violet Star',[132] and kept her updated with her activities. On one occasion she wrote:

> Violet Star,
>   Every new soul I teach I always feel it is your tender voice saying to my spirit – Elsa [Laura], it is the true life that I have given you to give . . . How glad I will be to see you all in Paris. Dear one, I feel that everything is going well, how could it be helped, when you are ever praying for your children.[133]

In another letter to May, Laura thanked God and said she believed that it was only through action that she felt nearer to the Beloved.[134] She told May that she had had some quiet time to teach and read to some believers and that she needed patience and prudence before sharing the message and the teachings of the Faith with others.[135] Laura continued admiring and adoring May Bolles, whose impact on her contemporaries was enormous. Moreover, she believed that it was May's fragility, her luminous and mysterious beauty that glowed with a soft light that attracted people to her.[136] May symbolized the love of the Cause to those early believers.

Perhaps it was while Laura was in 'Akká that she wrote to May, thanking her for her kind words and news of her work in Paris. She mentioned that she loved that city as the spot where she had received spiritual birth. Laura shared the news of the friends – that they were all striving to attain the good pleasure of the Master.[137]

It was around that time, 1902 or 1903, that Laura discovered that May had fallen ill. As soon as Laura heard the news, she wrote to May's husband, William Sutherland Maxwell, in Montreal. He and May had married in London on May 8, 1902. Out of her deep love and respect for May, Laura offered to help and even suggested that she go to Montreal to do so.

> I write to ask you to let me know if you think I could do anything for her. It would be very easy for me to go to Montreal and stay in a hotel for a couple of weeks if you think it would do her any good.
>
> I know you will not feel that I am intruding, for you above all others can understand my deep love for May. If I am to come, just wire me . . .[138]

Some years later, when Laura was again in 'Akká, she wrote to May and sent her greetings from the Master and the ladies of the Holy Family. Laura reflected that the last few months had given her peace and conviction, and she mentioned that she was grateful to May for leading her 'to the Water of Life'. She wished that May was with her, anticipating the time when she could share with May what she had received from the Master. Laura wondered if there was a way she could be of service to May.[139] In yet another letter, Laura promised to bring the Master's words to May. She stated that her 'path is lit by God's mercy and she is happy' and she had 'the priceless gem of existences – love for our Lord'.[140]

False News Reports and Effects on Laura's Family

It must have been difficult for Laura to return to the Washington society after her two pilgrimages to 'Akká. She did not mind supporting and accompanying an elderly oriental man wearing an *abá* in the streets of Washington. She believed wholeheartedly in Bahá'u'lláh's teachings, such as the oneness of God, the unity of religions, gender equality and the elimination of racial prejudice. And her faith never wavered. It must have been her firm belief that kept her going. She worked hard to further the Bahá'í Faith in Washington with her characteristic dedication and vision.

While in Washington Laura stayed with her parents. It was around that time that numerous newspaper articles reported her conversion to the Bahá'í Faith. Because of her family's social status, there were constant newspaper articles about the Barneys. The family's every action was followed closely in society pages of Washington's newspapers and others across the United States. The press chronicled their every move. Some articles gave incorrect information while others mocked Laura and her family. Only rarely did newspapers give accurate information. The Washington media was not particularly sympathetic when it learned of Laura's adoption of this new religion from the East and Alice's support for it. Of particular fascination to the news media was the presence of Abu'l-Faḍl in Washington. Laura and her family continued to be shocked by these newspaper articles and reports.

In 1901 *The Idaho Falls Times,* the *Greelay Tribune* of Colorado and the *Grand Valley* of Utah printed the same article under the heading 'Babist of Persia'.[141] They incorrectly named Natalie Barney as the one who had converted, reporting that Mrs Barney and Natalie had adopted Babism and that Natalie had donated all her jewelry to the poor.

An article was published in March 1902 in *The Washington Post* with the heading 'New Religious Cult' that was almost correct in its report on the Bahá'í Faith and Laura's conversion:

> Miss Alice [Laura] Barney, who is a Behaist, as are other members of A. C. Barney's family, says that at Acca one sees demonstrated, both in the family and the religious life, the harmony and love which is one of the pivotal principles of the teachings of Behaism. Miss Barney also states that while disciples do not give up their perspective creeds, each rises above all creed through the spirit of love. In speaking of what she considers the proof that Abbas Effendi is an inspired messenger of God, Miss Barney said: 'A true prophet's predictions are fulfilled, and such are also able to fulfill their own prophecies. Abbas Effendi is able to give both these evidences.'[142]

Also in March 1902, another short-lived gossip newspaper, *The Washington Mirror*, printed an article focusing on Laura's conversion to the Bahá'í Faith, calling it the family's 'latest fad' and giving a condescending impression of Abu'l-Faḍl's lessons: 'Dear knows, our American girls have done worse things in the past than to have embraced the teachings of Behah Ullah . . . Preachings of Mírzá Abul Fazel Gulpaygan may do good in its own peculiar way.' It concluded that it was perhaps better 'after all to spend the time in prayer and fasting than inhaling the perfume of green carnations in an incense laden room'.[143] Much to the dismay of the local clergy, as Alice's biographer points out, the teachings of the eastern scholar that there is only one God for all humankind and that His guidance is revealed through a number of prophets were attracting prominent and wealthy people.[144]

Two months later *The Washington Mirror* printed another inaccurate and condescending article about the Bahá'í Faith, depicting Laura as a medium conducting séances to contact Bahá'u'lláh while 'etherealized' in a 'receptive trance'.[145] The article ended with the address where the 'séances' were taking place, the result being large numbers of people turning up there to jeer at those attending.

One can easily imagine how Albert reacted to all of this – he was furious. He had an image to uphold and was highly sensitive to public opinion and fearful of the damaging effects of anything that was said or written about him or his family. He quickly took action to limit the damage, buying out the lease on Abu'l-Faḍl's rented house and stopping his lessons.[146]

Albert was also incredibly angry with Natalie, who had published a small soft cover book of poetry *Quelques Portraits – Sonnets de Femmes* (Some Portraits – Sonnets of Women), with poems dedicated to women. Alice had drawn the illustrations for this chapbook.[147]

Albert's ongoing anger with his wife, Natalie and Laura probably contributed further to his poor health. Having suffered one heart attack in mid-1900, he had a second in the spring of 1902 and, taking the advice of his doctors, sailed to Europe with Natalie a second time to recuperate in the healing waters of Nauheim.[148]

Further salacious news articles about the family and Laura were printed later in the year, including 'Miss Barney & Babism' on September 28 in the *Sun*; 'Rich Aid Behaist Sect' on September 29 as the headline of the *Chicago Tribune*; and 'Miss Barney & Babism' on

October 2 in the *Kansas City Star*.[149] Laura was not at all happy at the publication of these articles and the ignorance they revealed.[150] Far from weakening her devotion to the Faith, her perseverance was strengthened and she became an even more staunch believer. She was, however, deeply concerned about her father's health and wrote to Natalie, offering to travel to Europe: 'Natalie Dear: Is there anything that I can do for Father, from your letter he appeared most sad and ill. If I can help him, please let me know.'[151]

Death of Her Father

Albert's health deteriorated while he was in Monte Carlo and Natalie, who was in Paris, rushed to see her father on his deathbed. When she arrived, her father had already passed away. Albert died on December 5, 1902 at the age of 52. Alice and Laura, who were in America, were unable to be at his bedside. Laura had received a cable from her sister with the news of his passing.[152]

Laura had asked Abu'l-Faḍl and Khan about the Bahá'í teaching on cremation. She had also written to 'Abdu'l-Bahá on the subject and had asked if cremation would be acceptable, given the many advantages espoused by western scientists. 'Abdu'l-Bahá had responded to her in a Tablet in which He explained the order of transferences and journeys within the chain of life in the system of divine creation, which is 'mighty and without flaw'.

> And just as the composition, the formation, and growth and development of the physical body have come about by degrees, so too must its decomposition and dispersal be gradual. If the disintegration be rapid, this will cause an overlapping and a slackening in the chain of transferences, and this discontinuity will impair the universal relationships within the chain of created things.[153]

'Abdu'l-Bahá explained that physical bodies decompose into microscopic organisms which, according to the 'divine order and the driving forces of nature . . . will have an effect on the life of the universe, and will pass into other forms'. In other words, cremation converts the body to ashes and mineral form, and this process circumvents 'its natural journey through the chain of all created things'. 'Abdu'l-Bahá emphasized that the natural order must be honored, and that all creatures must proceed according to the natural order, divine rule and the laws of God 'so that no marring nor impairment may affect the essential relationships which arise out of the inner realities of created things. This is why, according to the law of God, we are bidden to bury the dead.'

'Abdu'l-Bahá also recognized how slowly family and friends accept the death of a loved one, as the earthly form is treasured. 'Never can the heart agree to look on the cherished body of a friend, a father, a mother, a brother, a child, and see it instantly fall to nothing – and this is an exigency of love.'[154] Laura learned that cremation was to be avoided except in special cases such a general epidemic.

Laura cabled a message to Natalie as soon as she received news of the passing of her father and she asked her not to cremate him but it was too late. Albert's body had been sent to Père Lachaise Cemetery in Paris for cremation. Natalie brought his ashes back to the United States, and Alice and Laura, wearing fashionable and elegant black dresses, went to New York to receive them. They then prepared for the burial of Albert's ashes in his hometown, Dayton.

Albert's funeral service took place at the home of his brother Eugene J. Barney on January 26, 1903, with only Albert's brothers, Alice, Laura and Laura's maternal cousin Ellen in attendance.[155] A number of newspapers printed respectful notices of Albert's death. *The Washington Post* reported among its Obituaries that he had been educated at Brown University and had been a prominent person in Washington society, mentioning his membership of several clubs in New York, Cincinnati and Washington, D.C.[156]

Another newspaper reported in its In Memoriam section: 'Mr Barney was a man of exquisite discrimination: of cultivated appreciations and of interesting personal attributes. He had the quality of refined sympathy which adds to best touch of gentle manners, and to younger people, to nieces and nephews he was a source of inspiration in the formation of taste and the guiding of their activities.'[157]

When Albert's will was executed, an article in *The Washington Post* reported that his estate was to be held in a trust with its income (except for his horses, carriages and stables) divided equally between his wife and two daughters.[158] Alice could draw out her portion of the principal after a year; Laura and Natalie would receive their portions when they reached the age of 30. It also reported that Albert's will included a statement that during his life he had always supported charities and he wished for his wife and daughters to continue the same practice, although he did not make this a condition of their inheritance.[159]

When Alice learned the extent of her inheritance, she realized that Albert's claim that she would bankrupt the family by building Studio House on Sheridan Circle was unfounded. He was an extremely wealthy man at his time of death, with over three million dollars in property and cash in banks. According to a Dayton newspaper, Albert left three million dollars for Alice and his daughters; and in 1902, there were no income or inheritance taxes.[160] Natalie's biographer, Susan Rodriguez, wrote that the estate was worth about nine million dollars (over $266 million in 2020). Either sum would certainly provide a 'considerable yearly income divided equally among them'.[161]

Before the passing of her father, Laura had called herself Elsa and sometimes Alice and Elsie, and used any of these names as signatures. After his passing, she started using the name Laura. Whether she preferred the name Elsa or Laura is not clear, nor is it clear whether she wanted to make her father happy by using Elsa while he was alive or if she wanted to honor him by using her given name Laura after his death. One account mentioned that she had been named as Laura in her father's will.[162] The author has not seen any letters from her father to her or his will so cannot verify how he addressed her. However, she did use Laura after the death of her father.

Keeping Her Mother Company in the United States

Laura stayed with her mother in Washington after the passing of her father. Life went on and her mother continued her painting. In mid-February of 1903 her mother submitted another pastel portrait of Laura to the annual juried exhibition of the Society of Washington Arts.[163] The show was successful and attendance increased greatly that year.

The following month Alice and Laura moved to Studio House on Sheridan Circle at 2306 Massachusetts Avenue. Alice had been involved in the architectural design of the house and in the smallest details of the work undertaken during its construction. Later, she designed its interior. A prominent architect of the time, Waddy Butler Wood, had built Studio House in the Spanish Colonial Revival architectural style. Compared to the imposing houses in its vicinity, Studio House was rather small and simple with an exterior of stucco and stone and a red-tile roof. The exterior of the house was Spanish Mission and the interior a mixture of American and European, as well as Art Nouveau. She filled the house with her paintings and those by her friends and with ornate furniture, oriental rugs and decorative objects.[164] Red damask fabrics were used on the first-floor walls and gold damask on the second.[165]

Alice organized a party at the new house, inviting the builders and workmen as well as the architect. Alice had hung her paintings on the walls and had a small concert of chamber music and singing, and a drama with Laura reciting excerpts of Victor Hugo's writings in French.[166] Alice took the opportunity of this first party to make the point that art and culture should not be elitist but were for everyone to enjoy.

The Washington Mirror reported in a long article news of the family and their move to Studio House: 'everything appertaining to the Barney's inclines to the unique and this entertainment planned for the "artisans" and their families proved an oasis in the social desert of the week.' Not all the workmen could be accommodated at this first reception so another was to be given later in the year. The article continued:

> However, of recent years, Mrs Barney and Miss Alice [Laura] have joined a theosophic cult known as the 'Babbists'. The brotherhood of man is part of this creed and social barriers are not recognized, Mrs Barney has allowed the believers to use her drawing-rooms for their meetings for nearly a year, and the people represented are not classed among the smart set. These meetings are presided over by a venerable old man of most striking aspect, a personation (*sic*), in fact, of some of the weird Indian priests so graphically described by Kipling. This man is known as the 'Master' and Mrs Barney and Miss Alice [Laura] spent hours daily, drinking in the mystic lore of Ind.[167]

The mother and daughter decided to spend that summer in Onteora, an artists' resort in the Catskill Mountains in New York, so that they could have ample time to mourn in a picturesque environment.[168] Writers and artists lived Onteora in a relatively simple manner. Laura spent her free time reading her books.[169] It was about this time that Alice painted a striking portrait of Abu'l-Faḍl, as well as one of Ali-Kuli Khan.[170]

Late that year of 1903 Natalie came to Washington to spend time with her mother, who was still grieving over the loss of her husband. Even though Alice had an unhappy marriage, she had spent almost three decades with Albert. It was soon after Natalie's arrival that Laura left for Egypt to meet with the Bahá'ís there and then went to 'Akká to spend more time with 'Abdu'l-Bahá. This was Laura's third visit to the Middle East.

While Laura was with her mother in Washington, she may have received from 'Abdu'l-Bahá a Tablet (partially excerpted below) before her departure.

O Maidservant of God!

If thou knewest how intently Abdu'l-Baha is entreating the Abha Kingdom for its help and favor, surely thou wouldst, out of sheer joy and delight, develop feathers and, with outspread wings, soar to the summit of ecstasy and exultation. I beseech God that at every instant thou mayest glimpse a fresh light of divine bounty and attract enduring confirmations. O thou beloved maidservant of Bahá, I will henceforth address thee as Amatu'l-Bahá [Handmaiden of Bahá] to signify that thou hast attained a special rank and that this title will be a crown of beneficence upon thy head, whose gems and pearls will shine forevermore! Reflect upon future centuries and ages and thou wilt know how precious a gift this is.[171]

After advising Laura that her services were accepted and approved at the threshold of God, 'Abdu'l-Bahá wrote that there were differences among some of the believers in New York. Would she go there with the 'utmost joy and fragrances of the confirmation of the Kingdom of God to remove those differences through the power of the Spirit and bring about perfect love among the Bahá'ís?'[172] Then in His own hand at the bottom of the Tablet He wrote in Persian:

O maidservant of Bahá! The Power of the Holy Spirit is confirmatory: Be thou assured! At every moment, I see heavenly Bounties, in the world of Spirit, in their behalf. Turn thy face into the Kingdom of God at early dawn, and thou wilt find 'Abdu'l-Bahá thy companion.[173]

'Abdu'l-Bahá hoped that Laura would organize Bahá'í meetings and teach about her faith. He had written a letter to her that said: 'I hope that the maid-servant of Beha (Miss Barney) has already organized and established the meetings of Washington.'[174]

Some years later her friend Mariam Haney recalled a series of events. She reminded Laura of the Bahá'í gatherings at the home of Arthur Dodge in New York City starting in 1900 and continuing for many years thereafter, where Laura had met Mariam in 1903. It seems that there was some discussion between them of a certain lady who was circulating a silly story about Christ being a Russian Jewish boy in Kansas.[175]

In one of her letters Mariam explained how Laura at one point wrote to 'Abdu'l-Bahá asking about the station of Jesus the Christ.[176] In reply, 'Abdu'l-Bahá revealed a Tablet that was sent to Laura and was later published. Mariam believed that this was the Tablet:

> Verily that Infant is born and exists and there will appear from His Cause a wonder which thou wilt hear in future. Thou shalt see Him with the most perfect form, most great gift, most complete perfection, most great power and strongest might! His Face glistened a glistening whereby the horizons are illumined. Therefore, forget not this account as long as thou art living, for as much as there are signs for it in the passing centuries and ages.[177]

It was around that time that the following Tablet was also revealed for Laura, which may have been the answer to her question and to which Mariam refers:

> As to [what thou hast heard concerning] the child born from Russian parentage, this is pure imagination. Yea, certain persons shall in this divine dispensation produce heavenly children and such children shall promulgate the teachings of the Beauty of ABHA and serve His great Cause. Through a heavenly power and spiritual confirmation, they shall be enabled to promote the Word of God and to diffuse the fragrances of God. These children are neither Oriental nor Occidental, neither Asiatic nor American, neither European nor African, but they are of the Kingdom; their native home is heaven and their resort is the Kingdom of ABHA. This is but truth and there is naught after truth save superstitions (or fancy).[178]

Laura Helping Atabak after Khan's Intervention

Laura and Ellen went to New York in October 1903. This trip may have been in response to the Master's request that she visit with the Bahá'ís of New York to assist them in overcoming internal difficulties. During this period, the Persian ambassador in Washington received a cable from Atabak, the deposed premier of Persia, stating that he would be arriving in New York from San Francisco on his way to Mecca for the Muslim pilgrimage.[179] Khan, who was serving as a translator and secretary at the Persian Legation, had also served as interpreter for Atabak several years earlier in Tehran. Atabak had arrived in San Francisco out of funds and the Persian Ambassador to the US had to arrange payment for the trip to New York. Learning about Atabak's financial difficulties, Khan consulted with Laura and suggested that as a gesture of friendship from the American Bahá'ís, a gift to Atabak might well be helpful to the Persian Bahá'í community later on, if and when Atabak and his people regained power.[180]

Khan went from Washington to New York. He was up early the day that Atabak was supposed to depart. Atabak's party needed to leave quickly for the ship or else they would miss it and be unable to reach Mecca in time for the Haj. But first Khan needed to introduce Laura and Ellen to Atabak, so he rapidly arranged a hurried visit in Atabak's suite. During the conversation Laura gave Atabak an envelope containing between eight hundred and a thousand dollars. Atabak was grateful for this kind gesture and thoughtfulness.[181] Khan then rushed the men and their luggage to the steamer.

The Story of the Exchanges Between Laura and Ali-Kuli Khan

Laura had first met Ali-Kuli Khan in 1900 in Haifa, then again in Chicago and later in Washington, D.C. By this time they had become close friends and saw each other often. Khan had little time to develop personal friendships, especially when in Washington, but he did see Laura every day when she went to see Abu'l-Faḍl and to attend classes. Undoubtedly observing all social proprieties outwardly, in Laura's mind it was not only perfectly reasonable but necessary for her to spend much time with Abu'l-Faḍl and Khan while they were in Washington. Perhaps Laura felt strongly drawn to Khan for some reason. Khan's daughter,

Marzieh Gail, wrote, 'I remember father's telling me that Laura was quite interested in him, & he spoke of seeing her one evening after she'd been to a dance at the White House. Ergo, it must have been somewhere in Washington, D.C. and I know it was before his marriage (1904).'[182]

Several times Laura invited Khan to her parents' home to teach her Persian and she spent considerable time with him. They saw each other frequently and she in turn would encourage him to share his troubles and ask her advice.[183] Marzieh later described their relationship in her memoir of her father.

> She was a very wise person, looked at a problem from all sides, and then offered a solution. She was young, dark, and strikingly beautiful (as her mother's portraits of her show) and a great comfort to him, but the love she inspired in him was, he said many years later on, that of a child for its all-wise grandmother.[184]

Laura left Washington for 'Akká at end of 1903, while Khan had been directed by the Master to remain in the United States.[185] It was during his stay in Washington that Khan met a young American girl from Boston by the name of Florence Breed. He had met her parents through a friend of his and was to teach them about the Faith.

Florence learned about Laura soon after meeting Khan. Florence wrote to Khan, 'very much with white gloves on', about the visit to New York of 'Miss B', most probably referring to Laura Barney, and 'Miss G', her cousin Ellen Goin: 'It was good of Miss B to come . . . She has a great deal of beauty and I found her greatly interesting. Miss G is so very pretty and charming . . . Miss B laughed and said she liked your enthusiasm, even if what you said were not always true, so I had to smile, as I then concluded she found me a disappointment . . .'[186]

Florence did not understand the relationship and was jealous of the friendship between Laura and Khan. She mentioned her jealousy in several letters, an emotion that is perhaps understandable from her perspective when one remembers Khan's many women admirers. However, her use of initials in her letters make it difficult to know exactly to whom she is referring. For example, in one letter to Khan she wrote, 'Can't you love Miss B more? I hope you can't.'[187] Khan must have reassured Florence that his love for Laura was platonic because Florence

wrote to Khan in February 1904, 'I fully understand that there is nothing dear heart between you and Miss B.'[188] The following month she
wrote:

> I only want to stay as near you this Summer as possible . . . my
> most beautiful joy – and I do not want to go away from you . . . I
> have just given up a chance to play Ophelia through the West, as a
> leading woman in a company . . . So this hopeless tragedy is avoided
> . . . You too will go to Acca ['Akká] some time; I wish you might go
> with Mírzá A[bu'l]-F[aḍl] or Miss B. How happy they must be.[189]

Florence may have had a confrontation that summer with Laura about
Khan, although as usual the identification of the woman is blurred. She
advised him 'to go to 'Akká while the lady in question [Miss B] is still
in America' and not to go to 'Akká, 'that Heaven' when she would be
there because 'Akká must be a 'Mecca of Peace' to his heart. Florence
wrote that 'tests are God's affairs' but that Miss B 'is *your* affair', and
the Master 'knows all things'.[190] Florence was concerned about Miss B
having a strong influence over Khan and asked him forthrightly if he
was in her power, and then reassured him that perhaps he was not.

Laura was in 'Akká most of 1904 and 1905, and shortly she after
arrived she wrote a letter to Khan that disturbed him. She suggested
that Khan would surely be happy to be in the Master's presence again
and to translate His replies to her questions. She had even asked Ellen,
who was back in America, to arrange Khan's travel. Marzieh Gail notes
that not only did Laura ask Ellen to reserve passage for Khan on a ship
to the Holy Land but Laura's mother, who went to 'Akká in 1905, also
wrote to Khan about this time from the Holy Land offering to pay all
his travel expenses.

Khan, however, had been instructed by 'Abdu'l-Bahá to remain in
the United States, and immediately wrote to Laura and Ellen that he
must obey Him and remain in America. But Laura was not to be dissuaded and she again wrote to Ellen asking her to assist in Khan's travel
arrangements, creating serious tests for Khan. He was also distraught at
the thought of leaving Florence, with whom he was deeply in love. He
and Florence discussed the situation and he then wrote to the Master
that if now 'Abdu'l-Bahá desired him to leave America, as Laura suggested, he would obey.

To complicate matters further, Khan's uncle in Persia wrote to Khan that he was aging, that his many children were still young and that wished Khan to return to Persia to help him and to marry his daughter. Surprisingly, Florence advised Khan to acquiesce with his family's wishes. To her surprise, Khan told her that he had already responded to his uncle that he could not leave at that time because he was preparing a book for publication. Even so, Florence told their daughter Marzieh Gail many years later that 'she felt as if an iron portal were clanging shut across her future'.[191] Khan and Florence would have to wait to learn 'Abdu'l-Bahá's wishes.

The response came soon. 'Abdu'l-Bahá wrote that Laura had wanted Khan to share her happiness in 'Akká but that His instructions to Khan that he stay and serve in America had not changed. Florence and Khan rejoiced.

Then two more letters came from Laura and Ellen still urging him to prepare to leave for 'Akká. Khan replied to Laura, again explaining what the Master had requested of him and writing that she should understand the situation.

Khan and Florence then made the decision that would prevent further obstacles from family and friends and that would also honor 'Abdu'l-Bahá's request that he stay in America. They got married. One evening they slipped away, marriage license in hand, and were married by a Protestant minister who lived nearby. It was the first marriage between a Persian Bahá'í and an American Bahá'í. One intention of this elopement was to spare her family the work and expense of a formal wedding. Another was to have some quiet time to themselves before the news spread, but that was not to be.

The very next morning local newspapers spread the word about this international marriage of a Boston society girl and a distinguished Persian. The story was picked up by newspapers around the nation. The newlyweds cabled the news to 'Abdu'l-Bahá, who was delighted and upon receiving the news clapped His hands and sent for sweets. He told the pilgrims and celebrated with them this fulfillment of Bahá'u'lláh's prophecy that one day East and West would embrace like two lovers. 'Abdu'l-Bahá blessed their marriage with a special wedding Tablet, wishing them a life of achievement in both the material and spiritual worlds. Soon after He sent a second Tablet, writing that even though He had already sent a wedding Tablet, this one was at the request of Laura.[192]

Laura's Visits in the Holy Land

In late 1903 Laura sailed to Europe then continued on to the Holy Land to spend time near the Master; she arrived in 'Akká in early 1904. Details of her travels between 1904 and 1906 are of great significance. Her visits to 'Akká during these two years became the center of Laura's life and the source of stimulation and inspiration.

The Master had asked Laura to come to 'Akká in 1904. She wrote about that visit years later:

> Five years ago, I arrived at Acca. I remained there but a few days, when 'Abdu'l-Bahá realized I had much to learn so little by little I received a fuller realization of his teachings. They are not of the Master but of the Spirit that speaks through him. This marvelous serenity in his difficulties is wonderful to behold.[193]

During this visit, Ethel Rosenberg assisted her as her secretary.[194] Ethel stayed in 'Akká from April 21 to December 24, 1904.[195] Laura wrote many years later:

> . . . it was on my third visit to 'Akká that I arrived with Miss Rosenberg. I spent the winter of 1904 there. I visited Egypt briefly and in the spring of 1905 paid a visit to my mother, after which we both returned to the Holy Land. I left again in the midsummer of 1905, returning to 'Akká in the fall of that year. I spent a part of that winter in Cairo and returned to 'Akká and Haifa by the end of spring [1906].[196]

It seems that Laura traveled to Port Said in March and again in July 1905.[197] Laura wrote many years later about her early travels to 'Akká and her impressions of the Master.

> Now just a few words about what those of us who saw the Master forty years ago (and even more) can remember, the simplicity and depth of the life that we all felt in the holy land in the early days. My first visit was a short one [1900]. The next a little longer [1901], when I was not even of the age when Bahá'ís are accepted into the Community now as adult members . . . 'Abdu'l-Bahá said at first

that I was to return to the United States with Mírzá Abu-l Fazl and that later I should go to Persia. But then He decided that I should remain in 'Akká, familiarizing myself there with the Persian language.[198]

Those early years of the 20th century were perhaps the most perilous for 'Abdu'l-Bahá during His many decades of Ottoman imprisonment. Still a prisoner of the Turkish government, He was confined within the walls of the prison city, 'subjected to continual surveillance, and confronted with the constant threat of further exile or of execution. It was 'dangerous for Him to receive visitors of any kind, let alone host prominent Western guests'.[199] It seems that when standing, one could see from the windows of the living quarters 'the military guard pacing up and down in front of some barrack-like buildings a little way from His house', which reminded visitors that 'the Master – unbelievable for one of His demeanor – was a prisoner'.[200] This period was described by Shoghi Effendi as 'the most troublous and dramatic of 'Abdu'l-Bahá's ministry'.[201] 'Yet 'Abdu'l-Bahá was determined to nurture the seeds of faith so recently germinated.'[202]

'Abdu'l-Bahá was faced with the hostility of Ottoman officials who believed the falsehoods that His enemies gave them, determined to destroy Him. A Commission of Enquiry was sent from Istanbul by the Ottomans to investigate the false charges, one of which was that the first stages of building the Shrine of the Báb was the erection of a military fortress. It was under these conditions that 'Abdu'l-Bahá was corresponding with Bahá'ís in Iran and with the new western believers, including Laura as she sought guidance and knowledge.

In 1904, an article in the *Washington Times* reported Laura's efforts to ease and improve the conditions of 'Abdu'l-Bahá in 'Akká. This was not confirmed and there are no records to corroborate it:

From the walled city of Akka, in far Syria, under the dominion of the Turkish Empire, there has come a story of the rescue from captivity of the head of the Babist faith by a prominent society girl of Washington. It is known that the Turkish government has realized its severe ruling against the person of Abbas Effendi, 'the greatest branch' of the Beha's faith, and that He is now permitted to visit the tomb of his father Beha Ullah, several miles beyond the walls of Akka, and to make short journeys in the neighboring parts of Syria, and rumor is insistent that the ottoman government has made these concessions because of the pressure brought by the European governments at the solicitation of Miss Laura Clifford Barney, of this city.

The story is neither affirmed nor denied, but it is known that Miss Barney made a round of the embassies and legations before her departure last spring. The British ambassador, Sir Mortimer Duran, and Chekib bey, the representative of the Turkish government, were among those visited. Since that time, Miss Barney has been in Akka and it is said that her efforts have been energetically continued and finally crowned with success . . .[203]

'Abdu'l-Bahá's conversations at this time concerned the approach of turmoil and upheaval, therefore, permission for visitors to enter 'Akká was extremely difficult to obtain. Laura was an exception, but she had to use great caution. One reason she was among the few allowed to visit was her 'extreme piety'. She also 'had an intense affinity for life' in 'Akká. Despite being used to wealth and comfort, she did not mind the difficult challenges of that city.[204]

Once she arrived, Laura seldom left the house of 'Abdu'l-Bahá except on certain occasions, such as to visit the Shrine of Bahá'u'lláh, which were undertaken with great caution.[205] She had perhaps planned to leave 'Akká earlier than she eventually did, since in an undated letter to her mother she explained that she was going to stay longer: 'Mother Dear: At present, I do not think I need leave Acca this fall. The Master wishes me to remain to pursue my studies: His teachings and Persian, so if nothing unforeseen happens I shall not be obliged to leave now.'[206] Laura explained her daily activities and life in 'Akká to her mother:

The other night we had such an interesting discussion about 20 or 25 Persian men pilgrims and Rosen [perhaps Rosenberg] and I. Many of us gave little talks and the meeting was most impressive . . .

It may interest you to know how we pass the days. I get up at five and after dressing generally read over one of the Master's lessons, at about half after six we go to Him and He talks to us or reads his letters, in the morning we do two or three hours of translation from the Master's lessons and in the after [afternoon] I have a Persian lesson & give an English reading lesson to one of the ladies. We see the Master at meals where He generally gives us instructions and sometimes in the afternoons.

In the evening, we talk & walk on the roof etc. You see it is a busy life & OK! So full of interest.[207]

Laura wrote to her mother of how bright and happy she was at the time and of her delight at living in the house where she was staying. She raved about the view and the beautiful sunsets over the sea that she could see from her balcony over an old fortified wall of stone.[208] In yet another letter to her mother she wrote: 'The Master's life is a marvel to me – never have I seen such a useful and perfect being.'[209]

It was during these most difficult years of 'Abdu'l-Bahá's life that Laura started writing down the 'expositions made by Him at His table talks to the pilgrims'.[210] Several years later, Laura referred to those times in a talk she gave:

When I saw the Master – a Prisoner in 'Akká, cut away from much of the world – and saw how He dictated to His scribes, I asked Him whether it would be feasible to have some talks written down when He honored us by coming to take a meal with us, or sometimes in the early morning when we were having tea . . . We never knew when we were going to have these talks. It was after a heavy day of visiting the poor or attending to some very difficult and complicated business that He would come, and sit, and rest; and it was the thought of you all, and the thought that perhaps it would save Him the cost of many Tablets, that gave me the courage to ask, when I wanted to remain silent.[211]

As she learned more and more about the Faith, she started posing her questions to 'Abdu'l-Bahá. As 'Abdu'l-Bahá revealed answers to her questions, she wrote down the answers. The ultimate result was her compilation of the book *Some Answered Questions*, which was first published in 1908.[212] Some years later she wrote:

When I realized that I was to remain in 'Akká for some time, I thought of gathering together the explanations on the Teachings about which there had been some confusion, for others who could not visit the Master themselves. As 'Abdu'l-Bahá dictated His Tablets it came to me to take down His explanations, then to have these corrected and His seal and Signature put on every one.[213]

At that time Dr Youness Afroukhteh was serving as a secretary and translator for 'Abdu'l-Bahá. A Persian, he served in those capacities and as a physician to 'Abdu'l-Bahá from 1900 to 1909. In his memoirs, *Memories of Nine Years in 'Akká*, Afroukhteh gives accounts of how he translated Laura's questions from English into Persian and then translated the Master's answers from Persian into English. He wrote of Laura:

> In the heat and confusion of 'Akká, she [Laura Barney] joyfully pursued her solitary task of collecting the Writings of the Master. And as she meditated and soared in the realms of spirit, she beheld the light of the celestial flame in the Sinai of her heart and discovered many divine realities.[214]

The talks were given in the dining room of the house of 'Abdu'lláh Páshá, where 'Abdu'l-Bahá was residing. This house was the main building of the former Governorate of 'Abdu'lláh Páshá and was rented to 'Abdu'l-Bahá in October 1896. It served as His and His family's residence for nearly two decades.[215] It was in the small dining room of this house that lunch was usually served. A room next to the Master's reception room, the dining room looked towards the sea.[216] Afroukhteh recalled that the Master would sit at the head of the dinner table and Laura sat on His left. Ethel Rosenberg sat to her left, while Afroukhteh would sit on 'Abdu'l-Bahá's right to translate. When Afroukhteh went on a trip to Paris, possibly in 1905, the daughters of 'Abdu'l-Bahá took on the task of translation.[217]

Often several pilgrims and friends were also present.[218] 'Abdu'l-Bahá often sacrificed His time to eat to answer Laura's questions, but to Him that was not a problem. On one such occasion when His meal was not only interrupted but He was fatigued, He stood up and happily said, 'It is encouraging that after all this labor, at least she understands the concepts. This is refreshing. What would I have done if after all this effort she still failed to comprehend the issues?'[219]

'Like the other Western friends,' Afroukhteh wrote, 'this lady received her share of spiritual education at the dinner table,' explaining that the Master's excessive workload only allowed time for question and answer sessions at lunch time, at about one o'clock p.m.[220]

Afroukhteh remembered that Laura 'was endowed with an avid enthusiasm for acquiring spiritual qualities and heavenly attributes', which is why 'Abdu'l-Bahá 'honored her with the title of Amatu'l-Bahá, the Handmaiden of Bahá'.[221] She was a 'very shy young woman, the quintessence of purity and piety'. She immersed herself 'in the ocean of divine knowledge, where she discovered many a precious pearl' and 'considered the Prison City of 'Akká and the small house of the Beloved of the world preferable to the most splendid mansions of Western countries'.[222] Laura's keen intelligence and inquisitive nature enabled her to make insightful observations. Her deep understanding of the Bahá'í Faith may have been a result of her studies with Abu'l-Faḍl, who helped her to ponder on deep philosophical and religious subjects. Laura's evolving spirituality was fostered by the Master, who seemed satisfied with the progress she was making to gain deeper understanding.

Laura had said that it was her intention from the beginning to have the words of 'Abdu'l-Bahá transcribed and therefore the English translation of His words was written down. As the talks continued, it was decided to also record the Persian words as they were spoken in order to preserve them in that language.[223] It was also Laura's wish to make sure that accurate records were kept of His replies, and therefore she made sure that one of the four people who were accustomed to performing secretarial work for the Master was present to take down His words.[224] These included Mírzá Munír (son of Mírzá Muḥammad-Qulí), Mírzá Hádí Afnán (son-in-law of 'Abdu'l-Bahá and father of Shoghi Effendi), Mírzá Muḥsin (another son-in-law of 'Abdu'l-Bahá) and Mírzá Núru'd-Dín Zayn.

Laura said that it was her intention from the beginning to have a Persian record:[225]

> While I desired from the very beginning that the Master's utterances be recorded in Persian, it was only when the Master mentioned that at some time these transcripts would have to be reviewed and corrected, that He made the decision that His utterances be also recorded in Persian.[226]

The Holy Family was also convinced of the significance of the precious gems coming to light and they too made sure that a secretary or other competent person attended the meetings to take down every word.[227] They realized that if Laura 'had not immersed herself in the depths' of this divine knowledge 'those heavenly jewels would have been left concealed in the depths of the storehouse of meanings. And now these hidden gems had come to light. What could be better than to record them in the Persian language so that they might remain intact and inviolate for prosperity in the annals of the Faith?'[228]

Dr Afroukhteh went on a brief trip to Beirut and when he returned to 'Akká he noted that Miss Barney was 'still persevering at 'Abdu'l-Bahá's dinner table with her question-and-answer sessions'.[229] He had earlier remarked that 'the discussions were concluded in an atmosphere of joy and amity'.[230] He also described a number of episodes when the Master's manner of expression utterly enchanted Laura and other listeners.[231]

Laura had become quite fluent in Persian because she had the opportunity to immerse herself in it, to speak it every day with members of the household and staff, and to study the holy writings in Persian. And because of her familiarity with Bahá'í terminology and Persian expressions, communication was easier for her than for most of the other western Bahá'ís who visited the Master in those years.

Laura wrote in the Preface to *Some Answered Questions* that one day the Master told her, as He rose from the table after answering one of her questions, 'I have given to you my tired moments.' So tired was He that sometimes weeks passed before she would receive instruction from Him. 'But', she wrote, 'I could well be patient, for I had always before me the greater lesson – the lesson of His personal life . . . In these lessons He is the teacher adapting Himself to His pupil, and not the orator or poet.'[232] She noted some years later, 'The Master had that wonderful patience in trying to get a few words over; He would use the Persian words that we understood, over and over.'[233]

Dr Afroukhteh noted that 'Abdu'l-Bahá gave nourishment of the spirit precedence over that of the body, so meals were often delayed. He described a humorous episode demonstrating 'Abdu'l-Bahá's concern for him:

The Master when elucidating the problems used to speak in such a manner that the hearer would be enchanted. One day when He was insisting that I should first eat and then speak, and I was deeply engrossed in the subject under discussion, He asked Laura what was the English word for 'mutarjim'; she said 'interpreter'. Again He asked what was the word for 'gorosneh'. She said 'hungry'. Thereupon 'Abdu'l-Bahá, pointing at me, exclaimed: 'Hungry interpreter! Hungry interpreter!'[234]

According to Ethel Rosenberg, the Master gave tremendous new insights into the Faith at these lunches. According to her biographer, in His answers,

> 'Abdu'l-Bahá dealt with the vast eternal questions about the nature and existence of God, the universe, the life of the soul, and the relations between science and religion. He spoke about esoteric matters – immorality, predestination, free will and reincarnation – as well as practical aspects of the Bahá'í teachings concerning labour and capital, law and order. Most importantly perhaps for Ethel, He dwelt on Christian subjects, the fulfillment of prophecies and explanations of biblical themes.[235]

Her Impressions and Experiences Living in 'Akká

Laura had unique and exceptional experiences living in 'Akká near 'Abdu'l-Bahá, and many years later she wrote about them for *The Bahá'í World*:

> . . . I was privileged to live in the prison town of 'Akká, near 'Abdu'l-Bahá. I have seen the seasons of the year pass over that medieval stronghold; I have seen the storm tossed waves of winter beat against the ramparts below my windows, and outside the walled city I have seen the great plains near the Mansion of Bahjí covered with myriads of bright spring flowers and, after the scorching sun of summer, the color of the plains matching the sand of the desert. I have seen many people from many parts of the world, different in ideas, customs and situations, enter 'Abdu'l-Bahá's presence and each and all felt that He understood their needs and purposes.[236]

In a talk that she gave in the United States a few years later, she covered many aspects of her life in 'Akká and her observations of 'Abdu'l-Bahá's character and His attributes: 'It is not what I think, is of much importance but what I saw, and such incidents as came to my notice and of the characteristics and habits of 'Abdu'l-Bahá.'[237] After talking about the household in 'Akká, she continued:

> As to 'Abdu'l-Bahá Himself it is very hard [difficult] to describe Him, owing to His diversity, so many aspects. Perhaps I had better give you the view as to how outsiders look upon and think of Him. All around the surrounding country of Acca He is known as Abbas Effendi. They look upon Him as a very wise man, likening Him to Solomon. They come to Him for advice and many difficult questions are put before Him for solution. They all trust Him, and even though a prisoner the Governor himself has come to Him for comfort and consultation. He is felt to be a wise and remarkable saint. He is extraordinary in His dealings with the poor, being their best friend.
>
> I have heard the stirring history of the Cause from those who lived the heroic days, for years I have been reading the written word which, through the centuries, will unfold wisdom to seekers. Above all, I have seen 'the Master' day in, day out, unfaltering and joyous in His mission of education and love. He is firm yet very kind, His position is most difficult, many governors have come to Acca while 'Abdu'l-Bahá has been imprisoned there. At first many have held aloof from Him but quickly signs of friendliness appear and many have admired Him. Looking upon Him now from the aspect of a teacher as a Centre of the Covenant . . .
>
> As the Centre of the Covenant His station is humility. He would be a brilliant being in any walk of life and would have made a success in any (material undertaking) walk of life because He depends wholly upon that force which is of God.[238]

She went on to talk about the Master's character and His seemingly limitless equanimity whether faced with the press of work or with danger.

> 'Abdu'l-Bahá is sensitive and poetical in the midst of all this activity. When He is about to answer a question, He is calm and meditative, and seems to be looking out on nature. He seems to forget your presence, and by and by when He answers all that which seemed

difficult for you to comprehend becomes easy to understand. All mysteries are imparted unto you. I remember one day He came in for lunch, looking weary and grieved. After a few moments, we asked had anything happened. Could we send a message to anyone? Then He related a heartbreaking experience which He had gone through that day. How He had been passing the barracks where they were enlisting soldiers.[239]

Laura recognized 'Akká as a gathering place for people from all places and backgrounds.

Acca is the centre of the world. It is the place of meeting for all pilgrims. Many of my dearest friends are pilgrims. Many of my dearest friends are people I have met there, Muhammadan, Jews, Zoroastrians, etc. Not only there do we feel that bond of unity. It is everywhere we meet the Bahá'ís. They are all connected with one another and like one great happy family. This bond of sympathy creates beautiful actions and it is really wonderful what we can accomplish in this world.[240]

Laura included in her talk the most important principles that the Master respected:

'Abdu'l-Bahá is wonderful in His example. He displays two principles which are very powerful. They are toleration and vigilance.[241]

When a pilgrim goes to Acca, 'Abdu'l-Bahá knows his true condition but He does not judge by the outward expression but judges by their inward self. He seems to know intimately the action of their secret minds. One of the questions is after personal welfare: Are you happy and have you rested? He has this kindly greeting for everyone.[242]

Laura found 'Abdu'l-Bahá's teaching style to be simple yet mystical. His straightforward way of expressing a concept would coalesce with the listener's inner being.

'It is difficult to condense into words the volume of force that radiated from His teachings,' she wrote. 'He spoke simply and His sentences became a part of one's inner thoughts seeking a worthy outlet in action.'[243]

She also remembered His words:

> I recall one day, when we were taking early morning tea, 'Abdu'l-Bahá sat looking out at the dawn-lit horizon; He spoke softly, as though to Himself. We must learn how to read the Universe; it is an open book.
>
> All the worlds, known and unknown, are ours if we are at one with the Spirit.[244]

Almost seven decades later, Laura shared her early experiences of meeting 'Abdu'l-Bahá with the Bahá'ís of Paris. She said there was only one thing that she wished to say:

> . . . the whole life of 'Abdu'l-Bahá radiated encouragement and spiritually to all those with whom He came in contact – be they high personages, or be they the simple, poor people He might meet in the street.
>
> Several times I have seen Him go up to discouraged persons and stop and speak to them. And when His word of guidance was expressed and the smile began to show on their faces, He would pass further on. I do not think He ever left any being sobbing, or deeply upset. When He parted, the person was sustained and encouraged.
>
> The above is not 'one' incident that you asked for: I have seen it in many forms and have been deeply impressed by the gift of encouragement He could pass on to others – especially the down and out. And all this took place during the years He was still a prisoner in the city of St Jean d'Acre ['Akká].[245]

With 'Abdu'l-Bahá's Household and Shoghi Effendi

Because of her long stays in the Holy Land, Laura became close with the women of the household of 'Abdu'l-Bahá. She included a description of 'Abdu'l-Bahá's household in 'Akká in her talk given back in the United States in 1909:

> First, the surrounding household of 'Abdu'l-Bahá. It is like a village. His family consists of the wives, sisters and daughters of many

Studio House, located on Sheridan Circle at 2306 Massachusetts Avenue, Sheridan Circle, Washington D.C.

Alice Pike Barney at Studio House, 1908

Room at Studio House

Smithsonian Institution Archives. Image # SIA2007-0149

*Laura Barney, Hippolyte Dreyfus and Mme Lacheny with Bahá'ís
at the Bahá'í Temple in 'Ishqábád, June 1906*

National Archives of the Bahá'ís of France

Smithsonian Institution Archives. Image # SIA2607-0149

Smithsonian Institution Archives. Image # SIA2015-00696

Laura Barney, Hippolyte Dreyfus and Mme Lacheny with Persian Bahá'ís in Iran

Smithsonian Institution Archives. Image # SIA2015-006924

Smithsonian Institution Archives. Image # SIA2015-00694

The cover, spine and title page of the first English edition of Some Answered Questions, *published in 1908*

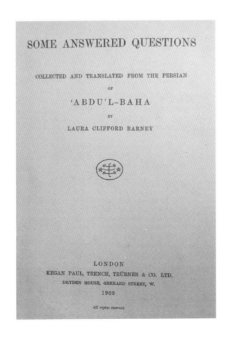

SOME ANSWERED QUESTIONS

COLLECTED AND TRANSLATED FROM THE PERSIAN

OF

'ABDU'L-BAHA

BY

LAURA CLIFFORD BARNEY

LONDON
KEGAN PAUL, TRENCH, TRÜBNER & CO. LTD.
DRYDEN HOUSE, GERRARD STREET, W.
1908
All rights reserved

Elizabeth Diggett, Susan Moody, Alice Barney, Laura Barney, Jean Masson and Marie Hopper at the site of the House of Worship, in 1909

Laura and Natalie, in 1910

Juliet Thompson, an American artist and friend of Alice Pike Barney and Laura Barney

Edwin Scott in front of the apartment building at 4 Avenue de Camoëns where 'Abdu'l-Bahá stayed while in Paris in 1911

Sara Louisa, Lady Blomfield, an early Irish Bahá'í in whose home in Cadogan Gardens, London, 'Abdu'l Bahá stayed while in England in September and October 1911 and on His return in December 1912 and January 1913

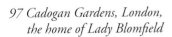

97 Cadogan Gardens, London, the home of Lady Blomfield

The house built by Hippolyte's family on Mont Pèlerin facing Lac Léman, across from Évian les Bains

National Archives of the Bahá'ís of France

Laura and Hippolyte in 1911 at Mont Pèlerin

Smithsonian Institution Archives. Image # SIA2015-006920

Laura and Hippolyte in 1911, some time after their marriage

Laura in 1913

Smithsonian Institution Archives. Image # SIA2015-006972

*'Abdu'l-Bahá in Paris, with Hippolyte, standing at far left rear,
and Laura Dreyfus-Barney, standing to the right of 'Abdu'l-Bahá*

National Archives of the Bahá'ís of France

Laura and Hippolyte, in 1915

Smithsonian Institution Archives.
Image # SIA2015-006972

A 1926 photo postcard depicting Laura Barney in a flying machine at the historic spa town Marienbad in Czechoslovakia (today's Czechia). The reverse of the postcard reads: 'Miss Barney, 200 Rue Jacob, Paris; Sailing along in the height of fashion! Laura'

Smithsonian Institution Archives.
Image # SIA2015-006967

Laura at Amilie-les-Boines during World War I, circa 1915

Smithsonian Institution Archives.
Image # SIA2015-006923

martyrs, all saintly souls, and many Bahá'ís find shelter there. There are a few young men who do the manual labor necessary and many children who have been sent to the Master to care for and bring up and many of those in the household have grown up splendid Bahá'ís and all are active in the service of El Abha. All those in the Household feel that any service they perform is an act of worship so they are always anxious to perform some kind of service for you.

The love that reigns here you have all heard of. Everyone smilingly performs the tasks set for them and everyone is an example of what spiritual education can accomplish. The household at Acca is all Union, Harmony in action of service. Acca is the center of all activity in the Bahá'í Cause owing to the example set by 'Abdu'l-Bahá's life which radiates to all Bahá'í centers in all parts of the world.[246]

In addition to 'Abdu'l-Bahá's only sister, Bahíyyih Khánum, and His wife, Munírih Khánum, the immediate holy family also included His four daughters, Díyá'iyyih, Túbá, Rúhá and Munavvar. Laura taught English to the daughters of 'Abdu'l-Bahá and other ladies of the holy family,[247] describing His household as 'the loving family who had taken me into their inner life'.[248] Her quiet and reserved manner impressed those near to 'Abdu'l-Bahá. Bahíyyih Khánum sent her greetings to Laura in a letter to an individual: 'To the honored handmaid of God, Miss Barney, give my many and fond wishes. I implore God to assist her and yourself to attain the greatest of all His favors in His Mighty Kingdom.'[249]

Laura held 'Abdu'l-Bahá's family in unshakable affection:

Laura's abiding devotion to the family of the Master, the Greatest Holy Leaf and Munírih Khánum, the wife of 'Abdu'l-Bahá, was repaid with trust, love and gratitude. 'Abdu'l-Bahá extolled the variety of her services in many Tablets, and the ladies of the household presented her with many gifts, mostly pieces of jewellery . . .[250]

By the way, several decades later, Laura returned the gifts that she had received from 'Abdu'l-Bahá and His sister to the Bahá'í World Centre. There are references to 'Abdu'l-Bahá giving gifts that had been given to Him to other Bahá'ís. Laura had given jewels to 'Abdu'l-Bahá and begged Him to accept them. He in turn gave some of those pieces of jewelry to a Bahá'í couple, Lua and Edward Getsinger, to sell so that they could use the money for their return to the United States.[251] Another example was a gold pen-holder, spiral-shaped with a pearl at one end, that she may have given to 'Abdu'l-Bahá and which He gave to Ali-Kuli Khan.[252]

Laura also met Shoghi Effendi, the grandson of 'Abdu'l-Bahá, when he was a young child. She remembered him in this way:

> I was permitted, at the beginning of this century [20th century], to visit the Master in 'Akká, which at that time was a Turkish province. This happened during the critical years 1904–5 when 'Abdu'l-Bahá was constantly under the menace of being exiled to the far-away desert of Fízán in Africa, and I was privileged to have my interviews and conversations with Him while I was living in His household. Shoghi Effendi was at the time a child of seven or eight years of age. He was rather small for his age, but very keen and attentive. When not engaged in his early morning studies, he followed his Grandfather ['Abdu'l-Bahá] wherever He went. He was almost like His shadow and passed long hours seated on the rug in the manner of the East, listening, quietly and silently, to every word He uttered. The child had a remarkably retentive memory and, at times when guests were present, the Master would ask him either to recite some passage from Bahá'u'lláh's Writings, which he had memorized, or to chant a prayer. It was very moving to hear the limpid, crystal chanting of that child, because all his being and soul were engaged in communion with God. Eagerness was ever present and animated him like a flame of fire in all he did.[253]

Soon after that first meeting, the young Shoghi Effendi became close to Miss Barney. He sent her notes that were delivered to her while she was in 'Akká and Haifa. Years later she found three of those little notes from Shoghi Effendi sent to her on fancy paper, one with a design of roses, doves and angels.[254] In one of these notes he stated that his French was not good enough yet but it gave him pleasure to work hard to improve it.[255] In another note written around the same time in French on a fancy paper, he expressed his joy in writing to Mademoiselle [Laura Barney]. He was disappointed that he did not have time to visit her more often because of his studies. He wrote, 'Mademoiselle, know that your little friend Choki [Shoghi Effendi] would like very much to see you.'[256]

Laura received another letter written in French from her little friend, Choki, after her return to Paris. He had again selected a fancy paper with designs, writing, 'I am very angry because I do not see you anymore. I hope that you return soon, I also hope that your health is good.' He then wrote about the different family members and told her that Rúḥá Khánum, the third daughter of 'Abdu'l-Bahá, had married Mírzá Jalál. He also sent Laura New Year wishes from Rúḥangíz, Rúḥí and himself for the coming year, writing that Bahíyyih Khánum, his mother and his aunts were sending a thousand salutations. 'Please accept, dear Mademoiselle,' he wrote, 'my very tender hugs.'[257]

Shoghi Effendi had an Italian governess, but Laura learned about 'Abdu'l-Bahá's interest in finding a tutor for His grandson to teach him English literature. It was Laura who secured the services of a cultured and refined English lady.[258] This was vital in the education of Shoghi Effendi, who possessed a keen talent for learning the English language. 'Abdu'l-Bahá wrote to Laura to inform her that a teacher had arrived, possibly referring to the English teacher that Laura had found for Shoghi Effendi.[259]

Laura as a Persian Translator for a United States Presidential Candidate

Laura met a most interesting person during her 1904–6 stays in 'Akká. The American Democratic Party's twice-nominated presidential candidate William Jennings Bryan (1860–1925) visited 'Akká in 1904. He was traveling internationally to share his ideas and to promote his plans, going to Japan and visiting London in 1905 and 1906. He would run for president a third time in 1908 and became the United States Secretary of State under President Woodrow Wilson from 1913 to 1915.

Bryan had developed a peace plan and campaigned tirelessly for its adoption. He had visited Tolstoy, the renowned author, just outside Moscow in 1903 to learn about his ideals for Russia. Tolstoy was keenly interested in the Bahá'í Faith and met and corresponded with some Bahá'ís.[260] It might have been Tolstoy who told Bryan about 'Abdu'l-Bahá. Bryan also visited Ottoman Turkey and much later he wrote about Him in his memoirs, somewhat erroneously:

Today Turkey has not only joined the great company of republics but has banished the spiritual head of the Church. While in Syria, where the family was exiled, we called on Abbas Effendi, who was then the head of the reform movement. Like Gandhi of India, he believed in moral persuasion rather than force.[261]

Years later Laura wrote that he was in 'Akká 'in connection with a mission to confer with celebrated individuals about of peace. He met with the great religious leader, Abbas Effendi ['Abdu'l-Bahá], who had been imprisoned by the Sultan, and I interpreted the Persian into English for Mr Bryan. I didn't speak Persian very well, but I understood it perfectly.'[262]

When 'Abdu'l-Bahá was traveling across America in 1912, He visited Bryan's hometown of Lincoln, Nebraska, and had tea at his home with Mrs Bryan and their daughter, as Bryan was on a tour campaigning for the future President Wilson. Before he left, 'Abdu'l-Bahá wrote a prayer for assistance for Bryan in a notebook.[263]

With Her Mother in 'Akká

While Laura was in the Middle East, she arranged for her mother to visit the Holy Land and she accepted. Laura was not sure if she should meet her mother in Egypt or ask her to come directly to 'Akká. She was extremely excited about this visit and even asked her mother to bring her painting materials.

> When you come bring plenty of painting materials for you will always be wishing to paint, of this I am sure for the East is the land of living picture, you will not need trouble about models & draperies and backgrounds, you will just simply have to paint. I have not yet asked the Master if you can paint Him better wait until the time arrives. Oh, I do hope that you will be able to do it.[264]

Laura raved about the pleasant weather at that time of the year and informed her mother that even though it was warm, it was far from being unbearable. She told her mother that she was 'in the best of health . . . and have not had one day one hour of sickness' since she had arrived.[265]

Laura must have traveled to Egypt to meet her mother in the early spring of 1905. They traveled from Cairo to 'Akká and stayed there for a month. During her stay Alice painted a portrait of the son of the governor of 'Akká.[266]

The Washington Post printed an article about the visit with the usual inclusions of incorrect information, such as giving their destination of 'Akká in Persia rather than in Palestine. Under the headline 'Mrs. Barney & Daughter on Visit to 'Akká, Persia', it reported:

> Just now Mrs Barney and Miss Alice [Laura] Barney are in 'Akká, Persia, the home of the founder of the Beha Ullah faith whom the believers in that faith call 'The Master' . . . That Mrs Barney and her daughter Alice [Laura] have been believers and followers in the faith for some time is well known, and at the time of their departure for Europe it was believed they under took the journey for the purpose of visiting 'The Master'.[267]

Alice Barney's Return to the United States and Her Conversion

Alice returned to the United States in November 1905 following her visit to Cairo and 'Akká and a tour of southern Europe.[268] Back in Washington, Alice became active in its Bahá'í community and opened her home, Studio House, for Bahá'í meetings.[269] Upon her return, Alice received a letter from 'Abdu'l-Bahá, which said in part:

> O thou who art honored and dear!
> Thy letter was received and was the source of pleasure, for thou hast not forgotten this imprisoned one and remembered Acca ['Akká]. Although thy days here were few, as they were pleasant, they will count as years; a real intimacy between thee and all the family was formed which will not be forgotten in the passing of years.[270]

Alice responded to 'Abdu'l-Bahá with thanks for His letter, saying that it brought her much joy, that she had framed it and that she would put it in a place where she could see it. She wrote that when she was in 'Akká they had had a splendid time together and she would never forget those days, since remembering them brought her happiness. She thanked the Master for His hospitality and begged to go back to 'Akká in the future.[271]

When Laura heard that her mother had received a Tablet from the Master, she wrote a letter to Mírzá Ahmad Esphahani (who later he took the name Ahmad Sohrab), a translator for 'Abdu'l-Bahá, saying, 'the Master's gracious Tablet has been secured by her [Alice]' and conveying her mother's gratitude for having received it.[272]

After her return, Alice decided to order velvet window hangings from Paris for the Shrine of Bahá'u'lláh, located a short distance outside 'Akká. Bahíyyih Khánum and the daughters of 'Abdu'l-Bahá started the task of measuring the various windows for this gift. When the rich curtains arrived, they were hung in the larger room at the entrance.[273]

Back in Washington, Alice also resumed her activities in promoting arts and culture by inviting accomplished artists and actors to perform at Studio House. She was virtually Washington's 'Queen of Culture'. Though unconventional and at times eccentric, Alice helped establish Washington, D.C. as a cultural center.[274] She was a woman of many interests. She was a prominent hostess, a civic leader, and a philanthropist. In 1901 she had served briefly as vice president of Associated Charities, a forerunner of the United Way, through which she became acquainted with and developed respect for its young executive director, Charles Weller, who was also the director of Neighborhood House.

At that time Washington's wealthy women customarily chose one charity to support. Alice chose Neighborhood House, a settlement house in the southwest area of Washington modeled after the successful English social movement begun in 1884. She chose it because she believed it could provide a model for the development of cultural awareness among blue-collar workers.[275] She bought a property in southwest Washington in 1905 and provided it rent-free to Neighborhood House, volunteering her time there and organizing many events throughout her life to raise funds for it.[276] 'Abdu'l-Bahá visited Neighborhood House in Washington in 1912 and showed much interest in it.[277] Years later the name was changed to Barney Neighborhood House, and as of 2018, over 110 years since its founding, this institution was still functioning in Washington.

Years later Alice was interviewed after the end of a fundraising event called The Mystery of the East that she had organized for Neighborhood House. It included readings and songs from three Eastern countries – Persia, India and Egypt. She had even been involved in the production of the hand-dyed Liberty silks used for this event that were made at classes taught at Neighborhood House. When Alice was asked why she was so involved in this project, she gave the same response that she had given a few years earlier in Boston:

> Work, good, honest toil is as much an obligation of the rich as it is a necessity to the poor. It is part of my creed. The Bahai faith teaches it. I believe that every man and woman should earn his or her place in the world by honest application to whatever trade, profession or art he or she is best fitted for.[278]

According to Alice's biographer, 'The Baháí Faith, which proclaimed full equality for women as a basic tenet, mirrored her [Alice Barney's] own values more closely.'[279]

Towards the end of the summer of 1906 as Alice was embarking on a visit to Stony Man Mountain in the Blue Ridge Mountains in Virginia, and then to Canada, Laura was completing her travels to Turkmenistan and to Persia, the native land of the Prophet-Founder of her faith.

Meeting Hippolyte Dreyfus

Laura was asked by 'Abdu'l-Bahá to travel to Persia, which she did in the summer of 1906. Her travel companion was Hippolyte Dreyfus.[280] She had met Hippolyte, who became an important figure in her future, some years earlier while attending May Bolles's gatherings in Paris.

Hippolyte Dreyfus Cardozo was born in 1873 to a prominent French Jewish family, the only son of a broker living in the eighth arrondissement of Paris. Though he was of Jewish descent, he was not related to Albert Dreyfus of the infamous Dreyfus Affair that shook France in the 1890s and lasted until 1906. He attended the Lycée Condorcet and was a classmate of Robert Proust, the brother of Marcel Proust, in a philosophy class in 1890. After successfully completing his thesis in law, *Des droits de succession du conjoint survivant,* in 1898, Dreyfus became the secretary of François Thévenet, a well-known lawyer.[281] He had studied law at the Institut des Sciences Politiques (Political Science Institute) in Paris, had completed a doctoral degree there, and was practicing law before the Paris Court of Appeals.[282] Some years later, Laura had this to say about Hippolyte:

He had all the advantages that could be obtained from a happy home and from an intellectual and artistic center such as Paris at the height of its culture. He grew up strong in appreciation of life and all that it has to offer. When he reached manhood his questing mind led him onward to ever-vaster horizons.

Law was the profession he chose and he became the secretary of one of the most prominent barristers in France. While he pursued his career with success, he came close to the problems and difficulties of many people, and his generosity of heart gave him a subtle understanding of human nature. He had the rare quality of being more interested in others than in himself.[283]

Like Laura, Hippolyte was introduced to the Bahá'í Faith in 1900 by May Bolles, who later wrote:

Day by day the believers and friends who still remained in Paris came to my little apartment, where the golden summer hours slipped by bathed in the burning rays of the Divine Revelation . . . Never shall I forget the overpowering impression of grace and power in the person of Hippolyte Dreyfus the first time he came to see me.[284]

May Bolles recalled that Hippolyte told her that he had come to discover how she had produced a remarkable change in Edith Sanderson, an American Bahá'í woman living in Paris.

'She is not the same – she has found joy, serenity and a deep purpose in life' – and with his charming smile – 'how did you do it'?

He asked to know the tenets of a Faith which had, he said, transformed a friend of his. With fervour, simplicity, and, conscious of my utter ignorance in the face of such a scholar, putting my full trust in Bahá'u'lláh, as the Master had bidden me in Acca to do – I told him all I knew! He listened with courteous attention, deep interest at times, searching questions, and over all, a light veil of humour and slight scepticism.[285]

May remembered that after the first visit Hippolyte had considered the Faith interesting but did not recognize its historic importance. He was touched by May's enthusiasm for the Faith but he did not believe in anything beyond natural forces, having never experienced anything that would lead him to believe in anything spiritual in nature. Yet Hippolyte returned a few days later, seemingly both amazed and unsettled. He had had a series of somewhat strange experiences that he could not explain within the context of natural forces, but he had argued with himself for some time to prove their natural origins. May commented:

> Frankly I was amused & delighted, having many times been an 'eye-witness' of the might, mysterious workings of Bahá'u'lláh, and I knew that this great soul was in the toils! Gradually, [he became] unable to resist his own experiences and the irresistible 'charm of faith'. Later, his rationalism being somewhat subdued, he began to read & study, and the priceless seed of faith germinated in his heart. And in due time he became the great beacon light of the Bahá'í Faith in France and in Europe.[286]

Hippolyte became the first French Jew to believe in Bahá'u'lláh and visited 'Abdu'l-Bahá in 'Akká in 1903. He later gave up his legal career to devote himself to oriental studies and comparative religion, and to learn Arabic and Persian with the intention of translating the Bahá'í writings into French. He was probably the only western Bahá'í of his generation to receive formal training in Persian and Arabic.[287]

Laura recalled her first encounter with Hippolyte:

> The first meeting with Hippolyte Dreyfus that I can recall was in 1900 in Paris on the threshold of May Bolles's apartment near L'École des Beaux-Arts. He was leaving; I was arriving to hear more of the Bábí epilogue. Though I was away from France almost constantly from 1901 to 1906, I knew that he had become an outstanding Bahá'í and that his father and mother, his sister and brother-in-law had all joined the Cause.[288]

Laura must have seen Hippolyte in 'Akká when he was on a five-day stop there on his way to visit the Master when traveling to India and Burma in March 1905.[289] She saw him again when she visited Port Said in July of that year. This may have happened by accident as he was returning from Asia to France.[290] Or maybe she knew that he would be there. Possibly the encounter was while Laura was in Egypt to accompany her mother to 'Akká. Perhaps Laura already knew that Hippolyte was not an ordinary man, that she had met an outstanding man, one of whom Shoghi Effendi would refer to as a person with 'qualities of genial & enlivening fellowship', with 'sound judgment and distinctive ability'.[291] His many services were also noted by Shoghi Effendi, who wrote that 'through his writings, translations, travels and other pioneer services, was able to consolidate, as the years went by, the work which had been initiated in his country'.[292]

Laura's Trip to Turkmenistan and Persia (Iran)

During Laura's long stays in 'Akká, she had become acquainted with the history of Persia and the conditions of the Bahá'ís there. 'Gradually,' she wrote, 'I became familiar with the past and existing conditions of Persia. This was in accordance with the wish of 'Abdu'l-Bahá. That I should see how the love of Bahá'u'lláh had enkindled the hearts of men. The spirit of Bahaism is tranquility and peace.'[293] She embarked on this trip to Persia at the request of 'Abdu'l-Bahá.[294]

As she was preparing for her travels, Laura consulted with her mother about a particular American male friend who might accompany her on the trip. Alice encouraged Laura to travel in the company of the young Frenchman and not the American because 'the other will always be thinking of himself'.[295] That French man was Hippolyte.

'Abdu'l-Bahá also reassured Laura that He respected her decision. It seems that Hippolyte also had requested permission to visit Persia. In a Tablet revealed for Laura possibly dated around early March 1906, 'Abdu'l-Bahá mentioned that Hippolyte Dreyfus had requested permission to go to Persia and He knew that Dreyfus had corresponded with her about this request. 'Abdu'l-Bahá stated that if she thought it a good idea, He would send Dreyfus to Persia in the spring.[296]

Laura made up her mind and decided to travel to Persia with Hippolyte and a chaperone, Mme Lacheny, as her companions.[297] Mme Lacheny was a French Bahá'í who had accepted the Faith perhaps around 1900 but little is known of her.[298] She may be the same Mme Emmanuelle Lacheny who was the Barney sisters' governess in Paris and might have worked for them until 1907. Ethel Rosenberg had wished also to join them on this trip but her poor health did not allow her to do so.[299]

The three embarked on their historic journey in the summer of 1906. This was the first visit by western Bahá'ís to Persia. The trip was made easier in that both Laura and Hippolyte spoke Persian and because some of the dignitaries may have spoken English or French.

Visiting the Bahá'ís in Turkmenistan and Russian Turkestan (Uzbekistan)

Laura joined Hippolyte and Mme Lacheny in Constantinople (today's Istanbul) and they left on May 24, 1906.[300] She must have come directly from the Holy Land. Hippolyte had left Paris a few days earlier on the Orient Express, the legendary train that ran between Paris and Constantinople with a stop in Belgrade. Mme Lacheny had arrived a day earlier. They traveled from Constantinople on a steamer that arrived in Odessa, Ukraine, the next day. There seems to have been some kind of a strike, perhaps a train strike, and they had to delay their departure by almost a week. Eventually they left for Baku, arriving on June 4, and visited the Bahá'ís there. This was during the tumultuous times of the reign of the last emperor of Russia, Nicholas II, and the disturbances in Odessa that had lasted for over a year.[301] Then they crossed the Caspian Sea and arrived at the port of Krasnovodsk (present-day Turkmenbashi). Their next stop was 'Ishqábád (present-day Ashgabat) in Turkmenistan, which at that time was called Turkistan, on June 8, where they visited the Bahá'í House of Worship which was being built there.[302]

Persian Bahá'ís, especially those from Isfahan, Yazd and Sabzivar, had started fleeing to 'Ishqábád, across the border from Persia, in the 1880s to escape persecution. In the late 19th century the Persian Bahá'ís were a small minority of the larger Persian immigrant population of Shí'í Muslims in 'Ishqábád. However, although the Persian Bahá'ís were denigrated by the Shí'ís, they were not as overtly persecuted as they had been in Persia.[303]

By the mid-1890s the Bahá'í community in 'Ishqábád had grown and prospered. The freedom of religion that the Bahá'ís experienced there motivated them to start setting up some of the institutions envisaged by Bahá'u'lláh and 'Abdu'l-Bahá. Construction on that most important edifice, the Mashriqu'l-Adhkár (literally, dawning-place of the mention of God; referred to as a House of Worship or Temple), was started in 1902, making it the first Bahá'í House of Worship ever built.

Bahá'í Houses of Worship are to be surrounded by humanitarian, educational and charitable institutions such as hospitals, homes for the elderly, schools and a university to serve the neighborhoods where these Temples stand. Even before the construction of the House of Worship was started, the Bahá'ís began building some of these, such as a public bath, a meeting hall, a travelers' hospice, a pharmaceutical dispensary and hospital, an elementary school for boys, and a cemetery. The foundation stone for the Mashriqu'l-Adhkár was laid by General Dmitrii I. Subotich, the Russian military governor of the region, at a ceremony attended by high-ranking Russian officials. Their participation was considered evidence of the official recognition of the Bahá'í Faith by the Russian government. Designed by the Iranian Bahá'í architect Ustád 'Alí-Akbar Banná Yazdí, the Temple's exterior was completed in 1906, while the exterior and interior ornamentation was not in place until more than a decade later, in 1919. When the Temple was completed, it was the largest house of worship of any religion in the city.[304] Its establishment was regarded by Bahá'ís as 'one of the most brilliant and enduring achievements in the history of the first Bahá'í century'.[305]

Further social institutions were established as time went on, including a school for girls, two kindergartens, a Bahá'í library and a reading room.[306] The Bahá'í community also initiated the establishment of the Bahá'í administrative order by electing a Local Spiritual Assembly, the local governing body of the Bahá'ís. The social and religious lives of the Bahá'ís were thus greatly enhanced by the House of Worship, the local assembly, and the auxiliary institutions. The House of Worship was central to Bahá'í community life.[307]

By the time Laura, Hippolyte and Mme Lacheny arrived in 'Ishqábád there were over a thousand Bahá'ís in the city. These first visitors from the West visited the Temple and met with the local Bahá'ís and dignitaries.[308] Laura described her visit to the Temple in a public talk a few years later:

> Here I had my first meeting, and the men were all seated and as I came in with M. Dreyfus they arose and greeted us with love and affection. After I had returned their greetings, I gave them news of Acca which they were longing for. The meeting was one of deep sincerity and emotion. This Temple was built by the people for the Love of Bahá'u'lláh to bring about the harmony of the different

races, religions, and mentalities of mankind. After the meeting, we drove to the top of the mountains near the Temple and from there had a magnificent view of the vast plains. A wonderful vision indeed of peace and tranquility. Here nature voiced a hope for future generations to be kind and generous.

Through this revelation we are not only practical but spiritual. Then I asked the men to have a real large meeting at the Temple to have their wives and daughters and children attend. The Persian women have had very little opportunity to understand the principles of our day. Shortly after this the meeting assembled and I will never forget the love witnessed there.[309]

Although the Bahá'í teachings include the spiritual equality of women and men and the right of women to participate openly in society, implementation of that principle was slow. Cultural attitudes towards women as lesser beings were deeply ingrained, in Europe and North America as well as throughout Islamic and Middle East culture, and these attitudes carried over into the Bahá'í community of 'Ishqábád, where many of the men had converted from Islam. Certain advances in attitude and practice were being made within the community, but it was considered wise that women 'defer to the customs of the surrounding culture to avoid provoking violent reactions'. It was therefore, not until after the Russian Revolution that women were elected to the Local Assembly, although veiling in public continued.[310] Even during the Bahá'í gatherings in the meeting hall adjacent to the Mashriqu'l-Adhkár, men and women were segregated, with the men seated on the ground floor and the women and children seated in an upper balcony.[311]

Laura and her chaperon wore long-sleeved dresses and hats during their visit, as was customary in the West at that time. She was always photographed wearing a long skirt and a hat. However, photographs taken of her in 'Ishqábád show her seated in the front row in the company of men, despite what was customary for women in those days, even the Bahá'ís. This was probably the first time that men and women had ever been publicly seated and photographed together in 'Ishqábád.

The trio took a side trip to the historical cities of Bukhara and Samarkand in Uzbekistan, possibly traveling by train. Laura wrote:

From there I went to Samarkand. This was once a great city but [is] now in ruins. All earthly might crumbles to dust. Many homes filled with Bahais are here. Joy was radiant in their faces and hearts.[312]

In Samarkand, they visited the tombs of Tamerlane and St Daniel and had dinner with the Bahá'ís.[313] The reason for visiting these cities must have been to meet the Bahá'ís and also to teach the Faith as opportunity allowed. Another reason may have been a recommendation of Abu'l-Faḍl, who had visited 'Ishqábád from September 1889 for eight months and then traveled to Bukhara in 1890 to spread the Faith. Between 1890 and 1894 he lived at different times in 'Ishqábád, Bukhara and Samarkand, and is considered 'as perhaps the single most formidable Bahá'í personality to shape the Bahá'í communities of Turkestan'.[314]

Arrival in Persia

Laura and her travel companions next continued to Persia (today's Iran). 'Abdu'l-Bahá had requested her to visit the native land of Bahá'u'lláh. The government stamps on Laura's passport show that she entered the country on June 23 and departed on August 31, 1906.[315] The three westerners were welcomed in every city. Laura stated some years later: 'Our joy cannot be estimated over the crowds that met us on our arrival at the different places we went to.'[316] She reflected on Persia in a talk that she gave a few years later, calling it 'this land of wonderful history',[317] and saying that while in Persia:

> I visited several of the Holy places including the house from which Qurraut'l'Ain [Ṭáhirih] escaped (where I spent a night) and also the cave where the Bab was originally imprisoned as well as the town where he was later executed – some distance away. I saw also the outside of the dungeon where Baha'u'llah had been confined.[318]

Laura found the country picturesque but exceedingly difficult to travel in.[319] Years later, she wrote in a letter to a Bahá'í friend: 'In 1906, during the Bloodless Revolution in Persia, I was the first foreign woman to be sent to that country by 'Abdu'l-Bahá, whom I had visited earlier.'[320] Laura's journey took place during the reign of Muẓaffari'd-Dín Sháh (1853–1907) of the Qajar dynasty. The 'Bloodless Revolution' was the

Constitutional Revolution, which began in Persia in 1905 and ended in 1911 and led to the establishment of a parliament.

Persecution of the Bahá'ís was frequent but sporadic and localized yet the Bahá'í community had grown steadily, drawing Zoroastrians, Muslims and Jews to the religion. The visit of the first western believers to Iran created a sense of optimism.[321] Hippolyte guessed the Bahá'í population in Tehran to be about 30,000, and the total in Persia to be between 100,000 and 200,000.[322] Accurate data was not kept, and another source considered that the size of the national Bahá'í community in Persia during the early 1900s was probably between 100,000 and 1,000,000.[323] Other Bahá'í scholars differ with Hippolyte's approximation of the number of Bahá'ís in Tehran, one of them estimating that there were between five and ten thousand in 1906.[324]

Accounts of the trip to Persia were reported in the Bahá'í news and in Bahá'í history books, memoirs and journals. One such report appeared in a Bahá'í memoir, under the title 'The American Travelers', even though two of the travelers were French:

> The first group of travelers who came to Iran to visit the Bahá'ís and discover the Iranians' general demeanor and temperament was composed of three individuals, two of whom were Bahá'í ladies and the third a Bahá'í gentleman, Mr Dreyfus, an American who is currently residing in Paris. Mr Dreyfus is a respected scholar and a distinguished member of the Bahá'í community. He is the author of a number of works, including a recent treatise in French, which has been published under the title 'Bahá'í History' and treats such subjects as Bahá'í history, philosophy and various conclusive proofs. One of the ladies was Miss Barney, who was well-educated and cultured.[325]

Another Bahá'í account stated:

> It was three years after the tragedy of Yazd, at a time when the prevailing conditions did not make it easy for a foreigner to visit Iran, that this group of three came to Iran and, despite the many hardships, found infinite happiness in visiting the birthplace of Bahá'u'lláh.[326]

Yet another account read:

> In the days which coincided with the Iranian Constitutional Revolution and Tehran was under military law, Mr Dreyfus and Miss Barney, accompanied by Madame Lacheny, arrived in Tehran. Despite the fact that the streets and avenues of the city were under the complete control of the military, yet the conditions were not peaceful and people remained uneasy and fearful.[327]

While in Persia they met with government officials and prominent people, some of whom were Bahá'ís, as well as with local Bahá'ís. They visited Tehran, Rasht, Qazvín, Isfahan, Káshán, Zanján, Tabríz and Máкú.[328] Several of these cities were historical and important sites for Bahá'ís. Everywhere Laura and her companions went they received a lavish yet dignified welcome.[329] One account of the visit stated:

> During her [Laura's] travels in Iran, she met with several distinguished and high-ranking individuals and explained to them the fundamental principles of the Bahá'í Faith, its emphasis on kindness and good deeds, as well as its spiritual character, human virtues and perfections, and its disregard of politics. She made great efforts to educate these individuals and carry out her mission to the best of her ability.[330]

Most of the details of the day-to-day activities of this trip come from Hippolyte's diary as he documented their daily travels. However, not all of his handwritten notes are legible.[331] Since there is no diary for Laura, one assumes that the three of them attended all the meetings together and all the photographs of their trip suggest this to be the case.

Continuing to Tehran, the Capital City

Laura, Hippolyte, and Mme Lacheny entered Persia via the border town of Astara near the northwestern Iranian province of Azerbaijan. From there they went to Rasht, a town situated near the southwest shore of the Caspian Sea. Laura wrote that in Rasht they had 'several beautiful meetings', perhaps with the local Bahá'ís, and then continued their journey onward and arrived at Qazvín.[332] She wrote that in Qazvín:

The homes are all singular being without outward windows. All windows opening on an inner courtyard. It is a frowning city looking rather like a fortressed town. They were indeed fortunate to have woman like Kurayt'Ain [Ṭáhirih] to awaken that city. The women are very much advanced in this community.[333]

Ṭáhirih was a poet, theologian and was a follower of the Báb. Ṭaráz'u'lláh Samandarí, a Persian Hand of the Cause[334] who visited Laura years later in Paris, mentioned that Hippolyte and Laura had visited his family's home while in Qazvín. He reminded her that when 'you visited us you spoke Persian very well'.[335]

The group arrived in Tehran on the evening of June 27 and stayed at the Hotel Europe. An account of Laura's travel to Tehran was given in her own words at a talk three years later: 'We then went our way and arrived at Teheran. Here the influence toward better conditions has become great through the Bahá'ís.'[336]

During their visit the travelers had two or three meetings a day with small groups. Both Laura and Hippolyte spoke Persian. 'Abdu'l-Bahá had thought it advisable for the meetings to consist of small numbers of people, less than 30, because of the unsettled conditions caused by the granting of the new constitution.[337]

Aziz'u'llah Azizi was an Iranian Bahá'í and a friend of Hippolyte. He accompanied the group on several occasions during their stay in Tehran, wrote about their visit in detail and explained conditions in Tehran, even the problems with garbage collection.

What added to the unsettled and chaotic state of affairs was Tehran's ever-growing garbage which was not being collected and disposed of. Tehran was a city of dirty and dusty air, lacking the basic requisites of life and devoid of the requirements for welcoming guests. Based on our knowledge of the European lifestyle, we were certain that these guests would not enjoy their stay since at that time Tehran did not have any hotels or restaurants and the only available guest accommodation was offered by a Romanian fellow who managed a few dirty and untidy rooms above a tailor's shop on Ferdowsi Street which, in his own view, was a 'hotel'. That is where Mr Dreyfus and his companions stayed. I went to visit them and asked about their living quarters and to my surprise I learned that not only were they not unsatisfied but were even happy to be visiting the Bahá'ís in Iran. They wished to meet more believers and their living quarters was not an issue for them. I accepted to be their guide and was able to host them on several occasions. I tried to create fun and entertainment for them so that they would not have a bad experience in Tehran, as they had come from Paris, the bride of the cities.[338]

Hippolyte took daily notes of where they went and the people they met with during their visit to every town in Persia. They went twice to Shemirán, a suburb north of Tehran. The first time they stayed at the home of A.-L.-M. Nicolas, who was stationed at the French Legation in Persia. Nicolas was a noted scholar on the Bábí and Bahá'í Faiths and later became the French Consul in Tabríz.[339] Many years later Laura wrote that they invited Nicolas to give talks at Bahá'í gatherings in Paris. He corresponded with Hippolyte regularly.[340] The correspondence between the two of them, including 15 original letters written to Hippolyte in the early 1900s, have been stored in the archives at the Bahá'í World Centre.[341]

They also met with Mr Bagherof, a prominent early Bahá'í, and Mr Arbáb. They managed to visit Tarbíyat School, a Bahá'í school for boys. They visited with Shamsu'd-Dín Beg, the Ottoman ambassador, on third of July.[342] Two days later, they were invited to a *majlis* (reception). One of the people they met was Arastú Ḥakím, the grandson of an early Bahá'í, Masíḥ Ḥakím.[343] They also met Mullá 'Alí-Akbar Shahmírzádí (1842/3–1910), who had the considerable responsibility of overseeing the teaching and administration of the Persian Bahá'í community during those years.[344] Another person they met was a Belgian called Naus. He must be Joseph Naus, who was recruited to modernize the Iranian customs and manage it. He arrived in Iran in 1898 and was dismissed in 1907.[345]

One day the group attended a dinner gathering hosted by Aziz'u'llah Azizi, who described the details of this party:

Jalál ud-Dawlih, the son of Ẓillu's-Sulṭán, was one of the wealthy and influential people of Tehran, was a friend of mine and was truly kind to me. He had a beautiful garden in the suburbs of Tehran called Jalálíyyih (where the University of Tehran is now located). I asked his permission to let me give a reception for my European guests at his garden and he accepted right away. I gave a glorious party at the

Jaláláyyih Garden where the distinguished guests and many of the Bahá'ís came to meet Mr Dreyfus, Miss Barney and Mme Lacheny. Talks were given about the contributions and services of Mr Dreyfus and Miss Barney and Mme Lacheny and the gathering was superb and sumptuous. This gathering created much joy and happiness for the western friends, especially as the garden was tidied and water in the pool was changed. The ambiance and charm of the garden and the rippling water beckoned M. Dreyfus to wade into the crystal clear water. He later told me that he had had such a good time that evening that he had written about it in his book about the history of his life and that he was indebted to the kindness and friendship of the friends in Iran.[346]

The group also met with the children of the Bahá'í martyrs. Some years later, Laura said in a speech:

> We also met in Teheran the orphans of many of the martyrs. Here was martyred the twelve-year-old boy who when his father had been killed was asked to recant his Bahá'í views and refused. He said you cannot separate me from my father. Only if I give up these views will I be separated. Death will only unite us in the spirit which joined us in life. He was immediately executed. The lesson teaches us the reasoning of the minds of these simple people, how they are filled with spiritual illumination.[347]

While in Tehran, Laura sent several letters to her mother reassuring her that she should not worry about them, stating that Persia was 'one of the most peaceful countries' that she had seen.[348] 'We are kept very busy seeing people,' she commented, 'and interesting people too.'[349] In another letter she said that the Bahá'ís there were 'wonderfully sincere and kind' and the people she met were among 'the most important people of Persia'.[350] She told her mother that she was going to visit Isfahan.[351] They left Tehran for Isfahan on July 10.[352]

Visiting Isfahan

The group left Tehran in carriages with fast horses, traveling for what must have been three grueling days through the desert to reach Isfahan.

On the way they stopped for a few hours in Qom, the holy city of Shí'í Islam and a significant destination for pilgrimage, and then headed towards Káshán. Laura commented on Káshán in an address that she gave a few years later: 'We held wonderful meetings at Tashan [Káshán]. One particularly at midnight (11:30). We walked through strange streets and arrived to meet these eager loving people.'[353]

Isfahan had been the ancient capital of Persia and was the scene of innumerable pogroms and martyrdoms of the Bahá'ís.[354] Those martyrs included the King of Martyrs, Ḥájí Siyyid Muḥammad Ḥasan, and the Beloved of Martyrs, Ḥájí Siyyid Muḥammad Ḥusayn, who were killed in 1879. Their tombs were demolished by a mob in 1920.

Some years later, Laura spoke of the people they met in Isfahan:

Here we met a relative of Mírzá Azalullah [perhaps Asadu'lláh Vazír] by name Zellah Sultan [Mas'ud Mírzá Ẓillu's-Sulṭán], Governor of Isfahan. Outsiders are not seen openly with Bahais in this town yet they are especially kind to them. I asked of the Governor why he objected to Bahais and he replied: 'They are communists and keep things to themselves.' He has since my trip been exiled from Persia and he's now in Paris and will there no doubt learn better the principles which govern Bahais and through the contact with the hardships of the world have his heart softened toward them.[355]

The westerners were hosted in Isfahan by Mírzá Asadu'lláh Vazír and Fátiḥu'l-Mulk.[356] Mírzá Asadu'lláh Vazír was a well-known Bahá'í who had been appointed to the post of Vazír of Isfahan in 1890, a position that entailed responsibility for government finances in that province. He was so powerful and well-respected in the town that the enemies of the Bahá'ís were unable to harm him. Fátiḥu'l-Mulk was one of the notables of Isfahan who had also become a Bahá'í.[357] The year before Laura's travel to Iran, 'Abdu'l-Bahá had asked her to stay with the family of Mírzá Asadu'lláh Iṣfahání, a Bahá'í scholar whom 'Abdu'l-Bahá had sent to Paris and America. He was the father of Aminu'lláh Fareed. They attended a reception in the garden of an Asadu'lláh in Isfahan which may have been the same family or Mírzá Asadu'lláh Vazír.

Upon arrival in the province of Isfahan, they first visited Julfa, the Armenian quarter near the city of Isfahan, and met with Père Pascal [Father Pascal]. Then they went to Bágh Arbáb (the garden of Arbáb) where they met Mírzá Asadu'lláh Vazír and Fátiḥu'l-Mulk. Hippolyte mentioned that they met with the Russian Consul and several other dignitaries. Then they visited historical sites of Isfahan such as Chihil Sutún, which means 40 columns. It is a pavilion with 20 columns in the middle of a park. When the columns are reflected in the pool they give the impression that they are 40 columns. According to Hippolyte's diary of this trip they also visited Hasht Bihisht (meaning Eight Paradises, an imperial palace built during the Safavid Empire in the 17th century), Chahár Bágh (meaning Four Gardens, a historical avenue constructed during the Safavid Empire in the 17th century) and the Jum'ih (Friday) Mosque.[358] Another place the westerners went to was Alliance Israelite, most likely the school founded in 1901 by the Alliance Israélite Universelle, a Jewish organization founded in 1860 in Paris.[359]

On their way back to Tehran they made another stop in Káshán, where they met some other Bahá'ís.[360] They visited the historical and famous Fin Garden where Amír Kabír, the Qajar prime minister, was murdered in 1852. It was he who ordered the execution of the Báb, the forerunner of Bahá'u'lláh. The travelers made a second stop in the city of Qom before returning to Tehran.

Back in Tehran

Returned to Tehran, the party went to Dawshan-tappih, an area southeast of Tehran, on July 26 for two days. In the capital, they had daily meetings with Bahá'ís and other friends. On July 31 they had dinner at 'Ayn us-Salṭanih, a Qajar prince. For a time he was governor of Tehran, then prime minister and head of the conservative anti-reform faction in government circles. He was also in touch with the Bahá'ís (for example Fá'izih Khánum) and was in correspondence with 'Abdu'l-Bahá.[361]

Hippolyte mentioned that on August 1 they went to the Garden of Arbáb. This Garden was named Jamshídábád and was in the suburbs of Tehran. It was the estate of Jamshíd Arbáb, a Zoroastrian businessman and merchant. Laura had this to say about her meetings at the end of her journey and referred to the Mr Arbáb:

> After all these meetings, we were constantly importuned by the messengers inviting us to additional meetings saying there were many

thousands who were anxious to meet us but our time was in a sense limited and we regretted our inability to stay on. We were informed that many had said: 'Here our Western sisters and brothers are going away and many of us have never met them.' This is a great Centre of Bahais. One half or one third of the Persians are Bahais. Perhaps I had better give you a view as how outsiders consider Bahais. There was here a wealthy Zoroastrian when we had a first meeting in his house. He was Arbad [Arbáb] Zawski. He is very near to our movement but not an acknowledged Bahai. He was asked his opinion of Bahais and replied: 'While I am not a Bahai yet, all my important affairs are taken care of by Bahais.'[362]

Laura and Hippolyte met Siyyid Aḥmad Músaví Hamadání known as Ṣadru'ṣ-Ṣudúr (1868–1907) in Tehran on July 7.[363] He was an Islamic scholar originally from Hamádán who had converted to the Bahá'í Faith.[364] The title Ṣadru'ṣ-Ṣudúr was given to him by 'Abdu'l-Bahá and means 'foremost authority'.[365] They visited him at least nine more times after their return to Tehran, at the end of July and in early August.[366] Laura described the meeting with him:

> In Teheran, I met a great teacher. He was like Mírzá Abul Fazil [Mírzá Abu'l-Faḍl]. Only he had the enthusiasm of youth . . . I said to him you have never made the journey to Acca? He replied: I have never taken the material road but I have often journeyed there in the spirit.[367]

The account of a gathering organized by the pupils of Ṣadru'ṣ-Ṣudúr reads:

> There was also an elaborate invitation made by the pupils of Ṣadru'ṣ-Ṣudúr to attend a grand reception in his presence. Of course, the spiritual quality and rarefied atmosphere of such heavenly assemblies where the distinguished members of the West and East gather together in such a loving environment can neither be described nor recorded. It should only be witnessed. The signs of the greatness and power of the Lord can easily be discerned.[368]

Laura spent long hours asking him questions on matters related to Islamic topics, spirituality and mysticism, and received satisfactory, coherent and convincing responses. Ṣadru'ṣ-Ṣudúr wrote a treatise which he dedicated to Laura and Hippolyte as a gift to remind them of their visit and especially Laura's deeply spiritual and heavenly journey.[369]

On August 6 they met a lady called Faeze Khanum.[370] Faeze most probably was the same Fá'izih Khánum who was born Fáṭimih Sulṭán Bígum, also known as Gul-i-Bígum, and was given the title of Fá'izih, which means prosper, by 'Abdu'l-Bahá. She was born in Isfahan about 1854 and became a Bahá'í through her brother, who lived in Tehran. Together with her husband, who became a Bahá'í several years after their marriage, they visited 'Abdu'l-Bahá in 1896. From then on, Fá'izih Khánum was an active teacher of the Bahá'í Faith in the cities of Káshán, Isfahan, and Najafábád. She converted many men and women to the Faith and even debated unveiled with a mullá, an Islamic cleric and teacher, in Káshán in 1916. She was active in assisting Bahá'ís who were imprisoned in Tehran, arranging food for them and submitting petitions on their behalf. Fá'izih Khánum became increasingly concerned with the welfare and education of women and with raising their status in the Bahá'í community. She taught Bahá'í women how to propagate the Faith after receiving a Tablet from 'Abdu'l-Bahá on this subject. She herself stopped wearing the chádur (veil) in 1914 after reading a Tablet of 'Abdu'l-Bahá to Lady Blomfield, and she promoted the discarding of the veil at mixed Bahá'í meetings.[371]

A Quick Stop in Qazvín and on to Tabríz

Laura, Hippolyte, and Laura's travel companion, Mme Lacheny, had lunch with Bagherof and then left Tehran for Tabríz on 9 August, briefly visiting Qazvín on the way. By coincidence they ran into Ali-Kuli Khan, who happened to be there, on his way to Tehran.[372] Some years later, Laura spoke about this, saying that on their way from Qazvín to Tabríz 'we met with Ali-Kuli Khan and his American wife Florence Khánum, who had quite the appearance of Orientals. We were going in different directions. It was wonderful this meeting and we did have a joyful reunion. But we had to proceed onward and shortly bade each other farewell.'[373]

They stayed for one night at the home of Dr Ḥakím I'tibár, who was perhaps a Bahá'í. They continued their trip, with brief stops on the way, including in Zanján where they met with the Bahá'ís before arriving in Tabríz on 18 August. Their visit to Tabríz must have been incredibly significant for them for it was here in the town square on July 9, 1850 that the Báb, the herald and the forerunner to Bahá'u'lláh, was executed. Laura spoke of the sacred ground of Tabríz, remembering the sad history of the Bahá'ís:

> In Tabriz while these martyrs were being persecuted many had taken refuge and fortified themselves. The hour of prayer, Azan [_adhán_] called by the Muezzin arrived and the besiegers surrounded them on all sides. There was no one going to the minaret to call the prayers so some of the Bahais volunteered. One went to the top and called the prayer and was made a target of and died ere he had half finished, undismayed a second Bahá'í took his place and shortly after met the same fate yet a third took his place and his life ended with the last of the prayer. You can imagine what our feelings were on this sacred ground. What imagining can bring to a realization of the difficulties and trials of the Bab and these blessed people.[374]

A Bahá'í in Tabríz, Ḥaydar-'Alí Uskú'í, wrote an account of the visit of the western Bahá'ís to his city, of which this is a summary:

> A droshky [a low four-wheeled open carriage] was hired to bring them, and some of the Tabríz Bahá'ís went as far as Zanján to greet and escort them. The Bahá'ís of Saysán came en masse to the village of Ḥájí Áqá on the main road to greet them as they passed. In Tabríz a house was rented for them in the Armenian quarter and meetings were held in different Bahá'í homes each day. Sayyid Riḍá Khwájih, representing the crown prince, and the employees of Niẓám us-Salṭanih attended these meetings. Ḥusayn Khán, the son of Niẓám us-Salṭanih, met with the visiting Bahá'ís and asked them many questions, including about the Bahá'í Faith. Ḥájí Mírzá Mahdí Khán Mufákhir ud-Dawlih, the Foreign Office agent in Tabríz, met with them and afterwards praised them greatly, commenting on how Barney, an American woman, could speak Persian better than many educated Iranians while other Americans (he was here probably referring to the missionaries) spent 40 years in Iran and still their heavy accent made them unintelligible to most Iranians.[375]

Uskú'í stated that before their arrival, his brother had sent him a picture of Laura, Hippolyte and Mme Lacheny taken in 'Ishqábád. The Bahá'ís thought it necessary to inform the crown prince, Muḥammad 'Alí Mírzá, before their arrival. Therefore Uskú'í visited him to tell him of their arrival. He showed the crown prince a photograph of the group, which the crown prince studied for some time and asked the identity of every person in the picture.[376] Muḥammad 'Alí Mírzá invited the group to an audience with him for a whole day. Uskú'í wrote that at the instruction of the crown prince and the governor, Niẓám us-Salṭanih, an informer came to every Bahá'í gathering.[377]

Laura spoke about the important Bahá'ís and dignitaries that she met:

> I had the pleasure of meeting the son of the then Shah (now become our present Shah [Muḥammad 'Alí Sháh]). His extreme friendliness was a good omen for the Bahá'ís.[378]

Laura, Hippolyte and Mme Lacheny remained nine days in Tabríz and then wanted to go to Mákú, despite the troubled conditions of the times. The city of Mákú is well known in Bahá'í history for its prison fortress, where the Báb was imprisoned for nine months from July 1847 to April 1848. He was executed by firing squad in 1850. The travelers had been requested by 'Abdu'l-Bahá to visit Mákú,[379] so Laura was determined to go there despite the unsettled circumstances. Niẓám us-Salṭanih provided them with an escort.[380] Uskú'í described their visit to Mákú:

> One day they decided to visit Maku. There was talk of the constitutional revolution. We explained that it was not safe to go there, but it was to no avail. They said, 'we don't know if we will ever come to Tabríz again; we have to visit this holy place.' We arranged for a phaeton [horse-drawn open carriage] to come and take them to Mákú . . .[381]

Laura later spoke about this visit:

> We visited many historical places (to the Bahais) among them the court of the Lord of the Age, where the martyrdom of the Báb had taken place. It was empty and our party were alone there. Coming

to our minds' eye was the picture of the wonderful figure of the Bab suspended on the wall being made a target of and shot to death for His beliefs. We journeyed to Maku, a desolate prison city near the frontier.

We visited the prison where the Bab had been confined for some time. Here He wrote His great work called the Seven Proofs, which is now translated in French and will shortly appear here in English. There are no Bahais in Maku except those who make the pilgrimage. This proves that personality is outside of the Spirit for the further away from where the Bab and Baha'u'llah resided, the most greatest number of Bahais can be found.

This very desolate grim prison place, houses of stone, made us realize what men [who] lived here tried to do to the Bab in the line of persecution. We shortly returned to Tabriz. Here we had many meetings. Peace and tranquility reigned over all and the sight was very impressive.[382]

Before departing Iran on August 31, Hippolyte noted in his diary that they met someone called Ezzatullah Khan [Izzatu'lláh Khán]. It is not clear who he was, perhaps a local Bahá'í. The three left for the Caucasus via Khúy and Julfa in Azerbaijan in the northwestern part of the country.[383] After crossing the Iranian border at Julfa in September, they arrived in Tbilisi (today's capital of Georgia) the following day and stayed in the Hotel Orient. The day after their arrival they visited the botanical garden and met with Maḥmúd Khán, for whom no last name was given. Laura and her companions traveled to Constantinople [today's Istanbul] on September 11. There they visited the old city and toured the bazaar and Hagia Sophia, as well as several mosques. And as they had done in most cities that they had visited, they met with the local Bahá'ís.

From there Hippolyte went to Switzerland and Laura may have stopped in Egypt in order to meet with the Bahá'ís there before traveling to 'Akká.[384]

The Effects of Laura's Trip to Persia and the Media Coverage

Laura discussed the outcome of her journey through Persia in a public talk in 1909:

It certainly was fortunate for me that I was acquainted with the Persian language. Radiating around these cities which we visited were smaller towns and villages the entire population of which were Bahais. It was not unusual to find entire communities of Jews who were all Bahais. This proves how great the teachings of Baha'u'llah were to them to turn these people into true philosophers and religious men. They were men of the fields and of menial labor and degree yet they were intellectual as well as spiritual.[385]

Laura had been impressed with how the teachings of the Bahá'í Faith had changed people of different religions and made them tolerant towards others.

Real toleration and wise vigilance: one could spend a lifetime to absorb these alone. It is privilege and responsibility to know this revelation. We must be tolerant to all mankind and vigilant not to harm. Journeying through Persia I realized how vividly these Bahai people understood that toleration. They never went to extremes but were always kind to Mohammedans [Muslims] and all people. The aspect of all truth is in this manifestation.[386]

This visit of Bahá'ís from the West must have profoundly affected the Bahá'í communities they visited, as well as the visitors themselves, by deepening their understanding of the universality of the teachings of their faith and how it was bringing the peoples of East and West together. It brought a new awareness that they belonged to an international community. *Najm-i-Bakhtar*, the Persian section of the *Star of the West*, noted: '[Laura's] journey to Iran brought much enthusiasm and passion to the hearts of the lovers of God and her services in the course of that visit were considered distinguished in the eyes of the Hands of the Cause.'[387] The travels of Laura and Hippolyte and others 'marked the beginning of the efforts by Occidental Bahá'ís, and especially by American Bahá'ís, to serve their religion globally'.[388] They opened the way for many other western Bahá'ís to travel to Iran, and correspondence between American and Iranian Bahá'í women began in 1908 or 1909. These letters motivated other western women to travel to Iran, including Susan Moody (1851–1934), who went to Tehran in 1909. Dr Moody was an American physician from Chicago who had become a Bahá'í. She went to

Iran, following an appeal endorsed by 'Abdu'l-Bahá, to work in a hospital being opened by Bahá'í doctors so that the new hospital's services would be available to women.[389] Iranian women lacked competent medical care at that time because the medical profession was male dominated and the culture made it difficult for women to be seen by men.

Laura had visited an Islamic country whose culture severely circum-scribed women's lives. Laura went as an unmarried, 27-year-old woman being accompanied by a young man. Perhaps the presence of a female chaperon had mitigated the scandal of an unmarried woman travel-ing with a man. Yet she was uniformly welcomed with respect. It took extraordinary courage for Laura to undertake this trip. The Persians had always looked up to westerners, and the group's impeccable manners and behavior must have given a silent message which resonated deeply: women, married or unmarried, could have public lives. Meeting with Laura must have opened the minds of some Iranian women when they learned how western women lived. Hearing about this educated, independent, devoted Bahá'í must have been exciting and thought-pro-voking. Harlan F. Ober, a Bahá'í pilgrim in 'Akká while Laura was there following her trip to Persia, wrote to a Bahá'í friend about Laura Barney and Hippolyte Dreyfus's journey: 'The effect of the trip through Persia by Miss B and Mr D has been wonderful,' he wrote, and he hoped and prayed that his own trip would also bring East and West closer together and would 'unify the world'.[390]

No mention or reference to the trip of Laura, Hippolyte and Mme Lacheny to Persia has been found in the Persian press of those days,[391] but several American newspapers later reported, though not always with correct information, that Laura had traveled there. These newspa-pers included *The Washington Herald*, *The Boston Globe*, *Chicago Sunday Tribune* and *The Washington Times*.[392] An article in *The Boston Globe* reported that Laura had gone to Persia and 'sat at the feet of Abbas Effendi, the present head of Bahaist movement'.[393] The *Chicago Sunday Tribune* under the heading of 'Bahaism Seizes Paris', wrote that Natalie and Laura had both gone to Persia.[394] *The Washington Times* reported that Laura had spent three years in Persia studying the language.[395] A few years after her return, in 1909, *The Washington Herald* reported:

Miss Laura Clifford Barney, the youngest daughter of Mrs. A.C. Barney, will arrive in this country on May 15. She has been abroad for a period of five years, during which time she traveled to Persia, Egypt, Syria . . . Miss Barney is a young woman of many gifts and is endowed with originality and executive talent. In addition to her perfect mastery of French, she has gained vast knowledge in the Persian language, in which she writes, reads, translates, and speaks fluently. Her devotion to the Bahá'í movement speaks for her broad-mindedness and proves her ardent desire to serve humanity. For this philosophy, she considers an efficient means to that end. Her house in Paris has been a delightful center and a gathering place for those interested in the higher problems of humanity.[396]

Return to 'Akká and Laura's Report to the Master about Her Trip

Laura had fulfilled her duties with great courage and brought happiness to the Bahá'ís in the different cities of Persia she visited. She soon returned to 'Akká to give her report to 'Abdu'l-Bahá, later noting, 'We left Persia and returned towards our home Acca.'[397] Some years later, she commented, 'We couldn't express to 'Abdu'l-Bahá our deep gratitude at what we had seen and heard. Little by little we spoke of it.'[398] She wept as she described to 'Abdu'l-Bahá the sacrifices, love, and devotion of the Persian friends, and of the joy and inspiration she had received.[399]

Following her return, Laura delivered to 'Abdu'l-Bahá a handwritten treatise: the responses of Ṣadru'ṣ-Ṣudúr to her questions.[400] In the Introduction of his treatise, Ṣadru'ṣ-Ṣudúr wrote:

> During this meeting, as a gesture of kindness to this essence of nothingness, two sanctified and heavenly souls expressed the blessed view that this evanescent one prepare a small compilation of Islamic verses and traditions establishing the truth of the Cause of the Primal Point and the most holy Abhá Beauty – glorified be their mention – and the station of Him who has demonstrated His unfailing servitude, the King of the Covenant, 'Abdu'l-Bahá – may the souls of all that dwell on earth and in the heavens be a sacrifice for His servitude and the wrongs He has suffered.[401]

Ṣadru'ṣ-Ṣudúr closes his treatise with a dedication to 'the sacred threshold of the two sanctified personages who are firm and immovable in the Covenant of 'Abdu'l-Bahá' and names Monsieur Dreyfus and

Miss Barney.[402] The treatise was published in 1975 with the title *Istid-láliyyih of Ṣadru'ṣ-Ṣudúr* (*Book of Proofs of Ṣadru'ṣ-Ṣudúr*).[403] It included a Tablet revealed by 'Abdu'l-Bahá to Ṣadru'ṣ-Ṣudúr with the salutation 'Upon you be the Glory of God'. The Tablet mentions the treatise and expresses 'Abdu'l-Bahá's 'delight in the wonderful quality of their journey to Iran'.[404] The Tablet dwelled on Laura's visit to Persia and how thrilled and touched she was after meeting the Persian Bahá'ís.

> O dove of the Eternal Paradise! Amatu'l-Bahá [Laura Barney] arrived with supreme glad tidings and eloquent speech, with teary eyes and a heart full with the spirit of joy, each day and night praising the friends in Iran and her devotion to that loving friend [Ṣadru'ṣ-Ṣudúr]. In truth, she is enthralled with those who have remained steadfast in the Covenant and enamored with the pure and noble friends. Whenever there is a mention of you, like an electric spark she bursts into laughter and like a cloud she weeps and declares that those friends are true and heartfelt lovers of the Blessed Beauty, are beguiled by that sublime face, attracted to those fragrant locks, aflame with the fire of the love of God, and free from any superstition . . .
>
> Thus Amatu'l-Bahá Barney was very happy with the Iranian friends and night and day praised them. Now she has traveled to the western world so she may recount the stories of the eastern friends, that the fire of the love of the Blessed Beauty may blaze and the hearts be filled with love from the wafting of the sacred breezes. Pray that she may succeed.[405]

It was during this trip to 'Akká that Laura encountered Hooper Harris and Harlan Foster Ober, both American Bahá'ís who were in 'Akká as pilgrims. Laura knew Hooper Harris from Washington, D.C.[406] She might well have shared her experiences with them and helped them to prepare for their forthcoming trip to India and Burma.[407] She also helped to translate 'Abdu'l-Bahá's words when Harris and Ober met with Him. Ober wrote: 'At every gathering there were exchanges of love and greetings that were wonderful in their beauty. Miss Barney interpreted for us, made our sojourn there very pleasant.'[408] The two men then left to teach the Bahá'í Faith in Asia.

Laura continued her services. Among them was 'the great labor' and 'inestimable service' of assisting with research and the translation of the Tablets of 'Abdu'l-Bahá from the original language of Persian into English, which she undertook in collaboration with several others.[409]

Back in the West

Before returning to Paris, Laura wrote to Natalie, who was at the time living in Neuilly-sur-Seine, a suburb of Paris, asking if she could stay with her for a month before sailing to the United States. She explained to her sister, 'Perhaps you cannot have me for so long, especially as I will be working with others.' Laura was going to finish her book. She must have been planning to complete her book *Some Answered Questions*, with questions that she had posed to 'Abdu'l-Bahá and His responses. Laura suggested she could stay either at the house of Eva Palmer, Natalie's American friend, or at the same hotel as Ethel Rosenberg, as Ethel was going to work with Laura. Laura had thought of staying in a hotel but she needed two bedrooms, one for herself and one for Ethel. Laura did not want to stay at Eva's home for several reasons, one being that she might return to Paris soon. Also, Neuilly was possibly too far away if Laura could not have the pleasure of seeing her constantly around the house. She apologized that she had to burden Natalie with her plans: 'Mille fois pardon chérie [A thousand pardons, my dear].' She sent her greetings to Hippolyte and asked Natalie to tell him that she had received the films and his letter.[410]

Laura arrived in Paris in early 1907 and did stay with Natalie in Neuilly-sur-Seine. Her mother and cousin Ellen were arriving in Paris too.[411] She had many stories to tell to the Parisian Bahá'ís about her trip and, in particular, about the sacrificial efforts and the happiness of the Bahá'ís of Persia.[412] Paris was home to Europe's first Bahá'í community, which included many expatriates from North America.[413] In those years many Bahá'ís lived there and many Bahá'ís passed though.[414] Among them were 'Hippolyte Dreyfus; an architecture student, Charles Mason Remey; the Englishman Thomas Breakwell' as well as artists such as 'the American Impressionist painter Edwin Scott; artists Juliet Thompson and Marion Jack; and Edith Sanderson, whose sister Sybil was a celebrated opera singer of her time – a muse of the composer Massenet, feted by Toulouse Lautrec and the first love of American newspaper magnet William Randolph Hearst, whose philanthropist mother [Phoebe Hearst] was one of the most prominent American followers

of 'Abdu'l-Bahá.' Thus the circles that the Bahá'ís moved in were mon-
eyed, 'culturally sophisticated and open-minded'.[415]

Laura got settled in Paris and worked on her book of the 'table talks'
of 'Abdu'l-Bahá, busily editing and finalizing it. In one of her talks she
made an interesting comment: 'They say women are marvelous smug-
glers; to get the book out of 'Akka, I asked the secretaries to copy the set
twice; they did; I smuggled it out and brought it to Paris.'[416] She had
the manuscript and started working on it

Ethel Rosenberg traveled from London and was in Paris by Easter
of 1907 to help Laura with the book.[417] Ethel's biographer commented
on the effectiveness of this collaboration: 'Laura and Ethel were coun-
terparts of each other, pioneer workers engaged in the same important
task of spreading the Bahá'í teachings in their respective countries.'[418]

It may have been around this time that Laura received a Tablet from
'Abdu'l-Bahá.

> O Amatu'l-Bahá
> No greater title than this exists in the divine Kingdom that I may
> choose to address you. News has arrived from Paris that you have
> spoken at a number of assemblies, which has imparted glad tidings
> and joy to those present. This news caused much rejoicing and
> jubilation since you were nurtured in 'Akká and were animated by
> the breezes of the spirit of life and attained the power of eloquent
> speech. Therefore, strive night and day so that each hour your flame
> may become greater and your speech more eloquent and thus begin
> to soar out of pure joy and delight.[419]

'Abdu'l-Bahá continued by writing about the difficulties in 'Akká but
He noted that they were not bitter but sweet, not darkness but light. He
ended the Tablet in His own handwriting:

> O Amatu'l-Bahá,
> Convey to the beloved of God and His handmaidens, one by one,
> loving greetings and regards, and also to your respected mother. Tell
> your sister that the divine song and the verses of the Kingdom and
> the strains of the heavenly harp are enduring and eternal and their
> melody fills the endless and limitless space, while all the beautiful
> songs of this earthly existence shall be extinguished.[420]

'Abdu'l-Bahá wrote in yet another Tablet to Laura:

O Amatu'l-Bahá,

Although it was my wish that you should have a share in My pain and torment and this, too, was your highest desire, yet your sacred purpose and the Cause of the Word of God are greater than our desire and that is why I sent you on your way. Therefore, be not distressed and despondent. The time has come that in this field of service you shall gain ascendance over all the prominent men. Deliver eloquent speeches, and guide the friends and handmaidens to the straight path and, like Mary Magdalene, guide the apostles to the service of the heavenly light, until its musk-laden breezes perfume all horizons and the light of truth shine upon that realm. Then will the light of bounty shine, heavenly blessings appear, the influence of the Word of God be discerned and the power of God's army become clearly established.

Yet perseverance and constancy are indispensable and firmness and vigor imperative. Gather together the friends in Paris, arrange an assemblage of God's lovers, and raise the melody of holiness. Console the friends, be loving to God's handmaidens and tell them that, for 'Abdu'l-Bahá, pain and suffering are His heart's desire and pain and faithlessness at the hands of the heedless are the joy of His soul and conscience, while suspension from the cross is His heavenly throne and violent death but a new life. The taste of deadly poison is but sweetness upon sweetness, and the venom of betrayal is sweeter than sugar and nectar. He sees immortality in annihilation and everlasting life in death; in utter joy He will hasten to the field of sacrifice and, at the moment of martyrdom, celebrate the day.

His suffering and pain should bring no sadness to your hearts or make you feel hopeless, do not grieve. Be not grief stricken but become illumined and afire. For the secret of sacrifice bestows everlasting life, and death and destruction in this field are the cause of life itself.

In short, bring joy to all hearts and become the cause of activity and action, such that hearts may be attracted to the Abhá Kingdom and souls receive life from the breezes of the denizens of the heavenly throne.

O Amatu'l-Bahá, raise such a burning flame that all feelings of aloofness and apathy may melt away, and become the cause of elevation of the Word of God.

Raise the banner of the love of God so that ultimately war and conflict may end; darkness, enmity and hatred may melt away; and the radiant day of the love of God may dawn and cause such feelings of harmony and kindliness among men that all may become the pearls of one sea and the roses of the same garden.

Be not astonished at such a claim. We are now at the outset, look to the end. The true farmer drops a few seeds but sees the future harvest of the field. We must not consider our own power and ability but concentrate on the bounty and blessing of the Kingdom. Take the first step, no matter how tiny and insignificant. Under the shining of the sun, it becomes great. No matter how small a drop of water, yet it is connected to the sea of seas. Therefore consider the bounty and blessing of the Abhá Beauty and arise to serve.

The ladies of the Holy Family remember you night and day and desire success and blessings for you. Convey to all the friends of God loving greetings and waft the breezes of benediction upon the handmaiden of the Lord.

Upon you be greetings and blessings.[421]

While in France, Laura saw her friend Ali-Kuli Khan and his wife Florence who had returned from their trip to Persia and stopped for a while in Paris. They attended a Bahá'í meeting at Laura's in Neuilly-sur-Seine where she was staying with Natalie.[422] Laura's mother, Alice, also arrived in Paris in this period and spent some of her time with Natalie at her home and some in London, where she was organizing an exhibition for the following year.[423]

Laura and her mother went to Évian-les-Bains in France, a spa town on the south side of Lac Léman (Lake Geneva), for a few weeks of treatment; and then to Mont Pèlerin, Switzerland, where Hippolyte's family had built a house on the mountain facing Lac Léman, across from Évian-les-Bains.

Compiling and Publishing *Some Answered Questions*

Laura went on yet another pilgrimage to 'Akká in October 1908 for a few weeks.[424] That was the year the Young Turk Revolution broke out in the Ottoman Empire. The sultan, who would be deposed in 1909,[425] was forced to activate the constitution, which he had earlier suspended, and to release all religious and political prisoners held under the old regime. After 40 years of imprisonment and confinement in 'Akká, 'Abdu'l-Bahá was freed in September of that year. Laura was among the first to visit 'Abdu'l-Bahá as a free man.

The year 1908 was also momentous for Laura because it was the year her manuscript *Some Answered Questions* was published. She had worked on it during her several visits to 'Akká from 1904 to 1906 and had worked further in Paris after returning from Persia. In 1906 'Abdu'l-Bahá had given permission for her corrected version of *Some Answered Questions* to be published.[426]

H.M. Balyuzi (1908–80), a prominent Iranian Bahá'í scholar and a Hand of the Cause who lived most of his adult life in the United Kingdom, wrote that it was during those several years from 1904 to 1908 that 'a book unique in the entire range of the Writings of the Founders of the Faith took shape. The book was *Some Answered Questions*. Questions came from Laura Barney and 'Abdu'l-Bahá answered them.'[427] The book was originally called *Table Talks*, and the Persian-language version had a subtitle: 'Talks During Luncheon'.[428] At first Laura had not intended to publish these questions and answers, writing in the preface of the book that 'these answers were written down in Persian while 'Abdu'l-Bahá spoke, not with a view to publication, but simply that I might have them for future study'.[429] However, she had desired early on to save the teachings of 'Abdu'l-Bahá for posterity.[430]

Years later Laura described the long, painstaking process from the initial note-taking to 'Abdu'l-Bahá's final approval for publication. She had to be patient, waiting for 'Abdu'l-Bahá to review the written answers to her questions. He admired her efforts in a Tablet to her:

O Amatu'l-Bahá,
Regarding the lessons, be assured that during the upcoming days, regardless of circumstance, I will attend to their review and correction. I consider you in such high regard that I want you to be happy always and to advance and progress each day so that you may attain to the knowledge of the Divine. Thus far no one has received this favor whereby such lessons were dictated and transcribed. You are the only one who has attained to such a bounty. This bounty will be

eternal, therefore be thankful to God and remain in utter happiness and joy.[431]

Laura selected material from among the transcripts she had gathered from many table talks given by 'Abdu'l-Bahá and chose some of them for inclusion in her book.[432] Then came the task of translating them, then comparing the Persian and the English, followed by correcting and rereading. These were arduous tasks for both the Master and Laura, especially when the time arrived to arrange the sequence of the segments for the compilation. 'Abdu'l-Bahá had decided early in the process that Laura's notes should be recorded in Persian as well as in English. However, they had not been recorded in Persian from the beginning and this factor made the compilation and finalization of the earliest texts from the English notes more difficult.

The Master would correct Mírzá Munír's first Persian draft and then review the corrections. Laura explained that the English and French versions of the book were translated from the Persian notes.[433] 'Abdu'l-Bahá altered the material as needed by adding or deleting a word here and there with His *nay* (reed pen). Then He would approve and sign each corrected segment and stamp it with His seal, the same seal that was used for His revealed Tablets.[434]

Some years later Laura explained how the book had been written over time, noting that 'Abdu'l-Bahá's explanations were corrected by Him and received His seal and signature.

> This is why 'Some Answered Questions' is as authentic as the Letters [Tablets] of 'Abdu'l-Bahá. This material was taken by me to Europe and brought back again so that although the book seems as one constant stream, it was really done in this piecemeal way. It shows how the Teachings fit together perfectly, for although weeks and even months elapsed between these different chapters, when completed, it is as one song.[435]

Laura confirmed the book's authenticity a few years later:

> . . . when 'Abdu'l-Bahá answered the questions printed in this book I always arranged for some able Persian secretary to be present to ensure that valuable teachings would not be lost or misinterpreted

. . . 'Abdu'l-Bahá would read every line of the original Persian text, and sometimes would correct a word or a line with His reed pen; He would then sign each lesson and stamp it with His seal; the same signature and the same seal as His Tablets.[436]

Laura will be long remembered in history as the person who, during lunchtimes, asked 'Abdu'l-Bahá all manner of questions and carefully recorded His answers. It was noted on its publication that the book was in 'the style of the great master, food alike for the learned and for the simple hearted'.[437] A writer commented that her questions were related to significant matters such as theology, materialism, the reality of the spirit and the interpretation of a number of Bible verses as well as issues such as the oneness of God and His creation, reincarnation and many other similar concepts. To these questions she received ample answers from 'Abdu'l-Bahá, which she subsequently collected, catalogued and, after approval, published in the form of a book which has since become a major text on various religious and spiritual topics.[438]

Laura noted in her preface:

In my case the teachings were made simple, to correspond to my rudimentary knowledge, and are therefore in no way complete and exhaustive, as the Table of Contents may suggest – the Table of Contents having been added merely to indicate the subjects treated of. But I believe that what has been so valuable to me may be of use to others, since all men, notwithstanding their differences, are united in their search for reality; and I have therefore asked 'Abdu'l-Bahá's permission to publish these talks.[439]

The first English edition of *Some Answered Questions: Collected and Translated from the Persian of Abdu'l-Baha* by Laura Clifford Barney was published by Kegan, Paul, Trench, Trübner & Company of London in 1908. She explained in a talk in 1944 that a Persian scholar had helped with the English translation.[440] She also collaborated with Hippolyte in translating it into French.[441] The French translation, which was carried out mostly by Hippolyte, was called *Les Leçons de St. Jean d'Acre* and was published, also that same year, by Ernest Leroux in Paris. The Persian edition, published by E.J. Brill in Leiden, Netherlands, also in 1908, was later titled *An-Núru'l-Abhá-fí-Mufáwaḍat Abdu'l-Bahá* (The

Light of Bahá Shining in Discourse with 'Abdu'l-Bahá) and had the subtitle 'Talks During Luncheon'. Thus three different language editions were published in one year.

The scholar Balyuzi explained why *Some Answered Questions* has no equal:

> Men who have devoted precious years of their lives to study and research – to the building of arguments, the laying of premises, and the marshalling of facts – have never presented the fundamentals of life and belief, the basic truths of the universe around them, and the mainsprings of action, with such lucidity and coherence as are here apparent. Nor can they hope to rival, much less to match 'Abdu'l-Bahá's all-encompassing wisdom. And these were words spoken without previous intimation of the nature and purport of the query. Not only do His answers arrest attention and compel thought, the strength wedded to the crystal clarity of the language enchant the mind. His statements are unencumbered, His similes most apt. His reasoning is flawless. His conclusions are unhedged and emphatic, informed with authority. *Some Answered Questions* has no equal, and the service rendered by its compiler has been characterized by the Guardian of the Faith as 'imperishable'.[442]

Shoghi Effendi explained how this book was published during 'Abdu'l-Bahá's 'troublous times, the most dramatic period of His ministry' and the wide range of the subjects covered:

> It was at this juncture that that celebrated compilation of His table talks, published under the title 'Some Answered Questions', was made, talks given during the brief time He was able to spare, in the course of which certain fundamental aspects of His Father's Faith were elucidated, traditional and rational proofs of its validity adduced, and a great variety of subjects regarding the Christian Dispensation, the Prophets of God, Biblical prophecies, the origin and condition of man and other kindred themes authoritatively explained.[443]

Laura wrote in the preface to the first edition of *Some Answered Questions*: 'This book presents only certain aspects of the Bahá'í Faith, which is universal in its message and has for each questioner the answer suited to his special development and needs.'[444] The questions and answers covered a wide range of topics. She later explained:

Questions which are considered: Is there a God? How can we know God? What of free-will? – remain unanswered or misunderstood for the minds of many. Here too, are commentaries and explanations of Biblical passages suited to our age.[445]

The book's section titles demonstrate the wide range of subjects covered by the book: 'On the Influence of the Prophets in the Evolution of Humanity', 'Some Christian Subjects', 'On the Powers and Conditions of the Manifestations of God', 'On the Origin, Powers, and Conditions of Man', and 'Miscellaneous Subjects'.[446] The book provides 'Abdu'l-Bahá's answers to 84 questions asked by Laura on a diversity of issues about such Christian topics as the resurrection of Christ and the meaning of the Holy Spirit and the Trinity, and about topical issues such as reincarnation, predestination, the modification of species, the advancement of human souls in other worlds, spiritual healing, the influence of the stars, the justice and mercy of God, and the punishment of criminals.

'Abdu'l-Bahá was also asked by Laura to comment on specific verses in the Books of Revelation and Isaiah and to describe the missions of Abraham, Moses and Jesus. An American Bahá'í researcher and writer, Robert Stockman, wrote, 'As a result of Laura Barney's probings, answers to many questions of eternal significance, as well as those reflecting a Western or Christian orientation, became a part of the Bahá'í sacred writings. The book has always been one of the most popular Bahá'í texts.'[447]

Ian Kluge, a Bahá'í student of philosophy, commented that *Some Answered Questions* reaches into academic areas that were relatively unknown at the time: 'This survey of SAQ [*Some Answered Questions*] has covered major subjects in ontology [the nature of being, or the relations within a set of concepts and categories in a subject area], onto-theology [the ontology of God or the theology of being], epistemology [the philosophical study of the nature, origin, and limits of human knowledge] and philosophical anthropology [a branch of philosophy that explores the individual and the collective nature of humankind]. Among Kluge's several conclusions is this:

SAQ's ideas on these four foundational subject areas are founded on and shaped by a consistent set of philosophical ideas. In other words, SAQ is more than a random collection of thoughts on various topics; instead it exemplifies a consistent underlying philosophy vis-à-vis ontology, ontotheology, epistemology and philosophical anthropology. In these areas, SAQ lays down basic principles from which considerable portions of SAQ (and the other Writings) may be deduced or to which they can be rationally related. Close analysis shows the seemingly unconnected parts are joined at an often implicit level by a coherent underlying philosophy.[448]

The value of Laura's work regarding *Some Answered Questions* and the book's importance were well recognized. 'Abdu'l-Bahá advised Juliet Thompson, a new Bahá'í at the time, to read it:

> You must read Miss Barney's book [*Some Answered Questions*] and Mírzá Abu'l-Faḍl's [*The Bahá'í Proofs*] a great deal, Juliet. I want you to progress spiritually and to be a real daughter of the Kingdom. I want you to be entirely severed from the world.[449]

Dr Afroukhteh wrote that Laura was 'able to complete the work and present this great service to the Bahá'í world, a gift that will cause her to be remembered eternally'.[450] Dr Ugo Giachery (1896–1989), who was appointed a Hand of the Cause of God in 1951 and would provide inestimable service to Shoghi Effendi in the completion of the Shrine of the Báb, recognized the book as 'unique in all religious literature' and Laura's 'most outstanding' achievement, 'one that has immortalized her name the world over'.[451]

Hippolyte described the contribution *Some Answered Questions* made in the West in the preface of his own book, *The Universal Religion: The Bahaism*, which was published in 1909:

> By this work, Laura Clifford Barney has powerfully contributed to placing within the reach of the public the teachings of the new religion, for she has given, in the very simple form in which they were held, the conversations she had with the 'Master of 'Akká'. Till now, in fact, considering the small number of works translated into any one of the European languages, the knowledge of the philosophy and theology of Bahaism was limited only to the Orientalists

who could read in the text the works of Bahá'u'lláh or of 'Abdu'l-Bahá, and to the adepts among whom the Master's Tablets are in circulation. *Some Answered Questions* therefore covers a deficiency particularly perceptible in the West.[452]

Shoghi Effendi, when recording the names of those persons who had been instrumental for the rise of the Faith in the West, mentions Laura Barney, 'whose imperishable service was to collect and transmit to posterity in the form of a book, entitled "Some Answered Questions", 'Abdu'l-Bahá's priceless explanations, covering a wide variety of subjects'.[453] The Foreword to the latest edition of *Some Answered Questions* (2014) notes, 'Shoghi Effendi observed that the book expounds the basic beliefs of the Cause in a simple and clear language and regarded its content as essential for grasping the significance and implications of the Bahá'í Revelation.'[454] In this book, he wrote, one 'will find the clue to all the perplexing questions that agitate the mind of man in his search after true knowledge. The more this Book is read with care and patience, the greater are its revelations, and the more complete the understanding of its inner truth and significance.'[455]

The publication of *Some Answered Questions* was announced at a book fair in 1908. On October 17 of that year *The New York Times*, under the heading of 'Literary News of Philadelphia', reported, not completely accurately, on the fall book fair and new books, mentioning Laura's new publication:

A curious book on Bahaism comes this week from the Lippincott Company. It bears the somewhat cryptic title, 'Some Questions Answered', and is the work of Laura Clifford Barney a Philadelphian who has made a study of this interesting Persian sect and its peculiar doctrinal system. The great teacher of this new religion, which claims its adherents in all countries and among Jews and Christians, Mohammedans and Zoroastrians and what not, was Abdu'l-Baha, who was born in Tehran in 1817, was one of the earliest followers of the Bab, and died in Acca, Palestine, in 1892. The material for the present work was collected in Acca, during the latter years of Abdu'l-Baha's life, the author writing from his dictation and afterwards translating them from the Persian. A French version of these teachings has already been published in Paris, and will be brought out in London.[456]

While the report in *The New York Times* did not get all the facts correct, *The Washington Herald* did get the details right and was laudatory in its reporting of the publication of *Some Answered Questions*:

> At Acca she [Laura Clifford Barney] paid extended visits to Abdu'l Baha, to receive special instructions concerning the Baha'i movement. In order to make the subject clear and intelligent to the West, she formulated a set of questions dealing with most vital problems of religious and social reform which are of interest to many thinkers in Europe and America. In his answers to these Abdu'l Baha embodies the higher philosophy of the movement and the means by which such Baha'i ideals are applied to the peace and unity of the race. Miss Barney's book, 'Some Answered Questions', gives a vivid and comprehensive exposition of these interesting points, coupled with interpretation of various prophetic chapters of the Bible. The book is vastly read here and abroad and is considered by authorities as the best work written by an American to make the Baha'i teachings intelligible to the Western mind.[457]

The French Nobel Prize winner novelist Romain Rolland (1866–1944) quoted from *Some Answered Questions* in his novel *Clérambault*. He also referred to the Bahá'í Faith in his book *La Vie de Tolstoï*.[458] He had learned about the Faith in Geneva:

> It is above all a religious ethic, which does not conceive of religion without putting it into practice, and which seeks to remain in accord with science and reason, without cult or priests. The first duty is that each has a profession; work is holy; it is divine benediction.
>
> I have noticed an analogy with Christian Science. In my spirit, I prefer Baha'ism, I find it more flexible and subtle. And it offers the poetic imagination a rich feast. Its roots are sunk in the great metaphysical dreams of the Orient. There are some luminous pages in the discourses of St Jean d'Acre [i.e. *Some Answered Questions*] of 'Abdul-Baha. Baha'u'llah, a prisoner, succeeded in writing and answering some 'tablets' of an admirable and moral beauty, under the name 'the Oppressed One'. . . .[459]

The year after the publication of the book, the *Springfield Republican* in Massachusetts reported: 'In America considerable interest has recently been aroused in the Mohammedan religious sect of Babis or Bahais. The greatest living teacher of their belief is Abdu'l Baha at whose feet Laura Clifford Barney received her instructions. The result of her studies is a book entitled *Some Answered Questions*.'[460] The article then discussed various topics that were covered by the book.

Soon after it was published, Laura sent a copy of *Some Answered Questions* to Edward G. Browne (1862–1926), the British Oriental-ist who had met Bahá'u'lláh.[461] Browne was a friend of Hippolyte and perhaps also knew Laura. In the bibliographical section of his book *Materials for the Study of the Bábí Religion*, Browne has an entry for 'Barney, Laura Clifford (now Madame H. Dreyfus)' and gives the details of the Persian, English and French editions of *Some Answered Questions* as well as her play *God's Heroes*.[462]

Laura also sent a copy to the British writer, scientist and Persian scholar Edward Heron-Allen (1861–1943). Upon receiving it, he replied by letter, addressing her in Persian, '*fadáyat shavam ru'yá-i dúr*' (May my life be a ransom for you, O Distant Dream): 'The pleasure of possessing, and also the charm of reading, your book, is increased a thousand-fold by its being received at your hands. I read it a great while under the Aurora Borealis last night.' He ended his letter by saying, 'Your book has given me a great deal of peaceful pleasure & is destined to give me a great deal more.'[463]

Copies of her book were sent to many prominent people, including John H. Patterson, a socially progressive businessman who founded the National Cash Register Company, whom she may have known through her family. He thanked her for the thought and wrote that it was a 'revelation' to him. 'It is a thing of beauty and a joy forever, but the greatest joy in this will be, not only the remembrance of your beautiful character, but also the philosophy which it contains.'[464]

Reflecting on Her Conversion

Nine years after learning about the Bahá'í Faith, Laura wrote a letter to a Bahá'í friend, perhaps Ahmad Sohrab, in which she reflected on her conversion:

Dear Mirza Ahmad –
I read your letters with deep interest & am glad to know that you are again able to begin such a useful work.

You have kindly asked me to tell you what I have been doing & seeing in the Cause since I became associated with this Universal Movement.

I have done little, but I have seen much, these 9 years, much for I have gone from city to city, from country to county & everywhere I have seen Bahaism broaden the minds & uplift the hearts of men.

In France, England, America I have seen these teachings impregnate themselves into the ever-increasing groups of Bahais & influence the western evolution of thought. The lectures, the publications, the efforts of individual Bahais & the natural springtime of reformation have brought this about under the direction of Abdu'l Baha.

In Egypt, I have lived among the native Bahais & seen the stimulus that is given to those who dwell in the land so near Acca ['Akká].

In Russia, I have seen the first Mashragu'l azkar [Mashriqu'l-Adhkár, House of Worship] which is reminder to humanity that God can be worshiped truly anywhere knowledge, charity & actively blended to prayer.

In Persia, I have seen the birth place of this Cause filled by the splendor of matured form of Bahaism. I have met thousands & thousands of Persians imbued with the spirit of brotherhood & progress. Throughout the land we came in contact with the leavening power of Bahaism & it is easy to track the new awakening of Persia to this mighty Cause.

In Acca I have witnessed that guidance & information radiate from that center to the world at large.

I have seen a simple man, through the assistance of God, closely in touch with the innermost lives of millions of fellow beings. In here I have seen the guidance of servitude & love.

At some future time, I hope to tell fully of life of 'Abdu'l-Bahá at Acca during the months I had the privilege of visiting Him in His imprisonment. I want to describe how His task is accomplished in the midst of storms & turmoil which leave his active spirit always serene.[465]

Laura continued her correspondence with 'Abdu'l-Bahá after the publication of her book and received numerous Tablets from Him. He wrote in response to one of her letters:

> The content of your letter was delightful, reflecting the love of God. I hope that God may bestow such favor that your face, like unto the moon, becomes radiant with the knowledge of God and you may become the cause of entry into the Cause of God by people of noble character and distinction.

Trip to Chicago with Her Mother

In Paris, Laura celebrated the Bahá'í Feast of Naw-Rúz, which is also the Persian New Year, at her home on March 21, 1909.[466] She then traveled to the United States, where she gave several talks about the Bahá'í Faith in different cities. It may have been at Lockwood Academy (presumably in New York City) that she gave a talk on May 16 reflecting on her conversion and her early experiences.[467] On June 24 she hosted a gathering that takes place on the first day of each Bahá'í month, that is every 19 days. *The Evening Star* reported that these are a '"feast of reason and flow of soul" rather than a banquet with appetizing viands'.[468] At that Feast, she chaired the meeting, arranged for readings from a recently published book, played some piano pieces and served refreshments to the 140 guests. She later gave a talk about 'Bahaism' at the People's Church-Pythian Temple in Washington, D.C., which was reported in the June 26 issue of *The Washington Post*.[469]

On July 8, together with her mother, she traveled to Chicago, where they were welcomed by the Bahá'í women and found that roses had been sent to their hotel room. They visited the grounds of the Bahá'í Temple with some of the prominent Bahá'í women. Laura also met with the Bahá'í friends and gave several talks, mostly speaking about her stays in 'Akká near the Master and His household, and her trip to Persia.[470] At one gathering, when asked to talk about 'Abdu'l-Bahá, she 'complied with the request most beautifully'.[471] She gave a talk one day at the Arts and Crafts Institute about her trip to Persia and another that same evening to a packed audience. One of the attendees wrote about her delivery and knowledge:

She is a very fine speaker and spoke with much earnestness and power. She has a fine intellect and is without a doubt a powerful instrument in this great Cause. There is a great work for her to do and she is doing it. She has a broad view of the Revelation and is practical, sensible – not emotional.[472]

She received a letter from 'Abdu'l-Bahá and she responded in Persian, saying that she was rejoiced that He was well-pleased with her trip, perhaps meaning her current trip to Chicago. Now, she wrote, she would make the same effort in Paris as she had in the United States. She also noted that from this letter it became clear to her what 'vafá' [faithfulness] means.[473]

Laura and her mother went to Bar Harbor, Maine, that summer, the first time after Albert's death that they had gone there. They stayed at a hotel since their house, Bar-y-Byrn, was rented out.[474]

Developments within the Barney Family

By 1910 Laura had returned to Europe with her mother. They had planned to visit Germany and then return to Paris for a few months.[475] Laura was finalizing the publication of her new play, *God's Heroes,* as a book while her mother was receiving her share of attention. Alice Barney had met a popular and handsome bachelor, Christian Dominique Hemmick, in Washington the previous year. The son of the US Consul to Geneva, Switzerland, he was at 24 years of age, 30 years her junior. It was love at first sight. Christian was a few years younger than her younger daughter, Laura. Alice had advertised a role for one of her plays and he had applied for it. Towards the end of spring of 1910, Alice announced that she had become engaged and planned to marry him.[476] While she was in Paris, Alice wanted to get the blessings of her daughters, to prepare them for the arrival of Christian in a few months and their possible upcoming marriage.

The two daughters were not happy. Both strongly opposed this forthcoming marriage. Laura, who managed the family's finances, was convinced that Christian was just a gigolo looking for financial support. She warned her mother that a marriage to Christian would bring her mother 'social humiliation, if not outright ostracism'. Natalie's objections took a more pragmatic and feminist perspective. She agreed that after years of marital imprisonment Alice was finally a free woman, so why would she accept the restrictions of marriage again after she had achieved many accomplishments as a single woman? However, in the face of their mother's happiness, Natalie and Laura acquiesced to the marriage.[477]

While in Paris, Alice first stayed with Natalie but she was not comfortable there. After a few weeks she moved to Laura's apartment at 20 rue de Vienne, although she did not find her stay with Laura as much fun as it had been with Natalie, since Laura was involved with more serious activities. Alice's biographer remarked, 'In some ways, Laura was as puzzling as Natalie. Alice often wondered how she could have produced a daughter who took every minute of life so seriously.'[478]

Natalie had lived in Neuilly-sur-Seine for almost ten years and Laura had stayed with her there a few times. In 1909 Natalie moved to 20 rue Jacob in Paris on the edge of the ancient Latin Quarter.[479] The house she occupied was an 18th-century villa with a Doric temple. Natalie continued her unconventional lifestyle and befriended prominent women artists of the time. Their mother did not approve of Natalie's disregard of societal norms, but accepted it since she believed it brought happiness to her daughter's life.[480]

Natalie started holding salons at her new home for prominent authors and poets in Paris. Over the years, the world's intellectual and artistic elite attended her salons, including T.S. Eliot, Ezra Pound, Paul Valéry, Gertrude Stein, Rabindranath Tagore, Isadora Duncan, Ida Rubenstein, Colette, James Joyce, F. Scott Fitzgerald, Alicia Toklas, Zelda and André Gide. One of the factors that contributed to the success of Natalie's salons was her wit, which was a combination of intelligence and humor.[481] One of Natalie's biographers wrote: 'Even Laura, known for her dour and humorless personality, was constantly laughing around her sister.'[482] Laura must have attended some of her salons and must have known some of the guests.

God's Heroes: A Drama in Five Acts

In 1910 Laura published *God's Heroes: A Drama in Five Acts*, in an effort to protect the Bábí and the Bahá'í Faiths from other dramatic productions which might portray them inappropriately.[483]

The Russian dramatist and playwright with the pen name Isabella

Grinevskaya (real name Beyle Friedberg, 1864–1944) had published a play in 1903 about the life of the Báb, the founder of the Bábí religion, and the life of Ṭáhirih (c. 1814/17–1852; sources differ on the year of her birth).[484] The drama, entitled *Bab: A Dramatic Poem of the History of Persia*, was translated into French and Tartar languages, caught the interest of educated people,[485] and had successful runs in St Petersburg in 1904.[486] Grinevskaya later met 'Abdu'l-Bahá in Egypt in 1910.[487]

Sarah Bernhardt, the best-known French actress of her time, had also become interested in the story of the Báb and had asked two authors, Catulle Mendès and Jules-Bois,[488] to write a play about Ṭáhirih and the Bábís, intending to play the role of Ṭáhirih herself. Mendès (1841–1909), the famous French poet, may have been Laura's mentor in Paris. According to a newspaper article: '[Mendès] was a friend and admirer of Miss Barney and was at the time of his tragic taking off [death] engaged in writing a play of which this beautiful young Bahá poetess was the heroine.'[489]

Laura was shocked by the thought of what they might show on the Paris stage about the life of the Báb and wrote her historical drama to protect the Báb and His Faith. Her publisher in the United States was J. B. Lippincott of Philadelphia[490] and in London was Kegan Paul, Trench, Trübner & Co.[491] The protocol among playwrights was that if someone were planning and working on a play, other playwrights would not use the same subject. Years later, Laura explained why she wrote the drama:

> When I was in Paris a few years before World War I, a noted French playwright was planning to use the story of Quarratu'l'Ain [Ṭáhirih] as the basis for a play for Sarah Bernhardt. Knowing that the empha-sis for such a celebrated actress would be less on the spiritual love than on the physical one and having myself had dramatic training under two of the outstanding French actors of the day, I decided myself to write such a play, and arranged for this playwright to be so informed; he then put aside his project.[492]

She later wrote:

> The cover and page designs of the 1910 edition of *God's Heroes* were done by a special firm in Baltimore, Maryland, and are lithographs

made from stone impressions. These designs were selected by me from a collection at the Rare Book Room of the United States Library of Congress, whose Librarian at that time was a family friend.[493]

George Herbert Putnam (1861–1955), who was the eighth Librarian of Congress at the time, had loaned her the book from which she chose the lithograph page designs.[494]

Laura explained, 'I first became acquainted with the story of Qurrat-i-Ayn (afterwards named Ṭáhirih – 'the Pure One') through the writings of Lord Curzon, Viceroy of His Majesty's Government of Great Britain, and those of Tolstoy and one or two other historians.'[495]

She had visited Qazvín, the birth city of Ṭáhirih, later writing, 'When I went to Persia at the request of 'Abdu'l-Bahá, I spent a night in the house from which Qurrat-i-Ayn [Ṭáhirih] escaped.'[496]

Ṭáhirih was born Fáṭimih Baragháni (Umm-i-Salmih) and was given an excellent education, which was unusual for a woman of her time. She received the name Qurratu'l-'Ayn, Solace of the Eyes, from her religious teacher. Her poetry showed keen, even mystical, understanding of complex theological matters and she became a renowned Islamic scholar. When she became acquainted with the teachings of the Báb, she immediately recognized His station and became a stalwart teacher of the Bábí Faith, defying many of the social restrictions on women to do so. She attended the conference of Badasht held in 1848 for the Báb's most eminent followers. The Báb named her Ṭáhirih, which means the Pure One, and this was confirmed by Bahá'u'lláh at the Badasht Conference, where she played a major role. It was at this Conference that Ṭáhirih unveiled herself, which caused tremendous consternation, as it was an absolutely unprecedented move for a woman of that time and culture. Ṭáhirih was executed in 1852 for her allegiance to the Bábí Faith. Before her execution she uttered these words: "You can kill me as soon as you like, but you cannot stop the emancipation of women.'[497]

Laura, who was most concerned that the history of the Bábí Faith be presented with accuracy and respect, yet also at the level of understanding of an audience unfamiliar with the Báb and Ṭáhirih, wrote in the preface to her drama:

Introductions should often be divided into two unequal parts – one for the reader of little patience; the other for the heroic investigator.

So, first I shall briefly say that this work portrays but a fragment of one of the most dramatic periods in history and is but a limited presentation of the most vast philosophy yet known to man. For the rest, beware! hasty reader, and turn over these pages, unless you feel the wish to know what my subject really is, and why I have chosen to express such a subject in drama . . . The writers of plays should always be true psychologists: then if they treat of the faults of men and women they will do so boldly and show them as they really are, and the result will be good; for when the mirror of truth is held before the gaze, he is blind indeed who can turn away uninfluenced by the sight of a disorderly reflection. Masters of the dramatic art always have been genuine moralists, Who, on seeing Shakespeare's plays, does not realize the evils of ambition, jealousy, and licentiousness; or, beholding the personages of Molière, perceive the folly of frivolity, hypocrisy and pedantry?[498]

Laura believed 'that the wave of regeneration, which is sweeping over the world, should take form also on the stage', and that she was 'trying, therefore, in this play, to bring before the public some of the most inspiring events of our epoch'.[499] She further explained that the founder of the Bahá'í Faith had called for

> . . . a general reform of all abuses in human society; and that the barriers of hate between castes, between nations, and between religions should be levelled, so that all men might unite in one great brotherhood under a universal code of love and of honour, free from superstition, division and dogma.[500]

The story was set in Persia between 1848 and 1852 and centered on the great Persian Bábí heroine, poet, early women's rights activist, and martyr, Qurratu'l-'Ayn. The book was illuminated in the style of Persian books.

The drama opened with a scene in a rose garden at dawn in Qazvín, the birthplace of Ṭáhirih, with the Islamic *adhán* (call to prayer). Laura depicted the scene as 'laid in the distant Orient, in a country full of archaic and barbaric customs – the Persia of over half a century ago; but the aspirations of my heroes are of all ages and of all lands.'[501] The play gives a brief history of the Bábí and Bahá'í Faiths in Persia and the banishment and exile of Bahá'u'lláh to different places and ending in 'Akká, and leaving His son 'Abdu'l-Bahá to spread His message to the world. She avoided depicting the roles of the Báb and Bahá'u'lláh in the play 'for certain beings cannot be adequately impersonated; their influence, nevertheless, will be felt throughout the play'.[502] This influence was depicted in the life of Qurratu'l-'Ayn who 'stands forth in history as an example of what the disciple of truth can accomplish despite hampering custom, and violent persecution.'[503] The characters of her drama were all historical figures who had lived during the time of the Báb and Bahá'u'lláh. The closing scenes portrayed historical events on which the play was based.

A footnote in *God's Heroes* mentions that the verses in Act 4 were translations by the orientalist E.G. Browne.[504] He later received a final copy of this work and thanked her for a wonderful book.[505]

Years later, in a letter to a friend, Laura clarified that some parts of the story were fictional.[506] In another letter to this friend she wrote, 'I was never able to be certain of the names of the characters that I used in the play but the events are those which were told to me.'[507]

'Abdu'l-Bahá sent a Tablet to Laura in which He appreciated her hard work: 'Thou art indeed striving with heart and soul, and I am well pleased with thee.'[508] He noted that though that facts in *God's Heroes* were correct, she could have expanded on the events of the Badasht Conference.[509] Perhaps the most defining moment of this significant conference was Ṭáhirih's removal of her veil while in the company of men. However, in several letters 'Abdu'l-Bahá commended Laura for her achievement:

> In short, thou hast indeed been most assiduous in writing this book. I beseech God that as day followeth day, thy spirit of endeavour, service, and sacrifice, and thy constancy and steadfastness in the Cause, may wax stronger so that thou mayest become a luminous star shining from the horizon of eternity.[510]

God's Heroes had been sent to Egypt to be translated into Arabic. 'Abdu'l-Bahá had read the Arabic version, was happy with the 'eloquent' translation and, if necessary, would send a copy to her.[511] It was also translated into Persian and titled *Dalírán-i-Rabbání* and deposited in the Iranian National Bahá'í Archives. A copy of that translation was sent to the Holy Land in 1956 and a limited number of copies were printed by the National Assembly of the Bahá'ís of Iran (the elected national administrative institution).[512]

Laura requested that the proceeds from the sale of *God's Heroes* go to the Persian girls' school in Tehran.[513] However, *Star of the West* records that the proceeds from the sale of the book would be given to the Mashriqu'l-Adhkár (House of Worship).[514]

Ethel Rosenberg referred to Laura's book in an advertisement included in her book *A Brief Account of the Bahai Movement*: 'The most expensive of all the books being advertised was a deluxe boxed volume of *God's Heroes*, a poetic drama about the early history of the Movement by Laura Clifford Barney which sold for twelve shillings and sixpence.'[515]

Laura contacted the manager of a theater on Broadway in New York City to consider her play for the stage. He replied that the play was 'written beautifully and its atmosphere was delightful and her knowledge of the country was marvelous'. However, he said that it would not make a successful stage production. Even though the theme was lofty and beautiful, it was 'above the heads of the people'.[516]

News of publication of Laura's book was reported in American newspapers.[517] A month before the publication of the play, *The Bar Harbor Record* ran a long article with the title 'The Amazing and Versatile Barneys of Washington', reporting on each of the Barney women and stating this about Laura:

> Under the inspiration of her religious belief, Miss Barney has written and will publish within the month a drama founded upon the cult of Bahaism. The scene is laid in Persia, the first being in a rose garden of Tehran. The heroine, 'Qurratu'l-Ain', is a believer in Bahaism, and owing to the fanatical hatred of the Mohammedans for her creed, she loses her life in martyrdom. It is a bold literary attempt, this setting forth in drama the inception of a new religion, but Miss Barney is said to have handled the subject with the talent and genius necessary to make it a success . . .
>
> Like her mother, Miss Barney is talented in the arts of sculpture and painting, but, it is said, will lay aside all these to concentrate her efforts on literary work for the good of the Bahaist propagation. The form of the book itself, aside from its literary contents, was designed by the author, and will be a most artistic production, the

binding and border beings handsomely ornamented with symbolic
Persian designs and each page being illuminated in original Oriental
coloring.[518]

Unfortunately, the rest of the article was incorrect:

It will be handsomely illustrated with engravings from original photographs of Miss Barney herself, who posed in costume for them in
the private studio of . . . friend in Washington for the purpose of
these illustrations.[519]

The New York Times recommended that its readers read *God's Heroes*,
saying 'the author humanized her heroine' and gave 'a living picture of a
great personage who laid the foundations of a great movement . . . The
book itself is an artistic production of great beauty, its Persian decora-
tions and traceries being especially noteworthy.'[520]

The Boston Globe ran its article with the title 'American Girl Startles
Paris', with the long subtitle 'Laura Clifford Barney of Washington, the
Author of "God's Heroes", a Theatre des Arts Production – Deals With
Great Religious Movement in Persia and the Martyrdom of "Consola-
tion of the Eye", the Most Wonderful Persian Woman on Record':

The Persian crisis has drawn much attention to the new play written
by an accomplished and learned American girl, Miss Laura Clifford
Barney, for the theatres des Arts this season . . . It is not an exaggeration to say, therefore, that this American family is one of the most
accomplished in the City of Light . . . Miss Barney knows Persian
almost as well as she knows French or English.[521]

The Indianapolis Star based its article on *The Boston Globe*'s with the
heading 'Girl Writes Persian Play for Parisians':

'God's Heroes' is a play dealing exclusively with the modern history
of Persia. The heroine is a woman who lived there some fifty years
ago. Her name is Quarratul-Ain, which means in Persian 'Consolation of the Eye'. I quote Dr Brown [*sic*], professor of Arabic of the
University of Cambridge, as to what manner of woman this marvelous Persian lady was.

'The appearance of such a woman in any country in any age,' he said, 'is a rare phenomenon, but in such a country as Persia, it is a prodigy, nay almost a miracle.'

The play, while dealing with a modern subject, is in a medieval spirit. It savors of the miracle or mystery plays. Miss Barney knows Persian almost as well as she knows French or English. Hence the rich oriental metaphors one finds in the play and the flights of imagination such as are seen in the 'Rubaiyat of Omar Khayyam'. Even the very shades of meanings are well brought out.[522]

Soon after the book's publication, a newspaper in San Francisco reported, under the title 'Persian Sect Led by American Girl', that Miss Laura Clifford Barney had recently cabled the newspaper informing it of the publication of her play. The article outlines the play's story and quotes Laura, who explained to the correspondent of the newspaper that this new Faith, the Bahai Faith 'is above all others, a religion for women, not only in spiritual affairs, but in things temporal. Its broad principles are universal brotherhood and peace.'[523]

As for the staging of Isabella Grinevskaya's play *Báb*, in the summer of 1912 Grinevskaya met with André Antoine (1858–1943), the director of the Odéon Theatre in Paris and with the theatre journalist and future premier Léon Blum (1872–1950), who was very taken with the play and which was tentatively advertised for the winter season. Information about this meeting was published in Russia.[524] Grinevskaya had come to Paris to consult with the French translator Nina Halpérine-Kaminsky (d. 1925/1926) about the French version of the play.[525] Years later the play found an even larger audience after the 1917 Russian revolution, when it was staged in the Folk Theatre in St Petersburg.[526]

There is another unpublished, undated manuscript by Laura titled 'Outlines & Shadows'. She may have written it around this time or perhaps later. It is a collection of 25 poems, anecdotes and short stories. Rather small in size with only 54 pages, the titles of the pieces are 'Cantine Maternelle', '"Artist in Hair"', 'The Chill of the Morning', 'M. & Mme Gros', 'The Syghia [temporary marriage]', 'A Photograph', 'Return', 'Hotel Moderne', 'The Better Part', 'Daughters of Joy', 'To Attain to Peace', 'The Midwife', 'Bridal Hour', 'An Eastern Song', 'Misunderstood', 'As Father as Son', 'A Night in the Harim [Harem]', 'Untrammeled', 'The Pilgrim in the Desert', 'Those Who Know', 'The

Dervish', 'Sincerity', 'Solace at Last', 'In the Grass' and 'Towards the Stars'.[527] Some are true stories and some fictional. It was Laura's usual literary and creative writing mind at work again. The characters as well as the stories are diverse. The characters varied from a Dervish to a Lady in London; from Zia, a Middle Eastern man, to the English Mrs Reynolds; while the venues ranged from Paris to London to the desert and somewhere in the Middle East or to somewhere in her imagination.

Nude Sculpture by Laura in Washington, D.C.

The newspapers, not only in Washington but in several cities across the United States, continued reporting the Barney family's activities. In the lengthy article about the family in *The Bar Harbor Record*, mentioned above, with the title 'The Amazing and Versatile Barneys of Washington' the newspaper remarked, 'So, when, as is admitted by those who know their Washington, the Barneys stand at the head of the list of notables, it behooves those who would know of the capital to know of the Barney family.'[528]

The New York Evening Telegram published an article headlined 'Well Known Daughters of Famous Men' in which it mentioned Alice Barney and her two daughters:

> They are devoted to an Oriental cult, Bahaism, which they encountered in Persia, and which in addition to its mystic teaching, encourages practical action in helping the weak and loving one's neighbor. Mrs Barney brought over from Persia one of the Bahaist priests to expound the doctrines in Washington.[529]

Much of the information was incorrect. Alice had never gone to Persia, the Faith was not a cult and it was not Mrs Barney who had brought the 'Bahaist priest', referring to Abu'l-Faḍl, to the United States but Laura. He was not a priest but a teacher and Laura did not bring him from Persia.

In 1910 yet another seemingly social scandal created a buzz for the press and rocked the Barney family. The cause was a sculpture by Laura of a reclining female nude that was accidentally set in front of Alice Barney's home, Studio House. Laura had always been the proper Barney, who only became controversial because of her embrace of the Bahá'í Faith and its activities. She was a woman of many talents who read, wrote and translated Persian, composed short stories and books, and was an accomplished public speaker. But it was her considerable ability as a sculptor that caused the trouble this time. A biographer of her sister wrote:

> In the summer of 1910 Laura shipped her latest sculpture from Paris to Alice's Washington home, Studio House. The work, *Reclining Nude*, was of an unclothed woman stretched out and cradling her right arm beneath her head. A note to the caretaker accompanied the statue. Laura asked him to keep it outside covered with canvas, and to sprinkle it every day with water (made of plaster of Paris and cement, it would harden each time it was wet down and allowed to dry). He did as asked, leaving the heavy sculpture to cure where it had been delivered near the front entrance of Studio House.[530]

Then one day the canvas cover was blown away by the wind, revealing the sculpture. It is difficult today to understand why a nude sculpture would be scandalous. But in the early 20th century American culture was staunchly conservative, and several states thought about bringing in laws requiring nude statues in museums to be clothed.

News of a sculpture of a nude body lying outside the home of a society doyen spread like wildfire. Tour guides, armed with megaphones, led legions of sightseers to the Barney home. Then the moralists got into the act. The biographer continued:

> Members of the Watch and Ward Society, a women's organization devoted to upholding the city's moral values, unanimously concluded that *Reclining Nude* was a moral threat and must be taken away – immediately. They brought their complaints to chief of police Richard Sylvester, who, hoping to stem the crowds, covered the statue with a pup tent. 'Barney Statue Shocks Artist Police Chief!' blared a headline in the *Washington Times*.
>
> Another paper reported that he had ordered the cover because 'his chivalrous nature revolted against letting the statue of a lady lie exposed to the wind and rain, and because he didn't think it was an out-of-doors work of art anyhow'. *The Press* observed that the statue 'has attracted the rabble as well as the art-loving, and the rabble is the most numerous among the sightseeing crowds. The comments

of the rabble are offensive to the ears of delicately natured women on Sheridan Circle, where the crowd is intensely objectionable.[531]

Newspapers reported that 25,000 people, likely an exaggeration, came the next day to view Laura's work which had been removed by drunks or mischief-makers from its pup tent to the pedestal of General Sheridan's statue. The story made the front pages of newspapers not only countrywide but in the Paris edition of *The New York Herald* and other English-language newspapers across Europe.[532] Some said that Natalie had posed for her sister but the family denied it. *The Bar Harbor Record* reported later that the family maintained that Natalie was not the model for all or any part of the art work, declaring, 'the original of the statue was a professional model of Paris'.[533] Alice made several denials that Natalie had posed for the sculpture and sent a letter to the editor of *The New York Herald* that was printed on October 12, 1910 under the heading 'Mrs. A. C. Barney Corrects Story from Washington: Denies That Nude Statue, Mentioned in Dispatch, Was Modeled from Her Daughter'.[534] Alice is reported as saying that the model was the well-known 'Marguerite Silvestre' and that the sculpture did not represent her daughter.[535] Laura also sent a cable to The *New York American* denying that her sister had posed for the work.[536]

The story of the nude sculpture would not go away. For years Alice continued to be linked to the 'nude statue' in newspaper articles, many of them filled with misinformation, for example reporting that she had turned her garage into a Greek Temple[537] or that the statue was being destroyed.[538]

When Laura was in her early eighties and visiting Washington to approve the new site for the statue selected by the Smithsonian, a photograph was taken in which she symbolically draped the work with a canvas cloth.[539] The sculpture still exists in the backyard of the Embassy of Latvia, the current owners of Studio House.

Laura and the Persian–American Educational Society

Laura was supportive of the Persian–American Educational Society (PAES) which was founded in Washington, D.C., in 1910 by a group of prominent American Bahá'ís. Ahmad Sohrab, a Persian Bahá'í translator who later would serve as a secretary for 'Abdu'l-Bahá from 1912 to

1919, had an important role in the founding of PAES. He had become interested in establishing an 'association dedicated to the educational, economic and commercial development of Persia and its Bahá'í community'.[540] As the primary goal of PAES was to assist Iran in its educational and economic development and it needed to cooperate with the Persian authorities to do so, the planning committee decided that PAES would serve all Persians, would be open to all, and that it would not be an official Bahá'í organization. Any benefits to the Bahá'í Faith, such as increased recognition and prestige, were only secondary.[541]

As soon as the mission and the structure of the Society were established, an inauguration was planned. More than 350 people, Bahá'ís and others, including the representative of Persia to the United States, attended this gathering on January 8, 1910 in Washington, D.C. The American minister to Persia, Charles Russell, who was still in Washington, also attended.[542] PAES solicited from publications and newsletters in the United States donations of books and supplies that could be sent to Persia for school libraries. They also asked for financial assistance internationally and urged American Bahá'ís to travel to Persia to teach in schools.[543]

The establishment of PAES had been prompted by the financial difficulties of the Tarbíyat Boys' School in Tehran, which had been established in 1899.[544] American Bahá'ís financed the school and oversaw its management and the teaching staff. This partnership between Persian and American Bahá'ís prompted the opening of a girls' school in Tehran in 1911 called Tarbíyat-i-banát, which meant the cultivation and moral education of girls.[545]

PAES had two types of membership – an associate membership to support the monthly newsletters and an active membership to support scholarships for Persian children at the Tarbíyat schools. The latter membership cost $18 a year and the member would receive a photograph of the child and copies of his or her progress report.[546] Laura's mother was an honorary vice president of PAES. It owed much of its formation and success to her because she had enlisted the services of Sydney Sprague, a former professor at Harvard University, for the school in Persia.[547] Sydney Sprague (1875–1943) was an American Bahá'í who was an author, lecturer and composer.[548] Laura herself supported PAES by paying for the scholarship of a young boy, 'Agha Habib', who was among the first beneficiaries,[549] one of the first 30 boys to be educated at the Tarbíyat Boys' School in Tehran. He finished school successfully and entered Dár ul-Funún, an institution of higher learning in Tehran. Laura then paid for a second boy, 'Mírzá Emad', who was one of the brighter boys at the school.[550]

Laura, who was living in Paris in 1910, was in regular contact with Ahmad Sohrab, who had been in Washington since the inception of PAES. She advised the committee members to be more organized, to specify goals, and to carefully select members of the committee, and she also gave advice on other organizational matters. In one of her early letters to the PAES committee Laura wrote:

> I am glad to see that you are also considering the girls' education, this I had not understood at first, and it interests me greatly. For years I have been preparing to be of use to the Persian women and girls, for they must have an education different from that of a regular school, for they must learn to care for their homes and health as well as learn how to read and write. But I think that I have already spoken to you about it.[551]

When PAES requested that Laura sponsor more students, she responded that she was already paying $1,100 for the education of several children and that she could not pay any more, especially since she had not been able to review carefully the plans and goals of PAES for this particular project.[552] Her correspondence also shows how outward-looking she was. She asked PAES to find people who were well known in the outside world and not only in Bahá'í communities to achieve a larger outreach. Perhaps the committee had discussed the idea of having an endowment for PAES, since she suggested that it was too early to have one and that it was also too early to rent facilities for the head office.

The first conference of the PAES in June 1911 discussed the merging of the activities of the PAES with the Orient–Occident Unity Society.[553] This Society was established at the request of 'Abdu'l-Bahá to expand the activities of the PAES.[554] However, it seems that the names were used interchangeably. The next year Laura was informed that 'Abdu'l-Bahá was going to give His very first public talk in Washington, D.C. to this Society at its second annual conference.[555]

PART 3

MARRIED LIFE, TRAVELS AND ACHIEVEMENTS

1911 – 1928

Passing of Hippolyte Dreyfus's Father

The year 1911 started with the sudden passing of Hippolyte Dreyfus's father, Lucien Dreyfus-Cardozo, at age 70, on January 4. He was buried at the Montmartre Cemetery. The service and burial were held in private at the request of the deceased, with only family allowed to attend.[1] Laura sent a letter to Ahmad Sohrab at the Persian American Education Society in Washington, D.C., and asked him to inform the friends in the East of the passing. She wrote that Mr Dreyfus had been a staunch Bahá'í and his sudden death had brought sorrow to all the family.[2] Lucien Dreyfus, his wife Lea Marie Cardozo, their daughter Yvonne and son-in-law Paul had become Bahá'ís shortly after Hippolyte. It was reported in *Bahai News* that the family were Bahá'ís, and this had 'enabled them to accept the separation with courage'.[3] His passing was also announced in *Najm-i-Bakhtar*, the Persian version of that magazine.

Hippolyte thanked those who had written to him through Ahmad Sohrab, saying that 'the sympathy of the friends has been in this great bereavement a mighty consolation, and it had made us feel even more than before the great unity of Al Abha'.[4]

Marriage of Laura Barney to Hippolyte Dreyfus

A few months later, a significant event occurred in Laura's life – her marriage. Laura had known Hippolyte for 11 years, during which they had discovered their common aspirations. It was through their collaboration on the translations of *Some Answered Questions* that she came to understand how well they worked together.[5] And it was on their travels that she realized how well matched they were. Hippolyte was a scholar and an active member of the Bahá'í community in Paris. An intellectual with a brilliant mind, he also had a wonderful sense of humor, was compassionate and gentle, and he also made Laura laugh.[6] They had known each other for several years, had traveled together and had worked together, particularly on translating and publishing *Some Answered Questions* in French. Their personalities complemented each other's, and their goals of serving their Faith and the humankind matched too.

Perhaps Laura had asked 'Abdu'l-Bahá about marriage and questioned Him if marriage would interfere with her activities and services, because 'Abdu'l-Bahá sent a Tablet to her mentioning the importance of service to the Cause of God as well as the importance of marriage. He stated: 'This [teaching and service] doth not preclude marriage. Thou canst take unto thyself a husband and at the same time serve the Cause of God; the one doth not preclude the other.'[7]

At the age of 32, Laura was married to Hippolyte, who was 38, on April 15, 1911 in Paris.[8] In a Tablet, 'Abdu'l-Bahá congratulated them and informed Laura that He was sending her a bottle of rose perfume from Iran.[9] The newlyweds received another Tablet congratulating them on their union:

> Your joyous and delightful letter just arrived. This wedding is truly blessed and is the cause of much happiness for all the lovers of God. Relying upon the bounties of Bahá'u'lláh, it is my hope that this becomes, for both of you, the cause of fervent longing and intense attraction to the love of God and becomes the cause of the happiness and exultation of the lovers of God. In the divine kingdom, you both are considered the denizens of nearness and, in the sight of 'Abdu'l-Bahá, are much esteemed. Thus, what could be better for you two than to be married, to become as one and to establish a generation of Bahá'ís in Paris, bringing joy and happiness to all.[10]

A wedding reception was held for Laura and Hippolyte several days later, on April 24; her mother sent out the invitations.[11] May Bolles Maxwell, Laura's spiritual mother, was invited but was not able to attend.[12] The day before the reception *The New York Times* reported the news of the wedding with the heading 'Miss Barney to Wed: Said to be Engaged to Hippolyte Dreyfus – Brahman Rites Wedding', stating that they still have to be engaged. The newspaper's incorrect understanding of their religious beliefs resulted in the story reporting: 'As Mr Dreyfus is the leader of the Brahmist Church here, the ceremony will be according to the rites of the Persian religion.'[13]

The wedding was also announced in *Najm-i-Bakhtar*, the Persian section of the *Star of the West,* under the heading 'Wedding of Mr Dreyfus and Miss Barney'.

> Recently the auspicious and joyful news of the wedding of Mr Dreyfus and Amatu'l-Bahá Miss Laura Barney reached the offices of

Najm-i-Bakhtar [*Star of the West*] from Paris and filled the hearts of Bahá'í friends with joy and delight. The wedding of these two servants of the Cause of God and steadfast devotees of the Covenant is regarded with much interest and great significance.

Amatu'l-Bahá Miss Barney is one of the long-standing and faithful believers of America and her name in the East and West of the Bahá'í world is regarded with great love and respect. The description of her wonderful services and ceaseless sacrifices for the Cause [the Bahá'í Faith] would fill a thousand books. The Bahá'í community of Washington owes its very existence to her ceaseless efforts, as well as to the endeavors of a few other friends.

Her journey to Iran brought much enthusiasm and passion to the hearts of the lovers of God and her services in the course of that visit were considered distinguished in the eyes of the Hands of the Cause.[14]

Laura and Hippolyte adopted the last name Dreyfus-Barney after their marriage. Hyphenated last names were not common in America at that time, although Natalie knew a few people who had adopted them.[15] In fact, hyphenated surnames were so unusual in those years that the couple's decision sparked criticism in newspapers, one of which blamed the 'Barney eccentricity', present in both mother and daughters. Another newspaper article remarked, 'Mr Hippolyte Dreyfus-Barney of Paris, who, in the foreign fashion, when the wife's name is better or as well-known as the husband's, has hyphenated his name with that of his bride, who was Miss Laura Ellis (*sic*) Barney of Washington and Paris.'[16] Hippolyte showed his wife love and support throughout their marriage and Laura had mutual feelings which she expressed during his lifetime and even many years after his passing. Laura and Hippolyte traveled for their honeymoon to his family's summer house called 'Daru'l-Salam' or 'Dar-Es-Selam', built by his parents in Mont Pèlerin, a small village town on a mountain overlooking Lake Geneva in Switzerland. This villa was a vacation home for the Dreyfus-Cardozo family.

The couple settled into their first home, an apartment at 15 rue Greuze, sixteenth arrondissement in Paris. If the article published in *The Washington Post* in 1902 is correct, Laura would have received her inheritance from her father at the age of 30 in 1909. She may have used that to purchase this apartment. Alice was able draw out her portion of the principal a year after Albert's death; Laura and Natalie received their portions of the principal when they turned 30.[17]

Laura and Hippolyte's lives, both before and after their marriage, were filled with activities and travels. Laura's Bahá'í activities intensified after her marriage. Kling commented that, for the first time, Laura was relaxed and 'seemed almost carefree'.[18] Rodriguez noted: 'A fervent Bahá'í adherent and a compassionate human being, Hippolyte's interests dovetailed perfectly with Laura's' and like Natalie, he was able to 'make the serious Laura lighten up'.[19] Laura and Hippolyte became a power couple in marriage, their ardent services to their Faith doubling as they worked together.

Her Mother's Wedding

Meanwhile, two years earlier Laura's mother Alice had met a young artist, Christian Hemmick, when he had auditioned for a role in her play, and they had decided to marry. The two sisters finally accepted their mother's wish, despite the age difference, since she was obviously very happy.[20] Alice had suggested that she and Christian be married the same day as Laura in a double ceremony and Laura accepted, agreeing to a joint civil ceremony out of her wish to share her happiness with her 'Little One', as she called her mother.[21] Fortunately, Hippolyte also agreed to the double ceremony. Laura's acquiescence with her mother's idea was an example of how she had feet in two different worlds, one foot in the world of her spiritual family and the other in that of her biological family. She was able to balance their different demands easily and functioned well in both.

The day of the wedding was eventful. Alice had converted to Catholicism for Christian's sake, and their Catholic wedding took place after the joint civil wedding. A headline on the front page of *The New York Times* blared 'MRS BARNEY WEDS YOUNG HEMMICK; Wealthy Widow of Albert Barney, Aged 61, Married to Youth of 26 in Paris' and reported that they were married at the Mairie (Town Hall) in the eighth arrondissement of Paris, noting that the witness for the bridegroom was Hippolyte Dreyfus.[22]

Alice followed the legal advice she received and had Hemmick sign a prenuptial agreement. She also transferred her inheritance from her first husband into an irrevocable trust for Natalie and Laura.

Invitation to a Special Guest: 'Abdu'l-Bahá's Journey West

A few months after her wedding, Laura was awaiting the arrival of the Master in Europe. She had invited 'Abdu'l-Bahá to visit Europe several times. He sent numerous letters to Laura prior to His first journey to the West, and she played a major role in making it possible.[23] He had traveled to Egypt in 1910 and stayed in Port Said for a month.[24] 'Abdu'l-Bahá mentioned in an undated letter to Laura, perhaps that same year, that initially He had not given much thought to traveling to Europe but only of going to Egypt. Now, however, He wished to meet '_shumá-há_', meaning Laura and Hippolyte, and He would soon arrive in France:

> O Amatu'l-Bahá,
> Your services in the path of the Abhá Kingdom are well recognized and the hardships and calamities that you bore in the days of 'Abdu'l-Bahá's imprisonment and your perseverance in dealing with countless tribulations are before the mind's eye. They will never be forgotten, since these trials took place at the time of the most severe tests and at the harshest times of captivity . . .
>
> I had not given the idea of a journey to Europe much thought as it was more likely for me first to travel to Egypt. However, in order to meet you, I decided to travel to Europe. I am hoping to reach Paris shortly.[25]

'Abdu'l-Bahá left Egypt for Europe on September 22, and a telegram was sent to Hippolyte stating that He would arrive in Marseilles. Hippolyte was in Munich at the time and left immediately for Marseilles to receive Him, but received another cable while on his way stating that 'the sea did not agree with Him'. He had postponed His trip to Europe and had returned to Egypt and was staying in Alexandria. His health had not allowed Him to continue. While in Alexandria, He sent a letter to Laura:

> O Amatu'l-Bahá,
> As I have been making plans for my upcoming travels, I have not written you in some time. Presently I am in Alexandria and am writing you this letter so that you may know that wherever I may be,

I bring you to mind and never forget you. I beseech limitless bounties for you from the Abhá Kingdom. Your services to the Divine
Kingdom are indisputable and absolute and your heartfelt effort
and endeavor are clear and confirmed. I am certain that heavenly
assistance will reach you from every direction . . .[26]

'Abdu'l-Bahá was now 66 years old and had suffered imprisonment and
exile from the age of nine, causing Him to suffer from poor health. In
an undated letter to Laura, He informed her that He would thus defer
His departure.[27] In another Tablet He stated that though His health
had much improved, He had decided to say longer in Ramleh as the
weather was 'very pleasant'.[28]

After gaining sufficient strength, 'Abdu'l-Bahá resumed His journey to
Europe in August 1911.[29] He left Egypt on August 11 on *L'Orénoque*.[30]
Hippolyte traveled from Vevey, Switzerland, for the port city of Marseilles
to greet 'Abdu'l-Bahá on August 16. After a few days' rest, Hippolyte
accompanied 'Abdu'l-Bahá and His entourage to Geneva by train and
spent a night there.[31] On August 21 they took the boat to Thonon-les-
Bains, a French town near the southern shore of Lake Geneva.[32] Hippolyte
had become very close to 'Abdu'l-Bahá since their first meeting in 1903.
According to Laura, 'Abdu'l-Bahá relied on Hippolyte to arrange His
stays in France and, later, His trips to and from England. There was no
restraint between them.[33] However, it was not only Hippolyte, but Laura
as well, who accompanied 'Abdu'l-Bahá during His visit to France. Laura
joined them when they arrived in Thonon.

The choice of the town of Thonon with its refreshing air, mineral
waters and Hôtel du Parc as the first place for 'Abdu'l-Bahá to visit must
have been at the suggestion of Hippolyte and Laura. Hippolyte had a
summer home in Mont Pèlerin, in Vevey, Switzerland across the Lake
from Thonon and he must have been familiar with the small resort
town. Laura also had visited Évian-les-Bains, another small town in
France, six miles from Thonon, where she had stayed with her mother.

Juliet Thompson and Laura

One of the friends who joined them in Thonon-les-Bains a few days
after 'Abdu'l-Bahá's arrival was Juliet Thompson. An American portrait
artist, Juliet had been a friend of Laura and Alice for several years. She

had moved to Paris to study the arts and had heard about the Faith from Laura in the United States. She had traveled to Europe to see 'Abdu'l-Bahá and recorded her memories of those days, which included several references to Laura and her husband.

'It was Laura who gave me the Message,' Juliet wrote in her diary, 'bringing to me the greatest of gifts in earth *and* heaven and changing the whole direction of my life.'[34] Her diary records that when she was recovering from a grave illness in Washington, possibly in 1900, she one day told her brother that she had been thinking that it was time for another 'Messenger of God' to appear. A few months previously, she had dreamed of a man she later identified as 'Abdu'l-Bahá. The following day, Laura visited Juliet on her way back from Bar Harbor, as she was traveling from New York to Palestine the next day. 'But I *couldn't* sail without first seeing you,' Laura told Juliet, 'to tell you why I am making this pilgrimage. Juliet, the Christ-Spirit is again on earth, and – as before – He is in Palestine.'[35]

Juliet went on pilgrimage in 1909 to visit the Master in 'Akká. She recorded one visit with 'Abdu'l-Bahá when she asked, 'My Lord, how can I tell? Thou knowest. And I should like to say this: though dear Laura Barney was Thine instrument, it was through Thee that the doors were opened for me to come home to Thee. So, when Thou wishest me to come again, I know that again Thou wilt open the doors for me.'[36] Juliet also mentioned to 'Abdu'l-Bahá Laura's beautiful goodness to her and prayed for blessings for her.[37] 'Abdu'l-Bahá asked Juliet to study *Some Answered Questions*.[38] Juliet wrote extensively about 'Abdu'l-Bahá's visit to Europe in 1911 and to America in the following year.

With 'Abdu'l-Bahá in France

Laura must have been excited to finally welcome her special guest, 'Abdu'l-Bahá, who had arrived at Thonon-les-Bains on August 21, 1911. He and Hippolyte had traveled by rail to Geneva, spent the night in that city, and taken a day boat to Thonon-les-Bains.[39] Laura was already there to welcome Him. 'Abdu'l-Bahá and the Dreyfus-Barneys stayed at Grand Hôtel du Parc, by the lake.[40]

Juliet wrote in her diary that they were either in His room or He was in their rooms 'in the most charming informality'.[41] She recorded that one day they 'did the most amazing thing: the Master, Laura, Hippolyte, and I went for an automobile ride! "Did you ever think, Juliet," said the Master, laughing, as we got into the car with Him, "that you and Laura would be riding in an automobile with me in Europe?"[42] They drove to a country inn where several children were selling bunches of violets and 'Abdu'l-Bahá bought all of them. The Master paid for the flowers but the children held out their hands for more money. Laura did not want the Master to be bothered. 'Don't let them impose!' cried Laura. The Master replied, 'Tell them, that they have taken.'[43]

Then 'Abdu'l-Bahá turned and walked into the forest to see 'the Devil's Bridge' which Hippolyte had told Him about. Hippolyte followed Him and since Laura couldn't walk far into the forest, Juliet stayed with her. The Master was enraptured by the beauty of the forest and the bridge.[44]

When they returned to the inn, the children again swarmed around 'Abdu'l-Bahá asking for more money, but Laura firmly ordered them to leave since she thought they were imposing. 'He would give away everything He has,' she whispered to Juliet. But the Master had seen a child much younger than the others, a newcomer with a very sensitive face, who was looking at Him. 'But,' He said, 'to this *little* one I have not given.'[45]

During their drive home, they passed a magnificent waterfall and, Juliet recorded,

> . . . the Master peremptorily stopped the car and with a sort of excitement got out of it; then walked to the very edge of the precipice. After standing there for some time, His eyes fixed on that long, shining torrent, which seemed to be shaking off diamonds in a fury, He seated Himself on a rock hanging over the deep abyss. I can still see that Figure of quiet Power perilously poised above the precipice, that still, rapt Face delighting in some secret way in the beauty of the waterfall. Tears came to Laura's eyes and mine.'[46]

During His stay in France, many visitors, reporters and Bahá'ís visited 'Abdu'l-Bahá. Laura and Hippolyte were His constant companions and were present during most of these visits. Some members of the Persian royal family, including Ẓillu's-Sulṭán (1850–1918) and his sons, were in exile in Geneva at that time.

One day while 'Abdu'l-Bahá was in Thonon-les-Bains, Ẓillu's-Sulṭán took a day trip to the town with his entourage and went to Grand Hôtel du Parc. At the hotel he saw a Persian nobleman on the terrace and, seeing Hippolyte, whom he had met in Persia, asked who the nobleman was. Learning that it was 'Abdu'l-Bahá, he asked to be taken to Him. 'If you could have heard the wretch mumbling his miserable excuses!' Hippolyte remarked later.

But the Master took him in His arms and said, 'All those things are in the past. Never think of them again.' Then He invited the two sons of Zillu's-Sultán to spend a day with Him.[47] Thus it was that the Master had lunch with Prince Bahram of Persia (1885–1916); the Dreyfus-Barneys were present.[48]

Prince Bahram was one of the 14 sons of Zillu's-Sultán, who was the eldest son of Násiri'd-Dín Sháh Qájár (1831–96). Zillu's-Sultán would have succeeded to the throne but for the fact that his mother was not of royal blood. He was the governor of Isfahan from 1872 to 1907. It was owing to Zillu's-Sultán's orders that two great Bahá'ís, Mírzá Muhammad-Hasan and his older brother Mírzá Muhammad-Husayn, were executed in 1879 because they had refused to recant their faith.[49] It was for these crimes that Zillu's-Sultán asked for forgiveness from 'Abdu'l-Bahá. Laura recalled years later that 'Abdu'l-Bahá had met Zillu's-Sultán while in Europe but was not sure if they had met in Geneva or during a sail on the lake.[50] There is also an account by Juliet Thompson of 'Abdu'l-Bahá taking a side trip to Vevey on which Laura did not recall accompanying them that day. She wrote that she would not have forgotten such an important experience.[51]

Trip to London to Assist the Master with Translation

The next stop on 'Abdu'l-Bahá's itinerary was a 29-day stay in Great Britain and the Dreyfus-Barneys also went there to assist with translations. They were among a number of Bahá'ís who arrived in London during His stay.[52] While in London, 'Abdu'l-Bahá stayed at the home of Sara Louisa, Lady Blomfield, an early Irish Bahá'í who lived in the fashionable Cadogan Gardens. She and her daughter Mary had heard about the Bahá'í Faith in Paris in 1907. Laura had 'made a profound impact on Lady Blomfield, who would come to love and greatly admire her as an outstanding Bahá'í'.[53]

Blomfield recalled the many people who came to visit 'Abdu'l-Bahá in her home and particularly her guests from Paris:

Foremost amongst our visitors were Monsieur and Madame Dreyfus-Barney, the brilliant French scholar and his no less brilliant American wife, who spoke Persian with 'Abdu'l-Bahá, translated for Him, and were altogether helpful, courteous, and charming.'[54]

During His stay, 'Abdu'l-Bahá met many visitors at His residence, gave addresses at churches and temples, met with Bahá'ís, visited a settlement, gave a talk at an Indian religious center and the Theosophical Society. Perhaps it was Laura who helped with translation at the Indian religious center of Keshub Niketon in Hampstead.[55]

Honored Guest in Paris

After London, 'Abdu'l-Bahá returned to France and went to Paris on October 3, 1911, staying with the Dreyfus-Barneys at their apartment at 15 rue Greuze in the sixteenth arrondissement. He may have stayed with them for a few days before moving to an apartment at 4 Avenue de Camoëns which they had found and prepared for Him. He was able to receive His guests at the apartment and some members of His entourage were able to stay with Him. The apartment was newly-built, comfortable, 'charmingly furnished, sunny, spacious', and situated by the Trocadéro Gardens in the area of Quai de Passy.[56]

The arrival of 'Abdu'l-Bahá in Paris was covered by several newspapers that picked up an article distributed by the International News Service in the United States. *The Washington Post* headlined its article 'WANTS FAITHS UNITED' 'Abdul Baha Abbas, head of the Bahaian religion, is visiting Mr. and Mrs. Hippolite Dreyfus, formerly Miss Laura Barney, and other co-religionists in Paris.'[57]

'Abdu'l-Bahá was accompanied by some of His followers from England and the United States as well as His own entourage.[58] Many meetings and gatherings, public and private, were held in Paris during His stay. He addressed many groups of people and met with innumerable individuals.

He spent a good deal of time at the Dreyfus-Barney home, which was not far from His apartment. As they had in London, Laura and Hippolyte again served as interpreters for Him and several other people. Laura translated 'Abdu'l-Bahá's addresses from Persian into English and Hippolyte into French.[59]

Something quite interesting happened during 'Abdu'l-Bahá's stay in Paris. Two prominent Persians, Muḥammad Qazvíní and Siyyid Ḥasan Taqízádih, who were also in Paris at the time, visited 'Abdu'l-Bahá. Qazvíní visited with Him several times at His place of residence at Avenue de Camoëns and at the Dreyfus-Barneys' home. He wrote that on several occasions he had lunch with 'Abdu'l-Bahá.[60] Taqízádih, a Persian politician and writer, visited Him on November 5, and recorded the following amusing incident:

Of the events of that night, after 'Abdu'l-Bahá's companions had left us to go for a walk, and he and I were left alone, at one point the French maid came in and informed him [in French] that he had a telephone call. He asked me, 'What is she saying?'

I translated.

He said, 'Find 'Azizu'lláh Khán, and tell him to take the call.'

I translated that, too. The maid said that he was not there.

He then said, 'Tamaddun [Tamaddunu'l-Mulk] should take the call.'

The maid responded that he was not there either. Finally, 'Abdu'l-Bahá himself had to take the call, which apparently was from an American Bahá'í woman who spoke Persian, and went to the phone. When he returned, he said to me, 'That was the first time in my life that I spoke on a telephone.'[61]

This first telephone call that 'Abdu'l-Bahá experienced, made by 'an American Bahá'í woman who spoke Persian', may have been from Laura.[62]

Natalie also visited 'Abdu'l-Bahá in Paris and brought her friend, the French poet, novelist and literary critic Remy de Gourmont (1858–1915), on October 20.[63] He had met her the year before and had dedicated his *Lettres à l'Amazone* (*Letters to the Amazon*) to her, thus immortalizing her.[64]

The American expatriate poet Ezra Pound, who knew the Dreyfus-Barneys and was a close friend of Natalie, had also met 'Abdu'l-Bahá in London that September.[65] Pound wrote a letter to Margaret Cravens, a friend of his in Paris, telling her that 'Abdu'l-Bahá was at the home of the Dreyfus-Barneys and that she could arrange to meet Him there if she were interested.[66]

On the afternoon of October 15 'Abdu'l-Bahá visited a settlement project started in a desolate quarter just outside of Paris by a poor Bahá'í couple, Victor and Fanny Élise Ponsonaille, for less advantaged children and those with no parents. Laura, Hippolyte who interpreted for Him, and Tamaddunu'l-Mulk, were among those who accompanied Him in a carriage for the return trip.[67]

A few days later, 'Abdu'l-Bahá recounted the following in a public address:

> Yesterday evening when I came home from the house of Monsieur Dreyfus I was very tired – yet I did not sleep, I lay awake thinking.
>
> I said, O God, Here am I in Paris! What is Paris and who am I? Never did I dream that from the darkness of my prison I should ever be able to come to you, though when they read me my sentence, I did not believe in it.[68]

The Dreyfus-Barneys held at their home the last meeting in Paris for 'Abdu'l-Bahá before He returned to Egypt.[69] He left Paris on December 2 after spending about two months there. It is possible that Laura was present at Gare de Lyon (the railway station) as He departed.[70] In addition to 'Abdu'l-Bahá's entourage, Hippolyte accompanied Him to Marseilles and then at a meeting at the Theosophical Society where He gave a talk on Dec. 6.[71] 'Abdu'l-Bahá's departure from France after an exhaustive but fruitful first journey to the West was likely on the ship *Le Portugal* from Marseilles to Alexandria on December 7.[72]

That year Laura met a number of other prominent Persian dignitaries in Paris. 'Abdu'l-Bahá referred to them in several letters to Laura and asked her to be kind to them, because some were distressed and living in exile.[73] Among these dignitaries was the Persian Ambassador to France. She also saw Jalál ud-Dawlih, whom she had first met in Thonon-les-Bains, and met with Mírzá Sultán-Husayn (1870–1913), another son of Zillu's-Sultán.[74]

During the time that 'Abdu'l-Bahá was visiting Europe, Laura's mother and her husband had returned to Washington from their honeymoon. They had been in Marienbad in West Bohemia (today's Czechia) during July and in August were in the Dolomites, a mountain range in northeastern Italy. While sailing back to the United States on the TSS *Lapland*, Christian sent a letter to Laura expressing his regret at not meeting 'Abdu'l-Bahá and effusively praised Laura's qualities:

Laura, you are wonderful – yes, a wonderful & splendid woman – and I admire you so – you don't mind me saying so to you do you – for I say it with all the sincerity of my heart – and I fell toward you as I do towards my dear old Father Confessor to whom I can talk my heart out – but alas! who is not worldly wise as you – and if I ever am in trouble of any kind I tell you right now I would come to you at once. It does a young fellow a world of good to know and feel he has a good friend in his life, doesn't it Laura.[75]

He closed the letter by asking Laura to convey his apologies to 'Abdu'l-Bahá for not being able to meet Him and repeated how genuinely sorry he was for not having had this honor.

Paris Talks

'Abdu'l-Bahá attended and spoke at many gatherings during His stay in Paris. His words were written down by several people. It was through the efforts of Laura and a few others that His addresses in 1911 were published in English in May of the following year under the title *Talks by Abdul Baha Given in Paris*, later known as *Paris Talks*.[76]

Laura assisted with the translation from Persian to French. Anne Lynch helped with the translation in 1939 and the French edition which was published in Geneva.[77] Anne Slastiona Lynch was born in Russia in 1892, became a Bahá'í in Italy in 1926, served her Faith during World War II in Geneva, and died in 1966. Years later Laura noted that there were some errors in the Preface to the French translation, which was titled *Causeries d'Abdu'l-Bahá* [*Paris Talks*]. She asked a Bahá'í friend to clarify to the National Spiritual Assembly of France that Lady Blomfield did not take notes of the talks. Laura explained that it was she who was present when 'Abdu'l-Bahá spoke in Persian and it was her husband Hippolyte who translated for 'Abdu'l-Bahá into French. According to Laura, one of the secretaries of the daughters of Lady Blomfield, who was not a Bahá'í, took notes of these double translations, meaning from Persian to French and then French to English, and sometime later the translation into English was made. 'Abdu'l-Bahá never saw the English text, but He had read the Persian one that was written by Maḥmúd Zarqání and Valíyu'lláh Varqá, who had accompanied Him. According to Laura, it was after seeing these notes taken in Persian that 'Abdu'l-Bahá gave permission for the Persian text to be published.[78] It seems that Lady Bromfield's daughters spoke French, though she herself did not.[79]

Another letter sent by Laura's Bahá'í friend to the National Spiritual Assembly of France conveyed her continuing concerns. She again stressed that Lady Blomfield had always asked Laura and her husband to correct the notes that were taken by the secretary. She had referred to a Persian book written by Maḥmúd Zarqání, in which he mentions the fact that the Dreyfus-Barneys were responsible for the translation of the *Paris Talks*. Before the translation of each phrase, Hippolyte first wrote it in French and then corrected it. According to the understanding of this Bahá'í friend, and based on what Laura had explained to him, the Dreyfus-Barneys were responsible for the interpretation and were best qualified in French. It seems that Laura did not find enough time to correct the notes of Lady Blomfield and that is why Laura and Hippolyte's names were removed when it was published in English. Laura was not blaming Lady Blomfield, but herself, for not completing that task due to lack of time. She had also expressed her concern that the names of the halls, houses and streets of the places that 'Abdu'l-Bahá had given His addresses were removed, as this information had historic value and should have been included.[80] She had sent a note which was attached to this letter, saying: 'Lady Blomfield and daughters always asked my husband and me to correct the notes taken and came to Vevey as we were spending the summer in Mont Pèlerin in his parents' home.'[81] Lady Blomfield and her daughters did work on the transcript of *Talks by 'Abdu'l-Bahá Given in Paris* while staying at the Hotel Belvedere in Mont Pèlerin.[82]

With 'Abdu'l-Bahá in the United States

On the other side of the Atlantic, the American Bahá'í community numbered about two thousand.[83] They were now eagerly preparing for 'Abdu'l-Bahá's visit.

Laura received a letter dated January 12, 1912 from the Persian–American Educational Society of Washington, from someone, possibly Mason Remey, who had returned from a trip to Paris earlier that year. He mentioned how much he appreciated what he had learned and suggested that this knowledge could be used to prepare for 'Abdu'l-Bahá's visit to the United States. The letter stated, 'I do not see how we could have arranged any organized or systematic plan if we did not know something, by actual experience, about His arrival and reception in European countries.' He also requested that Laura come to America to help the Bahá'ís receive 'Abdu'l-Bahá. Since his return to the United States, he said, he had visited several major cities such as New York, Boston, Chicago, Philadelphia, and Atlantic City, as well as Montreal, Canada, in preparation for 'Abdu'l-Bahá's trip. His preparations had also included interviewing the heads of various organizations and prominent societies in all of these cities.[84]

For 'Abdu'l-Bahá's historic journey to America, His admirers had sent Him thousands of dollars for first class travel on the RMS *Titanic*. They wished for Him to sail in great opulence. But He did not accept the money and returned it to them.[85] Booking passage on another ship, the steamer SS *Cedric*, 'Abdu'l-Bahá arrived in New York on April 11, a few days before the sinking of the *Titanic* on its maiden voyage. He stayed in America for 239 days and visited many cities across the United States as well Montreal, Canada.

'Abdu'l-Bahá arrived in Washington, D.C. by train on April 20. Laura was not in the country for this first visit.[86] But Laura's mother, who was then Mrs Alice Barney-Hemmick, and whom the Master had met in 1905 in 'Akká, was in Washington. She was living at Studio House with her second husband. She sent her car to Union Station to take 'Abdu'l-Bahá to the home of Agnes Parsons 'where he was entertained during his sojourn'.[87] Agnes Parsons (1861–1934) was a wealthy Washington socialite who had become a Bahá'í around 1908 and visited 'Abdu'l-Bahá in Haifa in 1910. Her husband, Arthur Jeffrey Parsons, was a Librarian at the Library of Congress.[88] She was asked by 'Abdu'l-Bahá to arrange a race unity convention, which was so successful it became the first of many across the United States.[89]

'Abdu'l-Bahá had lunch at Alice's home on April 21, the day after His arrival.[90] Two days later He went for a drive with Alice and the Turkish ambassador, Yúsuf Díyá Páshá, who seemed 'much interested in the conversation'.[91] On April 25, after a meeting with Theosophists in the home of Agnes Parsons, the Master was taken motoring during the afternoon and met with people at the homes of Alice Hemmick and Mrs Ali-Kuli Khan.[92] 'Abdu'l-Bahá's visits to these homes, as well as the fact that these gathering were open to everyone, attracted the attention of the newspapers. The *Washington Bee* published this account on April 27, 1921:

Its [the Bahá'í Faith's] white devotees, even in this prejudice-ridden community, refuse to draw the color line. The informal meetings, held frequently in the fashionable mansions of the cultured society in Sheridan Circle, Dupont Circle, Connecticut and Massachusetts avenues, have been open to Negroes on terms of absolute equality.[93]

'Abdu'l-Bahá's seven-day schedule in Washington was full, with 13 formal talks, a few informal ones and various visits.[94] On April 28, on His way to the railway station to travel to Chicago, 'Abdu'l-Bahá stopped His carriage at Studio House to say goodbye to Alice but she was out.[95]

In those days Alice was actively working for women's equality, which was a new interest of hers. Her biographer wrote that Alice had publicly affirmed her allegiance to the suffrage cause, as she supported the movement with the passion reminiscent of her days as an artist. Alice wrote two plays to promote the rights of women. One was called *The Woman*, in which she depicted famous women in history, including Ṭáhirih, who was a disciple of the Báb, an ardent teacher of the Bábí Faith, a poet, a reformer who defied the Islamic restrictions on women, and who ultimately became a martyr for her beliefs and activities. The play ended with the dance of the Maidens of Peace.[96]

As for the gossip magazines, the gatherings and meetings at Alice's home were reported as 'sedate', so reporters were 'forced to put a different spin' on the 'coverage of Studio House happenings in order to titillate' their 'readers'. Some of the Washington media grossly misreported 'Abdu'l-Bahá's visit. *The Washington Mirror* incorrectly announced that Christian had become a Bahá'í and was sitting on the floor to eat his meals, wearing Eastern clothes.[97]

Other newspapers did a little better. *The Washington Post* wrote:

All yesterday afternoon, women in automobiles and carriages arrived for private conversations with the aged leader. A few poorer people came, but most of the visitors were wealthy . . . Mrs Nicholas Longworth [Alice Roosevelt] occupied a seat far back in the audience with two other women and seemed greatly interested in the afternoon's entertainment.[98]

Laura and Hippolyte were in Europe during April and sailed from Cherbourg on April 17.[99] They must have been worried by and concerned over the fate of the *Titanic*, which had consumed the thoughts of every-one. They disembarked in New York and went straight to Washington.

When 'Abdu'l-Bahá arrived in Washington for His second visit on May 8, Laura and Hippolyte were staying with Alice and Christian at Studio House. Laura wrote to Afroukhteh that she 'had the honour of attaining His presence' during this visit, as did her husband.[100]

Laura and Hippolyte both went to the railway station to welcome 'Abdu'l-Bahá and accompanied Him in the car of Laura's mother to the home of Agnes Parsons for tea.[101] Hippolyte noted that 'Abdu'l-Bahá was in 'very good health' when He arrived.[102]

'Abdu'l-Bahá gave several talks during His second visit in Wash-ington. Two days after His arrival He addressed a group of women in the afternoon, speaking about the rights and education of women. He then visited Neighborhood House, a community center that had been established through the efforts of Alice Barney-Hemmick.[103] Laura was present on both occasions, then drove Him to Studio House, where He spoke and had a ten o'clock dinner.[104]

Laura and Hippolyte may have gone for a short visit to Cincinnati, Laura's birthplace.[105] Upon their return to Washington, they also spent time with the newlyweds, Alice and her new husband. It was the first time Laura had been back in Washington since her mother had remar-ried. The two couples went to Bar Harbor, which was busy with its usual social demands on the rich and famous who summered there. The Hemmicks 'whirled from one party to the next'. Laura and Hip-polyte attended a fancy dress party, dressing as pirates, and took part in a theatrical performance in which Laura was dressed as a Middle Eastern woman and Hippolyte as a sheikh.[106] But Laura had left the social trappings of her family's class for a simpler life, so the social scene may not have been her preferred way to spend her time and energy. She had never been a pleasure-seeking person and would rather have pre-ferred to spend her time on more worthy causes. However, as always, she managed to live in her two worlds graciously.

During the time when the Dreyfus-Barneys were still in the United States, 'Abdu'l-Bahá and His entourage were traveling across the coun-try, visiting different cities. Hippolyte received a letter from 'Abdu'l-Bahá written around the time He was leaving Philadelphia for New York in June. After giving Hippolyte the news of His meetings and addresses in Philadelphia, 'Abdu'l-Bahá wrote:

I hope both you and the maidservant of Bahá will be able to render important services on this journey and will become the cause of proclaiming the Word of God. Convey my respectful greetings to the maidservant of Bahá. I pray God for confirmations and assistance for her.

May the Glory of the All-Glorious rest upon thee.[107]

After their visit to Bar Harbor, Laura returned to Washington. She helped her mother with the house at 1629 Rhode Island Avenue and taking care of their affairs while Hippolyte was traveling. Then she went to Stony Man Mountain in Virginia and invited Natalie, who was in Paris, to join her in the house Laura and Hippolyte owned. Laura was enjoying the camp life; it was a rest between Washington and Bar Harbor. This was to be the last time Laura would host Natalie there, as they intended to rent or sell the house since Laura was not sure when they would return to Paris. If Hippolyte's mother stayed well, they planned to return to Paris the first week of September. Hippolyte, who had been traveling to several cities in the western United States, including Seattle and San Francisco and a visit to the Grand Canyon in Arizona, joined Laura in West Virginia to look after the land they owned.[108]

Hippolyte was present that July when 'Abdu'l-Bahá officiated at the marriage of Grace Robarts of Canada and Harlan Foster Ober (1881–1962) in New York City. 'Abdu'l-Bahá had suggested the marriage, and these two devoted Bahá'ís immediately and joyously were obedient to His wish. There was first a 'simple Bahá'í service' which was 'followed later that same day by a legal ceremony performed by the Reverend Howard Colby Ives (not yet a Bahá'í), in the presence of friends from East and West.' The marriage certificate was signed by 'Abdu'l-Bahá, Hippolyte, and the Reverend Howard Colby Ives.[109]

Hippolyte might have accompanied 'Abdu'l-Bahá when He met Kahlil Gibran in New York that July.[110] However, when 'Abdu'l-Bahá visited Washington for the third time from 6 to 11 November, the Dreyfus-Barneys were not there. They had returned to Paris.

Joining 'Abdu'l-Bahá in the United Kingdom

Laura and Hippolyte returned to Paris and then traveled to England when 'Abdu'l-Bahá visited there after His eight-month tour of North

America. Laura wrote that 'when the Master visited Europe I again gained admittance to His presence'.[111] Hippolyte was present with a dozen other people when 'Abdu'l-Bahá's ship docked in Liverpool on December 13, 1912 and accompanied Him on the train to London.[112] Laura, arriving from Paris and looking 'well and happy', joined them in London two days later. During this visit, she discussed with 'Abdu'l-Bahá His forthcoming trip to Paris.[113] Lady Blomfield, who 'much loved and admired' Laura, must have been delighted to see her again.[114]

Professor Edward Granville Browne, the orientalist who had met Bahá'u'lláh in 1890, knew the Dreyfus-Barneys. He was among the numerous people who visited 'Abdu'l-Bahá at 97 Cadogan Gardens to hear Him speak on the morning of December 18.[115] Two days later Hippolyte made the closing remarks following an address by 'Abdu'l-Bahá at a London gathering of 'scientists and diplomats, Oriental visitors and leading thinkers of the day'.[116]

'Abdu'l-Bahá and Natalie

Laura had discussed her faith and beliefs with Natalie soon after discovering the Bahá'í Faith but Natalie had not been receptive. It is not clear whether Laura encouraged her to visit 'Abdu'l-Bahá, or Natalie, who had already met 'Abdu'l-Bahá in Paris, had asked to do so. Natalie, who was in London at the time, visited 'Abdu'l-Bahá at the Blomfield home on December 19, 27 and 28, 1912.[117] She interviewed 'Abdu'l-Bahá at their first meeting. Ahmad Sohrab wrote about two of these meetings and recorded that 'Abdu'l-Bahá spoke with Natalie for some time and told her that God had given her fruitful seeds of great capacity but that she must sow them in (illegible, maybe fertile) soil to yield worthy harvests.[118] At their second meeting 'Abdu'l-Bahá gave her more guidance. He spoke with her 'about the darkness of the hearts and the souls [caused] by the gloom of matter and nature, encouraging her to work for the universal illumination of the world'.[119]

It seems that the relationship between Laura and Natalie was difficult during this period of their lives. They had each chosen a different path early in life. Laura told her mother that there had been some contention between her and Natalie but they had resolved it. She wished that Natalie could again be as nice as she had been one particular morning. Laura hated leaving Natalie when she was behaving nicely. 'Why cannot you and I be a comfort to one another always?' Laura asked her sister. 'Instead of such a constant source of unrest?'[120] Laura explained to her mother, 'She [Natalie] is the greatest pleasure and the greatest trouble in one person, but as pleasure is rarer than all things, it is only memory that remains.'[121]

The Master Back in Paris

Laura and her husband returned home and soon afterward hosted 'Abdu'l-Bahá. They welcomed Him at the Gare Saint-Lazare when He arrived in Paris for His second visit on January 21.[122] They had rented an apartment for Him at 30 rue St. Didier in the sixteenth arrondissement.[123] At the apartment 'Abdu'l-Bahá was served a traditional Persian meal that had been prepared at the Dreyfus-Barney home.[124] Again, numerous newspapers covered 'Abdu'l-Bahá's travels and wrote about the Barney family. The *Chicago Sunday Tribune* headline screamed, 'Bahaism Seizes Paris' and reported that 'Abdu'l-Bahá, the 'Prophet of Peace', had arrived in Paris, that Laura had embraced this new religion and that she had 'devoted her life to the gathering together of converts'. The article also mentioned that the apartment that Laura had rented for 'Abdu'l-Bahá was larger and more luxurious than the one of last season, and that His engagements for private conferences were 'many and important'.[125]

Again, Laura and her husband accompanied 'Abdu'l-Bahá to meetings and organized significant gatherings for Him in their home and helped with translation:

> Every Friday evening, he addressed an assemblage at M. and Mme. Dreyfus-Barney's, 15 rue Greuze and every Monday afternoon he visited a group at the studio of Mr [Edwin] Scott (an American artist), in the Latin Quarter, 17 rue Boissonade.[126]

These weekly meetings were attended by Bahá'ís, and seekers and inquirers were welcomed too. 'Abdu'l-Bahá attended the Dreyfus-Barneys' Friday evening meetings at least seven times.[127]

On Saturday, February 1, 'Abdu'l-Bahá attended dinner in the home of the Dreyfus-Barneys with several Persian dignitaries, including the Persian ambassador and the first secretary.[128] In early February, two

Baháʼís from Egypt, Ríyáḍ Salím Effendi and Dr Muḥammad Ṣáliḥ, arrived to visit Him.[129] On February 6 Laura and her husband took ʻAbduʼl-Bahá sightseeing to Versailles and driving Him to other historical places in and around Paris.[130] ʻAbduʼl-Bahá visited the Louvre on February 14. A cousin of Hippolyte, Carle Dreyfus, was a conservator of the Département des Objets dʼArt at the museum. Most likely Hippolyte accompanied Him there.[131] On March 9, Edward G. Browne and his wife, who knew the Dreyfus-Barneys, came to one of ʻAbduʼl-Baháʼs talks given at their home. ʻAbduʼl-Bahá spoke with Browne for almost three hours.[132] ʻAbduʼl-Bahá, who was tired from all His travels, talked about soon returning to the Holy Land.[133] Hippolyte was present at this meeting but Laura had to be excused to accompany Mrs Browne.[134]

Natalie, who was also back in Paris, invited ʻAbduʼl-Bahá to dine at her home at 20 rue Jacob. This is the same house where authors and members of Parisian high society attended salons for over 50 years.[135]

Laura and Hippolyte invited ʻAbduʼl-Bahá to speak at a meeting at their home on February 14. They also welcomed another guest, Mirra Richard (1878–1973), a French Hindu spiritual leader known to her followers as ʻThe Motherʼ, who gave an introduction to the Baháʼí Faith. This was her first documented meeting with ʻAbduʼl-Bahá, and though she may have met Him previously, there is no record of it. She saw Him again on March 10.[136] Born Blanche Rachel Mirra Alfassa in Paris to a Jewish immigrant family, the Mother believed she had been in spiritual communication with Sri Aurobindo (1872–1950), an Indian nationalist, yogi, poet, spiritualist and mystic, before actually meeting him. He had left his hometown in West Bengal in 1910 during the years of Indiaʼs struggle for freedom, and she joined him in 1911. Sri Aurobindoʼs essential message was that all nations were one and must live in harmonious diversity. Until her death, the Mother ran his ashram in Pondicherry in southern India, which became the world headquarters of the Sri Aurobindo movement. She married Paul Richard in 1911.

Anil Sarwal, who chronicled the Motherʼs life, quoted her own testimony that those years were ʻthe most important for her spiritual growthʼ.[137] Sarwal also recorded that the Mother was once again asked by ʻAbduʼl-Bahá to speak in His place on March 10 because He was not well. Even though she had given an introductory talk a few days earlier, she was not a Baháʼí and she did not feel prepared to do so. However, she did deliver a talk based on living the life, saying:

But 'Abdu'l-Bahá is not content to give us his teaching, he is living it, and therein lies all his power of persuasion . . . Indeed, who has seen 'Abdu'l-Bahá and not felt in his presence this perfect goodness, this sweet serenity, this peace emanating from his being?[138]

The Mother attended several meetings at the homes of the Dreyfus-Barneys, Edith Sanderson, and the Scotts. Later the Mother wrote in her 'Causeries' manuscripts that she had met these people and had herself given talks at their gatherings.[139]

Laura wrote to the Mother many years later and shared her grief at the loss of a mutual beloved friend, Suzanne Karpeles, with whom Laura had been close in many ways 'of thought and action'. She wrote that they had not been in touch in years but that she would not forget the special times they had been together and the spiritual work that she was carrying out.[140]

Laura met other prominent Persians in Paris that year. One was Muḥammad Valí Khán Tunukábuní, who was in France for medical treatment. One of his titles was Sipah-Salár-i-A'ẓam (Field Marshall). He had been the governor of Rasht from 1899 to 1903 and of Tabríz in 1912. From 1909 he was the leader of the Constitutionalist revolutionaries and forced the abdication of the shah, restoring the Constitution. Known as one of the greatest statesmen and military commanders in Persian history, he later became prime minister and held other important national posts. He met with 'Abdu'l-Bahá on February 28 and was perhaps the most notable and high-ranking Persian to meet Him in Paris.[141] Laura gave him a Persian copy of her book *Some Answered Questions*, the *Mufáwaḍát*. As a young man he had heard an eye-witness account of the execution of Badí', Bahá'u'lláh's messenger to Náṣiri'd-Dín Sháh, so when he came to that part of the book, he wrote a moving account of this on the margins of the page.[142]

Laura and her husband were in constant touch with their special guest in Paris. On March 19 they went to 'Abdu'l-Bahá's apartment and helped with His move to the Martha-Pension, 97 rue Lauriston, near Place de l'Étoile. 'Abdu'l-Bahá's meals were to be cooked at the home of Laura and Hippolyte and brought to the hotel. On the day of the move, Rúḥá, 'Abdu'l-Bahá's third daughter, and her husband arrived in Paris with her companion and 'Abdu'l-Bahá's nephew, Mírzá Ḥusayn Afnán.[143] 'Abdu'l-Bahá had asked Rúḥá to come for medical treatment.

Laura hosted 'Abdu'l-Bahá for lunch on March 20.[144] The next day, for Naw-Rúz, the Persian New Year, 'Abdu'l-Bahá hosted lunch at His hotel.[145] That afternoon Hippolyte accompanied Him to a reception at the Persian Embassy to celebrate the New Year, at which many Persian students and dignitaries were present. Later that evening He addressed the friends at a gathering at the Dreyfus-Barney home, as He had done on many occasions previously.[146] They arrived at 'Abdu'l-Bahá's hotel on April 1 then drove Him to the Gare de l'Est, where several people had come to say farewell as He departed for Stuttgart, Vienna and Budapest.[147]

While 'Abdu'l-Bahá traveled in Germany and Austro-Hungary during the whole month of April, His mail was being received at the Dreyfus-Barney home. Bundles of letters were delivered to Him when He returned to Paris in early May.[148] He stayed at the Baltimore Hotel situated at 88 bis Ave Kléber.

As was the local practice, Laura brought a large bunch of roses for 'Abdu'l-Bahá on May 19.[149] A few days later a celebration of 'Abdu'l-Bahá's birthday was held on May 23 at the Dreyfus-Barney home. The Bahá'ís arrived with bouquets of flowers all that day, but He told them that the day should be considered and celebrated only as the anniversary of the Declaration of the Báb, for that was why May 23 was a blessed day.[150] Two days later, 'Abdu'l-Bahá and Hippolyte went by carriage to a meeting with Paul and Mirra Richard, the Mother.[151]

On May 27, three weeks after His return to Paris, 'Abdu'l-Bahá moved from the hotel on Avenue Kléber to the more secluded one on Rue Lauriston where He had stayed before, so He could rest and regain his strength.[152] During that time the Dreyfus-Barneys were in constant contact with Him. They knew that the hotel meals did not suit Him and offered to have meals cooked at their home and taken to His hotel, but He refused.[153]

In a few days 'Abdu'l-Bahá regained His strength and the meetings again resumed. On May 30 He attended 'a noteworthy gathering at the home of the Dreyfus-Barneys', with people of diverse nationalities attending.[154] Consul Albert Schwarz of Germany, a Bahá'í and government official who had established a healing mineral bath in Mergentheim, spoke at this meeting.[155] In His talk 'Abdu'l-Bahá 'underlined the true import of that harmonious and loving association of people of so many origins, brought about by the power of Bahá'u'lláh'.[156]

'Abdu'l-Bahá visited or attended meetings at the Dreyfus-Barney home more than 11 times and Laura and Hippolyte accompanied Him to numerous meetings held in other locations. He met with Laura several times during His final stay in Paris and they discussed many matters. 'Abdu'l-Bahá and Laura visited Hippolyte's mother, who was very ill, on June 2.[157] Hippolyte lost his mother, Lea Marie Sophie Ines Dreyfus-Cardozo, four months later in Paris on October 2. As with his father's funeral, the service and burial were held in private at her request.

The Dreyfus-Barneys' special guest was to depart from Paris. On June 12 they drove the Master to Gare de Lyon in their car and bade farewell to Him at 8:00 a.m. 'Abdu'l-Bahá spoke with the Bahá'ís who had come to the station to say goodbye. He urged them to be united at all times. The train left at noon for the 12-hour run to Marseilles, where 'Abdu'l-Bahá spent the night at a hotel next to the train station. The next morning, He boarded the SS *Himalaya,* a British ship of the Peninsular and Oriental Steam Navigation Company, for Port Said.[158] While on board the ship, the Master received a radiogram from Laura and Hippolyte:

> A thousand regrets to see you parting, and not being able to accompany you. We hope that your voyage will be agreeable and we trust to find you again soon. Rooha [Rúḥá] is well. In thought she joins with us to send you affectionate greeting.[159]

Travels across America

Towards the end of 1913 Laura and her husband arrived in Washington, D.C., their first stop on their journey west to Japan, French Indochina (at that time the three states of Vietnam, Laos and Cambodia), Korea, China and perhaps Persia.[160] During this stay, they were busy with visiting, giving presentations on the Bahá'í Faith and attending dinners to which they had been invited. Their visits were mostly with diplomats, senators and guests that Alice invited for lunches and dinners.[161] One of their main meetings was when Laura and Hippolyte gave talks about the Faith at the Music Conservatory of Washington, D.C. on December 10.[162] Even so, this was a relatively quiet time for the couple.[163]

The Dreyfus-Barneys received an invitation to a diplomatic reception at the White House, to which they looked forward. Hippolyte did not wish to miss this event and changed the schedule of his forthcoming trip to Cuba to make their attendance at the reception possible. It was a party hosted by President Woodrow Wilson. Laura was among the few Bahá'ís of her era who had been received at the White House.[164]

The day after the reception, Hippolyte left for Cuba for a week while Laura stayed with her mother.[165] Laura informed him while he was in Cuba that her mother would join them on the trip west across the country while Christian would stay home to take care of his business.[166] In an undated letter to Alice, Hippolyte said how much they looked forward to her letters, adding, 'I love following you in your Washington life which you have made me know in such a pleasant way.'[167-]

Laura and Hippolyte went to New York for four days in January 1914, right after Hippolyte's return from Cuba. They were looking forward to seeing May Bolles Maxwell, the Mountfort Millses, and other Bahá'í friends, as well as Laura's cousin Ellen and her husband.[168] They had a pleasant time and returned to Washington on February 1, starting their trip west with Alice by taking a train the next day for New Orleans.[169]

They traveled to several new cities that they had not yet visited. Hippolyte, who had a respectful and admiring relationship with Laura's mother, must have enjoyed having her on this trip.

The trio traveled by train through Atlanta, New Orleans, San Antonio and El Paso in Texas, ending their trip in San Francisco.[170] They enjoyed this cross-country travel and visited attractive and significant places. Hippolyte commented that he found New Orleans a 'curious city' and San Antonio 'interesting'.[171]

They arrived in San Diego on February 9 and visited Katherine Augusta Tingley, a leader of the American Section of the Theosophical Society and the founder of the Point Loma Theosophical colony in San Diego. The Society was co-founded in 1875 by Helena Blavatsky, Col. Henry Steel Olcott, William Quan Judge and others to promote universal brotherhood, and to 'serve humanity by cultivating an ever-deepening understanding and realization of the Ageless Wisdom, spiritual Self-transformation, and the Unity of all Life'.[172] Its objectives are 'to form a nucleus of the universal brotherhood of humanity without distinction of race, creed, sex, caste or color; to encourage the comparative study of religion, philosophy, and science;

and to investigate the unexplained laws of nature and the powers latent in humanity'.[173]

Theosophy is a collection of occultist and mystical philosophies seeking direct knowledge of the mysteries of life and nature, the nature of divinity and the origin and purpose of the universe. After a few years, the founders of the Society moved to India and established their international headquarters in Madras (today's Chennai). Hippolyte and Laura were familiar with the commonalities of the Bahá'í Faith and Theosophy and wanted to learn more about its American version, aware that 'Abdu'l-Bahá had great respect for the Theosophists. When He had been asked if He recognized the good that the Theosophical Society had done, He had replied,

> I know it; I think a great deal of it. I know that their desire is to serve mankind. I thank this noble Society in the name of all Bahá'ís and for myself. I hope that by God's help these friends will succeed in bringing about love and unity. It is a great work and needs the effort of all the servants of God![174]

'Abdu'l-Bahá had given talks at Theosophical Societies in the United States and major European capitals. The previous year, Hippolyte had accompanied Him to the headquarters of the Theosophical Society of France in Paris, where He gave an address.[175] The Dreyfus-Barneys were aware that their belief in universal brotherhood was held in common with Theosophists but they also learned that the central beliefs of Theosophy were reincarnation and the occult, which are not compatible with Bahá'í teachings.

They had train reservations to continue onward to Los Angeles but had to change their plans because of flooding. Unfortunately, they witnessed the destruction and damage. When they finally arrived in Los Angeles, Laura, Hippolyte, and Alice had a short visit in Hollywood.[176] It was Alice's first visit to Hollywood and she was so impressed that she decided to move to California years later.

San Francisco, where there had also been floods that January and February, was their next destination. Their arrival was announced in the newspapers. Flowers inundated their hotel room, along with country club admission cards for Hippolyte.[177] They attended an event organized by the Bahá'ís of San Francisco at 165 Post Street and both Laura and Hippolyte addressed the gathering. Their talks were followed by a reading of the talk given by 'Abdu'l-Bahá during His visit the year before.[178]

The San Francisco millionaires Adolph and Alma Spreckels invited the Dreyfus-Barneys to their yacht and to visit a country club.[179] Adolph was a successful businessman who managed the Spreckels Sugar Company and donated the California Palace of the Legion of Honor to the city of San Francisco. The Hearsts (perhaps Phoebe and her family) and the Kohls also welcomed the guests and invited them. Hippolyte wrote to his sister raving about the hospitality of the people there. Flowers were brought for Laura every day and cigarettes for him.[180]

Alice was to remain in San Francisco. As Laura and Hippolyte departed San Francisco for the Far East and said farewell to her, Laura expressed her own adventurous personality:

We must part with my lady mother: she will not leave the States; and my spirit of wandering pushes me toward the East. What is this craving for distant lands which urges me away from the known and the loved?[181]

Beginning of Her Journey around the World

On March 5, 1914 Laura and Hippolyte boarded the SS *Mongolia* in San Francisco for Japan with a stop in Hawaii, embarking on a journey around the world in accordance with the wishes of 'Abdu'l-Bahá.[182] He had encouraged them to travel to China, India, Japan and other Asian countries and possibly return to Persia. Perhaps these places were destinations to teach their faith. Based on a manuscript written by Laura two years after her trip, they used the journey to explore those lands and its peoples and customs as well.[183] They had a letter of recommendation from Stephen Pichon, the foreign minister of France, addressed to the foreign ministries of various Asian countries, diplomatic agencies and French consular offices, especially the ones in the Far East where the couple planned to visit. This letter introducing the Dreyfus-Barneys and giving them credentials for the trip, read:

Although your fellow citizens are always assured of receiving the best possible welcome from you, I would, nevertheless, particularly like to recommend Mr. and Mrs. H. Dreyfus-Barney. I would be very grateful if you could kindly lend them, where appropriate, the support of your good offices.[184]

On the ship to Hawaii they had a superb cabin facing the pool, since they also had a letter of recommendation for the captain.[185] They reached Waikiki, a neighborhood of Honolulu, a few days later. The *Honolulu Star Bulletin*, a daily newspaper that announced the visits of the people of high society, reported their arrival.[186] Colonel Samuel Parker (1853–1920), who had been introduced to the Dreyfus-Barneys by the Spreckels, took them on a tour of Honolulu in his car. Colonel Parker was a landowner, businessman and politician serving in the last cabinet of the Kingdom of Hawaii. The Dreyfus-Barneys attended several conferences and gave talks addressing many Bahá'ís.[187] They managed to sail to several Hawaiian Islands before continuing their journey west.

'From the Peace of the East to the War of the West' and Their Arrival in Japan

Two years after the completion of her journey Laura wrote a travelogue in manuscript form called 'From the Peace of the East to the War of the West', chronicling impressions of her travels and the lands she visited, cultures she encountered and people she met.[188] She explained the manuscript in the Foreword:

> These notes are impressions, mere impressions. Can one really know any man? Can one really know any country? I am drawn to nations as others are attracted to individual beings. I find them complex, both lovable and imperfect, and I am made to realize that alone an intermingling of certain racial customs, of certain social aspirations, can form a civilization worthy of life and of the genius of man.[189]

Laura did not use Hippolyte's name in this manuscript but referred to an individual called 'X' who accompanied her on this trip and took care of her during her illness. She must have been referring to him. She used literary and flowery language and symbolic phrases. For example, describing a temple in Japan, she wrote: 'The curves of the temple are as graceful as the opened petals of a tulip descending from heaven.'[190] She rarely made references to her Bahá'í beliefs and referred to God as the 'Supreme Body'. She showed compassion and understanding towards the poor and the needy and those who suffered. In many instances in this manuscript she expressed her strong desire to see new sights, to visit new places, to learn and to observe. She did not name-drop and was discreet about the important people she met as well as her privileged mode of travel.

Laura recorded several incidents of the sufferings of women that she witnessed and expressed her compassion for them. While sailing from Hawaii to Japan she wrote about a woman and her three children who had left the mainland to return to her homeland to give birth because it would be cheaper there.

In the morning I heard that a Japanese woman had died in the steer-age. A square place near the railing of the after deck was roped off. The Captain and the ship's doctor stood there with the friends of the dead woman, who held her children − tots of one, three and four. The father had remained in San Francisco while she returned to Japan to give birth to the fourth child − life in the native land was so much cheaper!

I wondered if she would have died if she could have had the comfort that goes with a first-class cabin . . . If I had but known!

Three men advanced carrying the dead woman's body wrapped tightly in sack-cloth: it looked so slender, so tiny, so flexible! They placed it on a board, which was tilted against the open part of the railing, they covered the body with a Japanese flag and bound the whole firmly together. The bystanders sang the wistful heroic anthem of Japan; someone threw an orchid upon her, the command was given, the slab was thrust overboard. There was a splash, and the suction of the ship swallowed the body instantaneously!

The children of the dead woman looked straight ahead, uncon-scious of what they had lost. I looked down into the sea, the foaming waves impelled from the side of the ship were like the white mane of a fabulous horse, and there came into my mind something that I do not know how to express, and that Lafcadio Hearn should have written.[191]

Laura and Hippolyte arrived at the port city of Yokohama, south of Tokyo, where they spent one day touring. They saw the magnificent

Shinto temple and the famous statue of Buddha in the city of Kana Kura (Kamakura). Their next stop was Tokyo, where they arrived on April 10 and stayed for a week. They were welcomed by Mr and Mrs Philip H. Dodge, American Bahá'ís who had moved to Japan.[192] Hippolyte wrote to his brother-in-law saying they had met with the local Bahá'ís.[193] Several meetings were organized, and Japanese friends were invited to meet the visitors. They had the opportunity to introduce the Bahá'í Faith to many interested people. The Dreyfus-Barneys were not the first Bahá'ís to make the long voyage to Japan. Howard Struven and Charles Mason Remey had traveled to Japan in 1909 and Mrs Aurelia Bethlen in 1911.[194]

The Japanese were in mourning during the time the Dreyfus-Barneys were in Japan because the dowager empress (the mother of the emperor) had passed away. Empress Dowager Shōken (1849–1914) was the widow of Emperor Meiji (1852–1912). Laura recorded:

> We had hoped to be present at the Imperial cherry blossom garden party; but before that time the Court had gone into mourning for the death of the Dowager Empress. She died in Numazu, the ninth of April; but in accordance with the dictates of the past, royalty can only die in Tokyo. So, the Empress was not declared dead till three days after, when her corpse had been deposed in her Tokyo palace.[195]

In Tokyo the Dreyfus-Barneys were invited by the Ambassador of France for lunch and were joined by the military attaché Colonel and Mrs Lottin and their six daughters. They also met with an American friend who was in Tokyo at that time.[196]

After a week in Tokyo, they traveled to Nikko.[197] This was a popular destination for tourists, with the mausoleum of a shogun, the tomb of his grandson and a shrine that dates to the 8th century. They were fascinated by Nikko's beauty, its monasteries and tombs. They also visited Chusenji, and since the weather was foul, Laura went on a rickshaw and Hippolyte rode a horse.[198]

Laura was deeply concerned about the situation of Japanese women. She wrote in her travel journal that since the fall of the feudal system, Japan faced new problems, some of which were from the West. Japanese national solidarity still existed but Japan was being challenged by social and economic difficulties. Social unrest would disrupt the state unless Japan learned to deal with it. Laura saw that the health of women, the mothers of future generations, was being adversely affected. Women worked in dire conditions in factories, and their situation at home with their children was little better, since Japan was a strongly patriarchal society. She noticed that Japan was transitioning to an industrial society, but recognition of the welfare of women and children was not yet part of the process.[199]

They visited Yokohama and the Miyanoshita hot spring (near Mount Fuji) before arriving in Kyoto towards the end April. They absolutely loved visiting Kyoto, this quintessential Japanese city, and could not bear to leave it.[200] After a short daytrip to Nara, they were back in Kyoto and left for Kobe.

Hippolyte wrote to his sister that they were vaccinated. This is how he explained it: 'Since Laura learnt that there was smallpox in China, she had us vaccinated by a local Hippocrates [Greek physician]'.[201] This 'Hippocrates' did not speak English or German and they did not know exactly what virus he inoculated them with. But they well knew that in China, besides smallpox there were the plague and typhus.[202]

They were aware of all the rumors of an eminent war and did not know how to plan the rest of their trip. They had heard much contradictory news.[203] They left for Kobe and from there they took a little boat to Miyajima, located among the islands. A few days later, and after visiting Hiroshima, they left Japan for Korea, despite the rumors.[204]

Laura found the behavior of the Japanese towards Hippolyte and her pleasing. She noticed that there was 'no loud speaking, their demeanor was polite, content and unconscious'.[205] Her general impression of Japan was this:

> The national ambition impels the people to prepare for the struggles of our epoch. Japan acquires from all sources, but once she has absorbed her fill, she will reject restraint. Though she adapts new machinery to her needs, her mentality remains Asiatic and immovable.[206]

Korea, China and News of War

The Dreyfus-Barneys then visited Seoul and Moukden (Mukden; Shenyang today) in Korea.[207] As in Japan, Laura noticed the situation of women:

The Korean lady of the old regime only left the house once, when she went from her father's home to enter her husband's dwelling. She is not supposed to address her husband, but, after bearing him several children, she observes this etiquette less rigorously. Unlike the Japanese woman, who is her husband's head servant, the Korean lady lives apart with her own attendants. Prostitution is practically unknown, several wives and '*autres moeurs*' [other ways, as in mistresses and concubines] are not unusual.[208]

The next country they visited was the Republic of China. Laura wrote about Chinese traditions and customs, and again she was struck by the devastating consequences of some aspects of Chinese culture on women's lives. For example, she wrote about the drastic extreme to which three sisters went to save face, reflecting their lack of power to demand their rights:

Filial piety is still strong in China. That very week in the district of Yangtszepoo, three middle aged women finding that they had not enough money to conduct their mother's funeral, suitably hung themselves to the posts of her bed by long strips torn from their white mourning clothes. They left a letter to say that they were committing suicide to save their 'fame' and added that a relative was holding back a thousand dollars due to them; if the money could be forced from him, it was to be given to the Red Cross Society. This bequest shows that they were in touch with modern civilization.[209]

The Dreyfus-Barneys sailed to Qingdao, just across the Yellow Sea from Korea. They had planned to be in Peking (Beijing), China, between May 10 and May 15 but Hippolyte delayed their departure because of bad weather on the Yangtze River.[210] Also, the troubling news of European pre-war tensions spilling over into the Far East did not make travel decisions any easier. Qingdao was at that time a Chinese fishing village ceded by China to Germany at the turn of the century. The Germans declared martial law in Qingdao on August 1, 1914, and within a week the British vice consul ordered all allied visitors to leave immediately.

Rumors of impending war between Japan and Germany had followed the Dreyfus-Barneys from Japan to Korea and then to China. Just when Laura and Hippolyte were about to leave by boat on the

Yangtze River and go overland to Peking the rumors increased.[211]

Rumors turned into reality when Japan declared war on Germany on August 23 and landed troops in Shantung Province, putting Qingdao under siege on October 31. In Europe, Germany had declared war on France on August 3 and invaded Belgium on the same day. The French and Russian armies were mobilized and Britain declared war on Germany on August 4. By the end of the month the Great War had begun in earnest in both the West and the East.

Under these conditions, Alice, Christian and Natalie were worried about Laura and Hippolyte. Natalie sent Laura a letter from Paris on August 1 stating, 'Agitated time my Laura bird.' Natalie hoped the Dreyfus-Barneys would not come back to Europe and instead would stay somewhere safe like 'Egypt or something like that.'[212]

Laura was impressed by Hippolyte's 'adroitness' in getting them safely away from the German colony of Yunnan.[213] Through his negotiations with the Consulate, he managed to get tickets on a train from Qingdao going south to Shanghai.[214] When they arrived there, they realized that, sadly, a major war was inevitable. The next day, they left on a boat for Japan. Because of a typhoon, their trip was delayed while at sea. Finally they arrived in Nagasaki and passed through Kobe, Tokyo, Yokohama, and then sailed for Hawaii. They were in Washington, D.C. by the end of September. It was there, at the Embassy of France, that Hippolyte received an official notification of his assignment back in France.[215]

Return to Europe via the United States and Laura's Services in France

The Dreyfus-Barneys returned to the United States and traveled to New York because the only route to Paris was from the United States. They spent time in Washington, D.C. where Laura was able to give advice about a delicate situation relating to racial issues within the Bahá'í community that was causing disunity:

> When we had explained the whole matter to her [that some people did not like the fact that people from both races had been invited to the home of a white Bahá'í], she agreed with us that no public meetings could safely be held for white people only besides being contrary to the teachings but that meetings for prejudiced white

people might be held at an apartment house and at people's private homes . . .'[216]

After two months in America the Dreyfus-Barneys took the passenger ship SS *La France* on its last voyage to the continent, at Le Havre. Arriving safely by train in Paris, they found it calm compared to the perilous conditions they had left in China.

They returned to France in time for Hippolyte to assume his military service. Laura noted in a letter to her mother that he was serving as a railroad guard near Paris.[217] Laura visited Hippolyte twice a week during the war.[218] At the onset of the war, Laura, who would devote the rest of her life to bringing peace to the world, remarked in a letter to her mother: 'when men will see on one side: arbitration, prosperity, peace and friendliness, and on other: war and its results, they may have learnt the lesson of their epochs'.[219]

Soon after her return to France, Laura, along with many other wealthy American women who volunteered for the war effort, joined the American Ambulance Corps in Paris.[220] Several American women residing in France organized the American Ambulance Corps in Neuilly-sur-Seine and used in their nomenclature the French practice of applying the term ambulance to the type of military institution that Americans call a hospital. These women had pioneered the development of the Corps in the absence of American nurses in Paris. Among them were Mrs George Munroe, wife of an American banker in Paris, and Mrs William K. (Virginia) Vanderbilt.[221] These volunteers, through their generosity, elegance and cordiality, gave 'proof of what "ladies of society" are capable of in the way of fortitude and self-sacrifice, when they are resolved to meet the exigencies of a situation demanding that they be *women* in the highest acceptation of the term'.[222] These unofficial American volunteer groups, as well as individuals, rendered service to their future allies in order to serve humanity by assisting the doctors, surgeons and nurses. This was long before their country officially entered the war.

Laura got involved with the Corps to care for special medical cases at night.[223] During the first two years of the war she served as an auxiliary night nurse at Lycée Pasteur Neuilly-sur-Seine, a secondary school converted into a hospital on the outskirts of Paris.[224] She found her work there most interesting.[225] Natalie had correctly guessed that upon her return to Paris Laura might wish to nurse the wounded.[226]

The American colony in Paris established the American Ambulance soon after the war began and soon a volunteer field service section was added, which was developed by individuals who had used their own automobiles to remove the wounded during the first battle of the Marne, September 6–12, 1914.[227] The volunteers helped the war effort by driving ambulances, establishing funds for wounded soldiers, and delivering hospital supplies in the south of France, while other wealthy women funded and worked in the hospital. It is highly likely that Laura knew these women and for that reason joined this group.[228]

As well as volunteering as a night nurse, Laura, according to *Who's Who in America*, also served by assisting in the re-education of the mentally and physically disabled in the military hospital of Marseilles, spending much time there in 1915 and 1916.[229] During those years, Hippolyte's military duties 'were for the most part in censorship because of his military classification, linguistic abilities and legal training'.[230] As he was based in the south of France, Laura could visit him.[231]

The Opium Pipe: In the Land of Persia

While Laura was helping the injured and dealing with the war efforts in France, her mother was doing her best to promote peace and prevent the entry of the United States into the war by writing and presenting plays and by working on pageants and fundraising events. One fund-raising event was the staging of *The Opium Pipe: In the Land of Persia*, a three-act play originally written by Laura in 1912 on the death of Renée Vivien but not published. Vivien, a British poet who wrote in French, was a friend of Natalie who had died of anorexia and substance abuse in 1909. Laura and Alice had grown very fond of her. Renée had traveled throughout the Orient and the Middle East during the last years of her life.[232]

Alice reworked the play in 1916 and asked Christian to play the lead role of an oriental ruler who became addicted to opium and caused the death of his lover.[233] Alice hired Paul Swan, a protégé of the great actress Alla Nazimova, Natalie's friend, to dance in the opium den scene.[234] Swan was billed 'the most beautiful man in the world' by his agent.[235]

The play was set in ancient Persia, so Alice asked Ali-Kuli Khan, who was now the chargé d'affaires for the Persian Embassy, to assist her with a set design both authentic and sumptuous. While the local chapter of the Drama League of America dismissed the play as lacking literary merit, everyone wanted to be a part of what was expected to be the most lavish and bold production yet produced by Alice.[236] Alice described the play in an article in *The Washington Times*:

> The ultra-modern play, though highly moral and beautiful, intro-duces touches of oriental weirdness, fantastic snake dances, and strange light, with now and then a dash of tom-tom music.[237]

Despite the criticism of the Drama League, the play sold out for its four performances. A fifth one was scheduled as a benefit for the French Ambulance Motor Fund, one of Laura's favorite causes.[238]

It was during the same year that, through the efforts of Alice, Con-gress approved the funding for the first federally funded theatre in the United States, the National Sylvan Theater, an amphitheater located on the Mall near the Washington Monument.

Women's Rights in the United States and Laura's Mother

Alice had shown her allegiance to the women's suffrage cause in 1912 and actively supported it. Despite her support and the activism of thousands of other women, the 19th amendment to the United States Constitution, which gave women the right to vote, was not passed in Congress until 1919 and became law only in 1920.

As the National American Woman Suffrage Association needed new headquarters, Alice lent it her 26-room house at 1626 Rhode Island Avenue in 1916, just for a year, because the Barney-Hemmicks wanted to move back in. In the meantime, Christian had moved from that house to Studio House, where he was supposed to be studying.[239]

The news of the house rental was reported in newspapers such as *The Evening Star,* which ran a picture of the house under the headline 'New Home of National American Suffrage Association'. The article noted as 'a curious coincidence' that 'Abdul-Baha Abbas, the famous Persian reli-gious leader and mystic, has come out for increased rights for women in that far-off land', and reporting that 'Mrs Hemmick said yesterday she had frequently discussed the question of votes for women with the distinguished Persian . . . before the war broke out.'[240] However, the rest of the article, which stated that 'Abdu'l-Bahá had slept there as the guest of Mr and Mrs Hemmick and that Mrs Hemmick had visited Him in his native land, was not correct.

Laura's Work with the American Red Cross

Laura continued her volunteer work during the war and worked for the American Red Cross; she also became its delegate for the Refugees and Repatriation Service for three Departments in the south of France from 1916 to 1918.[241] The Bureau of Refugees and Relief sent representatives/delegates to set up headquarters in nearly all the main Departments in the south of France.

Laura saw an announcement about working with the Red Cross sometime in 1917. She had read in the newspaper that Natalie's friend Mrs Morganthau was sailing to Europe to assist Mr Henry Davison, Chairman of the War Council of the American Red Cross that was formed that May. Natalie's friend was going to assist the Red Cross cooperatives 'to work to better the lives of people all over the world'.[242] Laura was keenly interested in this announcement and wanted to work towards this goal herself. She asked Natalie to help her obtain a recommendation. Laura had already been in active service with the American Red Cross for 15 months and was responsible for three departments in France. All she needed now was an introduction from Natalie to the heads of the organization. The Red Cross personnel at that level were all very professional, and Laura wanted Mr Davison to know who she was.[243] It is not clear whether she got the job.

In April 1917 the United States entered World War I on the side of the Allies – France, Russia and Great Britain. Their war against the Central Powers – Austria-Hungary, Germany, Turkey and Bulgaria – was in its third year. When America entered the war, casualties mounted as the Germans were driven back.

While Laura and Hippolyte were living between Paris and Marseilles, and Natalie was in Paris contending with air raids, Alice was deeply concerned about the safety of her loved ones. She and Christian rented a house in New York. Even though she received regular letters from her daughters and heard of their well-being and safety, she did not stop worrying about them. She feared even more for her daughters when she heard the news of the heavy losses in several battles and the constant raids on Paris. In a letter to Christian written while he was in

Pittsburg, Alice shared her concerns and worries about her two daughters and how the events in Paris might be affecting their lives:

> Natalie with her beautiful mind torn from the quiet of her work to a realization that the world is sinking – that it is full of misery and fear. And Alice [Laura] – with the brave look I've seen so often when something must be met without flinching . . . You know that girl has been through Hell, and God knows I went with her . . . These two dear friends of mine are the only ones in the whole world who care for me and know me, and I am full of fears.[244]

She worried too for 'beautiful smiling Paris and the kindly warmhearted people'.[245]

Reprinting *Some Answered Questions*

Somehow during the last full year of the war in 1917, Laura found the time to correspond with the Bahai Publishing Society in Chicago about publishing a new edition of *Some Answered Questions*. The Society had asked Laura for permission to publish a new edition in the United States since the English publisher had sold all its copies and the book was very much in demand.[246] A reprint of the first edition in England planned for 1912 had not happened. During July 1917 Laura wrote to the Society and stated that she was happy to give the 'privilege' of publication of the second edition to the Society and asked that the price be kept as low as one dollar and for 1,500 copies to be printed.[247] The Society agreed to all her terms but later informed her that the cost of production had gone up and it was necessary to increase the sale price of the book. It promised her that the current print run would be as good as the first edition and that the Society would try to keep production expenses as low as possible because this was a book 'that no one should be without'.[248]

Laura told the Society that she would make some corrections and send them to the Society. She was not too happy that the price would increase.[249] She also asked for a printed version of the title page and discussed whether the pages should be plated or typeset. The Society responded that it would send her a copy of the title page, and it also gave her two estimates for publishing the book in the United States.

The price would be at least one dollar and fifty cents per copy.[250]

The Society reminded Laura in every letter that the demand for her book was brisk and urged her to act quickly so that it could start the publishing process. She promised to keep the Society as the publisher of her book for the next ten years and even longer if it used the same layout as the first edition. She wrote that the Society had 'proved its devotion to the Cause for many years'[251] – 'the Cause' is how Laura referred to the Bahá'í Faith. She submitted the corrections with the addition of 'one lesson'.[252] Though the copy that she mailed had gilt edges, she asked the Society not to incur that extra expense but asked that the copyright in the United States be put in her name.[253] The second English language edition of *Some Answered Questions* was published in 1918.

The Last Years of World War I

As noted above, during the last years of the war Laura worked in the south of France and was actively engaged mainly with refugee relief activities.[254] The American Red Cross Commission in France had two sections, a Bureau of Refugees and Relief, and a Department of Civilian Relief working in the Marseilles area, so it is most probable Laura worked with them both.[255]

When the Germans launched the first of five major offensives in March 1918, 'the refugee problem immediately assumed enormous proportions'.[256] Responding to the need, vast amounts of food and clothing were issued, farming implements were supplied so that crops could be grown to ease food shortages, and work was found for trained workmen.[257] During that summer more than 70 Red Cross representatives and assistants covered 58 of the 66 departments in France that had not been invaded.[258]

The housing stock in Marseilles that had accommodated 600,000 people in 1914 was wholly inadequate for the one million or more persons who flocked into the city in 1917.[259] Marseilles had always been a cosmopolitan city and now it had become a transient one. Soldiers, refugees and merchants of every race thronged the streets. Greeks and Italians established substantial colonies in Marseilles. Most French cities had homogeneous populations but Marseilles resembled many American cities with its multiple ethnicities, so its social service and public health needs were not unusual for experienced American personnel.[260]

Laura wrote to her mother about the wounded, the mix of people who made Marseilles look like a world's fair, and the English, Indians, Chinese, Serbians, Arabs and black men, 'all in different costumes walking and riding about the place . . . In a way all these horrors are a good thing for the future generations who see what war means, not simply chivalry and medals. I think that women will be a great help to get out of this horrible habit of the past.'[261]

Laura's letters to her mother during this period provided much information and insight into her work with the Red Cross. She wrote in one letter:

I am much occupied here with the Bureau of Repatriates and Refugees, up to the present no American Red Cross people are in this department, & we are organizing something with the Prefet, a personal friend of ours, the 3 French Red Crosses & the . . . wife, a delightful active Parisian. I have asked the American Red Cross to help too, but they are rather slow about starting things.[262]

Laura was the co-founder of the first children's hospital, L'Avenir des Enfants en Vaucluse, in Avignon.[263] She traveled between Paris, Avignon and Marseilles regularly in those years.

When the war ended in November 1918, Laura described the joyous celebration in Marseilles in her unpublished manuscript 'The Way Reopens':

I had been away for a few days visiting villages where there were groups of refugees and repatriates under the care of my French societies and the American Red Cross bureau to which I was attached. When returning to Marseilles, I was amazed to see the unusual animation of an always animated city at its most animated hour. It was evident that something joy-giving had occurred; and as my automobile slackened to push through the mass of people thronging the Canebière [the historic high street in the old part of Marseilles], I asked a man nearby if a great victory had been won. Before he could answer, a youth leapt on the top of A.R.C. [American Red Cross] car shouting: 'Vive l'Amérique qui se bat avec nous,' [Long live America which fights with us] and from all sides rang out exultant cheers of welcome.

Today man had ceased to fire against man. We, who lived through this period, know well that this moment of exultation was the apex of emotion. Not the peace treaty, nor the conferences, cut and dried and unsatisfactory, have been able to uplift us again to that state of enthusiasm. Now we realize that years full of debates and conferences will be necessary to accomplish the promise of that day's vision. Mistrust and financial problems complicate an already intricate puzzle. Alas, the fringes of war are still dragging on the earth.[264]

Contacts with Her Mother During the War Years

During the war years Laura remained in constant touch with her mother. She gave her updates, telling her that 'even the Holy Family in the Holy Land has been handled roughly by the times!' and commenting, 'It is remarkable how one has become adapted to the circumstances.'[265]

Laura sent some doilies and centerpieces to her mother in Washington to sell for the benefit of the refugees.[266] After a few months she sent some bags and asked her mother to sell them to raise funds.[267]

Laura shared with her mother some of the situations she had encountered:

I have come here [Avignon] to see what can be done with the Rapatriés [Repatriates] who are to arrive, for this department is on 'the black list'. Fortunately, there is a new Prefet [Prefect], and I think that if the American Red Cross stands by me we can do something worthy of these poor tired creatures. Mrs Metcalf [a family friend in the United States] continues her generosity, but her money is to go to special cases and what should be done here is the kind of effort that should be made by the American Red Cross.[268]

Laura also told her mother that she had some minor health problems but she said they did not interfere with her work.

In another letter, written from Marseilles, Laura told her mother about her activities there. The Préfet had nominated Laura to serve on a departmental commission to assist refugees. Her Red Cross responsibilities promised an active winter, and she gave credit to the French Army for giving her all the work she needed. She was touched by the appreciation of the refugees who were receiving assistance. She also asked her mother to tell Mrs Metcalf that over a thousand dollars of her contribution had bought many sewing machines. This was important because 'one sewing machine helps a whole family out of misery'.[269]

Not only was Laura worried and concerned about the war, the refugees and everything else going on around her during those years, she was also concerned about her mother and her marital problems. In one letter written in September 1918 Laura expressed hope that her mother was comfortable in her new apartment. She wrote comforting words to her, such as 'do not be too severe with yourself, keep a little comfort, for my sake'.[270] A few months later Laura told her mother not to worry and reassured her of the love of Hippolyte and herself. Alice had sent Laura a check and Laura responded that her life was simple, so her mother should not have sent her any money.[271]

Laura made only a few references to Hippolyte and his whereabouts in her correspondence during those years. It seems they were both in Marseilles in the latter part of 1918, living at 308 rue Paradis.[272]

Acknowledgments of Laura's Contributions During World War I

Numerous local newspapers printed acknowledgments of Laura Dreyfus-Barney's selfless contributions to refugee welfare during the war. The *Courant de Vaucluse* printed an article under the heading of 'Fête Américaine du 4 Juillet 1918 á Avignon et en Vaucluse' [The American Celebration of Fourth of July 1918 in Avignon and Vaucluse], reporting that the French government had decided to celebrate this occasion since the French celebration of independence, Bastille Day, would arrive ten days later, on July 14. It noted that in honor of this event the generous Mme Dreyfus-Barney, the philanthropist, charitable and untiring delegate of the American Red Cross, had decided to distribute useful objects and food to the unfortunate refugees in the area.[273] For this goodwill action, another newspaper, the *Le Républicain du Gard*, recognized her as 'the distinguished delegate'.[274] On July 14 Laura went to the region around Nîmes to give gifts and donations to refugees during the celebration of Bastille Day.[275]

On first of January 1919, soon after the end of the war, the monthly journal *Réfugié en Provence* paid homage to Laura and her contributions:

But one thing strengthens us: the heroism of our soldiers, who water our land with their blood as they regain it piece by piece. The presence of the Americans – and I am happy to now pay homage to Mme Dreyfus-Barney, the American Red Cross's delegate, who wishes by her presence to demonstrate to us her attachment to our cause (Mme Dreyfus-Barney is warmly applauded) – the Republic of the United States' presence, I'd like to say, alongside the French Republic – as these are peoples who do not consider what they have written as 'scraps of paper' and keep their word once given.[276]

Another refugee journal reported that at a gathering in '*une manifestation de reconnaissance envers la délégation de la Croix-Rouge*' (an expression of gratitude to the Red Cross delegation), a beautiful bouquet of flowers in the national colors of France and America was given to Mme Dreyfus-Barney, the devoted delegate. She then spoke on behalf of the Red Cross about a plan and promise to rebuild Marseilles and its factories, saying that they would be an ointment on the wounds of the exiled. The audience could not hold back its tears.[277] This celebration was also reported in several local newspapers.[278] These expressions of appreciation were generated by Laura's involvement in many of the Red Cross's events and by her financial support, which continued to the end of 1918.

It was through Laura's efforts on behalf of the American Red Cross that Christmas celebrations were organized in 1918. Over 1,500 refugee and repatriate children attended and were given gifts, and Laura joined the children in this event.

Travel to the Holy Land

Laura completed her assignments with the refugees and repatriates and put them 'in the care of the competent French committees' that she had had 'the good fortune to form' some 18 months earlier.[279] Her responsibilities as an American Red Cross delegate in Southern France ended as soon as the war was over. Now she was free! And so was her husband Hippolyte!

They planned to go on pilgrimage to the Holy Land first and applied for passports while in Marseilles. Hippolyte told a friend, 'We are leaving for the Holy Land the end of this week. If you have any messages for Abdul-Baha, send them to my address in Marseilles.'[280] He also wrote to another friend in the United States that they might meet in Palestine since they were planning to go in the spring too.[281] A normal mail service to Haifa resumed after the war. Perhaps it was in reply to a request from Hippolyte to visit the Holy Land with Laura that 'Abdu'l-Bahá wrote in a letter on February 7, 1919 that 'it is indeed highly opportune and, on our part, we await your arrival'. He continued that He was happy to hear from him and to know that he and 'Laura Khanum had been freed from severe hardships and had again attained rest and comfort'.[282]

Laura and Hippolyte sailed from Marseilles towards Port Said at the end of March 1919. The violent anti-colonial riots in Egypt threatened to prevent their ship from docking in Port Said. However, it seems that Hippolyte found a solution. Laura wrote to her mother that Hippolyte interpreted the saying 'Where there is a will, there is a way' to mean, 'Where there is a way, have the wits to find it', and they eventually landed in Port Said.[283]

As they were embarking on this voyage Laura wrote to her mother, saying that years and years before, 'Abdu'l-Bahá had warned Hippolyte and her of the horror of a coming war but she could hardly believe that it had happened within a century. She hoped that the struggle for international peace would be made in accordance with natural laws so that war would not occur again.[284]

The couple dispatched a telegram to inform 'Abdu'l-Bahá's household that they were arriving on Saturday April 5. Shoghi Effendi replied:

> Startling and unexpected at the news broke upon us, it nevertheless filled our hearts with joy and rapture for today at noon were to welcome two well-known friends of the Cause who are really the first to arrive from Europe, from belligerent countries, from a region that has been devastated by war and pillage and has undergone the severest trials.[285]

From Port Said they took the train to Cairo for a few days' visit. They were 'the only civilians that took the train for Cairo, passing through the stations which the insurgents had freshly burnt'.[286] They continued by train to Haifa on April 4, which was a much shorter journey than traveling by ship – that would have taken them 30 hours or more. The train itself had been constructed by the British for military purposes during their conquest of Palestine.

The memories of the war years, which were still fresh in Laura's mind, were renewed while traveling in Palestine:

Full well I know that all the wounded soldiers that I have seen have given me but a faint idea of the vast battlefields of hideous carnage, and now these barren plains are being covered by the wild flowers of spring! A few inches of earth, a flush of vegetation, and the bodily struggle disappears; but the mental, the moral achievements cannot be wiped out in the memory of man. The world of nature reabsorbs matter; the world of thought perpetuates action.

Displaced stones, broken wood, twisted metal, gaping streets give a dramatic realization of what villages and cities underwent during bombardment and loot. The emptiness of the ruins proclaims the calamity that has shattered the home. Civilians have suffered with the heroism of the bravest soldier. They have endured and witnessed every kind of horror, unflinching in the traditional honor of their race. With reverence, we must bow the head before the vast numbers of these lowly martyrs deserving the crown of praise. They may be homeless, desolate, broken, they may not even know how great was their stand; but they have done what the world craves for. Above the trampling of the brute they have uplifted the name of man.[287]

The Dreyfus-Barneys were the first pilgrims to arrive from the West after the war. Major Wellesley Tudor-Pole (1884–1968) had facilitated their visit through officials in Cairo and had issued passes for them.[288] Tudor-Pole had met 'Abdu'l-Bahá in Egypt in 1910 and became attracted to the Bahá'í teachings, although he later drifted away. During the war Pole served as a military officer in the British Directorate of Military Intelligence in the Middle East.

Shoghi Effendi personally welcomed them at the train station in Haifa and took them straight away to the house of 'Abdu'l-Bahá where they were staying. The Master arrived a few minutes later. Shoghi Effendi wrote:

Oh, how glad and grateful they were to meet Him, to speak to Him, to hear His voice, to sit beside Him and to feel the touch of His hand. What a terrible time they had both experienced, how uncertain were the conditions they had lived in, how strenuous was the

Red Cross Relief work for the Refugees that had been undertaken by Mrs Dreyfus throughout the war, how delicate and even perilous had been the situation in which Mr Dreyfus had often found himself, once taken to China and there falling into trouble with the Germans and the story of his return safely to Europe, once guard of the railway service and once the censor in one of the south of French Departments, at which latter post he had been of service to the Cause.[289]

All the friends gathered that evening at the request of 'Abdu'l-Bahá to welcome them. It must have been heartwarming for Laura and Hippolyte to be with the Master after the war years. The next morning the couple had a meeting with students from the American University who were there on their Easter vacation, and shared their experiences of the war years. That afternoon, Laura and Hippolyte and a few of the friends went to the middle room of the Shrine of the Báb, where 'Abdu'l-Bahá joined them. He gave a talk and later they all entered the interior of the Tomb. According to Shoghi Effendi, 'a most ardent and inspiring prayers of praise and thanksgiving was offered on the whole as Mrs. Dreyfus intimated it was a very lovely and spiritual meeting.'[290]

A few days later Laura and Hippolyte visited 'Akká and the barracks where Bahá'u'lláh and His 70 followers spent His first years of exile, and later prayed at the Holy Shrine, the resting place of Bahá'u'lláh at Bahjí before returning to Haifa.[291] They could not stay much longer but promised to return towards the end of that year.[292]

Laura wrote:

At the foot of Mount Carmel we spent a few precious days with the friends from whom the war had separated us for long terrible years. After basking in the warmth of this regained intercourse, we went on to Jerusalem to see the Zionist movement in the stronghold of Ancient Judea.[293]

After visiting Jerusalem the Dreyfus-Barneys left for Port Said and then sailed for France on May 1, 1919. They had to return rapidly to Paris to prepare for a visit with Laura's mother in the United States and then return to Europe to embark on their long journey to the Far East.[294]

Follow-up from Shoghi Effendi and 'Abdu'l-Bahá

Soon after Laura and Hippolyte left the Holy Land, Shoghi Effendi sent a letter to Laura. He addressed her as 'Dear Laura Khanom' and wrote, 'Now we miss you these days and tenderly remember the happy days you spent amidst us in the presence of the Beloved.'[295] A month later upon receipt of a letter from her, he again addressed her as 'My dear Laura Khanom' and wrote that he and 'Abdu'l-Bahá had read her letter repeatedly:

> I have exposed the contents of your letter to my Grandfather ['Abdu'l-Bahá] who was eager to hear of your news and to know of your whereabouts and health. He told me to write to you and convey on his behalf his greetings and tender remembrances. He prays that you may be successful and that your journey to America will be attended with important results and a remarkable success . . .
>
> I look eagerly forward to the time of meeting you and of associating again with dear Hippolyte who seems so enliven, so cheer up those who meet him.
>
> My affectionate greetings to dear Hippolyte. I shall not forget him & I trust he will not. The silence he is assuming, however, makes me rather pessimistic upon this point.[296]

Four days later Shoghi Effendi wrote to Laura confirming that he had received the three books that she had mailed to him. He was very busy with work and had hardly any time for personal study or work. However, he wrote that 'as I am sure they are good books for me to read and have been chosen by you, I shall make an effort to read them with attention.'[297] It is interesting to note the trust and respect that Shoghi Effendi demonstrated for Laura in this letter.

That June Laura received a Tablet from 'Abdu'l-Bahá expressing appreciation for her services:

> . . . your services are gratifying and acclaimed and your hardships and ordeals are noted and recognized. I beseech divine bounties that like unto a lighted candle you may light up every assembly, present eloquent speeches and stirring utterances and with the power of Kingdom cause joy and excitement in the hearts of the audience. Upon you may rest Glory of Glories. 'Abdu'l-Bahá 'Abbás[298]

Trip to the United States to Visit Her Mother

After a three-month stay in Paris and taking care of their affairs, Laura and Hippolyte left the continent to visit Alice, whom they had not seen for several years. They left Le Havre for the United States on August 9, 1919 sailing on the SS *France*, the same ship that had carried them back to Europe at the onset of World War I.[299] Laura was delighted to be back in the United States 'in God's own country' and to see her very dear 'Little One', to be near family and friends, and to thank those who had assisted her war efforts so generously.[300]

They stayed in America a few months, visiting New York, Chicago, Boston and Washington, D.C. They were busy with meeting the Bahá'í friends in these cities.[301] They managed to attend Bahá'í meetings, including a Unity Feast (forerunner of the Nineteen Day Feast) at the home of Pauline and Joseph Hannen in D.C.[302] During their visit to Chicago, Laura was accompanied by her mother and they visited the grounds of the Bahá'í House of Worship of North America in nearby Wilmette. 'Abdu'l-Bahá had laid the cornerstone of the Temple and been present for the ground-breaking ceremony during His visit to America in 1912. The construction of the building started in 1921.

To sail back to France, Laura and Hippolyte had to go to New York, their port of departure. There they met May Bolles Maxwell, who had traveled from Boston to see them because Laura and Hippolyte were her 'spiritual children'.[303] The Dreyfus-Barneys returned to France by way of North Africa and Sicily.[304] They visited the Bahá'ís of Tunisia, where Hippolyte had a mission to discuss the situation of the small community of the Bahá'ís with officials.[305]

Laura was awarded the Médaille de la Reconnaissance Française (The Medal of French Gratitude) in the spring of 1920.[306] This medal was created on July 13, 1917 by the French government to honor civilians who, without any legal or military obligation, had dedicated themselves to aiding victims of World War I in the presence of the enemy. There were three levels – gold, silver and bronze – but sources do not state which one Laura was awarded.

Visits with Shoghi Effendi in Paris

Back in Paris, Laura was in regular contact with Shoghi Effendi, who had come to France and was in a sanatorium in Neuilly-sur-Seine from mid-April to early July to regain his health.[307] He was 23 years old and Laura's affection for him had grown into 'an ever-deepening sense of admiration and respect'.[308] The Dreyfus-Barneys hosted him in Paris and also introduced him to several meetings that he attended after his health had improved.[309] Laura also arranged for her sister Natalie to meet him during his time in Paris.[310]

It was during this stay that Laura introduced Shoghi Effendi to an American Bahá'í artist, (Frank) Edwin Scott, and his wife, Joséphine, who were living in Paris and whose studio 'Abdu'l-Bahá had visited in 1911. This visit strengthened Shoghi Effendi's interest in the arts and he became captivated by the art world. Under the guidance of this renowned artist, Shoghi Effendi's interest in sculpture and paintings opened up a vast field of knowledge to him.[311] Their friendship deepened. Upon his return to Palestine, Shoghi Effendi sent a letter to Scott stating that he missed him greatly and that he had not heard from him since his departure. Shoghi Effendi promised to send Scott photographs that they had taken of the places that 'Abdu'l-Bahá had visited in Paris.[312]

Shoghi Effendi was not happy that he had had no news from home during his convalescence in Paris.[313] He was longing for letters from 'Abdu'l-Bahá and the Holy Family. Laura called Shoghi Effendi on July 4, just as he was leaving for a visit to Versailles, to inform him that a message had at last been received from the Holy Land and that everyone was well. This was the joyous news for which he had been waiting. In that letter, 'Abdu'l-Bahá instructed him to continue his education in England and to apply for admission to Oxford University.[314]

The next day Laura attended a large gathering held at the apartment of Mrs Loulie Mathews. Lady Blomfield, Agnes Parsons and Florence Khan were also present. A knock on the door announced the arrival of Shoghi Effendi. Florence wrote, 'What unspeakable delight ensued, amongst one and all, as we were individually greeted by him. He appeared so fresh and radiant, so powerful, and joy-inspiring!'[315] Shoghi Effendi was invited to address them, which he did in his perfect, flawless and cultivated English. He then read a Tablet of 'Abdu'l-Bahá that introduced him to the friends in Europe and elsewhere. 'Abdu'l-Bahá named and praised a number of believers in the Tablet, including first Ali-Kuli Khan and his wife Florence; then the Dreyfus-Barneys; Edwin and Joséphine Scott; and Mrs Mathews and her daughter Wanden, for whom 'Abdu'l-Bahá had written, 'They are faithful.'[316]

Alice's Marital Problems and Divorce

Not surprisingly, and quite in accord with the gossip columns, the marriage of Laura's mother and Christian was not going well. Alice learned that Christian was having an affair.[317] A rift developed between them and Alice and her second husband separated.

It again fell to Laura to deal with her mother's marital problems which occurred at such an inopportune time: just before she was to leave on her long-anticipated journey to the Far East. Laura was always her mother's comfort, support and counselor. She had known about her mother's issues with Christian and had consoled her from across the ocean through her wartime letters. Laura had begged her not to worry so much about Christian.[318] Neither she nor Natalie was happy with Christian's conduct. Christian had planned a visit to France and their hope for this trip was to 'whip him into shape', but that strategy had not worked, primarily because he changed plans and did not go to Paris.[319] Laura continued to send her mother comforting words, while Hippolyte hoped that she would not be fettered with the idea of a divorce.[320]

The couple's arguments worsened and Alice decided upon divorce, which she handled in her usual unorthodox manner. She telephoned Christian from Paris and told him that the marriage was over. Then she returned to Washington and 'set society on its ear by issuing dinner invitations signed Alice Barney'. The headline of an article dated January 18, 1920 in *The Washington Post* ran: 'How Mrs. Hemmick Astonished Washington Society'. The subhead read: 'She Sent Out "At Home" Cards for a Big Reception at her Rhode Island Avenue Home and Eliminated Her Husband's Name from the Invitations – Divorced? Oh, No, Just Her Way to Announce Her Estrangement.' The story covered the whole front page in eight columns and concluded: 'Alice certainly does do things differently.'[321]

Alice received letters from Laura and Natalie from across the Atlantic Ocean advising her on how to separate herself from Christian. Laura knew his character very well and encouraged her mother to move on with her life. By now Laura favored divorce and even suggested that Alice should pay Christian off to get him out of her life.[322]

Laura not only advised her mother on what to do about Christian, she also showed her love and support during those difficult times. In an undated letter, possibly sent when Laura was in New York and her mother was in Dayton in 1920, she commiserated with her mother about the difficult time she was going through. Laura promised to visit her if her distraught emotions did not improve:

I feel that you are surrounded by affection and good care; but remember dear I yearn to come to you to bring you home if you need and wish it. Sunday, I leave for home, so if I receive a letter from you instead of going to Washington, I shall go to Dayton, for heart of hearts you are my home.[323]

Natalie advised her mother to make 'a clean cold break, no matter the cost. Do it and don't be done by it.'[324] She invited her mother to join her in Paris until the gossip died down. Alice was not present to attend the divorce hearing that was scheduled later in the summer of 1920. She had sent him a check for the sum of ten thousand dollars that he accepted and she owed him nothing more.[325]

Alice sailed to Europe while her divorce was being finalized and stayed with Natalie, who was living with Romaine Brooks, an American painter she had met in 1916. Natalie's longest and most important relationship was with Romaine. After a few weeks with Natalie, Alice realized she should not have stayed with her. Alice would have liked to stay in Laura and Hippolyte's apartment but they had left on their extended voyage. She traveled back and forth between Paris and London pursuing producers for her ballets.[326]

Laura's Last Visit with 'Abdu'l-Bahá in the Holy Land

Laura and Hippolyte finally started on the journey to the Far East that they had been forced to cut short at the onset of World War I. They left Paris in the fall of 1920, stopped in Egypt, and then visited with 'Abdu'l-Bahá in Haifa.[327] Laura had much time with Him on this visit to discuss social issues, later writing about them, saying that these matters 'have come to pass and revolutionized the present social order'.[328] During this visit, which lasted ten days, the Dreyfus-Barneys also received precious advice and suggestions for their upcoming visit.[329]

While in Haifa, they were invited to the wedding of Badí' Bushrú'í, which was held on November 18, 1920. Badí' had been raised in Palestine in the household of 'Abdu'l-Bahá and Laura had helped fund his education, as well as that of other young Bahá'ís.[330] Laura lent the bride one of her dresses for the wedding, a pink dress made of satin and lace.[331]

The next day the Dreyfus-Barneys left for Port Said, from where Laura sent a letter to Natalie telling her that their visit with 'Abdu'l-Bahá had been 'delightful' and they were on their way to the Far East.[332]

Laura's Second Journey to the Far East

Laura and Hippolyte were looking forward to this journey. The itinerary included traveling to Indochina, Singapore, Burma, southern China and India at the request of 'Abdu'l-Bahá.[333] They were traveling to meet the Bahá'ís and to enable Laura to continue learning about the living conditions of people in different nations and to study their religions and cultures.

A cabin was secured for them on a pleasant Dutch ship that had arrived in Port Said and Laura was glad to finally start their adventurous journey, as she put it, to 'distant Asia as before us stretched the open way'.[334]

Laura regretted that while traveling she would not be getting news from Natalie and Alice as regularly as she wished and that she would miss her mother's birthday and the opportunity to wish her all the best. She wrote to Natalie, 'I am sorry that one cannot have everything at the same time: Little One & you & Oriental countries & warm sunshine, costumes, flowers, fruits fresh from the trees.'[335] She had arranged with Aḥmad Yazdí in Egypt to forward letters from her mother and sister to the various places they would be staying.

As Laura and Hippolyte were embarking on this epic journey, Laura shared with Natalie the excitement of sailing on the Arabian Seas, the fresh air on board, and seeing Asia on one side and Africa on the other. Laura talked about Hippo, her nickname for Hippolyte, and his popularity with their fellow travelers on the ship.[336]

Laura recorded the details of this trip in a travelogue journal the year after their return, in 1922. She wrote it for general readership even though it was never published. She said that she had written it with the intention of pleasing just 'two people', without naming anyone. Most fortunately, this journal was saved because it has provided most of what is known about this journey, as there are very few other sources of information about it. Also, it shows a part of Laura's character that she seldom showed. Laura was generally considered to be a serious person who was quite meticulous and systematic while performing her religious, humanitarian and other volunteer work. This manuscript shows her soft side. The travelogue, titled 'The Way Reopens', is also educational, as it recorded local cultural habits, customs, varieties of food, traditions, rituals and festivals as well her daily activities. Laura wrote respectfully about people of all religions and their rituals and traditions, reflecting the same consideration she had always shown in her life. She also wrote about the geography and the history of the places she visited, writing in the literary style of a cultured traveler and describing her experiences in a positive way. The manuscript is written in the first-person format and signed 'L.C.D.B.'

The Foreword offers her apologia for writing this unpublished journal:

> To certain people it may seem foolish to travel; but absolutely unpardonable to write about one's journeys. I have done both: still I appreciate this point of view; therefore, I am apologetic, most apologetic, for I well know that one should be able to imagine what one has not seen, and that impressions expressed are apt to present mere husks stripped of reality. But alack, alas, I have followed impulse to the detriment of wisdom. I am of family of the rolling stone, naked of the gentle stay-at-home that adds charm to the hard mineral.
>
> As to my excuse for writing at all, I have none; except perhaps my wish to please two persons, who have arbitrarily asked me for these impressions jotted down en passant. One of my lenient critics has suggested that, before starting my second journey, I should show how the way reopened and so complete the war memorandum which ended the notes of my first trip to the Far East. If I chance to have another reader, and if for any reason, he cannot stand hearing anything more about the war, he need only turn to page . . . to find himself landing with me in the Dutch Indies.[337]

Even though Laura did not use Bahá'í jargon or terminology or refer to her beliefs directly, she told her mother that they talked about the Bahá'í Faith to many people in China and Indochina and 'interest[ed] a certain number of people about the Cause' and that they planned to meet the Bahá'ís in India.[338] Even if Laura had talked about her beliefs, that would not have been mentioned in this manuscript. She must have talked about the Faith but rarely wrote about it in this manuscript. She did not impose her beliefs on others and kept them separate from her daily contacts with the public.

Laura met many important religious figures during this trip and visited many temples and religious sites. It seems that in some cases she knew more about their history than the local people did.

In the manuscript Laura referred to a 'Mr X' as the person who had accompanied her. This was a reference to her husband, Hippolyte. However, there are only a few references to him and she mostly wrote about her own experiences and her own impressions. She also referred to Mr Z, the husband of the couple who were with them for about eight months of the journey. During this trip, she did not have the luxury and comfort of her usual life but she rarely registered a complaint about any discomfort. They stayed at government rest houses, beautiful hotels and cabins but a few times they had to stay in tents. They traveled by train, small steamers, sail boats, row boats, canoes, sedan chairs, small planes, rickshaws, cars, elephants and other modes of transport. Sometimes they had to travel on treacherous paths during rainy and stormy weather. They met princes, sultans, religious figures and street people. They witnessed local traditions, such as cock fights, local market happenings, religious dances and Buddhist monastery festivals. She wrote in detail about the unusual animals they saw and the unfamiliar vegetation, flowers, smells and aromas they experienced.

Given Laura's experiences during the war working with the wounded and refugees, this trip must have been heaven for her. It was certainly a well-deserved respite. The adventure lasted over a year and took them to many parts of the Far East. She loved to travel and this was her dream trip.

Dutch Indies (Indonesia)

The Dreyfus-Barneys sailed from Egypt and traveled for almost a month before arriving at their first destination, Sabang, an island off the northern part of Sumatra in the Dutch Indies in December of 1920. It was the rainy season and it was hot and humid. But since Laura liked heat, that must not have bothered her much. She explained in detail the customs of the locals and the vegetation of the land. She believed that 'The Dutch, like all other white races, have abused the natives at certain periods of their colonization' but now they were humane.

They continued by train to Buitenzorg (today's Bogor), where they spent their first Christmas Eve away from home wandering about the Chinese quarter. Being the hot and humid rainy season, Laura wrote that sharpening a pencil made you perspire as though you had been chopping down trees. She had seen Christmas in deserts and in places with white snow and ice but this experience of seeing lush green vegetation everywhere at Christmas time was unique. It was an all-green Christmas.

To be in such beautiful surroundings after being on a ship for a month was an unparalleled experience. Laura described sitting on a veranda that Christmas morning:

> Seated by a lotus lake in the gentle air of this golden morning, I look at the great white or pink flowers as they rest between the large round leaves. Further off peacocks pass over a smooth lawn, and still further off herds of spotted deer graze in a meadow park adjoining the Governor's Mansion, for this peaceful, small country town is the seat of government for the Dutch Indies.

They boarded a train that took them through the terraces of rice fields and arrived in Garoet (today's Garut). There, watching little boys trying to sell batiks and playing bamboo harps was most enjoyable. They managed a side excursion to see a volcano. At Kraton, on the island of Java, they had permission to visit the enclosure of the Sultan's palace which was situated in the middle of the city and where the Sultan lived with his relatives. They visited Borobudur and the historical sites of Kawah Kamojang and Djokjakarta (Yogyakarta) as well as Surakarta, Tosari and Surabaya. In the last city, a friend of Hippolyte and his wife came to visit them after an eight-hour train journey. Laura regretted that she and Hippolyte were not able to visit them in their hometown since they had to sail to Bali the next day. So it was that they boarded a ship in Madura for the island of Bali, where they spent a week.

Bali and Singapore

One of the highlights of the visit to Bali was attending a cock fight. A bank manager had arranged the visit, giving them the use his car and driver to take them to Gianjar to watch it. The cock fight started at 11 a.m. and was to go on until sunset. Laura noted every little detail of the fighters, the cocks and the audience. She was relieved when she was able to follow her companion out of the hall. They then drove through villages, lunched at the government rest house, traveled to the beach, visited markets resembling each other, and passed by the smoking Batur volcano. They also found the groups of masked dancers performing in the street fascinating. In Kintamani, Laura and Hippolyte were invited to the home of a local prince who had arranged an opera performance for his guests at his residence. They were courteously received by the prince, who invited them into the dining hall where they sat at a table set out in the European fashion.

While she was in Bali, Laura recalled an episode that had happened there some years earlier. She wrote about the two daughters, 15 and 16 years old, of a Brahmin king who could not find husbands. They had to remain unwed, which was not acceptable. She remarked that for 'these people an unmarried life is nearly unheard of; the mission of a woman is wedlock and maternity'. Sometime later, two men in their father's court fell in love with the girls. This remained secret for several months until the scandal broke. The two men were charged with disregarding their caste and condemned. But the two princesses were so popular that no judge could condemn them. The sisters begged forgiveness but the king, who was law-abiding, did not accept their plea. The two men were sentenced to death. Since the two princesses were highborn and could not be killed by the hand of men, an old servant took them out to sea and cast them into the water. When he reported this to the king, the king stabbed the servant in the heart with a knife and killed him. After the death of his two daughters and the servant, the king, who was strict in all things that were sacred law, would rarely leave the palace.

The Dreyfus-Barneys traveled by boat from Bali to Singapore, the

British island colony off the coast of China. They visited a festival given by the Chitty (Chetty) community, a distinctive group of Tamil people in Malacca and Singapore, visited a museum and toured a botanical garden. They found the life in Singapore comfortable and easy. Laura wrote in her journal about the local living conditions, how their friends had settled in pleasantly and found Singapore to their liking.

The next stop was Saigon (today's Ho Chi Minh City). Laura and Hippolyte were likely the first Bahá'ís to visit Vietnam.[339] She wrote upon their arrival:

> I have been too well prepared by disparaging remarks to be disappointed in Saigon. Then we are here under agreeable circumstances. After four months traveling, we are in a real home, a home such as one could have in our countries a score of years ago, spacious, comfortable, peaceful, with a bevy of excellent servants.

They had a maid, a young servant, and a gardener to take care of them. She wrote about life in colonies and its comfort, ease and even the luxury that had disappeared from European countries. She noticed how Europeans found it much cheaper to live in these colonial countries but then they missed the intellectual exchanges and the development of the arts in their home countries.

Around the time of the Chinese New Year in February 1921, they traveled by train to Phan Thiet, a city on the southeast coast. She noticed the holiday attire of the local passengers and the bouquets of paper flowers they carried. Their car was moved from the train upon arrival at their destination and they drove to the mansion of the Duke de Montpensier, their host. On this part of the journey they were with some friends who enjoyed hunting.

Phnom Penh, Cambodia

The next destination was Phnom Penh, the capital of Cambodia, which was three long ferry rides away from Phan Thiet. She remarked about how the French were working hard to improve the soil for cultivation and had built splendid roads in that part of Indochina. She found Phnom Penh quite sympathetic with 'interesting native quarters, nice European houses, good bridges built consistent with the architecture of the county, and the Phnom (fort) dominating the town on a green hill'. They visited an industrial school and a museum where she purchased hand-woven materials made in the villages. Since their hotel was unsatisfactory, they moved to the mayor's house. The mayor was away and had left orders that they be welcomed.

The Dreyfus-Barneys were invited to the palace of the king of Cambodia together with other Europeans for artistic presentations where on 'one side were grouped all the Europeans and outside guests; on the other, the courtiers and members of the household. At one end sat the musicians; at the other were the dancers lined up waiting for their entrance.' Laura found the dancing to be 'a succession of artistic and characteristic attitudes [poses] but not dancing' and thought the artistic movements of Isadora Duncan more appealing than the disconnected posing of traditional Cambodian dance. The king did not attend this event owing to his 'delicate age'. However, the prince attended but wearied of the performance and left halfway through.

Reaching Angkor Wat, the famed temple complex of Cambodia, necessitated several hours of driving, then seven hours by launch and ferry, and finally another car drive to their government rest house. Laura noted while visiting Angkor Wat, 'When you wander through the archways, the corridors, the courts, the halls, you are bewildered by the proportions and the beauty of detail.' One night the temple was illumined by a hundred torches and another evening dancers performed on the terrace before the entrance to the temple. As Laura was departing, a group of torchbearers marched on either side to light the way. 'This scene of antique splendor', she noted, 'lighted by flickering torches is registered among the impressions that is ours forever.' Laura raved about this experience to Natalie, describing the hundreds of people marching with torches down the stairs and the dancers on the terrace.

She was excited about their travel companions, Colonel and Mrs Moore, whom she found to be cultured Americans.[340] Laura was happy that Mrs Moore was there with her daughters and that they were so nice. The Moores were continuing to Siam (Thailand) but Laura and Hippolyte had decided not to go there since it was similar to Cambodia.[341]

Back in Vietnam

Returning to Saigon necessitated going through Cap Saint Jacques (today's Vũng Tàu), a simple and ancient city that she called 'Deauville of Chochin China'. They were so captivated by Cap Saint Jacques that they remained there for a couple of weeks before leaving for Saigon.[342] They arrived in Saigon in March, staying at the Continental Palace Hotel.[343]

While they were enjoying their journey and the interesting places they were visiting, Laura was still concerned about her mother and their family affairs. Her mother, who was newly divorced, was in Monte Carlo at the time.[344] Laura was not happy that she had not heard any news from Natalie and complained to her about this in several letters.

As she did with every city they visited, Laura observed Saigon and wrote about its environment. She gave detailed descriptions of the historical places and wrote about the beauty of nature. A moonlight drive by the coast left a pleasant impression: 'How truly great are the appearances of beauty that belong to all and which money is incapable of confining and locking up in a safe. Should we not endeavor to cultivate humanity into the appreciation of the universal gifts?' She realized how important it was to 'understand that the priceless gifts become ours through our power of appreciation'.

They sailed from Saigon to Tourane (today's Da Nong), an important port city, where they went on a day's excursion to the Mountains of Marble. She commented on these mountains 'humped up like dark monsters in single file against the pale sky, a caravan of earth and rock resting in the sand before the stretch of green seas'. She was surprised to see a group of American missionaries in Tourane who did not feel the need to spread their teaching by works of social value: 'They denounce Buddhism, Confucianism and Catholicism. They have been unable to see the bond of brotherhood linking together the great teachers.'

From Tourane they drove to Hue, a provincial city in central Vietnam that was the colonial capital from 1802 to 1945. After visiting the stately tombs, they had a traditional Vietnamese dinner inspired by the culinary traditions of the east coast of Vietnam. 'To the sounds of 16-stringed zithers,' Laura wrote, 'we ate the sweetened pig with rice, perfumed by the famous sauce, Nuocmam, and many other native dishes.'

Tonkin, a French protectorate that encompassed northern Vietnam up to the Chinese border, was next. They arrived in Hanoi, the capital of Tonkin and of French Indochina in early April after a journey by boat and car. In a neighboring city to Hanoi, Hai Duong, they visited a factory, several model villages, and gardens. Tong-doc, the native governor, had arranged these visits for them. They dined with the governor in the evening and his three daughters played the piano for them. He also arranged for them to visit the famous pagoda at Huong Tich. They drove by car, rode on a barge on the river and then sat on primitive mountain chairs to traverse the treacherous path to a large cave. Though the path was difficult, the lunch spread on red-lacquered tables and the gigantic fans that blew cool air was a welcome respite.

These side trips had perils. The tires of their car burst near Hanoi while they were driving through a forest. They managed to get to a small village where the local people could protect them from wild animals and give them rooms for shelter. Again, they had a flat tire after leaving that village. However, Laura seemed not to worry about those mishaps and enjoyed the surroundings. During this trip, as usual, she accepted the drawbacks and problems with good spirits.

Laura wrote of one exceptionally interesting experience:

> This time it was dark, and I walked ahead to a little bridge overlooking a little valley and became enchanted by the sight. Fireflies by thousands were twinkling between me and the earth, between me and the skies. My fancy became elated; I forgot myself and became a part of this forest light.

Not long after, she was warned of the dangers of being taken by the tigers and she had to walk back.

The travelers were welcomed by the mayor of the next city they visited, Haiphong, located southeast of Hanoi on the coast. He had sent his carriage to meet them at the rail station and they dined at his residence before going on board a yacht for their three-day trip on Baie d'Along (Ha Long Bay). They were joined by another couple who were their friends. Laura found the water in a grotto 'deep emerald and the silence and beauty of the cliffs made it hard to leave'. 'Beautiful places', she wrote, 'are rapid dreams.' Their idyllic sail had come to an end.

Back in Hanoi, they stayed at the house of the Director of Public

Works, who was away for a month or two. The house was an important and comfortable one with servants, in an excellent location. She considered Hanoi the 'French intellectual center of Indochina . . . peaceful city with broad silent streets boarded by great trees and as we have already met several cultivated people, we have enjoyed our stay.'[345] They planned to visit Laos but it would have taken three weeks travel each way, mostly on horseback. Hippolyte wanted to fly on a small army airplane but Laura could not go because women were not allowed to fly on French army airplanes. They decided to give up that trip.[346]

The Dreyfus-Barneys continued north from Hanoi in two cars, one for the passengers and the other for the servants and suitcases. They stopped at gendarmerie quarters for dinner and were received in a 'most touching manner', and Laura was 'sure that a month's rations of delicacies' were used to fete their stay.

They continued by boat on the river and then a lake. Whenever they had a stop, the ladies were carried on sedan chairs by carriers and were deposited at the rest areas.

Upon arrival at their destination, they readied themselves for dinner at the house of the director of the zinc mines and his French wife. They stayed with them for three days. Laura had a slight fever but that did not stop her from visiting a mine where she enjoyed the sensation of being underground. She wrote of her experience while being carried on a sedan chair: 'the balancing of my chair, the hum in my head, the gallop of my circulation gave me deep sensations, and as I passed through the jungle and heard the murmur, I felt its echo in my head.' They visited the town of Cho Dien in northeast Vietnam the next day and then left by horses, chairs and rail lorries.

Laura had a high fever when they returned to Hanoi. It lasted for 27 days and the doctors did not know its cause. Fortunately, the fever gently left her after treatment. Even when suffering from the fever, though, she did not complain about it. Rather, she wrote,

It was rather wonderful. I had all the voices of the forest singing in my head and a great weakness like a swoon. At times, my whole body was drenched with fiery dampness, and again, I would feel cool and smooth like a stone. No pain, no sick feeling.

She had someone special to take care of her – Mr X. She referred to Mr X as one 'who was always there to care for me with solicitude and skill'. She gained her 'old state of health with a new-gained sense of appreciation' after a 'few days of immobile life'.

In the Republic of China

The Dreyfus-Barneys arrived in southern China in summer of 1921, seven years after their forced departure at the outbreak of World War I. A friend of Laura was kind enough to put a car at their disposal for the three-day trip to the capital city of the province of Yunnan, Yunnan Fu (today's Kunming). Another friend met them when they arrived at the house they had rented. Yunnan Province is located in the mountainous southwest corner of China and borders the countries of Laos, Vietnam and Myanmar of today.

Yunnan Fu was a walled city with seven gates that gave it a well-kept medieval appearance. Laura took much delight in the numerous shops and the streams of people passing through the narrow streets with their uneven stones, as well as the other everyday manifestations of life. She wrote in detail about the mode of dress and way of life of the local Chinese people. They visited the Pagoda of Confucius that had been erected by the great Muslim governor Seyyid Edjell (Sayyid Ajall Shams al-Din Omar al-Bukhari) in the 13th century.[347] It seems that Shams al-Din ordered the construction of Buddhist temples as well as two mosques.[348]

The use of opium was pervasive, Laura noticed. She remarked that 'when you go through the narrow streets at night, you smell the sweet, insinuating perfume of opium; opium, the companion of the coolie, of the merchant, of the mandarin, of the emperor – opium, the drug that stimulates intensity, to sap energy and lay man an idle dreamer in the world of active reality'. She wrote about the odors and others but noted, 'I have no doubt overlooked many aspects of Chinese life that could be taken from the quick, though I have promised myself to put in shadows as well as highlights, for I am tired of chromo [chromolithographic] appreciations of foreign countries.'

Laura noted the complexity of the political situation in Yunnan, which had been a German colony and was restored to China at the end of the war. There were soldiers everywhere. And to complicate matters further, opponents of the current governor had threatened to kidnap or kill as many foreigners as he could. Laura regretted having seen little of real Chinese life, how the 'vital existence' of the Chinese people 'remained hidden' from her observation.

Laura let Natalie know that while they were in Yunnan Fu they were living with Mrs Lochard, a delightful painter whose husband was one of the most important men in the government of French Indochina and who were friends of the Karpeles.[349] Many years later, Laura referred to her friend Suzanne Karpeles, to whom she was close in many ways 'of thought and action', and she must be from that family.[350]

Laura was delighted to finally hear from 'Golden Locks', Natalie's nickname, and receive news of their mother. She also learned that the crash of the Banque Industrielle had gone badly for the Barneys.[351] She was aware that the Banque had gone through a difficult phase but the Saigon agency had tried to reinvest millions of francs to the mother bank a few months earlier.[352] Unfortunately the negotiations fell through and the Banque closed the following year.

Laura and Hippolyte met new people on this trip. Laura commented, 'We have lived under the same roof with friends new in time, old in sympathy' for about three months.

Rain in Yunnan caused frequent interruptions in travel plans as Laura and Hippolyte waited until the roads were dry and reopened. Eventually they had to leave China and go back to Indochina. They left Yunnan by train and stayed in Ha Long Bay for a few days.

Laura was also sad to leave Indochina and found it difficult to say goodbye to their friends, noting in poetic imagery that when saying goodbye there were clouds about them, 'not like a shroud, for a shroud is a wound on a dead thing, while a cloud is made of the living vapors of earth; and we are sad, because from our intimacy there has risen something that would fall from our eyes in tears in landmarks traversed together.' She lamented, 'In a moment the friends, who had been our constant companions for months, were lost to sight.' They left by car from Ha Long Bay,[353] then sailed away on a yacht and later went by ship to Hong Kong.

Laura had already sailed several times across oceans and seas. While at sea Laura wrote in her journal, describing her feelings about being at sea and sailing.

The sea has been a personality in my life; it has been my companion during transitory periods. Often, I have left the hard shore with days of water faring ahead, expecting to reach another land where things would be different; and again, I would leave this land, and the sea would lull my sadness on the depths of its water and in the expanse of its horizons. Could I have taken up life anew without this transition? I doubt it.

Laura reminisced about the places they had visited:

There my thoughts returned to what I had really seen, the Tonkin, rich rice fields, lotus lakes, pilgrimages and pagodas – the great rivers, the River Black, the River Red, the River Clear – all the same tawny color – the emerald-toned Baie d'Along [Ha Long Bay] – the spacious pleasant city of Hanoi with our fairy-tale mansion, the wilds of the rugged North Tonkin with deep lakes and high mountains. It was here that I had inhaled with all my breath the fragrance of the strange giant flower torn away for me from the Buddha's shrine. Was it this desecrated offering that had laid me low on a bed of fever? And, above all, the jungle! The jungle was always omnipresent in my mind.

Hong Kong, Macao and Canton

The next place they visited was Hong Kong. Laura found this picturesque port city most pleasing. She noticed the preponderance of Chinese people and the sedan chairs and rickshaws but she also noted that Hong Kong was quite influenced by the English, who had colonized and governed it. There were summer resorts, racing events, tennis matches and dinner dances in the English manner. The Dreyfus-Barneys met interesting people there, including Sir Chatchick Paul Chater (1846–1926), an Armenian whose house held a bewildering collection of porcelain objects. They also met some Persians who gave them a tour of Kowloon and invited them to their home for a Persian dinner. Laura and Hippolyte were invited by a former governor of Yunnan for an evening at his home and they also managed to go on a day trip to Macao.

While in Hong Kong, Laura wrote to Natalie, who was in Capri, to discuss their mother's situation. Laura told her that she felt much stronger than she had when she was in Europe and reminded her that she had been ill with a fever for a long time when they lived in Washington, D.C. This had aggravated the weakness in her leg. Now, even though she had lost her 'long docile hair' for locks that gave her a 'Medusa' appearance, she did not consider this to be 'another drawback'.[354] She was referring to the pastel portrait that her mother had painted portraying Laura with her hair billowing around her face like snakes streaming from her head.

Laura also told Natalie she found that Mr Lochard was reading *Lettres à l'Amazone* by Remy de Gourmont. She thought Gourmont's study of Natalite helped Lochard to understand Laura! 'Iron', she wrote, 'has the same properties though sometimes solid and cold and at other times fiery and flexible.'[355]

Next on the itinerary was Canton, the capital city of Guangdong Province. They left for this charming city on the south coast of China in October.[356] She and Hippolyte went to the Office of Foreign Affairs to see Dr Woo Ting Fang, an 80-year-old man with a gracious manner whom they had met in Shanghai in 1914. They found him 'always a fervent theosophist and still interested in Bahaism, and it was with hope in our hearts for the welfare of China that we bade goodbye to this wise-living old man'.

While in Canton, they stayed in the Victoria Hotel and had a delightful week. Laura felt that it was wise that they had stayed for a week and had not rushed discovering this city.[357] During the week they went sightseeing, saw a play at a theatre, ate at a fancy Chinese restaurant and went for boat ride on the river to see the famous flower boats.

They decided to take a river steamer to Wuzhou, even though many had discouraged them because of the pirates. Leaving with a spirit of adventure in a small boat up the Pearl River, Laura and Hippolyte then continued by ferry and train. They were lucky to reach Wuzhou without misadventure since two ships before theirs had been fired upon. They visited the thousand-year-old city and the China of the interior. She realized 'deeply once more what strange places exist' in this world. They also visited two religious projects in that city, the Alliance Mission and the Baptist Mission Hospital and Dispensary. They had met one or two of the members of the Alliance earlier in their travels while visiting Tourane. It was in Wuzhou that Laura reflected: 'We have begun seriously as the Washington Conference attests; for to lessen armaments will lessen misery and mistrust and give us wealth and leisure to think out how to go to others with extended hand instead of the mailed fist.'

Back in Angkor Wat and Continuing Onward

Laura and Hippolyte craved for a more extensive tour of Angkor Wat and did not want to wait for another trip to the Far East before seeing it again, so planned another visit. They sailed on a small Japanese boat from Canton to Saigon and stayed at the Hotel Intercontinental, which had the buzz of city life. After a short stop in Saigon and some adventures, such as running out of gasoline on a road flanked by swampland and traveling through a flooded forest on a yacht, they arrived in Angkor Wat. 'High up of the upper sanctuaries', Laura wrote, 'we lay down in a stone balcony and looked below at this monument of carved splendor surrounded by the green jungle.' She expressed her excitement at seeing the temple in Bayon: 'We sat and felt the place grow into us. No wonder that it is considered one of the most extraordinary monuments in existence; you feel it; you sense it like the personality of an unusual being.' They visited and enjoyed Angkor Wat, 'one of the world's great wonders', exploring it thoroughly this time. Of course, they eventually had to leave this 'wondrous city of ruins' but the immensity of the monuments left an even deeper impression after this second pilgrimage.

They sailed towards Phnom Penh on the Gulf of Siam (today's Gulf of Thailand) but their yacht became entangled in the floating plants on the banks and they had to continue by car. On the way, they stopped for lunch at a beach with coconut palms. Some of them bathed in the sea first and then it was time to have lunch, which they ate with their fingers. Laura wrote: 'I was selected to carve the duck with nature's fork and knife and though I cannot pride myself on daintiness, I did no havoc to the bird or to myself and I laid large detached pieces on the plate before us.'

Before starting their travel to Saigon, they drove past a leper home. This prompted Laura to write, 'the desire of my girlhood came before me – my desire to share existence with the disinherited, to put my will on its best metal in forcing it to have daily commerce with ugliness and suffering. I do not know if I did wisely in giving up this vocation for a more usual life.'

On the way, they spent one night at a bungalow and another at the governor's villa. Laura remarked on 'an old-new sensation to be

'Abdu'l-Bahá

The dining room in the House of 'Abdu'lláh Páshá

Alice Pike Barney in her wedding dress

Alice Pike Barney, in Wedding Gown. Artist: Jared Bradley Flagg, 1876, oil on canvas, Smithsonian American Art Museum

Albert Clifford Barney

Albert Clifford Barney. Artist: Ottilie Wilhelmina Roederstein, circa 1900, oil on canvas, Smithsonian American Art Museum

Painting of Alice Pike Barney

Self-Portrait with Palette. Artist: Alice Pike Barney, circa 1906, oil on canvas, Smithsonian American Art Museum

Painting of Laura Barney as Medusa

Medusa (Laura Dreyfus Barney). Artist: Alice Pike Barney, 1892, pastel on canvas, Smithsonian American Art Museum

Ali-Kuli Khan

Ali Kuli Khan. Artist: Alice Pike Barney, 1903, pastel on fiberboard, Smithsonian American Art Museum

Mírzá Abu'l-Faḍl

Mirza Abul Fazl. Artist: Alice Pike Barney, 1903, pastel on paper, Smithsonian American Art Museum

Hippolyte Dreyfus

Hippolyte Dreyfus. Artist: Alice Pike Barney, pastel 1907, Smithsonian American Art Museum

(Frank) Edwin Scott

Portrait du peintre par lui-meme (Portrait of the painter by himself). Artist: Frank Edwin Scott, no date, oil on canvas, Smithsonian American Art Museum

Christian Hemmick

Christian. Artist: Alice Pike Barney, 1910, pastel on paper, Smithsonian American Art Museum

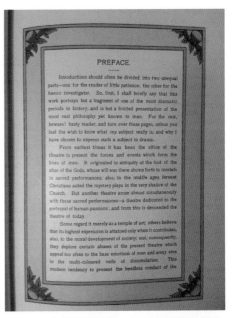

Cover of the first, 1910, edition of Laura Barney's God's Heroes: A Drama in Five Acts, *and illuminated pages from the book*

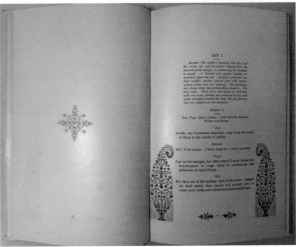

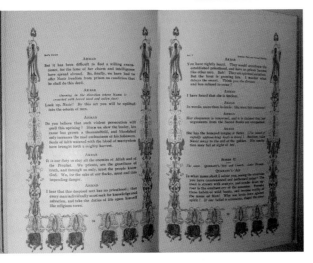

Laura in 1964, at her desk in her apartment at 74 rue Raynouard, Paris

Laura, perhaps in the mid-1950s

huddled in a soft, warmly covered bed . . .' In the morning, 'X' brought her 'a regal rose, pale, stately, fragrant'.

Now it was sadly time to separate from the friends they had met in Hanoi eight months earlier. Each couple went in different directions. Laura wrote that 'a flash of eye was the last that we saw of our friends who had been untiring in their hospitality'. Mr Z. (the man who had accompanied them on this part of their trip with his wife) had made their whole journey easy with his personality 'characteristic of solicitude and affection with which he had surrounded' them since the time they had met in Hanoi.

While traveling on the train to Saigon, Laura sensed that this was a goodbye forever to Indochina! Two days after arrival in Saigon, they sailed for Singapore on a tiny steamer. They stayed less than 24 hours in Singapore but managed to do some shopping for the New Year and send some mail to the family. Laura sent a letter to her mother in Europe, marveling at the interesting sites and the beauty of Indochina, and saying that they had been able to 'interest a certain number of people in the Cause [the Bahá'í Faith]'. Laura hoped to visit the Bahá'ís when they traveled to India. They planned to stay there for four months and then a couple of weeks in Syria before returning to France by the end of June 1922.[358]

They sailed towards Rangoon, Burma (today's Myanmar), had a few hours' stay at Penang, Malaysian Peninsula, and only managed to drive through the coconut groves. But she did not regret that they could not stay longer. She observed, 'I have learned through experience that often places, like people, cannot be correctly estimated by the first superficial glimpses. There is often a charm that reveals itself only to those who care to observe and give time to the unfolding of the outer wrappings.'

Visit to Burma (Myanmar)

Next stop was Burma. Laura had pictured the people and the temples of this place for many years. She conjectured, 'Who has not wished like me to visit Burma? Those perhaps who do not read, who do not dream, or those who are fettered by circumstances.' Soon after arrival they tried to find a Persian friend who had hosted Hippolyte almost 15 years earlier to find the local Bahá'ís. They knew that he had passed away, but they discovered that his sons were also deceased. They also found that the family home had been replaced with a garden and a public building. On their quest to find any Bahá'ís in the area, they went to a Persian restaurant, but no one there knew of the Bahá'ís. However, the Persian-Armenian manager of a hotel assisted in finding one or two Bahá'ís. He was extremely kind to the travelers when he heard that they had visited his homeland, Persia, which he had not seen in many years. He could not do enough for them. His carriage drove them to interesting places, his cook made them Persian rice, and his brother-in-law helped with their shopping!

Laura and Hippolyte spent their second Christmas away from family and friends in Rangoon (now Yangon). They managed to visit the Buddhist Shwedagon Pagoda; that she had not wanted to miss. She noted 'numberless pilgrims moving about in their picturesque attires' in this city of shrines. The city was getting ready for the visit of the Prince of Wales on December 31, and they could see from the windows of their hotel the rehearsal for the reception that was to be held on January 2, 1922. The royal visit inspired Laura to write: 'Let us hope that order and law will at least outlive royal popularity; that aristocracy of intelligence, experience, culture and high motives will have the ascendency over our civilization; that common sense and moral appreciation will save humanity from an ugly brutal debacle, that can only retard fearfully its revolution towards a better-balanced state of existence.'

Hearing in Rangoon the Sad News of the Passing of the Master

On December 27, in Rangoon, Laura and Hippolyte heard from two Bahá'ís of the passing of 'Abdu'l-Bahá about a month earlier, on November 28, 1921.[359] The two were a blind, aged Persian man and a young professor from Kashmir, who had not encountered any Bahá'ís in about a year. Laura and Hippolyte invited their guests for refreshment in a small private dining room of their hotel for ease of conversation. This is how Laura recounted the ensuing conversation:

> The old gentleman spoke of the time when X had been here years and years ago; the young man asked twice if we had received news from Haifa. I wondered at his insistence, as I had already answered that we had received our last mail the first part of November in Saigon.
>   'But you, you must have newer news?'
>   He began to weep and said, 'The Master is dead!'

The old man and the young professor had only heard the news of 'Abdu'l-Bahá's death the day before when they received a cable from Bombay.

A great sense of grief and loss must have gripped Laura and Hippolyte. This news was devastating and shocking for both, but the loss was definitively greater for Laura, who had spent months close to the Master in Palestine, Europe and the United States. Given that she did not write much about her beliefs in her travel memoirs because it was written for general readers, her words about the passing of 'Abdu'l-Bahá are powerful:

The Master has departed, finished the bodily link, finished the possibility of going into his presence, of hearing his living voice, for seeing his thoughtful eyes, finished – finished the expression of love, energy and patience that was personified in his form. To be with him now, we must turn to our own hearts; we must turn to our memory; we must turn to his written words; and we must fit ourselves to commune with his spirit. Time, space, are our limitations not his – now that he has passed out of the contingent world. The impulse to follow him was irresistible, to leave behind the triteness of earth. But he has told us not to keep for ourselves alone what he has entrusted to us for humanity. Then came upon me the resigned feeling of someone, who might have seen his dearest friend and councilor carried away on an express train that he had missed; and as he turned back into the city to put order in things left behind, found satisfaction in the certainty that he, too, would no doubt soon follow by the same road.

'It is best that you should assist the world with word and deed; but if this you cannot do, come to me, the shelter of love.' I recalled how often sadness had weighted upon me during the last few weeks. My heart had known what my ears had not heard and my eyes had not seen.

I watched the air bubbles in the glass of lemonade before the old blind gentleman. They detached themselves from a group of other bubbles, rushed up to the air and burst into a gentle spray. I turned to X, who had been stunned by the news, and together we wrote a cable to the loved family, expressing understanding sympathy, asking if we were to go to them immediately or if we should take time to see the friends in India. The answer will reach us in Calcutta and this city is therefore all that we shall see of Burma.

It must have been consoling to them to be with other Bahá'ís during their grieving times. They managed to visit the home of a Bahá'í in Rangoon for a meeting. Laura wrote: 'Everyone had the firm composure of those who know where their duty lies and how their love and loyalty can be expressed.' Yet another meeting was arranged for them out of town before they sailed to India. Laura reflected:

> Could we be surprised by the news of the Master's departure: had he not said that, when the far-away countries had received the message, his task in the body was finished. In the last few years, others as well as we had journeyed to untouched lands; we were freeing Him of his earthly bond. Were we to regret it?
>
> How vast is our inheritance! Not hearsay and legends, but the written word; and the stress that the Master has put on Unity gives us the key to all things. Aspects are numerous, but the joining force is one. We must safeguard the inheritance, keep it as it was given to us clean, clear, living, universal. We must prepare our hearts to reflect the love of the one eternally desirous to remain in our midst.

Travel to India

They decided to continue their trip to India because it was Laura's third attempt to get there, but they shortened it. The first cancellation was caused by political turmoil in southern Persia and the second was caused by the outbreak of World War I while they were in the Far East. This time they had planned to stay in India for three months because there were many interesting people to meet there, but they stayed only one month. They traveled quickly from the eastern side of India to the western on their way to Haifa.

In Calcutta (today's Kolkata) they stayed in the Grand Hotel where, upon arrival, they received several cables from Haifa. Perhaps those cables included the one from Shoghi Effendi inviting them to join him in Haifa for consultation in February 1922. If so, that is another reason why they hastened through India. They visited with Sir Rabindranath Tagore (1861–1941), a Bengali polymath, a person of wide-ranging and encyclopedia knowledge. He had reshaped Bengali music and literature as well as Indian art and was the recipient of the Nobel Prize for Literature in 1913. However, the details of the visit of the Dreyfus-Barneys with him are not known. While in Calcutta they also visited the Marble Mansion, Jain temples and a market.

The owner of a store next to their hotel recognized Laura and Hippolyte when they paused to look at some Persian miniatures. He had seen them in Julfa, near Isfahan, Persia, in 1906 at the telegraph service. He even asked them about the other lady, Laura's chaperone during that trip.

Laura wrote to her sister from Calcutta. It is not clear what Natalie had written that prompted Laura to state that 'your account of having to ask everyone you know to decorate me, it is your idea and I discourage you. You must see now that your "wonderful sister" is a miserable little owl, beautiful only to its near of kin.' She shared with Natalie the news of the passing of the Master that they had heard in Rangoon:

> It was in this land [Burma] of bright colors and gay laughter that one month later we heard of the departure of the Master. You know it is hard for us not to be able to see him again, still he must be relieved to have finished with the bodily world, so in this thought I find consolation. The world now has started on a new evolution and has broken its crystallization.[360]

Next they traveled by train to Benares (today's Varanasi). Laura wrote:

> It is as difficult to describe Benares as it would be to give to someone the impression on awaking of an extraordinary, mad dream. Words are inadequate when worlds of unbelievable strangeness are to be expressed.

She described in detail the street scenes of men, cows and goats mingled together and the different rituals carried out by and in the Ganges River. She saw the Ghats where corpses were placed on the funeral pyre for cremation and then the ashes scattered in the Ganges River. They saw corpses ready to be placed on the wood and even saw dead bodies floating in the water. Her experience of Benares was so strong that she wrote, 'Still, Benares haunts me, in its force of strangeness.'

The next city they visited was Lucknow, with its public buildings of 'immense construction in Indian Moslem style'. They had a short visit in the bazaar and a stay of a few hours at Kanpur. Laura was happy to have visited one more city in India while rushing through the country.

Their next stop was Fatehpur Sikri where they visited the Mary-amuzzamani Palace. Fatehpur Sikri is a fascinating city founded in the 16th century about 23 miles from Agra, the site of the beautiful Taj Mahal built by Shah Jahan. While visiting the Taj Mahal, she wrote sensitively about Shah Jahan's love of Mumtaz Mahal:

> His appreciation of her womanhood is evident to all ages, and you understand that she was his affinity in the vast sense of the word, for he was able to erect a memorial unparalleled in beauty in the edifices of history, an inspiration springing from a lover's heart, and requiring solid marble to confront the ages with its power.

Next was Delhi, where they stayed at Maiden's Hotel.[361] They had just a few days before they had to leave India, as 'Abdu'l-Bahá's family missed having them near.[362] They did have time to visit several historical tombs, Hindu monuments and mosques, including the Red Fort, the historical residence of the emperors of the Mughal dynasty. Laura noted:

> The audience halls are surpassingly splendid, but the throne has been borne away; and when you look at the spot where the famous peacock throne used to stand until Nadir Shah, the conqueror, carried it away to Tehran, you realize that power rises and falls like waves of the sea. These days the actual Shah has hurriedly left his capital for Europe as he does not feel safe on this throne of ancient grandeur; and the peacocks, if they could reflect, would no doubt consider men not more substantial than the fleeting shadows cast on earth by passing clouds . . . the past is powerful enough to impose itself upon the modern trivializations. The Mughal presence stands upright in architectural triumph, a stable landmark in the shifting sand.

They visited Jaipur, a predominantly Hindu city, and its attractions, and then Rajasthan with its Amer Fort (Amber Fort), which they approached by elephant. Inside the fort is a palace of sandstone and marble. They drove to Ajmer and Puskar in Rajasthan and even went to

Mount Abu in a Hupmobile, an automobile made by Hupp Motors in the United States, to visit the Jain temples and two mosques.[363]

Visiting Ahmedabad and Meeting Gandhi

Ahmedabad is a large city in western India. Laura wrote upon her arrival there:

> My experience has generally taught me that it is your preparedness of mind which causes you to be surprised, disappointed or delighted with what you come across in life. It is the same with impressions of cities.

After visiting more gateways, tombs of kings and queens, a citadel, Jain temples and Hindu arts, she could not absorb any more:

> This rapid tourist manner of seeing countries is not my forte. I like to remain in places and associate them with my changing feelings with the changing light and when time is generous, to see them in changing seasons. I like to live in the world – not travel around it. I like to detach myself from trains and ships and become initiated by staying in a country, which unfolds its wonders before my patient, attentive gaze. As we look long into the heavens, new stars are born to our eyes!

She did, however, rave about the architecture of the Sidi Saiyyed Mosque and the Masjed Jome (Masjid Jum'ih, Friday Mosque), which she considered to be one of the finest mosques in the East.

One of Laura's desires during her visit to India was to meet Mahatma Gandhi. It was in January 1922 that Laura and Hippolyte requested a visit with him and it was granted. As the owner of the hotel where they were staying was a friend of Gandhi, he wrote a letter of introduction.[364] They also had a letter of introduction from Gandhi's friend Sir Jagadish Chandra Bose (1858–1937), another polymath – a physicist, biologist, botanist and science-fiction writer.

They drove to Gandhi's simple house, the home of the 'opponent of the British rule'. They were accompanied by Elizabeth Goodspeed Chapman (1893–1980), who was a patron of the arts and an art collector who later became the president of the Arts Club of Chicago (1932–40).[365]

They entered a small, plain room. Gandhi was sitting on one side on a floor mat with a pile of books and papers in front of him. The guests sat on a bench after he graciously asked them to do so. Unfortunately, the day of their visit was Gandhi's silence day. He could receive guests but could not talk. His guests could ask questions and he had to give his answers in writing. Laura found 'him sincere – the type of sincerity that does not see danger and irony any more than a somnambulist looks where he places his feet'.

The questions came from Hippolyte, which Gandhi answered in writing. Gandhi apologized that it was his silence day. Hippolyte asked about different societal and political questions related to India such as his movement, his campaign, the question of the Khalifat movement, the Punjab, the retirement of the president of the Congress, and civil disobedience. Gandhi wrote his answers and then permitted them to take his picture, provided they did not ask him to take up a position. They took a picture of him carrying on his day.[366] The questions asked were not about religion or the Bahá'í Faith. It is not clear if Gandhi was informed that they were Bahá'ís or if they discussed the Bahá'í teachings with him, but Gandhi later said, 'The Bahá'í Faith is a solace to humankind.'[367]

They visited Gandhi's ashram and saw his spinning and weaving projects. Laura hoped that Gandhi's principles would not

> . . . lead him and India to hate the advanced skill of our civilization but merely to condemn the abuses of power and greed. Most forces must be divided, one part cherished, the other killed; the operation is delicate and dangerous as the one required to separate the Siamese twins.

Laura's desire to meet him had been fulfilled but not her desire to hear him speak.

Their last stop in India was Bombay (today's Mumbai) which she found to be 'an English town well built with many greatly official buildings'. One evening they were invited to the home of a Persian acquaintance, perhaps a Bahá'í. They visited the five Parsee (Zoroastrian) Towers of Silence[368] that are 'curious features of Bombay', where the vultures 'perched upon the towers make one realize the finality of our frail life'.

They drove along the Back Bay Road and enjoyed the view of the 'boat-lit harbor'. Laura, who loved being at sea, noted as they sailed away from Bombay the next day, 'Ocean life unwrinkles one from the cares of earth. It blows away the stuffiness of housed-in habits.' Their 'looping the loop' in the Far East was finished, at least for that time.

They landed in Port Said on February 12:

> I am back again. I have lived in this golden beauty so long that it is one of the parts of the world that seem more especially my home. I know these countries too well to dare describe them. There is a diffidence born of intimacy – a fear that, if you speak of the cherished, words may not do justice to the confounding movements [monuments] of Ancient Egypt, the striking life in the streets around the splendid mosques; the poetry of the Nile stained by the red wound of the dying sun; and the desert, which by day is a blinding challenge to our fragileness, by night an unlimited dreamland where moonbeams unite with the thrill of our reverie.
>
> And Palestine and Syria – Syria that contains the much-sung mountains of Lebanon, the great ruins of Baalbek and those of Palmyra; and Damascus, the city that has throughout the ages kept its oriental fascination and the many spots that have grown familiar to us through the Bible. Jerusalem, still powerful of character; Nazareth, insignificant as it must always have been; and all the names that bring before our vision the prophets of old.

In 'Akká after the Passing of 'Abdu'l-Bahá

Then the Dreyfus-Barneys traveled to the Holy Land. They both had revered the Master and had a special relationship with Him devoting their time and energy to the principles of the Cause that He promoted. E. G. Browne wrote of their devotion to 'Abdu'l-Bahá:

> Ample materials exist even in English for the study of the remarkable personality who has now passed from our midst and of the doctrines he taught; and especially authoritative are the works of M. Hippolyte Dreyfus and his wife (formerly Miss Laura Clifford Barney), who combine intimacy and sympathy with their hero with sound knowledge and wide experience.[369]

Laura expressed her own feelings and thoughts about visiting 'Akká again:

> Days, weeks, months, years I have lived in this land. I have watched the red light of the light tower of Acca ['Akká] shine out in the night like a heart of flame, a warning of love to prevent disaster and to show the way.

Upon arrival she wrote:

> In the folds of this gentle mountain lies the body of my best friend and counselor, 'The Master'. Somehow it would seem that there is more life outside of this life – more world out of this world! Death is the way that we will all take smiling or grimacing. The law of evolution hurls man into eternity. The stream has only currents; tides belong alone to the ocean and to the seas!

And about Mount Carmel she wrote:

> At all hours of the day I have wandered over Mount Carmel. I have felt an emanation rising from this sacred hill, an emanation that would lift one upward, upward to spheres where man's thoughts become serene, where actions spring into life with the power of achievement.

Laura and Hippolyte had cut their trip short in India to be in Haifa. Not long after the passing of 'Abdu'l-Bahá, Shoghi Effendi had invited a number of capable and experienced Bahá'ís to Haifa to consult on the future of the Bahá'í Faith. The Dreyfus-Barneys were among the invited representatives, a group that included Lady Blomfield, who had returned with Shoghi Effendi from England; Ethel Rosenberg and Major Tudor-Pole from England; Emogene Hoagg, with whom Laura had traveled to 'Akká in 1901, Roy C. Wilhelm, Mountfort Mills (a lawyer by profession) and Charles Mason Remey from America; and Consul Albert and Mrs Alice Schwarz from Germany.[370] He discussed with them the need to develop the administrative foundation for the eventual election of the Universal House of Justice, the international governing body of the Bahá'í Faith.[371]

It must have been consoling to Laura and Hippolyte to be among these western Bahá'ís, the majority of whom were close friends, who gathered in Haifa. They must have been especially happy to see their old friend Lady Blomfield. All these western Bahá'ís now shared their grief in the company of friends and consoled Shoghi Effendi.[372]

Laura wrote to her sister that the Master's family was 'filling the great vacancy left in their lives by continual activity in carrying out His wishes' and that some friends from different countries 'have gathered here to consult with them and with Shoghi (the grandson that you met in Paris over a year earlier) for the Cause must now enter a new phase'.[373] It was in the Will of his grandfather that Shoghi Effendi was appointed the Guardian of the Bahá'í Faith.

During her visit, Laura attended the memorial meeting for Helen Goodall of California on February 26. Shoghi Effendi, Emogene Hoagg and Lady Blomfield were also present on that occasion, during which there were prayers, the reading of Tablets and a touching address about Mrs Goodall's life.[374] On March 24, Laura and Hippolyte together with several other western friends organized a celebration for around 50 Persian friends, among whom were 12 pilgrims from the province of Khurasan, Iran.[375]

A Short Expedition with Friends

Shortly after their consultations with Shoghi Effendi were concluded in late March, Hippolyte, Laura and Lady Blomfield left Haifa on an expedition in a Buick.[376] Since it was the first visit of Lady Blomfield, Laura and Hippolyte were going to show her Palestine and Lebanon.[377] Hippolyte drove the car, which at one point became grounded in the desert sands. After being rescued, they continued their trip and arrived in Beirut, where they spent two nights at the Grand Hôtel d'Orient on the seafront. 'Laura and Hippolyte are ideal travelers,' wrote Lady Blomfield, 'capable, calm, restful, no fuss whatever transpires.'

They met up with a few young Bahá'í men who were studying at the American and Jesuit colleges. One of the college students took them sightseeing around Beirut and a Bahá'í lady doctor visited them. 'They all know Laura and Hippolyte,' Lady Blomfield wrote, 'and positively adore them, small wonder! I know of none to equal them.'[378]

They then visited the Roman ruins in Baalbek northeast of Beirut, famous as home to some of the largest and most magnificent temples of the empire. Despite the mechanical problems with their car and a 12-hour delay getting there, the Dreyfus-Barneys and Lady Blomfield enjoyed this excursion to the historic site.

They returned south to Damascus the next day. The Persian Consul General, who looked very dignified, was waiting for them in his car, which sported a Persian flag. A Bahá'í, he tried to persuade them to stay with him at his home but Laura graciously yet determinedly refused the offer. They did, however, have dinner with the Consul and his family at his residence.

The next day the Consul General's car was put at their disposal as they visited the city and its mosque and attended a gathering of Bahá'ís, including Arabs, Persians, French, English and Indians. The western guests shared stories and news from the Bahá'í world center, which was much appreciated.

The travelers hoped to take a trip to Palmyra but could not, owing to security concerns. They returned to Haifa with their car transported on the train and with a sendoff by the Bahá'ís, who escorted them to the train platform and presented them with a large basket of fruit.

Back in Haifa, Laura noticed that Shoghi Effendi did not have a room of his own since his return from Oxford and was sleeping in his childhood room in his mother's house; his mother, Ḍíyá'íyyih Khánum, was the eldest daughter of 'Abdu'l-Bahá. Bahíyyih Khánum, 'Abdu'l-Bahá's sister, had built two rooms for Shoghi Effendi in the Holy Family's house but he had not wished to spend any money on furnishing them. They stayed bare until the day Laura went downtown and bought some furnishings and a floor covering. Because they were from her, Shoghi Effendi accepted them.[379] Afterwards he sent her a thank you letter: 'May I, before concluding, express my belated thanks to dear Laura Khanum for the admirable furniture she has arranged in my study of which I am now making full and constant use.'[380]

Sadly, the time for the Dreyfus-Barneys to leave the Holy Land arrived. Lady Blomfield was also saddened at their departure:

They are darlings – and the best Baha'is in the world I think from the mental as well as the spiritual plane . . . I could tell you reams of their adventures in Indonesia – always working for the Divine Cause of Peace and Unity without the narrow sectarianism which is

likely to be a danger in the future – a real pitfall to be avoided . . .
The Dreyfuses' adventures also broadened out to Jungles and Tigers
and things.[381]

Laura and Hippolyte returned to Europe after an absence of a year and
a half.

Laura's Interest in the League of Nations and the International Council of Women

Soon after her return from the Far East, Laura became interested in the
League of Nations, to which she gave great importance. The League
of Nations was the first international inter-governmental organization.
Its principal mission was the prevention of war and the maintenance
of world peace and Laura found that its social and humanitarian principles aligned with her own. It was established on January 10, 1920
as the outcome of the Paris Peace Conference convened at the end of
World War I which created the League's Covenant. The League was
later replaced by the United Nations after World War II.

The headquarters of the League of Nations were moved from London
to Geneva on November 1, 1920. Its mission of world peace was near to
Laura's heart. She started working with the League of Nations in 1924,
if not earlier. One of her first trips for the League of Nations may have
been to Denmark, since she sent a postcard to her sister from there on
May 24, 1924 stating that she was quite absorbed in her work.[382]

Another organization that drew Laura into its orbit was the International Council of Women (ICW).[383] The ICW brings women and
women's organizations from around the world together. From its beginning in 1888, its purpose was not only for the cause of suffrage but
also for other progressive movements. In that year women leaders from
professional organizations and different walks of life had come to Washington, D.C., to participate in its establishment. Founding members
included Susan B. Anthony, May Wright Sewall and Frances Willard
and 53 women's organizations from nine countries were represented
at the first gathering. National Councils of the ICW were formed to
make themselves heard at the international level. In 1899 the ICW
began to take on major issues and formed an International Standing
Committee on Peace and Arbitration. In 1925 the ICW convened its

first coalition, the Joint Standing Committee of Women's International Organizations, to lobby for the appointment of women to the League of Nations. Since its inception, the ICW's aims have been consistent – the unification of women's organizations for action to promote human rights, the equality of women and men, peace and the participation of women in decision-making at all levels.

The ICW's aim was to promote human rights, equality, peace and women's involvement in all spheres of life through the establishment of an international federation, or umbrella organization, of National Councils of Women, one council for each country. From time to time the ICW created standing committees, for example, to study and promote women's interests in the areas of child welfare, employment, legislation, hygiene (health), peace, the press, literature and education.

During the time of the League, the principle of the equality of women and men was a primary concern of the ICW. It collaborated with the League of Nations throughout the League's existence. In the 1920s Laura became the ICW representative to the League of Nations and played important roles in different capacities, serving on its agencies and committees.[384] Having been through a world war and seen the human suffering and destruction that war brings at first hand, and believing in world peace and the goals of the newly formed League, she certainly was well qualified to serve in different roles. Two major issues – the horrors of war and the rights and responsibilities of women – were major areas of concern to her. In one letter she wrote: 'In a way, all these horrors are a good thing for the future generations who see what war means, not simply chivalry and medals. I think that women will be of great help to get out of this horrible habit of the past.'[385]

She wished to devote her time to the League's work and also to help women's organizations such as the ICW. Years later she wrote that she had decided to take part in the feminist movement on the express recommendation of her husband.[386] She had his support throughout their life together.

Travel to the United States to Visit Laura's Mother

Laura and Hippolyte traveled on board the SS *France* to New York in January 1925.[387] They had sailed on the same ship at the onset of World War I when they were returning to France. Soon after their arrival she wrote to Natalie that she had to dodge the reporters and photographers. She dreaded to think what they would say when she gave public talks to promote the League of Nations. She believed that controversy would ensue, truths would be considered dull and virtues would be exaggerated to catch the eye as she lived in a whirl of League of Nations activities.[388]

Washington was like home to Laura, but they had to stay in a hotel now that her mother had moved to California. This time they stayed at Shoreham Hotel.[389] While in Washington Laura must have attended the Sixth Quinquennial Convention of the International Council of Women which took place from May 4 to 14 of that year. After short stays in New York and Washington, Laura and Hippolyte traveled to California to visit Alice, who had moved to Hollywood in the spring of 1923 after her return from Europe and her divorce.[390]

While visiting Alice, they attended an important Bahá'í gathering. Their visit to California was reported in the *Baha'i News Letter*:

> The friends will be delighted to learn of the arrival in this country of Monsieur and Madame Dreyfus-Barney from Paris, their plans including a visit of several months in California with Mrs Dreyfus-Barney's mother. The world-wide Baha'i experience of Mons. and Madame Dreyfus-Barney, their intimate knowledge of the history and teachings of the Cause, and their unique proficiency in the Persian language, bring to the American believers a mental and spiritual reinforcement that will assist us greatly.'[391]

The Bahá'ís of several communities in the Hollywood area had organized a fellowship dinner to welcome the distinguished Persian Bahá'í teacher and scholar Mírzá Asadu'lláh Fáḍil Mázandárání, known as Jináb-i-Fáḍil (1880–1957). More than 250 people attended the dinner. Hippolyte was the toastmaster. He welcomed everyone and spoke about constructive ideals for world unity. Laura, who at the time was a member of the Peace Committee of the ICW, was at the head table with leaders of different churches and synagogues and other prominent people.[392]

Shoghi Effendi asked Laura to attend and chair the Convention of the Bahá'ís of the United States, to be held from July 5, 1925 at Green Acre Bahá'í School in Eliot, Maine but her health did not allow her to attend.[393] It seems she was receiving care at the Washington Sanitarium and Hospital during June that year. Hippolyte was with her and was not sure if he would be able to attend any of the sessions either.[394] It seems, however, that Hippolyte was finally able to attend the Convention and was elected as one of the honorary delegates, representing France.[395]

Horace Holley, an American Bahá'í who was a friend and coworker, deeply regretted Laura's illness and hoped that the rest she was taking in Washington would be sufficient to 'bring her back to perfect health'.[396]

Back on the Continent and Further Accomplishments

It was back to France later that summer and then to Mont Pèlerin in Vevey for Laura to continue her rest. Her ill health, which had started in March and may have been related to her leg, fortunately seemed to be improving. She had to decline an invitation from Mme Avril de Sainte-Croix, who was President of the National Council of French Women, to attend the Universal Congress of Peace in Paris that year.[397]

Back on the European continent, it was on July 23, 1925 that Laura was appointed Chevalier de la Légion d'Honneur (Knight of the Legion of Honor) from the French Republic for her outstanding service during the war, on the recommendation of the Ministry of Foreign Affairs.[398] Created by Napoleon Bonaparte in 1802, it remains the highest order of merit of the French government.[399] It was awarded to Laura for her outstanding service and work among the wounded.[400]

Because Laura had developed excellent public speaking skills, she was invited to speak at many events. Natalie must have made fun of her activities and meetings, since Laura wrote to her that she did not accept every invitation, as Natalie had imagined. She told her sister that she accepted most of the speaking invitations but she refused to be one of the six women to give a talk at a big public event to be held in Geneva on August 28. She was doubtful of the capability of the women who were organizing the affair and was worried that it was not going to be particularly professional. The organizers may have been several Bahá'í representatives who were in Geneva at the time. Most of the Bahá'ís who were serving on these projects were volunteers with little experience. Laura wrote to Natalie: 'But I will attend the congress there of my cherished University boys and girls. So, you see I am only doing exactly what pleases me. But Mrs Aberdeen is throwing a big welfare conference and has gone to my hotel so we can work easier when I arrive.'[401]

When Laura went for a short visit to Geneva in September, Natalie was in Vevey, about 57 miles away. Laura wrote to her, excited at the possibility of spending time with her sister in the first week of October. She was going to Mont Pèlerin after a day in Geneva as Hippolyte was there already.[402] But it is not certain that she and Natalie managed to see each other.

Laura also told Natalie that Mrs Spreckels, whom she had met in San Francisco over a decade before, had an art collection that Laura believed to be unbalanced. She thought it best if Natalie asked their mother about museums in Washington. Referring to a particular museum, she wrote, 'I have not put my foot down into that museum since I was twenty and then there was room for improvement and I have heard that there has been an effort in the right direction.'[403] Laura was knowledgeable about the art world and museums because of her exposure to them from early childhood and she carried on a correspondence with authors, poets and other artists throughout her life.

A talk Laura gave at the American Women's Club in Paris was reported in the newspapers. One newspaper account on December 16, 1925 stated that she was a member of the Peace and Arbitration Section of both the French and the International Commission of Intellectual Cooperation that met in Paris under the aegis of the League of Nations with the purpose of protecting and stimulating the finer powers of the minds of all races. It noted how Laura used photographs, documents and maps to illustrate the magnitude of the task the League of Nations faced in working for peace.

Since her war relief work came to an end, Mme Dreyfus-Barney, who is a Knight of the Legion of Honor, has devoted herself to working for peace. Her efforts are mainly directed to the building of a new psychology among young people. We must make the youth of the world realize that the moral code of the individual must be applied to the relations between nations. She declares: 'Theft, attack, rapine between nations, all the crimes for which the laws of a country penalize the individual, must be dealt with in identical manner by a court of arbitration, world court, League of Nations or what you will.' She was one of the delegates from the National

Council of French Women to the Quinquennial Congress of the International body of Washington.[404]

After writing about her childhood and privileged life, the article continued:

> A woman as gifted as she is striking in appearance, she is a writer, sculptor, Persian scholar, and student of sociological and philosophical questions. Her studies have been practical as well as theoretical.
>
> Women, she believes, have the great opportunity, through their position in homes and in the schools, to bring about a new attitude and a real understanding between people. 'Let the child learn', she writes in one of her articles, 'that true patriotism is not opposed to universal cooperation. On the contrary, universal cooperation is the sole means of ensuring peace and prosperity, so interdependent had the modern world become.'[405]

Her talk was published under the title 'Consultation and Reconciliation versus Conflict' in the bulletin of the American Women's Club and she also sent it to be printed in *Bahá'í News*.[406]

Laura Continues Her Bahá'í Activities

While at home in Paris, Laura always helped with the affairs of the local Bahá'ís and assisted with the treasurer's work whenever needed.[407] Hippolyte was also actively serving the Faith in his own right. He traveled to Haifa and Egypt in 1926 to assist in securing the civil and religious rights of Egyptian Bahá'ís. He also traveled to Baghdad three times between 1923 and 1926, one of these with Laura.[408] The visits were made at the request of the Guardian and concerned the house of Bahá'u'lláh.[409]

Martha Root, an active Bahá'í teacher, visited the British Isles in 1926 for five months to help spread the Bahá'í Faith and to generate the interest of the media. Prominent Bahá'ís joined her in a series of events. Both Hippolyte and Laura went there to assist.[410] They both also joined forces with other Bahá'ís in giving a series of talks in Europe.[411] Martha Root visited Professor R. A. Nicholson, who had been appointed Professor of Oriental Languages at Cambridge University after Edward G.

Browne's death. She was accompanied by some prominent Bahá'ís: Lady Blomfield, George Townshend, Mountfort Mills and Hippolyte.[412] Laura joined her at a talk organized by the Religious and Ethics Committee of the League of Nations and the ICW.[413]

When Martha Root was in Geneva during August and September of 1926 organizing several meetings to present the Bahá'í Faith, she had hoped that the Dreyfus-Barneys would join other prominent Bahá'ís she had invited to speak about the League.[414] However, it seems that they were not able to do so. Laura and her husband were also expected to be among the speakers at a meeting in Geneva at which a proposal on education was to be presented to League of Nations officials who were interested in the Bahá'í message.[415]

The International Bahá'í Bureau was established in Geneva in 1925. Its purpose was to assist the expansion of the Bahá'í Faith in Europe. It served as a secretariat to the Bahá'í communities around the world and was a distribution center for information on the Bahá'í Faith. After some deliberation, the Bureau was in 1925 admitted to the membership of a group of international associations in Geneva on the strength of the international scope of its work. The Bureau was recognized by the League of Nations and became a member of the Fédération des Mouvements Internationaux. In 1930 the Bureau was registered as an international working unit governed by a committee under the direct supervision of Shoghi Effendi but later in the 1930s this aspect of its work declined.

The Bureau had a formal relationship with the League of Nations from 1926. Jean Stannard, Julia Culver, Emogene Hoagg and Helen Bishop were some of the women who served the Bureau – the longest serving was Anne Lynch, who served from 1928 to 1857.[416] Laura assisted and advised this Bureau over many years.

Laura's Involvement in Diverse Humanitarian Activities and Using Cinema as an Educational Tool for Peace

The driving force in Laura's life was her vision of a unified world, world peace and women's rights, which intensified after the war, and she supported the institutions that fostered these principles. It was after her return from Asia that she concentrated her efforts on institutions that promoted her ideals, one of which was the International Commission on Intellectual Cooperation (ICIC).

Laura was a member of the ICIC, the precursor to the United Nations Educational, Scientific and Cultural Organization (UNESCO). The ICIC was established with 12 members in Geneva in January 1922 and remained active until 1946. It was an advisory organization for the League of Nations promoting international exchanges among scientists, researchers, teachers, artists and intellectuals; encouraging common standards in science and librarianship; promoting the spread of major scholarly achievements; protecting intellectual property; and facilitating student exchanges based on Geneva.[417] The first session was held in August 1922 under the chairmanship of Henri Bergson. During its lifetime, the committee attracted a variety of prominent members and speakers, including Albert Einstein, Marie Curie, Kristine Bonnevie and Jagadish Chandra Bose.[418]

One of Laura's characteristics was her adamance about the educational role of cinema in bringing peace and understanding between peoples of the world. As a member of ICIC, she pushed hard for it. It was in January of that same year that she reported to the ICW that an International Bureau of Cinematography was to be established at the League of Nations under the ICIC. It would be composed of highly competent specialists and technicians 'with the mission to establish, among other things, an analytical catalogue of all currently existing educational and teaching films and that this catalogue be kept up to date'.[419] She wrote to the members of the ICW's Cinema Sub-Committee:

> If you were among the delegates who took part in the meetings of the Cinema Sub-Committee at Geneva, you will remember the earnestness that was brought to the work by women all anxious to further the development of the Cinema. If, however, you were among those who were not able to be present, you will see by the resolutions which were adopted unanimously, which were the points which seemed to us most deserving of our attention. In either case, we count upon you to help to get these resolutions put into effect.[420]

Several months later she wrote to the sub-committee members urging them to cooperate with the ICW:

> There are about twenty Councils who have not yet appointed a member on the ICW Cinema Sub-Committee, but I know perfectly

well that the Councils who are not interested in this important question do not number anything like twenty and I hope that shortly
effective cooperation will be established with all the Councils.[421]

Lady Aberdeen asked Laura to include her in all correspondence concerning the ICW because she was especially interested in matters related
to the International Bureau of Cinematography and the ICW's Cinema
Sub-committee.[422] Laura stayed in touch with her and they were in discussion about the development of the use of cinema in the education
of youth.

Lady Aberdeen was Ishbel Hamilton-Gordon, Marchioness of
Aberdeen and Tamair (née Isabel Maria Marjoribanks, 1857–1939),
an author, philanthropist and advocate of women's interests. She took
comfort in the fact that even though Laura was not able to attend the
Assembly meeting of the League of Nations in Geneva, a member of the
ICW office in Geneva had been very active there and another person
had given Lady Aberdeen all the news.[423]

Laura had been a little preoccupied with Hippolyte's health issues
but while she was caring for Hippolyte she continued to correspond
with Lady Aberdeen about their mutual interests and ongoing work.
Laura had sent her report on the ICW's Cinematography Sub-Committee to arrive in time for the League's meeting.[424] Lady Aberdeen was
concerned about Hippolyte and wrote to Laura on October 7, 'I earnestly hope that M. Dreyfus-Barney is daily gaining strength, and that
you find your present resort suits him.'[425]

Laura's collaboration with Lady Aberdeen, who was president of the
International Council of Women from 1922 to 1936, lasted several
years, even after Lady Aberdeen's presidency of ICW ended.

Hippolyte's Health

Hippolyte went to Cairo in January 1927 to assist with the effort to
obtain recognition for the rights of the Egyptian Bahá'ís. He told Laura
he was going to proceed to Assam in southern Egypt and then to Wadi
Halfa, a city on the southern Egyptian border with Sudan. From there
he was planning to return to Port Said and then to Paris as soon as
he could find a cabin on a Nile ship. Laura was also busy, attending a
conference in Ireland in May and then presiding at another conference,

writing reports, and attending meetings before going to Geneva.[426] In June, Laura told her sister about Hippolyte's back pain.[427] A month later Hippolyte was still having pain and she wrote to Natalie, 'Hippo has a little back pain today, ups and downs like life itself.'[428] By July Hippolyte was not any better and had to stay in bed, so they cancelled their planned trip to America.[429] By the following month he still had a temperature and they could not make any further plans.[430] She told her sister that Hippo had received Natalie's note and kept it on his little table for over a day while all other papers were taken out of his room. A few weeks later his temperature was almost normal and the doctor said that he would be convalescing by the end of the month.[431]

They finally decided to go to St. Moritz les Bains in Switzerland later that month and stayed at the Grand Hotel Stahlbad for some rest.[432] From there, they went to Vernet-les-Bains in the Pyrenees (a commune in southern France) around September 12. Arriving in Vernet, Laura considered the place fine but the food problematic because it was 'a great resort for the English people'. They could not meet Natalie until November since her 'haunting grounds' were far away from where they were. Hippolyte stayed for a few weeks for the benefit of the mountain air, but Laura had to return to Paris for a quick visit.[433]

A few months later, in February 1928, Laura and Hippolyte were at the Hôtel de Provence in Cannes, near mountain walks. While there they drove to several places nearby in southern France to find a suitable place that Hippolyte liked where he could continue his rest. One day when they had traveled to another commune (civil township or municipality), they wanted to drive to Beauvallon to visit Natalie but it got dark and they had to return.[434] They were still in Cannes in March and Hippolyte was convalescing.[435]

Promoting the Mission of the League of Nations at Teacher Training Colleges

Laura tirelessly and with detachment continued her humanitarian work, even while Hippolyte was not well. She arranged to be with him as needed and at the same time handled her other responsibilities. Laura sent the minutes of the Comité d'Entente (Liaison Committee) of Women's International Organizations to Lady Aberdeen. The Comité d'Entente was the parent committee of the Peace and Disarmament

Committee. Laura was happy that branches of the Liaison Committee had been established in two new countries, Belgium and Bulgaria, and wondered if these member countries could assist the League of Nations in South American countries. Since Laura was rather new to the ICW and its committees at the League, she was not sure if it could undertake to work in certain countries to assist with the work of the League of Nations. If it could, then she would write to Elizabeth Mary Cadbury, an English philanthropist who was active with the ICW.[436] Cadbury was the first chair of the Peace and International Relations Committee of the ICW. Together with Lady Aberdeen, Millicent Fawcett and Mrs Corbett Ashby, she had pressed, with minimal success, for the inclusion of women's issues on the agenda of the negotiations at the Paris Peace Conference that resulted in the Treaty of Versailles, the major peace treaty that set the terms of peace and was signed on June 28, 1919. The Treaty did include a clause enabling women to participate in all organizational positions of the League of Nations.

Yet another interest of Laura's in the early years of the establishment of the League of Nations was the promotion of its mission, which she began to do as early as 1925. It seems that it was through Laura's efforts that the discussion of the education of youth on the aims of international organizations such as the League of Nations was added to the agenda of the conference of the World Federation of Education Associations. The Association, which had been established after the war and which had education as its sole concern, was nonpolitical and nonsectarian and was separate from the League of Nations. The education of youth was considered at the first meeting of the Association, held in Edinburgh from July 20 to 27, 1925. The issue was in harmony with the decision of the Fourth Assembly of the League of Nations to ask the governments of member countries to acquaint children and youth in their respective countries of the existence and aims of the League of Nations and the terms of its Covenant.[437]

In line with the same idea of promoting the mission and goals of the League of Nations, Laura worked tirelessly to establish a competition for the students of the Teacher Colleges (Écoles Normales). This project was a result of her initiative as a member of the National Council of French Women. This Council had been established in 1902 to promote women's rights, was affiliated with the ICW and had about 125,000 members in 1925. The project that Laura spearheaded was supported by the Rector of the Academy of Paris for the French national education districts.[438] She prepared a report for the Teacher Colleges of France on subjects related to the League of Nations.[439] The competition would be held in several French educational districts (academies) including those of Aix, Dijon, Grenoble and Lyon on May 24 and 25, 1928. It would be for third-year students in sociology and history classes and would take the form of two written essays. The first essay was to be written in French about the League, and the second one was to be a lesson plan of about 20 minutes prepared for primary school students. The winners would receive a trip to Geneva to visit the various offices of the League of Nations, with six top winners each receiving a monetary prize.

Laura met with Mr Georges Oprescu, Secretary of the International Commission of Intellectual Cooperation (ICIC). She also sent him a letter describing the progress of the preparations for the competition being made by the National Council of French Women for the Teacher Colleges of France and explaining her desire to see this letter, or parts of it, sent to the members of the ICIC and its Sub Committee of Experts.[440] She also needed him to send a letter to Madame Avril de Sainte-Croix, the President of the National Council of French Women, to encourage her organizational assistance in these efforts: 'I do want to point out that I'm not asking for any special favors (or anything unethical) and that if you should have any objections to make, please believe that I will appreciate you being frank with me.'[441] She wanted her suggestion to be passed up to the ministerial level; the Minister of Public Education (today's Ministry of National Education, Higher Education and Research) was Mr Édouard Marie Herriot (1872–1957).[442]

An internal letter confirmed that Laura had talked to Mr Oprescu and was planning to organize a competition for about 40 Teacher Colleges on the theme of the League of Nations. Mr Albert Dufour-Féronce, the Under-Secretary General and Director of the Section of the International Bureau who had accepted her suggestions, forwarded the letter of the Minister to the ICIC.[443] Laura's tireless efforts and perseverance paid off. They accepted her suggestion. She promised that the National Council of French Women would make every effort to make sure that the younger generations understood the goals of the League.

Mr Dufour-Féronce congratulated Laura for the interesting and wonderful news, which made him very happy, that this competition had been organized at the Council's initiative and with the help of

the Minister of Education, saying that the information was to be forwarded to several subcommittees.[444] The League of Nations announced
its approval in late March 1928.[445] Dufour-Féronce also sent a letter of
gratitude to Mme Avril de Sainte-Croix, the President of the National
Council of French Women, as promised, expressing his delight with
the news. He could not stress how happy he was to see this endeavor,
which gave future teachers the opportunity to learn about the activities
of the League of Nations and the guidelines for international cooperation.[446] Laura remained active with her work with the League of
Nations despite her family preoccupations.

Another project of hers was the League's Child Welfare Committee.
One aspect of this endeavor was to place relevant books and publications in libraries. Laura realized that it was important for young people
to learn about the work of the League of Nations and she addressed her
concern in many letters to League of Nations offices while serving on
different subcommittees.[447] When she was informed that her suggestion
to put materials and publications in the libraries would require funding and therefore could not be approved, she suggested that a group of
competent people at the League of Nations Secretariat be appointed to
find funding through generous donors and volunteers who were interested in the League. She stressed that in order to achieve this goal, they
first had to discover which countries put emphasis on education and
then worry about finances.[448]

Laura suggested to the Secretariat of the League of Nations that a
draft report be prepared summarizing the efforts made up to that time to
support and provide educational and cultural activities and opportunities
to numerous unemployed men and women. She reported that studies
had shown that most children left school before the age of 12 because
of financial difficulties and were thus ill-qualified for the job market.
Long-term job prospects were bleak for those with little education. She
suggested that her committee produce a summary of all the efforts made
so far to advance the education of all children, such as extending school
attendance, providing adult education, and using libraries, cinema, radio,
clubs and games. A summary of all new suggestions made to the ICIC
should be submitted and given to the League's General Assembly. Laura
was convinced that governments had to take in hand the dangers posed
by masses of idle, unemployed people, particularly youth, who would
likely be attracted to the 'forces of disorder and desperation'.[449]

Laura was informed that the Sub Committee of Experts had adopted the recommendation to ask the Secretary General to review the possibility of preparing a periodic report of the activities of the League with the intention of initiating a major pedagogical review. This recommendation, which had been made by the ICIC in 1927, was implemented in 1928.[450]

Laura was not able to attend the last few meetings of the League of Nations held in June and July, though she did not mention the reason in her correspondence. She did state she was hoping to go to the League of Nations Geneva office at the end of August 1928. The Secretariat of the ICIC was keeping her up to date by sending reports of its subcommittee.[451] Laura did not mention anything about her husband or his health during this time when she was both working and caring for Hippolyte.[452]

The Passing of Laura's Husband, Hippolyte Dreyfus-Barney

Towards the fall of 1928 Hippolyte's health started to deteriorate. Perhaps he knew the severity of his illness, because at the end of September that year he resigned from the Cercle des Ch. defer (perhaps Chemin de Fer, which may be the Circle of Friends of the veterans of the railway during the war, of which he was a member).[453] It seems he had an operation at the American Hospital in Neuilly-sur-Seine in early October 1928. Natalie was concerned about his operation and his health and wanted more news from Laura. Romaine Brooks was distressed too and sent her sympathy to Laura.[454] Laura had told her sister earlier of Hippolyte's *état grave stationnaire* (serious but stable condition), which had made Natalie even more concerned. Natalie asked Laura if she wanted her nearby and requested constant news of Hippolyte. She closed a letter to Laura by sending her 'tender and solicitous thoughts' towards him and her and signed 'ever your loving sister'.[455]

By November, Hippolyte's condition had become more serious and they were anticipating a long and weary road of recovery ahead. Laura shared with May Bolles Maxwell that the thoughts and prayers of friends would make dealing with her husband's illness easier.[456]

It is not clear from surviving letters and records what the nature of Hippolyte's health problem was. He was released from the hospital and it was hoped that he was getting better but his health worsened. Laura and Mountfort Mills, who had become close friends of Hippolyte and were in Paris at the time, were at his bedside during the last hours of his life. They said prayers while Hippolyte's body lay before them, 'calm and beautiful bathed by the spirit'.[457] Hippolyte Isidore Dreyfus-Barney passed away peacefully on December 20, 1928 at the age of 55. He was buried at Montmartre Cemetery (Cimetière du Nord) in the Meyer-Dreyfus family chapel.[458]

The news of Hippolyte's passing was shocking for everyone who had hoped that he would recover. Those who had visited him a few months earlier had believed he was getting better. Their friend Lady Blomfield, who had visited him the previous July, wrote, 'I had hoped and thought that he was recovering.'[459] Even his doctor at the American Hospital in Paris was surprised. 'Little did I dream that such remarkable progress would be cut short so soon after leaving the hospital.'[460]

Laura had lost her 'Hippo', her life partner, her devoted husband and her collaborator. Her grief was deep. They had collaborated on so many different projects and had traveled together extensively. Laura wrote a tribute to Hippolyte's life and achievements, mentioning his eight visits to the Holy Land. The last three trips were made after the passing of 'Abdu'l-Bahá, when Hippolyte 'wished to be with Shoghi Effendi, whom he had known as a youth and for whom he bore a deep and understand-ing love'. 'He never "borrowed trouble",' she wrote, 'he faced situations with ease and when the occasion demanded with unflinching courage. He was rapid in decision but deliberate in manner.'[461]

He spoke little of the past. What I know of his life before 1900 has come to me through outside channels. For instance, it was his sister who told me of his fondness for mountain climbing. Again, at his death a friend wrote me that in the whirl of a Parisian life he founded with her a welfare society for home visiting, and was untiring in his support of those who had so little of that of which he had so much.

The Dreyfus family used to give musicales frequented by people of taste, including many artists. It was at one of these entertain-ments that he met Mrs Sanderson and her daughters, Sybil of opera fame and Edith who became later a leading Bahá'í in France. It was through May Bolles that both Edith and Hippolyte entered the Faith a short time after she had given me the Message. It was really May, our spiritual guide, who started the Bahá'í group in France; though the Bábí and Bahá'í movement was known to an elite through the writings of several distinguished French authors . . .

Hippolyte Dreyfus was a well balanced and independent person. He liked both thought and action. He could sit at his desk and translate and read all day and late into the night. Or he could go for a swim or horseback ride with friends or alone. Though ready of speech and eloquent he preferred talking of the Bahá'í Message to individuals and to small groups rather than addressing large audiences.

What he did, he did with pleasure. He never grumbled. He took life as it came. In suffering he showed the simple fortitude which manifested a mature soul. He was ready to die.[462]

The accomplishments of Hippolyte were many. He wrote significant books about the Bahá'í Faith in French and gave great service to the Faith by translating some of the Bahá'í writings into French and English together with Laura.[463] Among the translations were some of the most important Bahá'í books such as Bahá'u'lláh's Kitáb-i-Íqán (The Book of Certitude), The Hidden Words and Epistle to the Son of the Wolf. His own major works included *Essai sur le Béhâisme: Son Histoire, Sa Portée Sociale* (*The Universal Religion: Bahaism, Its Rise and Social Impact*).[464] He was named a Disciple of 'Abdu'l-Bahá by Shoghi Effendi, the Guardian of the Bahá'í Faith, one of 19 Bahá'ís who had been thus honored.[465] Disciples of 'Abdu'l-Bahá were eminent western Bahá'ís designated by Shoghi Effendi for their steadfastness in the covenant.

Hippolyte Dreyfus was 'greatly respected' by 'Abdu'l-Bahá, 'who encouraged him in his travels and relied on him in various delicate matters'.[466] In 1902 Hippolyte and Lua Getsinger had presented a petition 'personally to His Majesty', 'Muẓaffari'd-Dín Sháh' (reigned from 1896 to1907) 'at the Elysée Palace Hotel in Paris'.[467] Hippolyte had traveled to India and Burma in 1905 and visited the Bahá'í communities there. He was called to undertake special missions using his legal and linguistic skills to represent the Bahá'ís in legal conflicts, for example in the conflict over the status of the Bahá'í holy places in Palestine, in the matter concerning the seizure of Bahá'u'lláh's house in Baghdad and in the maltreatment of the Bahá'ís of Egypt.[468]

There was an outpouring of sympathy for Laura. In the weeks following Hippolyte's death she received more than three hundred letters, cards and telegrams of condolence and sympathy from all over the world, from dignitaries, government officials, lords and ladies, friends and family, and colleagues.[469] Shoghi Effendi, now the Guardian of the Bahá'í Faith, who had seen Hippolyte for the last time when he visited Haifa in 1926, sent telegrams and letters of condolence to Laura, sharing the extent of his grief in a telegram sent the day after Hippolyte's passing: 'FAMILY FRIENDS GRIEF STRICKEN PROFOUNDLY FEEL HIS LOSS OFFERING HEARTFELT CONDOLENCES PRAYING FOR HIS BELOVED SOUL.' SHOGHI.'[470] Not only had Shoghi Effendi known Hippolyte since his childhood, but Hippolyte had used his legal qualifications and his other skills and experience to assist him greatly after he became the Guardian. A member of his immediate family wrote to Laura that Shoghi Effendi had cried much on hearing the tragic news of the death of Hippolyte.[471] In a letter addressed to 'My dear Laura Khanum', the Guardian wrote:

> I can confidently assert, among the Bahá'ís of the East and the West, combined to the extent that he had the qualities of genial and enlivening fellowship, of intimate acquaintance with the manifold aspects of the Cause, of sound judgment and distinctive ability, of close familiarity with the problems and condition of the world – all of which made him such a lovable, esteemed and useful collaborator and friend . . . Needless to say how overpowering is the sense of his loss to me, in particular, who received from him such comfort and support in perhaps the darkest days of my life, and cherished the fondest hopes for his further contributions to the advancement of the international work of the Cause.[472]

Shoghi Effendi wrote that Hippolyte

> . . . achieved a standing which few have as yet attainted . . . His gifts of unfailing sympathy and penetrating insight, his wide knowledge and mature experience, all of which he utilized for the glory and propagation of the Message of Bahá'u'lláh, will be gratefully remembered by future generations, who, as the days go by, will better estimate the abiding value of the responsibilities he shouldered for the introduction and consolidation of the Bahá'í Faith in the Western world.[473]

Soon afterwards Shoghi Effendi asked Laura for a photograph of Hippolyte saying, 'I very much desire to have a good portrait of my departed friend to keep in my study wherein we have spent delightful hours conversing and collaborating with regard to the affairs of the Cause.'[474] In his letter of December 21, 1928, addressed to the Bahá'ís of the West, Shoghi Effendi expressed his 'deep sorrow' at the passing of Hippolyte Dreyfus-Barney and mentioned his many years of 'inestimable services'. He declared that Hippolyte Dreyfus-Barney's 'brilliant gifts of mind and heart', as well as the 'divers achievements of his life,' had 'truly enriched the annals of God's immortal Faith'.[475]

The loss of Hippolyte must have been shocking news for Laura's mother, too. She and Hippolyte had had a respectful relationship and Hippolyte addressed her as 'My very dear Little One' in several of his letters. He had mentioned many times that he had enjoyed her hospitality and looked forward to receiving her news. Alice sent a telegram to Laura the day after his passing: 'HEARTBROKEN DEEPEST SYMPATHY LOVINGLY MOTHER'.[476] Alice, who was living in Hollywood, could not join her daughter. A week later she wrote that it was a shame that Hippolyte had died at the peak of his life, when he had so much to live for, when lesser men live on. Laura must feel comforted by her devotion to him, her mother said, knowing that everything possible had been done. Alice wished that she could be with Laura to share her grief but, she wrote, at least Natalie was close by in Paris and she was dependable and sympathetic when needed. Alice observed that Hippolyte's family must also be in great grief.[477]

Alice suggested that maybe Laura could go to Los Angeles to be close to her and stay in an apartment nearby. She even offered to build a little home for Laura on the adjoining lot that she had bought. 'I suppose you feel bewildered', she wrote ' – not knowing how to adjust your life but you with your large interest must find consolation in work. I am thankful that I've given you that energy (which I had from my own dear father).'[478]

Natalie wrote a tribute to Hippolyte on the passing of her brother-in-law, commenting on his position between the two sisters:

Hippolyte, my brother-in-law, a gentle bearded man with smooth skin over cheekbones that were a bit Asian, with slightly slanted eyes and a predilection for the Orient – a passive force set between two

American sisters like an insulator between two batteries. He accepted us as we were but his presence kept our overly tense nerves from short-circuiting, and when he could not prevent it, he remained, with a small swirl of wrinkles on his forehead, on the sidewalk from which some scheme or sudden decision had just torn us. He did not try to understand – and even less to follow – us and firmly walked off like a man who knows that walking is restful.[479]

Natalie noted his other qualities such as not changing his tastes and not imposing them on others; his love of good food and knowing the best food at excellent restaurants; horseback riding and swimming. Natalie would miss receiving from him little bottles of *attar de roses* (rose water) that he would bring for her when he returned from his trips to Persia, Egypt and other countries of the Middle East. These bottles reminded her of his travels. She finished the tribute:

> And on his final one (voyage), when my sister and I were following his simple funeral procession, she told me the only compliment that he had ever paid me, but one of such grandeur in his friendly slang that I felt I had just been crowned by one of the only beings from whom I would have accepted such a distinction.[480]

Munavvar, one of the daughters of 'Abdu'l-Bahá, who knew Laura from her many visits to 'Akká, wrote: 'Dear Laura, though your loss is very great, yet I am assured that your brave nature and deep wisdom will take it most peacefully and courageously and this knowledge alone will ease my heart about you at this great sorrow.'[481]

May Bolles Maxwell, in whose house in Paris Laura and Hippolyte had met almost 30 years earlier, and who knew both very well, wrote to her at three o'clock in the early morning of the New Year and poured out how her heart and mind were so full of Laura and 'dearest Hippolyte' that she could not sleep:

> Although I sent you a cablegram Laura, I have not been able to write – I seemed to feel too deeply for you for any other expression – although my love and prayers have flowed unceasingly. Thoughts of the beautiful life you have had together, of your great and rare love which found such sublime expression in service to the Cause

and to mankind; thoughts of the early days, of your books and of translations, of your travels, your teachings . . . the manifold expressions of your noble lives are vividly present, and touch my heart, with infinite tenderness devotion and gratitude. I cannot feel that Hippolyte is gone but rather that his peerless spirit is with you . . . and is working more potently than ever. Oh! Laura – my whole heart is with you – my soul cleaves unto you in this supreme hour. Only when you can let me have a word.[482]

Edith Sanderson, who had known Hippolyte for many years in Paris, sent Laura a message: 'You know your grief is my grief.' And, 'In spite of everything it came as a great shock. My heart goes out to you. At last our Hippolyte is out of his struggle and his great mystery opens before us.'[483]

Lady Aberdeen, who had collaborated with Laura and was a friend to her, sent her a telegram of condolences in the name of both herself and her husband and commented that Hippolyte 'was such a true and kind friend'.[484] A comforting letter of condolence from Mary Dingman, a colleague with the ICW, shared with Laura her own experience of losing a husband:

The saddest news I could possibly receive came to me thru Lady Aberdeen, I had hoped that your dear husband might have been spared. But it was not to be. I shall never forget the infinite love with which he regarded you as you were sleeping upon our way from Geneva. The concern at your exhaustion and anxiety. It took me some time after my husband's death to realize that I had a personal duty to life as my own possession and that I must regard the gift as one which no one else could use for me – left alone with our own purposes, our own responsibilities to take our own way [weep] on it so difficult but at the same time holds a reward.[485]

Laura received a letter from Lucie Delarue-Mardrus (1874–1945), the French novelist, poet and journalist, who remarked that Natalie had sent her a gift on behalf of Laura but did not mention Laura's 'irretrievable loss' that had 'befallen her' and that this action was expected of Natalie! [486] Delarue-Mardrus had heard the news from a mutual friend. She continued: 'Is it possible that your husband has died – so young – and that you are in mourning for a companion who seemed so perfect? My heart is heavy thinking about you and how you must be suffering. I understand that Hippolyte Dreyfus' parting was noble and serene. But you? You?'[487]

Laura also received a letter from the Ministry of Foreign Affairs: 'We have just learned, with great sadness and deep sympathy for your pain, of the very cruel loss that you have just suffered, after your husband's long illness. My wife joins me in expressing our feelings of sorrow and our most sincere condolences.'[488]

Salomon Reinach, a famous archeologist, sent Laura a letter of condolence. They had last seen each other in St. Moritz les Bains in Switzerland where Hippolyte was recuperating in August of the previous year.[489] He was also a friend of Natalie. He was incredibly surprised to read in the newspaper this sad news since he had received reassuring words from Natalie about Hippolyte's health:

Through the originality of his work and his alert curiosity, your husband was able to take – and will keep – his place in the small phalanx of historians of Eastern religions; you assisted him with that and, by associating yourself in his research, you fully deserved your position alongside him. This is, no doubt, small consolation for the sudden end to such a long and close relationship; but we must, in such instances, consider those men and women who find no consolation in their pasts and who die completely.[490]

Lady Blomfield, their close friend and admirer, wrote to Laura referring to a statement Hippolyte had made earlier that year: 'When he said "younger ones must henceforth carry on the work, I have done what I could", he looked so vital and so young, that he could continue to render to the Cause greater service than ever, that only he could achieve! And now!! The loss to the world is terrible, as to you unspeakable . . . This mortal world is the poorer for his passing from it, as it is the richer for his life's work, which is immortal![491]

Martha Root wrote to Laura:

When you think of your loved companion of all these years being free of pain, going into this great new spiritual adventure of the Abha Kingdom of Light, of love, then you are brave, you are willing to give him to Baha'u'llah, you are happy that he is with the Supreme Concourse . . . A part of you has passed into the other mysterious world of love . . . You will never cease missing him, Laura, life will never be the same but Hippolyte will be with you in a new and even more glorious comradeship. Spiritually when you may, when you meditate in the silent times, and when in the midst of your greatest activities, your husband will flash to you his faithful presence. He will help you. You loved him and he loved you and this love goes on through all the worlds of God . . . There is no separation of the spirit Laura . . . You and he both . . . are not candles, you are fixed stars in His Firmament.[492]

Martha Root then encouraged Laura to go to the International Educational Congress to be held in Geneva the following summer to meet some of the crowned heads and presidents. She ended her letter by saying: 'I know of no Bahá'í in Europe so trained and with such capacity and gifts as you, Laura. You are our most brilliant jewel among His treasures.'[493]

Soon after Hippolyte's death, Laura decided to establish a scholarship for a Bahá'í student in his name in Persia. She consulted Shoghi Effendi about this, who responded that she should write to the Local Spiritual Assembly of Tehran (the local elected administrative institution of Bahá'ís, in this case, in Tehran). Shoghi Effendi acknowledged her 'noble and generous action':

> I am deeply appreciative of your generous offer of a scholarship in memory of your dear husband, and I feel that the best procedure would be to send the pamphlet you sent me to the Teheran Assembly who will be acquainted thereby with the nature of the work of the university and will be better qualified to appoint the suitable student.[494]

He suggested that he would communicate with them and would ask them to write to her so that she could have direct contact for any matters arising in the future. Furthermore, he remarked that a direct connection with the recognized representatives of 'the Bahá'ís of Persia, would I feel, be more appropriate & closer to the wish of Hippolyte himself.'[495]

This was the end of the long and productive chapter of Laura's life with her husband Hippolyte, together as collaborators and as partners in life and work. In a letter to a friend Laura said, 'he was ready to go on as he had been ill'. Then she wrote: 'Strange how the pain of separation is a binding [*sic*] link of presence!'[496] Laura, after a period of bereavement and mourning, had to accept her sorrow and loneliness and proceed into the last, long chapter of her life alone.

PART 4

LAURA ON HER OWN

1929 – 1964

Life after the Death of Hippolyte

The passing of her husband brought Laura overwhelming sadness and sorrow; she had lost the closest person in her life. She had known or been with Hippolyte for most of her adulthood and they had had a rich life. Not only had they been dedicated to serving their Faith, but they had also simply enjoyed life together. She was not yet 50 years old when she became a widow. A Bahá'í friend who lived in Paris in the 1950s and 1960s, commented, 'To be alone in a city like Paris, after her husband died, and with an infamous sister was difficult for Laura . . . Laura Barney and Hippolyte Dreyfus were devoted to one another.'[1]

However, time would show that Laura was quite as strong after Hippolyte's death as she had been during other difficult times, and continued her activities with zeal and persistence. She tried to overcome her loneliness by intensifying her efforts on behalf of the Bahá'í Faith, women's activities and the cause of peace.[2] Though her devotion to promoting human cooperation and bringing people together had perhaps begun the day she became a Bahá'í, it increased after the loss of her husband. Now, to fill in the emptiness, she was even more devoted to translating the principles of her faith and ideals into action by working with like-minded organizations. The key to her amazing resilience seemed to be keeping her personal life separate from her professional work.

While Hippolyte's life had been fully devoted to his faith, Laura's life was devoted to her faith through her humanitarian activities. Her life was a nexus between religion and humanitarian action, in which the principles of her faith continued to play a central role. The vision of a just and peaceful civilization and the equality of women and men gave her much opportunity to blend her ideals with secular associations that shared them. Her goals and purposes in life were reflected in her tireless work for the International Council of Women (ICW), the League of Nations and her faith. She picked up her activities soon after Hippolyte's death and quickly had no free time. She once wrote, 'Except [when] on sea I am really never "off duty".'[3]

Outpourings of love and sympathy continued to surround Laura throughout the year after Hippolyte's passing. A comforting letter of condolence from Mary Dingman showed how well she knew Laura's character and commitment:

I am concerned for your health but not for your strength of purpose. And I do hope that what you may see before you that you can accomplish for the good of humanity will be a support and comfort.[4]

A year after Hippolyte's passing, the stock market crashed in October. Incredibly, the Barney family fortune was not affected by the crash or the ensuing Great Depression as were the fortunes of so many other wealthy Americans. Laura, her mother Alice and her sister Natalie continued to receive substantial income from the seemingly inexhaustible, depression-proof trust set up by Albert Barney so many years before.[5] Laura was a wealthy expatriate living in Paris and each of the Barney sisters was 'among the very few non-European heiresses in France in complete control of her own wealth and life, choosing to live outside the confines dictated for women by society in America or Europe'.[6] One of Natalie's biographers wrote that Natalie lived in style, with a housekeeper, a chauffeur, a chambermaid and two Indochinese who worked as cook and *maître d'hôtel* (butler).[7] There are records that show that both sisters had housekeepers and drivers for most of their adult lives.[8] Laura also had someone who acted as her secretary during the last decades of her life.

After Hippolyte's death, Laura's mother told her that the apartment where she had lived with Hippolyte at rue Greuze was too large and lonely.[9] Laura followed her mother's suggestion that she should move to a smaller place and started looking for another apartment and purchased one on the fifth floor of 74 rue Raynouard, sixteenth arrondissement, moving into it in 1930. It seems that each apartment in that building had been custom-designed according to the needs of the owner, and the one for Laura was likewise prepared in accordance with her needs and desires.[10]

Despite her many responsibilities in Europe, Laura stayed in touch with family and friends in North America. In the spring of 1929, in a letter to her spiritual mother, May Maxwell, she assured May that she would keep in touch and mentioned how much she was missing Hippolyte, although feeling his presence. Laura was going to visit her mother before long and suggested that the two of them must meet in the United States.[11]

A few months later when she was in southern California visiting her mother, Laura received a letter from May asking her to alter her route when traveling east to spend a few days in Montreal at her home. Laura was unable to change her itinerary but May hoped that Laura might be able to see her 'old-time friend' before she left the United States. May referred to a Washington newspaper article about Laura speaking at a public meeting on October 24 and also at another larger one on November 6. May had hoped to be in New York in order to hear Laura speak at the meeting but was unable to do so.[12]

Reflections on 'Abdu'l-Bahá

In early 1930 Laura took time off from her busy schedule of traveling, organizing conferences and attending meetings to write an article for *The Bahá'í World* in which she expressed her memories of and deep feelings about 'Abdu'l-Bahá:

> I would like sometime, to step out of the whirl of my present life to describe how 'Abdu'l-Bahá appeared to me as I observed His majestic sensitive beauty, His life, active and human, forceful and inspired. Without doubt, He saw beyond the present – 'the wise man sees the tree in the seed'. Step by step, event after event, have led to His conclusions. Men have followed short-sighted passions – economic disorder, war, revolution, mass suffering.
>
> 'Abdu'l-Bahá spoke also of another time, when the mind and the heart, united, should establish true civilization. Ah! when will this time be the present? Perhaps when men understand the lessons of the past and the purpose of existence.
>
> We, who have lived through this last half century, have witnessed the world knitted closely together by many interests; science has compassed time and space and given us power to turn darkness into light, cold into warmth, scarcity into plenty; but are we not further away from content and peace, and friendliness? . . . Why this present misery, this disorder, this enmity? Perhaps high purpose and generous sentiment have been brushed aside in the material onrush of progress; and now, material civilization itself cries out to be saved from the destruction which is inevitable unless some guiding power comes to the rescue.
>
> We are again at the crossing of the ways. The choice of the road of progress should be made clear by the Word of Bahá'u'lláh enjoining

His followers to consider that world affairs are home affairs, to mingle with all men in helpful understanding, to penetrate and disclose the secret forces of civilization.[13]

Efforts with the League of Nations and the International Council of Women

Laura took on more responsibilities with the ICW and the League of Nations while still grieving the loss of her husband. Her vision of a unified, peaceful world was shown through her ongoing support of the ICW, the League of Nations and institutions that fostered those ideals to bring understanding and collaboration between peoples of the world. It was the fact that the network of the ICW had become 'a potent symbol of intercultural dialogue and cooperation, certainly a prerequisite for global peace and security' that attracted Laura.[14]

Laura continued to concentrate her efforts on causes dear to her heart. One of the major responsibilities she had accepted was serving on the International Committee on Intellectual Cooperation (ICIC) from the mid-1920s. The ICIC collaborated closely with the International Educational Cinematographic Institute (IECI) that was established in Rome in 1928 by the Italian government while Mussolini was in power. The IECI was created to consider radio and cinema as means to reinforce intellectual cooperation between countries. It worked closely and collaborated with a sub-committee of the ICIC, whose main objective was to encourage the production, distribution and exchange of educational films.

As the president of the sub-committee, Laura initiated several projects, one of which was an international competition to promote the mission and further the understanding of the League of Nations to young people. One of these was her sponsorship of competitions held at Teacher Colleges and starting another competition in 1929. She sent information about this competition to Professor Georges Oprescu, the Secretary of the ICIC who also served on the board of administration of the ICEI.[15] Based on her suggestion, the League of Nations decided to send information about the competition to all the member countries. Even some daily newspapers received copies. In addition, the information was sent to the headquarters of every member association of the Comité d'Entente (Liaison Committee), the parent committee of the

Committee on Peace and Arbitration of the ICW. It seems that plans were also being made for other member countries of the League of Nations to hold similar competitions.[16]

In May 1930 Laura asked the office of ICIC to provide her with 'a report of memorandum describing the ways in which Governments had provided for instruction in the aims of the League of Nations in the schools'.[17] As a result of her persistence, her request was finally fulfilled despite an initial unwillingness on the part of the ICW to assist. She believed that by presenting these reports to the delegates at the important ICW conference that was taking place in Vienna that year, the delegates might be influenced by this valuable information and act on these suggestions upon return to their countries.[18]

The following year, Laura made valuable suggestions to this Sub-Committee, including the preparation of a documentary report on school books; the establishment of an educational information center; contacts with the directors of educational museums; liaison with libraries; publication of more materials about the League of Nations; the use of cinema and broadcasting for promoting the aims of the League of Nations; and the promotion of the exchange between students of secondary schools.[19] All her suggestions were approved and followed up by ICIC.[20]

Early in the summer of 1930 Laura met with a Mr Rosset at the French Ministry of Public Education and discussed among other matters the work of the Sub-Committee of Experts.[21] She strongly recommended to the Sub-Committee that he be invited to its next meeting. Given his status in the world of education, she thought they should discuss it with the Under-Secretary and invite him, even if that meant he would take Laura's place on the committee.[22] A very supportive response was received, stating that Mr Dufour-Féronce, the Sub-Secretary of the Secretariat of the League of Nations, 'has the utmost esteem for the energy and devotion you have shown on the sub-committee, is sure that you will be invited to take part in the sessions as a full member'.[23] She thanked Mr Dufour-Féronce for his encouraging words: 'I would like to assure you that my very active desire is to be useful for the cause of peace insofar as I am able in whatever way I can.'[24]

Preparations for the First Conference of Women Specializing in Motion Pictures

Zoë Druick notes that the 1920s and 1930s represented an important period for both film and politics. Film offered new experiences, perceptions and forms of sociality, while the mass media played an important role in education and marshalling popular opinion for a variety of nation- and empire-building philosophies, for example in the Soviet Union and Germany.[25]

The IECI shared some common goals with reformist women's groups. Those groups with mandates for social reform lobbied the Motion Picture Producers of America and agitated for higher standards of morality in films. Some women's groups also worked with the IECI on issues of morality in cinema.[26] These activists believed that the family was the basic unit of civilization and, therefore, women were responsible for regulating the effects of movies on family life.[27] A press release issued by the ICW described the work of its Cinema Sub-Committee:

> In 1925 several countries – particularly faraway countries – asked that the issue of cinematography be studied. A Cinema Sub-Committee was created in 1926 under the aegis of the Standing Committee on Education. In 1930, it added Radio Broadcasting to its study and action program. Many of the members of this sub-committee have been serving for a number of years on the official censure committees of their respective countries.[28]

Laura served on the Cinema Sub-Committee and was its convener at the Meeting of the Executive and Standing Committees of the ICW that was held in London on April 29, 1929. She recognized the role of cinema and radio in promoting peace rather than war. On behalf of the ICW, she told her colleagues about the meeting and asked them to prepare reports of activities in their respective countries for the Sub-Committee.[29] Soon after the conference Laura informed the members of the Sub-Committee of the positive reviews she had received from various countries about the excellence of the conference. She also shared these communications on several occasions in her dealings with the League of Nations. After giving the report on activities in June, she wrote, 'It is now our duty to see what practical steps we can take to bring about the application of the resolutions which our Committee has had under consideration.'[30]

Laura asked the Cinema Sub-Committee members to send her short reports, before their next meeting in Vienna, showing the results of their actions on the resolutions or any difficulties encountered in connection with this work. The list of resolutions that they had discussed were those of two years earlier. However, one rider to a resolution was 'to avoid presenting foreign nations or races in a degrading light on the screen'.[31] She then discussed other aspects of cinema, which formed the subjects of their resolutions, which were of vital importance, such as 'a study of the psychological effect of films on children, the development of recreational films and the suppression of inflammatory films, often the cause of terrible disasters'.[32] Various aspects of the work some members of the Sub-Committee were carrying out were listed:

> . . . watching the enforcement of regulations regarding the admission of minors to cinema performances, also those dealing with safety and health, and the suitability of the posters; working for the appointment of women on the Boards of Censors, and at the same time stressing the supreme importance of the production of the right type of films; urging the reduction of customs dues and other taxes on educational films; patronizing all films which tend to develop the spirit of international understanding; combating the abuses of block booking opposing films likely to have a demoralizing effect on certain classes or certain races; pressing for the regulation of the employment of children in the cinematograph industry; enquiring into the effect of certain films upon the spectators, especially upon children and young people, such as war films, historical films, passionate films and those dealing with crime.[33]

The Sub-Committee hoped to bring improved conditions to the cinema and highlighted the 'necessity of each country grouping the individuals, and, above all, the organizations, interested in the development of the cinema as a civilizing agency'.[34] Laura concluded her report:

> To sum up, our main object [objective] must be to work together for the application of the resolutions passed at our meetings in Geneva and London, and to bring all the forces of our respective countries

to bear for improving the Cinema. As members of the ICW, we shall be able to do useful work for encouraging popular interest in art, and with perseverance we may be sure of success.[35]

Working hard for adoption of the declaration of the Sub-Committee by the ICW, Laura asked its president, Lady Aberdeen, to speak about the Declaration of the Cinema Committee and asked her to have the ICW adopt it. The Council of French Women had already adopted it.[36] She also wished that the ICW could persuade Mrs Cadbury to remain in office for a few years, as her name carried significant weight for their Peace Commission. Cadbury had been the Convener of the Peace and International Relations Standing Committee the year before. She had met Laura in Washington in 1925 and they had begun their international work together at that time. She wrote to Laura some years later: 'What a happy time we had there [Washington] in 1925, staying in the Mayflower Hotel. That was when we first began to work together internationally.'[37]

Pushing for the goals of this sub-committee, Laura went to Rome to work out the details of a conference to take place at the venue of the IECI there. The IECI had been established as an international institute under the League of Nations. A press release stated: 'In October 1930, Mme Dreyfus-Barney, President of the Sub-Committee of Cinematography, visited the Institute and in agreement with Mr [Luciano] de Feo, its eminent director, the Marquise Aberdeen, President of the ICW, and with the regrets of Comtesse Spalletti-Esponi, President of the National Council of Italian Women, she decided to hold at the Institute a study conference with a program of intensive action for education in Cinematography'[38]

Laura hoped to meet with the members of the ICW Council of Rome. She had the support of Professor Rocco, the President of the ICEI, but she also needed the involvement of the National Council of Italian Women. Progress was made during this visit to Italy, and the Council of Rome agreed upon the conference, scheduled for October 1931. Upon her return to Paris, the National Council of Italian Women contacted her and expressed that it would be delighted to host the Cinema Conference of the ICW in Rome. Laura must have been relieved. In addition, Mr Rocco and Mr Luciano de Feo, the Director of the Institute, supported her plans.[39]

Laura explained to Lady Aberdeen her vision for this conference. Her plan was to have the three-day commission address different aspects of cinema and radio. Mr de Feo was to assist by sending the delegates a report of the actual conditions concerning the different points, to be studied and discussed in advance so that they would be well prepared.[40] He even arranged discounts for the delegates' travel on trains and ships.

The conference program created innumerable details to attend to, but Laura had thought them through and believed that the conference was vital for the ICW and the progress of women. She knew the task was immense, but she assured Lady Aberdeen that many people at the Secretariat of the League of Nations supported and backed her plan for the conference.[41] Lady Aberdeen believed that Laura's plans were quite splendid and predicted a great success.[42] Laura was already becoming an expert in this field. She had given a talk at the request of Mme Avril de Sainte-Croix on the topic of cinema in Strasburg and the audience seemed to be keen on the subject. Mme de Sainte-Croix lived in Paris and was the president of the National Council of French Women from 1922 to 1932.

After a meeting of the Sub-Committee in Vienna, Laura sent a letter to its members in December 1930 advising them that the Sub-Committee had decided to add radio to its agenda, the challenges of which were related to those of cinematography. The name of the Sub-Committee was changed to the Cinematograph and Radio Sub-Committee. It was in this letter that she informed the members of this Committee that with the approbation of the Lady Aberdeen and the National Council of Italian Women, the conference to study cinematography and radio would be held in Rome from October 6 to 8, 1931.

> These members will remember the cordial invitation of Mr Oprescu, Secretary of the International Institute on Intellectual Cooperation and also of the Board of Administration of the Institute, for us to always cooperate more closely with this Institute of the League of Nations. In order to adopt the best method of collaboration, I went to Rome last October to meet the President of the Institute, Mr Rocco, as well as its Director, Mr de Feo.[43]

A draft of the conference program was enclosed. Laura asked members to prepare for the conference and to suggest ideas for its agenda.

Expressing her gratitude to the Councils, she continued, 'I take this opportunity to thank the Councils for the confidence they have shown to the Countess Apponyi in choosing her as Vice President and to myself in renewing my mandate of President and so entrusting us with the care of their interests.'[44]

In a letter to Lady Aberdeen, Laura explained that 'this is the first time that a meeting of the kind is called under the auspices of the Institute and we are the only Women's International Society attending to the Cinema problems'.[45] She wrote that at the Secretariat of the League of Nations 'we should act as a focus for all the important women's organizations'.[46] Laura had become close to Lady Aberdeen as the result of their collaboration. She was delighted to hear that her friend had been honored with the Dame Grand Cross of the Order of the British Empire, and congratulated her.[47] During those years Laura remained in constant touch with Lady Aberdeen.[48]

A secretary was needed for the Rome conference. In addition, it was necessary for a member of the British Council to attend and act as a rapporteur (a person who gives reports), but the intended person had declined with a response that made Laura think that some Council members considered this conference in Rome to be something separate from the work of the ICW! She reiterated to Lady Aberdeen that her greatest desire was the success of this conference, for which credit would go to ICW, the only women's organization that was responsible for it.[49]

Soon after the New Year of 1931 Laura contacted Lady Aberdeen, who was in Scotland, to discuss Sub-Committee matters pertinent to annual fees and the need to confer with the Executive of the British National Council of Women about a new nominee, a Miss Sharples, to act as the Secretary.[50] Laura gave her updates about the plans for the conference in October including the news that several people had accepted to be *rapporteurs*.[51] However, Laura was perplexed that the British National Council of Women was not collaborating with the efforts for the conference. She asked for Lady Aberdeen's confidential opinion and inquired if the British could not come up with a representative. Laura needed an English-speaking secretary who also had a good command of French. Lady Aberdeen addressed Laura's concerns in a letter to a colleague at the British Council: 'I think you know that Madame Dreyfus-Barney is arranging for the ICW Cinema Committee to hold a special meeting and Conference at Rome under the direct auspices of the League of Nations Cinema Institute at Rome. In fact, the Director of the Institute is arranging for all the meetings to be held in the Institute itself, and the Italian Government are giving 50 per cent reduction on Italian trains and steamers to our delegates.'[52] She continued that Mme Dreyfus-Barney was disturbed that the British Council was not sending a representative since she had hoped that one of the two possible representatives could take responsibility for the translation of resolutions and other papers into English.[53]

By April Laura was getting quite concerned and distressed with the situation. She wrote to Lady Aberdeen again: 'Unless I have a reliable secretary for the recording of the transactions and translation of the recommendations who could also attend to the printing form of whatever publication we can make after this meeting, I am reluctant to undertake this conference, for it will be impossible for me to attend to everything and this part is a serious matter.' She continued that she had her own secretary who could do the 'whole correspondence connected to the organization of this meeting'.[54]

Laura was experiencing doubts about the conference and she was exhausted. She was also concerned about the high cost and lack of help. But at the same time, she had received exceptional cordiality and support from the Institute of the League of Nations on the significant goal of the conference and advancing the important cause of ICW and the rights of women.[55] She was looking forward to having Lady Aberdeen with her in Paris and she could not imagine how much she would appreciate seeing her. Laura was truly delighted and expressed her extreme joy in seeing her.[56] They must have continued their discussions about the conference when Lady Aberdeen visited Laura at her home in Paris for lunch on June 2.

By that time it was well understood that Laura would continue to manage the organization of the conference. She was grateful that Lady Aberdeen and her office were committed to the conference's success. Lady Aberdeen tried to assist Laura further by writing to a Dr Thomas, perhaps of the International Labour Bureau of the League of Nations, informing him of the conference in Rome that was to be held with the cooperation and under the direct auspices of the IECI. She mentioned how Mr de Feo had been extraordinarily kind in offering all possible facilities and other assistance for the success of the endeavors.

'Representations of different uses to which the Cinematography may be put,' Lady Aberdeen wrote, 'and interesting visits to different places in Rome, are also to be arranged for those who can give the time to such expeditions.' She also asked for a favor.

> I therefore feel that although this is only a meeting of one of our Committees, yet I may venture to ask you to send a representative from the International Labour Bureau to this meeting and Conference. I believe it is a fact that the I.C.W. is the only women's international organization which is devoting its attention to the Cinematography and all its possibilities, and it is for this reason mainly that Mr de Feo is giving us so much valuable help . . . Mme Dreyfus-Barney hopes to be able to bring out a handbook in which the resolutions and recommendations accepted at the meeting together with other items of importance brought forward at the Conference will be embodied. I will ask her to enclose in this letter the Program of the Conference and Mr Lucian de Feo's Memorandum together with any other information which I may have omitted.[57]

Lady Aberdeen reassured Laura in June, 'Please remember that I am earnestly anxious to support you in all your efforts to make this Conference the brilliant success which I am sure it will be.'[58] She would write again and send an opening message for the conference, which she asked Laura to deliver.[59]

The Conference in Rome

The conference was to be held at the headquarters of the IECI of the League of Nations in Rome in October 1931. At the time of this conference, the ICW consisted of 43 national councils representing more than 40 million women of all races. This was an effort of the ICW to focus on motion pictures and their effect on human relations.[60] The conference date was fast approaching and challenges continued, one after another. Even though the governor of Rome had accepted to receive the delegates on October 7, unfortunately, the Countess Apponyi, the vice-convener, who had planned to attend the conference, had passed away. Also, Princess Cantacusene had declined to address the conference since she had to be in Bucharest. Another person who was going to help them could not render her services because she was recovering from an illness. Further, a few weeks before the conference, Dr de Feo, the Director of the Institute of the League of Nations, became sick and needed an operation.

Because of the financial crisis in many countries at that time, numerous members were not able to attend, even with the reduction in transportation fares that the Italian government provided. But all these women had asked to be kept informed of the current work and had committed to making every effort to implement approved programs of action in their respective countries. They were convinced of the important role of cinematography and its force in supporting or destroying basic moral standards.[61]

Reformist women's groups seemed to find a welcome reception at the IECI in Rome. Their vision of a domestic woman fighting to improve the nation one family at a time dovetailed with the Italian fascist vision of women as mothers of the nation, as well as moral censors. Although only Italy mandated that a mother be included as one of three members of the national film censorship board, other western nations gave women pride of place as moral regulators when it came to film and children.[62]

Despite these last-minute challenges, Laura's efforts paid off and the event went well. Dr de Feo recovered in time and the conference was opened with his words. As the co-convener of the conference, Laura had to address it; she emphasized the role that women play as censors.[63] Newspapers reported the conference's success. Laura was interviewed by about 20 journalists about the work of the ICW and the Sub-Committee and several articles were printed before the conference and after.[64] An Italian newspaper under the title of 'Una conferenza romana pel Cinema: Delegate di tutto il mondo' (A Conference in Rome about Cinema: Delegates from all over the World) printed a picture of Laura with the caption 'la delegate della Francia' (delegate from France) with a report of the conference.[65]

The French newspaper *Minerva* printed an article about the success of the conference in Rome entitled 'Madame Dreyfus-Barney, Présidente du Comité International du Cinématographe et la Radio-Diffusion' (Madame Dreyfus-Barney, President of the International Committee of Cinematography and Radio). The article stated that an extremely important conference of women, that of the ICW, had gathered in Rome at the headquarters of the IECI located at the splendid Villa Torlonia to examine problems related to cinema and radio transmissions:

Four days of diligent effort would not have been enough to examine all the many points included in the program had the greatest punctuality not been observed by all the participants and had the chairwoman of the Congress, Mme Dreyfus-Barney, always pleasant and smiling, not been able to lead the debates with a foresight, rigor and, at the same time, courtesy that were truly praiseworthy.[66]

After the conference, a letter was sent from Prof. Rocco, President of the IECI, to Laura and Mrs Louise van Eeghen, the new co-convener of the conference. He thanked them for organizing the conference and stated that it was their responsibility to help the ICW influence the development and betterment of the cinema, in particular its use as a tool of education.[67]

Dr de Feo also sent a letter to Laura and Mrs van Eeghen stating that Laura's letter of October 11 had touched him deeply. Perhaps she had expressed her appreciation for his assistance in making the conference successful. It was because of their direction and management of the IECI, he wrote, that the conference had been successful. He thanked them for choosing his Institute as the conference venue and was grateful for this collaboration.[68] In fact, Dr de Feo was so impressed by Laura's organizational skills that he later asked her to organize the Evening of Cinematography to be held in Stockholm in July 1933, and put himself at her disposal to help with this event.[69]

While she was still in Rome Laura reported the success of the conference to Lady Aberdeen. She had overcome several obstacles, the pioneering conference was relatively well attended and it had fostered interesting debates and discussions. She wrote that she was indeed pleased to see that her efforts had aided the work of the ICW and had advanced a useful cause, the use of cinema. She had decided to stay a few more days in Rome to assist with translations as Dr de Feo had decided to publish the proceedings in five languages.[70]

Before leaving Italy, Laura had a private audience with Pope Pius XI. She wrote to her sister about this meeting, '. . . strange to see the (illegible, possibly Monsieur) of the Vatican! He is kind, looks good & high-minded.'[71] She was also happy to share the success of the conference with Natalie and asked if she had seen the newspaper articles about it.

Farewell to Her Mother

There were only a few days for Laura to enjoy her happiness after the end of the conference before she received the sad news that her mother had passed away on October 12. Upon receiving this news, Laura told Natalie that it would be nice to be together in Santa Margherita, Italy, where Natalie was staying.[72] However, it seems that they did not get together as Laura had wished and she returned directly to Paris.[73] She stayed in touch with her sister by letter, even though this was one of the rare occasions she was upset with her: Laura had asked Natalie to write to their trust to sort things out and she had not done so.[74] Despite her grief and loneliness, Laura continued her work and meetings with members of the ICW.[75] She wrote to Lady Aberdeen about her mother's death, remarking that her mother had had a life of art and beauty and 'no doubt was well prepared to go onward beyond the veil!'[76]

Laura explained to Natalie how she had received the unexpected news of their mother's passing. She was driving in either Italy or Switzerland when she saw a newspaper notice about her mother's will.[77] She was hoping to receive a letter from her mother but instead she learned of her death through newspapers. 'Still I have seen another clipping speaking also of her sudden death and letters from California saying that her death was sudden . . .'[78]

The sisters had lost their 'Little One'. Earlier in the year, Alice had written to Natalie saying that she had had an 'attack' and that her sister Hester (Aunt Hessie to Laura and Natalie) had taken her to see a doctor. The diagnosis was angina and arteriosclerosis but she was getting better. Alice had been looking forward to the visits of her two daughters that November but fate intervened.[79] She was proud of her daughters and had described them as 'the two dearest girls that ever lived'.[80]

The day that Alice passed away, she was to attend a concert after a busy day. When she walked into the concert room, she felt a little faint and sat down on a lounge to rest before going to her seat. It was there that her life came to a sudden end. Alice collapsed and died before help could arrive. Neither of her daughters was able to attend the burial.[81] Commercial air travel was not yet available for trans-Atlantic journeys and crossing Atlantic by steamship plus land travel to California would have taken two or three weeks. Laura and her sister cancelled their plans to return to the States in November since there was now no reason to go.[82]

Alice had not purchased a burial plot but had accepted Hester's offer to share hers in Dayton.[83] Her body was sent for burial in Hester's plot at Woodland Cemetery, separated from the Barney plot by a few feet of grassy path.[84] Thus she was buried with her sister rather than her former husband, Albert Barney, who was interred not far from her resting place. Alice had selected the engraving for her burial stone: Alice Pike Barney, The Talented One.[85]

The passing of this famous woman was, of course, reported in the newspapers. *The Evening Star* ran the heading 'FAMED SOCIETY WOMAN HERE, MRS ALICE PIKE BARNEY DIES' with the subheading 'Wealthy Artist, Who Gathered Celebrities at Her Salon, Expires at 70 Years', and noted her extraordinary social salons and her many accomplishments.[86]

Alice passed away one month after presenting her ballet *The Shepherd of Shiraz* at the Hollywood Bowl, the prestigious outdoor amphitheater in Los Angeles.[87] The ballet was performed by Norma Gould, a famous dancer who pioneered modern and oriental dance, who was also its choreographer. The story was written by Alice and may have been the same as that of *Road to Shiraz*, a play she had presented several years before. *The Shepherd of Shiraz* tells the story of a shepherd who came to the Sacred Pool of Love on the road to Shiraz, Persia, to watch the world go by, bent on pleasure or business. As he rests there, he is urged by the vendors of sandals, scarves and masks to purchase their wares. He pleads with each vendor to give him money as he has none. When they refuse, he prays to the goddess of the Sacred Pool of Love for gold and she sends him the purest gold of all, a loving heart.[88]

The arts were Alice's mode of conveying her messages. As we have seen, among her many endeavors to show her allegiance to the suffrage cause was her play *The Woman*, which consisted of several tableaux and a dance for peace concluding the program. Her dedication to the cause of peace prompted her to develop a free artistic program called *The Awakening* comprising ten tableaux on the theme of war and peace that was performed in Washington, D.C., in 1915.[89]

An early supporter of feminism and women's rights during the suffrage movement, we saw how Alice had allowed the National Women's Suffrage Association to use her Rhode Island house in Washington for free for its headquarters. Concerned about the well-being of the poor, she had established Neighborhood House to support from 1901 until the end of her life, believing its programs could 'provide a model for the development of cultural awareness among blue-collar workers'.[90] The name was changed in 1933 to Barney Neighborhood House and Social and Industrial Settlement.[91]

Laura had lost the last person to whom she was truly close, the dearest person in her life. She shared some of her mother's aspirations and goals in life though Alice's lifestyle was more flamboyant and eclectic than Laura's. She had adored and worshipped her mother and often expressed her love for her, as in the following undated letter to her 'Dear Little One' as she was sailing away.

From where I am seated, I can see your ship leaving harbor. I cannot express what joy it means to me to be with you, and what an emptiness is on my life when you are far. You are so tolerant, so sympathetic, so amiable, and so wise behind your misleading blue eyes.

Heart of hearts, thank you for coming to us, thank you for the willingness with which you permit me to remain and above all, thank you for your tender love.[92]

In July 1906 she wrote to her mother:

I always think of you, for that thought gives me pleasure and happiness. It seems unbelievable to express to you my affection and devotion; but sometimes I must say a (illegible) of what I feel and that is the profoundest love and admiration for you.[93]

And another letter to her 'Dear Little One', probably written in 1920, expressed the same loving sentiments:

Though we cannot be together for Christmastide, my deep wish is that the New Year will bring us together, for no one is dearer to my heart than my talented & charming Little One.[94]

An In Memoriam article in *The Bahá'í World* noted the death of Alice Barney:

Mrs Alice Barney, gifted poetess, painter, dramatist, musician, architect and craftswoman, who passed away in Los Angeles in 1931, lived as her friends and contemporaries attest, in a world of beauty. She became interested in the Bahá'í Cause shortly after her daughter Laura (now Mme Dreyfus-Barney of Paris) visited Haifa in 1900. The Washington home of Mr and Mrs Barney was open for Bahá'í meetings on many occasions . . . She was always a generous patron of the arts and offered her encouragement especially to members of the colored race, assisting them to develop their talents with sympathetic understanding.

The well-known settlement [house] 'Neighborhood-House' was her gift to the city of Washington, and this splendid institution interested 'Abdu'l-Bahá very much when He visited Washington in 1912.

Mrs Barney was particularly attracted to the Bahá'í Cause because of its broad teachings of tolerance, its humanitarianism, its love of the beautiful and fruitful action.[95]

Alice Barney, an eccentric and unconventional person, was respected by the Master. 'Abdu'l-Bahá asked Laura in numerous letters to give His greetings to her respected mother. For example, in one letter 'Abdu'l-Bahá asked Laura to 'convey to your respected mother greetings . . . '[96] In another He wrote 'from the passionate [captivating] and delightful [engaging] Amatu'lláh, your mother, write news of her whereabouts and her general well-being'.[97]

Years later Laura wrote to Natalie:

Yes, she took pleasure in whatever she wished to express. She never seemed harassed in accomplishing something she had decided to do; she handled situations with denominative and good humor & felt responsible in a light-hearted manner which achieved her aims. We were sometimes surprised to see how she could stand certain people. I think that they were to be a part of an ensemble needed for the moment![98]

Vice President of the Disarmament Committee of the Women's International Organisations

The Peace and Disarmament Committee of the Women's International Organisations was founded in September 1931. It was informally called the Women's Disarmament Committee (formally the Disarmament Committee of the Women's International Organisations); and changed its name in 1935 to Peace and Disarmament Committee of the Women's International Organisations. The PDCWIO was formed to promote the Conference for the Reduction and Limitation of Armaments and called itself the 'greatest concerted action for peace ever undertaken by women'.[99]

In 1925 the League of Nations established a Disarmament Commission whose main objective was to organize an international disarmament conference. The importance of forming a committee to represent women's international organizations was recognized. An eight-member bureau was created with the task of closely monitoring the work of the conference. Its mandate was drawn from more than 45 million women. Countless petitions, sent in from all parts of the globe, approved the decision, thereby affirming the committee's authority.[100] The standing committee of Women's International Organisations emerged, with the objective of working unitedly for the appointment of women on bodies of the League of Nations where it was thought women's opinions should be represented.[101]

In 1931 the Disarmament Committee of the Women's International Organisations was established as the Joint Committee of the Women's International Organisations. With headquarters in Geneva, it worked to promote the Conference for the Reduction and Limitation of Armaments, gathering support from different countries for disarmament. Laura served as the vice president of the Committee, which was composed of between 12 and 14 of the major women's organizations representing millions of women, and coordinated peace work throughout the 1930s. Despite its short life, the work of this Committee in Geneva marked an important aspect of the commitment of that generation of women to social welfare, as these leading women and their organizations negotiated international politics by developing transnational activism.

It was in 1932 that as vice president of the Disarmament Committee Laura went to Geneva to attend the World Disarmament Conference and the General Assembly meeting of the League of Nations on March 3.[102] The representatives of the member states were active in the proceedings of the conference. The Bahá'ís were active at this conference too. Martha Root, the American Bahá'í teacher wrote:

One of the very impressive moments at the Conference was when the delegation representing 45 million women of the world from fifty-six countries, presented resolutions adopted at that time for actual limitation of armaments and for moral disarmament. Mrs Laura Dreyfus-Barney took an active part in the work of this delegation.[103]

In May of that year Lady Aberdeen and all the board members of the ICW, including Laura, were present at a meeting in Geneva of the Disarmament Committee of the Women's International Organisations. It had met for a study conference and was chaired by the two vice presidents of the Committee, Laura and Kathleen D. Courtney.[104] Laura made the opening remarks.

Around the same time, Laura on behalf of the Committee organized a dinner to honor Arthur Henderson, the Chairman of the Disarmament Conference. The President of the Disarmament Committee attributed the success of this particular event to Laura and stressed that it 'was unusually well attended yet had a delightful intimate character due largely to the graceful manner at which it was presided over by Madame Dreyfus-Barney'.[105]

About this time in Geneva Laura was contacted by Mr de Montenach of the Secretariat of the ICIC to attend, on a voluntary basis, the meetings of the delegates of the Sub-Committee of Experts for the Instruction of Youth in the Aims of the League of Nations. He noted that Laura had in the past accepted to attend the meetings on a volunteer basis and he hoped she would continue, as the Chair felt her participation was vital.[106] Laura was understanding of the situation and did not mind that she had not been 'officially' invited. She replied that she would change her plans for a trip to the United States in the summer and join the delegates in Geneva at end of July.[107] As usual, she went out of her way to meet the demands of her responsibilities. She had served on this Sub-Committee and had attended its sessions since 1930. She always made valuable suggestions and interesting proposals. At one particular meeting, all her suggestions were accepted and sent to all the members.[108]

According to *Who's Who in America*, by that time, Laura had the following titles and achievements – Knight of the Legion of Honor; Expert and Liaison Officer of the Intellectual Committee of International Cooperation of the League of Nations; Vice President of the Disarmament Committee of the Women's International Organisations;

President of the Cinematography and Broadcasting Committee of the International Council of Women; and Treasurer of the International Commission on the Social and Educational Use of Films and Broadcasting.[109] Until 1938 Laura also served as a member of the Sub-Committee of Experts for Instruction of Youth of the League of Nations, which dealt with international radio broadcasting problems and relationships between peoples.[110]

Travels and Lectures across Canada

Next, in 1932, Laura was off to Canada to give a series of talks. Lady Aberdeen was supportive of this journey and told her that the ICW Councils of Winnipeg and Montreal were looking forward to her visit.[111] A press release was prepared before her departure, providing information about her background, the topics that she planned to cover in her lectures, her experiences and some of her titles:

> She had made a special study of international questions, and after the World War, during which she took an active part in hospital service and refugee relief, she turned her activity to serve the constructive efforts being made toward better understanding between classes and various peoples, such as those undertaken by the League of Nations.[112]

She declined to take fees for lectures but she appreciated 'the entrance fees or collections being applied, whenever possible, to the relief of the unemployed'.[113]

Mme Dreyfus-Barney, as she was professionally addressed, gave her lectures in Canada in September of that year. Her busy itinerary of talks throughout that month was announced before her arrival and included:

> 12: Montreal – a joint meeting with business and professional women and the local ICW Council, an address called 'Cooperation of Nations or World Disaster'.

> 16: Ottawa – a lunch at the Women's Canadian Club followed by her talk 'Intellectual Cooperation' and a visit to the national office of the Associations of Canadian Clubs.

17: Toronto – luncheon with the Toronto ICW Council, followed by her talk 'Intellectual Cooperation', then a tea at the University Women's Club followed by her talk 'Problems of the Cinema'.

[no date given]: Winnipeg – joint meeting with [the Winnipeg] Council of Women [the ICW], the Women's Canadian Club, the University Women's Club, and the Business and Professional Women [with the talk] 'Problems of the Cinema', and meetings with Prof. Osborne at Alliance Française and Mr John W. Dafol not confirmed.

26: Vancouver – tea with the Women's Canadian Club, evening meeting of the University Women's Club.

27: Vancouver – Local council of women [with the talk] 'Problems of Cinematography' and an unconfirmed meeting with Mrs Archibald of Alliance Française.[114]

Canada welcomed Laura warmly. While in Ottawa she wrote to Natalie, 'the official people turned out to have me' and in Toronto also 'all went off well and I am feted with bouquets, flowers & looked after with cars etc. in every stop. I feel like a singer or cinema actress . . . The hotels are excellent as the banquets are generally held in my hotel, the hotel people give me a splendid room as they know I am being received by the "notables".'[115]

When in Jasper, Laura shared with Natalie the thrill of enjoying the natural beauties of Canada. She missed having Natalie close to her and wanted to share her joy and accomplishments with someone. Laura sent her only a few of the newspaper clippings in order not to bore her. She wished that her sister was with her in that lovely place, writing: 'In this beautiful place, I have thought a great deal of our "Little One" and appreciative of Nature . . . News of you awaits me soon I hope.'[116] One senses the loneliness that Laura was feeling. The warm welcomes and gracious hospitality she experienced in Canada could not compensate for the loss of her husband and her mother within the previous three years.

Her last stop in Canada was on Victoria Island. On September 28, she wrote to Lady Aberdeen:

Here I am at my last stop in Canada, and it has been a most satisfactory trip: I have seen many people and spoken from 2 to 3 times
a day in the cities where I have stopped in and the press has given
excellent report and their articles have appeared I am told in many
local papers that I have not seen except by chance in picking up a
paper in the train.[117]

Laura also wrote about the delightful people she had met, a public
meeting given in a large church, lunch at the government house and
an evening talk to professional and businesswomen. She raved about
the fact that the name of the ICW had been widespread in Canada and
that questions of peace, education, intellectual cooperation, cinema
and publications were discussed. She closed her letter by saying: 'On
all sides people have experienced this admiration for you and Lord
Aberdeen. I am delighted with my journey – splendid scenery, cordial
people. When I return to the U.S.A. I shall have more breathing space
& will then write you in detail.'[118]

Her trip was successful and Lady Aberdeen was most appreciative
of her efforts in Canada. She responded: 'Dear Mme Dreyfus-Barney:
I was so glad to hear of your triumphant tour through Canada, and I
have received so many testimonies of the appreciation with which your
visits and your addresses were received at your various stopping places
. . .'[119] Laura had indeed undertaken activities to serve 'the constructive
efforts being made toward better understanding between classes and
peoples, such as those undertaken by the League of Nations' as was
heralded in the press release prior to her trip.[120]

Arrival in Los Angeles and Managing Her Mother's Estate

Laura had been appointed the executrix of her mother's estate. Now it
was time for her to face the reality of her family responsibilities, that of
handling her mother's estate and her sister's financial affairs. This is how
she expressed her feelings to Natalie when she arrived in Hollywood in
October 1932: 'How can I begin, everything is as Mother left it, and
one feels that she might return at any moment. It is best that she does
not return today as she has gained all that can be taken from life.'[121]

Before her arrival, Laura had informed their California Trust in Los
Angeles and the American Security and Trust in Washington, D.C.,

that she would be coming.[122] Upon arrival, she met with a representative of her mother's trust and an attorney to get the 'best advice to proceed in the arrangement of the estate' of her dear mother.[123] It was the Depression and Laura had to handle the sale of some of the inherited properties during this time. The sisters had inherited apartments on Doheny Drive, property in Garden Grove and the Old Garden Cottage, as well as Theatre Mart, all in southern California. Alice had bought Theatre Mart, a Spanish-architecture playhouse, in 1929 and used it to start a production company to stage her own plays, as well as other new productions.[124] As for their other properties, Laura decided to extend the lease of one of the houses, which was being used as a private girls' school. The house in Hollywood was rented to a friend of theirs to whom they decided to give life tenancy, which was common in France, since he had been gassed during World War I.[125] The sisters had also inherited a property in Cincinnati and other houses including Studio House in Washington, D.C.[126] And as always, there was substantial principal and income from the Barney trust.

The Barney sisters had lived off the interest from their trust and not the principal, which remained intact. But their mother 'had repeatedly nipped away at her foundation over the years in support of her many interests and charities'.[127] As a result, the financial estate that was meant for Natalie and Laura had diminished. When Natalie and Romaine had visited Alice a few years earlier, they had to confront her about this situation. They had been deputized by Laura 'to curtail Alice's outlandish spending until the financial markets stabilized'.[128] When Alice had decided to write her autobiography in Washington some years earlier, she had hired a university sophomore, William E. Huntington, to produce the typescript.[129] According to Huntington, 'Alice spent right up to every penny she had.'[130] Despite their mother's extravagance that necessitated dipping into the trust's capital, the sisters were still rich.[131]

It was a relief to know that many of the people Laura dealt with had known her mother and that she was deeply appreciated by different kinds of people who were devoted to her charming memory.[132] Laura wrote to Natalie: 'Mother is loved here by everyone I see. People realized that she was a rare and lovely woman, too bad that she did not have certain success that she wanted along theatrical lines.'[133]

Laura wished to be alone with her memories of her mother now that she was in her hometown. She shared her feelings with Natalie: 'I do not want to be disturbed during my stay in Mother's house, so full of her. I know that when I begin my work it will be hard.'[134] When she learned that a few of Natalie's friends were arriving in Los Angeles soon, she hoped not to meet them. Those days were deeply emotional for her, with the memories brought by going through her mother's belongings. She wrote to Natalie, that their mother was 'of those that must be (illegible) with veiled eyes; but not with a heart of desolation & misery'.[135]

Always supportive of Natalie who was the spender, Laura was the saver. Laura told Natalie that she had sent her money and would send more, even if it came from her portion of the trust income.[136] During her stay in Hollywood, she longed to receive letters from Natalie because she found them heartwarming. She was disappointed that she had not heard from Natalie before she left Paris for North America, except for a letter sent by express mail with the news of Natalie's arrival with Romaine Brooks in Beauvallon, at the north shore of the bay at Saint-Tropez. She had received no other news.[137] But that had not stopped Laura from writing to her sister, saying: 'Your letters keep me company in my strange life here.'[138] She discussed renting Studio House in Washington and their finances and accounts.

Their mother's estate also included her works of art and decisions had to be made as to where they should go. Laura suggested that perhaps they could be donated to the Dayton Museum.[139] Whistler's painting of Alice also needed an appropriate home.[140] Many years before, a museum in California had sent its staff to look at their mother's paintings and old embroideries, and the museum personnel had agreed to take some objects of value on loan.[141]

While in Los Angeles, coping with her loss and the memories of her mother, and managing her estate, Laura attended some work-related meetings and pursued other activities. Always in control of her emotions, Laura was able to give several talks at the University of Southern California. She wrote to Natalie: 'The deputy director has taken me under his wing and wants me as an impresario, having me invited to many important functions – on your birthday I am to do the after-dinner speech with Mr Rubio former president of Mexico.'[142] Pascual Ortiz Rubio was the President of Mexico from 1930 to September 4, 1932. The Deputy Director of the University of Southern California also asked Laura to help with creating studies on intellectual cooperation that the university was planning. He even offered her an important post that required Laura to be in Los Angeles only six months of the year. Laura would have considered the offer had her mother been alive but not under the current circumstances.[143]

Laura visited her Aunt Hessie [Hester], who had been devoted to her mother. Aunt Hessie was quite frail at that time and in later years she also became depressed and discomforted, but she was grateful to Laura for her kindness. She wrote to Laura some years later: 'God bless you for all you have done.'[144]

Laura had been planning to leave Los Angeles before Christmas after finalizing arrangements with the California Trust but she had to extend her stay in the United States to handle additional responsibilities regarding her mother's estate.[145] She told Natalie, 'As I have to attend to Mother's things and fixtures, I can't gallop; but I am counting a return end of January, though it will be hard to lease her little last house.'[146]

Laura gave several talks that were arranged by organizations and were given to Professional and Business Women, the National Councils of the ICW, the League of Nations Society in California, and the University of Southern California.[147] In December, Laura attended a session of the World Affairs Council held in San Diego, a two-hour drive from Los Angeles.[148] She told Lady Aberdeen that she had gone to a 'most interesting place' to speak at this event, saying: 'Circumstances have permitted me to do a solid bit of work for the League [of Nations] in this region also for the Council [International Council of Women] . . .'[149]

She also wrote about other meetings and conferences: 'Yes, since the night I spoke with the ex-president of Mexico, I have given conferences 2 to 3 times a week but after today – I spoke in a large Canadian Club – I shall again enter my circle of silence for some days.' She again noted how happy she was when people came to her and talked about her darling 'Little One' and how loved she was, writing, 'after all these people felt that she was unusual and her charm was there to be'.[150]

Later that December, when Laura went to visit her mother's resting place in Dayton, she left some memorabilia from Lady Aberdeen on her mother's graveside. She wrote to Lady Aberdeen that the gift of 'white leather' ended its journey there.[151] Two months later she wrote: 'Did I tell you that the white leather you sent me on the steamer after my trip through Canada and stay in California was laid on my lovely Mother's earthly resting place?'[152] Laura's relationship with Lady Aberdeen was a special one. They were not only co-workers for the same cause, that of the advancement of women, but they had become close friends.

Exhibition of Her Mother's Paintings

Laura arrived in Washington in January 1933 and stayed at the May-flower Hotel.[153] Staying at luxury hotels was one of her rare indulgences. She went on a quick trip to New York, but in neither Washington nor New York did she accept any speaking engagements, since she planned to return to Europe by spring.[154] She had to attend to matters concerning the Barney trust, taxes and the renting of Studio House.[155] The house needed repairs because it had not been touched since her mother had moved to California. Another problem was that it was not a practical family home. Natalie suggested that it be turned into a museum with their mother's and Romaine Brooks' paintings displayed together with Romaine's collection of works of Monet, Degas, Stevens and others. But they could not agree on this idea.[156]

While in Washington Laura decided to organize an exhibition of her mother's artwork and again had to postpone her return to Europe. She wished to show the entirety of her mother's paintings and pastels before they were distributed to various museums across the country. The exhibition was to be held in Studio House at the end of that January.[157] The exhibition was organized and the press, friends of her mother, and the public were invited to view her mother's artwork one last time at Studio House, Alice's old home. Hundreds attended the exhibition and savored the artistic accomplishments of this talented and sometimes controversial woman who had known and hosted many famous persons.[158] *The Evening Star,* a Washington newspaper, reported:

The famous home of the late Mrs Alice Pike Barney Studio House 2306 Massachusetts Ave will be thrown open to artists, collectors, students and her friends Friday, Saturday and Sunday, January 27, 28 and 29 from 11 am to 3 pm. Her large collection of pastel and oil paintings will be on view for the last time before being sent to various museums and art galleries throughout the country where they will be placed in permanent collections . . . Mrs. Barney's older daughter Natalie Clifford Barney, a noted writer, is in Paris. A younger daughter, Mme Dreyfus-Barney, is in Washington now and will be present at the exhibit of her mother's paintings.[159]

Laura shared the exhibition's success with Natalie: 'The exhibition is great news, people crowd into Studio House, and are deeply impressed by the pictures in this setting.'[160] One afternoon more than five hundred people attended the exhibition so she decided to keep it open for two more days. Her cousin Ellen, with whom she had traveled to 'Akká in 1900, and her husband, Manuel Rionda, came from New York to visit the exhibition. Juliet Thompson, the American artist who was a friend of Alice and Laura, also came. Laura shared this news with Lady Aberdeen: 'I have just closed an exhibition of my mother's pictures, ever a success that had to leave it open two more days than scheduled – and now most of those pictures are being sent to museums – much detail is connected to all these.'[161] Lady Aberdeen, who was aware of Laura's untiring work and was always supportive of her, responded: 'I trust you have now had a restful time amongst old associations, although it must necessarily have been sad for you to close up your dear mother's old home associated with so many dear memories. You will now soon be turning your face towards Europe again, and there will be many to welcome you back, for you have been much missed during this anxious time.'[162]

Laura had informed May Maxwell earlier of her itinerary as she was more than anxious to see May and her daughter Mary, who was 21 years old at the time.[163] It may have been during this visit that she saw the two of them in New York. She wrote to her sister: 'May Maxwell is looking lovely and is most tender when she speaks of you.'[164] When Laura was back in New York before sailing to Europe, she received a bouquet of flowers from May. Laura wrote to her, thanking her and saying she was grateful for the flowers, which she had placed on her desk, and that her thoughts had often gone out to both May and Mary. Laura had been charmed by Mary's qualities of grace, fire and spirituality.[165]

As Laura was about to sail back to Europe, she reflected on her trip to North America. She wrote to Natalie, 'All this trip I have been near our dear "Little One", from the onset it has been a kind of pilgrimage and I hope that I have done what she wished done.' She told Natalie that she had taken a state room on the USS *Manhattan* and was arriving home in France on March 2, 1933.[166]

It had been an exhausting trip for Laura both physically and emotionally and she hoped to get some rest during the voyage home.

Continuing Her Activities Back on the Continent

Back in Europe, Laura had to travel to Geneva in October 1933 to spend a few days dealing with how 'organizations and most of the governments wish to stand firm and, by means of a convention, further the issue of the reduction of armaments'.[167] Then she traveled to Rome for the IECI to 'work with the directors of this organization about a most interesting question: The effects of the film on different races.'[168]

It was during this time that Laura, who was vice president of the ICW's Standing Committee on Peace and Arbitration and the ICIC's Sub-Committee of Experts for Instruction of Youth of the League of Nations, wrote an article entitled 'Peace through Intellectual Co-operation':

> Our much-loved Peace Convener wishes this supplement to include a few lines on international co-operation because she is well aware that this constructive force is indispensable if Peace is to live, develop and take root.
>
> For many years, the International Council of Women has realized the power of those spiritual values of thought and feeling which cut through the frontiers of nations, races and classes, by which all distinctions and even differing opinions are welded together to build a harmonious and complete whole.
>
> For this reason, the International Council of Women welcomed with deep satisfaction the creation by the League of Nations of the International Committee of Intellectual Co-operation, knowing that the aim of this organization is to produce an atmosphere favorable to the solution of vital problems and to the development of a system of co-operation between countries, Institutes, organizations and individuals, for the enrichment of intellectual and spiritual life. As the Great French author Paul Valéry expressed it: 'A League of Nations implies a League of Minds.'[169]

Back in Paris, Laura remained active in the Bahá'í community by hosting at her home monthly meetings of the Local Spiritual Assembly, the locally elected Bahá'í institution. In those years, regular Bahá'í meetings were held every fortnight at Scott Studio, Local Assembly meetings once a month at Laura's home, and monthly meetings for Persian students at Edith Sanderson's home.[170]

The First Congress of Educational and International Cinematography in Rome

Yet another conference was in the works and Laura was responsible for it. During the spring of 1934, Laura organized the First International Congress of Educational and Instructional Cinematography (IECI) under the auspices of the International Educational Cinematographic Institute of the League of Nations in Rome.[171] The Secretary of the Institute in Geneva wrote to his colleagues at the League of Nations about Laura and her responsibilities: 'Mme Dreyfus-Barney, who as you know takes the very greatest interest in the work of the Secretariat and especially in the collaboration of women in the international field, is now in Rome for the preparation of the Congress on Educational Cinematography.'[172]

Laura went to Rome and went to the Institute to work every day. She wrote to her sister: 'My study has been interesting: reports from Syria, Palestine, and lower Africa, India, Siam, Indo China, Dutch Indies, Philippines, China, Korea, Japan, etc. a good brush up in geography! China is to be represented at our congress. Many countries are sending officials and important delegations.'[173] She mentioned that Dr de Feo, with whom she had worked on the previous conference, was most appreciative of her work and had published in full five of her reports in five languages.[174]

The inaugural meeting of the Congress took place in the capital and Benito Mussolini (1883–1945), prime minister of Italy, and other dignitaries spoke. Major international organizations were invited on the suggestion of Laura but she was the only woman delegate to the Congress.[175] The primary importance of cinematography in shaping the mindset of races, and especially of young people, was discussed. The Congress itself, which was held at the IECI, was divided into three sections, each further divided into various committees in which the several hundred participants enrolled according to their interests and particular specialties. The sections were Teaching, Education and

Cinematography, and Educational Films in the Lives of Peoples.[176] Laura noted in closing the report of the Congress: 'In conclusion, let us come to what is the fundamental preoccupation of our Committee: Peace and mutual understanding between peoples . . . We certainly will do all in our power to make the Cinematograph[y] demonstrate more and more clearly the necessity for the human races to stand together, by showing that so many catastrophes, revolutions and wars are the outcome of a lack of mutual understanding.'[177]

Laura wished Natalie were there with her and wrote to her several times during the Congress. As always, she needed to share her joy and excitement with someone close. She was now relieved and had a light moment with her sister. At the end of the Congress she told Natalie about the meeting with Mussolini:

The Congress is over and I have this moment returned from the Palais de Venice where S. E. [His Excellency] Benito Mussolini received our Board of Officers . . . We were all taken together in a photo. I hope that I will not look like a scare crow besides the Duce![178]

Mussolini was known as Il Duce (the Leader). Laura's hotel was situated by the Gardens of Villa Borghese and she shared the same park with Mussolini.[179]

Travels and Talks in Egypt and Visit to Haifa

As the vice president of the Disarmament Committee, Laura embarked on travels to several countries early in 1935 for a series of talks and lectures on behalf of a number of committees of the League of Nations and ICW, including the ICIC and its Disarmament Committee. As soon as she started her trip in Marseilles, she wrote to her sister, 'It seems always so strange to be in Marseille without Hippo!'[180]

On her way to Egypt, perhaps in Marseilles, Laura was interviewed by Jeanne Arcache, a journalist from a French language newspaper. A remarkably interesting article under the heading of 'MME DREYFUS-BARNEY' was printed. After covering her childhood and what had inspired her in life, the journalist wrote:

It was not just the speaker (whom I had) heard under the auspices of the (Association of) French Women University Graduates, the Chairwoman of the International Women's Council's Cinema and Radio Broadcasting Commission, the expert from the League of Nations Commission on Intellectual Cooperation whom I wished to approach, but the woman, the vibrant great artist Madame Dreyfus-Barney, who, in addition to all the above titles, holds that of Chevalier (Knight) of the French Legion of Honor.

I knew that she had been involved in the whole Franco-American literary movement illustrated by such names as Stuart Merrill and Viélé-Griffin. I knew that her life had first been dedicated to art, sculpture, poetry, and how dearly I wished to hear her speak of Remy de Gourmont, that Benedictine of letters, and of the mysterious figure of Renée Vivien, that muse of the violets, who died so young!

It was she, the American woman transplanted to France, who was able to put her roots down to serve a greater homeland, that of men of goodwill, whose prestigious 'adventures of the spirit' I wanted to know.

But the clock showed us that time was short before her departure for Cairo. Fortunately, Madame Dreyfus-Barney was born in a country where each minute has greater value than elsewhere and that reassured me.

In the lobby of her hotel, Madame Dreyfus-Barney welcomed me with charming and convincing simplicity. Her still youthful face glows with intelligence and kindness. Her clear gaze holds you and seems to see right through you. Madame Dreyfus-Barney speaks French in a refined voice, without any foreign accent; when one hears her speak, one doubts her American origins.

'I have never had to choose between different homelands,' she told me. 'When I was six, my mother, who was French, took my sister and me to Paris. She went there to study painting. This led us very early to live in a setting of artists, intellectuals,' she explained.

Frequent stays in Washington, the city of legations, allowed her to renew her contacts with the writers and creators of the United States, because there are no borders between countries for those who think and work. On both sides of the ocean, the same current of ideas comes to those who are ready to receive it. Americans (is this because of the astonishing mixtures of races that reigns there?), have, more than others, a mindset that consists of sympathetically taking on the best of every people. And what wonderful liaisons between nations these women ambassadors of letters can be as they travel, not as idle folk or as dilettantes, but in order to work with others to bring about intellectual rapprochement.

In Paris, Madame Dreyfus-Barney surrounds herself with elite figures. She is friends with Lucie Delarue-Mardrus. She is interested in both the work of Jean Painlevé and Brunschvicg's research. Her sister, Natalie Clifford Barney, did not create a 'salon' with all that worldliness that word can bring, but rather, as she herself likes to call it, 'a temple to friendship'. She is the Amazon that inspired Remy de Gourmont to write one of the most beautiful books that a man has ever dedicated to a woman.

A never-tiring traveler, Madame Dreyfus-Barney has circled the globe several times, which allowed her to study close up the living conditions of the peoples of all nations and to look into their daily problems. Then the war came.

'It caught up with me in China, where I was accompanying my husband, an Orientalist scholar.'

'And it was the horror of that tragedy that pushed me to act, to collaborate, as far as I am able, with the work of peace and reconstruction that I spoke to you about yesterday. Everyone can contribute. I wasn't prepared but action had to be taken. If I had known that one day I would be giving speeches, I would have studied French more,' she added with charming modesty. Oh, how far we are from the 'Précieuses de Genève' and how misleading irony can be even when used by intelligent people!

Madame Dreyfus-Barney's astonishing personality and her lucid intelligence are self-evident. I admire this elite woman who knows 'how to think globally' at a time when so much hatred and so many minds make brothers into enemies and, once again, the threat of war returns. The example of this life devoted to art and action can show the way to so many beings 'born in exile', who are trying to find themselves. Because one is never without roots when one can serve the greater homeland where intellectuals, artists and those whose utmost wish is to work for peace can be found. That is the beautiful message that Madame Dreyfus-Barney came to bring us.[181]

Laura sailed from Marseilles to Alexandria, Egypt, where she arrived in a hotel room so overflowing with flowers that she could barely turn around.[182] After a few presentations, she traveled to Cairo for further talks. Dozens of Easter lilies were sent to her room at Shepheard's Hotel in Cairo. She had always liked Egypt on her many visits there because she found the Egyptians to be exceptionally kind. But this was her first stay in Egypt without her mother or her husband, and this made for a bitter-sweet experience.[183] She was missing her 'Hippo' and sent a note to her sister: 'I often yearn for Hippo and when I look at his dear suitcase that I have taken on this trip sometimes I forget . . . But it is best so; those who are out of sight seem a magnet drawing us onward to better things!'[184]

Receiving three letters from Natalie during the Egyptian stay did much to lift Laura's spirits.[185] She told her sister that she had met some people at the home of her hosts who had asked her if she was related to Natalie Clifford Barney. As always, she was immensely proud of Natalie and wrote that people knew her everywhere.[186] She sent copies of the newspaper articles to her sister, who was now the only close relative with whom she could share her happiness.

Laura's visit and talks were covered in the local newspapers. *The Egypt Mail* ran an article on March 10, 1935 using the title of Laura's talk as the heading: 'International Co-operation or World Chaos'.

Mme Dreyfus-Barney began her lecture by pointing out that we lived nowadays in a world of abundance, with unheard of facilities for a better and easier life but we had not yet learned how to guide and control the great machine we had created. If we were to organize the modern world with success, cooperation was essential, and in many spheres international cooperation was steadily growing. The League of Nations was the great modern symbol of international cooperation, and she proposed to deal with some of the various ways in which League cooperation worked.

After referring to political cooperation among Governments, their fear of putting what they could not advance ahead more quickly than public opinion would allow, Mme Dreyfus-Barney discussed the work of the International Labour Office, declaring that if it had not existed, there would have been far more chaos in the world of labour, giving more scope for the work of Moscow. The great and sad problem of the future was 'Youth and Unemployment'. The speaker then dealt with the Institute of Intellectual Cooperation, the clearing-house for international ideas set up by the League, which had Bergson as its first President, and numbered people like Gilbert Murray and Einstein among its helpers, the committees of investigation into the radio and the cinema, and the attempts made by the League to enlist the press in its work. Mme. Dreyfus-Barney was particularly illuminating on the subject of the newsreels and animated cartoons shown in the ordinary commercial cinema, and the opportunities they afforded for subtle reactionary propaganda of the worst kind. She told an interesting story of an animated cartoon delicately ridiculing disarmament, showing weapons of war, which, upon investigation, was found to have been financed and placed upon the market by an armaments firm.

The speaker concluded her lecture by likening the work of all those interested in the maintenance of peace today to a net pulling something very heavy, very fatiguing, to land. 'But the net', she declared, 'must above all be strong, if we are to pull our poor wracked civilization to safety.'[187]

Yet another article was printed in the *Egypt Mail*. Under the heading 'Poetry and the Influence Wielded by the Radio', it noted that radio was far more accessible to populations than the cinema and that governments had finally realized the enormous influence that the cinema and radio wield over the masses. Therefore, governments were coming to understand the necessity of not only checking the abuse of cinema and radio but also of encouraging the educational opportunities they presented. A challenge was issued to act:

Now that the technique of filming and broadcasting has reached such a high standard, the world awakens to the fact that both should be put to some more worthy use. Already the moral side is supervised by censors, but censors are not concerned with the perfection of the thing as a work of art or an educational masterpiece. The days of 'wild historical films' are now over and Hollywood parties are doomed to be lost to the screen.

The work of the Commission for Intellectual Cooperation, of which Mrs Barney is president, may be divided into three parts. In the first place, they are unanimously agreed that the cinema and the radio need teachers and professors to expand and explain what they provide. In the second place, they are concerned with the use of films in medicine and surgery, many delicate operations being taught by actual demonstrations. And lastly, they study the 'Life of the People', the different mentalities of races, cultures, and ages, and the resulting influence of various presentations of a subject.

Mrs Barney concluded by saying that although the road was full of difficulties, it had infinite possibilities, so great that it made any work worthwhile. Films and radios were soon going to be very appreciable influences in the affairs of nations, and it was a privilege to be in a responsible position for the organization of an International agreement in the use and abuse of the camera and the wireless.[188]

Laura made a quick visit to Haifa and 'Akká about the end of March on her way to Beirut, Lebanon.[189] Perhaps she met with Shoghi Effendi during this visit. Laura noticed how much Haifa had grown, 'from a village to a city, and one has to go to Akka to find surroundings of the past'. She was having a pleasant stay and was on her way to Beirut where she would spend 'a few ever-busy days' before going to Damascus and Turkey.[190]

Continuing Her Talks and Lectures in Lebanon, Turkey and Greece

Laura arrived in Beirut where the Lebanese National Committee of the ICIC had organized a talk for her at the Bibliothèque Nationale on April 2 as the Expert from the ICIC of the League of Nations.[191] Her presentation was covered by the Beirut newspapers. One French language newspaper, *L'Orient,* had the headline 'La Coopération Intellectuelle: La Conférence de Mme Dreyfus-Barney'.[192] It reported that the conference was held in the magnificent hall of the National Library and was attended by the President of Lebanon, the country's Director of Public Education and many dignitaries. Laura's fluent French drew compliments: 'Although the speaker was American, she spoke French with truly remarkable fluency and purity of both style and diction.'[193]

As this talk was the first of its kind in Beirut, Laura explained the history of the ICIC and how the initial idea of intellectual cooperation took had taken root in the noble mind of Léon Bourgeois, France's

Permanent Delegate to the famous Hague Conference and one of the main leaders of foreign policy. She explained:

> Léon Bourgeois believed that economic exchanges would not suffice to produce between the nations that brotherhood of souls and that 'understanding which is essential for proper understanding between peoples whose interests are forcibly different and often contrasting'. This led to the idea of establishing the Institute of International Intellectual Cooperation [*sic*], whose first president was the great thinker Bergson, who was then succeeded by M. Laurents of the Netherlands, and then by Professor Gilbert Murray of the University of Oxford, the current President.
>
> The Institute's Headquarters are in Paris. Among its collaborators, it has included scholars of the highest order such as Painlevé, Mme Curie, and, today, Einstein, the however rather unpersuasive apostle of relativity.
>
> The Goals of Cooperation: International cooperation attempts, wherever possible, to remedy the current isolation of most countries, which are hiding behind their own Great Walls of China.
>
> We must not, the speaker said, be confused about patriotism. Being patriotic is a very good thing, because understanding civic issues is a key condition for resolving global ones.[194]

Laura emphasized the leading role of the press and its invaluable contribution to ensuring universal harmony.

> So the speaker fully supports H. H. Pius X's beautiful and noble declaration to the French Press Delegation, whose head at the Vatican is the veteran Saint-Brice: '*You are knights of the Word. The scope of your influence in this world is incalculable. Always exercise it in service of justice and the truth . . .*'[195]

The article stated that Laura listed other activities of this 'beneficent' institution, such as use of the cinema, documentary films, and radio programs to transmit important intellectual and educational information. The failure of these modes of communication could mean that they would commit harm against society. In addition, all efforts should be directed towards moral disarmament, the prerequisite for general disarmament. She was quoted as saying, 'This goal will be achieved through surveillance of scholastic education and the distribution of high-level works such as Einstein's *Why War?*.[196] The topic of intellectual unemployment was also mentioned:

> In collaboration with the League of Nations International Labor Office, the Institute is also studying practical ways of offsetting international intellectual unemployment.
>
> In the meantime, special and very useful attention is being paid to giving unemployed or underemployed laborers intellectual activities and entertainment via books, the cinema, and so forth, leading them to a healthy vision of life and thereby preventing discontent and the war of unequally endowed social classes.
>
> Finally, Mme D. Barney summed up the ideal of Intellectual Cooperation through this short and noble synopsis: 'Preserving and developing the heritage already acquired, the fruit of the intellectual activities of the past, all that is currently being produced, and everything the future holds for us . . .'[197]

Another French language newspaper, *Syrie*, under the heading 'La Coopération Intellectuelle: La Conférence de Mme Dreyfus-Barney', also reported the talk she had given at the National Library on April 2, mentioning that the President of Lebanon had attended, along with delegations from the universities and teacher colleges, and other dignitaries.[198] A summary of her talk was given and the journalist reported:

> In extremely charming and well-educated language, Mme Dreyfus-Barney explained the intellectual cooperation undertaking, whose main unit is in Geneva; the exchange and contact mechanism that it has arranged, and the support of national agencies in various countries. She noted, in that regard, that the Lebanese National Committee had fully taken on the spirit of international cooperation and she recalled a few passages from the talk given by its President, Mr Camille Eddé, who had clearly understood and explained the horizons of this work.
>
> Through very comprehensive documentation, she demonstrated the actual results already achieved, the goals of scholastic education, the direction of human culture, the use of cinema and

radio-broadcasting. She expressed the Geneva Commission's concerns about the intellectual unemployment of young people, and she indicated the best ways, in her opinion, for ensuring a permanent mechanism of exchanges and collaboration between peoples.

Mme Dreyfus-Barney's talk was punctuated by enthusiastic applause from the audience. The article continued that Mme Camille Eddé, Chairwoman of the Lebanese National Intellectual Cooperation Committee, immediately stood up to thank the speaker:

> We were already aware, through the reports of the Geneva Intellectual Cooperation Commission and the many talks that you have given in America, of all the efforts and all the talent you have devoted, over the past few years, to spreading the doctrine of the League of Nations, aimed at achieving an understanding between peoples through an understanding between minds.
>
> A fertile doctrine, without which peace is impossible, since, to use André Maurois's expression, war and persecution are never caused by armies but by the dogmatic elite! 'Arms give battle but brains instigate.' We had also surmised, dear Madame, that as well as being a woman of thought, you must be a woman of action and an apostle.
>
> But what we were not yet familiar with but what you have revealed to us this evening, is that it is not only the magic of your words and their force of persuasion, but the faith that gives them life, in spite of the difficulties and pressing concerns that exist.
>
> You quite properly thought that it is at critical moments that true faith must show itself to be even more active and you felt that it is at the very time when the international spirit seems most threatened within the political order that we must redouble our efforts to preserve it at the intellectual level.
>
> We especially thank you, Madame, for having allowed us [to] share this faith in the Geneva ideal with you. More than any other, the Lebanese people, who, for centuries, have been the objects of and victims to the desires of stronger peoples, needs to believe and have hope in an ideal of universal justice and equality, whose reign is the sole means for ensuring their physical and moral independence . . .[199]

Laura also addressed the students at the American University in Beirut. She wrote to her sister, 'I have just returned from giving a talk to the students of the American University. Nice place and nice audience . . .' Despite her satisfaction with her activities and talks, she hoped that her travels would soon be over and that she could 'take the vacation to Racing Club and play Ping Pong with l'Amazone!'[200]

The French language newspaper *La Liberté*, under the headline 'Le féminisme au service de la paix', printed an article based on a long interview with Laura about the Disarmament Committee and real mission and aspirations. The interviewer started by stating that the two current issues peace and the rights of women were, global public opinion, seemingly not related. The article explained that ties of moral solidarity existed between these two issues because of feminism's contribution to the cause of peace, a contribution that takes many forms and intends to remain relevant. One proof of this was the formation, at the very onset of the Disarmament Conference, of a Disarmament Committee representing the most important international women's organizations. The interviewer wrote that Laura 'recorded her substantive responses, endowed with the force of conviction not because they were based on vain rhetoric but by the effect of the mark of total faith and sincerity, together with a tone of serene gravity that can only be displayed by those who have a firm belief in the truth of their opinions'.[201]

Laura gave a history of the Disarmament Conference and explained to the interviewer that several delegates maintained ongoing relations with various aspects of the Conference. A series of conferences had been held under its auspices and with the support of international specialists attached to the work of the Disarmament Conference, they had addressed several topics related to the issue of peace, such as arms manufacturing and trafficking. She explained that the committee's work consisted of keeping the international organizations of women from which it arose aware of events and initiatives that had been undertaken. Those organizations, in turn, were to share these reports with their various national sections. Laura continued:

> This implies work upstream to explain and refine it since the arms issue, which was the focus of the Disarmament Conference, is first and foremost a national issue. Given that, feminism's collaboration in resolving this problem cannot be based on universal data; each

country, each region requires appropriate actions.

I would also like to emphasize the remarkable spirit of cooperation that drives all the members of our committee, the mutual and
never-failing harmony that characterizes our work. This cooperation
and harmony must undoubtedly be put down to a common factor
in my colleagues' activities, that is, consideration for the realities (of
the situation). Is that not the key condition for understanding the
endlessly debated problem of arms reduction?'

How many have had such an understanding – comprehensive,
fathoming all the facets of the issue – even among the statesmen in
charge of resolving these problems? And should not the blame for
the delay in coming to an agreement taken by the delegates assembled in Geneva be attributed to the lack of an all-embracing view, to
the absence of a plan broad enough to eliminate, to the satisfaction
of all, the contradictions of interests and power?[202]

Laura provided brilliant responses to the interviewer, who wrote, 'This
eminent feminist' explained:

The delegates at the Disarmament Conference should never have
lost track of, e.g. the interdependence of issues related to arms
reduction, namely mutual assistance, ensured security, a safeguards
oversight system. Going hand in hand with such questions, which
correspond to physical realities, an issue that is just as vital, if not
more so since it involves the grounds on which the coming international agreements will be built: moral disarmament. Conceived
not as a negative process but as an educational task requiring effort,
sacrifice, the conciliation that is so difficult to bring into being.

Moral disarmament is the basis for material disarmament. This
definition, which forms the overarching principle of a paper that the
women's organizations committee sent to the Disarmament Conference in the month of March, 1932, cannot be repeated often enough.
The concept appears in all the main passages of that concise and
very clear document and takes on its full significance in this weighty
sentence: 'moral disarmament is not merely the ending of the spirit
of strife but also the beginning of the spirit of understanding'.

This statement shows the educational aspect of moral disarmament. Education is necessarily slow and calls on preserving efforts, as

in a great many cases it involves bringing about a change in concepts passed on from one generation to the next, the first and foremost of which is patriotism.[203]

Patriotism, and especially its element of aggressiveness, is often seen as an impediment to moral disarmament, a cause of hate and dissension, Laura reflected. However, she suggested a higher purpose of patriotism:

> Patriotism is a natural principle, necessary to human beings, in the same way as love for one's family or home. It seems that patriotism must, in fact, lead to sharing, beyond one's borders, the very best elements of a country's soul, those that are unique to it and make it outstanding. Assisting this type of sharing by strengthening it is the very goal of the International Committee on Intellectual Cooperation that the Geneva Committee is doing its best to promote.
>
> In that way, sustainable *entente* [agreement] may be established between the diverse populations of the world, each respecting the material and moral heritage of the others. Such an attitude, far from minimizing the national good, enriches it, through the contributions of foreign cultures.
>
> 'Should this concept become widespread, the reign of peace will be ensured.' . . . How many antagonisms, when subject to such an analysis, simply vanish as they were only based on a misunderstanding?
>
> Is it not so for the great feminist quarrel? Arguments both 'pro' and 'con' have been exchanged and continue to be exchanged in an atmosphere of intransigence. Have sufficient explanations been given of the mutually upheld positions, the rights put forth by the one side and contested by the other?[204]

Laura was reported as seeing feminism as a movement that arose naturally from modern life, which often required women to enter the fray of public life far beyond the traditional confines of the home. The narrow view that women belonged at home, secluded from public life, was no longer feasible.

> What feminism is aspiring towards is in no way that women overwhelm all the professions, without any exception, nor is it absolute egalitarianism. But rather that the ability to choose, in regard to a

profession, be reserved to each woman and that no insurmountable barriers to certain professions be erected for her simply because she is a woman.

Let us admit for a moment that this concept is a reality. Has not science been able to claim a Mme Curie and in aviation a Ruth Elder?

So, no fast and firm partitions, no prohibitions on principle. Let women do what they want and we will realize that of their own accord, women will eliminate from their programs of action whatever they don't feel capable of doing.

What's more men themselves, or at least a large majority of them, have realized that fact. They perceive that women, who are less attached than their companions to everything that forms the outside framework of life, only seek through all their activities to bring more joy, well-being and happiness into the home. The proof of that is that most of the great feminists have been urged into action . . . by their husbands, women such as Mme Brunschvicg, Mme Corbett-Ashby, Mme Malaterre-Sellier, Mme Siegfried. I myself only decided to take part in the feminist movement on the express recommendation of Mr. Dreyfus.[205]

The interview then turned inexorably to the subject of politics, perhaps a natural progression after women had won the right to vote in most western countries. Laura pointed out that politics do not consist only of agitation, electoral struggles and parliamentary battles:

There exists a more profound level of politics that does not have any need for a partisan tent. It consists of carrying out major projects on health, social well-being, mass education, aspects of which are, in the end, the very basis for the sustainable prosperity of a nation. And in that sphere of activity, women have, for a very long time, proven their skills, their organizational gifts.[206]

Laura's next stop was in Damascus and from there she continued to Ankara, Turkey. She noticed how much Turkey had changed since her last visit there in 1908. She met with the Minister of Foreign Affairs and expressed her hope that Turkey would consider creating a committee of intellectual cooperation. She noted: 'The whole country is backing this leader Kamal Pasha [Ataturk], and the Turkish are a well-balanced solid people and the women take this sudden freedom most naturally.'[207] She was in Ankara when Ataturk identified the women who were to become members of the government, and Laura was invited to meet all of them in an 'outstanding general's home'.[208] There were about 25 lady deputies who were doctors and teachers; many of them already had important responsibilities. Laura asked to know their feelings about being included in the government and they said, 'as this was the first session, they would just sit and listen to what the men had to say – they would voice their opinion later.'[209]

The next country on her speaking circuit was Greece and then back home to Paris after a triumphant but grueling few weeks of travel and lectures. Soon after her return, she had to travel to Geneva, where she attended a meeting of the League of Nations on July 7 and an ICIC meeting on July 11, then staying in Brussels for the summer.[210]

Corresponding with May Maxwell, Laura's Spiritual Mother

Laura and May Maxwell continued to correspond, maintaining a regular and loving relationship. They shared news about Bahá'í activities and the general happenings of their lives. In some letters Laura would convey the affection of Natalie to May and vice versa, and May expressed her wish to see Natalie.[211] Laura shared with May the news that friends were passing through Paris during the summer of 1933 and provided details regarding May's request for Bahá'í books in French.[212] May wrote to Laura in March 1934 expressing her joy at receiving from her the good news about the Bahá'í Faith in Paris that was 'so dear to my heart!'[213] Knowing that Laura loved her daughter Mary, May told Laura about a 'very beautiful play' that Mary had written about Persian life and the martyrs at the time of the Báb and mentioning that Mary was giving a course of lectures in Montreal that the friends had described as 'remarkable'. May fondly reminisced about 'the sacred beauty of the early days in Paris and the spiritual lessons learned there'.[214]

Laura hoped to see May and Mary when they came to Europe the end of 1936. She mentioned that if the visit was going to coincide with a gathering of students, everyone would be ecstatic to meet them.[215] When May Maxwell visited Paris, she attended the Union of Bahá'í Students of Europe. Laura was not present but she had donated books to the group.[216] May was in Marseilles in July 1937 and was delighted to have heard from Laura but not surprised, as she had thought of her constantly the day before and dreamed of her in the night. May was going to travel to Lyon to meet with the Bahá'ís for two or three weeks and then go to Paris afterward and she was looking forward to seeing Laura then. May expressed her love for Paris as 'the first and dearest center of my Bahá'í life'.[217]

Unfortunately, Laura was in Geneva when May went to Paris that September. She was happy that their Bahá'í group in Paris had seen May and hoped that the Maxwells might remain longer in France and Europe. She had shared with May in July 1937 how she was in a whirl of international problems in Geneva, but that it was 'deeply moving to see people directing themselves toward the constructive action so clearly laid down in the Cause [the Bahá'í Faith]'. However, Laura also realized that the 'outer word is of no avail unless the heart and spirit is willing'.[218] That December, Laura received affectionate Christmas and New Year greetings from May and her husband, Sutherland Maxwell, from Montreal.[219] Years later, Laura was not sure if she had seen May in Paris in 1938 or 1939.[220]

The great news that Laura had received was that May's daughter Mary had married Shoghi Effendi on March 24, 1937. Laura had seen Mary grow into a beautiful, intelligent and devout young woman, which must have brought Laura immense joy. Immediately after her marriage she was given by Shoghi Effendi the title Amatu'l-Bahá Rúḥíyyih Khánum (*Amatu'l-Bahá* means 'Handmaiden of Glory'). Thereafter Mary Maxwell signed her name Rúḥíyyih Rabbani.

The Convener of the Peace and Arbitration Committee of the ICW

Laura had some concerns about the mission of the League of Nations.[221] She shared her concerns with William Huntington:

> I am leaving this very day for Geneva and agree heartily with you that the League of Nations cannot perform its mission until it is stably supported by the big nations. Up till now one never can tell what attitude these big nations will take. Also, they have other problems to study, most actively, in common, such as: immigration, overproduction, etc.[222]

Despite her concerns, Laura continued her efforts and updated League of Nations officials on a regular basis. And because of her unwavering support of these efforts, she received wonderful news from the French Legion of Honor. By Decree of January 31, 1937, she was promoted to the rank of Officer in the French Legion of Honor because of the report by the Minister of Foreign Affairs about her work as chair of the ICW's Committee on Peace and Arbitration.[223] Laura wrote to Natalie about how some people had congratulated her: 'The Trust has sent me 2 cables, strange I dreaded an accident to you . . . I opened both envelopes before having courage to take out the messages . . . Then I was relieved it was from friends to congratulate me for my position in the Légion d'Honneur . . .'[224] Previously Laura had been made a Chevalier (Knight) of Honor in the French Legion of Honor.[225] She later was appointed a member of the Legion's board and became an officer of the American Society of the French Legion of Honor in New York, where she had established a trust fund for the benefit of the Legion's schools for girls in France.[226]

When the League of Nations Advisory Committee on Teaching and the representatives of the ICIC met in Paris in July 1937, Laura was among the participants as a special expert. Laura was among the few members, in fact one of only three, who never claimed anything for expenses.[227] She had become the president of the Committee on Peace and Arbitration of the ICW and was the liaison between Women's International Organizations and the ICIC. The ICW had formed its first Standing Committee on Peace and Arbitration in 1899, with Lady Aberdeen as its first convener. This committee consisted of the representatives of the IECI, special invited guests, assessors, observers from the Secretariat of the League of Nations and a few members of the ICIC.[228]

Laura was the convener of the International Committee on Peace and Arbitration Conference to be held in Edinburgh in July 1938. A few months before the conference, she updated the committee members by sending them a list of the 24 ICW Councils that had responded. She expressed the hope that after the Edinburgh conference this initial list would be lengthened by submissions from new, active collaborators.[229] At the conference, the Peace and Arbitration Committee met with the Education Committee and they agreed to collaborate on these points: distribution of appropriate publications; education of public opinion in order to make every country realize that it cannot, any more than the others, be sufficient unto itself; and civic education based on a more equitable understanding of other nations; ideas should be given regarding the best method of establishing peace.[230]

After the conference, as the convener, Laura prepared two documents: 'Summary Edinburgh Report' and 'Resolutions Edinburgh'. In her cover letter, she emphasized that the ICW from its foundation and its very nature was bound to the cause of understanding and collaboration between peoples.[231] She recalled that the first permanent commission of the ICW had been the Committee on Peace and Arbitration, which conferred on the ICW a birthright and therefore grave obligations for the eminent women who had directed it, such as Lady Aberdeen, Mrs Mary Wright Sewall and Dame Elizabeth Cadbury.[232] She closed the report to her colleagues with these words: 'The Convener heartily thanked her colleagues both present and absent for their valuable collaboration and voiced the hope that their common task in promoting all the factors of Peace will be steadily pursued.'[233]

In the general report of the conference, Laura listed the resolutions and tendencies: 'responsibility towards the younger generations; disarmament of the mind through mutual understanding; settlement of all conflicts between nations by peaceful negotiations; respect of international laws, which must be improved and strengthened; protection of security by collaboration of nations; restoration of faith in the League of Nations and in international obligations through the action of member governments; development of technical services of the League of Nations; energetic efforts to attain fuller economic justice in the life of nations; cessation of competition in armaments that is the ruin of states; an effective condemnation of war, even under its modern synonyms, primarily that of air raids; and the cooperation of women for the molding of public opinion to the idea of peace and equality not only in view of personal, limited interests but for the development of genuine civilizations.'[234]

Laura recognized that those years were probably leading to armed conflict. 'In the hours of agonized suspense through which the whole world is living now, we are all united in the same spirit and our common efforts are being continued to avoid war and establish peace.' She stated that in Edinburgh it had been decided that 'a common program, wide in scope and based on the following main points, be adopted:

the role of woman in preventing war and establishing peace, economic interdependence of peoples, and the restoration of confidence in institutions working for peace'.[235] The following month, Laura wrote to her collaborators:

> The courageous sacrifice made by a little country [Great Britain, the Munich Agreement] has saved the lives of millions of human beings. Statesmen have assumed their responsibilities. At the eleventh-hour humanity was saved from an irreparable catastrophe: God be praised! May it be confirmed that a new step forward has been taken in the onward march to Peace . . . Among the many actions and speeches of these last few days, let us not forget the words uttered by the Prime Minister of Great Britain: 'Peace is not won by being content merely to remain with folded arms. It is also a positive and active effort.' Let the password of our present endeavor and of our campaign for 1939 be to do all in our power to continue to create a watchful and enlightened public opinion that shall act without delay in favor of the development of Peace, for war is still continuing on several continents.[236]

As soon as the conference in Edinburgh was over and 'after a whirl of work', Laura was to return home to Paris.[237] She had met many interesting people at the conference but had to give up visiting several important people such as Dame Elizabeth Cadbury since at the last minute her dear friend and co-worker in the ICW of Paris, the 84-year-old Mme Avril de Sainte-Croix, had decided to travel with her from Edinburgh to Paris. Laura could not let her return alone to Paris and Mme Avril did not wish to journey with anyone else but Laura!

Laura and the Outbreak of World War II

By December of 1938 Laura was concerned about Nazi Germany aggressively taking over some European countries.[238] A year later, following Germany's invasion of Poland, she expressed her concern about the effect of seeing history form about them in this great war.[239] Shortly before the outbreak of World War II, nearly 30,000 Americans were living in or near Paris.[240] The Americans who did not have vital business in France were advised in 1939 by the American Embassy officials to leave the country. At least 5,000 Americans ignored this advisory and stayed for different reasons. The love affair of Americans with Paris was described by Abigail Adams (wife of John Adams), who famously said, 'No one leaves Paris without a feeling of *tristesse* [sadness].'[241]

As American citizens, Laura and Natalie were included in the warning to leave. They had more reason to leave than most Americans because of their one-quarter Jewish heritage, and because Laura had been married to a man from a Jewish background. Her married name of Dreyfus was not helpful either. So Laura decided to leave for Washington and pleaded with Natalie to join her. But, as usual, Natalie had her own priorities and decided to join Romaine Brooks in Florence, Italy.

Laura had reservations for a train leaving Paris for Le Havre in the early morning of April 12, 1939 and then for a single cabin on the S.S. *Île de France* departing from Le Havre for the United States the same day and returning from New York to Le Havre at the end of June of that year.[242] She rushed her visit to the US when she went to California, then back for a few days in Washington, New York and Alpine, New Jersey, before returning home that year. In a letter written while she was in the US, Laura confirmed that she had traveled to America and would return to Paris. She also wrote to Natalie, 'War and rumors of war echo in the United States.'[243]

Back home in Paris, Laura commented about the effect of seeing history in the making as the great war was unfolding around them.[244] She left Paris at the onset of war with trepidation. She had to say goodbye to everything and everyone, including her housekeeper, Yvonne, who stayed in Paris.[245] Yvonne remained faithful to Laura and stayed with her for the rest of her life.

Safe Arrival and Continuation of Her Humanitarian Services in the United States

It was in June of 1940 that Germans marched into Paris and France fell to its knees before the Nazi invaders. Laura sailed to the United States and safely arrived at the end of June of that year.[246] On the first night of her transatlantic crossing, she listened on the radio to Churchill's call to the United States to arm and come to the rescue of Europe.[247]

Laura stayed at the luxury Hay Adams Hotel and later in a suite in the Wardman Towers in Washington, D.C., and remained in constant touch with ICW boards and members around the world. She wrote to a colleague, 'It was with a heavy heart that I left France, but there is little that I could do there now.'[248] Laura and Mary Dingman, who was the president of the Disarmament Committee before the war, corresponded during those years. In a letter to Laura, Mary addressing her as 'My dear dear Friend', wrote that she was very disappointed that she was not in New York to greet her after her sad and 'doubtless very uncomfortable journey'.[249] She had had some family obligations that forced her to leave New York a week earlier. Mary invited Laura to visit her and her sister while she was at a camp in Pennsylvania.[250]

ICW colleagues were updating their activities and trying to get news of their colleagues in Europe. Laura informed the Executive Secretary of the ICW in Geneva that Mary Dingman was with her sister at the seashore and Laura had to remain in Washington and New York to see many people connected with her usual activities. She continued to send money to the ICW, knowing that funds might be short for the office. In closing her letter, she wrote: 'You and I who believe in spiritual forces can but hope that their hour has come to put a halt to the destructive onward rush of brutal forces.'[251]

Laura was distressed about the situation in Europe. She had worked for many years promoting peace and arbitration, and seeing that the destruction of war was now beginning was hard and unfathomable to her. She wrote about the tragedy that was unfolding: 'I, too, am more grieved than words can express. Causes that are worthwhile cannot be destroyed, but most certainly, periods of trials and tribulations are still ahead of those working and living for a more human and evolved civilization.'[252] She wrote to a colleague in England, 'You must know that not a day passed – I might even say an hour, without my thoughts going toward all of you living in such imminent danger.'[253] She wrote to yet another ICW colleague, 'The suffering of many friends, to say nothing of their countries, is heartbreaking, more especially since we had hoped to settle controversies by other means than aggression and destruction.'[254] To a colleague in New York she wrote, 'Yes, it is all too dreadful even to fully realize, and week by week one understands better the disaster and suffering that has fallen upon countries which were so highly civilized. This war seems to have a character quite its own.'[255]

The war had disrupted not only the work of the ICW but also that of other humanitarian and service organizations. A colleague from the international ICW headquarters in Geneva wrote to Laura: 'In Geneva life is very dull. The Labour Office will soon be closed, all our friends from international organizations have already left or are leaving for other countries.'[256]

Laura stayed as active as possible in the United States during the war years. She visited a photography exhibition in 1940 at the Library of Congress and then wrote a report titled 'In a Library', which included this statement:

> During this cruel period we know that we must remain united in our service to others; then the end of the war will find us strong before the realities of life. The bigger purpose of life appears in art and science, in civics and religion. Cannot these forces, well directed, conquer tyranny and ruin? Civilization may be halted for a period, but it cannot be destroyed.[257]

Towards the end of September, Laura went to New York for two weeks and stayed at the Hotel St Regis.[258] She met with Mary Dingman and they had delightful conversations.[259] Mary hoped to see Laura again at a meeting of the ICW to be held in Washington on November 25 of that year. The following year, Mary, who had become an international lecturer, wrote to Laura from New York to thank her for all her 'kindness and to pay my honest debts'.[260]

Laura truly missed the ICW meetings held in Europe and her annual trips to Geneva she had made prior to the war.[261] One of her colleagues, Dr Renée Girod, the interim President of the ICW from 1940 to 1945 who resided in Geneva, wrote to her that they all missed seeing Laura in January, the month that she would usually arrive. Laura sent monthly letters to Dr Girod at the ICW headquarters and sometimes enclosed news clippings of the activities of the Institute on World Organization, an organization she had co-founded in Washington. She corresponded with friends and ICW members in Hungary, South Rhodesia, the United Kingdom, France and Switzerland. Dorothy M. Arnold, the Executive Secretary of the Peace and Disarmament Committee (previously Women's Disarmament Committee) of the ICW wrote to Laura from Geneva thanking her for a gift and saying that she had never accepted 'so large a sum from anybody before'.[262] It must have been a personal gift. Once World War II erupted, the Geneva office became difficult to maintain and the Committee was disbanded for good. Except for the materials preserved by individual women active in the organization, its documents were lost when it was forced out of Geneva.[263] Laura, who was the ICW representative on the Committee for most of the 1930s, was the person who later collected the surviving records.[264]

During the war, Laura learned that the French hospital that she had co-founded in 1920 was desperate to purchase milk.[265] She donated Swiss Francs to the hospital for whatever it needed, especially the purchase of milk.[266]

An important responsibility during November 1941 was Laura's service as a member of the United States delegation to the second American Conference of the ICIC held in Havana, Cuba.[267]

Co-founding and Co-sponsoring the Institute on World Organization

While in Washington during World War II, Laura co-founded and was one of the sponsors of the Institute on World Organization, which was established in August 1941.[268] She wrote to a friend, 'You have heard from Mrs Puffer Morgan that she and I are actively engaged in preparing for an Institute on World Organization which will treat the balance sheet of the Great Experiment – the League of Nations.'[269] The Balance Sheet of the Institute stated in part:

> This is an Institute unique in character, organized by a small Committee as the first step toward establishing a permanent center in Washington for the study and dissemination of the principles and methods of world organization. It is sponsored by a group of distinguished men and women known for their interest in international affairs, more than twenty of whom are representative of universities throughout the country.[270]

The first conference of the organization was held at the American University in Washington from September 21 to 23, 1941.[271] The Institute's ultimate purpose was 'the discovery of practical solutions for the problem of future world organizations'. Two reasons were stated for the decision to review the League of Nations experience. 'First, we must enter the future through the gateway of the past. Only by knowing what has happened, and why, can we proceed intelligently to constructive work for the future.' The second reason was:

> . . . we have now in the United States, and especially in Washington, an unparalleled opportunity to obtain this knowledge at first hand from men and women who have themselves been a part of the work, who have helped create the machinery and who know it from the inside, some of whom are still officials of the services that now are being carried on from Montreal, from Princeton, and from Washington itself. There will be a chance for the first time in this country to get a complete picture of the first comprehensive experiment in international organization.[272]

Laura may have continued her sponsorship and membership with the Institute until 1961.[273]

Other Endeavors while in the United States

Laura was involved with many projects and activities during the war years. She established a portraiture prize in her mother's name for the annual exhibition of the Society of Washington Artists and arranged several retrospectives of her mother's work. She had organized an exhibition of her mother's artwork in 1933 but this was the first of what would be annual exhibitions of Alice's work. It was held in Neighborhood House in 1941 and was attended by First Lady Eleanor Roosevelt, who had visited Studio House in 1913 when her husband was the Assistant Secretary of the Navy.[274] The opening of the exhibition was reported in the newspapers, including *The Evening Star*.[275]

Laura had plans to go to South America for the work of the ICW in 1942 but had to postpone them. She wrote to a friend, 'Unfortunately I have been forced to postpone my trip to South America on account of the uncertainty of transportation, but I am very interested in life in Washington at the time where so much is being studied in connection with the great questions of the moment.'[276] She never did manage to travel to South America.

In October 1943 Laura went to New York to take part in an important meeting of '*The New York Times* Forum of the 27th'.[277] Between the years 1942 and 1945 she served as an advisory chairman and director of training for the Information Service of the War Hospitality Committee in Washington, which provided recreational activities for servicemen on leave. She was a board member of the American Society for the French Legion of Honor in New York and trustee and president of the James Monroe Memorial Foundation in Fredericksburg, Virginia. In 1946 she was a representative on the Coordinating Committee for Better Race Understanding of the National Council of Women of the United States.[278] She also served on several other boards.

Laura was able to attend several of the events and celebrations held at the Barney Neighborhood House during her six-year stay in the United States.[279] This was the charity that her mother had started to support in 1901 and for which she later bought a house which she provided rent-free for the use of the charity; the name of the charity had been changed in 1933. The House had long been a center of community life and Laura became an honorary board member during the war years.

The executive director of the Barney Neighborhood House described its wartime contributions. 'Our all-important war time job, which we also consider our most vital peacetime one, is our concentration on making better citizens for the immediate present.' The House was a major center of civic activity in urban Washington during the war: in just one year between 75,000 and 80,000 people participated in its various activities.[280] News of events and celebrations at the House were always covered by area newspapers. An article in *The Washington Post* stated: 'In the crowd for tea was the woman whose mother, Mrs Alice Pike Barney, made the home possible. Mrs Laura Dreyfus-Barney with her mother gave the settlement its early financial start; helped shape its policies.'[281]

The Star reported on the celebration of the forty-second annual spring festival of the House. Laura later hosted a luncheon, entertaining members of the Board of Directors of the Barney Neighborhood House at the Shoreham Hotel. After the luncheon, the members discussed plans for one of the May Festivals that was to be held that weekend in the grounds of the House.[282] One newspaper published Laura's picture, along with an article about the celebration titled 'Milestone for Neigh-borhood House', reporting that at 48 years old, Neighborhood House was celebrating its birthday at 470 N. Street SW.[283] The caption named the people in the picture including Laura but the article incorrectly stated that Natalie had given the settlement house to the community. Others in the picture were Board members and a volunteer who had worked at Neighborhood House for 28 years![284] The House was still operating in 2018.

Contact with Shoghi Effendi and His Wife during World War II

Before May Maxwell's departure for the United States in 1939, Laura expressed her happiness to her that Shoghi Effendi and Rúḥíyyih Khánum had returned to Palestine from a trip.[285] Soon afterwards, in March 1940, May passed away in Argentina. May was Laura's spiritual mother and they had continued their cordial and respectful relationship. Laura had visited the Maxwells in Canada and had visited with them several times in Paris and the United States. The Maxwells and Laura had had a close relationship and were in regular touch with each other. May's death must have been a great loss for Laura. However, she had developed a loving and mutual connection with May's daughter, Mary, Rúḥíyyih Khánum.

Soon after the war broke out, Shoghi Effendi and Rúḥíyyih Khánum worried that did not know where Laura was.[286] In a letter addressed to 'Dearest Laura' dated April 26, 1941, Rúḥíyyih Khánum expressed her anxiety about Laura's whereabouts earlier that year, adding, 'You will always be an added bond with mother because you were so extremely dear to her and your name was so often on her lips. She told me such lovely stories of those early days in Paris and of you, your sister and Mr Dreyfus. How foolish I was not to write them down at that time.'[287] She said that the Guardian would pray for the protection and welfare of her sister.[288] They were happy and relieved when they found out that Laura had left for the United States almost a year earlier.[289]

Rúḥíyyih Khánum became Shoghi Effendi's principal secretary in 1941 and this enabled more regular exchanges between them Laura. Rúḥíyyih Khánum would write on behalf of both of them and then Shoghi Effendi would add a postscript. Laura also provided them regular updates of her activities in America. Shoghi Effendi was happy that she was aiding the Bahá'í work and helping the American friends. He knew that she had so much to give, not only to the seeking and intelligent people 'who are becoming more and more Bahá'ís in their thinking but also to the believers themselves'.[290] He deeply valued her assistance with the production of French Bahá'í publications and also her support of the Bahá'í Bureau in Geneva, for which he had also expressed his appreciation in the past.[291]

In the early years of the war Laura had shared her concern about the functioning of the Bahá'í Bureau with the National Spiritual Assembly of the United States and Canada. She feared that there would be an interruption of the transfer of funds between the two continents and that the Bureau would not be able to receive money from North America. In the spring of 1941 she instructed her Swiss bank to transfer funds for the Bureau's rent until the National Assembly could figure out the best way to help the Bureau.[292] She continued her support of this office during the war years.

Shoghi Effendi prayed for Hippolyte's sister, who had passed away, and also for the protection of Laura's sister, as Laura's letters reflected her concern for Natalie, who was in Italy.[293]

On one occasion Shoghi Effendi wrote: 'It is, indeed, encouraging to see so many progressive movements with platforms that incorporate our teachings!' He was 'glad to hear' that Laura was as 'strong and active as ever'.[294] He asked Laura to attend the celebration of the centenary of the birth of the Bahá'í Faith that was to be held at the Bahá'í House of Worship in Wilmette, Illinois, from May 19 to 25, 1944, which she did.[295] A brilliant speaker, she gave a moving address at this event:[296]

> Two months ago I was hesitating whether or not to attend the Convention. I felt this to be a moment of rejoicing, and I so attuned to the war-torn world, because I have been so much in Europe and the Far East, that I would bring a note of sadness which should not appear here. But Shoghi Effendi wrote me that he wished me to come to this Centenary gathering. So here I am, in full appreciation of what has been done. I felt I should pay tribute here to the strength that is growing from the Americas. Though not an accredited delegate, I feel I can speak for France and Switzerland and the other countries, and greet you, and say they are expecting much from this part of the world.[297]

The Guardian and Rúḥíyyih Khánum were happy that Laura had been present at 'the glorious Centenary Convention'.[298]

Rúḥíyyih Khánum hoped that Laura had news of her sister and the Paris Bahá'ís. Shoghi Effendi asked her not to confine her work to France and advised that she 'should not feel that your work is nearing an end'.[299]

The three continued their close correspondence until the war was over. Laura informed them that she might return to Paris in the spring of 1946. At the end of the summer of 1946, Rúḥíyyih Khánum addressed her as 'Laura Khánum' and wrote that Laura's suggestions for the Geneva office were the same as Shoghi Effendi's and that he had conveyed them to the National Spiritual Assembly of the United States and Canada. They were glad that Laura was returning to France and would lend a hand to the Bahá'ís of Paris, who had held the fort during the war years. Shoghi Effendi was happy to hear that Laura's sister had gone through the war unscathed and that the two sisters would soon be reunited.[300] Rúḥíyyih Khánum sent her a telegram from Basel, Switzerland, and asked her to call her back the next day.[301] She wanted to hear Laura's voice after her return to Paris.

Contact with the Bahá'ís of Paris and Geneva during the War

Laura had maintained as close a correspondence with the European Bahá'ís as was possible during the war years. She had especially kept in touch with the Bahá'ís of Paris, spending long hours writing letters and giving them advice concerning their affairs and decisions. They also gave her regular updates about the friends and their activities in the city.

Most of the Bahá'ís in Paris had been expatriates and had moved away before or soon after France collapsed to the Nazis. A few small meetings continued to be held for the Bahá'ís who were left, thanks to Edith Sanderson, who had remained.[302] Another Bahá'í who had stayed in Paris was a Miss Tabrizi, who helped Edith Sanderson with Bahá'í affairs. Laura had known her as a young girl in Haifa where she had spent her childhood and in about 1923 had sponsored her when she wanted to study nursing in France. Miss Tabrizi became an excellent nurse and worked for several years in that profession.[303] Some years earlier, Laura trusted Miss Tabrizi to take some important Bahá'í documents that were in her possession to the Holy Land.[304]

The scarcity of French-language Bahá'í books during the war years was of concern to Laura, who felt that the propagation of the faith would be hampered in francophone countries because of this lack. The situation for publishers in wartime France had made it impossible to find copies of certain French-language books. Laura sent letters to various individuals for assistance and searched for copies of Bahá'í books in French. She finally came up with a list of people who had appropriate copies of these books and discussed this matter in several letters with the National Assembly of the United States and Canada in 1942.[305] She also gave suggestions about matters that were of concern to the French community, such as the printing expenses for the French edition of *Bahá'u'lláh and the New Era* by J. E. Esslemont. She also offered her funds at the Swiss bank to be used to compensate individuals who were helping with the Bahá'í work, such as Miss Tabrizi. She suggested to the Local Assembly of Paris to keep using Miss Tabrizi for Bahá'í work and she would provide her with an income.[306]

While in the United States, Laura sympathized deeply with those Bahá'ís who had to stay in Paris during the war and then chose to remain during the post-war years. Even though Paris had been liberated from the Germans in August 1944, she was still concerned about their welfare. As a result, in 1946 she prepared a list of the Bahá'ís who had remained to handle the affairs of the community and tried to find ways to help those who needed support. The list had details of every person's services to the Bahá'í community and their needs and she sent the list together with her recommendations to the Local Assembly of Paris.[307] She was aware of their sacrificial efforts and asked the Local Assembly, 'Will you give each of the friends my cordial greetings and to you the assurance of my appreciation for what you continue to do for our Paris group of pioneers in world civilization.'[308] Yet in another letter to the chairman of the Local Assembly, she expressed her concern for the Bahá'ís' hard work and difficult times: 'Winter must be hard in France and I feel deeply for you all so tried there long years and still facing so many financial and material difficulties!'[309]

Return to Europe after World War II

Laura returned to Paris in March 1946 and this was reported by a newspaper in Washington, which stated that Mme Dreyfus-Barney, who had lived most of her life in France, had bought a one-way ticket and was returning soon to her beloved Paris. 'Mme Dreyfus-Barney is looking forward to a reunion with her sister, Natalie Barney, whose artistic gifts lie in the field of poetry.'[310]

The Paris that Laura returned to had been devastated by the war.

Parisians were exhausted from the occupation and now were coping with shortages of food, adequate housing and other necessities of life. This once vibrant city, the city of light, had been brought to its knees and the grayness of a slow recovery. It had been pillaged by the Nazis and Laura's home had not escaped the thefts.[311] Being one-fourth Jewish, having the last name Dreyfus, which was a common Jewish name from Alsace, and having an apartment in a wealthy part of the city probably targeted Laura for Nazi searches and thefts. She had simply locked her apartment and left and the Nazis had come in and taken whatever they could.[312]

Nazi agents did a clean sweep of almost all Laura's books, records and files of the ICW; documents of other international organizations that she was active with and her belongings were stolen. The most significant of her losses, though, were invaluable only to herself – the handwritten memoirs and notes from her early trips to the Holy Land.[313] She had written many priceless notes during her several visits in the Holy Land in the early 20th century, recounting her personal witness to early Bahá'í history. Laura's notes about her time spent near and with 'Abdu'l-Bahá and His family were of inestimable value. She had intended to compile them and send them to Shoghi Effendi before publication and distribution but that had not proved possible.[314] They also included notes of the visits to Haifa and her visit to Iran and Russia.[315]

Years later, a Bahá'í friend found in a Parisian book stall a copy of an important Bahá'í book, the *Kitáb-i-Íqán* (*The Book of Certitude*, revealed by Bahá'u'lláh in 1862 in Baghdad), autographed by Shoghi Effendi for Laura. Shoghi Effendi had translated this work into English. Its finder was dismayed that Laura would give away such a valuable book to be sold.[316] But Laura would never have parted with such a valued gift. It was asked why Laura, who throughout her life saved all the letters she received, copies of all the letters she sent, and even envelopes and invitations, would give away a significant book signed by someone so dear to her? She had not. This signed copy of the *Kitáb-i-Íqán* was undoubtedly one the books stolen from her home which had somehow found its way to a used-book stall. A Bahá'í book would have been of little value to Nazi agents except for a small sum in the used book market.

Most unfortunately, few of Laura's other notes, books, documents or belongings were recovered, despite searches by the present author. The state archives in Berlin were researched revealing that, in most instances, confiscated Bahá'í documents had been destroyed on the spot.[317] Holocaust Museums in Washington, D.C. and Los Angeles, as well as the German Embassy in Washington, D.C. were contacted with no success.[318] It is very unlikely that her notes would have been saved and archived since they had no material value. However, in 2017, some items that Laura had owned were located by the author in an archive in Munich. These included some of her rare French-language books and two valuable Persian-language books written by the renowned Iranian poet Sa'dí (1208–92) of Shiraz – a 1932 edition of *Gulistán* (The Flower Garden) written in 1258, and *Bustán* (The Orchard). Both were rare poetry books, accounts of the poet's travels, and his analysis of human psychology, with leather covers and illuminated pages. Also included in this recovery was a pair of pearl and gold earrings.[319]

Back in the United States

After a short stay in Paris, and catching up with her personal affairs, Bahá'í work and some meetings, Laura returned to the United States. She had to stay longer than planned to attend an important conference of the ICW that was held in Philadelphia from September 3 to 13, 1947.[320] The ICW became one of the first non-governmental organizations to obtain consultative status with the new United Nations (UN) and some of its agencies. The conference was a great success, even though the war had caused tremendous disorganization in the American Council. This Council had met the previous year in Philadelphia to refocus its efforts to recover its former unity.

Laura was also active with the transition from the League of Nations to the early beginnings of the UN in New York. After World War II, the United Nations was established on October 24, 1945. The League of Nations had lasted for 26 years, being formally disbanded on April 19, 1946, its powers and functions having been transferred to the UN.[321] In a letter to the chairman of the Local Spiritual Assembly of Paris, she wrote: 'I have been busy spending much of my time with matters of the United Nations a step forward in the right direction . . . It is surprising to witness the great trend throughout the world and how now the Press and Statesmen express Bahai ideas.'[322]

While in the United States, Laura stayed in touch with Edna True (1888–1988), whom she had known for some years. Edna was an

American Bahá'í who was elected to the National Spiritual Assembly of the United States and Canada in 1946 and to the newly formed NSA of the United States in 1948, serving a total of 22 years. She also served as the chairperson of the European Teaching Committee for the entire duration of its existence (1946–64). Laura reminisced about the times they had spent together. As she wrote to Edna, 'I always recall Yuletide in Chicago some years ago when you drove me out for a family dinner; you and your dear ones came often to my thoughts through cherished memories.'[323] In 1949, three decades after visiting the Bahá'í Temple in Wilmette with her mother, Laura reminisced with Edna True about it: 'In looking over some very old papers, I came across the enclosed – you must have it; still you may not remember it. How well I recall the day Mother and I and a few Bahá'ís went to see the grounds, it sounds so far away from everything . . .'[324]

Laura shared with Edna that she had been able to help a mutual Bahá'í friend, Helen Elsie Austin (1908–2004), to serve on the 'delegation of the International Council [of] Women at the United Nations Conference of International Voluntary Organizations to be held at Lake Success [New York] in February'.[325] Elsie was an African-American attorney, a United States foreign service officer, and at different times in her life a member of the National Assemblies of the United States and of North West Africa.

Laura regretted that she was not able to go to Chicago before sailing back to Europe early in April 1948. She wrote that it would have been 'a joy to see old Bahá'í friends and again meditate in the Temple that I have seen rise up from a country meadow!'[326]

Laura's Bahá'í Activities after the War

Back home in Paris, Laura continued to fulfill her responsibilities. She resumed an active Bahá'í life by guiding the Bahá'ís and meeting with the prominent people of the Bahá'í Faith. She had plans to go to Zurich and then attend meetings in Geneva and to meet the Bahá'í friends who had gathered there. She learned that the Bahá'í European Teaching Committee (ETC) had organized its first European teaching conference to be held in Geneva in May. She hoped that Edith Sanderson would attend the conference, as it would be a nice change for her after living in Paris during the war years.[327]

The Europe-wide teaching conference had been called by Leroy Ioas, who was one of the four members to the ETC. He and Edna True were active participants, joined by long-term, notable Bahá'ís such as Laura as well as newer Bahá'ís, thus bringing the old and new European Bahá'í communities together. This conference presented an opportunity for intense consultation and friendship-building among the pioneers living in Europe and the other European Bahá'ís. (The term 'pioneers' is used by Bahá'ís for persons who have left their native countries and relocated to another to teach the Faith and assist with its activities.) Ninety-two Bahá'ís from 19 countries attended, and Laura attended as an invited guest. The conference took place from May 22 to 26, 1948 in Geneva. The conference was 'hailed by the Guardian as a landmark in the European campaign'.[328]

As the Chairperson of the ETC, Edna True wrote to Laura afterwards that it had been a 'definite drawing together of the different Continental and British Bahá'í Communities since the Geneva [ETC] conference . . . Although we expressed our appreciation to you personally, the European Teaching Committee wishes to tell you again how very deeply we appreciate all the assistance you gave us during the sessions of the Geneva Conference. Your contribution was a very rich and unique one and we can never adequately express our thanks.'[329]

Edna True was also thankful to Laura for her generous financial contribution for the improvement of the Bahá'í international library at the Bahá'í Bureau and for devoting her time to addressing and resolving the Bureau's various problems.[330] During her visits to Geneva, Laura often went to the Bureau. The Bureau had remained active after the war, long after the League of Nations had ceased to function, and had started to work with the UN in 1945. It was registered as a non-governmental agency three years later. In time the Bureau had a new office in the Quai Wilson area, which Laura visited in 1948, giving some suggestions to its personnel.[331] She agreed to continue contributing to the upgrade of the Bureau. She also visited Brussels and Luxembourg and managed to give talks for the Bahá'í youth in those countries whenever she could.[332]

Laura had continued to correspond with Rúḥíyyih Khánum. Rúḥíyyih Khánum's father, Sutherland Maxwell, had visited Paris in 1948, and she was happy that Laura had helped him with his stay. She wrote, 'You were so very dear to my mother and are indeed close and dear to Shoghi Effendi and me.'[333] Shoghi Effendi continued to add his remarks to Rúḥíyyih Khánum's letters in postscripts, sending her encouraging and supporting words. He enthusiastically approved of her humanitarian work. One letter written by Rúḥíyyih Khánum on his behalf stated, 'There is no doubt believers whose inclinations are along those lines would do well to show a cooperative interest in many of the non-political aspects of . . . work, but such contacts should always be considered a means of bringing our Baháʼí teachings to the attention of progressive-minded people.' And the Guardian himself added, 'May the Almighty bless your efforts, remove all obstacles from your path, aid you to contribute effectively to the promotion of this Faith and the consolation of its institutions.' He also suggested that Laura find a capable translator to translate *Gleanings from the Writings of Baháʼuʼlláh* into French, leaving this matter to her discretion. He felt that Baháʼí literature was much needed in France.[334]

When home in postwar Paris, Laura hosted many visitors. One was Ugo Giachery (1896–1989), a prominent Italian Baháʼí who translated many Baháʼí works into Italian. Giachery thanked Laura for her gracious hospitality and hours of conversation at her home.[335] They remained close friends until the end of her life. He was appointed a Hand of the Cause of God by Shoghi Effendi in 1951.[336]

The second ETC conference, which Laura attended, was held in Brussels, Belgium, in August 1949. After the conference, the ETC received Laura's notes and comments about the gathering. Its members appreciated her contributions and wrote to her that they 'went over very carefully your helpful constructive comments and recommendations and wish to express their appreciation and gratitude for your report and remarks'.[337] She also sent some suggestions about the ETC conference to Shoghi Effendi. Rúḥíyyih Khánum replied on his behalf that the friends had been very happy to see Laura and Mason Remey in Brussels and noted her active participation in the conference. She further noted:

> He [Shoghi Effendi] was pleased to learn through Mrs Haney that you put some of your papers in her hands to go over. Your long association with our beloved Faith must have brought much material of historic value into your hands and it is very important that it should be preserved for the Cause.[338]

After the passing of ʻAbduʼl-Bahá, and as the Baháʼí Faith was expanding, it seems that Laura was consulted by different Bahá'í individuals and institutions, who asked for her advice. She was in constant communication with the National Assemblies of the United States, Canada and France, and with the ETC.[339] Her experiences, her well-trained mind and her faith were invaluable assets, and she was revered and respected by Bahá'ís for having spent long periods of time close to the Master and for compiling an important book. One Bahá'í who knew her during those postwar years in Paris was Hassan Ali-Kamran from Belgium. He was a long-time member of the National Assembly of Belgium, and he and his family provided the initial funding and then for years the operating budget for the Anis Zunuzi Bahá'í School near Port-au-Prince, Haiti. He reminisced:

> Mme Barney was compassionate and very ladylike. While being serious, she maintained her characteristic kindness. She had two different sides to her personality or character; she was serious and she was kind. Humanity will never understand or appreciate her true importance. She was very much influenced by living close to 'Abdu'l-Bahá, who had recommended to the Greatest Holy Leaf (His sister) to be kind to Laura Barney. At Bahá'í Feasts, she would ask for the prayers to be chanted in Persian. She was stubborn. Whatever 'Abdu'l-Bahá had said was the ultimate verdict for her. I believe she was inspired to ask the questions for *Some Answered Questions*.[340]

Another person who had met her in the postwar years was Professor Amin Banani, an Iranian American Bahá'í who achieved scholastic distinction in Iranian and Islamic studies. He stated in an interview that 'one cannot doubt her faith and closeness to 'Abdu'l-Bahá. She would have sacrificed everything to please Him.'[341]

Staying in Touch with Natalie

At the onset of the war, the sisters would not have been safe in German-occupied Paris owing to their one-quarter Jewish heritage. Laura heeded the warnings of the United States Embassy and left, but Natalie had a different idea. Up to the last minute before her departure, Laura pleaded with Natalie to accompany her to the United States. Instead, Natalie went to Florence, Italy, to be with Romaine Brooks. Natalie hoped to return to Paris soon but in June 1940 Italy declared war on France. Foreigners in Italy were advised to return to their native countries, but it had become impossible to obtain travel permits. So Natalie and Romaine were forced to stay in Italy.

Laura was concerned and worried about Natalie. Even though she rarely mentioned anything about her personal life in her correspondence with the ICW board and its members, in a few letters she showed her concern for her sister. Laura must have been very lonely despite her active life handling numerous responsibilities and maintaining correspondence with friends and professional contacts. Throughout the war, Laura urged her sister in vain to leave Florence for America.

Borders were finally opened and travel restrictions slowly eased soon after the war in Europe ended in May 1945. When Japan was defeated and the war was truly over, Laura suggested to Natalie ways to travel to the United States. A few months later, she suggested that Natalie contact the American consulate in Florence to see if she could get a visa for travel via France to the United States.[342] Laura had talked to several friends who had contact with that consulate but she could not help her much.

Laura had not seen, and perhaps not even talked with, her sister in several years. When she returned to Paris after the war, she was finally able to talk with Natalie on the phone in early May 1946. Laura subsequently wrote to Natalie: 'Your telephone call gave me a thrill as it seemed to bring you nearer.' She updated Natalie about their mutual friends in Paris, Natalie's maid Berthe [Cleyrergue]'s well-being, and how her rented home at rue Jacob had deteriorated. Laura told her of life in Paris after the war and how she was learning to use the buses and the metro. 'When most people seem less well off,' she wrote, 'one does not think of complaining. Paris itself is beautiful & the slower tempo is becoming.'[343]

The good news for Laura was that she was finally reunited with her sister in Paris on May 24, 1946, after a six-year separation. Laura's friends and colleagues were happy that the two of them were reunited. Shoghi Effendi was also happy to learn that Laura and her sister were together after so many years.[344] Natalie stayed at her sister's home at 74 rue Raynouard since her own home at rue Jacob was in 'abysmal condition'.[345]

In 1947 Laura was trying to find a way for Natalie to join her in the United States.[346] Having seen each other only briefly in Paris after six years of separation, Laura missed her sister. Finally Natalie and Romaine came to the United States in the fall of that year, and Laura was with them in Washington, D.C. Staying at Studio House, the sisters had to decide what to do with that property and their mother's paintings. They had to make a final disposition of their mother's artwork, most of which had remained in storage over the years, although a few pieces had been on loan to museums and government organizations.

Laura returned to Europe in 1947 but she stayed in touch with Natalie, who had remained in the United States. She planned to go to Arles and then to Avignon after her meetings.[347]

Serious Laura sometimes shared her lighter moments with Natalie in her letters. When back in Paris, she wrote, 'I wish that my "official week" had been some days ago; but alas I still have a full week of obligations, it is a real temptation to "play hokey" [sic] . . .'[348] While traveling at sea, she had seen some people whom she knew and 'some agreeable men at my table in dining room'.[349]

Laura had been a widow for more than 20 years when in 1949 she expressed her feelings about Hippolyte to her sister: 'How well I recall the first days of Hippolyte's passing away, you used to come & we would take little walks near la Cascade, also I went to concerts with Mountfort Mills of Wagnerian music which Hippolyte cared for, and looked over opened books he cared to read or study. I have always felt in absence the presence of dearest ones, often more vividly than in the routine of daily life.'[350]

Establishing a Memorial Fund for Alice Pike Barney at the Smithsonian Institution

Finally, and at long last, Laura and Natalie made up their minds and decided what to do with their mother's paintings. They agreed to donate them to the Smithsonian Institution. Perhaps the suggestion and idea for this came from Laura. It was through her efforts, her connections and many discussions and meetings that this was made possible. It was also during her six-year stay in Washington that she had become more interested in the activities of the various research and educational endeavors of the Smithsonian, which had been founded in 1846 under terms of the will of James Smithson of London. Smithson had bequeathed his fortune for the purpose of creating 'an establishment for the increase and diffusion of knowledge among men'.[351] She had become particularly interested in the National Collection of Fine Arts (renamed the National Museum of American Art in 1980 and the Smithsonian American Art Museum in 2000).

Laura informed Dr Alexander Westmore, Secretary of the Smithsonian, of her mother's paintings that were being donated by her sister and herself. She wrote that there were 224 paintings and pastels and about 54 paintings by other artists that were on loan to a number of educational and philanthropic institutions. The collection also included many sculptures and objets d'art. They included works by Edwin Scott, the American painter living in Paris with whom Alice had exhibited several times. Laura also expressed her desire 'to continue the usefulness of these in decorating public buildings and those semi-private ones dedicated to the use of the public, and to further encourage appreciation of creative graphic expression in the United States'.[352] In order to achieve this, she wrote, 'I wish to give this collection to the Smithsonian Institution together with an initial sum of Fifteen Thousand Dollars to establish the Alice Pike Barney Memorial Fund for the use of the National Collection of Fine Arts [today's Smithsonian American Art Museum] for maintaining and increasing such a loan collection and for the encouragement of American artistic endeavor.' She planned to increase this amount to 30,000 dollars every year for several years to memorialize her mother's artistic attainments and civic interests.[353] Arrangements would be made to continue this bequest after her death. Over the ensuring two decades the works of art that had been on loan to federal buildings and cultural centers at the time of the initial gifts were subsequently donated to the Smithsonian, including many of Alice's paintings and pastels.

The Alice Pike Barney Memorial Collection established by Laura was the 'nucleus of a loan collection for the embellishment of Federal buildings, museums, libraries, colleges, and other educational institutions in the United States'.[354] At the beginning about 130 of Alice's paintings and drawings were donated to the National Collection of Fine Arts and they were accepted as the basis of a Smithsonian lending service. The Fund was set up in 1951 to 'encourage the appreciation and creation of art, and to maintain the loan collection and to organize and circulate traveling arts exhibitions in the United States'.[355]

Laura later wrote to Natalie about her mother and her paintings, and the way she used to paint. Her 'Little One' painted for her own pleasure until she had to use glasses. Alice later gave up oils and painted only pastels occasionally. She would rent a studio off and on in Paris or New York and would go to classes given by Jean-Jacques Henner and Carlos Duran, or she would give a class herself in Normandy or Brittany. She gave away her paintings at will and kept those that she liked at Studio House.[356] Her mother liked to change painting styles and follow those of James McNeill Whistler or Claudio Castelucho (a Spanish-born painter living in France). Even though it rather bored Alice to have exhibitions, she had two exhibitions in London, three in France, one in Los Angeles and a number of them in New York and Washington. After her death, her paintings were shown through the agencies of the Smithsonian. Laura wrote to her sister that 'we have done nothing but carry out what she did herself; but in a more permanent way'.[357]

It seems that Laura had been in touch with Mr Henri Bonnet, the French Ambassador to the United States. She received a letter from him in which he thanked her for her gift of linen: 'I have been aware for a long time of all you do for Franco-American friendship in every field. My compatriots cannot help being touched by this new proof of your delicate concern and thoughtfulness.'[358]

Laura's Activities while in Europe

Back in Europe, Laura had remained active while the League of Nations was still in existence and then continued her work under the auspices of the UN.[359] She attended the Conference of Non-Governmental Organizations convened by the UN and held in Geneva from May 12 to 23, 1948. She was always happy to see her old friends and colleagues in Paris after the few years of separation. She wrote to her sister that year, 'I am interested in my work and meeting old colleagues.'[360] She was appointed to two of the UN's subcommittees.[361] The UN had inherited several agencies and organizations founded by the League of Nations.

Laura explained her responsibilities in those years to a Bahá'í colleague: 'My non-Bahá'í occupation – if one can call it so – was to attend to the Economic and Social Council of the UN, also the Interim Committee of Non-Governmental Organizations which met in Geneva the end of July and early August, as I am on the board. I will be connected to the development of this promising work for months to come.'[362] In those years, she was a senior liaison officer of the ICW with the United Nations and its specialized agencies – the United Nations Educational, Scientific and Cultural Organization (UNESCO), the Food and Agriculture Organization (FAO), and the United Nations Economic and Social Council (ECOSOC) – and was sometimes chairman of study groups and organizations of other international associations working for peace and international understanding.

The bulk of her time in those years was devoted to her work with the ICW. A noted Bahá'í who had met Laura many times accepted assignments to represent the Bahá'í community in its status as a non-governmental organization at UN conferences starting in the late 1940s. While attending one of these meetings, he wrote, 'Laura Barney happened to be there as the representative of an international women's organization. We had a friendly meeting.'[363] Another prominent Bahá'í who met Laura in Geneva in those years was Shapour Rassekh, who was then a student but would become an eminent scholar:

> When Mrs Dreyfus Barney came to Geneva in those years, I knew that this is the same person who had asked philosophical questions from 'Abdu'l-Bahá and had published *Some Answered Questions*. We were in the presence of a historic heroine of our faith but did not permit ourselves to talk to her about her services. She would attend the Nineteen Day Feasts [Bahá'í meetings of worship, community consultation and fellowship] in Geneva whenever she could and sometimes would attend with Miss Sanderson, who was one of the early Bahá'ís in Paris. Mrs Dreyfus was very distinguished, cordial and elegant and perhaps a little tall compared to Miss Sanderson.[364]

In September 1952 Laura attended an executive meeting of the ICW that was held at Reading University in England. The National Spiritual Assembly of the British Isles looked forward to her trip and prepared the following draft of a press release for this event:

> Madame L. Dreyfus-Barney . . . has just attended the executive meeting of the International Council of Women at Reading University in her capacity as liaison officer for the UN. While Madame L. Dreyfus-Barney is in England she hopes to attend the Commemoration of the Martyrdom of the famous scholar and poetess Tahirih

who perished in Persia in 1852, a forerunner of the emancipation of women, and a reformer in her own right, known to Lord Curzon and other noted historians of that period, a woman who spoke of a new freedom for women, a freedom that is only now, 100 years later, becoming a possibility. Madame L. Dreyfus-Barney, a believer in social and spiritual progress, salutes the woman of Persia who died 100 years ago for these beliefs.[365]

Visits to the United States

Laura continued her regular visits to the United States and remained active during those stays. As a result of being appointed to two subcommittees of the UN in 1948, she had to travel to New York often.[366] Mr Huntington was still available to assist her with her affairs on these visits.

It was at a dinner party during one of these trips in 1952 that Laura met John Alexander Pope, the new Director of the Freer Gallery of Art at the Smithsonian Institution. She showed him copies of paintings and drawings of Romaine Brooks that she had received earlier. He seemed to appreciate them and was quite fascinated by her drawings.[367] Another guest was the head of the Rare Book Section of the Library of Congress, who had agreed to give Laura a list of places for distribution of Romaine's books of drawings.[368] Laura also asked the Smithsonian to check on her mother's and Edwin Scott's paintings. Three of her mother's paintings were at that time on loan from the SI and graced the walls of three judges' homes.[369]

Responsibilities connected with her mother's estate never ended. Laura was still managing the house she and Natalie had inherited, Studio House, which had not yet been rented. She was still going through her mother's jewelry and belongings, and she shipped a tapestry for Natalie to France.[370]

While in the United States, Laura was kept informed of the activities of the Bahá'í community of France and the Local Assembly of Paris through her correspondence with Bahá'ís.[371] She also managed to go to the House of Worship situated in Wilmette, a northern suburb of Chicago, for the Jubilee Celebration and the All-American Intercontinental Bahá'í Teaching Conference, staying for over a week. The construction and the landscaping of the House of Worship had finally been completed. She did tell Natalie about her trip to Chicago but not that it was for a Bahá'í event.[372]

Laura managed to see her cousin Ellen, her closest relative after Natalie, almost every time she visited the United States, stopping in New Jersey either coming or going to New York. She spent the Easter of 1953 and then again in 1955 at Alpine, New Jersey, with Ellen in her new house.[373] Ellen helped her whenever she could and was very supportive of her. Laura also stayed in touch with other relatives, who by this time were mostly cousins such as James Perrine Barney, who lived in Princeton, New Jersey.[374] Laura had suggested to Natalie that they help Perrine's son with a financial gift for his new home and they subsequently made a gift of one thousand dollars to him.[375] Their cousin Perrine was touched by this gift and he thanked Laura and Natalie for being so wonderful.[376]

Supporting Joséphine, Wife of Edwin Scott

Laura had known Edwin and Joséphine Scott for many years in Paris. Edwin had had a studio outside of Paris that 'Abdu'l-Bahá visited during His stay in 1911. Laura had introduced Edwin to Shoghi Effendi while he was in Paris. Bi-monthly Bahá'í meetings were held at the Scotts' home, which Joséphine continued hosting after Edwin passed away in 1929.[377] In 1947 Laura gave Joséphine the good news that a museum was interested in accepting two of the beautiful paintings by her husband and would be in touch with her. A few years later, she also informed Joséphine that she had talked with Smithsonian personnel about Edwin's paintings.[378]

When Laura first heard in February 1947 that Joséphine was not well, she wrote to the Local Assembly of Paris asking that Joséphine's case be discussed, as her difficult situation had evidently been known for a while.[379] Declining health forced her to move into a nursing home the following year. Laura also became aware of Joséphine's financial difficulties and contributed towards her living expenses and paying part of the cost of the nursing home where she lived. Laura had found this nursing home in a convent in Versailles and every year paid for part of its charges. She decided in 1951 to maintain Mrs Scott the rest of her life.[380] The board of the American Aid Society of Paris authorized payment for the balance of her expenses.

It seems that Laura was a member of the American Aid Society of

Paris, since she wrote that she would miss attending its annual meeting to be held on February 16, 1951.[381] The President of the Society was grateful to Laura for financially assisting Mrs Scott. After receiving one of the payments for Mrs Scott, the President wrote, 'It is indeed generous of you to assume this responsibility once again . . .'[382] The members of the European Teaching Committee as well as the Bahá'ís of Paris were also thankful for her kindness and generosity towards Joséphine.[383]

Towards the end of 1955 Laura learned of Joséphine Scott's death. A letter from the American Hospital of Paris confirmed the sad news.[384] Laura wrote a lovely tribute to Joséphine, published in *The Bahá'í World*, recounting her activities and how Joséphine had held special programs a few times a year from 1932 to 1938 for the Iranian students in Paris and invited notable speakers and historians. Altogether, she had hosted meetings at her home in Paris from 1907 to 1948 and had received 'Abdu'l-Bahá two or three times during His visits to Paris.[385]

As for her husband Edwin Scott, he had studied at L'École des Beaux-Arts and was made a Chevalier de la Légion d'Honneur for his 'recognized ability as an artist'.[386] He was a distinguished member of la Société Nationale des Beaux-Arts and five of his paintings were purchased by the French Government.[387] Posthumously Scott achieved high distinction when one of his works was hung in the Salle du Jeu de Paume in the Museum of State in Paris.[388] Laura donated many his paintings to the Smithsonian. In addition, Edwin Scott's paintings could be found in several museums and official establishments for the fine arts in Washington.[389] Years later, in the fall of 1970, Laura was instrumental in organizing an exhibition of Scott's paintings at one of the museums of the Smithsonian Institution.[390]

The Bust of 'Abdu'l-Bahá and other Bahá'í Happenings

Early in January 1954 Rúḥíyyih <u>Kh</u>ánum wrote to Laura that it would be nice to have the bust of 'Abdu'l-Bahá that Laura and her mother had seen in a Parisian studio sent to Haifa. This bronze bust had been sculpted in Paris around 1934.[391] Laura arranged for its safe shipment to Haifa. Leroy Ioas, an American Bahá'í who was serving as Secretary-General of the International Bahá'í Council, thanked Laura from Haifa for sending it. After its delivery Rúḥíyyih <u>Kh</u>ánum realized they already had one. It had been sent sometime earlier and she had thought that this bust was different from the one she had asked Laura to send. She also remembered the day she had gone with Laura and her mother to see the sculptor at his Parisian studio.[392]

Laura attended the dedication of the new Baháʼí Center of Paris together with Edith Sanderson in 1953.[393] They were the last remaining of the early Baháʼís of Paris.[394] The new Baháʼí Center was located at 11 rue de la Pompe in the same arrondissement where Laura lived. She later suggested to the ETC that it allocate funds for the Baháʼí Center and it welcomed her suggestion.[395] She supported the Center financially until the end of her life. Shoghi Effendi deeply appreciated ʻLaura Khánum' for her generous support of the Baháʼí Center.[396]

Laura also attended the ETC meeting held in Lyon in August 1955.[397] She continued holding some meetings at her home but a few years earlier had requested that the meetings should end at 10:15 p.m.[398] She was now 76 years old.

Since the early 1950s, when the headquarters of the Food and Agriculture Organization (FAO), an agency of the UN, had been transferred from Washington to Rome, Laura traveled to Rome for the meetings.[399] Laura may have gone to the headquarters of FAO of the UN as the liaison officer of the ICW. She visited Rome often and was welcomed at the home of her Baháʼí friends Ugo and Angeline Giachery.[400] She often managed to meet the Baháʼís and give talks whenever she traveled for work. Early in November 1955 she managed to address a group of Baháʼís gathered at the Baháʼí Center in Rome when she was in the city for one of the FAO meetings.[401]

Farewell to Edith Sanderson

Laura lost a close friend in September 1955, Edith Sanderson, who was the second convert to the Faith in 1900 in Paris after Edith McKay de Bons (of a French mother and North American father). The two remained friends in Paris and Edith gave Laura updates and news of the Baháʼís, their activities and herself whenever she was away. Her passing left Laura as the only early Baháʼí of Paris from the 1900s. A memorial service was held for Edith at the new Baháʼí Center in Paris.

Edith was born in California and her father was the Chief Justice of the state's Supreme Court. He died when Edith was a child and her mother took her four young daughters to Paris to finish their education.

The eldest, Sybil, became a great opera singer. Edith became a Bahá'í in 1901 and visited the Holy Land several times, living with the family of 'Abdu'l-Bahá. She remained in Paris during both world wars and tried to keep the Bahá'í Faith alive in France during those tragic times. Many Bahá'í meetings were held at her house.[402] Ugo Giachery expressed his deepest condolences to Laura for the passing of Edith, writing: 'I believe you were one of her closest friends.'[403]

Laura was asked to write a tribute to Edith in French. She was later informed that it was going to be translated into English and published in the 'In Memoriam' section of *The Bahá'í World*.[404] She felt this idea was very 'worthy of Edith Sanderson's loyal service throughout many, many years in times of war as in times of peace'.[405] The tribute reads in part:

> During the two world wars, Edith Sanderson did everything in her power to preserve in France the flame of the Bahá'í Faith. Her study of the teachings of the Báb, of Bahá'u'lláh, and of 'Abdu'l-Bahá was continuous and profound, and with her growing knowledge of Persian she achieved an ever more direct comprehension of Their Writings. Although fragile in appearance, she had rare will-power and fidelity, had displayed a courage almost heroic in spreading the Bahá'í Faith in a country where it found little response . . . She was a force in these uncertain times, a hope in hours of desolation; she gave to the point of exhaustion of her time and her means.[406]

Her Friends from Long Ago

The year 1956 must have been difficult for Laura because another friend of hers, the well-known American Bahá'í artist Juliet Thompson (1873–1956), also passed away that year. Laura had known Juliet since her childhood; they had become good friends and remained so whether they were in New York, Washington or Paris. It was Laura's mother who had met Juliet in Washington in 1889, had become very close to her and encouraged her to paint. In an undated letter, Juliet invited Laura, who was in New York, to visit later and wrote:

> Darling, I can never tell you what those days with you in that beloved house, among those beloved pictures meant – still mean and will always mean to me. I don't have to try to tell you. A life-time

of loving your mother and adoring her genius and being inspired by her, by it, make it possible to share your feeling, dear, and the sacredness and joy of that memorial and to feel her closeness. Thank you with my whole heart, dearest Laura, for giving me such a happiness and such a memory and for all your sweetness and loving thoughtfulness to me.[407]

The National Assembly of the United States was aware that it was Laura who had introduced Juliet to the Faith and asked her to write a tribute to Juliet's Bahá'í life to be read at her memorial.[408] Her words were read at Juliet's memorial service held on February 9, 1957 in the Foundation Hall of the Bahá'í Temple in Wilmette and were appreciated by the National Assembly.[409] Laura reminisced about how she had met Juliet through her mother and their time together in Thonon-les-Bains, France, with 'Abdu'l-Bahá.[410]

A tribute in *The Bahá'í World* reads in part:

Around the turn of the century the mother of Laura Clifford Barney invited the young artist to come to Paris for further study. Juliet went accompanied by her mother and brother. It was there that she met May Bolles – the first Bahá'í on the European continent – and through her, accepted this new Faith. Mrs Barney wrote of Juliet that she had accepted it 'as naturally as a swallow takes to the air'.[411]

Another friend who had stayed in touch with Laura was Mariam Haney, who had met Laura decades ago, perhaps in 1903 or 1904 while attending Bahá'í meetings in New York. The two remained friends for 55 years. Mariam was given her name by 'Abdu'l-Bahá after she became a Bahá'í. She went on pilgrimage with her husband to 'Akká in 1909. The Haney family was residing in Washington when 'Abdu'l-Bahá visited in 1912 and Laura tried to visit them every time she came to town.

When in 1953 Mariam had had no news of Laura for some time, she wrote to her. 'The last time I saw you was when we came home from Chicago together, and you looked after me so beautifully. You were kind and thoughtful.'[412] When Laura was in the United States in 1955, she visited Mariam in Washington. Mariam was thankful for the visit and the time Laura had spent with her. It seems that Mariam was recovering from an illness at that time.[413]

At age 84 Mariam reminisced to Laura, 'We have both been in the Most Great Prison with 'Abdu'l-Bahá. Eight of us are left of those years! My memory is good. Juliet Thompson was my age.'[414] Mariam informed Laura that her son Paul was in Haifa serving as a Hand of the Cause of God, having been appointed to this position in 1957.[415] She loved and respected Laura very much, as she wrote in another letter that year: 'Deep love from my heart to my dear friend and sister and you become more dear as the years pass into history.'[416]

In one of her last letters to Laura in 1959, Mariam wrote, 'To think of and reading your loving kindness and your interest in me really filled me to overflowing with something more than deep gratitude, an enlarged vista opened before me as I fully realized to the extent of my capacity the bond Eternal between us and which will continue on and on down the ages – a bond never to be broken – a bond which is not dependent on anything connected with this world.'[417] After giving news of herself and her son who was in Haifa, she closed her letter by saying, 'Thank you with all the sincerity that is within me and at this moment I put my arms around you and deeply yearn. Always your devoted, Mariam.' She added in a postscript: 'I have always realized this bond but it is growing stronger with the years.'[418] Mariam died in early 1965 at 93 years of age.

Another person Laura had met in Haifa years back was Badí' Bushrú'í (1892–1973), an intelligent man who had been raised in the household of 'Abdu'l-Bahá from a young age and then received higher education with Laura's financial assistance.[419] When Badí' was married a few decades earlier in Haifa, Laura had loaned the bride her wedding dress. Now a grown-up man, Badí' Bushrú'í came across Laura's name in 1953 while he was perusing the list of non-governmental organizations affiliated with the social and cultural activities of the UN. He wrote to her in 'utmost joy': 'In recognition of your untold kindnesses to me I could not but take pen and paper in order to express my heartiest appreciation for all that you have done for me.' He continued, telling about his wife and five children in Alexandria, Egypt, where they had taken residence.[420]

Laura and Romaine Brooks

Laura had met and known Romaine through Natalie and saw Romaine every time she visited her sister in France, Italy and Switzerland. Whenever Laura wanted to see Natalie while she was with Romaine, she had to be with both. She had spent several summers with both at Beauvallon and many other holidays with them and became fond of Romaine over the years. Whenever Laura wrote to Natalie, she gave her greetings to Romaine and at times she corresponded with her directly.[421] She even advised Romaine about her investments, through Natalie or directly. Laura and Romaine had apartments in the same building in rue Raynouard in Paris, with Romaine's apartment one floor above Laura's.[422] Romaine never returned to her apartment after World War II and it was Laura who managed it. Laura not only assisted Romaine with the care of her apartment but with her mail, payment of bills and preparation of taxes when she was away. Laura remained close to and supportive of Romaine in her life and work.

Laura tried to help Romaine with her books of drawings and paintings whenever she could and suggested ways to promote her work. Romaine had largely specialized in portraiture and used subdued palettes of grays and blues. She mostly painted people close to her and her subjects ranged from unknown models to famous aristocrats. During one of her visits to Washington, D.C., Laura showed pictures of some of Romaine's drawings to Mr John Pope, the Director of Freer Gallery at the SI.[423] During another visit, Laura met with Mr Thomas M. Beggs, the curator for fine arts at the Smithsonian in 1952, who later became the Director of the National Collection of Fine Arts at the SI. She informed her sister that a Mr H (perhaps Mr Huntington) had received 200 copies Romaine's brochures through Mr Beggs, that over a hundred had been returned to a Mr Herman and that she was waiting for responses.[424] A few weeks later, she told Natalie later that Mr Herman had received 60 acknowledgments regarding Romaine's brochures.[425] She arranged for the brochures of Romaine's paintings to be sent to leading galleries.[426] Several years later, during a visit to Washington in 1957, Laura checked with the Library of Congress and informed Natalie that Romaine's books of drawings were not there.[427] It was her firm idea that they should be sent to suitable libraries rather than just letting copies sit in the storage room at Romaine's apartment.

Passing of the Guardian, Shoghi Effendi

Shoghi Effendi passed away in London on November 4, 1957. As for so many, his passing must have been a devastating loss for Laura. She urged the National Spiritual Assembly of the British Isles to inform her about the passing and the details of funeral services.[428] Much to her regret, however, she was unable to attend the funeral, possibly because of health issues that had started the previous year. She must have sent a letter of condolence to Shoghi Effendi's wife that November since she received a reply and was touched deeply to hear so quickly from her. Laura sympathized with her.

> To a certain extent I can appreciate your heart-breaking situation, still we both believe in the power of the spirit and it is only through this power that you can continue to live your share of the allotted plan which the courageous Guardian has made possible through his sacrifices, projects and achievements.[429]

Laura had met Shoghi Effendi when he was a little boy. She had seen him every time she visited 'Akká and Haifa and he visited her and Hippolyte in Paris. She had watched him go through the different stages of life, growing from a child of five or six to become the Guardian of the Bahá'í Faith. Their correspondence had continued throughout the years. Shoghi Effendi respected and admired her greatly. Once, in 1955, Laura received a one-line telegram from the Guardian that simply said, 'Laura Barney: LOVING REMEMBRANCE SHRINES. SHOGHI.'[430] It was dated the evening of Naw-Rúz, the Persian and Bahá'í New Year celebrated in March, and was forwarded to her in Washington by the National Assembly.[431]

After Shoghi Effendi was married, his wife, Rúḥíyyih Khánum, would correspond with Laura. Laura was always delighted to hear from her as well as reading the few lines added by Shoghi Effendi. In a letter written in January 1948 she expressed her joy at receiving a letter from Rúḥíyyih Khánum that touched her. Laura had shared with them the letters she had found that Shoghi Effendi had written to her in 1904 and 1905, which reminded her of the years she lived in 'Akká.[432] Laura was always obedient to Shoghi Effendi's requests and he was appreciative of her services. In a letter written in April 1953 he had expressed his happiness on hearing that Laura would be attending the Jubilee Celebration and the All-American Intercontinental Teaching Conference in Wilmette, Illinois, from April 29 to May 6 of that year.[433]

Laura's Health

Laura walked with a limp all her life because of the injuries to her leg caused by a childhood fall from a pony cart. She experienced pain and discomfort in that leg, though she rarely complained about it. In 1953 she wrote to Natalie: 'My winter has passed well with only a few twinges in my left leg but right knee has behaved excellently and in this elevator century it is small hardship not to be able to go up and down stairs normally.'[434] She was more concerned about Natalie's health than her own.[435] Laura felt that since Natalie had rarely been sick in her life, it was therefore more difficult for her to live with a health problem than it was for Laura. She wrote to Romaine that she had had a 'long life of restrain[t] and adapted' herself to her handicap.[436]

Soon after, Laura was seriously ill and thereafter lost a little of her balance.[437] She was 77 years old at the time and wrote to Romaine, 'Unfortunately my condition is more complicated, still with insistence I hope to better my present state though it will take time.'[438] She defined her illness as 'tuberculosis of her body' but her health improved the following year.[439]

Laura was able to attend a meeting on January 19, 1958 but a few months later she had to excuse herself from attending another meeting.[440] It was perhaps for health reasons that she decided not to attend. She went to a place that was quite 'restful: attentive service, spacious park and healthy food' and she stayed for about six weeks. While there she tried to keep herself up-to-date by following world events.[441]

Sharing the Stories of Her Early Bahá'í Years and Preserving Them

Laura, or Madame Barney as she was known in those years, was now revered and respected by the Bahá'ís around the world. The Bahá'í community appreciated her decades of service and contributions to the Faith, and the fact that she had been in the presence of 'Abdu'l-Bahá several times during her life. There were scarcely any people left like her. She continued receiving invitations to attend Bahá'í meetings, summer schools and conferences to talk about her early experiences in the Faith, and these invitations kept coming, even though by the mid-1960s traveling had become difficult for her. For example, a person who invited Laura to attend a Bahá'í school even offered to fly her by private plane to an airport near the venue to make the trip easy for her.[442] Another person invited her and insisted that she should attend because she believed that 'there is no one else but you who can do this. We have no one else.'[443] Laura was the last of her Bahá'í generation in Paris.

Laura had safeguarded her early memories by recording them, especially those of her early visits to 'Akká and the Master, and the early Bahá'í community of Paris. She had been planning in 1958 to write the history of this community but found it difficult since her copious notes, files and most of her books had been confiscated during the Nazi occupation of France. She had to depend on the memories of other Bahá'ís of that period, and everyone was advancing in years.

The Local Assembly of Paris was not able to find anyone to help Laura with research and writing about this early history. Laura asked Kathleen Javid to help her. Kathleen was an American Bahá'í who had moved to Paris with her husband Farhang. When the Guardian had asked the National Assembly of the United States to send Bahá'í pioneers to Finland and France in preparation of the formation of the National Assemblies of those two countries, the Javids had come to Paris in response to that request.[444] They had moved from Ohio to Paris to assist and stayed for one year. The first National Assembly of France was established in 1958.[445] They were introduced to Laura at a Feast held at the Paris Bahá'í Center soon after their arrival. Kathleen's husband recounted his impressions:

> As she walked to the Feast it was evident to me that she came from a distinguished family. She was not accompanied when she came to the Center. It was a total surprise to meet the person who was the author of *Some Answered Questions* and had spent so much time with 'Abdu'l-Bahá. She was a very impressive lady, tall and slender with natural beauty, charm, well-dressed, and limping when walking straight even with a cane.[446]

Farhang remembered that she went to greet them, and continued: 'She actually was quite kind to the new visitors from America and asked

Kathleen to go to her home and help her type some letters.'[447] He had also heard that Laura generously contributed to the Paris funds and that she had a secretary working at her home.

Laura asked Kathleen to review the evolution of events in Paris at the time of 'Abdu'l-Bahá's visit that eventually led to the official formation of the National Assembly of France. The review included a listing of the events and people in the history of the Bahá'í Faith in Paris and France through researching the Bahá'í archives and history books.[448] Kathleen completed a detailed report.

The Bahá'ís also wished to interview Laura and record her words for posterity; this was done by a member of the National Assembly.[449] Two other Bahá'ís also wished to record her memories and suggested that they take a tape recorder to her home. Laura could give the same talk that she had given in French sometime earlier at the National Convention in France but this time she would speak in English. After the interview, John McHenry, one of the interviewers in 1959, wrote to her, 'As I listen to this tape, I am impressed over and over again with the enthusiasm with which you speak.'[450]

Laura also asked her Bahá'í friend Agnes Alexander, whom she had known since 1901 in Paris and who was residing in Japan, to help her to write a brief history. Despite her other responsibilities and engagements at the time, Agnes was finally able to write a short article about how she found the Bahá'í Faith while visiting Italy in 1900 and the gatherings of the early Bahá'ís in Paris in 1901.[451] Agnes had attended May Bolles's meetings during her three-and-a-half-month stay in Paris. The National Publicity Committee of the National Assembly of France also asked Laura to write news articles for the press about the first Bahá'ís in Paris and 'Abdu'l-Bahá's visits to the city in 1911 and 1913.

Whenever well-known Bahá'ís or dignitaries arrived in Paris, the Bahá'í institutions or individuals would inform Laura of their arrival and request that she make arrangements to meet them. Laura was also asked to invite dignitaries and important people to her home several times. When Mark Tobey (1890–1976), an America painter who embraced the Faith in 1918, was in Paris, she was asked to receive him in her home.[452] She also informed the Bahá'ís in Paris whenever a dignitary or important person was going to be in Paris. For example, when her friend Richard St Barbe Baker (1889–1982), a forester and environmental activist, was coming to Paris May 1954, she arranged a talk for him at the Bahá'í Center.[453] He had become a Bahá'í in London in 1935.[454] The Bahá'ís in return would visit her and give her updates and news of the Local Assembly of Paris and the National Assembly of France.[455]

Further Developments with *Some Answered Questions*

While Laura was involved for years with humanitarian work, her book *Some Answered Questions* was being read all over the Bahá'í world. It had been translated into several languages and more were being added. Shoghi Effendi had written years earlier that the book provided a wealth 'of knowledge regarding basic spiritual, ethical, and social problems'.[456] Another letter written on behalf of Shoghi Effendi stated: 'Those talks of the Master that were later reviewed by Him and corrected or in some other form considered authentic by Himself, such as "Some Answered Questions", these could be considered as Tablets and therefore be given the necessary binding power.'[457] In a letter to the National Assembly of Germany dated June 28, 1950, Shoghi Effendi addressed the urgent importance of a new edition being issued: 'In regard to certain matters you raised in your letters: he does not consider it necessary to publish at present "This Earth One Country"; there are other books more urgently needed by the German friends such as "Some Answered Questions" and the "Paris Talks" of the Master.'[458] In yet another letter written on his behalf in March 1951 is this statement: 'He thinks that "Some Answered Questions" is more important in the teaching work than "Paris Talks", and recommends to get "Some Answered Questions" out first.'[459] A few years later in 1957, Shoghi Effendi wrote that he felt 'the urgent need now is to get out "Some Answered Questions", which is one of the most important books for a proper study of the Faith. When this has been printed, the next publication of the Master's Works can be considered.'[460] He also advised an individual that the two books he recommended be studied were '"Some Answered Questions" and the "Dispensation of Bahá'u'lláh" which help you to grasp these questions'.[461]

American Bahá'í Farrukh Ioas (1920–60), the daughter of Leroy Ioas, moved to Paris in 1956 to assist the community. She was born Mary Lorraine Ioas but the name Farrukh, meaning 'the joyous one', was bestowed upon her by 'Abdu'l-Bahá and was a name she loved.[462]

She wrote to Laura about the importance of *Some Answered Questions* to herself and others. She stated how truly privileged she felt to have met Laura, then continued:

> You have been one of the great almost mystical figures of the Faith to me and I am delighted to know the real person. Your work *Some Answered Questions* has long been one of my favorite Bahá'í texts. In fact, it is the one Bahá'í book I carried in my suitcase; all others being in the trunk. It truly fills a place no other book we have does, for it deals with such deeply significant questions in an orderly, uniform pattern such as no other book we have in English does. I know all the Bahá'ís are grateful to you for this precious treasure which will always be an original source for explanations of these vital subjects by the Master.[463]

As the copyright owner of the book, Laura was contacted whenever there were questions about it. In 1953 she was contacted by the Secretary of the National Assembly of the United States who asked her if she had any corrections to make to *Some Answered Questions* as that institution needed a new edition of the book.[464] Since Laura was in Washington, D.C., the secretary sent her his own copy so that she could work out of that but he requested that she return the book because 'he would be lost without it'.[465]

Another letter to Laura indicated that paper size was to be reduced because paper had become very expensive.[466] When a new edition of the book was to be issued by the Bahá'í Publishing Committee in 1958, she wrote to the Secretary of the National Assembly saying that she was not happy with the Introduction that the Publishing Committee had placed in the last edition of the book. She felt that she should have been consulted and stressed that she did not consider *Some Answered Questions* as 'my book' but that 'it is in my trust'.[467] She added that she believed that the length and character of the Introduction did not 'harmonize with the text that follows, and no point is made of the authenticity of the material which is that of a signed and sealed Tablet'.[468]

She later explained that when writing the short Preface to the first edition in 1908, she had also been afraid for the safety of 'Abdu'l-Bahá and for that reason did not include all the details in that section. She felt that the book needed an Introduction and asked Hippolyte to write a short history of the Faith in French titled *Essai sur le Bahá'isme* that proved to be most helpful in certain countries.[469]

When Laura received a copy of the new edition in March 1958 she was not happy with various statements on the dust jacket of the book either. She clarified in a letter to the National Assembly that all the talks had taken place in 'Akká, not in Haifa; that 'Abdu'l-Bahá was a prisoner and was leading too busy a life to entertain at lunch and dinner; that there were only a few pilgrims at Laura's lunch meetings with Him; and that when they came, they could remain only for a day or two. She also clarified that when posing questions and obtaining the answers, she had not wished to trust her notes and that was why at least four people were present during the sessions.[470]

Laura believed that the new Introduction by Annamarie Honnold, an American Bahá'í, was more like a thesis than an Introduction and was overly long.[471] She believed that an Introduction should be written either by an outstanding personality whose name would bring public attention to the book, or someone who had intimate knowledge of the facts presented, or in the case of *Some Answered Questions,* someone who had concise historical knowledge. In her letter, she stated that when she gave the copyright to the Bahá'í Publishing Committee it did not occur to her that it would reprinted without her foreknowledge. She insisted that 'there must be assurance, also, that after my death nothing inappropriate will be placed in any new edition in any language'.[472] It is not clear how she gave the copyright to the Publishing Trust, which was established in 1955 by Shoghi Effendi. There must have been an understanding that she expected to be consulted on matters related to this book at that time, even though she had given copyright to the Publishing Trust.

The National Assembly assured her that it would make the necessary corrections.[473] It advised her in March 1959 that it had forwarded her letter to the Bahá'í Publishing Trust with 'instructions to bring it up for mutual conference as soon as the Publishing Trust is ready to bring out a new edition of *Some Answered Questions*'.[474] The purpose of the conference was to ensure that proper action was taken in accordance with her wishes. They continued discussions. The following year, the secretary of the National Spiritual Assembly responded by acknowledging that the needed changes would be made on the dust jacket and in the Introduction and agreed that the Introduction should have been submitted to her for her comments and approval. It was explained that 'this is a courtesy due to the author' and promised to fix the Introduction in the next edition.[475]

It was later clarified that Honnold had written the Introduction to *Some Answered Questions* at the request of the National Assembly, who revised it in accordance with Honnold's suggestions, and then the book was published.[476] The National Assembly explained that it was aware that Laura had been in touch with Honnold, but it seemed that she had not reviewed the final version and that that version had not been sent to Laura for her approval. Three hundred copies had been printed and it would cost 2,000 dollars or more to eliminate the Introduction and the dust jacket. The assembly considered it impractical to get rid of these copies but would consider her suggestion for the Introduction for future editions.[477]

After consulting with Laura in Paris, Honnold did her best to revise the Introduction in a way that seemed fitting to Laura. Honnold hoped that Laura and the National Assembly would approve the next edition and regretted that she had written something that Laura did not like. At the end of a letter to Laura she wrote: 'And I am so sorry it has caused you so much trouble. But your efforts long ago have given the world a book that will be treasured for years, so indeed, you should be happy that you have so well contributed to the new spiritual civilization.'[478]

Laura stayed in touch with the National Assembly as well as with Annamarie Honnold, who was rewriting and updating the Introduction of the book in 1960. She was closely involved in the publication of another revised English edition of *Some Answered Questions* and with various details such as minor punctuation and corrections, some footnotes, the transliteration of Persian names, the Introduction and even the capitalization of some words. She advised Honnold to condense the information and suggested that the Introduction be divided into two parts, 'a brief introduction to the book, and an historical summary of the Faith, which could follow one another'.[479] As for a proposed leaflet to be inserted into *Some Answered Questions*, which Laura had approved, the National Assembly suggested that it pay for the cost of printing and inserting it. The National Assembly thanked her for her kind offer to send the leaflet insertion to various National Spiritual Assemblies, but it was most happy to proceed with doing so as soon as the leaflet was printed.[480]

Laura was also concerned about the transliteration of oriental names in *Some Answered Questions* and discussed them with several knowledgeable Bahá'ís and the National Assembly of France. She wrote to an Iranian-French Bahá'í, 'Your assistance is most opportune, as I need the transliteration according to current Bahá'í practice of the names on the attached sheet.'[481] Some years later, she was still concerned with the Persian names of those who had helped with writing down 'Abdu'l-Bahá's answers to her questions during her visits in 'Akká. She also asked for help from another member of the National Assembly of France who was Persian-French to read the Persian text of *Some Answered Questions*.[482]

Laura was adamant that the book be the way she wanted it, in accordance with her high standard. When *Some Answered Questions* was translated into German in 1959, Laura was again not happy with the Introduction because of the changes that the National Assembly of Germany had made in it. She wrote to the Hands of the Cause Residing in the Holy Land, known as the Custodians of the Faith,[483] and made several suggestions for the way Introductions to Bahá'í books should be written and prepared. As Shoghi Effendi had passed away in 1957, the Hands of the Cause were the head of the Faith until the election of the Universal House of Justice. They responded by saying that they were considering and reviewing her suggestions and, in the meantime, she should write to that National Assembly and ask them to omit the Introduction that she had not approved.[484] She did write to that National Assembly of Germany on March 13, 1960 recommending that the English translation of the French Introduction be translated for use in the German publication and the Assembly assured her that it would abide by her request.[485]

Some Answered Questions had been translated into several languages over the years. In 1960 Laura was informed that the first nine chapters of the book had been translated into Korean and published. Agnes Alexander, her Bahá'í friend in Japan, wrote to her: 'How wonderful it is that God assisted you to make it possible for the Bahá'í World to receive those precious Talks from the Master!'[486]

The book was translated into Italian in 1961 under Laura's supervision.[487] Prior to its publication she was contacted for her suggestions to ensure that the Italian edition was as satisfactory as possible; Laura updated the Introduction of the Italian version. Ugo Giachery, the Secretary of the Italian Translating and Publishing Company of the National Spiritual Assembly of Italy and Switzerland, wrote to Laura, 'It is with great pleasure that I express to you in the name of the National Assembly, the Committee and all the Italian friends, our deepest gratitude for your remarkable and unique labors in producing this valuable Bahá'í text and in permitting us to produce it in its Italian translation.'[488] Mrs Giachery thought Laura might be interested to know that there was a mention of her book *Le lezioni di San Giovanni d'Acri* in the monthly book review of Italian books and periodicals of a government publication.[489] Laura later requested a copy of this review.[490]

In 1962 the Custodians of the Faith congratulated Laura for the latest edition of *Some Answered Questions*: 'It is a source of satisfaction to us that *Some Answered Questions* is being so widely circulated throughout the Bahá'í world and made available in different languages. It is a book of great importance. You must be very happy.'[491]

Her New Concern

Laura was 80 years old when she took an interest in the Convention on the Prevention and Punishment of the Crime of Genocide. The UN had adopted the Genocide Convention on December 9, 1948 and it became effective on January 12, 1951. The Convention gave legal definitions of the crime of genocide and all signatories to it were to prevent and punish instances of genocide in times of both war and peace.

Laura had asked the ICW in 1959 to send Mr Raphael Lemkin (1900–59) a copy of a study in which prominent mention was made of the Genocide Convention. He was grateful to receive it.[492] Lemkin was a Polish-American Jewish lawyer who coined the word 'genocide' in 1943 or 1944 by joining the words 'genos' (race or tribe) and 'cide' (a person or agent that kills). In 1933 he had started working for legal safeguards of ethnic, religious, and social groups in Europe, but met with no success. He fled Poland when the Nazis invaded and found refuge in the United States. After teaching at Duke University, he joined the War Department in Washington, D.C., in 1942 as an analyst. After the war Lemkin worked with the American team that prepared for the Nuremberg trials of Nazi war criminals, specifically as an adviser to Robert H. Jackson, the Chief United States Prosecutor for the Nuremberg trials. He returned from Europe and lobbied at the UN for the legal inclusion of genocide in international law. He initiated and co-wrote the Genocide Convention adopted by the UN.

There are no records of any previous correspondence between Laura and Lemkin but it seems that Lemkin knew of Laura's work and achievements and the fact that she was a Bahá'í. He wrote in his letter to Laura dated April 20, 1959:

> This letter brings both good and bad news about the Genocide Convention, from the enclosed statement issued on April 10 by the International Bahá'í Community, you will see what a splendid endorsement has come from the Bahá'ís. In the same document, you will find a statement by the Ambassador of Ceylon [today's Sri Lanka], who is Chairman of the Human Rights Commission, in which he deplores the fact that efforts are being made to weaken the Genocide Convention by having its concept included in other documents which are unenforceable.[493]

Lemkin also stated in this letter that Dr Jeanne Eder, President of the ICW from 1947 until her death in 1957, had defended the Genocide Convention against many onslaughts, with the ICW files speaking for themselves. He enclosed the text of the Convention so that Laura would see for herself. He wondered if he could impose on her to talk about it with Mme Lefaucheux, the president of the National Council of French Women.[494] Lemkin closed his letter, 'I know that you occupy, among the women of the world, a position of an "elder statesman", and I know that if you approach influential women they will listen to you.'[495]

Rescuing the Archives of the International Council of Women

One of Laura's last projects as she was entering the ninth decade of her life was to rescue the documents of the ICW for posterity from their loss during the war. In her personal life Laura had meticulously saved everything she received, including letters and their envelopes, invitations, newspaper clippings and other documents. She had realized the importance of these materials for future research. With that background, she understood the importance of collecting, cataloguing and housing materials dealing with the activities of the ICW and she took responsibility for helping to restore the archives of the ICW that had been removed or misplaced during the war.

It was known that some materials were being kept at the Library of Congress in Washington, D.C., and in the United Nations office in Geneva. In 1952 at the ICW's conference in Reading, England, the board officially agreed to have an archives program, which was already underway. In 1959 Laura prepared a resume of the activity of ICW since end of the WWII and wrote a long historical report on the process enabling the archives to be restored:

A year has passed since Mme. Lefaucheux asked me at the January Board meeting in Paris to write an account of our archives activity which was first undertaken 12 years ago. I regret that circumstances have not permitted me to accede to her request until now, and I hope that the following concise history of the project will interest those who would like to know something of its beginning, its accomplishments, and the plans for its continuation in the future. Mme. Lefaucheux and others have understood how our archives will serve as a valuable source for research work and for theses in the years to come. The unique character of the ICW gave our archives program special significance, for at the time we were founded (1888) the ICW was one of the very first international organizations, and it concerned itself not with one, but with a variety of subjects – peace, education, health, social justice and improvement, and abolishment of discrimination in the broadest sense of that term: class, sex, racial, and religious. The organization of the ICW had also a special character as it was formed of National Councils which in turn included both national and local groups of diverse nature.

It was the loss of so many important records during World War II that gave full perspective to the serious impact upon an outstanding organization when its written records, whether published or manuscript, that form its history are irretrievably lost, sometimes before their contents have been carefully studied in the light of changing conditions: documents that cover its early meetings and the objectives decided upon, growth and modifications in policies and procedures, and accounts of the outstanding personalities of the movement through various periods.[496]

Laura reported that during World War II significant collections of ICW materials kept at the Brussels headquarters were carried away by the

'Authorities of Occupation', as were records kept elsewhere: 'Most of my own books, records, and files of the ICW, along with documents of other international organizations in which I had long been active were taken too, as I discovered on my return to Paris in the spring of 1946.'[497]

According to Laura's report, the next steps would be 'to continue to find out what still exists and in what quantities, to insure a continuing program, and to keep ICW Headquarters collection as complete as possible, and augment collections that exist in important world libraries, and establish collections where none exist'. She further explained, 'There is under way a further project to make a general survey of ICW publications and to prepare a reference book which will give in concise but readable form those events and matters of particular interest that are now to be found only by referring to a series of books, pamphlets, bulletins and brochures.' Laura had begun the search by asking those National Councils that had records to forward them to her. Some years later, efforts were still underway to locate, preserve, place and utilize the publications and documents of the ICW. The main two institutions that were interested in having the ICW documents were the UN Library at Geneva and the Library of Congress in Washington, two highly specialized research centers.[498] The Library of Congress ultimately received from Laura all the ICW documents that had been found and sent to her.

Laura stayed in touch with the Archives Committee of the ICW for the next few years. She was sorry that three members of the Committee had resigned in 1964. She attended the ICW conference held in Interlaken in the summer of that year but regretted not having had a chance to talk with the archivists who attended because of her daily board meetings.[499] A condensed history of the ICW was about to be published in 1964.

Laura's Devotion and Obedience to the Faith and Its Leadership at a Time of Crisis

During her long life, Laura had seen the leadership of the Faith progress; she had shown her obedience to 'Abdu'l-Bahá (1844–1921), to the Guardianship of Shoghi Effendi (1921–57), and the interim leadership of the Hands of the Cause of God Residing in the Holy Land, the Custodians of the Faith (1957–63), leading to the permanent leadership

Laura Dreyfus-Barney's passport, issued in 1919

Laura and Hippolyte Dreyfus-Barney in the Holy Land with 'Abdu'l-Bahá and other Bahá'ís, 1919. Shoghi Effendi is seated to the right of Hippolyte.

Some of the Bahá'ís called to Haifa for consultation by Shoghi Effendi in February 1922: From left to right: Curtis Kelsey, Emogene Hoagg, Mountfort Mills, unknown, Shoghi Effendi, unknown, Laura Dreyfus-Barney, unknown, Ethel Rosenberg, behind her (?), Lady Blomfield, behind her Roy Wilhelm, Saichiro Fujita, behind him Ruth Randall

Palais Wilson, Geneva, the headquarters of the League of Nations from 1920 until 1936, when the League moved to the Palais des Nations

The Palais des Nations, Geneva, built between 1929 and 1938 to serve as the headquarters of the League of Nations; since 1946 it has been the home of the United Nations Office in Geneva

The First Congress of Educational and International Cinematography in Rome, 1934, organized by Laura. Far left, Director of the Institute Luciano de Feo; front row, second from left, Madame Dreyfus-Barney, President of the International Committee of Cinematography and Radio; to her right, Prime Minister Benito Mussolini. Laura was the only woman delegate to the Congress.

Smithsonian Institution Archives.
Image # SIA2015-006962

Lady Aberdeen, Ishbel Hamilton-Gordon, Marchioness of Aberdeen and Tamair (née Isabel Maria Marjoribanks, 1857–1939), in 1925

Laura Barney in Los Angeles, 1929

Mary Maxwell (Rúḥíyyih Khánum), daughter of May Maxwell and wife of Shoghi Effendi, Guardian of the Baháʼí Faith, the year of her second pilgrimage, 1926, when she was 16 years old

Anita Ioas Chapman, who lived in the same building as Laura

Laura in New York, in 1935

Smithsonian Institution Archives.
Image # SIA2015-006970

*Shepheard's Hotel, Cairo,
where Laura stayed in 1935*

Laura Barney, seated second from right, in Washington, D.C., 1935

Smithsonian Institution Archives. Image # SIA2015-006962

The Smithsonian Institution, Washington, D.C.

Laura in 1960

Laura, aged 85, at a reception given in her honor, with the former Director of the National Gallery of Art David Finley (left) and S. Dillion Ripley, Secretary of the Smithsonian Institution (right), at Studio House, Fall 1964

Smithsonian Institution Archives. Image # SIA2015-006982

Studio House was purchased in 2001 by the Government of the Republic of Latvia for its Embassy in the United States. The plaque bearing the name of Laura's mother can be seen on the right corner of the building.

Grave of Natalie Clifford Barney and Laura Clifford Barney in Passy Cemetery in the sixteenth arrondissement of Paris

of the Universal House of Justice, which was first elected in 1963 after the establishment of 56 National Spiritual Assemblies by that year. She also witnessed tests within her beloved Faith.

A crisis arose within the Faith when in 1960 the National Spiritual Assembly of France accepted the claim of one of the Hands of the Cause, Mason Remey, to be the second Guardian, the successor to Shoghi Effendi.[500] A majority of the Assembly members followed Remey. Within days, in May 1960, Abu'l-Qásim Faizi, one of the Custodians of the Faith, was dispatched to France to investigate the Remey matter. Faizi questioned all who were involved and then submitted his report. Remey was expelled from the Faith by the Custodians. The National Assembly of France was dissolved and the French Bahá'ís then elected a new Assembly.[501] The Bahá'í world was thrown into turmoil for a while, as each Bahá'í was tested in his or her firmness in the Faith. This attempted schism in the Faith on the part of Mason Remey and his expulsion from the Faith were a test for Bahá'ís everywhere.

The heart of this matter was obedience to the Bahá'í Covenant, the means instituted by Bahá'u'lláh that 'preserves the unity and integrity of the Faith itself and protects it from being disrupted by individuals who are convinced that only their understanding of the Teachings is the right one'.[502] It designated the succession of authority from Bahá'u'lláh to 'Abdu'l-Bahá and Shoghi Effendi. Shoghi Effendi had not been able to designate a second Guardian, which is why the Custodians of the Bahá'í Faith were managing the affairs of the Faith until the Universal House of Justice could be elected. The Bahá'í Faith was the first religion to stipulate the succession of its leadership in written documents that could not be repudiated. The unity of the Faith was inviolable. Those persons who retain their Bahá'í identity, yet oppose the authorized leadership of the Faith, are known as Covenant-breakers.

'Abdu'l-Bahá wrote: 'These [violators of the Covenant] do not doubt the validity of the Covenant but selfish motives have dragged them to this condition. It is not that they do not know what they do – they are perfectly aware and still they exhibit opposition.'[503] 'Thus a cardinal factor in Covenant-breaking is considered by 'Abdu'l-Bahá to be willful and conscious opposition to the divine will as manifested in the Covenant.'[504]

The claim of Mason Remey to be the second Guardian, and the loyalty of his followers, was perhaps the worst crisis to afflict the Faith since the days of Bahá'u'lláh and 'Abdu'l-Bahá. Remey's old friends were shocked. Laura's close friendship with Remey had spanned almost six decades. She had known him from her early days in Paris and in Washington and they had remained close friends. Like Laura, Remey had been introduced to the Faith by May Bolles in Paris. They had been in Haifa at the same time in 1901 and had attended many Bahá'í meetings and conferences together, such as the 1955 European Teaching Committee meeting held in Lyon.[505]

However, Laura remained firm in the Faith. She had had many tests in her Bahá'í life and this was just one more, although a most painful one. She supported Faizi and the decision of the Custodians of the Faith.[506] Agnes Alexander wrote to Laura that she had been in her thoughts since Remey's proclamation. Agnes had heard that all was well by that time, the end of January 1961. 'You and I probably are the oldest Bahá'í friends of Mason, as I met him in Paris after my arrival there in the spring of 1901. He was the second Bahá'í whom I met, as May was the first. He had just returned from his first pilgrimage to the prison in 'Akká and he told me of the Master. I can never forget that time.'[507]

The Custodians admired Laura's steadfastness, the way she 'arose to uphold the Covenant of God at the time of attack against the Faith by Mason Remey', and expressed their appreciation to her in a letter dated November 30, 1960: 'Your deeds of the devotion and assistance to the firm friends in France at this time call for our expression of appreciation and admiration.'[508] They also expressed gratitude for her assistance and support for the progress of the work of the Faith in France and abroad.[509]

The following year Laura became concerned about the safety of funds in a bank account for the French Bahá'ís that she had created and was under her trust. The National Assembly of the United States expressed its deep appreciation for her concern and the action she had taken with the bank to ensure that the Bahá'í bequest be moved to the National Assembly of the US, so that neither Mason Remey nor his followers could access the funds.[510] The Assembly also thanked Laura for her suggestion to consider contacting the editor of *Who's Who* to make sure that Mason Remey did not add his assumed title in the next edition. It agreed with her that the dignity of the Cause should be safeguarded.[511]

Another example of Laura's protective nature for the Faith was her concern that some Christian missionaries in Italy might write something derogatory about the Faith for public distribution. She warned Ugo Giachery and his wife in Rome about this matter in a letter in July 1962 and sent copies of the letter to the Bahá'í World Centre and the National Assembly of the United States.[512]

Donating Studio House to the Smithsonian Institution

Finalizing the affairs of Laura's mother required several trips to the United States over the years.[513] Laura had managed to sell the house at 1626 Rhode Island Avenue in Washington, D.C., the property she and Natalie had inherited, some years earlier.[514] They now had to take care of Studio House on 2306 Massachusetts Avenue, the house that their mother had built and the sisters had also inherited. Their mother loved living in this house that she had helped to design.[515] As interesting as this house was because of its architecture and history, it was not a successful rental project. It was during one of her last visits to Washington, D.C., in 1960, that Laura made a large donation. When Laura and Natalie had begun thinking about writing their wills, they had decided to give the majority of their assets to artistic and charitable organizations.[516] One of these donations was Studio House and its contents, given to the Smithsonian's National Collection of Fine Arts (now the Smithsonian American Art Museum) in memory of Alice Barney.[517] It seems that Laura paid Natalie her share of the value of Studio House before transferring it to the Smithsonian in both their names.[518] Natalie's signed acceptance of sale of Studio House was sent to Los Angeles the following year.[519]

In a letter to the Secretary of the Smithsonian, Laura expressed the hope that Studio House would be used as an arts and cultural center, as this was the purpose for which it was given. She ended her letter: 'With deep appreciation for your concern with the realization of this project, and for your proposal of a plaque so thoughtfully worded to acknowledge the gift . . .'[520] The plaque, given by her daughters in 1960, mentions that the House was donated in memory of Alice Pike Barney, an artist, civic leader and philanthropist.

Laura gave regular updates to Natalie about Studio House. For example, she wrote about a meeting held on October 17, 1961: 'Mr and Mrs Carmichael, friends of the Bruces [their second-cousin] and he is the overall director of the Smithsonian, met with me and a few friends in the dining room of Studio House and we spoke of the use of the dwelling for a center of people interested in the arts who come to the city for cultural development of the country, also most suitable for certain foreign visitors.'[521]

In June, a year after the bequest was made, the American Association of Museums (now known as the American Alliance of Museums) moved into Studio House, as reported in *The Museum News*. The article noted that this was 'the building Mrs [Dreyfus] Barney's mother, Alice Pike Barney, built in the early 1900s as an artists' studio'.[522] Of course, it was also her home.

Newspapers reported the donation. *The Evening Star* ran the heading 'Famous District Mansion is Given to Smithsonian' and reported that Laura was in Washington to make final preparations for the gift to the Smithsonian before her return to Paris. It quoted Laura, who said, 'My sister and I are very happy to give our mother's Studio House to the Smithsonian to be prepared for use as a center where persons concerned with arts and letters can meet and exchange points of view, or participate in cultural activities.'[523] The article also quoted Dr. Carmichael, the Secretary of the Smithsonian Institution, who was appreciative of the donation and the possibilities that it held for certain departments of the Smithsonian as well as for the American Association of Museums. After listing the number of artworks donated and the names of some of the artists, the article continued:

> Studio House was known as the place where an Oriental religion came to the attention of America. It emphasized the peace principle and was known as Bahá'í. It originated in Persia and was founded by a philosopher named Bahá'u'lláh. His eldest son, 'Abdu'l-Bahá, had come to the United States as interpreter and exemplar of the Bahá'í Faith, He was sponsored by the elder Mrs Barney, daughter of Samuel Nathan Pike, builder of Pike's Opera House in Cincinnati and the Grand Opera House in New York.[524]

Anita Chapman wondered why Laura had 'left Studio House not to the Bahá'ís of Washington but to the Smithsonian'. After some reflection, Anita thought that Laura gave financial support to organizations when there were businesspeople in charge, persons capable of managing the assets. A donation of this size required good management. The Bahá'í community of Washington, D.C. was still small in numbers in those years. Also, half of Studio House was owned by her sister – Laura was not the only owner. According to Chapman, under such circumstances it was not feasible to give it to the small Bahá'í community.[525]

Writing Articles and Reprinting Books by Hippolyte

Laura had been active throughout her life and now stayed active arranging for the reprinting of major Bahá'í books, both in English and French – not only *Some Answered Questions* but also the books Hippolyte had written and those he had translated. She also wrote articles for encyclopedias. The Local Assembly of Paris approved her suggestion in 1951 that she write an article about the Bahá'í Faith for the 1952 edition of *Larousse*.[526] Two years later she helped with an article about the Bahá'í Faith for the *l'Encyclopédie de l'Islam*, working with its translation committee.[527]

In 1954 the Local Assembly of Paris thanked her for reprinting *Les Leçons de St Jean d'Acre,* the French edition of *Some Answered Questions* translated by Hippolyte, and her donation to cover the expenses of the reprint.[528]

Since the passing of Hippolyte, Laura had promoted *Essai sur le Bahá'isme*, an introductory book on the Faith written and published by Hippolyte in 1909. She undertook the responsibility of publishing a new edition of it in 1960 and was in touch with the Presses Universitaires de France to do so. She consulted with the Bahá'í Publishing Trust of the United States to incorporate its suggestions about its reprinting.

Laura reprinted *Essai sur le Bahá'isme* in 1962 and personally sent copies of it and the French version of the *Kitáb-i-Íqán* (Book of Certitude), which had been translated into French by Hippolyte, to most of the National Spiritual Assemblies in the world. Many of them wrote letters of thanks and gratitude to her, including the National Assembly of France, which expressed the community's deep appreciation for her help and assistance.[529]

Laura also contacted the library of the National Ministry of Education of France and asked that it distribute to all municipal libraries of France copies of *Essai sur le Bahá'isme*. The ministry agreed to do so and asked her to have the publisher send 50 copies of the book.[530] The Director of the School Organization of the National Ministry of Education also asked her to send 250 copies of the book to be forwarded to professors of establishments that offered modern classic studies.[531] She had prepared a list for 'the distribution of certain Bahá'í publications to the libraries of teachers colleges through the Ministry of Education, and to the municipal libraries of Paris through the mayor'.[532]

Concerns about Natalie's Health and Visiting Her in Switzerland

In 1955, the Barney sisters, as they were known, had aged and when Laura was 76, she began to worry about the health of her sister, 79 and living in Nice.[533] Five years later, it seems that Natalie was not in touch with her sister and Laura had decided not to write to her directly, as she did not wish to reveal to her sister her concern. Instead she wrote a letter to Romaine: 'I am worried about Natalie as it will be hard for her to be careful.'[534] Laura asked for the address where Natalie was staying and for news of Natalie, as she did not want to bother her sister, even though she was 'eager and anxious for news'.[535]

As always, Laura was still proud of her sister. While at a medical and therapeutic clinic, perhaps in Switzerland, in 1960, Laura wrote to Natalie about a lady there who had read a newspaper article about Natalie's recent book. Laura believed that if people knew about her book that far away in a 'medical home', as she called the facility where she was resting, it would get good publicity in the summer.[536] Natalie was close by in Switzerland, but Laura was not sure if Natalie would have liked to see her. Their relationship seems to have been one-sided most of their lives and it got worse as they aged. Yet Laura was still loving, as always, towards Natalie and while she was at a clinic not far away, she wrote, 'It will be so nice to feel you nearer before long.'[537] In 1961 Laura wished to see Natalie, even for just two days. From Paris Laura wrote to Natalie in Nice: 'Maybe before or after I go to my date in Rome, seeing you will probably be in Easter Tide so I am especially happy to have had at least two days near you in Paris.'[538] Laura herself had to go to Rome for ICW work in May 1962.[539] However, it is not certain that she managed to see Natalie.

In 1963 Laura went for her annual retreat to Clinique Lignière in Switzerland. She was worried about Natalie and her heart problems.

Natalie, now 87, was nearby, also in Switzerland. After a phone conversation with Natalie in that year, Laura wrote to her:

> Your voice was clear even in giving me sad news that your heart was demanding attention and rest. I am and feel helpless; I see no way to add to your comfort; by reading, or aiding you hasten in some useful manner . . . Thoughts and feelings seem helpless under the present circumstances.[540]

Laura offered to bring Natalie Swiss Francs when she went to visit her and wanted to know how many thousand Francs she needed. She did manage to visit her sister at Janine's home and afterwards she wrote, 'Time to reach you was long and time with you doubly short.'[541] Laura, who managed their finances, also gave her sister an update as to how much money they had in the Swiss banks and what amount Natalie would need again.[542]

Last Visit to Her Country of Birth in the First Half of the 1960s

Laura continued traveling to the United States every year in the early 1960s. Her past innumerable trans-Atlantic trips by steamer were over because now she could fly between the continents. Voyage by ship took five to six days but, though the trip was long, offered first class passengers all manner of luxuries, social activities and entertainments. But eventually, commercial air service that took only a day was available. Time had been moving along inexorably for the sisters, from the Gilded Age, through two World Wars, and into the Cold War and the 1960s emphasis on personal freedoms regardless of social class. The sisters had both aged and had seen much. When a relative published a book, Laura wrote to Natalie: 'I cannot think that he is publishing the family origin? And that is for his future studies? Now we have entered history!'[543] She came across some old family documents and saw one with the date of Natalie's birth. 'On October the 31st,' she wrote, 'you will be 85 and a credit to our ancestry & to your wit to have dominated the traditional ills of age'.[544] Because she was still in the United States, Laura was going to miss Natalie's birthday. A few days after her birthday Laura wrote to Natalie, 'Natalie dear: I regret not being nearer in person for my thought right now is in your room rue Jacob.'[545]

During her visit to the United States in 1961 Laura did not go out much but managed to take care of the work that she needed to do. She wrote, 'I do not accept to go out for my meals at present.'[546] But she was able to attend the Barney Neighborhood House board meeting.[547] Her ties were maintained with this House and she managed to visit it every time she was in Washington. She had attended the May Festival and had served on the board during the last decade.[548] She was later made an honorary board member.[549]

While in the US Laura took care of the family safe deposit box at the bank and made arrangements to send some jewelry to Natalie. William Huntingdon was there to help Laura with her affairs. She asked him to go to the Library of Congress to make sure it had copies of all the books written by Natalie.[550] Laura then went to New York and visited her cousin Ellen in New Jersey, spending Thanksgiving with her.

When Laura flew back to the United States in June 1963, she had asked the financial official in charge of their investments to prepare an up-to-date document about Natalie's investments. Laura had reported faithfully to Natalie on her investments, securities, and financial interests. She was happy with the furnishing and care of Studio House and the furniture was placed the way their mother would have wished. She was also happy to see friends and acquaintances of her mother. She wrote to Natalie: 'It is always a joy to meet people who knew "Little One".'

At the age of 85, in the fall of 1964, Laura made her last trip to her country of birth and to Washington, D.C., the city that was like her hometown. She was planning to stay about six or seven weeks.[551] During this last visit she stayed at the Jefferson Hotel. William Huntington was around to help her with whatever he could from the minute she arrived in Washington.[552] For many years he had been extremely helpful to Laura in different capacities.

A reception was given in Laura's honor at Studio House. She was welcomed by the Secretary of the Smithsonian, S. Dillion Ripley, and the former National Gallery Director, David Finley, as well as other Smithsonian officials and members of the American Association of Museums. *The Museum News* under the heading of 'Mrs Barney Honored' reported that 'the guest of honor felt very much at home when the Association gave a candlelit reception' for her at its northwest Washington headquarters. The article continued: 'Smithsonian officials and members of the Association staff were on hand to welcome Mrs. Barney "home" from her permanent residence in Paris. She was able to review the restoration work to Studio House by Smithsonian and gave her advice for the future plans.'[553]

Laura did not go out or see many people while in Washington during this final stay.[554] She only did what needed to be done, such as attending to the publication that the Smithsonian was bringing out as a memorial to her mother, Alice Pike Barney.[555]

PART 5

THE LAST YEARS OF HER LIFE
IN PARIS

1965 – 1974

Last Return to Paris

Laura returned to Paris from her final trip to the United States in 1965. This was the last time she crossed the Atlantic, the last time she saw her country of birth and childhood, and where her parents were buried. She had traversed the Atlantic innumerable times since 1883, the first time when she was only four years old. At the beginning of the 20th century, she left her homeland to live in France. Now at the age of 86 she was returning to France, a country that had become her main home. Even though she had followed the same ideals and goals as an adult on both sides of the Atlantic, this last trip back to Paris may have been a bittersweet experience for her.

About three decades earlier she had written to Natalie explaining why she preferred to live in France: 'As I am more in sympathy with French policy than with the USA foreign policy, I expect to remain French, also I am a bit of a (illegible), and perhaps my American nature has been transported to Europe for better results than if I had remained rooted completely in 'God's own land'.[1]

Back in Paris, Laura continued living in her apartment at 74 rue Raynouard where she had moved after the passing of her husband, Hippolyte Dreyfus-Barney, so many years before. She had Yvonne, who was her housekeeper and assistant, for companionship. Her only travels during this last part of her life were for medical appointments and the physiotherapy clinic in Gland, Switzerland, once a year. She mostly stayed home and corresponded with those people whom she had met during her earlier years and some whom she had never met but who knew of her through her achievements. Her travels had taken her to faraway lands and her reputation had reached people around the world. Now it was time to savor all those memories. It was her letters that now traveled around the world. The only family member living near her was her sister. A reporter who visited the sisters in Paris had this to say about them in 1965:

Though the Barney sisters have remained close friends over the years, their attitudes and occupations have separated them diametrically. 'Dream noble deeds, Laura, don't do them all day long,' Natalie once said jokingly to her sister. But she continued that Laura has continued to do her noble deeds, and the world is richer for them.[2]

Laura did continue her deeds, even with diminished mobility. She was revered by the Bahá'ís for her accomplishments and the fact that she was one of the few who had been in the presence of 'Abdu'l-Bahá in the early years of the century, spending many days, weeks and months with Him. Many Bahá'ís and Bahá'í institutions stayed in touch with her. The young and the old who visited Paris would ask to have the honor of visiting her.

Her Health and Treatments

Laura had a limp that had stayed with her since her childhood fall and was perhaps a side effect of the operation she underwent. She never complained about this condition, neither in her formal nor in her private and personal correspondence. When she was older, arthritis and rheumatism set in, forcing her to decline some invitations. When she was invited to attend the first Bahá'í World Congress in the Albert Hall in London in 1963, she had to decline. Her frailty made it impossible for her to attend, although she had been promised a special reserved seat in a location whose accessibility required no stairs.[3] This momentous event was held to commemorate the centenary of the Declaration of Bahá'u'lláh and to announce the result of the election of the first Universal House of Justice. About 6,000 Bahá'ís attended.

In 1965 Laura consulted a doctor in Lausanne, Switzerland, about the discomfort in her hip and explained that as a young girl she had had a problem with her hip. The small bone between the hip and the femur had disappeared and the femur had grown into the hip. Ten years earlier she had been given strong doses of streptomycin. Since then she had been experiencing an increasing loss of balance. She had no pain but she needed an arm support when she walked and could not walk for long.[4] Laura also consulted her own Parisian doctor who had been taking care of her for a number of years. This doctor thought that the suggested treatment by the Swiss doctor could not be recommended for her case. Laura accordingly informed the Swiss doctor that she would not undergo any new treatment.[5]

Laura continued going to her usual Swiss clinic for dietary care and physical therapy. When she went to the clinic in August 1966, her doctor asked her to stay there for at least two months and not to leave the clinic sooner, as she had planned.

Arthritic hands had also made it increasingly difficult for Laura to write, so she dictated while William E. Huntington, her assistant who was now living in Paris, typed. She was happy that Huntington was such a great help in handling her correspondence.[6] He had been with her mother since the time she had been planning to write her autobiography and he was a student at George Washington University. He stayed loyal to the family and remained with Laura until the end of her life.

The International Council of Women and One More Trip to Iran?

Laura stayed active with the ICW as a board liaison officer. While she was in the United States in June 1963, she was planning to attend the ten days of meetings of the ICW.[7] She stated in an interview, 'I am very busy organizing and editing two books, one of them an historical account of the International Council of Women, and I'll be doing some traveling shortly, to various conferences . . .'[8] Two years later, when a reporter interviewed her, Laura again said that she hoped to travel to attend some conferences.[9] Perhaps she had wanted to go to Iran for the ICW conference and take other trips. In August 1965 the Universal House of Justice was informed that Laura had been invited by Princess Ashraf Pahlavi, the sister of the Shah of Iran, to attend the conference of ICW to be held in Tehran the following summer. It was to be chaired by the princess.[10] The Universal House of Justice wrote to Laura, 'This is a great honor and we congratulate you on your constant service.'[11] It told her that for some time the friends from the West had been required to obtain permission before visiting Iran and therefore the House of Justice had cleared her trip with the National Spiritual Assembly of Iran. It also asked Laura to mention that she was a Bahá'í, particularly to the ICW officers, if she attended the conference, as that would be a great service.[12]

Laura was planning to attend this conference, which was to be held in 1966. It had been 60 years since she had visited Iran, then called Persia, and she was hoping to attend the conference and visit some of her old friends there. However, as it got closer to the date, her doctor recommended that she not take this journey because of her health issues.[13] She wrote to a Bahá'í friend:

The twin sister of the Shah [of Iran] is greatly interested in the advancement of women; she is [the Honorary] President of Council of Women, of which you may recall I have been a member since many years. The International Council of Women was created in 1888 in Washington DC and is now active in each of the continents and among all classes in treating of education and world unity which, as you and I know are among the principal precepts of the Bahá'í Cause.[14]

Laura was updated of the happenings at the Conference after it was over. She later shared that news with Rúḥíyyih Khánum:

I have just received the enclosed brochure of a Conference of the International Council of Women held in Tehran last May under the auspices of Princess Ashraf, who is a Council member. This pamphlet will show you that the ICW began in 1888 its existence – to work for the goals earlier advanced by the Báb and Bahá'u'lláh. The organization works closely with the UN and its Specialized Agencies. Since many years, I have acted as the ICW's Board Liaison Officer to the United Nations.[15]

In 1930 Lady Aberdeen, the president of ICW at the time, had asked Laura if she had any plans to go to Persia, having known about her trip there and her contacts among the Persians. Laura replied that she did not have any such plans but that she knew the Persian Minister in Paris and his distinguished wife, who were her friends.[16] Lady Aberdeen had given Laura the names of several Persian ladies who had corresponded with her. The following year Lady Aberdeen asked Laura for some information regarding the prospect of the formation of a Persian Council, which would have been the predecessor of the National Council of Women of Persia. Laura had informed her that unfortunately the wife of the Persian Minister in Paris at that time, who was a highly cultured and influential woman, had not been able to follow up with Laura. It seems she was 'on the verge of a confinement'.[17]

Laura was often asked for her advice and counsel. Some years earlier the program director at the first and only Iranian television station, who seems to have been in touch with Laura and had consulted with her, told her that the station had been able to show a film about the aims of UNESCO and the emancipation of women and other related films. She wrote to Laura from Iran, '. . . all these could not be achieved without your initial guidance'.[18]

After many years of handling various responsible positions and serving as a board member of the ICW, Laura was still trying to help in any way possible. In those late years of her life she helped compile and edit a book about the history of ICW in order to safeguard and preserve the information. She also took the responsibility of overseeing the publication of, and collaborated as an editor on, the publication of two books, *Certainties* and *Women in a Changing World*.[19] The latter book was a history of 75 years (1888–1963) of the ICW and was published in 1966.[20] Also when she found out that the president of the National Council of Women of the United States was planning its eighty-fifth anniversary celebrations in Washington, D.C., where the National and International Councils had been founded, and needed a place to hold its festivities, she did not hesitate. She requested the Under Secretary of the Smithsonian to allow the delegates from these two organizations to hold their meetings in one of its buildings. The delegates also wished to visit Studio House and she asked him to assist and accompany them.[21]

Her Closest Cousin, Ellen Goin-Rionda

One of the closest relatives to Laura during her lifetime was Ellen Goin, her maternal cousin, the daughter of Aunt Nettie (Jeanette). She had traveled with Laura in 1900 on her first trip to visit 'Abdu'l-Bahá in 'Akká, and soon afterwards she became a Bahá'í. Laura stayed in touch with Ellen throughout her life and visited her in New York or New Jersey almost every time she returned to the United States over the years and spent some of her holidays including Easter and Thanksgiving with her and her family.

Ellen had married Manuel Enrique Rionda in 1911 in New York City and they lived in Alpine, New Jersey.[22] Manuel was orphaned at a young age and was raised by his uncle, Manuel Rionda, a sugar baron from Spain whose family had emigrated to Cuba in 1870. Laura was touched to hear, some years later, that Ellen's husband had provided for a gift to the Bahá'ís through his wife.[23] A few years after her husband died in 1943, Ellen gave some shares of the Francisco Sugar Company to the Bahá'í Fund, to be used either for the Shrine of the Báb in Haifa or the House of Worship in Chicago.[24] Ellen supported the Bahá'í fund for many years.[25] In mid-November 1949, when Laura saw her cousin Ellen in Alpine for a short time, it seems that Ellen was not very well.[26] Laura visited her again in April of the following year.[27]

Ellen gave to the Bahá'í Archives of the National Assembly of the United States documents related to the Faith and some memorabilia from her days in 'Akká when she had visited with Laura in 1900.[28] Ellen passed away in January 1966 in her hometown of Alpine.[29]

Baron von Blomberg of the World Fellowship of Religions

In 1967 Laura informed Anita Chapman that Baron von Blomberg, whom she had met ten years earlier in Washington, was in Paris. He was the co-president of the World Fellowship of Religions and was returning from its regional conference held in Tehran in June of that year. Interestingly, the conference had been held in the birthplace of the Prophet of the Bahá'í Faith. Attendees included members of the Muslim, Jewish, Zoroastrian, Sikh, Hindu, Protestant, Orthodox Christian and Catholic Christian faiths, but the Bahá'í Faith was not represented.[30] On his way back from Tehran he had stopped in Haifa to meet with the Bahá'ís and now that he was in Paris, he was interested in meeting the Bahá'ís there too.[31] The World Fellowship of Religions had been founded in 1957 and had held its initial conference the same year in Delhi. Sant Singh was elected as its President and held that position for 14 years. Other conferences were held in Calcutta in 1960, in Delhi in 1965 and Tehran in 1967.[32]

Baron von Blomberg had told his cousin, Baroness Martha von Blomberg, a great deal about Laura 'in highest terms' and the Baroness wanted to visit her while she was in Paris.[33] The Baroness was the Secretary of the World Advisory Committee of the World Fellowship of Religions and she informed Laura that she had also returned from Tehran. Laura arranged for Baron von Blomberg and Baroness von Blomberg to meet with the chairman of the National Assembly of France.[34] A meeting was also arranged for Laura to meet Baroness von Blomberg, who enjoyed her visit and expressed that the World Fellowship of Religions had the same beliefs that Laura had. The Baroness wrote to Laura, 'As you intimated, life only has true meaning when one lives in a world-wide vision and has wideness of heart and mind, taking all peoples, all good, into one's affection.'[35] The Baroness wished she had more time to discuss deeper matters with Laura. She asked Laura to honor them by allowing her name to be added to their World Advisory Board and Laura invited her to attend a meeting at the Bahá'í Center of Paris. However, Laura declined to become a member of the World Fellowship of Religions.[36]

Laura's Support of Others

Anne Lynch

Laura was as loyal to those who had tirelessly rendered services for the Bahá'í Faith as she was to her principles. One of these people was Anne Slastiona Lynch, who was born in Russia in 1892 and had fled to England and become a Bahá'í in 1926. She spent many years in service to the Faith, including work at the International Bahá'í Bureau in Geneva for 18 years.[37] Laura probably met Anne during her visits to Geneva on behalf of the League. Anne must also have visited Laura in Paris. She was one of the people Laura saw soon after her return to Paris after the war in the summer of 1946.[38]

The two corresponded for many years, especially during World War II, when Anne was working at the Geneva Bureau as a volunteer. During the early years of the Faith in Europe, the Bahá'ís had to learn to function efficiently. Almost all the staff of the Bureau and other Bahá'í organizations were volunteers who received little remuneration. Like other Bahá'ís who were impacted by the hard work and difficult years of the war, Anne was concerned about the amount of work and her health.[39] As was Laura's nature, she would listen to her grievances and offer her advice.

By the late 1940s Laura was worried about Anne's well-being.[40] Anne was appreciative for the genuineness of Laura's friendship and grateful for the support she received from her.[41] Laura even showed her kindness to Anne's brother. Laura's financial support of Anne continued for several years. In the 1950s Laura assisted with the cost of Anne's medical treatment.[42] She also asked the National Assembly of the United States that her contributions to the Bureau be put at Anne's disposal.

In one of her letters to Laura, Anne addressed her as 'My very dear Friend, Mrs Barney', and thanked her for her donation and for her 'thoughtfulness and kindness.'[43] In another letter, Anne again thanked her for her help: 'I often think of you and bless you for your aid. Only the Guardian and yourself have had that care and providence for me.'[44]

In early January 1966, Laura made yet again another contribution for Anne, who was ill in a hospital.[45] The next month Laura was informed that Anne has been discharged as incurable, that her strength was waning and that she had difficulty moving around but was in good spirits.[46] Laura asked Mona Haenni de Bons, another Bahá'í friend in Geneva, to take care of Anne during her last days.[47] Anne died that year, and the Universal House of Justice requested that memorial services be held for her at the Bahá'í Temples in Frankfurt, Germany, and Wilmette, Illinois, and at the Bahá'í Center in Berne, Switzerland.[48]

Lucienne Migette

Another person Laura appreciated and helped was Lucienne Migette (1903–83) from France. Lucienne shared with Laura what she had heard about her before they met, writing to Laura that 'our spiritual mother' [perhaps May Maxwell] had told her that the more she got to know Laura, the more she would appreciate her 'own particular way of working . . . of unusually high ideals . . .' and realize that there was 'nothing petty or limited about her'. Lucienne wrote that these were almost the same words she would have used herself. She had also heard that Laura was 'a credit to the Faith for her literary contributions both in English and in French' and 'a priceless gem for her years of sacrificial service and devotion to the Beloved'. Lucienne expressed her own gratitude, saying, 'I would myself like to tell you of my admiration and gratitude for the tender thoughtfulness that marks everything you do.'[49]

Over the years Laura and Lucienne wrote to each other about all sorts of Bahá'í matters, such as the welfare of its institutions and translations of its books. Lucienne felt close to Laura because of Laura's 'vast life and comprehension'.[50] She addressed Laura as 'Chère Madame Barney, grande amie' or 'Tres Chère Madame Barney' or 'Bien Chère Madame et Amie', always in an affectionate and admiring way.

Lucienne also shared her difficulties with Laura, who continued to support her over the years.[51] Laura assisted Lucienne financially and promised her that she would continue to receive this money even after Laura's death.[52] Laura also emotionally supported her during the difficult times, especially while Lucienne was taking care of her mother.[53] When Lucienne lost her mother, she received a thoughtful letter of condolence from Laura.[54]

By February 1972, Laura was receiving only a few people at her home. But when she heard that Lucienne was not well, she informed her that it 'would give her great pleasure' to see her again if she was well enough to travel to Paris.[55] Again, during those difficult days when Lucienne was gravely sick and could not sleep, eat, write or read, she was very surprised to receive 'a big check' for her unexpected expenses from Laura.[56]

Laura herself had a big loss that year when the dearest person in her life, her sister Natalie, passed away. Despite her own sorrow, she sent a loving letter to Lucienne. This was quite typical of Laura, who stayed strong and detached and able to control her emotions during times of grief and still think of others and what needed to be done. She had shown the same behavior when she had lost her mother. Lucienne wished to see Laura later that year and wrote to her, closing her letter, 'Á bientôt, mon bien affectueux souvenir, chère Amie (See you soon, my very affectionate remembrance, dear friend).'[57] It is not clear if Lucienne managed to visit Laura in Paris.

Mona Haenni de Bons, Daughter of the First French Bahá'í Woman

Another friend of Laura was Edith McKay de Bons (1878–1959), along with her daughter, Mona. She had received the notice of Edith's death on the first day of spring 1959. Edith had heard about the Faith from May Bolles in 1900 and was the first French woman to become a Bahá'í. She married a Swiss man and moved to Switzerland in the early part of the century. Upon her death, her daughter, Mona Haenni de Bons (1904–91), who was living in Geneva, thanked Laura for her kind act of writing a tribute for her mother in the French Bahá'í Bulletin and another one for The Bahá'í World.

Mona and Laura had become close and corresponded over the years until the end of Laura's life. Mona was grateful to Laura for her generous financial assistance. She visited Laura several times in Paris and in La Lignière, the therapeutic clinic that Laura used to go in Switzerland, annually for some years. Mona admired Laura and had great confidence in her judgment and counsel. She was touched by the talent that Laura had for Bahá'í work. Even when it had become difficult for Laura to have visitors, she asked Mona to make sure to visit her the next time she was in Paris.[58]

Mona kept Laura informed of her Bahá'í activities, news of Bahá'ís and the Bahá'í schools she attended, and the progress of the Faith.[59] Laura continued her financial support for Mona and for the work she was doing for the development of the Bahá'í Faith in Switzerland until 1973.[60] Mona Haenni de Bons remained grateful to Laura for her continued support and her precious affection until the end of Laura's life.[61]

Gravesite of Edwin and Joséphine Scott

Laura had known the Scotts from her early years in Paris. Edwin Scott was an American artist living in Paris. He had died in the early 1930s and his wife died in 1955. Both were buried at Sceaux Cemetery. Laura must have felt a responsibility towards the couple for she was worried about their graves. In the late 1960s Laura was concerned that the grave next to those of Edwin Scott and his wife might sink, thus threatening the Scotts' monument. In those years she was not able to leave her home without considerable assistance, so she asked Mr Selzer, a Frenchman, and his wife to take care of the graves. Mr Selzer checked the Scotts' graves and made sure that their monument was not in danger of collapsing.[62] He assured Laura that there were no threats and she should not be concerned.[63] She thanked the Selzers, writing, 'As I move about with difficulty, it means a great deal to me to have dependable friends such as yourselves to undertake a mission such as you did.'[64] The Selzers kept watchful eyes on the graves again the following year at her request.[65]

David Bruce, Her Closest Relative

Another person that Laura was close to was her second cousin David Kirkpatrick Este Bruce. David Bruce (1898–1977) had been an American intelligence officer with the Office of Strategic Services during WWII and then a state-level politician before serving as the United States Ambassador to France, to the Republic of Germany and to the United Kingdom. In 1973 he became the first Chief (or Head) of the United States Liaison Office to the People's Republic of China.[66]

Natalie had first met David Bruce and his wife Evangeline at a reception at her Paris home in July 1951. Perhaps they had accompanied one of the guests, or they may have attended because of his literary inclinations or perhaps because of his interest in the prize that was being awarded that evening to Germain Beaumont. Bruce was the United States Ambassador to France at that time and Natalie described him and his wife to Laura as 'the most official and yet most charming and human-y [sic] cousins'. Natalie and Laura were delighted to have met their newly-found cousin and his wife. They had discovered that his great-grandmother, Louise Miller Ester, and Laura and Natalie's grandmother, Ellen Miller Pike, were sisters.[67]

Laura became close to David Bruce over the years. Other than Natalie, David was Laura's only relative in Europe for some years and that may be why they became close. Laura stayed in touch with the Bruces and would visit them when they moved to Washington, D.C. He was appointed the Ambassador to the United Kingdom in 1961, and Laura chose him to represent her at the Smithsonian when she and Natalie donated Studio House to it.

Bruce visited his cousin Laura in Paris in late 1968. Laura wrote to him after his visit, 'One meditates these somber months, and I am more eager to talk with you on many subjects: past, present & future. All are demanding, especially for one who has lived around our changing world the way we have.'[68] It seems Laura had promised to give him a painting by Edwin Scott and a tapestry. This little *peinture à l'aiguille* (a type of tapestry that stresses lifelike images) was one that she had bought with Hippolyte in 1920 from an isolated monastery on a high mountain in China. Bruce, who had enjoyed his visit with her, wrote, 'It was a delight to visit you in Paris. I have not for years so much enjoyed a conversation; I do wish I could have sustained my part of it as engagingly as you did.' He was enamored by the gift of the painting, which would be put aside for them, and he promised to have a good home for the tapestry, which they would cherish.[69]

In 1973, Laura congratulated him on his appointment by President Richard Nixon as the first United States emissary to the People's Republic of China, a position he held from 1973 to 1974, and referred to this honor as 'again evidence of the high esteem in which you are held both at home and internationally'.[70]

Romaine Brooks' Artwork at the Smithsonian Institution and Her Death

It was through Laura's contacts with the Smithsonian throughout several years that officials there awakened their interest in Romaine Brooks' artwork. She showed the book of Romaine's drawings and paintings to the then new director of the Smithsonian and his assistants in 1963. They were 'very interested in her paintings and drawings'.[71] They needed to find out if Romaine's paintings were in Nice and Laura helped them locate her artwork.[72] In 1964 Laura gave the good news to Natalie: 'the outlook for her beautiful paintings is satisfactory'.[73]

The following year, Laura explained to Dr David Scott of the National Collection of Fine Arts at the Smithsonian (today's Smithsonian American Art Museum) how Romaine's artwork could be seen or found at various universities and museums. She also wrote to Dr Scott, 'I am very happy to hear of the appreciation of your staff for the paintings of Mrs Romaine Brooks, a remarkable artist too little known in the United States as she spent most her life in Italy and France. Her art is unique.'[74] She informed him that Carle Dreyfus, Hippolyte's cousin, who was a conservator at Musée Nissim de Camondo in Paris, had also published a book on Romaine.[75] Perhaps Laura was instrumental in helping this publication become an actuality. She asked Natalie, who was with Romaine at the time, to show Dr Scott's letter to her. Laura was aware that Romaine wished to keep her paintings during her lifetime.[76]

In 1966 Laura received a letter from Dr Scott stating that he had received five paintings by Romaine. He planned to visit her in Nice and was interested in seeing her work.[77] He did visit her the following year and selected additional work.[78] Two years later Laura informed Romaine that the men at the Smithsonian 'are most interested in placing your drawings to their advantage' in the new building which was to be completed next year.[79]

Years later, Charles Eldredge, the Director of the National Museum of American Art, gave the credit for making this possible to Laura.[80] It was after Laura's patronage that Romaine decided to donate her drawings and paintings, 60 in total, to the National Collection of Fine Arts.[81] Eldredge wrote:

Perhaps so difficult an art was destined to follow its maker into oblivion, except for the intervention of another American expatriate, Laura Dreyfus Barney – friend of Brooks and daughter of Alice Pike Barney, Washington's cultural *doyenne* – who (with her sister Natalie) had made a significant gift to the Smithsonian Institution . . . Intrigued by the example of the Barney family's benefaction, Brooks donated 23 paintings and 37 drawings to the national collection shortly before her death.[82]

Adelyn Dohme Breeskin, who was curator of the National Collection of Fine Arts at that time, organized an exhibition of Romaine Brooks' works the year after her death in Washington in 1971. The exhibition then traveled to the Whitney Museum of American Art in New York City.

It seems that Breeskin had an interview with Romaine in Nice. After visiting her and viewing her paintings, Breeskin went to Paris, saw the Barney sisters and found this meeting interesting. 'Natalie was living at the Hotel Maurice [Meurice],' she said, 'and Laura had her same old apartment which was in the building where Romaine Brooks had an apartment, also. Beautiful apartment. So, it was a good trip seeing Romaine and seeing the Barney sisters.'[83]

The Barney sisters were also instrumental in making sure Romaine's works would be put safely in museums. By 1968 three of her portraits had been sent to Yale University for restoration. The newly opened Yale Center for British Art had been founded two years earlier by Paul Mellon, the brother-in-law of David Bruce, Laura and Natalie's cousin.[84]

Romaine's last years were sad. She became increasingly reclusive, had abandoned painting years earlier, and was sinking into depression and paranoia. She died in Nice on December 7, 1970 at the of age 96. It must have been difficult for Laura, as she had been a close friend of Romaine for decades.

Laura's Contact with Natalie in Their Late Years

Laura had been lonely since the deaths of her husband and her mother, but she managed to live on her own with dignity and rectitude. Natalie was her only close family and Laura yearned for her sibling's love, affection and approval more than ever after the death of Hippolyte and Alice. Still, she was often disappointed by Natalie's failure to get together, to arrange meeting places and trips together and to show up when she had agreed upon the arrangements. Despite all these, Laura was always considerate, kind, and warm towards her sister.

Over the years, Laura had stayed in touch with Natalie despite their differences, and even when she was completely in a different world, literally and metaphorically. Laura had discussed her beliefs and way of thinking with her sister long before but ceased doing so when there was no approval or understanding. Laura learned early not to discuss her spiritual beliefs with Natalie – ever.

Throughout their lives, the Barney sisters both traveled extensively and had relentless schedules. However, their travels went different ways. The volume of letters between Laura and Natalie suggests that they spent almost all their time away from each other. As the years went on, they saw each other less and less. This state of affairs worsened progressively, probably because of the lukewarm relationship that Natalie had with Laura. This contrasted with Laura's careful handling of their estates, from which, thanks to Laura's efforts, Natalie received a regular income in trust money.

Laura's relationship with her sister had become more than a little distant despite her wishes. A newspaper article published after a reporter visited them in Paris in 1965 stated that they were both over 80 and were 'as different as can be . . . The sisters have lived in Paris well over 60 years and come from the same ancestry, but here the similarity ends.'[85] Laura had told the reporter, 'My sister and I have remained very good friends, but her life and mine have little in common.'[86] The reporter concluded: 'Natalie Barney and her sister Laura have come a long way since the early Dayton and Cincinnati days. Their lives led them on very different paths. But they have both taken and given the best of the two worlds.'[87]

Now in the eighth decade of her life and back in Paris after a trip to Switzerland, Laura spent most of her time inside her apartment with her documents rather than going out.[88] Through Huntington, Laura continued helping Natalie with their finances. Laura was still responsible for managing their investments. This had started upon the death of their mother, when Laura had been named as executor of the estate. Laura had competently handled the paperwork and correspondence with banks and various agents of their assets, and problems never arose between Natalie and Laura in this respect. Even though they had their disagreements, they never argued about money. They were both content with the situation. Laura believed that it was best to sell two inherited properties, Orange Grove and Old Garden Cottage, when a propitious time arrived.[89] She did sell the Old Garden Cottage a few years later.[90]

Laura rarely criticized Natalie for her lifestyle, even though she may not have approved of it. She always addressed Natalie with endearing words such as 'Dear One', 'Golden Locks' and 'Natalie dear'. For one of Natalie's birthdays, Laura addressed her as 'Dear Golden Locks' as she almost always did, and referring to their birth months of October for Natalie and November for Laura:

> . . . I am thankful that to me the 30th [31st] of October is not like many other days of the year – simply a numerical measure of time – October and November are side by side in the year – you and I are side by side in life, may we become as splendid as are the days of October and November.[91]

Their long lives gave Laura many opportunities to wish her sister well. For Natalie's sixtieth birthday, Laura wrote: 'Your sixty years seem light to your childhood companion . . . Birthday greetings to only "Golden Locks" – even when they will be silver to me, they will always be "golden locks".'[92] Laura sent a letter to her sister for her eighty-eighth birthday: 'To you my deep love for the many years we have gone through before.'[93] In 1968 Laura sent a loving note to her sister on her birthday, remembering their mother, years after her death: 'Mother also joined in your birth, so I enclose mother's ornament which is detached from its twin, which I keep. Thus, we share this souvenir of "Little One".'[94] She signed it 'Laura Alice', which was the full given name she had not used since childhood. Perhaps Laura wished to remember their mother and childhood in those years when Natalie was distancing herself.

Never failing to find different occasions to express her love and affection towards her sister, Laura wrote to her:

> My first letter of the year is to you, the last one of the year was from you . . . I do not know what you wish for the coming year, at least let it be what will be agreeable to you if you know it or not.[95]

In one letter around Christmas, Laura said that she had not changed much over the years and her love for Natalie had not changed since childhood. She remembered their lives at Christmastimes and the toys they received, stockings, holiday excitement, the joy of new possessions, and surprises in the New Year in those early childhood years:

> We have changed little; I have changed even less than you. Our childhood with snow, animals, adventures, fairy tales, certain sensations. My old childhood love goes to you tonight. It has not changed. I have changed so little.[96]

One time, Laura was so happy to have received two letters from her sister that she responded, 'I was very appreciative of your 2 letters . . . perhaps you are an angel in disguise?'[97] She often praised Natalie for everything she did and achieved. After having lunch with a friend of Natalie and their cousin, she wrote: 'we spent 2 or 3 hours singing your praises'.[98] When a friend of theirs had watched Natalie being interviewed on television, Laura commented to Natalie, 'you were more competent than the questioner'.[99] She even complimented Natalie for her looks, writing that she was 'smart tailored' when she had seen her a few days earlier.[100]

Laura continued living at 74 rue Raynouard on the north side of the Seine River and Natalie was at 20 rue Jacob on the Left Bank for an even longer period. In late 1969 or early 1970, Natalie moved to the Hôtel Le Meurice, also on the north side of the Seine since her house at rue Jacob was undergoing renovations before its sale.[101] Laura continued her communications with her sister despite getting unwelcoming responses while Natalie was at the hotel.[102]

They had taken different and separate paths in life as early as 1900, and perhaps even before. Two newspaper reporters from *The Club-Fellow* and *The Washington Mirror* observed that the sisters 'agreed to disagree and to live separate and apart'.[103] They were more than different – usually on opposite ends of a scale. Laura was tight with her money whereas Natalie was a spender. Laura was serious and rather shy, and Natalie was carefree. Even Laura herself once wrote how different they were in their social interactions: 'Natalie is sociable like her parents were, I am the only recluse of the family.'[104] Laura liked solitude to a certain level. In one letter to Natalie, soon after the death of their mother, she wrote: 'As numbers of interesting people are passing through Paris, so I shall have more visits than my solitude likes.'[105] Some even believed that 'As they aged, they had little to do with one another for neither sister accepted the direction the other's life had taken.'[106] Kling, their mother's biographer, wrote: 'Throughout the majority of their adult lives, the Barney sisters lived near one another in Paris . . . Psychically, however, they were far apart.'[107]

> Toward the end of their lives, communication between them was primarily through letters and messages carried by mutual friends or through errands run by William Huntington . . . While money kept them in communication, by the end of their lives their memories of Alice seemed their only emotional link, and even there they did not always agree.[108]

Kling further commented on the differences between the sisters. 'Where Laura sought satisfaction in intellectual pursuits and accomplishing good works, Natalie aspired to happiness by surrounding herself with stimulating people and writing pungent aphorisms.'[109] A major reason for Laura's letters to Natalie, the best open door for staying in touch it seems, was to inform Natalie of her whereabouts during the many years of constant travel. Rarely would she boast about her achievements even though Natalie was the only one with whom she could share her joy, which she did a few times by enclosing newspaper articles written about her.

Interestingly, though, early on even Natalie herself believed that Laura was the wise one of the two of them.[110] Huntington believed that Natalie had spent every single penny of her money and that Laura was the richer one. He believed that Laura 'was generous with organizations and Natalie was generous with individuals'.[111] And Alice Pike Barney's biographer believed, 'While Laura kept tight rein on the principal of their inheritance, Natalie spent her share of the interest as rapidly as possible.'[112]

A five-part series of articles about the Barney sisters was published in an Ohio newspaper late in their lives in 1965. One of these articles commented:

> They are over 85 and as different as can be . . . Laura Dreyfus-Barney, a romantic, dark-haired beauty in her youth, married a prominent

French lawyer and scholar, Hippolyte Dreyfus, and found her calling mainly in social work and travel, her leadership and outstanding contributions to society have won her various honors and a long column in *Who's Who*.[113]

In this day and age when everyone clamors for a university degree, their formal education might seem on the sparse side, yet both Barney sisters were to become famous in their separate ways: the younger one in the international peace movement and humanities and religion; the older one in the literary field, with an awesome mastery of the French language. In common they had their international background that was to shape their very different destinies.[114]

Their connection was also that they were forever the Barney Sisters, perhaps because neither of them had a family of her own. Laura lost her husband at an early age and Natalie never married. Neither having had children, they were considered Alice Pike Barney's daughters and the 'Barney Sisters' all their lives.[115] Another article commented:

> Yet, beneath the bickering was a deep, unbreakable bond forged from their earliest years. Natalie loved Laura, confided in her about everything, and relied on her in countless ways. Laura, in turn, admired her big sister's outgoing personality and ability to attract others. She was also proud of Natalie's accomplishments as a writer and literary salonist, constantly scissoring articles about her from newspapers to paste into scrapbooks or mail to friends and relatives. Laura once described Natalie as 'the greatest pleasure and the greatest trouble rolled into one person, but as pleasure is rarer than all things it is the only memory that remains'.[116]

Laura may not have approved of Natalie's pleasure-loving ways, but she never disliked and never stopped adoring her except, perhaps, when the usual sisterly family matters got out of hand. Natalie was a constant presence in Laura's life, from her birth to Natalie's death. Laura's emotional connection with Natalie was the strongest and the longest relationship she had. Laura remained in contact with Natalie and her love for her never diminished, despite a rocky relationship at times and the separate paths they had selected. There was not mutual dislike, at least not on Laura's part. Perhaps there was dislike of the other's direction but not an absence of affection. Perhaps this relationship with Natalie would have been different had Laura's husband lived longer. According to Chapman, after the passing of her husband, Laura was strongly influenced by her sister.[117] This was not because she agreed with Natalie's life style but to keep her happy in the relationship.

Even though Laura was the money manager for the two sisters and had to discuss those matters regularly, she never stopped expressing her love and adoration to her sister. She always conveyed her respects to all those that were associated with Natalie and appreciated everything she had accomplished. Natalie's biographer Rodriguez believed 'They took a practical approach, often discussing tax considerations and almost never resorting to sentiment.'[118] However, this was not how Laura approached their relationship.

Although they had distinctly different characters, there were some commonalities between the two sisters. Their shared genealogy gave them an interesting mixture of a little bit of 'French delicacy, taste and refinement combined with the American pioneer ingenuity and endurance'.[119] They were raised in the same family, went on the same family vacations and experienced the family feuds. They had shared the same boarding school, which may have had a long-term effect on both. They both took after their independent-minded, eccentric mother and shared the same international exposure, cultured upbringing and introduction to the artistic world. Both were childless and after the passing of their mother had no other close family. However, these commonalties contributed differently to each of them distinctly, giving them different directions in life.

The Passing of Natalie Barney

Laura lost her sister in 1972. Natalie had had two heart attacks previously before she died of heart failure in the arms of a nurse in Paris in the early hours of February 2 of that year. She was 95 years old at the time of her passing and was buried at Passy Cemetery near Place du Trocadéro in the sixteenth arrondissement. Her body was taken to the American church on Avenue George V and was then transferred to Passy Cemetery. No prayers were said when her coffin was lowered into the ground, in accordance with her wishes.[120] According to her biographer and friend, Chalon, she did not believe in God.[121]

Laura was too weak to attend her only sibling's funeral.[122] She must have been heartbroken and distressed at having lost her closest family member. But by then she was not even able to leave her apartment. Natalie had been given one plot at the Passy Cemetery in the mid-1950s and had requested another person be buried with her – either her sister or Romaine Brooks.[123] However, Brooks had died in 1970 and been buried in Nice.

It is said that even after death the sisters disagreed. Laura wished that Natalie's stone be simply inscribed 'American poet and writer' but Huntington was not happy with this. He asked for help from Natalie's friend Chalon. The two men met with Laura and tried to convince her to respect Natalie's wishes. To their surprise, Laura accepted without any further discussion. She told Chalon, 'I don't want her getting angry over something written on that tomb.'[124] The tombstone read:

Natalie Clifford Barney

Ecrivain

1876 – 1972

Elle fut L'Amazone de Remy de Gourmont

Je suis cet Être Légendaire

Ou je revis N.C.B.

Natalie had never accepted her sister's Faith but had met some of its important figures during her lifetime. 'Abdu'l-Bahá had met Natalie in London in 1911 and asked about her in numerous letters to Laura. 'Convey greetings to your sister,' He wrote in one such letter.[125] In another one sent from Haifa, He inquired about 'the whereabouts of your sister and her well-being and amenity'.[126] Shoghi Effendi, who had met Natalie in Paris, and his wife Rúḥíyyih Khánum were concerned about Natalie during World War II and were relieved when the two sisters were reunited after six years. The National Assembly of the Bahá'ís of France sent Laura a letter of condolence on the passing of her sister.[127]

Natalie was a playwright, poet, novelist and an adventurer. She was recognized as an immensely talented intellectual writer from France. She had created a salon in her home, an 18th-century villa in rue Jacob in Paris, which attracted the world's greatest writers who formed a small literary circle that flourished around her. Natalie was one of the great literary hostesses of her time, and her salons were held continuously until the late 1960s, except during the German occupation of World War II. Those who frequented her salons included Auguste Rodin, Marcel Proust, Colette, Anatole France, Robert de Montesquiou, James Joyce, Gertrude Stein, Alice B. Toklas, Somerset Maugham, Radclyffe Hall, T. S. Eliot, Isadora Duncan, Edna St. Vincent Millay, Virgil Thomson, Ezra Pound, Israel Zangwill, Gabriele d'Annunzio, Paul Valéry, Paul Morand, Jean Cocteau, Scott and Zelda Fitzgerald, Pierre Louÿs, William Carlos Williams, Nancy Cunard, Peggy Guggenheim, Mina Loy, Caresse and Harry Crosby, Marie Laurencin, Oscar Milosz, Paul Claudel, Adrienne Monnier, Sylvia Beach, Emma Calvé, Sherwood Anderson, Hart Crane, Mary McCarthy, Sinclair Lewis, André Gide, Wanda Landowska, George Antheil, Rabindranath Tagore, Ida Rubenstein, Truman Capote, Remy de Gourmont and Françoise Sagan.[128]

Natalie's correspondence and unpublished works were given to Bibliothèque Jacques Doucet in Paris to be archived. Laura also sent various documents and letters in her possession to this literary library.[129]

Further Editions of Laura's and Hippolyte's Books and Translations

One of Laura's activities that she continued in her old age was the reprinting of her own and Hippolyte's books. Given her editorial and writing capabilities and high standards, these ventures were right up her alley. She had the literary skills, the discerning eye, and the patience for meticulous work that made her an expert at preparing books for new editions. She had been involved with her own book, *Some Answered Questions*, since its initial publications. This compilation had its own success story and is discussed separately.

Regarding her other book, *God's Heroes*, she had contacted the National Bahá'í Archives in England in 1927 and informed the National Assembly that she had George Routledge and Sons, the publisher, send her one hundred copies. She asked that the proceeds go to the fund for the Bahá'í House of Worship in the United States. She also asked for suggestions as to how the book could be used in teaching the Cause.[130]

More recently, Horace Holley, an American Bahá'í, had suggested that she bring out a new edition of *God's Heroes*. He also suggested that the National Assembly of France sponsor the new edition.[131] Laura thought that the French version could be adapted for a radio broadcast in France. She felt that because of the writings of Comte de Gobineau, who had been an ambassador in Iran at the time of Qurratu'l-'Ayn, her story would be better known in France than in other countries.[132]

As for Hippolyte's books that she had financed, the National Assembly thanked her for reprinting them in 1965. She continued to send Bahá'í books authored by her husband to different institutions. She must have sent the corrected version of the third edition of *Livre de la Certitude* to the Director of the Library of Presses Universitaires, as it accepted to print the third edition in 1965. Laura was also involved in a new edition of the French translation of the *Kitáb-i-Íqán*. She distributed this new version to various National Spiritual Assemblies and communities worldwide.[133]

In 1965 she also reviewed the book *l'Épître au Fils du Loup* (*Epistle to the Son of the Wolf*) before the printing of a new edition.[134] She wanted to bring out a new edition of this book, which had been translated into French by Hippolyte. The book was written as a single letter by Bahá'u'lláh in which He described the persecutions He suffered and is an anthology of His own writings.[135]

Another of Hippolyte's books was *Essai sur le Bahá'isme (Essay on Bahaism)*; Laura had the copyright to the English language edition during her lifetime. Upon her death it would be passed on to the National Assembly of the United States. In 1966 she gave George Ronald, Publisher, permission to bring out an English version of this book, and asked it to send her the text and the layout for her approval before it was printed.[136] Laura was happy that *Essai sur le Bahá'isme* was going to be published in Spanish in 1970.[137] The National Assembly of Spain had contacted her to obtain permission and had asked for any corrections that she might have.

In 1972 the National Spiritual Assembly of France asked Laura for permission to reprint *Essay on Bahaism* and *Le Livre de la Certitude*, since she was the copyright holder for both books.[138] Until almost the last year of her life, she paid for the reprinting and publication of the French books authored by her husband and herself. It was only in 1973 that the National Assembly asked Laura's publisher, Presses Universitaires de France, not to charge her for any further reprints of the books.[139]

Laura's Will, Precious Documents and Valuables

Laura's longevity and sharpness of mind until almost the end of her life gave her ample time to plan how best to distribute her assets, her possessions and important documents. She donated her files and correspondence to the appropriate archives – letters to and from Bahá'ís to the relevant Bahá'í institutions, arts-related materials and her mother's papers to the Smithsonian, and documents related to the ICW to the Library of Congress and the Archives of the United Nations in Geneva.

Laura had informed the National Assembly of the United States as early as 1936 of the provisions in her will regarding her Bahá'í documents.[140] She had sent many of these precious documents to Shoghi Effendi for the Bahá'í Archives when someone that she trusted, Mrs Angiz Tabrizi, traveled to Haifa in the winter of 1937.[141] She later sent the original signed copies of *Some Answered Questions*, the Tablets from 'Abdu'l-Bahá to Hippolyte, and ones to herself, as well as a *cachet* (stamp or seal) of Bahá'u'lláh that 'Abdu'l-Bahá had given to her.[142] She said some years later:

> I never felt quite at ease while the original manuscript remained in Paris, but I didn't do much about it because my logic didn't tell me which way I was to go. Then a Persian woman was returning to see her family in the East; I said: Will you take these to Shoghi Effendi? I included, with the manuscript, all my Tablets and Mrs Tewkesbury Jackson's too, so that all these documents are in Shoghi Effendi's hands. I wonder if it isn't that deeper sense of Guardianship that makes us turn to him when we don't know quite what to do . . .[143]

In 1966 Laura sent some materials to the Universal House of Justice including original Tablets of 'Abdu'l-Bahá to different people that she had in her possession, Tablets of Bahá'u'lláh that Hippolyte had copied from the British Museum in London, copies of other Tablets of 'Abdu'l-Bahá, and some books. The Universal House of Justice informed her that it had received most of the materials that she had sent, but not all the documents related to *Some Answered Questions* with 'Abdu'l-Bahá's corrections.[144]

Twice in 1970 she sent letters and more 'precious contents' to the

Universal House of Justice.[145] Since she still had some objects given to her by 'Abdu'l-Bahá and His sister, the Universal House of Justice asked Ugo Giachery to obtain them from her if he visited Paris.[146] 'Abdu'l-Bahá had often received precious gifts, but He always passed them on to pilgrims and visitors or sold them for money to sustain the work of the Faith. The gifts that Laura had received included a gold chain and a gold bracelet; a gold ring with a ruby and two diamonds in a Lalique setting made from the precious stones given to her by 'Abdu'l-Bahá; a gold ring with emerald given to her by 'Abdu'l-Bahá's sister; a gold ring with 'sardonyx having incised symbol' given to her by 'Abdu'l-Bahá or His sister; a silver locket with four emeralds and two diamonds (Laura had mounted the stones and added a Bahá'í inscription); and pen boxes.[147] By March of the following year these items had been delivered by Ugo Giachery to the National Spiritual Assembly of the British Isles for safe keeping.[148] Laura was informed that the precious objects had been received by the Bahá'í World Centre by April 24, 1972.[149] She was happy that these precious documents and objects were being kept in the International Bahá'í Archives by the Universal House of Justice.[150]

New Developments with *Some Answered Questions*

Laura continued to oversee the publication of various editions of *Some Answered Questions*. A new English edition was released in 1964. This edition had some corrections on the book jacket. In mid-June 1966, Guy Murchie (1907–97), an American Bahá'í and writer in the fields of philosophy and science, wrote to Laura saying he and his wife were in Paris and would love to meet her. He had some questions about *Some Answered Questions*, 'something of importance to the Faith', and was a writer who was going to write, in the future, about the very principles that she had asked 'Abdu'l-Bahá about. He thus wanted to meet her to discuss the book.[151] They did meet in Paris. The following month, when he moved to a suburb of Paris, he offered to assist her with his proposed changes to the book.[152]

Laura checked *Some Answered Questions* with Chahab Ala'i, the chairman of the National Spiritual Assembly of France at that time. She believed that some technical terms used in the 1960s were not in usage when she first worked on the book. She wanted the National Assembly of the United States to approve minor corrections for a later edition.[153] She then wrote to Murchie, 'As you may no doubt realize, many technical terms in use today were not known in 1906 . . . also there are no technical words in the Persian language.'[154] She suggested again that certain terms could be added in the footnotes if the National Assembly approved them.[155]

Laura was proud of her achievement in compiling *Some Answered Questions* and gave updates to her friends of the numerous editions and the number of languages into which it had been translated. She also received news of its use and the high demand for it, and that it was being used in Bahá'í classes for their study.[156] In 1968, Laura was happy to learn that this book had been translated into Finnish. She wrote to a Bahá'í in Finland, 'It is encouraging to learn that *Some Answered Questions* has been translated into Finnish by your friend Greta Jankko. I know it is also in Persian, Arabic, Esperanto, Italian, German, English and French, and I believe in Japanese.'[157] She learned from the World Centre in 1969 that the book had been published in 16 languages in addition to five 'manuscript editions' and one in Braille.[158] There was also a great demand for the French version of *Some Answered Questions* in 1968.[159]

That year, in a letter to her dear friend Rúḥíyyih Khánum, addressing her as 'My very dear Mary Rúḥíyyih', Laura stated that there were 4,000 copies of the fourth edition of *Les Leçons de St. Jean d'Acre*.[160] She was working on a new edition to be sent to Presses Universitaires de France, which was subsequently submitted in June 1969.[161] Laura shared the news with her friend Anita Chapman in the United States that 500 copies of the latest edition of the French version of *Some Answered Questions* had been given to the Paris Bahá'í Center for sale.[162] She was happy that her book was very much in demand.[163]

While Laura remained involved with all the updates, revisions and reprints of *Some Answered Questions*, she was also concerned about future revisions of the book by people who might have good intentions but perhaps not the necessary knowledge and expertise to uphold her standards. Therefore she gave the responsibility for the book to the Universal House of Justice. In January 1973 she wrote,

> I took the precaution of writing to Wilmette administrative office [where the offices of the National Assembly of the United States are located] and also to Haifa [where the seat of the Universal House

of Justice is located] that I would like changes in future editions of
SOME ANSWERED QUESTIONS to be submitted to the Universal House of Justice, before publication, for approval.[164]

The National Assembly assured Laura that her wishes would be carried
out and that any proposed revisions for a new edition of *Some Answered
Questions* would be submitted to the House of Justice for approval.[165]
The House of Justice had also received a copy of a letter of January 27,
1973, to the National Assembly about a new edition of *Some Answered
Questions.* The House of Justice responded to Laura and thanked her
for her 'constant care for the protection of these precious talks from the
Master', and they assured her that they would review and 'if necessary,
edit any revisions which may have to be made from time to time'.[166]

That same year, Huntington also met with the National Assembly
of France to assist it with fulfilling Laura's wishes. He reported that she
wished to give the copyright of her publications to the National Assembly of the United States and that her books be published by reputable
publishers and the income from sales be used for financing her books.[167]
She never accepted reimbursement of her expenses for the publication
of her Bahá'í books. When publishers needed money for reprinting, she
would send whatever amount they needed.[168] As for the copyright of
the French version of *Some Answered Questions,* the Universal House of
Justice in a letter to the National Spiritual Assembly of Belgium wrote
that 'probably' it 'resides with Mrs Dreyfus-Barney and therefore will
continue for the prescribed period after her passing'.[169]

In appreciation for Laura's hard work, Marzieh Gail, whose father,
Ali-Kuli Khan, had been a close friend of Laura during the early years of
the 20th century, wrote to her in 1973, 'You have now done all that can
be done to protect the invaluable text of *Some Answered Questions.*'[170]

Appreciations from Around the World

Laura continued to receive many letters, visits and calls from people
around the world during her later years. She was immensely respected for
her inestimable services and this appreciation helped to keep her going.
A letter written on behalf of the Universal House of Justice in 1963 conveyed the greetings from the friends in Persia, who knew her name well
because of *Some Answered Questions.* They remembered her husband's

distinction, as well as their visit to Iran.[171] The National Assembly of the United States noted that it was aware of her 'distinguished services'.[172] The National Spiritual Assembly of France was grateful to have in its community such a respected individual with a reservoir of memories of her close association with the Master, 'Abdu'l-Bahá.[173]

In the early 1960s Laura received a letter from a Bahá'í woman from Nice who had wanted to take flowers to the hotel where she was staying but was informed that Laura had already left. She thanked Laura for her presence at a gathering and wrote, 'Your personality, your wise words, and your brilliant spirit will stay with me and I shall never forget.'[174] Another expression of appreciation came from May Bolles Maxwell some years earlier, who had stated that Laura was 'a girl so gifted and brilliant that her name is imperishably recorded in the early annals of the Faith'.[175]

In 1967 the administrator of *La Pensée Bahá'íe*, a Swiss Bahá'í journal, wrote to Laura:

> We are happy to take this special opportunity to tell you of our great esteem and admiration for that wonderful book, 'Les Leçons de Saint-Jean d'Acre.' It is the book we keep on our bedside tables. Every time we immerse ourselves in it, we think about its author and the extraordinary adventure you experienced with 'Abdu'l-Bahá, about all those marvelous and unique circumstances. And for every Bahá'í, old or new, what treasures you have gathered together on its weighty and irreplaceable pages. Words may fail us but not the sincere gratitude of your friends throughout the world.[176]

In 1970 the Local Assembly of Washington, D.C., thanked Laura for her continued support of the Washington Bahá'í Center over the years and acknowledged that she had been a young girl when she went to meet 'Abdu'l-Bahá and said, 'Now we have a lot of young people. You are an example to them.'[177]

The National Teaching Committee of the North of France also wrote to Laura:

> The legacy which you have bequeathed to all Bahá'ís, present and future, especially those who did not have the occasion to meet 'Abdu'l-Bahá, is precious beyond our imaginings. One will never know how

many hearts have been calmed and assured by the responses of 'Abdu'l-Bahá recorded in your 'Some Answered Questions'.[178]

One Bahá'í couple sent Laura a note: 'To our dear and precious Madame Dreyfus-Barney who gave great enlightenment to the world of mankind with her beautiful book "Some Answered Questions". May the Beloved guide you, protect you and love you through all eternity.'[179] A Bahá'í who had been a young man in Paris, Ezzat Zahrai, many years later remembered Laura as a 'very charming and elegant' lady: 'We all respected her deeply for herself and the services she had rendered to our Beloved Faith.'[180] Angeline Giachery, a Bahá'í who with her husband Ugo was close to Laura, wrote to her: '. . . you are always in our hearts and in our prayers. Your precious life of service to the Cause of Bahá'u'lláh is a constant inspiration to us and to countless believers who love and admire you.'[181]

Laura Dreyfus Barney Remembered

The American Bahá'í Anita Ioas Chapman knew Laura in her later years. When interviewed by the author, Anita did not remember exactly where they had met in Europe – perhaps they met at the first European Bahá'í Conference, held in Geneva in 1948. Anita lived in Paris from 1950 to 1955 and returned with her husband and three children to live there a second time from 1965 to 1967. Her family rented an apartment two floors below Laura's at 74 rue Raynouard. Anita recalled that Laura had been an active member of the Bahá'í community of Paris but in those later years she was not easily able to attend gatherings at the Bahá'í Center.[182]

Anita reflected on her years living close to Laura. Two years after her return to the United States, she wrote to Laura: 'Words cannot say; it is one of the choice memories to have lived two floors below and been able to participate in long conversations full of Bahá'í history and full of wisdom.'[183] Laura was in turn happy to have had Anita and her family living in the same building, where she had lived since 1930.[184]

When interviewed by the present author, Anita remembered that Laura was uncomfortable around children in her later years.

Laura Barney would invite us [the Chapmans] to tea in her apartment. She was very austere and was not cuddly. Laura was shrewd and intelligent. She was extremely active in those years, always a very devoted Bahá'í. She devoted much of her time to international organizations. It was very important to her. She was comfortable with people of her sort. Her network was with international organizations and she was very highborn . . . She had married an outstanding man. Her life would have evolved very differently vis-à-vis the Bahá'í Faith if her husband had lived. I am very convinced of that. But left alone, she almost took refuge in all those international organizations' work which she considered very important . . . As a woman alone and as a widow, it was very difficult for her. Nonetheless, she was close to her sister, she was family. Everyone associated the name Barney with Natalie Barney and she was Mme Dreyfus-Barney.[185]

Anita stayed in touch with Laura until her death. In 1988 she assisted in the planning of a tribute for Laura at Studio House.

Staying Home, Welcoming Visitors and Corresponding with Friends

During the last few years of Laura's life rheumatism restricted her body but her mind was still sharp and brilliant. She had traveled tirelessly and extensively when young and had once written, 'I wonder if I am not part "nomad" as I feel at home on the move.'[186] In 1914 she traveled with her husband to Japan and China, and in 1920 they traveled to the Middle East, Indochina, China and India for a year and a half. Her lectures on disarmament and peace for the ICW took her from eastern to western Canada in 1932. In 1935 she journeyed to Egypt, Palestine, Lebanon, Syria, Turkey and Greece for a series of talks. In March 1947 she was in Washington and New York, and upon her return to Paris in April went to meetings in Geneva, Zurich and Brussels before returning to the United States in the summer. She took annual trips to the United States and regular trips to Geneva for her meetings.

But that was the past. Now mobility was difficult, Laura remained active through corresponding with her old friends, completing projects, reprinting her books and staying in touch with the Bahá'ís from around the world who wrote to her, and with some who wanted to visit her. With her mind still alert and active, Laura stayed inside her apartment living with her memories and spending time with her documents rather than going out.[187] While at home, she kept a copy of *Some Answered Questions* by her side and would proudly show it off to those who visited her.[188] She still had Yvonne to assist, who, according to Laura, had continued 'firm in her many roles: secretary, economist, nurse, housekeeper'.[189]

In her correspondence with Rúḥíyyih Khánum she recalled with fondness past events and times with her mother and longed for news of Khánum.[190] Laura had known Mary (Rúḥíyyih Khánum) since an early age and wrote, 'You have been dear to me since the age of five or six, and I received the message of the Cause through your mother when she was May Bolles.'[191] Rúḥíyyih Khánum also continued to write to Laura. She addressed her in a letter in 1965 as 'My very dear Laura' and wrote, 'I think of you with regrets I did not – and do not have – more time to see you in this life. The evening in your home was a great consolation to me.'[192] She had received a beautiful tablecloth from Laura and was going to use it at the House of 'Abbúd in 'Akká.

In 1969 Rúḥíyyih Khánum wrote to Laura, who was then 90 years old, again regretting that they could so seldom visit, but also with an important request:

> It is a source of great regret to me that, because of distance and the fact that I always seem to be travelling in the opposite direction, I so seldom have been able to see you. It would be great pleasure if I could visit you frequently and we could talk of those we love and of the past, which you have such a rich store of memories. I do hope, Laura, that you have written down your memories? There are few left in the world today who can recall the early history of the Faith in the West as you can and to me it would be a great and tragic loss if this dies when you are sent to the Abhá Kingdom, which I hope will not be for a long time.[193]

Despite her health problems Laura managed to accept some visitors during specific times of the day. One of those visitors was Jack McLean, a young Canadian Bahá'í who was studying in Paris from 1965 to 1968 and met her in 1967. He was 21 years old at the time of his visit. He wrote of this first meeting:

Madame Barney was 88 years old and very frail. A formal, unsmiling Spanish maid opened the door of her apartment on rue de Ranelagh [Raynouard] and invited me to sit down. I cannot say she welcomed me, for I had the impression that she considered my visit as a sort of inconvenience, if not an intrusion. She withdrew for a moment and returned to notify me that Madame Barney was ready. The maid led me to the door of the bedroom. I entered and saw Laura sitting propped up in bed . . . Madame Barney was not loquacious. She spoke economically, keeping things simple, perhaps because of her age . . .

When the hour was up, I took my leave, thanking the maid as I left. As I descended the carpeted stairs of the apartment in the affluent 16th *arrondissement,* I realized that I had been graced by the presence of a great soul, one who met other great souls, one who had seen great things, and done great things in the service of the Greatest Servant of humanity.[194]

Laura regretted that her health did not permit her to go out or attend the meetings at the Paris Bahá'í Center.[195] In past decades she had attended many gatherings and had given many talks there.[196] But by 1969 she could no longer hold meetings or attend long ones. When she was unable to attend the wedding of the daughter of a Bahá'í, she asked the wedding party to visit her afterwards, saying she looked forward to meeting the bride and groom.[197]

Throughout her life, Laura was respectful to people of all faiths, creeds and religions. She supported and welcomed all those who worked for world peace. She wrote to a Quaker couple in 1968 that people like them 'have been tireless in their efforts to contribute to world harmony'.[198] Some years later she wrote to the same couple saying that she had enjoyed having interesting discussions with them.[199]

Laura was well aware that her years were coming to an end. She wrote to a friend who had visited her that she regretted not being able to say 'we shall meet again', since she was well on in years and they might 'not meet again; but there are no limits in the realms of thought'.[200] Around her 90th birthday Laura reflected on her life, writing, 'And the coming end of this year I shall be an old person who has had great spiritual aid through a great part of her life.'[201] Bahá'í friends visited her on her 90th birthday, among them Mr and Mrs Bolibaugh, an American

Bahá'í couple from California who visited her often.[202] The Bolibaughs had settled in Paris and gave her news of the French Bahá'ís on a regular basis.

Laura was happy that her friends the Giacherys, who were now residing in Monaco, visited her in Paris in 1970. She told them that Hippolyte's book would be published in Spanish and was happy and encouraged that the Faith was spreading throughout the world.[203] That same year she wrote to another friend, 'Friends from the Paris Assembly and also pilgrims passing through Paris on their way to or from Haifa keep me informed of the encouraging news of the spread of our Faith throughout the world. Here in Paris the meetings are well attended.'[204] She also had a visit from Enoch Olinga, a Hand of the Cause, and his wife.[205]

A young Iranian woman found Laura to be elegant and aristocratic even in her old age. Manijeh Zibahalat visited her in the summer of 1970:

> We sat in the living room and after a few minutes Mrs Barney entered the room in a wheelchair with her nurse. I felt like being in the presence of a queen. Her presence had such a dignity and special appeal. She had a very penetrating look with a sweet smile. She said: 'Khush ámadíd' [You are welcome, in Persian.] I thought she only knew this one sentence in Persian. I said in French that it has been my wish to meet her in person since she has been in the presence of the Master for days and days. She replied in Persian that the best days of her life had been in the presence of the Master. I admired the beauty of the way she spoke Persian and I thought her accent was the one of 'Abdu'l-Bahá. She asked about the Bahá'ís in Iran. She served tea and cookies the way the Persians do and then with a serious voice said that it is most important that the young people read and study the Writings and teach the Faith. At the end, I asked her to sign a copy of the *Some Answered Questions* that I had taken with me and she did.[206]

Laura wrote the following year that 'with me things have not changed, although the years are passing. Fortunately, Paris weather is improving and I am once again able to walk with Yvonne's help on the balcony of my apartment.'[207] In another letter she wrote, 'I no longer leave my apartment now that I am 91 years old, but I keep in touch with Bahá'í friends who come to Paris from time to time and of course with those at the Center here.'[208]

However, Laura's painful rheumatism had affected her temperament. A Bahá'í who was asked to visit her to talk about her early years described her as being in advanced age and not always in a good mood.[209] But she never complained.

At the age of 94, she wrote, 'My health remains satisfactory and I am comfortable in my apartment which is well-heated. And of course, I have the good care of Yvonne.'[210] She was content with her condition, that her life in Paris had remained tranquil, and that she was well cared for and comfortable.[211] Mr and Mrs Bolibaugh continued to call on her and keep her in touch with developments, with news of the Bahá'í Center and of people that she knew.[212]

Supporting Bahá'í Funds, Activities and Institutions

Among the many causes that Laura supported financially throughout her life were the many Bahá'í institutions and projects besides numerous individuals who needed help. She had helped with the purchase of the land at 7 Haparsim Street in Haifa and made contributions to Shoghi Effendi to cover the expenses of various Bahá'í projects. In 1938 she made a donation for Shoghi Effendi through the Bahá'í Fund of the National Spiritual Assembly of the United States and Canada.[213] She made a generous contribution in the name of Hippolyte for the work on the Shrine of the Báb on Mount Carmel and also made a donation towards the purchase of land surrounding Bahjí, the resting place of Bahá'u'lláh.[214] Among her other donations was the chandelier, comprising nine cone-shaped oil containers that was placed in the shrine of 'Abdu'l-Bahá, hung from a circular fitting suspended from the ceiling by chains. Similar chandeliers, smaller in size, were installed in the prayer rooms.[215]

When she adjusted her Trust, Laura realized the need of the Bahá'ís for funds to support their work and she made provisions for this assistance. In 1960 she wrote to Ellen:

Recently I adjusted my Trust to give more substantially to the Bahá'ís who are attending efficiently to carrying out the Master's work which is so needed . . . I have found that the most practical way (now that Shoghi Effendi is no longer with us) is to make one's bequest to The National Spiritual Assembly of the Bahá'ís of the United States for the development of the Faith throughout the world.[216]

Over many years Laura not only continued to assist individuals, she also made contributions to several Bahá'í institutions such as the National Assembly of France, the National Assembly of the United States, and the Bahá'í Bureau in Geneva.[217] They were all grateful for her donations. In 1948 she designated a particular donation for the Geneva Bahá'í Bureau in accordance with a request from the beloved Guardian.[218] In 1955 Laura supported the Bahá'í International Community, both financially and through her productive suggestions. As the Bahá'í institutions grew, Laura continued to support the increasingly expanding work of the Faith, including repairs to the Temple, through her contributions, which she sent through the National Spiritual Assembly of the United States.[219] The National Assembly of the United States thanked her in April 1955 for her donation to this office and for her services: 'Your record of service to the Faith over a period of many years has been most outstanding and meritorious.'[220]

Laura was greatly generous to the Local Assembly of Washington, D.C., and made a donation to it every year.[221] The Assembly thanked her for her donations.[222] In 1967 she helped the Washington Bahá'ís purchase a Bahá'í Center on 16th Street NW.[223] When she made further donations for this Center, the Washington Bahá'ís thanked her again and mentioned that the Center was attracting many people and serving as a venue for various activities.[224] The Assembly remained thankful for her 'constant generosity towards' its community.[225]

Laura had continuously supported the National Bahá'í Center of Paris at rue de la Pompe in the sixteenth arrondissement from its opening until the end of her life. She paid for its taxes, maintenance, utilities and renovations over the years.[226] In 1973 she increased her contribution to this Center.[227] She even made provision for contributions to the National Center of France to be continued after her death.[228]

Another area of financial support was covering the costs of reprinting Bahá'í books both in French and English, especially hers and Hippolyte's. While in Washington, she gave funds for the publication of several other Bahá'í books including John Esslemont's *Bahá'u'lláh and the New Era* and reprints of *Gleanings from the Writings of Bahá'u'lláh*.[229] She also made contributions to a quarterly magazine for the franco-phone Bahá'í world.[230]

Living with Her Memories and Finding Ways to Safeguard Them

During her last years of life, Laura was not only proud of her accomplishment in compiling *Some Answered Questions*, but reflected upon her days visiting the Master in 'Akká, her many travels to distant lands, her lectures and talks, and the many trips she made on behalf of the organizations to which she had devoted her life. When she was 86 years old, she reflected in a letter to her sister, 'I can hardly realize that you and I have lived in the midst of two World Wars, we have been in violent situations and somehow we have stood them without great harm, though we have felt them deeply in many ways, before, during and after.'[231]

The Bahá'í institutions realized that time was getting short for the preservation of Laura's valuable memories. In 1966 the National Assembly of the United States asked her to prepare a narrative on her contacts with 'Abdu'l-Bahá during her 1900 visit to 'Akká with her cousin Ellen. The Assembly felt that 'Such historical records by all means should be written, since they impart the unique flavor of the opportunities enjoyed by some exceptional few who shared the presence of the Master.'[232] The National Assembly of France was also eager that she write about her experiences of the early days of the Faith.[233]

Laura had stayed firm in her belief in the Bahá'í Faith, as evidenced by this letter to a Bahá'í friend: 'We Bahá'ís believe that understanding is possible but cannot be obtained while Continents are still in a state of evolution. That is why helpless though we may seem, knowing the Great Message we face our tasks with determination – realizing the objective cannot be achieved in a limited time.'[234]

From 1969, she could no longer leave her house except to travel by train to a Swiss health clinic for her annual stay, where she spent two months. That year she acknowledged the length of time she had known a Bahá'í colleague, and how they have both worked 'towards certain Bahá'í goals in diverse countries . . . Although I may have seemed a bit surprised to have seen a few youthful Bahá'ís at my apartment for my 90th birthday, their sincerity touched me deeply as I realized I could speak to them of the life at Saint Jean d'Acre ['Akká].'[235] In another letter she wrote about her happiness at having news of the progress of the Faith: 'It is a satisfaction to see how the Cause is spreading in a world which needs the guidance of the Holy Land.'[236] She wrote to another friend, 'The Cause continues to expand throughout the World, and the Message is brought not only to those in the cities but also to those in the rural areas and to many of the underdeveloped countries.'[237]

Laura was happy to see the teachings of her faith materializing through the work of the UN and UNESCO. She wrote to Rúhíyyih Khánum, 'In my contacts with the United Nations, especially with UNESCO in Paris, I am seeing how teachings of Bahá'u'lláh are being realized in part and are helping to bring world consciousness to the importance of education and brotherhood throughout all the continents.'[238]

Her years of visits and pilgrimages were another source of nostalgia. She wrote to Kathleen Javid, who had just returned from Haifa, 'It has been some years since I had the privilege of being in Haifa, but the visits I have made there are ever present in my memory.'[239] Laura also reminisced with Rúhíyyih Khánum about her early visits to 'Akká, seven decades after they had taken place. 'What wonderful days were those when I was in Acca ['Akká] and Haifa with the Master and the family.'[240] The memories of her second trip to 'Akká must have been especially poignant, as she continued, 'Did I ever tell you that on my second trip to the Holy Land, when seated with the Holy Family at the break of dawn, the Master turned to a lovely little boy of four (who later became your husband) and said: "Sing the Morning Prayer".'[241]

The Last Year of Laura's Life

How Laura must have yearned to return to the Holy Land for a pilgrimage. One of her last wishes was to visit Haifa and the Bahá'í Holy Places one more time. She had expressed that wish to the Universal House of Justice in 1973 and a letter written on its behalf extended an invitation for her to do so, and saying that, fortuitously, her visit would coincide with a situation with which she could be of service.[242] There was an opportunity to buy the house of 'Abdu'lláh Páshá in 'Akká, where Shoghi Effendi had been born, and in which Laura Barney had been received by 'Abdu'l-Bahá and she had posed her questions. Her memories would be helpful with the renovations, furnishings, and the disposition and arrangements of the rooms.[243] This house has immense historical significance for the Bahá'ís.

The invitation Laura received to visit Haifa and 'Akká was quite accommodating. She would be a guest of the Universal House of Justice and would have an appointed companion.[244] Despite her desire, and after deep contemplation she decided that she had to forgo the trip. Perhaps her advanced age and her poor physical health contributed to this decision. In turn, she extended an invitation to the members of the House of Justice to visit her in Paris.

The House of Justice later sent Laura photos and plans of the house of 'Abdu'lláh Páshá with a request for her memories of details about the furnishings and the arrangement of the rooms.[245] Her assistant, Huntington, responded that unfortunately Laura was not able to hold a pen or she would have written the letter herself. She was in reasonably good health but did not remember the details of those years in 'Akká or Haifa.[246]

Towards the end of the summer of 1973 Angeline Giachery informed Laura that her husband Ugo was publishing a book about Shoghi Effendi. Because of Laura's association with Shoghi Effendi during his childhood and her long association with him later, a page of her memories would be included. This one page was based on Ugo Giachery's stories that Laura had shared with him during her many visits to Rome and his visits to Paris. Giachery's book was to published a few months later.[247] By May of the following year, Laura had received a copy of the published book titled *Shoghi Effendi: Recollections*. It included one page of Laura's recollections.[248]

One of Laura's last letters, dictated to her assistant on May 8, 1974, was about *Some Answered Questions*. She gave permission to the publisher of a book by Adib Taherzadeh, *The Revelation of Bahá'u'lláh*, to use a paragraph from *Some Answered Questions*.[249]

Laura was also delighted to receive news of the proposed design of the building that would serve as the Seat of the Universal House of Justice in Haifa. In her letter to Marion Hofman, a Bahá'í friend at George Ronald, Publisher, Laura commented that the description of the 'proposed new Universal House of Justice building at Haifa, with the 24 fluted Corinthian columns facing 'Akká is most interesting'.[250] Laura was happy to have heard from Marion and invited her to visit if she had the opportunity to pass through Paris. However, that visit would not be possible since Laura suffered a stroke a few days later, on May 12.

Laura's doctor gave her only a few days to live but she lived for more than three months, until August 18, 1974. It was a Sunday, late afternoon, and she was in bed waiting for her night nurse. Yvonne, her faithful housekeeper, was reading to her when Yvonne noticed that her regular breathing had stopped. The nurse arrived and so did a doctor. Laura Clifford Dreyfus-Barney's earthly life had come to an end at the age of 94. Laura had no relatives in Paris. Huntington flew from Madrid immediately and, with the help of some friends, a burial was arranged within a couple of days.[251] She was buried in the Passy Cemetery in the sixteenth arrondissement of Paris near Place du Trocadéro and not far from where she had lived most of her life.[252] Even in death Laura was surrounded by artists, intellectuals and cultured people who were buried nearby. She had requested that, in lieu of flowers as expressions of sympathy, contributions be made to the Parents' School for Atypical Children in Chatham, Massachusetts.[253]

As Laura had wished, she was buried in the same plot as her sister Natalie. Natalie had suggested years earlier that they share a burial site, just as their mother had shared a grave with her sister Hester and not with her former husband.[254] Laura had noted seven decades earlier, in her youth, that two of them would be 'side by side in life' like October and November (their birth months) were side by side in the year'.[255] This had come true for Laura in death. She did not leave the sister she adored, even in death. She had decided to be buried with her sister rather than with her husband. Natalie's biographer believed this showed her lifetime of attachment to Natalie and their 'sisterly union'.[256]

Details of Laura's death were added below Natalie's on their shared gravestone:

Et Sa Soeur
Laura Clifford Barney
Officier de La Légion d'Honneur
1879 – 1974
Veuve d'Hippolyte Dreyfus
Membre
de
La Communauté Bahá'íe

Almost ten years earlier, Laura had requested that she be buried close to the place where her death occurred, which is a requirement for Bahá'í burial, and that her burial be simple and not costly. She also had specifically asked for a Bahá'í burial.[257] One of requirements for Bahá'í burial is that the body is not to be embalmed or cremated, unless required by law. The washed body should be wrapped in white cloth, and a Bahá'í burial ring placed on a finger of the deceased. The body is then placed in a coffin. The only other requirement for the funeral service is the recitation of the Prayer for the Dead. Other prayers may also be chosen. Laura's preference had been for a subdued service with readings from the Gospels and the Bahá'í writings, and music played if possible.[258] Bahá'í prayers were to be read at her gravesite.[259]

Laura, this multifaceted woman, was buried in France, the country where she had put down her roots several decades earlier. She was transplanted there and stayed eternally. This was the final resting place for this never-tiring traveler.

Announcements of Her Death, Obituaries and Acknowledgments of Her Services

The death of Laura Clifford Dreyfus-Barney was widely reported in French and English newspapers on both sides of the Atlantic.

Her obituaries were as diverse and varied as was her life, and they covered a variety of her activities and contributions to the betterment of society.[260] The commonality among them was the factual information about her life. *The Washington Star News*, under the headline 'Laura Barney, 94, Dies; Gave Home to Smithsonian', wrote that Laura Dreyfus-Barney, the last of Washington's Barney sisters, had died at her home in Paris. The obituary mentioned her family and Studio House, listed her activities during both world wars and noted that she was a member of the Bahá'í Faith.[261] The obituary in *The Washington Post* reported her death under the headline 'Laura D. Barney, 94, Delegate to Geneva, Cuba Conferences': 'Laura Dreyfus Barney, whose interests extended from the International Council of Women to local philanthropic projects by her family in Washington, died Sunday at her home in Paris.' It also covered her services during World War I and noted, 'She was the only woman delegate to the International Congress of Educational Cinematography at Rome.' It mentioned her achievements in

Europe and in the United States, her membership of the Bahá'í Faith and her role as compiler of *Some Answered Questions*, a book about that religion.[262]

The French daily *Le Monde*, under the heading of 'Ancienne représentante du Conseil International des Femmes à l'O.N.U.' (the Former Representative of the International Council of Women at the United Nations), wrote about her contributions in France and mentioned that in 1941 she was a member of the American delegation for cultural cooperation in Havana.[263]

Le Figaro, another French daily newspaper, reported the death of the widow of H. Dreyfus-Barney, born Laura Clifford Barney and a member of the Bahá'í international community. It wrote that she had wished for a private ceremony at Passy Cemetery. The article gave the names of directors and presidents of almost all the organizations in which she had been involved as well as the names of her family members, including the former US ambassador to Paris, David K. E. Bruce, and her cousins, nieces, and nephews by marriage.[264]

The obituaries section of the *International Herald Tribune*, under the heading of 'Laura D. Barney', remembered her as the author of books on religion. It also mentioned that she was a cousin of the United States Ambassador David K. E. Bruce, who was serving as the ambassador in Peking (Beijing), China.[265]

The New York Times, under the heading 'Laura Barney Dies: Served U. N. Groups', wrote:

> Paris – Laura Dreyfus Barney, a member of the International Council of Women, died yesterday at her home here . . . After the war [WWI], Mrs Barney became a consultant to the League of Nations and other international bodies concerned with education. After World War II, she held similar positions with specialized organizations of the United Nations, notably as liaison officer for the International Council of Women.
>
> During the war, Mrs Barney was cofounder of the Institute of World Organizations in Washington DC, served as director of training for the information service of the war Hospital Committee also in Washington, and represented the National Council of Women of the United States on the coordination committee for Better Racial Understanding. She was an officer of the French Legion of Honor.[266]

The headline of a newspaper in Laura's home state of Ohio read: 'Her Noble Deeds Enriched World'. The article stated: 'Trying to get a complete outline of Mme Dreyfus-Barney's life is like trying to put together all the intricate design in a Persian carpet.'[267] Another article wrote: 'Mme Dreyfus-Barney teaches by example: are not the very tone of her advocacy, the nature of her arguments the very proof of this?'[268] At the onset of World War II, it was said that this elite woman knew 'how to think globally' at a time when so much hatred and so many minds made brothers into enemies and, as once again, the threat of war was returning.[269]

A tribute to Laura in *The American Bahá'í* news magazine read:

Laura Dreyfus-Barney stands as a pioneer in the international women's movement and must be considered among its great unsung heroines. Her activities ranged from humanitarian service with the Red Cross in World War I to groundbreaking efforts in representing the cause of women before the United Nations and other international organizations through the 1930s, 1940s and 1950s . . . In addition to the peace and women's movements, Mrs Dreyfus-Barney was active in conferences and organizations to improve cross-cultural cooperation and harmony.[270]

An appreciative cable message was sent by the highest governing body of the Bahá'í Faith, the Universal House of Justice, recognizing her outstanding achievement during the Heroic Age of her Faith.

PASSING OF LAURA DREYFUS-BARNEY, COMPILER OF *SOME ANSWERED QUESTIONS*
22 AUGUST 1974
TO THE NATIONAL SPIRITUAL ASSEMBLY OF THE BAHÁ'ÍS OF FRANCE ASCENSION DISTINGUISHED MAIDSERVANT LAURA DREYFUS-BARNEY FURTHER DEPLETES SMALL BAND PROMOTERS FAITH HEROIC AGE. MEMBER FIRST HISTORIC GROUP PARIS TAUGHT BY MAY MAXWELL SHE ACHIEVED IMMORTAL FAME THROUGH COMPILATION SOME ANSWERED QUESTIONS UNIQUE ENTIRE FIELD RELIGIOUS HISTORY. OFFERING ARDENT PRAYERS SACRED THRESHOLD PROGRESS HER SOUL ABHA KINGDOM URGE ALL COMMUNITIES FRANCE HOLD MEMORIAL GATHERINGS GRATITUDE OUTSTANDING ACHIEVEMENT.[271]

Ugo Giachery, who had known Laura for many years, wrote the following tribute:

> With her keen intelligence, logical mind and investigating nature, she devoted her whole life, from adolescence, to improving human relations, bringing together peoples of different races, classes and nations. She was a brilliant speaker and made several trips around the world lecturing on the impelling necessity of a united world. She was a true pioneer in this field of activity at a time when the world was still geographically and politically divided and quite insensible to the call of spiritual unity. Her enthusiasm for this ideal [improving human relations, bringing together peoples of different races, classes and nations] never lessened. Her services were rendered joyfully with steadfastness and perseverance. Those who had the rare privilege of knowing her over a period of many decades can testify that her undaunted zeal for the objective of the brotherhood of man remained alive and glowing to the very last day of her life on earth.[272]

EPILOGUE

Years after her passing, Laura Dreyfus Barney continues to be remembered for two distinct contributions, one material and the other spiritual.

Laura Barney, or Mme Barney as she was known had no next of kin; she had no children and her only sibling had none either. The closest family member was a distant cousin, David Bruce. Maybe that is one reason why she donated her properties and assets to cultural institutions, charities and her faith community. She had donated all the paintings of her mother plus her own collection and some of her jewelry to the Smithsonian Institution during her lifetime.

Of her properties, the most important one was Studio House at 2306 Massachusetts Avenue, which Laura and Natalie had donated also to the Smithsonian Institution. It was later called the Barney Studio House and was opened to the public on November 7, 1979, with the building being used for the Smithsonian offices and to house visiting dignitaries. Public tours were given and seasonal cultural programs were held there.[1] The house was administered by the National Museum of American Art and was renovated to 'evoke its original mood and intent as a place of artistic enjoyment'.[2] However, owing to budget constraints, the Smithsonian's Board of Regents considered selling the building. By 1980 a group called Friends of Alice Pike Barney Studio House was working with the Smithsonian officials to develop a restoration and fund-raising partnership to save the edifice and stop the sale.[3] Anita Chapman, who objected to its sale because of its significance to the Bahá'ís, wrote to the Smithsonian on behalf of the Bahá'í community:

> Let us hope that the fascinating Studio House will remain in Smithsonian hands. It is a building that means a great deal to Bahá'ís, not only as the center of Alice Pike Barney's activities during her years in Washington, but also as one of the buildings visited on several occasions by 'Abdu'l-Bahá, son of the founder of the Bahá'í Faith, during His visits to the city in 1912.[4]

However, owing to structural deterioration and the increased cost of maintenance, Studio House was closed to the public in 1991 and was sold in 1999 to a private buyer. The contents of the house were auctioned in 2000. After a few unsuccessful attempts, the house was purchased in 2001 by the Government of the Republic of Latvia and the deed was transferred for use as its Embassy in the United States.[5] The Embassy has taken good care of the building and has renovated parts of it. It has also kept the plaque on the outside wall of the Embassy with the name of Laura's mother and the date the house was donated to the Smithsonian Institution, 1960. It also owns Laura's sculpture which in 1910 made headlines in Washington, D.C. and elsewhere in the US. The sculpture sits in the backyard of the Embassy.

In 1995 Studio House, which is located within the Sheridan–Kalorama Historic District, was designated as a District of Columbia Historic Landmark and was listed in the National Register of Historic Places. Its official listing name is Barney Studio House (and Interiors) according to the D.C. Government.[6] It is also listed on the register itself as 'Studio House' with 'Alice Pike Barney Studio House' as its 'other' name.[7] The house has great architectural and historical significance and both its exterior and interior are protected by District of Columbia Historic Preservation laws.[8]

As to her apartment in Paris at 74 rue Raynouard, according to Anita Chapman, Laura donated it to the Legion of Honor. However, the author has not been able to confirm this.[9]

Regarding her other assets and belongings, Laura had finalized her will and testament in 1964 during her last visit to the United States.[10] According to William Huntington, a lawyer who was the executor, the terms of her will directed that the assets of one of her trusts be given outright to the American Bahá'ís, perhaps through the National Spiritual Assembly of the Bahá'ís of the United States. Another trust was probably a living trust from which she received income during her lifetime. At her death, one-third of the income of this trust was to go to the Barney Settlement House in Washington and two-thirds to the Smithsonian Institution. Huntington oversaw these funds during his lifetime. According to Laura's will, after Huntington's death or in the year 1999, whichever came earlier, these funds would go outright to these two institutions.[11] Everything that was not mentioned in her will was to be given to Huntington and to Yvonne, her faithful housekeeper and companion in Paris.[12]

While Laura was alive, she had arranged for almost all her Bahá'í documents to be sent to the Bahá'í World Centre in Haifa. In 1973 she requested Huntington to give the remainder of her Bahá'í books and papers to the National Spiritual Assembly of France, which would appoint a committee to decide which papers would be sent to the Bahá'í World Centre.[13] Huntington informed the National Assembly a month before Laura's death that her books, which included her extra copies of Bahá'í publications, books on the Bahá'í Faith and books of interest to Bahá'ís, had been transferred to the Bahá'í Center of Paris together with three cartons of records.[14] The last shipment of documents was sent to the Paris Center four years after her death.

Laura's spiritual contribution and her most enduring legacy, her 'imperishable service',[15] was the book *Some Answered Questions*, a gift to humanity from which generations will gain insight and spiritual guidance. In it can be found 'the clue to all the perplexing questions that agitate the mind of man in his search after true knowledge'.[16] The profound significance of this book, brought about through Laura's foresight, dedication and perseverance, has yet to be fully realized.

However, there was a minor misunderstanding about some of Laura's papers relating to *Some Answered Questions*. In 1975 Ugo Giachery, who had been assigned to take care of these papers on behalf of the Universal House of Justice, advised that institution that Laura Dreyfus-Barney's 'secretary' had said that Laura had taken many papers from 'Akká to Paris, including parts of *Some Answered Questions* that were not included in the published book.[17] He did not say exactly who that 'secretary' was, but it was perhaps Huntington. At the request of the Universal House of Justice, the National Assembly appointed two Bahá'ís to examine the inventory of Laura's papers to see if anything related to *Some Answered Questions* could be found and promised that the National Assembly would inform the House of Justice and would ask Huntington.[18] It seems that it was not intended that *Some Answered Questions* would include everything that Laura had garnered from her many table talks with 'Abdu'l-Bahá but only selections from them.[19] Three years later the Universal House of Justice thanked the National Assembly of France for some books from Laura Barney's estate and asked the Assembly to keep copies of whatever it sent to ensure against loss and to 'maintain the integrity of this historically important collection'.[20] The matter was cleared.

The Universal House of Justice informed the National Assembly of France by letter on June 19, 1978, that it had received the original letters of the Guardian and other documents from Laura Dreyfus-Barney's collection, which also included five original letters sent to her before

Shoghi Effendi's guardianship, and letters sent by him to Hippolyte.[21] Huntington informed Anita Chapman years later that he had given all the papers concerning the Bahá'ís to the Bahá'í Center of Paris (which must have meant the National Assembly of the Bahá'ís of France).[22]

Two events in 1988 marked Laura's contribution and her work to bring understanding among the people of the world and to advance the status of women. One took place at the centennial celebration of the International Council of Women in Washington, D.C., when the Bahá'í International Community and its United Nations Office jointly 'sponsored a prestigious luncheon' for the Executive Board of the International Council of Women (ICW) honoring 'Madame Laura Dreyfus Barney, known to Bahá'ís as the compiler of *Some Answered Questions*, and a distinguished member of the ICW'. The second was a reception in New York on July 6 co-sponsored by UNICEF and United States Office of the Bahá'í International Community to commemorate Laura's work with the United Nations and UNICEF.[23] A press release for these two events prepared by this office was titled 'Pioneer of International Women's Movement Honored'.[24] It was reported that from the 1930s through the 1950s Laura worked tirelessly to increase the influence of women in international affairs and to assist those in diplomatic and government circles to understand how feminine values could advance the cause of peace. It seems that Mary Craig Schuller (McGeachy), who lived in Princeton, New Jersey, and was the President of ICW from 1963 to 1973, also wrote a tribute to Laura for these two events.[25]

The luncheon in Washington honoring Laura's memory was held at the Smithsonian Institution's Studio House on June 26 and was attended by the presidents and board members of the ICW and the National Council of Women of the United States among the 55 guests. Tributes were made to Laura Barney. The speakers were Dr Sookja Hong, president of the ICW and the first woman presidential candidate in the Republic of Korea; Mrs Merrinelle Sullivan, president of the United States National Council of Women; and Dr Wilma Brady for the Bahá'í International Community. Dr Brady said in a statement:

> We are honoring Mme Laura Dreyfus-Barney because of her pioneering work in the international women's movement. Her activities representing the cause of women and peace before the League of Nations, and later in the United Nations, surely classify her as one

of the movement's great activists, foreshadowing the tremendous involvement of women in peace and justice issues today.[26]

Shapour Rassekh, who had met Laura in Geneva when she traveled there for her work with the UN, wrote about her reputation and her work with that organization:

Years later when my wife [Dr Mehri Rassekh] was a member of the National Council of Iranian Women in the 1970s, she told me that often at the United Nations, the experts and responsible people in those fields talked highly of Mrs Clifford Dreyfus-Barney and her great services for women's equality and education. These stories were told years after she had retired.[27]

'Abdu'l-Bahá had wished that the book Laura compiled be a source enlightenment: 'I am always eagerly waiting to receive good news from thee, indicating that thou art holding *Some Answered Questions* in hand and, with that proof and testimony, art filling the friends and the hand-maidens of the All-Merciful with ecstasy, joy, and fervor, inasmuch as thou hast been singled out for this favor.'[28] 'In her service to the Cause', Laura had 'left as a memento for future generations a significant book from the utterances of 'Abdu'l-Bahá'.[29]

A Committee at the Bahá'í World Centre revised the English translation of *Some Answered Questions* rendered decades before and the resulting new edition was released in 2014. Its Foreword states:

Over the years since the original publication of *Some Answered Questions*, it has become increasingly clear that the translation would benefit from a careful and thorough revision. Miss Barney, as she herself stated, was a student of the Persian language and, however able, could not have entirely mastered its intricacies; and she could not of course have taken advantage of the brilliant illumination that was later to be cast upon the Sacred Texts of the Faith by the authoritative translations of Shoghi Effendi. Moreover, only a few necessary corrections had been made to the English translation during the course of its many reprintings, leaving it largely unchanged from the text of the first edition.

. . . The main objective of this retranslation has been to better represent the substance and the style of the original, in particular by capturing more clearly the subtleties of 'Abdu'l-Bahá's explanations, approximating more closely a style that is at once conversational and elevated, and by rendering more consistently the philosophical terms used throughout the text. While not bound by the original translation, this version nevertheless strives to retain many of its elegant expressions and felicitous turns of phrase.[30]

The Foreword states that the 'centenary of 'Abdu'l-Bahá's journeys to the West' was 'a fitting occasion both to honor Laura Clifford Barney's imperishable contribution as the primary catalyst and first translator of this volume' and to provide an 'improved translation of the "priceless explanations"'.[31]

Some Answered Questions was the first book to clarify the teachings of the Faith for the western world and is still as important as it was when it was first published in 1908. It has been 'an authoritative repository of 'Abdu'l-Bahá's profound insight' and its content is 'essential for grasping the significance and implications of the Bahá'í Revelation'.[32] It is 'unique' in the 'entire field' of 'religious history'.[33]

Its place in Bahá'í sacred literature is the same as a Tablet written by 'Abdu'l-Bahá Himself and has the same 'binding power'.[34] Thus the compilation *Some Answered Questions* is included in the body of the Bahá'í sacred writings.[35]

At the time of writing, the Library at the Bahá'í World Centre has copies of every translated and published version of *Some Answered Questions* in 40 languages, with selections of the text in an additional eight languages.[36] Laura had desired early on to save the words of 'Abdu'l-Bahá for posterity and, watching over her book for several decades, she accomplished her mission.

This distinguished woman, born into wealth and privilege, was enthralled by 'Abdu'l-Bahá's heavenly attributes and her life thus became one of service to humanity. She was inspired by His sanctity, by His wisdom, His majesty, His humility, by the manifestation of all the great qualities in such a simple, natural way, and she became His disciple. She had seen Him day in and day out, steadfast and joyous in His mission of education and love. She was taken by His firmness yet His very kindness. The hope and happiness that she found after meeting Him and hearing His words at an early age stayed with her for the rest of her life. "Abdu'l-Bahá is wonderful in His example,' she wrote. 'He displays two principles which are very powerful. They are toleration and vigilance.'[37] She had also learned from Him, 'We must be tolerant to all mankind and vigilant not to harm.'[38] Laura always remembered that 'Abdu'l-Bahá 'spoke simply and His sentences became a part of one's inner thoughts seeking worthy outlet in action'.[39] She always remembered what He had advised her and those near Him: 'not to keep for ourselves alone what He has entrusted to us for humanity'.[40] Laura Clifford Dreyfus-Barney believed that it was only through action that she felt nearer to the Beloved.[41] She followed these principles in her life, and her deeds followed her beyond this life. 'Abdu'l-Bahá prayed that she 'mayest become a luminous star shining from the horizon of eternity',[42] and she had become one.

When 'Abdu'l-Bahá was asked, 'What is a Bahá'í?', He replied: 'To be a Bahá'í simply means to love all the world; to love humanity and try to serve it; to work for universal peace and universal brotherhood.'[43]

Laura Clifford Dreyfus-Barney was a true Bahá'í.

APPENDIX A

A Brief Introduction to the Bahá'í Faith[1]

In the middle of the 19th century – one of the most turbulent periods in the world's history – a young merchant announced that He was the bearer of a message destined to transform the life of humanity. At a time when His country, Iran, was undergoing widespread moral breakdown, His message aroused excitement and hope among all classes, rapidly attracting thousands of followers. He took the name 'the Báb', meaning 'the Gate' in Arabic.

With His call for spiritual and moral reformation, and His attention to improving the position of women and the lot of the poor, the Báb's prescription for spiritual renewal was revolutionary. At the same time, He founded a distinct, independent religion of His own, inspiring His followers to transform their lives and carry out great acts of heroism.

The Báb announced that humanity stood at the threshold of a new era. His mission, which was to last only six years, was to prepare the way for the coming of a Manifestation of God Who would usher in the age of peace and justice promised in all the world's religions: Bahá'u'lláh, meaning the 'Glory of God'.

Bahá'u'lláh (1817–92) is the Promised One foretold by the Báb and all the divine Messengers of the past. Bahá'u'lláh delivered a new revelation from God to humanity. Thousands of verses, letters and books flowed from His pen. In His writings He outlined a framework for the development of a global civilization which takes into account both the spiritual and material dimensions of human life. For this He endured 40 years of imprisonment, torture and exile. Today, His life and mission are becoming increasingly well-known across the planet. Millions of people are learning to apply His teachings to their individual and collective lives for the betterment of the world.

In order to guarantee that His revelation would achieve its purpose of creating a united world – and to safeguard the unity of the Bahá'í community – Bahá'u'lláh appointed His eldest son, 'Abdu'l-Bahá (1844–1921), as the Centre of His Covenant. Following Bahá'u'lláh's passing, 'Abdu'l-Bahá's extraordinary qualities of character, His knowledge and His service to humanity offered a vivid demonstration of Bahá'u'lláh's teachings in action, and brought great prestige to the rapidly expanding community throughout the world.

'Abdu'l-Bahá devoted His ministry to furthering His Father's Faith and to promoting the ideals of peace and unity. He encouraged the establishment of local Bahá'í institutions, and guided nascent educational, social and economic initiatives. After His release from a lifetime of imprisonment, 'Abdu'l-Bahá set out on a series of journeys which took Him to Egypt, Europe and North America. Throughout His life, He presented with brilliant simplicity, to high and low alike, Bahá'u'lláh's prescription for the spiritual and social renewal of society.

In the early years of the 20th century, 'Abdu'l-Bahá was the Bahá'í Faith's leading exponent, renowned as a champion of social justice and an ambassador for international peace. In turn, 'Abdu'l-Bahá established principles for the operation of the Universal House of Justice and stated that after His passing, the Bahá'ís must turn to His eldest grandson, Shoghi Effendi, whom He named Guardian of the Bahá'í Faith.

For 36 years, with extraordinary foresight, wisdom and devotion, Shoghi Effendi systematically nurtured the development, deepened the understanding, and strengthened the unity of the Bahá'í community, as it increasingly grew to reflect the diversity of the entire human race.

Under Shoghi Effendi's direction, the unique system designed by Bahá'u'lláh for administering the affairs of the community evolved rapidly throughout the world. He translated the Bahá'í Scriptures into English, developed the Faith's spiritual and administrative centre in the Holy Land, and, in the thousands of letters he penned, offered profound insights into the spiritual dimension of civilization and the dynamics of social change, unveiling an awe-inspiring vision of the future towards which humanity is moving.

Both the Guardian and the Universal House of Justice were tasked with applying the principles, promulgating the laws, protecting the institutions, and adapting the Bahá'í Faith to the requirements of an ever-advancing society.

The Universal House of Justice is the international governing council of the Bahá'í Faith. Bahá'u'lláh ordained the creation of this institution in His book of laws, the Kitáb-i-Aqdas.

The Universal House of Justice is a nine-member body, elected every five years by the entire membership of all national Bahá'í assemblies. Bahá'u'lláh conferred divine authority upon the Universal House of Justice to exert a positive influence on the welfare of humankind, promote education, peace and global prosperity, and safeguard human honour and the position of religion. It is charged with applying the Bahá'í teachings to the requirements of an ever-evolving society and is thus empowered to legislate on matters not explicitly covered in the Faith's Sacred Texts.

Since its first election in 1963, the Universal House of Justice has guided the Bahá'í world community to develop its capacity to participate in building a prosperous global civilization. The guidance provided by the Universal House of Justice ensures unity of thought and action in the Bahá'í community as it learns to translate Bahá'u'lláh's vision of world peace into reality.

APPENDIX B

Listing for Laura Dreyfus-Barney in *Who's Who in America*

Who's Who in America of 1974–1975 printed the list of accomplishments and activities of Laura Dreyfus-Barney and the responsibilities she had undertaken (abbreviations in the list have been spelled out by the author for clarity):

Dreyfus-Barney, Laura (Mme. L. Dreyfus-Barney)

Served with American Ambulance at Lycée Pasteur as auxiliary night nurse, Paris, France, 1914–15; engaged in re-education of mentally and physically handicapped, Military Hospital in Marseilles, France, 1915–16; American Red Cross, delegate for Refugee and Repatriate Service for 3 departments of Southern France, 1916–18; co-founder of the first children's hospital, L'Avenir des Enfants de Vaucluse, Avignon, France, 1918; formed under aegis of the League of Nations, liaison committee of major international organizations to promote better understanding between peoples and classes, 1925–47; Appointed by Council of League of Nations to consultative committee of Organization of Intellectual Cooperation, 1926–39, active in establishment of the National Agricultural Center, Salon, France (near Marseilles), 1928; organizer for the International Council of Women under auspices of the International Institute of Educational Cinematography of League of Nations, 1931–37; elected member of the board of Congress, Rome, 1934; member of the Committee of Experts of League of Nations, dealing with international radio broadcasting problems and relationships between peoples, 1937–38; vice chairman of Committee of Women's International Organization for Control and Reduction of Armaments in Geneva, 1931–46; member of the U.S. delegation Second American Conference National Committees of Intellectual

Cooperation. Havana, Cuba, 1941; sponsor and member of the Institute on World Organization, Washington, 1941–61. Advisory chairman and director of training and volunteer for information service of War Hospitality Committee, Washington 1942–45; also representative of National Council of Women on Coordinating Committee for Better Race Understanding, 1946; senior liaison officer International Council of Women with United Nations and its specialized agencies, UNESCO [United Nations Educational, Scientific, and Cultural Organization], FAO [Food and Agriculture Organization], ECOSOC [Economic and Social Council], others; sometime accredited various international organizations from non-governmental Organizations; sometime chairman of study groups and organization of international associations. Founder of Alice Pike Barney Memorial Trust, Smithsonian Institution, 1951 for development of art in the United States; donor (with sister) Studio House Cultural Center, Smithsonian Institution; honorary president of Barney Neighborhood Settlement, Washington. Member of the board of American Society of French Legion of Honor, New York; officer of the French Legion of Honor; trustee and President of James Monroe Foundation, Fredericksburg, Virginia. Author or co-author of books, articles and monographs.[1]

ABBREVIATIONS

Archives

AAAMSI   Archives of American Art Museum, Smithsonian
              Institution

ABDF   Archives Bahá'íes de France. All the references are from
              Laura Dreyfus Barney Papers unless otherwise noted.

BAWDC   Bahá'í Archives of Washington, D.C. All references are
              from Laura Clifford Barney Papers unless otherwise
              noted.

BWCA   Bahá'í World Centre Archives

DMLA   Dayton Metro Library Archives

Doucet   Bibliothèque littéraire Jacques Doucet. All references are
              from Letters of Laura Dreyfus-Barney, Natalie Clifford
              Barney Collection.

LSEA   London School of Economics Archives. All references
              are from International Council of Women Papers.

NMWAA   National Museum of Women in the Arts Archives. All
              references are from Alice Pike Barney Papers.

SIA   Smithsonian Institution Archives. All references are
              from Alice Pike Barney Papers unless otherwise noted.

UNA   United Nations Archives in Geneva, Switzerland. All
              references are from Laura Dreyfus-Barney Papers of the
              League of Nations Collection.

USNBA   United States National Bahá'í Archives. All references
              are from Laura Dreyfus-Barney Papers unless otherwise
              noted.

Names

ACB	Albert Clifford Barney
APB, APBH	Alice Pike Barney, Alice Pike Barney Hemmick, Alice Barney
LCB, LDB, L.C.D.B.	Laura Alice Clifford Dreyfus-Barney
HD, HDB	Hippolyte Dreyfus, Hippolyte Dreyfus-Barney
NCB	Natalie Clifford Barney

Organizations, Institutions, Cities

BWC	Bahá'í World Centre
ICIC	International Committee of Intellectual Cooperation
ICW	International Council of Women
LSA	Local Spiritual Assembly
NSA	National Spiritual Assembly
SI	Smithsonian Institution
UN	United Nations
WDC	Washington, D.C.

BIBLIOGRAPHY

'Abdu'l-Bahá. *Le lezioni di San Giovanni d'Acri: Risposte a quesiti, raccolte e tradotte dal persiano da Laura Clifford Barney*. Roma: Casa Editrice Bahá'í, 1976.

—— *Light of the World: Selected Tablets of 'Abdu'l-Bahá*. Haifa: Bahá'í World Centre, 2021.

—— *Makátíb-i-Ḥaḍrat 'Abdu'l- Bahá* (Tablets of 'Abdu'l-Bahá). 8 vols.: vols. 13 Cairo (1910–22), vols. 4–8. Tehran: Mu'assasiy-i Millíy-i Maṭbú'át-i Amrí, 121–34 BE. https:/reference.bahai.org/fa/t/ab/ (accessed Oct. 2021).

—— *Paris Talks*. London: Bahá'í Publishing Trust, 1995.

—— *The Promulgation of Universal Peace*. Wilmette, IL: Bahá'í Publishing Trust, 1982.

—— *Selections from the Writings of 'Abdu'l-Bahá*. Haifa: Bahá'í World Centre, 1978.

—— *Some Answered Questions*. Compiled by Laura Clifford Barney. Haifa: Bahá'í World Centre, 2014. https://www.bahai.org/library/authoritative-texts/abdul-baha/some-answered-questions/

—— *Tablets of Abdul-Baha Abbas*. Chicago: Bahá'í Publishing Society; vol. 1, 1909; vol. 2, 1915.

Abdul Baha on Divine Philosophy. Boston: The Tudor Press, 1918.

'Abdu'l-Bahá in London. London: Bahá'í Publishing Trust, 1982.

Abu'l-Faḍl, Mírzá. *The Bahá'í Proofs*, translated by Ali-Kuli Khan. Wilmette, IL: Bahá'í Publishing Trust, 1983.

—— [Mírzá-Abul-Fazl]. *Hujaj'ul Beheyyeh* (*The Behai Proofs*). New York: J.W. Pratt Co., 1902.

Adler, Kathleen, Erica E. Hirshler, H. Barbara Weinberg (eds.) *Americans in Paris 1860–1900*. London: National Gallery, 2006.

Afroukhteh, Youness. *Memories of Nine Years in 'Akká*. Oxford: George Ronald, 2005.

Alexander, Agnes Baldwin. 'An Account of How I Became a Bahá'í and My Stays in Paris in 1901 and 1937: Written at the Request of Mrs. Laura Dreyfus-Barney. 1958. https://bahai-library.com/alexander_linard_autobiography (accessed Nov. 2015).

Ali-Kuli Khan and Marzieh Gail. 'Mírzá Abu'l-Faḍl in America'. *The Bahá'í World*, vol. 9 (1940–1944). Wilmette, IL: Bahá'í Publishing Committee, 1945, pp. 855–60.

Alice Pike Barney: Pastel Portraits from Studio House. Washington, D.C.: Smithsonian Institution Press for the National Museum of American Art, 1986.

Amanat, Mousa. *Bahá'iyán-i-Káshán* (Noura Amanat-Samimi, ed.). Madrid: Nehal Foundation, 2012.

'Apostles of Bahá'u'lláh'. *The Bahá'í World*, vol. 4, New York: Bahá'í Publishing Committee, 1933, pp. 108–9.

Arbáb, Furugh. *Akhtarán-i-Tábán*, vol. 2. New Delhi: Mir'at Publications, 1990.

Armstrong-Ingram, R. Jackson. 'Moody, Susan', 1998. https://bahai-library.com/armstrong-ingram_encyclopedia_susan_moody (accessed June 2021).

'Arúsí-yi-mistir dreyfus va mís barney' ['Wedding of Mr Dreyfus and Miss Barney'], *Najm-i-Bakhtar* (*Star of the West*), vol. 2, no. 4 (May 17, 1911), pp. 4–5, translated by Riaz Masrour.

Ávarih, 'Abdu'l-Ḥusayn. *Kavákib ud-Durriyih*. 2 vols. Cairo: al-Sa'ádah, 1923.

'Azízí, 'Azízu'lláh ['Azíz'u'lláh]. *Crown of Glory: Memoirs of Jináb-i-Azíz'u'lláh Azízí*, translated by Christopher and Nahzy Buck; Hamid and Sandra Azizi, eds.). North Vancouver: privately published, 1991. https://bahai-library.com/pdf/a/azizi_crown_glory.pdf (accessed Dec. 2020).

— (Dhabíḥu'lláh 'Azízí, ed.). *Táj-i-Vahháj: Kháṭirát-i Jináb 'Azízu'lláh 'Azízí,*.1st ed. Tehran: Mu'assisih-yi Millí-yi Maṭbú'át-i Amrí, 133 BE; 2nd printing with some changes. Privately published. March 1988/144 BE.

The Bahá'í Faith: The Official Website of the Worldwide Bahá'í Community. https://www.bahai.org/. The Báb – Herald of the Bahá'í Faith. https://www.bahai.org/the-bab; Bahá'u'lláh – The Divine Educator. https://www.bahai.org/bahaullah; 'Abdu'l-Bahá – The Perfect Exemplar. https://www.bahai.org/abdul-baha; Shoghi Effendi the Guardian of the Bahá'í Faith. https://www.bahai.org/shoghi-effendi; The Universal House of Justice. https://www.bahai.org/the-universal-house-of-justice (all accessed Oct. 2021).

Bahá'í International Community. https://www.bic.org/ (accessed Oct. 2021).

'Bahá'í International Community Representation: The United Nations Office of the Bahá'í International Community 1986–1992'. *The Bahá'í World*, vol. 20 (1986–1992). Haifa: Bahá'í World Centre, 1998, pp. 521–36.

Bahai News, vol. 1. no.11 (Sept. 27, 1910), p. 7 (Announcement of availability of *God's Heroes*).

Bahá'u'lláh. *Epistle to the Son of the Wolf.* Wilmette, IL: Bahá'í Publishing Trust, 1988.

— *The Hidden Words.* Wilmette, IL: Bahá'í Publishing Trust, 1990.

— *Kitáb-i-Íqán (The Book of Certitude).* Wilmette, IL: Bahá'í Publishing Trust, 1989.

Bahíyyih Khánum, the Greatest Holy Leaf: A Compilation from Bahá'í Sacred Texts and Writings of the Guardian of the Faith and Bahíyyih Khánum's Own Letters. Haifa: Bahá'í World Centre, 1982.

Ballanger, Yann (in collaboration with Parivash Ardeï Amini). *Hippolyte Dreyfus-Barney: Premier Bahá'í Français.* Paris, France: Librairie Bahá'íe, 2021.

Balyuzi, H. M. *'Abdu'l-Bahá: The Centre of the Covenant of Bahá'u'lláh.* Oxford: George Ronald, 2nd ed. with minor corr. 1987.

— *Bahá'u'lláh: The King of Glory.* Oxford: George Ronald, 1980.

— *Edward Granville Browne and the Bahá'í Faith.* Oxford: George Ronald, 1970.

Bámdád, Mihdí. *Sharḥ-i-Ḥál-i-Rijál-i-Írán dar Qarn-i-12 va 13 va 14 Hijrí.* Tehran: Zuvvár 1347 AHS – 1353 AHS [1968–75], 6 vols., vol. 5, p. 291.

Banani, Amin. *Ṭáhirih: A Portrait in Poetry. Selected Poems of Qurratu'l-'Ayn.* Los Angeles: Kalimát Press, 2005.

[Barney, Alice]. *Stanley's 'Lady' Alice By One Who Knew.* Unpublished MS in Record Unit 7473, SIA. https://siarchives.si.edu/collections/siris_arc_217626 (accessed Jan. 2020).

Barney, L.D. 'Edith Sanderson'. *The Bahá'í World*, vol. 13 (1954–1963), Haifa, Israel: The Universal House of Justice, 1970, pp. 889–90.

— 'Joséphine Scott'. *The Bahá'í World*, vol. 13 (1954–1963). Haifa, Israel: The Universal House of Justice, 1970, pp. 899–900.

Barney, Laura Clifford (published as Laura C. Dreyfus-Barney) and Shoghi Effendi (Thomas Linard, ed.). 'Biography of Hippolyte Dreyfus-Barney'. 1928. https://bahai-library.com/dreyfus-barney_biography_hippolyte_dreyfus-barney (accessed June 2017).

Barney, Laura Clifford. *God's Heroes: A Drama in Five Acts.* London: Kegan Paul, Trench, Trübner & Co., 1910.

Beede, Alice R. 'A Glimpse of 'Abdu'l-Bahá in Paris'. *Star of the West,* vol. 2, no. 18 (Feb. 7, 1912), pp. 7, 12.

Bishop, Helen. 'Geneva Scans the European Community'. *The Bahá'í World*, vol. 6 (1934–1936). New York: Bahá'í Publishing Committee, 1937, pp. 130–5.

Blomberg, Baron Richard Fritz von. Report of the World Fellowship of Religions, Second Regional Conference. Tehran, Iran. June 10–16, 1967. ABDF.

Blomfield, Lady [Sitárih Khánum; Sara Louise]. *The Chosen Highway.* Oxford: George Ronald, rpt. 2007.

Braun, Eunice. 'Farrukh Ioas'. *The Bahá'í World*, vol. 13 (1954–1963). Haifa, Israel: The Universal House of Justice, 1970, pp. 919–21.

— 'From Strength to Strength: The First Half Century of the Formative Age of the Bahá'í Faith'. *The Bahá'í World*, vol. 16 (1973–1976), pp. 63–100.

Breeskin, Adelyn D. *Romaine Brooks.* Washington, D.C.: Smithsonian Institution Press, 1986.

'A Brief History of the International Council of Women: 1888–1980'. National Council of Women of Great Britain (Aug. 1982), p. 5, LSEA.

Brooks, Romaine. Romaine Brooks papers, 1910–1973. https://www.aaa.si.edu/collections/romaine-brooks-papers-6290 (accessed Nov. 2016).

Browne, Edward G. *Materials for the Study of the Bábí Religion*. Cambridge: Cambridge University Press, 1918.

— 'Sir 'Abdu'l-Baha 'Abbas: Died 28th November, 1921. *The Journal of the Royal Asiatic Society of Great Britain and Ireland*, no. 1 (Jan. 1922), pp. 145–6. https://www.jstor.org/stable/25209873 (accessed Oct. 2021).

Bryan, William Jennings and Mary Baird Bryan. *The Memoirs of William Jennings Bryan*. Philadelphia: The John C. Winston Co., 1925.

Buck, Christopher. *Alain Locke: Faith and Philosophy* (Studies in the Bábí and Bahá'í Religions). Los Angeles: Kalimát Press, 2005.

'Builders of Wooden Railway Cars'. http://www.midcontinent.org/rollingstock/builders/barney-smith2.htm (accessed Feb. 2020).

Bulletin des Réfugié du Pas de Calais. 'A Marseille: La 'Croix-Rouge Américaine' et les Réfugiés'. https://gallica.bnf.fr/ark:/12148/bpt6k4533614v/f2.item (accessed Oct. 2021).

Chalon, Jean. *Portrait of a Seductress: The World of Natalie Barney*. New York: Crown Publishers, 1979.

Chapman, Anita Ioas. *Leroy Ioas: Hand of the Cause of God*. Oxford: George Ronald, 1998.

Clifford (Dreyfus) Barney, Laura. *Dalírán-i-Rabbání* (*God's Heroes*, translated by 'Azízu'lláh Shírází), vol. 54. Iran National Bahá'í Archive. Tehran: private printing, 1977. http://www.afnanlibrary.org/docs/persian-arabic-mss/inba/inba-vol-054/ (accessed Feb. 2021).

'Consul Albert Schwarz'. *The Bahá'í World*, vol. 4 (1930–1932). New York: Bahá'í Publishing Committee, 1933, pp. 264–6.

'The Convention', in *Bahá'í News Letter*, July–Aug. 1925, no. 6, pp. 3–4. https://bahai.works/Baha%27i_News_Letter/Issue_6 (accessed Oct. 2021).

Das, Nolima (ed.). *Glimpses of the Mother's Life*, vol.1. Pondicherry, India: Sri Aurobindo Ashram, 1978.

Day, Michael V., *Coronation on Carmel: The Story of the Shrine of the Báb*, vol. 2: 1922–1963. Oxford: George Ronald, 2018.

The Diary of Juliet Thompson. Los Angeles: Kalimát Press, 1983.

Diehl, Ambrose A. 'The Moral Effect of the Cinema on Individuals'. *International Review of Educational Cinematography* 3.12 (December 1931), 1123. http://www.jstor.org/stable/24408070 (accessed Oct. 2018).

Dock, Lavinia, *et al. History of American Red Cross Nursing*. New York: McMillan, 1922. https://archive.org/details/historyofamericaooameriala (accessed March 2021).

Dreyfus, Hippolyte. 'Les Béhaïs et le mouvement actuel en Perse'. *Revue du Monde Musulman*, 1 (1906), pp.198–206.

— *Essai sur le Bahá'ísme: Son Histoire, Sa portée Sociale*. Paris: Ernest Leroux, 1973.

—— *The Universal Religion: Bahaism* – Its Rise and Social Import. Chicago: The Bahai Publishing Company; London: Cope and Fenwick, 1909. Electronic edition: Sandy, UK: Afnan Library, 2017.

Dreyfus-Barney, Laura. 'Only a Word'. *The Bahá'í World*, vol. 5 (1932–1934). New York: Bahá'í Publishing Committee, 1936, p. 667.

—— 'Peace through Intellectual Co-operation', in 'World Peace', a Supplement to the *International Council of Women Bulletin*, Oct. 1933, p. 5.

—— 'The Way Reopens', unpublished manuscript, 1922, p. 4a, ABDF.

'Dreyfus-Barney, Laura (Mme. L. Dreyfus-Barney)'. *Who's Who in America,* 38th edition (1974–1975), vol. 1, p. 844. Chicago: Marquis Who's Who, Inc., 1974.

Druick, Zoë. 'The International Educational Cinematograph Institute, Reactionary'. *Canadian Journal of Film Studies*, vol. 16, no. 1 (Spring 2007), pp. 80–97.

Egea, Amín. *The Apostle of Peace: A Survey of References to 'Abdu'l-Bahá in the Western Press*, vol. 1. 1871–1911. Oxford: George Ronald, 2017.

Esslemont, John E. *Bahá'u'lláh and the New Era*. Wilmette, IL: Bahá'í Publishing Trust, 1980.

'Finding Aid to The Friends of Alice Pike Barney Studio House, Inc. Collection, 1992–2001, Archives of Women Artists'. National Museum of Women in the Arts, 2020. Finding-Aid-to-Friends-of-Alice-Pike-Barney-Studio-House-Inc.pdf (accessed May 2021).

French, Nellie S. 'A Notable Fellowship Dinner'. *The Bahá'í Magazine*, vol. 16, no.4 (July 1925), p. 504. USNBA.

'Friends of Alice Pike Barney Studio House, Inc. Collection'. National Museum of Women in the Arts. Aug. 2004. https://nmwa.org/ (accessed May 2021).

Gail, Marzieh. *Arches of the Years.* Oxford: George Ronald, 1991.

—— 'Impressions of the Centenary'. *Bahá'í News*, no. 170 (Sept. 1944), pp. 10–18.

https://bahai.works/Baha%27i_News/Issue_170 (accessed Aug. 2020).

—— *Summon Up Remembrance.* Oxford: George Ronald, 1987.

Garis, M. R. *Martha Root: Lioness at the Threshold.* Wilmette, IL: Bahá'í Publishing Trust, 1983.

Gaubatz, Piper Rae. *Beyond the Great Wall: Urban Form and Transformation on the Chinese Frontiers.* Stanford, CA: Stanford University Press, 1996.

Giachery, Ugo. 'Laura Clifford Dreyfus-Barney'. *The Bahá'í World*, vol. 16 (1973–1976). Haifa: Bahá'í World Centre, 1978, pp. 535–8.

—— 'Laura Clifford Dreyfus-Barney: Une Appréciation'. *La Pensée Bahá'íe*, no. 56 (June 1976), pp. 20–30.

—— *Shoghi Effendi: Recollections.* Oxford: George Ronald, 1973.

Glass, Charles. *Americans in Paris: Life and Death under Nazi Occupation 1940–44.* New York: HarperPress, 2010.

Hall, Delight. *Catalogue of the Alice Pike Barney Memorial Lending Collection*. Washington, D.C.: National Collection of Fine Arts, the Smithsonian Institution, 1965.

Hands of the Cause in the Western Hemisphere. Letter from the Hands of the Faith in the Western Hemisphere (Corinne True, Hermann Grossmann, William Sears) to All National Assemblies in the Western Hemisphere, and to all Members of the Auxiliary Board, May 31, 1960. https://bahai-library.com/true_grossman_sears_remey (accessed Feb. 2018).

Haney, Mariam. 'Mrs Agnes Parsons'. *The Bahá'í World*, vol. 5 (1932–1934). New York: Bahá'í Publishing Committee, 1936, p. 410–14.

Hannen, Joseph H. 'Abdul-Bahá in Washington, D.C.'. *Star of the West*, vol. 3, no. 3 (April 28, 1912), pp. 6–24.

Hannen Moe, Judy. *Aflame with Devotion: The Hannen and Knobloch Families and the Early Days of the Bahá'í Faith in America*. Wilmette, IL: Bahá'í Publishing, 2019.

Hardy, George (ed.). 'The Search for the Authentic and Spiritual: Americans in Paris and the French Countryside in the Second Half of the Nineteenth Century'. *Americans in Paris 1850 –1910*. Oklahoma City, OK: Oklahoma City Museum of Art, 2003.

Hassall, Graham. 'Notes on the Bábí and Bahá'í Religions in Russia and Its Territories'. *Journal of Bahá'í Studies*, vol. 5, no. 3, 1993, pp. 41–80. http://bahai-library.com/hassall_babi_Bahai_russia (accessed Dec. 2020).

Hatch, Willard P. 'Sydney Sprague'. *The Bahá'í World*, vol. 9 (1940–1944). Wilmette, IL: Bahá'í Publishing Committee, 1945, pp. 633–5.

'History'. International Council of Women. http://www.icw-cif.com/01/03.php (accessed March 2021).

Hoagg, H. Emogene. 'Short History of the International Bahá'í Bureau'. *The Bahá'í World*, vol. 4 (1930–1932). New York: Bahá'í Publishing Committee, 1933, pp. 257–61.

Hofman, Marion. 'Leroy C. Ioas'. *The Bahá'í World*, vol. 14 (1963–1968). Haifa, Israel: The Universal House of Justice, 1974, pp. 291–300.

Hogensen, Kathryn Jewett. *Lighting the Western Sky: The Hearst Pilgrimage and the Establishment of the Bahá'í Faith in the West*. Oxford: George Ronald, 2010.

Holley, Horace. 'Survey of Current Bahá'í Activities in the East and West: Extension of Teaching Activities in Europe'. *The Bahá'í World*, vol. 6 (1934–1936). New York: Bahá'í Publishing Committee, 1937, pp. 34–47.

Holley, Marion. 'May Maxwell'. *The Bahá'í World*, vol. 8 (1938–1940). Wilmette, IL: Bahá'í Publishing Committee, 1942, pp. 631–42.

Hollinger, Richard (ed.). *'Abdu'l-Bahá in America: Agnes Parsons' Diary*. Los Angeles: Kalimát Press, 1996.

Hutchinson, Sandra, and Richard Hollinger. 'Women in the North American Baha'i Community.' Skinner Keller, Rosemary, Rosemary Radford Ruether and Marie Cantlon, eds.). *Encyclopedia of Women and Religion in North America: Native*

American Creation Stories. Bloomington: Indiana University Press, 2006, pp. 776–82.

International Council of Women. (M.-H. Lefaucheux, *et al.*, eds.). *Women in a Changing World: The Dynamic Story of the International Council of Women since 1888*. London: Routledge and Kegan Paul, 1966.

Ishráq-Khávarí, 'Abdu'l-Ḥamíd. *Núrayn-i-Nayyirayn*, vol. 2. Tehran: Mu'assasiy-i Millíy-i Maṭbú'át-i Amrí, 1968.

Jasion, Jan Teofil. *'Abdu'l-Bahá in France 1911 & 1913*. Paris: Éditions bahá'íes France, 2016.

'Juliet Thompson'. *The Bahá'í World*, vol. 13 (1954–1963). Haifa, Israel: The Universal House of Justice, 1970, pp. 862–4.

Keshavmurti (Sri Aurobindo). *Sri Aurobindo: The Hope of Man*. Pondicherry, India: Dipti Publications, 1969.

Khadem, Riaz. *Prelude to the Guardianship*. Oxford: George Ronald, 2014.

Khademi, Mona. 'Laura Dreyfus-Barney and 'Abdu'l-Bahá's Visit to the West'. Negar Mottahedeh (ed.). *'Abdu'l-Bahá's Journey West: The Course of Human Solidarity*. New York: Palgrave Macmillan, 2013, pp. 15–38.

King, Charles. *Genius and Death in a City of Dreams: Odessa*. New York: W. W. Norton, 2011.

Kling, Jean L. *Alice Pike Barney: Her Life and Art*. Washington, D.C.: Smithsonian Books, 1994.

Kluge, Ian. '*Some Answered Questions* – A Philosophical Perspective', in *Lights of 'Irfán*, Book Ten. Darmstadt, Germany: 'Asr-i-Jadíd Publisher, 2009.

Langer, Cassandra. *Romaine Brooks: A Life*. Madison, WI: The University of Wisconsin Press, 2015.

'Laura Clifford Dreyfus-Barney'. *The Bahá'í World*, vol. 16 (1973–1976), pp. 535–8.

'Letter from Mr. Sprague'. *Bahai News*, vol. 1, no. 6 (June 24, 1910), p. 6.

Lights of Guidance: A Bahá'í Reference File. Compiled by Helen Hornby. New Delhi: Bahá'í Publishing Trust, 5th ed. 1997.

Maḥmúd-i-Zarqání. *Mahmúd's Diary*. Oxford: George Ronald, 1998.

'Mashriqu'l-Adhkár'. The Bahá'í Encyclopedia Project. https://www.bahai-encyclopedia-project.org/index.php?option=com_content&view=article&id=70:mashriqul-adhkar&catid=36:administrationinstitutions (accessed Jan. 2021).

Mavaddat, Rochan. 'Abdu'l-Bahá en France'. *Bahá'í France*, no. 15, Winter 1988.

May, Steven. 'The House that Alice Built'. *Historic Preservation*, vol. 46, no. 5 (Sept.–Oct. 1994).

Mázandarání, Asadu'lláh Fáḍil. *Táríkh-i-Ẓuhúru'l-Ḥaqq*, vol. 8, part 2. Tehran: Tehran: Mu'assasiy-i Millíy-i Maṭbú'át-i Amrí, 131 BE.

McClullough, David. *The Greater Journey: Americans in Paris*. New York: Simon and Shuster, 2011.

McLean, Jack. 'My Interview with Laura Dreyfus-Barney (Paris 1967)', 2007. http://jack-mclean.com/laura-dreyfus-barney/ (accessed May 2021).

Mehrábkhaní, Rúhu'lláh. *Zindigání-i-Mírzá Abu'l-Faḍl-i-Gulpáygání.* Hofheim-Langehain: Bahá'í-Verlag, 1988.

Metelmann, Velda Piff. *Lua Getsinger: Herald of the Covenant.* Oxford: George Ronald, 1997.

The Ministry of the Custodians, 1957–1963: An Account of the Stewardship of the Hands of the Cause. With an Introduction by the Hand of the Cause Amatu'l-Bahá Rúḥíyyih Khánum. Haifa: Bahá'í World Centre, 1992.

Momen, Moojan. 'ABU'L-FAŻL GOLPĀYEGĀNĪ'. *Encyclopædia Iranica*, vol. 1. London: Routledge and Kegan Paul, 1985, pp. 289–90. http://www.iranicaonline.org/articles/abul-fazl-or-abul-fazael-golpayegani-Mírzá-mohammad-prominent-bahai-scholar-and-apologist (accessed Jan. 2014).

— *The Bábí and Bahá'í Religions, 1844–1944. Some Contemporary Western Accounts.* Oxford: George Ronald, 1981.

— *The Baha'i Communities of Iran, 1851 –1921*, vol. 1: *The North of Iran.* Oxford: George Ronald, 2015.

— 'Baha'i Community of Ashkhabad: Its Social Basis and Importance in Baha'i History'. Shirin Akiner (ed.). *Cultural Change and Continuity in Central Asia.* London: Kegan Paul International and Central Asia Research Forum, SOAS, 1991, pp. 278–305.

— 'Covenant, The, and Covenant-breaker'. 1995, http://bahai-library.com/momen_encyclopedia_covenant (accessed Feb. 2018).

— 'Gulpáygání, Mírzá Abu'l-Fadl'. 1995. https://bahai-library.com/momen_encyclopedia_abul-fadl_gulpaygani (accessed June 2021).

— 'Russia'.1995. https://bahai-library.com/momen_encyclopedia_russia (accessed Feb. 2016).

Momen, Wendi. *A Basic Bahá'í Dictionary.* Oxford: George Ronald, 1989.

The Mother. *Words of Long Ago: Collected Works of The Mother*, vol. 2. Pondicherry, India: Sri Aurobindo International Centre for Education, Sri Aurobindo Ashram Publications Department, 1978.

'Mr. Edwin Scott'. *The Bahá'í World*, vol. 5 (1932–1934). New York: Bahá'í Publishing Committee, 1936, pp. 418–19.

'Mrs. Alice Barney'. *The Bahá'í World*, vol. 5 (1932–1934). New York: Bahá'í Publishing Committee, 1936, pp. 419–20.

Mu'ayyad, Ḥabíb. *Kháṭirát-i-Ḥabíb*, vol. 1. Hofheim: Bahá'í-Verlag, 1998.

Nakhjavání, Bahíyyih. *Asking Questions: A Challenge to Fundamentalism.* Oxford: George Ronald, 1990.

Nakhjavani, Violette. *The Maxwells of Montreal*, vol. 1: *Early Years 1870–1922.* Oxford: George Ronald, 2011.

'News of the Cause'. *Baha'i News Letter*, no. 2 (Jan. 1925), p. 3. https://bahai.works/ Baha%27i_News_Letter/Issue_2/Text (accessed March 2021).

'News from the Holy Land: Letter from Major W. Tudor-Pole'. *Star of the West*, vol. 10, no. 3 (April 28, 1919), pp. 36–7.

'News Notes'. *Bahai News*, vol. 1, no. 18 (Feb. 7, 1911), p. 9.

Ober, Elizabeth Kidder, Matthew W. Bullock and Beatrice Ashton. 'Harlan Foster Ober'. *The Bahá'í World*, vol. 13 (1954–1963). Haifa, Israel: The Universal House of Justice, 1970, pp. 866–71.

'Orient–Occident Unity'. *Star of the West*, vol. 2, no. 1 (March 21, 1911), p. 6.

Payám-i-Bahá'í (in Persian), no. 326 (Jan. 2007). Lyon: l'Assemblée spirituelle nationale des bahá'ís de France.

Peace and Disarmament Committee of the Women's International Organisations Collected Records, Swarthmore College Peace Collection. http://archives.tricolib. brynmawr.edu/resources/scpc-cdg-b-switzerland-peace_and_disarmament_ commi (accessed June 2021).

'The Persian–American Educational Society'. *Bahai News*, vol. 1, no. 5 (June 5, 1910), p. 2; and *Bahai News*, vol. 1, no. 13 (Nov. 4, 1910), p. 6.

Pound, Omar, and Robert Spoo (eds.). *Ezra Pound and Margaret Cravens: A Tragic Friendship 1910–1912*. Durham: Duke University Press, 1988.

Qazvini, Muhammad. "Abdu'l-Bahá's Meeting with Two Prominent Iranians', translated by Ahang Rabbani. *World Order*, vol. 30, no. 1 (Fall 1998), pp. 35–46. https://bahai-library.com/qazvini_abdulbaha_prominent_iranians (accessed June 2017).

Qobil, Rustom. 'Uzbekistan: Land of a thousand shrines'. BBC Uzbek, 15 Sept. 2018. https://www.bbc.co.uk/news/world-asia-44685414 (accessed Jan. 2021).

Rabbani, Rúḥíyyih. *The Priceless Pearl*. London: Bahá'í Publishing, 2000.

Rassekh, Shapour. 'Laura Clifford Dreyfus-Barney'. *Encyclopedia Iranica*, vol. 7. Costa Mesa: Mazda Publishers, 1997, pp. 552–3. http://www.iranicaonline.org/articles/ dreyfus-barney (accessed May 2021).

Reich, Jacqueline. 'Mussolini at the Movies: Fascism, Film, and Culture'. Reich, Jacqueline, and Piero Garofalo (eds.) *Re-viewing Fascism: Italian Cinema 1922– 1943*.

Rodriguez, Suzanne. *Wild Heart: A Life: Natalie Clifford Barney and the Decadence of Literary Paris*. New York: HarperCollins Publishers, 2002.

Root, Martha L. 'Disarmament Conference and the Extraordinary Session of League of Nations'. *Bahá'í Magazine*, vol. 23, no. 1 (April 1932), p. 18. USNBA.

— 'Russia's Cultural Contribution to the Bahá'í Faith'. *The Bahá'í World*, vol. 6 (1934–1936). New York: Bahá'í Publishing Committee, 1937, pp. 707–12.

— *Ṭáhirih the Pure*. Los Angeles: Kalimát Press, rev. ed. 1981.

Rose, Janet Fleming. *A Seed in Your Heart: The Life of Louise Mathew Gregory*. Oxford: George Ronald, 2018.

Rostam-Kolayi, Jasamin. 'The Tarbiyat Girls' School of Tehran: Iranian and American Baha'i Contributions to Modern Education'. *Middle East Critique*, Feb. 2013, vol. 22, no 1, pp. 77–93. DOI: 10.1080/19436149.2012.755298.

Ruhe, David S. *Door of Hope: The Bahá'í Faith in the Holy Land*. Oxford: George Ronald, 2nd rev. ed. 2001.

Ruhe-Schoen, Janet. *Champions of Oneness: Louis Gregory and His Shining Circle*. Wilmette, IL: Bahá'í Publishing, 2015.

Rutstein, Nathan. *Corinne True: Faithful Handmaid of 'Abdu'l-Bahá*. Oxford: George Ronald, 1987.

Ṣadr uṣ-Ṣudúr. *Istidlálíyyiy-i-Mukhtaṣar-i-Ṣadr uṣ-Ṣudúr*. Tehran: Mu'assasiy-i-Millíy-i-Maṭbú'át-i-Amrí, 132 BE [1975/6]; and Melbourne, Victoria: Century Press, 2004. http://www.afnanlibrary.org/wp-content/uploads/2017/01/INBA_v025.pdf (accessed Aug. 2020).

Safar, P.G. 'La Coopération Intellectuelle: La Conférence de Mme Dreyfus-Barney' ['The Conference of Mme Dreyfus-Barney']. *L'Orient*. Beirut, in French, April 6, 1935, Doucet, translated by Sheryl Mellor.

Samandari-Khoshbin, Parivash. *Ṭaráz-i-Iláhí. Hand of the Cause of God Mírzá Taráz'u'lláh Samandarí*. vol. 2. Hamilton, ON: Association for Bahá'í Studies in Persian, 2004. https://reference.bahai.org/fa/ (accessed Jan. 2020).

Samarkand Tours. http://www.samarkandtour.com/en/attractions/dostoprimechatel nosti_samarkanda/mavzoley_doniyor-paygambar.html (accessed Jan. 2021).

Sanderson, Edith. 'An Interview with A.L.M. Nicolas of Paris'. *The Bahá'í World*, vol. 8 (1938–1940). Wilmette, IL: Bahá'í Publishing Committee, 1942, pp. 885–7.

Sarwal, Anil. 'Sri Aurobindo Movement and the Bahá'í Faith'. 2001. http://bahai-library.com/sarwal_sri_aurobindo (accessed June 2018).

Shahvar, Soli. 'The Baha'i Faith and Its Communities in Iran, Transcaspia and the Caucasus'. Shahvar, Soli, Boris Morozov and Gad G. Gilbar (eds.). *The Baha'is of Iran, Transcaspia and the Caucasus*, vol. 1: *Letters of Russian Officers and Officials*. London: I. B. Tauris, 2011.

— *The Forgotten Schools: The Baha'is and Modern Education in Iran, 1899–1934*. London: Tauris Academic Studies, 2009.

Shoghi Effendi. *Bahá'í Administration*. Wilmette, IL: Bahá'í Publishing Trust, 1968.

— *God Passes By*. Wilmette, IL: Bahá'í Publishing Trust, 4th ed., 1995.

— *High Endeavors: Messages to Alaska*. [Anchorage]: National Spiritual Assembly of the Bahá'ís of Alaska, 1976.

— 'Hippolyte Dreyfus-Barney: An Appreciation'. *The Bahá'í World*, vol. 3 (1932–1934). New York: Bahá'í Publishing Committee, 1930, pp. 210–11, 214.

— *Japan Will Turn Ablaze!* Compiled by Barbara R. Sims. n.p. [Japan]: Bahá'í Publishing Trust, rev. ed. 1992.

— *The Light of Divine Guidance: The Messages from the Guardian of the Bahá'í Faith to the Bahá'ís of Germany and Austria*. 2 vols. Hofheim-Langenhain: Bahá'í-Verlag, 1982/1985.

— *The Unfolding Destiny of the British Bahá'í Community: The Messages of the Guardian of the Bahá'í Faith to the Bahá'ís of the British Isles*. London: Bahá'í Publishing Trust, 1981.

— *The World Order of Bahá'u'lláh*. Wilmette, IL: Bahá'í Publishing Trust, 1991.

Smith, Peter. 'Tolstoy, Leo', in *A Concise Encyclopedia of the Bahá'í Faith*. Oxford: Oneworld, 2000.

Smithsonian Institution. 'Annual Report' for the years 1951, 1953 and 1980. https://siris-sihistory.si.edu (accessed May 2021).

Sohrab, Mírzá Ahmad. 'With Abdul-Baha in London'. *Star of the West*, vol. 3, no. 19 (March 2, 1913), pp. 3–7.

'Some Answered Questions'. Advertisement in *Bahai News*, vol. 1, no. 3 (April 28, 1910), p. 20.

Star of the West, vol. 3, no. 12 (Oct. 16, 1912), p. 8.

Stockman, Robert H. *The Bahá'í Faith in America: Origins, 1892–1900*, vol. 1. Wilmette, IL: Bahá'í Publishing Trust, 1985.

— *The Bahá'í Faith in America, Early Expansion, 1900–1912*, vol. 2. Oxford: George Ronald, 1995.

— 'Remey, Charles Mason'. 1995. http://Bahai-library.com/stockman_remey (accessed Feb. 2015).

Stöckmann, Jan. '90 Years of Intellectual Cooperation: The Forgotten History of UNESCO's Predecessor'. Oct. 12, 2016. https://afus-unesco.org/assets/files/unesco-75-ans/unesco-avant-unesco-eng-stockmann.pdf (accessed Feb. 2019).

Sulaymání, 'Azízu'lláh. *Maṣábíḥ-i Hidáyat*, vol. 5. Tehran: Mu'assasiy-i Millíy-i Maṭbú'át-i Amrí, 118 BE/1961.

Taherzadeh, Adib. *The Revelation of Bahá'u'lláh*, vol. 4. Oxford: George Ronald, 1987.

Táhirzádeh, Habíb. 'Dr. Youness Afrukhtih [Afroukhteh]'. *The Bahá'í World*, vol. 12 (1950–1954). Wilmette, IL: Bahá'í Publishing Trust, 1956, pp. 679–81.

'The Tarbiat School, Persia'. *Bahai News*, vol. 1, no. 7 (July 13, 1910), pp. 3–7.

Taylor, Joshua C. *National Collection of Fine Arts*. Washington, D.C.: Smithsonian Institution, 1978.

Theosophical Society of America. https://www.theosophical.org (accessed April 2018).

Theological Society in England. https://theosophicalsociety.org.uk/ (accessed March 2021).

'A Tribute to Laura Dreyfus-Barney'. *The American Bahá'í*, Jan. 1989.

The United States Army Ambulance Service: American Ambulance Service in France

Prior to April 5, 1917. https://achh.army.mil/history/book-wwi-fieldoperations-chapter6 (accessed Oct. 2021).

United States Department of the Interior, National Park Service. National Register of Historic Places. https://www.nps.gov/subjects/nationalregister/database-research. htm#table (accessed May 2021); https://www.historicwashington.org/docs/ Historic%20Landmark%20Application/Alice%20Pike%20Barney%20Studio% 20House.pdf (accessed May 2021); and 'Studio House.' https://www.nps.gov/ subjects/nationalregister/database-research.htm#table (accessed May 2021).

The Universal House of Justice. 'Mason Remey and Those Who Followed Him', enclosure in a letter from the Universal House of Justice to National Spiritual Assemblies, Jan. 31, 1997. http://bahai-library.com/uhj_mason_remey_followers (accessed Feb. 2018); and revised statement 2008. https://bahai-library.com/pdf/ uhj/uhj_mason_remey_followers.pdf (accessed May 2021).

— *Messages from the Universal House of Justice 1963–1986: The Third Epoch of the Formative Age*. Wilmette, IL: Bahá'í Publishing Trust, 1996.

Ward, Allan L. *239 Days: 'Abdu'l-Bahá's Journey in America*. Wilmette, IL: Bahá'í Publishing Trust, 1979.

Weinberg, Robert. *Ethel Rosenberg: The Life and Times of England's Outstanding Bahá'í Pioneer Worker*. Oxford: George Ronald, 1995.

— *Lady Blomfield: Her Life and Times*. Oxford: George Ronald, 2012.

Whitehead, O.Z. *Some Bahá'ís to Remember*. Oxford: George Ronald, 1983.

Wickes, George. *The Amazon of Letters: The Life and Loves of Natalie Barney*. New York: G.P. Putnam's Sons, 1976.

Young, Roz. 'Barney Name Means More Than a Dinosaur to Dayton'. Dayton History Books Online. http://www.daytonhistorybooks.com/youngbarney.html (accessed Jan. 2016).

NOTES AND REFERENCES

Part 1 Family and Childhood 1879 – 1899

1 The hotel was completely destroyed by the Cairo fire of 1952.

2 Some of this information is based on an unattributed newspaper article by Jeanne Arcache, undated (perhaps 1935), Doucet, translated by Sheryl Mellor.

3 For further reading, see Rodriguez, *Wild Heart* and [Barney], *Stanley's 'Lady' Alice*, SIA. https://siarchives.si.edu/collections/siris_arc_217626 (accessed Jan. 2020).

4 [Barney], *Stanley's 'Lady' Alice*, p. 21, SIA. https://siarchives.si.edu/collections/siris_arc_217626 (accessed Jan. 2020).

5 Rodriguez, *Wild Heart*, pp. 2–5. Many of the details of Laura's family background are based on Rodriguez unless otherwise noted.

6 More information about Alice Pike can be found at Young, 'Barney Name Means More Than a Dinosaur to Dayton'. Dayton History Books Online. http://www.daytonhistorybooks.com/youngbarney.html (accessed Jan. 2016).

7 Rodriguez, *Wild Heart*, p. 15.

8 Adler, *Americans in Paris 1860–1900*, p. 11.

9 ibid.

10 Rodriguez, *Wild Heart*, pp. 15–16.

11 [Barney], *Stanley's 'Lady' Alice*, p. 54, SIA. https://siarchives.si.edu/collections/siris_arc_217626 (accessed Jan. 2020).

12 Rodriguez, *Wild Heart*, p. 17.

13 ibid. p. 11.

14 Kling, *Alice Pike Barney*, p. 66.

15 Rodriguez, *Wild Heart*, p. 18.

16 See Young, 'Barney Name'. http://www.daytonhistorybooks.com/youngbarney.html (accessed Jan. 2017). *These articles appeared in the Dayton Daily News on Jan. 28, Feb. 4, 11, 18, 25, March 4, 11, 18, and 25, 1995.*

17 [Barney], *Stanley's 'Lady' Alice*, p. 261, SIA. https://siarchives.si.edu/collections/siris_arc_217626 (accessed Jan. 2020).

18 See Young, 'Barney Name'. http://www.daytonhistorybooks.com/youngbarney.html (accessed Jan. 2017).

19 [Barney], *Stanley's 'Lady' Alice*, p. 262, SIA. https://siarchives.si.edu/collections/siris_arc_217626 (accessed Jan. 2020).

20 Kling, *Alice Pike Barney*, p. 70.

21 ibid. p. 81.

22 Rodriguez, *Wild Heart*, p. 27, n. 15; Barney, Natalie, 'N.C.B. sur sa mère Alice Barney', SIA.

23 Unattributed Dayton newspaper clipping, Dec. 1902, SIA.

24 'Builders of Wooden Railway Cars'. http://www.midcontinent.org/rollingstock/builders/barney-smith2.htm (accessed Feb. 2020).

25 Young, 'Barney Name'. http://www.daytonhistorybooks.com/youngbarney.html (accessed Jan. 2016).

26 Rodriguez, *Wild Heart*, p. 35.

27 Chalon, *Portrait of a Seductress*, p. 4.

28 Kling, *Alice Pike Barney*, p. 81.

29 Rodriguez, *Wild Heart*, p. 33.

30 ibid. p. 35.

31 Afroukhteh, *Memories*, p. 150.

32 Kling, *Alice Pike Barney*, p. 115.

33 ibid. p. 116.

34 Chalon, *Portrait of a Seductress*, pp. 3–4.

35 ibid.

36 Letter from Alice [LCB] Barney to Albert Clifford Barney, August 16, 1888, Doucet. Laura used Alice and Elsie as her first name for the several years during her childhood, according to her letters at Doucet.

37 Rodriguez, *Wild Heart*, p. 39.

38 Letters from Laura Alice Barney (LCB) to ACB and APB, 1888 and 1889, Doucet.

39 ibid.

40 Letters from Alice [LCB] to ACB, no month or day given, both 1888, Doucet.

41 Letter from Laura Alice [LCB] to ACB, no date, Doucet.

42 Letter from Alice [LCB] to APB, Dec. 3 and Dec. 14, 1891, Doucet.

43 As indicated in note 36, Laura used both Alice and Elsie as her first name during her childhood.

44 Rodriguez, *Wild Heart*, pp. 47–8.

45 Kling, *Alice Pike Barney*, pp. 83–4.

46 Adler, *Americans in Paris 1860–1900*, p. 12.

47 Hardy, 'The Search for the Authentic and Spiritual', p. 74.

48 McCullough, *Greater Paris,* statement on the flap of the book's front cover.

49 Adler, *Americans in Paris 1860–1900*, p. 11.

50 ibid. p. 12.

51 Mary Cassatt's nephew became Natalie's fiancé, according to Rodriguez, *Wild Heart*, p. 43.

52 Chalon, *Portrait of a Seductress*, pp. 3–4.

53 [Barney], *Stanley's 'Lady' Alice*, p. 235, SIA. https://siarchives.si.edu/collections/siris_arc_217626 (accessed Jan. 2020).

54 Kling, *Alice Pike Barney*, p. 88.

55 Rodriguez, *Wild Heart*, p. 44.

56 Kling, *Alice Pike Barney*, p. 90.

57 ibid. 101.

58 Unattributed newspaper clipping, c. 1889, SIA.

59 For information on the school, see http://en.wikipedia.org/wiki/Georgetown_Visitation_Preparatory_School; http://www.newadvent.org/cathen/15483c.htm (accessed May 2016).

60 Rodriguez, *Wild Heart*, p. 61.

61 ibid. p. 63.

62 Kling, *Alice Pike Barney*, p. 102. The name of the school may also be Misses Ely's. See 'Private, Boarding Schools for Young Ladies: 1893–1894'. http://www.thehistorybox.com/ny_city/society/articles/nycity_society_pvt_schools_article0018.htm (accessed Feb. 2020).

63 Wickes, *Amazon of Letters*, p. 25.

64 Rodriguez, *Wild Heart*, p. 55, n. 8.

65 Chalon, *Portrait of a Seductress*, p. 12.

66 Wanda M. Corn, Introduction to Kling, *Alice Pike Barney*, p. 14.

67 Rodriguez, *Wild Heart*, pp. 46–7.

68 Letter from Alice [LCB] to ABC, Friday 29, no month given, in 1890s, SIA.

69 Letter from LBC to ACB mailed April 18, 1898, SIA.

70 Letter from Alice [LCB] to ACB and APB, 1890s, Doucet.

71 ibid.

72 Chalon, *Portrait of a Seductress*, p. 35.

73 Letter from LDB to NCB, Jan. 14, 1937, Doucet.

74 Letter from Alice [LCB] to APB, Dec. 3, 1891, Doucet.

75 Letter from LCB to ACB, 1898, SIA.

76 Letter from LCB to ACB, Easter, 1898, SIA.

77 Letter from LCB to ACB, 1898, SIA.

78 ibid.

79 Kling, *Alice Pike Barney*, p. 112.

80 ibid. p. 120.

81 ibid. p. 132.

82 Chalon, *Portrait of a Seductress*, p. 25.

Part 2 Faith from the East and Life-Changing Effects 1900 – 1910

1 See Appendix A, 'A Brief Introduction to the Bahá'í Faith'.

2 *New York Times*, Oct. 23, 1910.

3 Young, 'Barney Name'. http://www.daytonhistorybooks.com/youngbarney.html (accessed Jan. 2017).

4 Rodriguez, *Wild Heart*, p. 109.

5 ibid. p. 141.

6 Nakhjavani, *Maxwells*, vol. 1. p. 67.

7 Nakhjavani, *Maxwells*, vol. 1. pp. 69–70.

8 For May Bolles's conversion and pilgrimage, see Stockman, *Bahá'í Faith in America*, vol. 1, pp. 141, 145–6; and Nakhjavani, *Maxwells*, vol. 1, pp. 68–70, 72–8.

9 For further reading about the details of this trip, see Hogenson, *Lighting the Western Sky*.

10 Stockman, *Bahá'í Faith in America*, vol. 2, p. 151; Nakhjavani, *Maxwells*, vol. 1, pp. 91–102, 134.

11 Stockman, *Bahá'í Faith in America*, vol. 2, p. 154.

12 ibid. p. 152; Stockman, 'Remey, Charles Mason', 1995. http://Bahái-library.com/stockman_remey (accessed Feb. 2015).

13 Typed extract of a talk given by Laura Barney, Chicago, Oct. 1901, and the short-hand text of a letter from LCB to Mírzá Abu'l-Faḍl, Oct. 27, 1901, USNBA; Nakhjavani, *Maxwells*, vol. 1, p. 106.

14 Typed extract of a talk given by LCB in Chicago, Oct. 1901, and the shorthand text of a letter from LCB to Mírzá Abu'l-Faḍl, Oct. 27, 1901, USNBA. In a letter written by LCB the year after her first pilgrimage, she referred to her companion as Emma Trouvé. However, in a report of her travels written years later, on Aug. 31, 1951, she named Mme Lacheny as her companion on her first trip.

15 Handwritten report of LDB to Mariam Haney, Aug. 31, 1951, ABDF.

16 See Ruhe, *Door of Hope*, pp. 191–5; Gail, *Summon Up Remembrance*, p. 110.

17 Gail, *Summon Up Remembrance*, p. 110.

18 ibid. p. 145. Ali-Kuli Khan ('Alí-Qulí Khán) Nabílu'd-Dawlih was a prominent Bahá'í and diplomat. During her childhood, Laura called herself Alice, Elsa and Elsie.

19 Gail, *Summon Up Remembrance*, p. 145.

20 Extracts from a talk by LCB given in Chicago, IL, Oct. 27, 1901, USNBA.

21 ibid.

22 Letter from Ellen Goin Rionda to LDB, March 17, 1957, ABDF.

23 Gail, *Summon Up Remembrance*, pp. 110–11.

24 ibid. p. 111.

25 ibid. p. 112.

26 'Words of the Master, 'Abdu'l-Bahá to Miss Barney', Oct. 19 to 24, 1900, USNBA.

27 Extracts from a talk by LCB on Oct. 27, 1901 in Chicago, IL, USNBA.

28 Letter from an unknown person (perhaps a Bahá'í) to Corinne True, July 11, 1901, Gertrude Buikema Papers, USNBA.

29 Weinberg, *Ethel Jenner Rosenberg*, p. 39.

30 Giachery, 'Laura Clifford Dreyfus-Barney', *Bahá'í World*, vol. 16 (1973–1976), p. 535. Ugo Giachery was appointed a Hand of the Cause of God by Shoghi Effendi and was a friend of Laura Barney.

31 Handwritten letter from LCB to Mírzá Abu'l-Faḍl, Oct. 27, 1901, USNBA.

32 Hogenson, *Lighting the Western Sky*, p. 322.

33 Nakhjavani, *Maxwells*, vol. 1, p. 130.

34 Handwritten report from LDB to Mariam Haney, Aug. 31, 1951, ABDF.

35 ibid.

36 Momen, 'Gulpáygání, Mírzá Abu'l-Fadl'. https://Bahái-library.com/momen_encyclopedia_abul-fadl_gulpaygani (accessed June 2021).

37 Momen, 'ABU'L-FAŻL GOLPĀYEGĀNĪ. http://www.iranicaonline.org/articles/abul-fazl-or-abul-fazael-golpayegani-Mírzá-mohammad-prominent-bahai-scholar-and-apologist (accessed Jan. 2014).

38 Letter from LCB to Mírzá Abu'l-Faḍl, 1901, USNBA.

39 ibid.

40 Handwritten report from LDB to Mariam Haney, Aug. 31, 1951, ABDF.

41 According to Nakhjavani, *Maxwells*, vol. 1, p. 180, n53 Aḥmad Yazdí was responsible for the translation of the Tablets of 'Abdu'l-Bahá.

42 Hogenson, *Lighting the Western Sky*, p. 317.

43 Gail, *Summon Up Remembrance*, p. 148.

44 Remey, 'Reminiscences of my Religious Life' in 'Reminiscences and Letters', vol. 88, 1933, p. 68, Charles Mason Remey Papers, USNBA.

45 Stockman, Robert, 'Charles Mason Remey', 1995. https://Bahái-library.com/stockman_remey (accessed Feb. 2015).

46 Remey, 'Reminiscences of My Religious Life', in 'Reminiscences and Letters', vol. 88, p. 68, 1933, Charles Mason Remey papers, USNBA.
47 ibid.
48 Weinberg, *Ethel Jenner Rosenberg*, p. 39.
49 Letter from LCB to Mírzá Abu'l-Faḍl, Oct. 27, 1901, USNBA.
50 ibid.
51 Gail, *Summon Up Remembrance*, p. 119.
52 Ruhe, *Door of Hope*, p. 56.
53 Remey, 'Reminiscences of My Religious Life', in 'Reminiscences and Letters', vol. 88, p. 73, 1933, Charles Mason Remey papers, USNBA.
54 'Miss Barney and Babism', *Sun* (New York), Sept. 28, 1902.
55 ibid.
56 Handwritten report from LDB to Mariam Haney, Aug. 31, 1951, ABDF.
57 Dreyfus Barney, 'Only a Word', *Bahá'í World*, vol. 5 (1932–1934), p. 667.
58 Giachery, *Shoghi Effendi*, pp. 14–15.
59 Giachery, 'Laura Clifford Dreyfus-Barney', *Bahá'í World*, vol. 16 (1973–1976), p. 536.
60 Letter from LDB to Rúḥíyyih Khánum Rabbani, June 21, 1969, ABDF.
61 Handwritten report by LDB to answer Mariam Haney's questions, Aug. 31, 1951, ABDF.
62 Mázandarání, *Táríkh-i-Ẓuhúru'l-Ḥaqq*, vol. 8, part 2, p. 1194.
63 Gail, *Summon Up Remembrance*, p. 143.
64 Handwritten report from LDB to Mariam Haney, Aug. 31, 1951, ABDF.
65 Anton Haddad was an Egyptian who became a deepened Bahá'í after meeting 'Abdu'l-Bahá.
66 Handwritten report by LDB to Mariam Haney, Aug. 31, 1951, ABDF.
67 Nakhjavani, *Maxwells*, vol. 1, p. 97. 'Abdu'l-Bahá reimbursed them for the construction work after its completion.
68 Giachery, 'Laura Clifford Dreyfus-Barney', *Bahá'í World*, vol. 16 (1973–1976), p. 537.
69 LDB, quoted in ibid.
70 *Payám-i-Bahá'í* (in Persian), no. 326, Jan. 2007, p. 8.
71 Giachery, 'Laura Clifford Dreyfus-Barney', *La Pensée Bahá'íe*, no. 56 (June 1976), n2, p. 25.
72 Handwritten report by LDB to Mariam Haney, Aug. 31, 1951, ABDF.
73 Stockman, *Bahá'í Faith in America*, vol. 2, p. 150.
74 Gail, *Summon Up Remembrance*, letter from Khan, June 11, 1901, p. 150.
75 Stockman, *Bahá'í Faith in America*, vol. 2, pp. 153–4.
76 Nakhjavani, *Maxwells*, vol. 1, p. 139.
77 Gail, *Summon Up Remembrance*, pp. 148–9.
78 ibid. p. 150.
79 Agnes Alexander, quoted in Holley, Marion, 'May Ellis Maxwell', *Bahá'í World*, vol. 8 (1938–1940), p. 634; and Nakhjavani, *Maxwells*, p. 135.
80 Juliet Thompson, quoted in Holley, Marion, 'May Ellis Maxwell', *Bahá'í World*, vol. 8 (1938–1940), p. 634; and Nakhjavani, *Maxwells*, p. 135.
81 Nakhjavani, *Maxwells*, vol. 1, p. 135: Stockman, *Bahá'í Faith in America*, vol. 2, p. 467, n298.
82 Gail, *Summon Up Remembrance*, p. 151–3.

83 Hogenson, *Lighting the Western Sky*, p. 223.
84 Handwritten report by LDB to Mariam Haney, Aug. 31, 1951, ABDF.
85 Gail, *Summon Up Remembrance*, p. 163.
86 Ali-Kuli Khan and Marzieh Gail, 'Mírzá Abu'l-Faḍl in America', *Bahá'í World*, vol. 9 (1940–1944), p. 856.
87 Stockman, *Bahá'í Faith in America*, vol. 1, pp. 100-4.
88 ibid. p. 163; Rutstein, *Corinne True*, p. 24.
89 Stockman, *Bahá'í Faith in America*, vol. 1, pp. 32–3.
90 ibid. pp. xxxvii–iii, 3–26.
91 ibid. vol. 2, pp. 35–6; Rutstein, *Corinne True*, p. 25.
92 Weinberg, *Ethel Jenner Rosenberg*, p. 59; Handwritten report by LDB to Mariam Haney, Aug. 31, 1951, ABDF.
93 Handwritten report by LDB to Mariam Haney, Aug. 31, 1951, ABDF.
94 Gail, *Summon Up Remembrance*, p. 167.
95 Hogenson, *Lighting the Western Sky*, p. 223.
96 Ali-Kuli Khan and Marzieh Gail, 'Mírzá Abu'l-Faḍl in America', *Bahá'í World*, vol. 9 (1940–1944), p. 857.
97 Gail, *Summon Up Remembrance*, pp. 156–7.
98 Hannen Moe, *Aflame with Devotion*, p. 25.
99 Alma Knobloch, personal recollections, 'How I Became a Bahá'í', Hannen Knobloch Collection, BAWDC, cited in ibid. pp. 25–6.
100 Handwritten report of LDB to Mariam Haney, Aug. 31, 1951, ABDF.
101 Young, 'Barney Name'. http://www.daytonhistorybooks.com/youngbarney.html (accessed Jan. 2017).
102 Kling, *Alice Pike Barney*, p. 170.
103 Hannen Moe, *Aflame with Devotion*, p. 21.
104 Stockman, *Bahá'í Faith in America*, vol. 2, p. 463, n265.
105 ibid. p. 81. See Mírzá Abu'l-Faḍl, *Bahá'í Proofs*.
106 Gail, *Summon Up Remembrance*, p. 167.
107 The copyright holder was 'A.P. Barney of Washington, D.C.', most likely Laura's mother. Gail, *Summon Up Remembrance*, p. 178.
108 Mírzá-Abul-Fazl [Abu'l-Faḍl], *Hujaj'ul Beheyyeh (The Behai Proofs)*, p. 21.
109 Handwritten report from LDB to Mariam Haney, Aug. 31, 1951, ABDF.
110 Stockman, *Bahá'í Faith in America*, vol. 2, p. 81.
111 Gail, *Summon Up Remembrance*, pp. 169.
112 ibid. pp. 167–70; Ali-Kuli Khan and Marzieh Gail, 'Mírzá Abu'l-Faḍl in America', *Bahá'í World*, vol. 9 (1940–1944), p. 858.
113 Mehrabkhani, *Zindigání-i-Mírzá Abu'l-Faḍl-i-Gulpáygání*, pp. 273, 275.
114 Gail, *Summon Up Remembrance*, p. 213.
115 Momen, 'Gulpáygání, Mírzá Abu'l-Faḍl'. https://bahai-library.com/momen_encyclopedia_abul-fadl_gulpaygani (accessed June 2021).
116 'Mrs. Alice Barney', *Bahá'í World*, vol. 5 (1932–1934), p. 420.
117 Weinberg, *Ethel Jenner Rosenberg*, p. 40.
118 Author's interviews with Anita Ioas-Chapman, who lived in Paris in 1950-5 and 1965-7 and was a friend and neighbor of Laura Dreyfus Barney.
119 Kling, *Alice Pike Barney*, p. 170.
120 ibid. p. 234.
121 Buck, *Alain Locke*, p. 46.

122 Kling, *Alice Pike Barney*, pp. 234–5.

123 ibid. p. 167.

124 ibid. p. 168, n5; unidentified newspaper clipping, APB, Scrapbooks, National Museum of American Arts (today's Smithsonian American Art Museum), Curatorial Office, SI, WDC.

125 Kling, *Alice Pike Barney*, p. 168.

126 Letter from Lua Gestinger to May Bolles, in Nakhjavani, *Maxwells*, vol. 1, p. 185.

127 Letter from Marie Squires to May Bolles, Nov. 24, 1901, in Nakhjavani, *Maxwells*, vol. 1, p. 159.

128 Nakhjavani, *Maxwells*, vol. 1, pp. 155–6.

129 Letter from LCB to May Bolles, undated; a summary of this letter was sent to the author by the Bahá'í World Centre, May 16, 2012.

130 Two undated letters from LCB to May Bolles; a summary of these letters was sent to the author by the Bahá'í World Centre, May 16, 2012.

131 Nakhjavani, *Maxwells*, vol. 1, p. 155.

132 ibid. p. 154.

133 Nakhjavani, *Maxwells*, vol. 1, p. 156.

134 Letter from Elsa Barney [LCB] to May Bolles, undated; a summary of this letter was sent to the author by the Bahá'í World Centre, May 16, 2012.

135 Letter from Elsa Barney [LCB] to May Bolles, 15 [month not given], 1901; a summary of this letter was sent to the author by the Bahá'í World Centre, May 16, 2012.

136 Juliet Thompson, cited in Nakhjavani, *Maxwells*, vol. 1, p. 154.

137 Letter from Elsa [Laura] Barney to May Bolles, undated; a summary of this letter was sent to the author by the Bahá'í World Centre, May 16, 2012.

138 Nakhjavani, *Maxwells*, vol. 1, p. 203.

139 Letter from Elsa [Laura] Barney from 'Akká to May Bolles, Nov. 24, year not given; a summary of this letter was sent to the author by the Bahá'í World Centre, May 16, 2012.

140 Letter from LCB to May Bolles, undated; a summary of this letter was sent to the author by the Bahá'í World Centre, May 16, 2012.

141 *Idaho Fall Times*, July 11, 1901; *Greelay Tribune*, July 4, 1901; and *Grand Valley*, Aug. 9, 1901.

142 'New Religious Cult: The Behaism Already Has Over Six Million Adherents', *Washington Post*, March 23, 1902.

143 *Washington Mirror*, March 29, 1902, cited in Kling, *Alice Pike Barney*, p. 169.

144 Kling, *Alice Pike Barney*, p. 170.

145 *Washington Mirror*, vol. 10, no. 10 (May 3, 1902), p. 3, cited in ibid. p. 171.

146 Rodriguez, *Wild Heart*, p. 141.

147 Kling, *Alice Pike Barney*, pp. 136, 145.

148 ibid. p. 172.

149 *Kansas City Star*, Oct. 2, 1902; *Sun*, Sept. 28; and *Chicago Tribune*, Sept. 29, 1902.

150 Kling, *Alice Pike Barney*, p. 170.

151 Letter from LDB to NCB, undated, perhaps 1902.

152 Gail, *Summon Up Remembrance*, p. 174.

153 ibid. pp. 174–6, n106; translated by the Research Department of the Universal House of Justice, original translation by Khan.

154 ibid.
155 Kling, *Alice Pike Barney*, p. 175.
156 'Albert Clifford Barney Dead: Stricken Down in South of France While in Search of Health', *Washington Post*, Dec. 9, 1902.
157 'In Memoriam. Albert C. Barney', Jan. 5. 1903, unattributed newspaper article, perhaps from Dayton, Ohio, SIA.
158 'Stricken Down in South of France While in Search of Health', *Washington Post*, Dec. 27, 1902.
159 *Washington Post*, Dec. 27, 1902.
160 Young, 'Barney Name'. http://www.daytonhistorybooks.com/youngbarney.html (accessed Jan. 2017).
161 Rodriguez, *Wild Heart*, p. 150.
162 Gail, *Summon Up Remembrance*, p. 177.
163 Kling, *Alice Pike Barney*, p. 178.
164 National Museum of American Art Smithsonian Institution brochure, 1983, SIA.
165 Kling, *Alice Pike Barney*, pp. 181–2.
166 ibid. p. 182.
167 *Washington Mirror*, July 11, 1903, SIA.
168 Kling, *Alice Pike Barney*, p. 184.
169 Letter from LCB to NCB, July 1902, Doucet.
170 Document dated 1986, SIA. The paintings of Alice Barney were donated by her daughters to the National Museum of American Art (today's Smithsonian American Art Museum) of WDC, SI.
171 'Abdu'l-Bahá, Tablet to LCB, Sept. 12, 1903, BWC, provisional translation by Riaz Masrour.
172 ibid.
173 'Abdu'l-Bahá, Tablet to LCB, Sept. 12, 1903, translated by A. K. Khan, Oct. 29, 1903, ABDF.
174 Typed translation of a letter from 'Abdu'l-Bahá to Mírzá Ahmad, translated by Ahmad Esphahani [Sohrab], Dec. 30, 1903, BAWDC.
175 Letters from Mariam Haney to LDB, Mar. 1 and March 11, 1957, ABDF.
176 Letter from Mariam Haney to LDB, Mar. 1, 1957, ABDF.
177 'Abdu'l-Bahá, *Tablets of 'Abdu'l-Bahá*, vol. 2, p. 484.
178 ibid. vol. 3, pp. 647–8, translated by A.K. Khan, March 12, 1904; typed copy in USNBA.
179 His name was Mírzá 'Alí Aṣghar Khán also known as Amin al-Soltan (Trusted of the King) and Atabak (Minister). He was the prime minister under Náṣiri'd-Dín Sháh Qájár in Iran. He was dismissed from this position in 1896.
180 Gail, *Summon Up Remembrance*, p. 183.
181 ibid. p. 184.
182 Letter from Marzieh Gail to Anita Chapman, March 3, 1981, Anita Chapman's Papers given to the author.
183 Gail, *Summon Up Remembrance*, pp. 171–2.
184 ibid.
185 ibid. p. 213.
186 ibid. p. 200.

187 ibid. p. 203.

188 ibid. p. 204.

189 ibid. p. 207.

190 ibid. p. 212.

191 ibid. p. 214.

192 This story is related in ibid. pp. 214–15.

193 LCB, transcript of talks, May 16, 1909, Frank Osborne Papers, USNBA.

194 Afroukhteh, *Memories,* pp. 314–15.

195 Weinberg, *Ethel Jenner Rosenberg,* pp. 73–4

196 Afroukhteh, *Memories,* p. 343, letter from LDB to Afroukhteh, Aug. 7, 1937.

197 Diary of HD, 1905, ABDF.

198 'Record of the First Bahá'í European Teaching Conference', held in Geneva, Switzerland, May 22–7, 1948, pp. 31–2, ABDF.

199 Foreword, 'Abdu'l-Bahá, *Some Answered Questions,* p. xi.

200 Gail, *Summon Up Remembrance,* p. 235.

201 Giachery, 'Laura Clifford Dreyfus-Barney', *Bahá'í World,* vol. 16 (1973–1976), p. 536.

202 Foreword, 'Abdu'l-Bahá, *Some Answered Questions,* pp. xi–xii.

203 'A Washington Society Girl's Romantic Pilgrimage to Syria to Rescue the Beha', *Washington Times,* Oct. 30, 1904.

204 Afroukhteh, *Memories,* p. 315.

205 ibid. p. 328.

206 Letter from LDB to APB, undated, perhaps summer of 1904, Doucet.

207 ibid.

208 Letter from LCB to APB, undated, USNBA.

209 ibid.

210 Weinberg, *Ethel Jenner Rosenberg,* p. 74.

211 Gail, 'Impressions of the Centenary', *Bahá'í News,* no. 170 (Sept. 1944), p. 13. https://bahai.works/Baha%27_News/Issue_170 (accessed Aug. 2020).

212 For additional commentary on this work, refer to Shoghi Effendi's statements in *God Passes By,* pp. 107, 260, 268, 305 and 383.

213 'Record of the First Bahá'í European Teaching Conference', held in Geneva, Switzerland, May 22–7, 1948, pp. 31–2, ABDF.

214 Afroukhteh, *Memories,* p. 315.

215 ibid. n28, p. 455.

216 Gail, *Summon Up Remembrance,* p. 230.

217 ibid. p. 319.

218 Afroukhteh, *Memories,* p. 316.

219 ibid. p. 316.

220 ibid. p. 315.

221 ibid. p. 314.

222 ibid. pp. 314–15.

223 ibid. pp. 318, 342–4, letter from LDB to Afroukhteh, Aug. 7, 1937.

224 Letter from LDB to Horace Holley, Jan. 21, 1959, ABDF.

225 Afroukhteh, *Memories,* pp. 316–18.

226 ibid. pp. 342–3, letter from LDB to Afroukhteh, Aug. 7, 1937.

227 ibid. p. 318

228 ibid.

229 ibid. p. 332.

230 ibid. p. 317.

231 ibid.

232 'Abdu'l-Bahá, *Some Answered Questions*, p. xix.

233 Gail, 'Impressions of the Centenary', *Bahá'í News*, no. 170 (Sept. 1944), p. 13. https://bahai.works/Baha%27i_News/Issue_170 (accessed Aug. 2020).

234 Weinberg, *Ethel Jenner Rosenberg*, p. 74, and n85: Táhirzádeh, 'Dr. Youness Afrukhtih [Afroukhteh]', *Bahá'í World*, vol. 12 (1950–1954), p. 680.

235 Weinberg, *Ethel Jenner Rosenberg*, p. 75.

236 Dreyfus-Barney, 'Only a Word', *Bahá'í World*, vol. 5 (1932–1934), p. 667.

237 LCB, transcript of talks, May 16, 1909, Frank Osborne Papers, USNBA.

238 ibid.

239 ibid.

240 ibid.

241 ibid.

242 ibid.

243 Dreyfus-Barney, 'Only a Word', *Bahá'í World*, vol. 5 (1932–1934), p. 667.

244 ibid.

245 Typed letter from LDB to Ezzat Zahrai in France, July 16, 1968, ABDF.

246 LCB, transcript of talks, May 16, 1909, Frank Osborne Papers, USNBA.

247 ibid. p. 315.

248 Letter from LDB to Ruhiyyeh Rabbani, Jan. 1958, ABDF.

249 *Bahíyyih Khánum, The Greatest Holy Leaf*, p. 111.

250 Giachery, 'Laura Clifford Dreyfus-Barney', *Bahá'í World*, vol. 16 (1973–1976), p. 537.

251 Gail, *Summon Up Remembrance*, p. 148.

252 ibid. p. 116.

253 Giachery, *Shoghi Effendi*, pp. 14–15.

254 Letter from LDB to Horace Holley, March 31, 1958, ABDF.

255 Letter from Shoghi Effendi in French signed Choki to LCB, undated, ABDF.

256 Letter from Shoghi Effendi to LCB, 'Akká, May 27, 1904, ABDF.

257 Letter from Choki Baháey [Shoghi Effendi] to LCB, 'Akká, Dec. 20, 1905, ABDF.

258 Giachery, 'Laura Clifford Dreyfus-Barney', *La Pensée Bahá'íe*, no. 56 (June 1976), p. 21.

259 'Abdu'l-Bahá, Tablet to LCB, 1909, BWC, AC1/1/192.

260 Momen, 'Russia'. http://Bahai-library.com/momen_encyclopedia_russia (accessed Feb. 2016).

261 Bryan and Bryan, *Memoirs of William Jennings Bryan*, p. 318.

262 'Laura's Noble Deeds Enrich World', *Journal Herald*, Dayton, Ohio, Dec. 28, 1965, DMLA.

263 Maḥmúd-i-Zarqání, *Maḥmúd's Diary*, p. 281.

264 Letter from LCB to APB, undated, perhaps 1905, Doucet.

265 ibid.

266 'Mrs. Alice Barney', *Bahá'í World*, vol. 5 (1932–1934), p. 419.

267 'Mrs. Barney & Daughter on Visit to 'Akká, Persia', *Washington Post*, July 10, 1905.

268 Kling, *Alice Pike Barney*, p. 195.

269   Stockman, *Bahá'í Faith in America*, vol. 2, p. 155.

270   'Abdu'l-Bahá, *Tablets of 'Abdu'l-Baha Abbas*, vol. 2, p. 357.

271   Historical information pertaining to LDB, received by the author on June 11, 2017, from the Research Department of the BWC.

272   Letter from LCB to Ahmad Sohrab, Aug. 31, 1907, USNBA.

273   Gail, *Summon Up Remembrance*, p. 280.

274   Kling, *Alice Pike Barney*, p. 197.

275   ibid. p. 190.

276   ibid. pp. 202, 206.

277   'Mrs. Alice Barney', *Bahá'í World*, vol. 5 (1932–1934), pp. 419–20.

278   'Women Worth While, Their Frivolities, Interests and Hobbies', *Evening Star*, Jan. 17, 1914, p. 7.

279   Kling, *Alice Pike Barney*, p. 230.

280   For further reading, see Ballanger, *Hippolyte Dreyfus-Barney*.

281   'Note Sur Hippolyte Dreyfus', HDB Papers, ABDF, translated by Sheryl Mellor.

282   Rassekh, Shapour, 'Dreyfus-Barney'. DREYFUS-BARNEY – Brill (brillonline. com) (accessed May 2021). Hippolyte was named after his maternal grandfather. He had one sister, Yvonne, who later married Paul Meyer-May.

283   LDB, 'Hippolyte Dreyfus-Barney', 1928, ABDF.

284   Nakhjavani, *Maxwells*, vol. 1, p. 145.

285   ibid. pp. 145–6.

286   ibid. p. 146.

287   Rassekh, 'Dreyfus-Barney, DREYFUS-BARNEY – Brill (brillonline.com) (accessed May 2021).

288   LDB, 'Hippolyte Dreyfus-Barney', 1928, ABDF.

289   Ballanger, *Hippolyte Dreyfus-Barney*, pp. 47–8.

290   HD, Diary of the Trip to Russia and Iran with Miss Clifford in 1906, HDB Papers, ABDF.

291   LDB and Shoghi Effendi, 'Biography Hippolyte Dreyfus-Barney'. http://Bahái-library.com/dreyfus-barney_biography_hippolyte_dreyfus-barney (accessed March 2016).

292   Shoghi Effendi, *God Passes By*, pp. 259–60.

293   Letter from LDB to Guy Murchie in NH, USA, Nov. 11, 1968, ABDF.

294   Letter from LDB to Mr Danjon (a Bahá'í), Nov. 11, 1973, ABDF.

295   From an anecdote told by Laura to Mark Hofman in 1971, cited in Nakhjávání, *Asking Questions*, p. 136, n7.

296   The date of March 5, 1906 associated with this Tablet is an estimate based on information on the envelope in which it was apparently received. Research Department of BWC, Sept. 22, 2008 to the author.

297   Mme Lacheny had replaced Miss Patridge, an earlier governess of the Barneys, in 1901. In Sanderson, 'An Interview with A.L.M. Nicolas of Paris', *Bahá'í World*, vol. 8 (1938–1940), p. 886, her name is given as 'Lacheney'; however, 'Lacheny' seems to be the more common spelling of this name.

298   Jasion, *'Abdu'l-Bahá in France*, pp. 3, 506 and n1198.

299   Weinberg, *Ethel Jenner Rosenberg*, p. 81.

300   HD, Diary of the Trip to Russia and Iran with Miss Clifford in 1906, HDB Papers, ABDF. Hippolyte adds LB's name in the diary from Constantinople.

301 King, *Genius and Death in a City of Dreams*, p. 164.

302 The cornerstone of the temple was laid on Dec. 2, 1902. Hassall, 'Notes on the Bábí and Bahá'í Religions in Russia and its territories', in *Journal of Bahá'í Studies*, 5:3, pp. 41–80. http://Bahai-library.com/hassall_babi_Bahai_russia (accessed Dec. 2020). HD had already visited the temple in April 1905. HD, Diary of his travels in 1905, HDB Papers, ABDF.

303 Shahvar, 'Baha'i Faith and Its Communities in Iran', in Shahvar (ed.), *Baha'is of Iran*, vol. 1, pp. 26–31. Information about the 'Ishqábád Bahá'ís and the House of Worship is largely based on this book unless otherwise noted. See also, 'Mashriqu'l-Adhkár', Bahá'í Encyclopedia Project. https://www.bahai-encyclo-pedia-project.org/index.php?option=com_content&view=article&id=70:mashr iqul-adhkar&catid=36:administrationinstitutions (accessed Jan. 2021).

304 Momen, 'Baha'i Community of Ashkhabad', in Akiner (ed.), *Cultural Change and Continuity in Central Asia*, p. 286.

305 Shoghi Effendi, *God Passes By*, p. 300.

306 Momen, 'Baha'i Community of Ashkhabad', in Akiner (ed.), *Cultural Change and Continuity in Central Asia*, p. 286.

307 The House of Worship was taken from the Bahá'ís in 1938 and turned into a museum, was damaged by an earthquake in 1948 and was finally demolished in 1963.

308 HD, Diary of the Trip to Russia and Iran with Miss Clifford in 1906, HDB Papers, ABDF.

309 LCB, transcript of talks, May 16, 1909, Frank Osborne Papers, USNBA.

310 Shahvar, 'Baha'i Faith and Its Communities in Iran', in Shahvar (ed.), *Baha'is of Iran*, vol. 1, p. 31.

311 ibid.

312 LCB, transcript of talks, May 16, 1909, Frank Osborne Papers, USNBA.

313 Daniel is an Old Testament prophet who is 'revered by three world religions. He is one of the four great Israel prophets in Judaism, the prophet, whose book is included in the Old Testament of the Christian Bible, and the prophet in Islamic tradition.' Samarkand Tours. See also, Qobil, 'Uzbekistan: Land of a thousand shrines', BBC Uzbek, 15 Sept. 2018.

314 Shahvar, 'Baha'i Faith and Its Communities in Iran', in Shahvar (ed.), *Baha'is of Iran*, vol. 1, p. 35.

315 Travel document (passport) of LDB issued by the Embassy of the USA in Paris, France, SIA.

316 LCB, transcript of talks, May 16, 1909, Frank Osborne Papers, USNBA.

317 ibid.

318 Letter from LDB to Guy Murchie in NH, USA, Nov. 11, 1968, ABDF.

319 Letter from LDB to Alice Dudley, Oct. 30, 1968, ABDF.

320 Letter from LDB to Guy Murchie in NH, USA, Nov. 11, 1968, ABDF.

321 Momen, *Baha'i Communities of Iran*, vol. 1, p. 86.

322 Dreyfus, 'Les Behaïs', p. 203.

323 Shahvar, *Forgotten Schools*, p. 202, n138.

324 Momen, *Baha'i Communities of Iran*, vol. 1, p. 89.

325 Ávárih, 'Abdu'l-Ḥusayn, *al-Kavákib ud-Durriyih*, pp. 160–1, passage translated by Riaz Masrour.

326 Arbáb, *Akhtarán-i-Tábán*, vol. 2, p. 37.

327 'Azízí, *Táj-i-Vahháj*, p. 101, passage translated by Riaz Masrour.

328 HD, Diary of the Trip to Russia and Iran with Miss Clifford in 1906, HDB Papers, ABDF.

329 Mázandarání, *Zuhúru'l-Ḥaqq*. 9 vols. vol. 8, part 2. Tehran, n.d., p. 1194.

330 Ávárih, *al-Kavákib ud-Durriyih*, pp. 160–1, passage translated by Riaz Masrour.

331 HD, Diary of the Trip to Russia and Iran with Miss Clifford in 1906, HDB Papers, ABDF.

332 LCB, transcript of talks, May 16, 1909, Frank Osborne Papers, USNBA.

333 ibid.

334 Hands of the Cause of God were outstanding individuals appointed by Bahá'u'lláh and later by Shoghi Effendi to protect and propagate the Bahá'í Faith. After the passing of Shoghi Effendi, no further Hands of the Cause could be appointed and there are no Hands of the Cause now living.

335 Samandari-Khoshbin, *Taráz-i-Iláhí*, p. 241. reference.bahai.org/fa (accessed Jan. 2020).

336 LCB, transcript of talks, May 16, 1909, Frank Osborne Papers, USNBA.

337 ibid.

338 'Azízí, *Táj-i-Vahháj*, p. 101, passage translated by Riaz Masrour. They also met 'Akkás-báshí.

339 See Momen, *Bábí and Bahá'í Religions*, pp. 36–40; Jasion, *'Abdu'l-Bahá in France*, p. 310.

340 Ballanger, *Hippolyte Dreyfus-Barney*, p. 56.

341 Letter from the Universal House of Justice to the National Spiritual Assembly of France, June 19, 1978, ABDF.

342 HD, Diary of the Trip to Russia and Iran with Miss Clifford in 1906, HDB Papers, ABDF. They also met a Dr Schneider.

343 Momen, *Baha'i Communities of Iran*, vol. 1, p. 58.

344 He was one of the four Hands of the Cause of God appointed by Bahá'u'lláh and was named an Apostle of Bahá'u'lláh in 'Apostles of Bahá'u'lláh', *Bahá'í World*, vol. 4, pp. 108–9; and Afroukhteh, *Memories*, p. 429.

345 Email response from Moojan Momen to the author, Jan. 20, 2018.

346 'Azízí, *Táj-i-Vahhaj*, pp. 101–3, translated by Riaz Masrour.

347 LCB, transcript of talks, May 16, 1909, Frank Osborne Papers, USNBA.

348 Letter from LCB to APB, July 4, 1906, SIA.

349 Letter from LCB to APB, July 9, 1906, SIA.

350 Letter from LCB to APB, July 5, 1906, SIA.

351 Letter from LCB to APB, July 9, 1906, SIA.

352 HD, Diary of Trip to Russia and Iran with Miss Clifford in 1906, HDB Papers, ABDF.

353 LCB, transcript of talks, May 16, 1909, Frank Osborne Papers, USNBA.

354 ibid.

355 ibid.

356 Mázandarání, *Táríkh-i-Zuhúru'l-Ḥaqq*, vol. 8, part 2, p. 1194. English summary of extracts from an account by Ḥaydar-'Alí Uskú'í around 1322 AH.

357 ibid. Ishráq-Khávarí, *Núrayn*, p. 223. His full name was Mírzá Aḥmad <u>Kh</u>án. He became a Bahá'í through the afore-mentioned Mírzá Asadu'lláh Iṣfahání in 1874. He was well known to be a Bahá'í.

358 HD, Diary of Trip to Russia and Iran with Miss Clifford in 1906, HDB Papers, ABDF.

359 Alliance Israélite Universelle. https://www.jewishvirtuallibrary.org/alliance-isra-elite-universelle (accessed Jan. 2021).

360 Amanat, *Bahá'íyán-i-Káshán*, pp. 177–8.

361 Email from Moojan Momen to the author, Jan. 20, 2018.

362 LCB, transcript of talks, May 16, 1909, Frank Osborne Papers, USNBA.

363 HD, Diary of the Trip to Russia and Iran with Miss Clifford in 1906, HDB Papers, ABDF.

364 Afroukhteh, *Memories*, p. 441.

365 Email to the author from Stephen Lambden, Dec. 2, 2017, translated by Stephen Lambden. It can be translated as 'leader of leaders' or 'heart of hearts'.

366 HD, Diary of the Trip to Russia and Iran with Miss Clifford in 1906, HDB Papers, ABDF.

367 LCB, transcript of talks, May 16, 1909, Frank Osborne Papers, USNBA.

368 Rastegar, quoted in Sulaymání, *Maṣábíḥ-i Hidáyat*, vol. 5, pp. 32–3, translated by Riaz Masrour.

369 ibid.

370 This is the only woman whose name is mentioned in the HD, Diary of the Trip to Russia and Iran with Miss Clifford in 1906 and is legible.

371 Momen, *Baha'i Communities of Iran*, vol. 1, pp. 81–3.

372 HD, Diary of the Trip to Russia and Iran with Miss Clifford in 1906, HDB Papers, AFDB.

373 LCB, transcript of talks, May 16, 1909, Frank Osborne Papers, USNBA.

374 ibid.

375 Momen, *Baha'i Communities of Iran*, vol. 1, pp. 381–2, citing Uskú'í, Táríkh-i Amrí-yi Ádharbáyján', MS A, Part 1, Section 4, pp. 85–6; and Mázandarání, *Táríkh-i Ẕuhúr ul-Ḥaqq* 8a:78.

376 From Bahá'í Research Department to the author, Sept. 6, 2009.

377 A reference to this individual may be found in Bámdád, *Sharḥ-i-Ḥál-i-Rijál-i-Írán dar Qarn-i-12 va 13 va 14 Hijrí*, vol. 5, p. 291.

378 LCB, transcript of talks, May 16, 1909, Frank Osborne Papers, USNBA.

379 Weinberg, *Ethel Jenner Rosenberg*, p. 88.

380 Momen, *Baha'i Communities of Iran,* vol. 1, p. 382.

381 From the Bahá'í Research Department to the author, Sept. 6, 2008.

382 LCB, transcript of talks, May 16, 1909, Frank Osborne Papers, USNBA.

383 From the Bahá'í Research Department to the author, Sept. 6, 2008. A note is added that Ḥaydar 'Alí wrote this many years later and that is why the year is not correct.

384 HD, Diary of the Trip to Russia and Iran with Miss Clifford in 1906, HDB Papers, ABDF; and LDB in her letter to Afroukhteh in *Memories*, p. 343.

385 LCB, transcript of talks, May 16, 1909, Frank Osborne Papers, USNBA.

386 ibid.

387 'Arúsí-yi-mistir dreyfus va mís barney' ['Wedding of Mr Dreyfus and Miss Barney'], *Najm-i-Bakhtar (Star of the West)*, vol. 2, no. 4 (May 17, 1911), pp. 4–5, translated by Riaz Masrour. *Star of the West* (originally titled *Bahai News*) was a Bahá'í periodical published between 1910 and 1935. It contained transla-tions of some of the Tablets of 'Abdu'l-Bahá and writings of Shoghi Effendi. It

also featured news of the Baháʼí world. This periodical was mostly in English but usually had a Persian language section with its own content.

388 Stockman, *Baháʼí Faith in America*, vol. 2, p. 353.

389 Armstrong-Ingram, 'Moody, Susan', 1998. https://bahai-library.com/armstrong-ingram_encyclopedia_susan_moody (accessed June 2021).

390 Letter from Harlan F. Ober from Port Said, Egypt, to Charles Mason Remey, Dec. 12, 1906, BAWDC.

391 Letter from Nooshin Mohajerin to the author, in response to the author's request that a search be made in Tehran libraries, Sept. 7, 2010.

392 *Washington Herald,* April 28, 1909; *Washington Times,* Oct. 15, 1910; *Chicago Sunday Tribune,* March 2, 1913 and *Boston Globe*, Nov. 27, 1910.

393 *Boston Globe*, Nov. 27, 1910.

394 *Chicago Sunday Tribune,* March 2, 1913.

395 *Washington Times,* Oct. 15, 1910.

396 *Washington Herald,* April 28, 1909.

397 LCB, transcript of talks, May 16, 1909, Frank Osborne Papers, USNBA.

398 ibid.

399 Arbab, *Akhtarán-i-Tábán*, vol. 2, p. 38.

400 Rastegar, quoted in Sulaymání, *Maṣábíḥ-i Hidáyat*, vol. 5, pp. 32–3.

401 Ṣadruʼṣ-Ṣudúr, *Istidláliyyiy-i-Mukhtaṣar-i-Ṣadruʼṣ-Ṣudúr*, p. 13, translated; and http://www.afnanlibrary.org/wp-content/uploads/2017/01/INBA_v025.pdf (accessed Aug. 2020).

402 ibid. p. 114.

403 ibid. The original handwritten book by *Ṣadruʼṣ-Ṣudúr* is kept at the Baháʼí International Archives in Haifa, Israel.

404 Rastegar, quoted in Sulaymání, *Maṣábíḥ-i Hidáyat*, vol. 5, pp. 32–3, translated by Riaz Masrour. According to Rastegar, a copy of that compilation was part of the possessions that Ṣadruʼṣ-Ṣudúr left in a box for safekeeping, all of which along with other remnants of his scholarly works were subsequently forwarded to ʻAbduʼl-Bahá.

405 Arbáb, *Akhtarán-i-Tábán*, vol. 2, p. 38, provisional translation by Riaz Masrour.

406 Letters of ʻAbduʼl-Bahá to William Hooper Harris through Miss Barney in Washington, D.C., translated by Ali-Kuli Khan, April 12, 1902, BAWDC.

407 Stockman, *Baháʼí Faith in America*, vol. 2, p. 268.

408 Letter from Harlan Ober in Port Said, Egypt to C.M.R. [Charles Mason Remey] in Washington, D.C., Dec. 12, 1906, BAWDC; and Ober, Bullock and Ashton, 'Harlan Foster Ober', *Baháʼí World*, vol. 13 (1954–1963), pp. 868–9.

409 ʻAbduʼl-Bahá, *Tablets of Abdul-Baha*, vol. 1, pp. v–vi. 'The great labor of translating these Tablets from the original language has been entrusted to the following translators, whose inestimable service is hereby gratefully acknowledged: Anton Haddad, Mírzá S. M. Raffie, Mírzá Housein Rouhy, Ali Kuli Khan, Dr Ameen U. Fareed, H. S. M. Taki Manshadi, Mírzá Ahmad Esphahani, Mrs Getsinger Miss Barney and Mírzá Moneer Zane.' Ahmad Esphahani is Ahmad Sohrab.

410 Letter from LCB to NCB, perhaps end of 1906, Doucet.

411 Gail, *Arches of the Years*, p. 34.

412 Arbáb, *Akhtarán-i-Tábán*, p. 38.

413 Weinberg, *Lady Blomfield*, p. 36.

414 Gail, *Arches of the Years*, p. 34.

415 Weinberg, *Lady Blomfield*, p. 37.
416 Gail, 'Impressions of the Centenary', *Bahá'í News*, no. 170 (Sept. 1944), p. 13. https://bahai.works/Baha%27i_News/Issue_170 (accessed Aug. 2020).
417 Weinberg, *Ethel Jenner Rosenberg*, p. 85.
418 Weinberg, *Lady Blomfield*, p. 43.
419 'Abdu'l-Bahá, Tablet to LBC, AC1/1/315, ABDF, provisional translation by Riaz Masrour.
420 ibid.
421 'Abdu'l-Bahá, Tablet to LCB, AC1/1/320, ABDF, provisional translation by Riaz Masrour.
422 Gail, *Arches of the Years*, p. 34.
423 Kling, *Alice Pike Barney*, pp. 203–4.
424 Balyuzi, *'Abdu'l-Bahá*, p. 82; and letter from LCB to Mr Dealy (a Bahá'í in Chicago), Oct. 5, 1908, USNBA.
425 The sultanate was abolished in November 1922 and the caliphate in 1924.
426 Balyuzi, *'Abdu'l-Bahá*, p. 82; Afroukhteh, *Memories*, p. 343, letter from LDB to Aoukhfrteh, Aug. 7, 1937.
427 Balyuzi, *'Abdu'l-Bahá*, p. 82.
428 ibid.
429 LCB, Author's Preface to the First Edition, 'Abdu'l-Bahá, *Some Answered Questions*. https://www.bahai.org/library/authoritative-texts/abdul-baha/some-answered-questions/ (accessed Jan. 2021).
430 Afroukhteh, *Memories*, p. 342, letter from LDB to Afroukhteh, Aug. 7, 1937.
431 'Abdu'l-Bahá, Tablet to LCB, March 3, 1908, sent from BWC to the author, June 22, 2008, provisional translation by Riaz Masrour.
432 Email from the Department of the Secretariat of the Universal House of Justice to the author, Aug. 31, 2018.
433 Afroukhteh, *Memories*, p. 342, letter from LDB to Afroukhteh, Aug. 7, 1937.
434 LDB replied in a letter dated Aug. 7, 1937 to a letter she had received from Afroukhteh in 1935, clarifying and correcting some of the historical references in the notes for *Memories*, see ibid. p. 328; and 'Abdu'l-Bahá, *Le lezioni di San Giovanni d'Acri*, pp. 374–5, in the closing remarks, translated by Kiumars Mazlum.
435 'Record of the First Bahá'í European Teaching Conference', held in Geneva, Switzerland, May 22–7, 1948, pp. 31–2, ABDF. See also Foreword to the 2014 edition of 'Abdu'l-Bahá, *Some Answered Questions*.
436 Letter from LDB to Horace Holley in the US, Jan. 21, 1959, ABDF.
437 'Some Answered Questions', advertisement in *Bahai News*, vol. 1, no. 3 (April 28, 1910), p. 20.
438 Ávarih, *Kavákib ud-Durriyih*, vol. 2, pp. 160–1, translated by Riaz Masrour.
439 LCB, Author's Preface to the First Edition, 'Abdu'l-Bahá, *Some Answered Questions*. https://www.bahai.org/library/authoritative-texts/abdul-baha/some-answered-questions/ (accessed Jan. 2021).
440 LDB in Gail, 'Impressions of the Centenary'. *Bahá'í News*, no. 170 (Sept. 1944), p. 13. https://bahai.works/Baha%27i_News/Issue_170 (accessed Aug. 2020).
441 Giachery, 'Laura Clifford Dreyfus-Barney', *Bahá'í World*, vol. 16 (1973–1976), p. 536.
442 Balyuzi, *'Abdu'l-Bahá*, p. 83.

443 Shoghi Effendi, *God Passes By*, pp. 267, 268.

444 LCB, Author's Preface to the First Edition, 'Abdu'l-Bahá, *Some Answered Questions*. https://www.bahai.org/library/authoritative-texts/abdul-baha/some-answered-questions/ (accessed Jan. 2021).

445 Attachment to a letter from LDB to Mrs John O. Honnold (Annamarie) in Pennsylvania, USA, March 2, 1960, ABDF.

446 'Abdu'l-Bahá, Table of Contents, *Some Answered Questions*. https://www.bahai.org/library/authoritative-texts/abdul-baha/some-answered-questions/ (accessed Jan. 2021).

447 Stockman, *Baháʼí Faith in America*, vol. 2. p. 238.

448 Kluge, '*Some Answered Questions* – A Philosophical Perspective', *Lights of Irfan*, vol. 10, p. 260.

449 *Diary of Juliet Thompson*, p. 93.

450 Afroukhteh, *Memories*, p. 319.

451 Giachery, 'Laura Clifford Dreyfus-Barney', *Baháʼí World*, vol. 16 (1973–1976), p. 536.

452 Dreyfus, *Universal Religion*, pp. 9–10. The Foreword of Dreyfus's book *Essai sur le Baháʼísme* contains the same passage in French; Dreyfus, *Essai sur le Baháʼísme*, pp. xiii–xiv. It was first published in 1909.

453 Shoghi Effendi, *God Passes By*, p. 260.

454 'Abdu'l-Bahá, *Some Answered Questions*, p. xvi.

455 From a letter of Shoghi Effendi to the Baháʼís of Australasia, March 13, 1923, cited in ibid. pp. xvi–xvii.

456 'Literary News of Philadelphia', *New York Times*, Oct. 17, 1908.

457 *Washington Herald,* April 28, 1909.

458 Weinberg, *Lady Blomfield*, p. 111.

459 Romain Rolland, quoted in Momen, *Bábí and Baháʼí Religions*, p. 54.

460 *Springfield Republican* [of Massachusetts], Sept. 13, 1909.

461 Letter from E.G. Browne to LDB, Sept. 2, 1908, SIA.

462 Browne, *Materials for the Study of the Bábí Religion*, pp. 177–8; see also Balyuzi, *Edward Granville Browne and the Baháʼí Faith*, p. 116.

463 Letter from Edward Heron-Allen in London to LCB, July 2, 1908, AFDB.

464 Letter from John H. Patterson (1844–1922) of Dayton, Ohio, to Mrs [Laura] Barney, June 14, 1912, ABDF.

465 Letter from LCB to Mírzá Ahmad [must be Sohrab], April 30, 1909 (Marked: Received May 8, 1909), USNBA.

466 *Washington Herald,* April 28, 1909.

467 LCB, transcript of talks, May 16, 1909, Frank Osborne Papers, USNBA.

468 *Evening Star*, July 11, 1909. https://chroniclingamerica.loc.gov (accessed Aug. 2020).

469 *Washington Post*, June 26, 1909.

470 Letter from unknown (perhaps a Baháʼí) to Corinne True, July 11, 1901, Gertrude Buikema Papers, USNBA.

471 ibid.

472 ibid.

473 Excerpt from a letter from LDB to 'Abdu'l-Bahá, likely early 1910, letter from the BWC to the author, May 14, 2010. The BWC has five undated letters written by LDB in Persian to 'Abdu'l-Bahá.

474 Kling, *Alice Pike Barney*, p. 209.
475 Letter from LDB to Ahmad [probably Sohrab], Nov. 27, 1909, USNBA.
476 Kling, *Alice Pike Barney*, p. 213–14.
477 Rodriguez, *Wild Heart*, p. 209.
478 Kling, *Alice Pike Barney*, p. 220.
479 Rodriguez, *Wild Heart*, pp. 171–4.
480 Kling, *Alice Pike Barney*, p. 220.
481 Rodriguez, *Wild Heart*, pp. 182, 246–8.
482 ibid. p. 182.
483 Author's interviews with Anita Ioas-Chapman.
484 Smith, 'Tolstoy, Leo', *Concise Encyclopedia of the Bahá'í Faith*, p. 340.
485 Hassall, 'Notes on the Bábí and Bahá'í Religions in Russia and its Territories', *Journal of Bahá'í Studies*, 5:3, pp. 41–80. http://Bahai-library.com/hassall_babi_Bahai_russia (accessed Feb. 2016).
486 Shahvar, 'Baha'i Faith and Its Communities in Iran', in Shahvar (ed.), *Baha'is of Iran*, vol. 1, p. 17.
487 Jasion, *'Abdu'l-Bahá in France*, p. 285.
488 Banani, *Táhirih: A Portrait in Poetry*, p. 16.
489 'The Amazing and Versatile Barneys of Washington', *Bar Harbor Record*, Nov. 2, 1910.
490 Announcement of availability of *God's Heroes*. *Bahai News*, vol. 1. no.11 (Sept. 27, 1910), p. 7.
491 Since its first publication the book has been republished/reprinted in 1946, 2009 and 2013.
492 Letter from LDB to Guy Murchie, Nov. 11, 1968, ABDF.
493 Letter from LDB to Guy Murchie, May 29, 1970, ABDF.
494 Letter from LDB to Guy Murchie in Spain, Nov. 29, 1966, ABDF.
495 Letter from LDB to Guy Murchie, Nov. 11, 1968, ABDF.
496 Letter from LDB to Mr Danjon, Nov. 11, 1973, ABDF.
497 Shoghi Effendi, *God Passes By*, p. 75; Root, *Táhirih the Pure*, p. 98.
498 LCB, *God's Heroes*, pp. v–vi.
499 ibid. p. vi.
500 ibid. p. vii.
501 ibid. p. vi.
502 ibid. p. viii. The prohibition on the depiction of the central figures of the Faith was not explicitly written down in those early years. Later, the Bahá'ís came to understand that the depiction or direct representation of the Manifestations of God in any form is not permitted, for reasons of dignity and general respect. (From a letter written on behalf of Shoghi Effendi to the National Spiritual Assembly of the United States and Canada, Jan. 27, 1935, in *Lights of Guidance*, no. 342; and from a letter written on behalf of Shoghi Effendi to an individual believer, July 25, 1936, in ibid.
503 LCB, *God's Heroes*, p. viii.
504 ibid. cited in n.b., p. 106.
505 Letter from Edward G. Browne to HDB, Nov. 6, 1920, HDB Papers, ABDF.
506 Letter from LDB to Guy Murchie in Spain, Nov. 29, 1966, ABDF.
507 Letter from LDB to Guy Murchie, June 20, 1970, ABDF.

508 'Abdu'l-Bahá, *Light of the World*, p. 42.

509 ibid.

510 ibid. p. 43.

511 ibid. p. 42.

512 Clifford (Dreyfus) Barney, *Dalírán-i-Rabbání*. http://www.afnanlibrary.org/docs/persian-arabic-mss/inba/inba-vol-054/ (accessed Feb. 2021).

513 Letter from LDB to Paul Haney, Aug. 29, 1912, USNBA.

514 *Star of the West*, vol. 3, no. 12 (Oct. 16, 1912), p. 8.

515 Weinberg, *Ethel Jenner Rosenberg*, pp. 111–12.

516 Letter from David Belasco, manager of Belasco Stuyvesant Theatre in NY to LCB, June 11, 1909, SIA.

517 *Boston Globe*, March 14, 1911; *Sunday Oregonian*, Nov. 20, 1910; and *Washington Herald,* April 28, 1909.

518 'The Amazing and Versatile Barneys of Washington', *Bar Harbor Record*, Nov. 2, 1910. From Bar Harbor Historical Society Archives.

519 ibid.

520 *New York Times*, Oct. 8, 1910.

521 'American Girl Startles Paris', *Boston Globe*, Nov. 27, 1910.

522 'Girl Writes Persian Play for Parisians', *Indianapolis Star*, Dec. 25, 1910.

523 'Persian Sect Led By American Girl: Former Washingtonian Abandons Sculpture to Teach Creed of Baha Uliah', *Call of San Francisco*, Jan. 1, 1911.

524 Jasion, *'Abdu'l-Bahá in France*, pp. 284–5, n656, n657.

525 Root, 'Russia's Cultural Contribution to the Bahá'í Faith', *Bahá'í World*, vol. 6 (1934–1936), p. 712.

526 Shahvar, 'Baha'i Faith and Its Communities in Iran', in Shahvar (ed.), *Baha'is of Iran*, vol. 1, p. 17.

527 Must be LCB, 'Outlines & Shadows', unpublished manuscript, SIA.

528 'The Amazing and Versatile Barneys of Washington', *Bar Harbor Record*, Nov. 2, 1910. From Bar Harbor Historical Society Archives.

529 'Well Known Daughters of Famous Men', *New York Evening Telegram*, Jan. 11, 1911, SIA.

530 Rodriguez, *Wild Heart*, p. 207.

531 ibid. citing *The Press*, Oct. 10, 1910.

532 ibid. pp. 207–8.

533 'The Amazing and Versatile Barneys of Washington', *Bar Harbor Record*, Nov. 2, 1910. Bar Harbor Historical Society Archives.

534 'Mrs. A.C. Barney Corrects Story from Washington', *New York Herald*, Oct. 14, 1910.

535 ibid.

536 Rodriguez, *Wild Heart*, p. 208.

537 Unattributed newspaper clipping, SIA.

538 *Sheboygan Press*, Jan. 8, 1912.

539 Rodriguez, *Wild Heart*, p. 208.

540 Stockman, *Bahá'í Faith in America*, vol. 2, p. 354.

541 ibid. p. 355.

542 ibid.

543 Rostam-Kolayi, 'The Tarbiyat Girls' School of Tehran', *Middle East Critique*, Feb. 2013, p. 7.

544 'The Persian–American Educational Society'. *Bahai News*, vol. 1, no. 5 (June 5, 1910), p. 2; 'Letter from Mr. Sprague'. *Bahai News*, vol. 1, no. 6 (June 24, 1910), p. 6; 'The Tarbiat School, Persia'. *Bahai News*, vol. 1, no. 7 (July 13, 1910), pp. 3–7.

545 Rostam-Kolayi, 'The Tarbiyat Girls' School of Tehran', *Middle East Critique*, Feb. 2013, p. 1.

546 Stockman, *Bahá'í Faith in America*, vol. 2, pp. 357–8.

547 Undated and unattributed newspaper article, LDB Papers, BAWDC.

548 Hatch, 'Sydney Sprague', *Bahá'í World*, vol. 9 (1940–1944), pp. 633–5.

549 'The Persian–American Educational Society'. *Bahai News*, vol. 1, no. 13 (Nov. 4, 1910), p. 6.

550 A note and a photograph of Mírzá Emad, ADBF.

551 Letter from LCB to Ahmad Sohrab, handwritten, March 6, 1910, USNBA.

552 Letter from LCB to Ahmad Sohrab, handwritten, Feb. 2, 1910, USNBA.

553 Stockman, *Bahá'í Faith in America*, vol. 2, p. 358.

554 'Orient–Occident Unity', *Star of the West*, vol. 2, no. 1 (March 21, 1911), p. 6.

555 Letter from PAES to LDB, March 4, 1912, USNBA. The name of the organization where 'Abdu'l-Bahá gave His first talk in April 1912 was referred to by one source as Orient Occident Unity (Hannen, Joseph H. 'Abdul-Bahá in Washington, D.C.', *Star of the West*, vol. 3, no. 3 (April 28, 1912), p. 7), and by another as the Persian American Society (Ward, *239 Days*, p. 38).

Part 3 Married Life, Travel and Achievements 1911 – 1928

1 Announcement about Lucien Dreyfus-Cardozo's death, HDB papers, ABDF.

2 Letter from LCB to Ahmad Sohrab, envelope postmarked Jan. 20, 1911, USNBA.

3 'News Notes', *Bahai News*, vol. 1, no. 18 (Feb. 7, 1911), p. 9.

4 Letter from HDB to Ahmad Sohrab, envelope postmarked Jan. 20, 1911, USNBA.

5 LDB in Gail, 'Impressions of the Centenary'. *Bahá'í News*, no. 170 (Sept. 1944), p. 13. https://bahai.works/Baha%27i_News/Issue_170 (accessed Aug. 2020).

6 Kling, *Alice Pike Barney*, p. 223.

7 'Abdu'l-Bahá, *Selections*, p. 100.

8 'The marriage [of Alice Barney and Christian Hemmick] took place on April 15 in a Catholic ceremony at the Church of Saint Joseph, Avenue Hoche, following a joint civil ceremony for Laura and Hippolyte.' Kling, *Alice Pike Barney*, p. 224.

9 'Abdu'l-Bahá, Tablet to LDB, undated, perhaps 1911, AC1/1/170, BWCA. In this Tablet 'Abdu'l-Bahá asked a Miss Mathew (perhaps Louise Mathew, who later married Louis Gregory) who was visiting Egypt in April 1911, to take back a copy of *God's Heroes* translated into Arabic and a bottle of Âtre (perfume).

10 'Abdu'l-Bahá, Tablet to LCB, undated, AC1/1/172, BWCA, provisional translation by Riaz Masrour.

11 Letter from BWC to the author, May 16, 2012.

12 ibid.

13 'Miss Barney to Wed', *New York Times*, April 23, 1911.

14 'Arúsí-yi-mistir dreyfus va mís barney' ['Wedding of Mr Dreyfus and Miss Barney'], *Najm-i-Bakhtar* (*Star of the West*), vol. 2, no. 4 (May 17, 1911), pp. 4–5, translated by Riaz Masrour.

15 Rodriguez, *Wild Heart*, pp. 210–11.

16 'In the World of Society', *Evening Star*, June 3, 1912, p. 7.

17 *Washington Post*, Dec. 27, 1902.

18 Kling, *Alice Pike Barney*, p. 223.

19 Rodriguez, *Wild Heart*, p. 209.

20 Kling, *Alice Pike Barney*, p. 216.

21 ibid. p. 223.

22 'MRS. BARNEY WEDS YOUNG HEMMICK; Wealthy Widow of Albert Barney, Aged 61, Married to Youth of 26 in Paris', *New York Times*, April 16, 1911.

23 For further information, see Khademi, 'Laura Dreyfus-Barney and 'Abdu'l-Bahá's Visit to the West', in Mottahedeh (ed.), *'Abdu'l-Bahá's Journey West*, pp. 15–38.

24 Balyuzi, *'Abdu'l-Bahá*, p. 136.

25 'Abdu'l-Bahá, Tablet to LCB, undated, AC1/1/145, ABDF, provisional translation by Riaz Masrour.

26 'Abdu'l-Bahá, Tablet to LDB, from Alexandria, BWC, AC1/1/177, ABDF, provisional translation by Riaz Masrour.

27 'Abdu'l-Bahá, Tablet to LDB, from Alexandria, undated, AC1/1/137, BWCA.

28 'Abdu'l-Bahá, Tablet to LDB, from Ramleh, undated, AC1/1/175, BWCA.

29 Balyuzi, *'Abdu'l-Bahá*, 139.

30 Jasion, *'Abdu'l-Bahá in France*, p. 6.

31 Ballanger, *Hippolyte Dreyfus-Barney*, p.136.

32 Barney and Shoghi Effendi, 'Biography of Hippolyte Dreyfus-Barney'. https://bahai-library.com/dreyfus-barney_biography_hippolyte_dreyfus-barney (accessed June 2017).

33 ibid.

34 *Diary of Juliet Thompson*, p. 159.

35 ibid. pp. 159–60.

36 ibid. p. 105.

37 ibid. p. 27.

38 ibid. p. 93.

39 Letter from LDB to Horace Holley, Oct. 25, 1943, USNBA.; Jasion, *'Abdu'l-Bahá in France*. p. 12.

40 ibid.

41 *Diary of Juliet Thompson*, p. 167.

42 ibid. pp. 173–4.

43 ibid. p. 174.

44 ibid.

45 ibid. p. 175.

46 ibid. p. 176.

47 ibid. pp. 172–3.

48 ibid. p. 173.

49 Taherzadeh, *Revelation of Bahá'u'lláh*, vol. 4, p. 79.

50 Letter from LDB to Horace Holley, Oct. 25, 1943, USNBA.

51 *Diary of Juliet Thompson*, pp. 184–6, 195; Letter from LDB to Frances B. Jones in Switzerland, Nov. 10, 1962. ABDF.

52 Weinberg, *Ethel Jenner Rosenberg*, pp. 130–1.

53 Weinberg, *Lady Blomfield*, pp. 36, 41, 43.

54 Blomfield, *Chosen Highway*, p. 151.
55 Egea, *Apostle of Peace*, p. 121, n76, n77.
56 Blomfield, *Chosen Highway*, p. 179.
57 *Washington Post*, Nov. 19, 1911, in Egea, *Apostle of Peace*, p. 171.
58 Weinberg, *Ethel Jenner Rosenberg*, p. 140.
59 Weinberg, *Lady Blomfield*, p. 95.
60 Qazvini, "Abdu'l-Bahá's Meeting with Two Prominent Iranians". *World Order*, vol. 30, no. 1 (Fall 1998), pp. 35–46, translated by Ahang Rabbani. https://bahai-library.com/qazvini_abdulbaha_prominent_iranians (accessed June 2017).
61 ibid.; Jasion, *'Abdu'l-Bahá in France*, p. 160.
62 Edith Sanderson also spoke Persian.
63 Jasion, *'Abdu'l-Bahá in France*, p. 95.
64 Breeskin, *Romaine Brooks*, p. 32.
65 Ezra Pound met 'Abdu'l-Bahá in Paris on Sept. 28, 1911.
66 Pound and Spoo (eds.), *Ezra Pound and Margaret Cravens*, p. 95.
67 Beede, 'A Glimpse of Abdul-Baha in Paris', *Star of the West*, vol. 2, no. 18 (Feb. 7, 1912), pp. 7, 12; Jasion, *'Abdu'l-Bahá in France*, pp. 76–7.
68 'Abdu'l-Bahá, *Paris Talks*, p. 40.
69 Balyuzi, *'Abdu'l-Bahá*, p. 167.
70 Jasion, *'Abdu'l-Bahá in France*, p. 246.
71 Ballanger, *Hippolyte Dreyfus-Barney*, p. 147.
72 ibid. p. 255.
73 'Abdu'l-Bahá, Tablets to LCB, C1/1/190, C1/1/192, possibly Jan. 10, 1909, ABDF; *Makátíb-i-Ḥaḍrat 'Abdu'l- Bahá*, pp. 314–16.
74 Blomfield, *Chosen Highway*, p. 151.
75 Letter from Christian Hemmick from T.S.S. *Lapland* to LDB, Sept. 1911, SIA.
76 Weinberg, *Ethel Jenner Rosenberg*, p. 140.
77 Blomfield, *Chosen Highway*, pp. 180--1n.
78 Letter from Dr Barafroukhteh to the NSA of France, Sept. 16, 1962, ABDF.
79 Email from Robert Weinberg to the author, Dec. 25, 2017.
80 Letter from Dr Barafroukhteh to the NSA of France, Oct. 12, 1962, ABDF.
81 Note from LDB attached to ibid.
82 Weinberg, *Lady Blomfield*, p. 107. According to Weinberg, Lady Blomfield, her daughters Mary Esther and Rose Ellinor Cecilia, and their former governess Beatrice Marion Platt collaborated on this project.
83 Stockman, *Bahá'í Faith in America*, vol. 2, pp. 382–3.
84 Letter from the Persian–American Educational Society, possibly from Mason Remey, to LDB, Jan. 12, 1912, Ahmad Sohrab Papers, USNBA.
85 Balyuzi, *'Abdu'l-Bahá*, p. 171.
86 Gail, *Arches of the Years*, states that Hippolyte was there, p. 79.
87 Hannen, Joseph H. 'Abdul-Bahá in Washington, D.C.', *Star of the West*, vol. 3, no. 3 (April 28, 1912), pp. 6–8.
88 Hollinger (ed.), *Agnes Parsons' Diary*, p. 152.
89 Haney, 'Mrs Agnes Parsons', *Bahá'í World*, vol. 5 (1932–1934), p. 413.
90 Hollinger (ed.), *Agnes Parsons' Diary*, p. 16.
91 ibid. p. 35.
92 ibid. p. 47.
93 *Washington Bee*, April 27, 1912, quoted by Ward, *239 Days*, p. 37.

94 See 'Abdu'l-Bahá, *Promulgation*, Table of Contents; Hollinger (ed.), *Agnes Parsons' Diary*, pp. xiv–v.

95 Hollinger (ed.), *Agnes Parsons' Diary*, p. 58.

96 Kling, *Alice Pike Barney*, pp. 234–5.

97 ibid. p. 230.

98 'Persian Priest Attracts Society Women to the Cult of Bahaism', *Washington Post*, April 26, 1912. It is worth mentioning that many press accounts of the time used the term 'cult', which had a different meaning and was not quite as negative as the contemporary use of the term.

99 Ballanger, *Hippolyte Dreyfus-Barney*, p. 148.

100 Letter from LDB to Afroukhteh, August 7, 1937, in Afroukhteh, *Memories*, p. 344.

101 Hollinger (ed.), *Agnes Parsons' Diary*, p. 61.

102 Letter from HDB in WDC to 'Dear Friend', May 9, most probably 1912, USNBA.

103 Maḥmúd-i-Zarqání, *Maḥmúd's Diary*, p. 87; Kling, *Alice Pike Barney*, p. 299: The House was still functioning in 2018. She organized many events throughout her life to fundraise for the Neighborhood House. On Dec. 12, 1933, Neighborhood House changed its name to Barney Neighborhood House.

104 Hollinger (ed.), *Agnes Parsons' Diary*, p. 65.

105 Ballanger, *Hippolyte Dreyfus-Barney*, p. 150.

106 Kling, *Alice Pike Barney*, pp. 231–3.

107 Maḥmúd-i-Zarqání, *Maḥmúd's Diary*, pp. 126–7; see n132, explaining that the events described for this day took place on 10 June.

108 Letter from LDB on Stony Man Mountain, Virginia, stationery to NCB, 'Season 1912' is printed on the stationery, Doucet; Ballanger, *Hippolyte Dreyfus-Barney*, p. 151. Hippolyte traveled to Minneapolis, Lake Louise, and then to Grand Canyon (June 30) as well as to San Francisco, Portland, Seattle and Vancouver.

109 Ober, Bullock, Ashton, 'Harlan Foster Ober', *Bahá'í World*, vol. 13 (1954–1963), pp. 866–7.

110 *Diary of Juliet Thompson*, p. 345.

111 Letter from LDB to Afroukhteh, August 7, 1937, in Afroukhteh, *Memories*, p. 344.

112 Weinberg, *Lady Blomfield*, pp. 123–4.

113 Mírzá Ahmad Sohrab, 'With Abdul-Baha in London', *Star of the West*, vol. 3, no. 19 (March 2, 1913), p. 4.

114 Weinberg, *Lady Blomfield*, p. 126.

115 ibid. p. 127.

116 Weinberg, *Ethel Rosenberg*, p.148.

117 Jasion, *'Abdu'l-Bahá in France*, p. 301.

118 Letter from Ahmad Sohrab to Harriet, Dec. 27, 1912, USNBA. Copies of the digitized handwritten letters given to the author by Stephen Lambden.

119 ibid. Dec. 28, 1912.

120 Letter from LDB to NCB, undated, Doucet.

121 Letter from LDB to APB, Aug. 5 (must be before 1931), USNBA.

122 Ballanger, *Hippolyte Dreyfus-Barney*, p. 158.

123 Balyuzi, *'Abdu'l-Bahá*, p. 373.

124 Ballanger, *Hippolyte Dreyfus-Barney*, p. 158, n375.

125 'Bahaism Seizes Paris', *Chicago Sunday Tribune*, March 2, 1913.

126 *'Abdu'l-Bahá, Divine Philosophy*, p. 27

127 Jasion, *'Abdu'l-Bahá in France, passim.*

128 ibid. p. 335.

129 Balyuzi, *'Abdu'l-Bahá*, p. 376.

130 ibid.; Rochan Mavaddat, ''Abdu'l-Bahá en France', *Bahá'í France,* no. 15, Winter, 1988, p. 6.

131 Jasion, *'Abdu'l-Bahá in France*, pp. 388–9.

132 ibid. p. 477.

133 Balyuzi, *'Abdu'l-Bahá*, p. 379.

134 Jasion, *'Abdu'l-Bahá in France*, p. 477.

135 ibid. p. 300.

136 Sarwal, 'Sri Aurobindo Movement and the Bahá'í Faith'. http://bahai-library. com/sarwal_sri_aurobindo (accessed June 2018).

137 Keshamurti (Sri Aurobindo), *Sri Aurobindo: The Hope of Man.*

138 Sarwal, 'Sri Aurobindo Movement and the Bahá'í Faith', quoting The Mother, *Words of Long Ago'*, vol. 2, p. 104.

139 ibid.; Das (ed.), *Glimpses of the Mother's Life*, vol. 1.

140 Letter from LDB to the Mother in India, Nov. 22, 1968, ABDF.

141 Momen, *Baha'i Communities of Iran*, vol. 1, pp. 322–4. He also held the titles of Naṣru's-Salṭanih and Sipahdár-i-Aʿẓam.

142 Balyuzi, *Bahá'u'lláh*, pp. 307–9 and Momen, *Baha'i Communities of Iran*, vol. 1, p. 324, n166.

143 Jasion, *'Abdu'l-Bahá in France*, p. 498.

144 ibid.

145 Balyuzi, *'Abdu'l-Bahá*, p. 379.

146 ibid.

147 Ballanger, *Hippolyte Dreyfus-Barney*, p. 167.

148 Jasion, *'Abdu'l-Bahá in France*, p. 543.

149 ibid. p. 611.

150 Balyuzi, *'Abdu'l-Bahá*, p. 394.

151 Jasion, *'Abdu'l-Bahá in France*, p. 635.

152 Balyuzi, *'Abdu'l-Bahá*, p. 394; Jasion, *'Abdu'l-Bahá in France,* p. 638.

153 Balyuzi, *'Abdu'l-Bahá*, p. 394.

154 ibid. p. 395.

155 ibid. Consul Albert Schwarz [1871–1931] was the chairman of the NSA of Germany some years later. 'Consul Albert Schwarz', *Bahá'í World*, vol. 4 (1930–1932), pp. 264–5.

156 Balyuzi, *'Abdu'l-Bahá*, p. 395.

157 Jasion, *'Abdu'l-Bahá in France*, p. 647.

158 ibid. p. 667.

159 Letter from Sohrab to Magee, June 13, 1913, USNBA, in Ballanger, *Hippolyte Dreyfus-Barney*, p. 170.

160 Giachery, 'Laura Clifford Dreyfus-Barney', *Bahá'í World*, vol. 16 (1973–1976), p. 537.

161 Letter from HDB in WDC to Paul Meyer-May, Dec. 13, 1913, ABDF.

162 Ballanger, *Hippolyte Dreyfus-Barney*, p. 178.

163 Letter from HDB in WDC to Yvonne Meyer-May, Nov. 30 (must be 1913), ABDF.

164 Marzieh Gail, in *Diary of Juliet Thompson*, p. xviii.

165 Letter from HDB in WDC to Yvonne Meyer-May, Jan. 12, 1914, ABDF.

166 ibid.

167 Letter from HDB to APB, undated, SIA.

168 Letters from HDB in WDC to Yvonne Meyer-May, Dec. 23, 1913 and Feb. 2, 1914, ABDF.

169 Letter from HDB in WDC to Yvonne Meyer-May, Feb. 2, 1914, ABDF.

170 Kling, *Alice Pike Barney*, p. 236.

171 Letters from HDB to Yvonne Meyer-May, Feb. 5 and 8, 1914, ABDF.

172 International Mission Statement of the Theosophical Society. See, for example, Theological Society in England. https://theosophicalsociety.org.uk/ (accessed March 2021).

173 Theosophical Society of America. https://www.theosophical.org (accessed April 2018).

174 'Abdu'l-Bahá, *'Abdu'l-Bahá in London*, p. 61.

175 Jasion, *'Abdu'l-Bahá in France*, p. 375.

176 Kling, *Alice Pike Barney*, p. 237.

177 Letter from HDB to Paul Meyer-May, Feb. 21, 1914, ABDF.

178 Talks given by HDB and LDB, in San Francisco, Feb. 28, 1914, USNBA.

179 Letter from HDB in San Francisco to his niece Valentine, Feb. 28, 1913 (must be 1914), ABDF.

180 Letter from HDB in San Francisco to Yvonne Meyer-May, March 4, 1914, ABDF.

181 L.C.D.B., 'From the Peace of the East to the War of the West', 1916, p. 13, ABDF.

182 Giachery, 'Laura Clifford Dreyfus-Barney', *Bahá'í World*, vol. 16 (1973–1976), p. 537.

183 L.C.D.B., 'From the Peace of the East to the War of the West', 1916, p. 13, ABDF.

184 Letter from S. Pichon, Ministère des Affaires étrangères, on the stationery of République Française, Oct. 26, 1913, ABDF, translated by Sheryl Mellor.

185 Letter from HDB in SF to Paul Meyer-May, March 4, 1914, ABDF.

186 Ballanger, *Hippolyte Dreyfus-Barney*, p. 184, n473.

187 Letter from HDB in Waikiki to Yvonne Meyer-May, March 15, 1914, ABDF.

188 L.C.D.B., 'From the Peace of the East to the War of the West', ABDF.

189 ibid. p. 13.

190 ibid.

191 ibid. pp. 28–9.

192 Ballanger, *Hippolyte Dreyfus-Barney*, p. 185.

193 Letter from HDB from Tokyo to his brother-in-law Paul, undated, ABDF.

194 Barbara Sims, in Introduction to Shoghi Effendi, *Japan Will Turn Ablaze!*, p. 5.

195 L.C.D.B., 'From the Peace of the East to the War of the West', p. 6, ABDF.

196 Letter from HDB in Yokohama to Yvonne Meyer-May, April 17, 1914, ABDF.

197 Letter from HDB in Tokyo to Yvonne Meyer-May, April 10, 1914, ABDF.

198 Letter from HDB in Yokohama to Yvonne Meyer-May, April 17, 1914, ABDF.

199 L.C.D.B., 'From the Peace of the East to the War of the West', p. 50, ABDF.

200 Letter from HDB in Kyoto to Yvonne Meyer-May, April 25, 1914, HDB Papers, ABDF.

201 ibid.

202 ibid.

203 Ballanger, *Hippolyte Dreyfus-Barney*, p. 187.

204 Postcard of HDB in Niyajima to Yvonne Meyer-May, May 6, no year given, HDB Papers, ABDF.

205 L.C.D.B., 'From the Peace of the East to the War of the West', p. 33, ABDF.

206 ibid. p. 40.

207 Letter from HDB in Kyoto to Paul Meyer-May, May 2, no year given, HDB papers, ABDF.

208 L.C.D.B., 'From the Peace of the East to the War of the West', pp. 60–1, ABDF.

209 ibid. p. 68.

210 Letter from HDB in Kyoto to Yvonne Meyer-May, April 27, 1914, HDB Papers, ABDF.

211 Barney and Shoghi Effendi, 'Biography of Hippolyte Dreyfus-Barney'. https://bahai-library.com/dreyfus-barney_biography_hippolyte_dreyfus-barney (accessed June 2017).

212 Letter from NCB to LDB, Aug. 1, 1914, AAAMSI.

213 Barney and Shoghi Effendi, 'Biography of Hippolyte Dreyfus-Barney'.

214 Ballanger, *Hippolyte Dreyfus-Barney*, p. 190.

215 ibid. p. 191.

216 Letter from Louise Gregory to Agnes Parsons, Dec. 21, 1914, in Rose, *Seed in Your Heart*, p. 81.

217 Letter from LDB to APB, Oct. 20, perhaps 1914, SIA.

218 Letter from LDB to APB, Nov. 25, year not given, Doucet.

219 Letter from LDB to APB, Oct. 24, USNBA.

220 See 'The United States Army Ambulance Service: American Ambulance Service in France Prior to April 5, 1917. http://history.amedd.army.mil/booksdocs/wwi/fieldoperations/chapter6.html (accessed March 2021).

221 *History of American Red Cross Nursing*, p. 536. https://archive.org/details/historyofamericaooameriala (accessed Oct. 2018).

222 *Bismarck Tribune*, Nov. 5, 1914, p. 4.

223 Letter from LDB to APB, Nov. 25, year not given, Doucet.

224 'Dreyfus-Barney, Laura (Mme. L. Dreyfus-Barney)', *Who's Who in America,* vol. 1, p. 844.

225 Letter from LDB to APB, Dec. 5, year not given, Doucet.

226 Kling, *Alice Pike Barney*, p. 240 and a letter from NCB to LDB, Aug. 1, 1914, AAAMSI.

227 United States Army Ambulance Service: American Ambulance Service in France Prior to April 5, 1917.
http://history.amedd.army.mil/booksdocs/wwi/fieldoperations/chapter6.html (accessed March 2021).

228 Email from Red Cross to the author, April 1, 2016.

229 'Dreyfus-Barney, Laura (Mme. L. Dreyfus-Barney)', *Who's Who in America,* vol. 1, p. 844.

230 Barney and Shoghi Effendi, 'Biography of Hippolyte Dreyfus-Barney'. https://bahai-library.com/dreyfus-barney_biography_hippolyte_dreyfus-barney (accessed June 2017).

231 Letter from Shoghi Effendi to unknown, April 5, 1919, Hannan Papers, USNBA.

232 Kling, *Alice Pike Barney*, p. 244.

233 ibid. pp. 245, 247.

234 Young, 'Barney Name'. https://www.daytonhistorybooks.com/youngbarney.html (accessed Jan. 2017).

235 Kling, *Alice Pike Barney*, p. 247.

236 ibid. p. 245.

237 Florence E. Yoder, 'Forty Members Quit Drama League, Back Mrs. Hemmick, Non-Endorsement of "The Opium Pipe" Leads to Formation of New Body in Capital', *Washington Times*, May 23, 1915, p. 8.

238 Kling, *Alice Pike Barney*, p. 247.

239 ibid. p. 249.

240 'New Home of National American Woman Suffrage Association', *Evening Star*, Dec. 1, 1916.

241 'Dreyfus-Barney, Laura (Mme. L. Dreyfus-Barney)', *Who's Who in America*, vol. 1, p. 44.

242 Letter from LDB to NCB, perhaps 1917, Doucet.

243 ibid.

244 Letter from APBH to Christian Hemmick, no date, National Museum of American Art.

245 ibid.

246 Letter from the Bahai Publishing Society of Chicago to LDB, June 8, 1917, USNBA. The Bahai Publishing Society had been in existence since 1902.

247 Letter from LDB to the Bahai Publishing Society of Chicago, July 20, 1917, USNBA.

248 Letter from the Bahai Publishing Society of Chicago to LDB, Aug. 10, 1917, USNBA.

249 Letter from LDB to the Bahai Publishing Society of Chicago, Sept. 13, 1917, USNBA.

250 Letter from the Bahai Publishing Society of Chicago to LDB, Oct. 24, 1917, USNBA.

251 Letter from LDB to the Bahai Publishing Society of Chicago, Nov. 18, 1917, USNBA.

252 ibid.

253 ibid.

254 Giachery, 'Laura Clifford Dreyfus-Barney', *Bahá'í World*, vol. 16 (1973–1976), p. 537; and 'Dreyfus-Barney, Laura (Mme. L. Dreyfus-Barney)', *Who's Who in America*, vol. 1, p. 844.

255 Email exchange between the American Red Cross Archivist and the author, April 2016.

256 *History of American Red Cross Nursing*, p. 831. https://archive.org/details/historyofamericaooameriala (accessed Oct. 2018).

257 ibid.

258 ibid. p. 840.

259 ibid. p. 791.

260 ibid.

261 Letter from LDB to APB, Jan. 17, 1918, USNBA.

262 Letter from LDB to APB, Dec. 15, perhaps 1917, Doucet.

263 'Dreyfus-Barney, Laura (Mme. L. Dreyfus-Barney)', *Who's Who in America*, vol. 1, p. 844.

264 L.C.D.B., 'The Way Reopens', p. 4a, ABDF.

265 Letter from LDB to APB, Jan. 17, 1918, USNBA.

266 Letter from LDB to APB, Jan. 29, perhaps 1918, Doucet.

267 Letter from LDB to APB, May 12, 1918, Doucet.

268 Letter from LDB from France to APB, Jan. 26, perhaps 1918, Doucet.

269 Letter from LDB to APB, Sept. 23, 1918, Doucet.

270 ibid.

271 Letter from LDB to APB, Dec. 24, 1918, Doucet.

272 Hippolyte was in Marseilles at 308 rue Paradis, according to a letter dated Oct. 12, 1918, USNBA.

273 'Fête Américane du 4 Juillet 1918 à Avignon et en Vaucluse', *Courant de Vaucluse,* July 4, 1918, ABDF.

274 'La Croix-Rouge Américaine et les Réfugiés,' *Le Républicain du Gard*, July 13, 1918, ABDF.

275 'La Croix-Rouge Américaine et la Société Nîmoise de Secours aux Réfugiés', *Le Républicain du Gard*, 13 Juillet, 1918, ABDF.

276 'Comment aider le pays-envahi à renaître de ses ruines?', *Réfugié en Provence*, Jan. 1, 1919, translated by Sheryl Mellor.

277 'A Marseille: La 'Croix-Rouge Américaine' et les Réfugiés', in *Bulletin des Réfugiés du Pas de Calais*, Aug. 18, 1918, translated by Sheryl Mellor. https://gallica.bnf.fr/ark:/12148/bpt6k4533614v/f2.item (accessed Oct. 2021).

278 *Petit Provençal* , Dec. 21, 1918; *Soleil du Midi*, 23 Dec. 1918; *Petit Marseillais*, 23 Dec. 1918; *Radical*, 23 Dec. 1918; and *Le Memorial d'Aix*, Dec. 29, 1918.

279 L.C.D.B., 'The Way Reopens', LDB papers, ABDF.

280 Letter from HDB to someone in Paris, must be around Naw-Rúz 1919, HDB papers, ABDF.

281 Ballanger, *Hippolyte Dreyfus-Barney*, p. 194, n506.

282 'Abdu'l-Bahá, Tablet to HDB, Feb. 7, 1919, HDB Papers, ABDF, translated by Shoghi Effendi.

283 L.C.D.B., 'The Way Reopens', p. 4a, ABDF.

284 Letter from LDB to APB, March 27, must be 1919, Doucet.

285 Shoghi Effendi to Ahmad, April 5, 1919, Hannen-Knobloch Family Papers, USNBA.

286 ibid.

287 L.C.D.B., 'The Way Reopens', p. 11a, ABDF.

288 Balyuzi, *'Abdu'l-Bahá*, p. 433; 'News from the Holy Land: Letter from Major W. Tudor-Pole', *Star of the West*, vol. 10, no. 3 (April 28, 1919), p. 37.

289 ibid.

290 Shoghi Effendi to an unknown recipient, April 6, 1919, Hannen-Knobloch Family Papers, USNBA.

291 Shoghi Effendi to Ahmad, April 14, 1919, Hannen-Knobloch Family Papers, USNBA.

292 Shoghi Effendi to Ahmad, April 15–18, 1919, Hannen-Knobloch Family Papers, USNBA.

293 L.C.D.B., 'The Way Reopens', p. 5a, ABDF.

294 Letter from LDB to APB, April 26, 1919, Doucet.

295 Letter from Shoghi Effendi to LDB, May 8, 1919, ABDF.

296 Letter from Shoghi Effendi to LDB, June 11, 1919, ABDF.

297 Letter from Shoghi Effendi to LDB, June 15, 1919, ABDF.

298 'Abdu'l-Bahá, Tablet to LDB, June 20, 1919, no. AC1/1/150, BWCA, provisional translation by Riaz Masrour.

299 L.C.D.B., 'The Way Reopens', p. 11a, ABDF and copy of the passport of LDB, ABDF.

300 ibid.

301 Ballanger, *Hippolyte Dreyfus-Barney*, p. 210.

302 Ruhe-Schoen, *Champions of Oneness*, p. 195. Pauline Knobloch and Joseph Hannen were a married couple who were active members of the small but growing Washington, D.C. Bahá'í community.

303 Nakhjavani, *Maxwells*, vol. 1, p. 349.

304 L.C.D.B., 'The Way Reopens', p. 12a, ABDF.

305 Ballanger, *Hippolyte Dreyfus-Barney*, p. 211.

306 Rodriguez, *Wild Heart*, p. 219.

307 Khadem, *Prelude to the Guardianship*, p. 135.

308 Giachery, 'Laura Clifford Dreyfus-Barney', *Bahá'í World*, vol. 16 (1973–1976), p. 536.

309 Khadem, *Prelude to the Guardianship*, p. 134 and Gail, *Arches of the Years*, p. 185.

310 Letter from LDB to NCB, Feb. 27, 1922, SIA.

311 Giachery, 'Laura Clifford Dreyfus-Barney', *La Pensée Bahá'íe*, no. 56 (June 1976), p. 27, translated by the present author; see also Rabbani, *Priceless Pearl*, pp. 358–9.

312 Khadem, *Prelude to the Guardianship*, p. 135.

313 ibid.

314 ibid. p. 136.

315 Gail, *Arches of the Years*, p. 185.

316 ibid.

317 Kling, *Alice Pike Barney*, pp. 247, 275.

318 Letter from LDB, on American Red Cross Service des Refugees stationery from Marseilles, to APB, Dec. 24, 1918, Doucet.

319 Letter from LDB to APB, Sept. 23, 1918, Doucet.

320 Letter from LDB to APB, Dec. 24, 1918, Doucet.

321 *Washington Post*, Jan. 18, 1920, p. 1.

322 Kling, *Alice Pike Barney*, pp. 275–6.

323 Letter from LDB to APB, undated, USNBA.

324 Rodriguez, *Wild Heart*, pp. 235–6.

325 ibid. pp. 235–6.

326 Kling, *Alice Pike Barney*, p. 282.

327 'News from the Near East – Letter from Elizabeth H. Stewart', *Star of the West*, vol. 12, no. 2 (April 9, 1921), p. 39.

328 Letter from LDB to Afroukhteh, August 7, 1937, in Afroukhteh, *Memories*, p. 344. LDB says 1921 but they were in Indochina in 1921, so it must be 1920.

329 Ballanger, *Hippolyte Dreyfus-Barney*, p. 216.
330 Mu'ayyad, *Khátirát-i-Habíb*, vol. 1, p. 60.
331 Interview with Naz Bushrui-Pakzad, Badí' Bushrú'í's daughter, in Washington, D.C, Feb. 7, 2012.
332 Letter from LDB to NCB, Nov. 27, probably 1920, SIA.
333 Giachery, 'Laura Clifford Dreyfus-Barney', *Bahá'í World*, vol. 16 (1973–1976), pp. 536–7.
334 L.C.D.B., 'The Way Reopens', p. 13a, ABDF.
335 Letter from LDB to NCB, Nov. 28, year not given, perhaps 1920, Doucet.
336 Letter from LDB to NCB, Dec. 6, 1920, Doucet.
337 L.C.D.B., 'The Way Reopens', p. 2a, ABDF. All the references below to this journey by the Dreyfus-Barneys are taken from 'The Way Reopens', unless otherwise indicated.
338 Letter from LDB to APB, Dec. 21, 1921, USNBA.
339 Giachery, 'Laura Clifford Dreyfus-Barney', *Bahá'í World*, vol. 16 (1973–1976), pp. 536–7.
340 Letter from LDB to NCB, Feb. 24, 1921, Doucet. It may be that the Col. Moore LDB is referring to is Joseph Haines Moore (1878–1949), an American astronomer born in Ohio and president of the Astronomical Society of the Pacific in 1920 and 1928. He was married to Federico Chase, the daughter of Joseph Emory, in 1907 and had two daughters.
341 Letter from LDB to NCB, Feb. 28, 1921, Doucet.
342 Letter from LDB to NCB, March 13, 1921, Doucet.
343 Letter from LDB to APB in Paris, March 16, 1921, Doucet.
344 Letter from LDB to NCB, April 2, 1921, Doucet.
345 Letter from LDB to NCB, April 20, 1921, Doucet.
346 ibid.
347 L.C.D.B., 'The Way Reopens', p. 131, ABDF.
348 Gaubatz, *Beyond the Great Wall*, p. 78.
349 Letter from LDB to NCB, July 8, 1921, Doucet.
350 Letter from LDB to the Mother, Nov. 22, 1968, ABDF.
351 Letter from LDB to NCB, Aug. 25, 1921, Doucet.
352 Letter from LDB to NCB, April 2, must be 1921, Doucet.
353 Letter from LDB to NCB, Sept. 30, 1921, Doucet.
354 Letter from LDB to NCB, Oct. 9, 1921, Doucet.
355 ibid.
356 ibid.
357 Letter from LDB to NCB, Oct. 22, 1921, Doucet.
358 Letter from LDB to APB, Dec. 21, 1921, USNBA.
359 Letter from LDB to Afroukhteh, August 7, 1937, in Afroukhteh, *Memories*, p. 344.
360 Letter from LDB to NCB, Jan. 5, 1922, Doucet.
361 Letter from LDB to NCB, Jan. 18, 1922, Doucet.
362 Letter from LDB to NCB, Jan. 18 (must be Feb. 18), 1922, Doucet.
363 Hupmobile was an automobile built between 1909 and 1939 by the Hupp Motor Car Co. in Detroit, Michigan.
364 Ballanger, *Hippolyte Dreyfus-Barney*, p. 225.

365 *Bombay Chronicle*, May 24, 1944.

366 Notes of the interview with Mahatma Gandhi, winter of 1922, SIA.

367 *Bombay Chronicle*, May 24, 1944.

368 Zoroastrians generally do not bury their dead but expose them to the elements to avoid contamination of the soil by their decay. The Tower of Silence (*dahkma*), a circular, raised structure, is constructed for this purpose. Vultures and other scavengers would eat the flesh, leaving the skeletons. The practice was brought by Zoroastrians to India, where they were known as Parsees, from Iran.

369 Browne, 'Sir 'Abdu'l-Baha 'Abbas'. *Journal of the Royal Asiatic Society*, no. 1 (Jan. 1922), pp. 145–6.

370 Rabbani, *Priceless Pearl*, p. 55.

371 Weinberg, *Ethel Jenner Rosenberg*, pp. 207–9.

372 ibid. p. 207.

373 Letter from LDB to NCB, Feb. 27, 1922, SIA.

374 Weinberg, *Ethel Jenner Rosenberg*, p. 206.

375 Ballanger, *Hippolyte Dreyfus-Barney*, p. 230.

376 This story is largely summarized from Weinberg, *Lady Blomfield*, pp. 238–44.

377 Ballanger, *Hippolyte Dreyfus-Barney*, p. 231.

378 Letter from Lady Blomfield to Mary Basil Hall (her daughter), March 30, 1922, United Kingdom Bahá'í Archives, cited in Weinberg, *Lady Blomfield*, p. 240, n59.

379 Gail, *Arches of the Years*, p. 285.

380 Letter from Shoghi Effendi to Dreyfus-Barneys, Dec. 17, 1922, ABDF.

381 From a letter of Lady Blomfield to Mary Basil Hall, April 2, 1922, United Kingdom Bahá'í Archives, cited in Weinberg, *Lady Blomfield*, p. 243, n68.

382 Postcard from LDB to NCB, May 24, 1924, Doucet.

383 See 'History', International Council of Women. http://www.icw-cif.com/01/03. php (accessed March 2021).

384 Giachery, 'Laura Clifford Dreyfus-Barney', *Bahá'í World*, vol. 16 (1973–1976), p. 537.

385 Letter from LDB to APB, Jan. 17, no year given, USNBA.

386 *La Liberté*, 'Le féminisme au service de la paix', 1935, Doucet, translated by Sheryl Mellor.

387 Letter from LDB to NCB, Jan. 11, 1925, Doucet.

388 Letter from LDB to NCB, Jan. 24,1925, Doucet.

389 ibid.

390 Alice moved to LA in 1923, returned to D.C. for a while and then returned to LA in late fall of 1924.

391 'News of the Cause', *Bahá'í News Letter*, Jan. 1925, no. 2, p. 3. https://bahai. works/Baha%27i_News_Letter/Issue_2/Text (accessed March 2021).

392 French, 'A Notable Fellowship Dinner', *Bahá'í Magazine*, vol. 16, no. 4 (July 1925), p. 504, BNAUSA.

393 Giachery, 'Laura Clifford Dreyfus-Barney', *La Pensée Bahá'ie*, no. 56 (June 1976), p. 27.

394 Letter from HDB in MD, US to Horace Holley, June 12, 1925, USNBA.

395 'The Convention', in *Bahá'í News Letter*, July–Aug. 1925, no. 6, pp. 3–4. https:// bahai.works/Baha%27i_News_Letter/Issue_6 (accessed Oct. 2021).

396 Letter from Horace Holley to HDB, US, June 15, 1925, USNBA.

397 Letter from LDB to NCB, Aug. 26, 1925, Doucet.

398 Letter from the Chief of the Office of Legion of Honor of Grand Chancellerie de la Légion d'Honneur, to the author, Feb. 14, 2012.

399 The Legion of Honor ranks, from lowest to highest, are Chevalier (Knight), Officier (Officer), Commander, Grand officier (Grand Officer) and Grand-croix (Grand Cross).

400 Kling, *Alice Pike Barney*, p. 264.

401 Letter from LDB to NCB, Aug. 1925, Doucet.

402 Letter from LDB to NCB, Sept. 18, perhaps 1925, Doucet.

403 Letter from LDB to NCB, Sept. 21, perhaps 1925, Doucet.

404 'Mme Laura Dreyfus-Barney', perhaps in *The Parisiennes*, Dec. 16, 1925.

405 ibid.

406 Letter from a Bahá'í institution to LDB, Jan. 13, 1926, USNBA.

407 Letter from LDB to Miss Culver, Jan. 14, 1924, USNBA.

408 Letter from Mountfort Mills to LDB, April 19, 1943, ABDF.

409 Ballanger, *Hippolyte Dreyfus-Barney*, p. 246.

410 Weinberg, *Ethel Jenner Rosenberg*, pp. 242–3.

411 Garis, *Martha Root*, p. 256.

412 Weinberg, *Lady Blomfield*, p. 277.

413 ibid. and Garis, *Martha Root*, p. 256.

414 Garis, *Martha Root*, p. 283.

415 Weinberg, *Lady Blomfield*, p. 258.

416 Hoagg, 'Short History of the International Bahá'í Bureau', *Bahá'í World*, vol. 4 (1930–1932), pp. 257–61; Bishop, 'Geneva Scans the European Community', *Bahá'í World*, vol. 6 (1934–1936), pp. 130–5; Hutchinson and Hollinger, 'Women in the North American Bahá'í Community', in *Encyclopedia of Women and Religion in North America*, pp. 776–82.

417 Stöckmann, '90 Years of Intellectual Cooperation'. https://afus-unesco.org/assets/files/unesco-75-ans/unesco-avant-unesco-eng-stockmann.pdf (accessed March 2021).

418 Einstein resigned in 1923, protesting publicly the committee's inefficacy; he rejoined in 1924 to mitigate the use German chauvinists made of his resignation.

419 Letter from LDB to Colleagues at the ICW's Sub-Committee on Cinematography, Feb. 5, 1927, translated by Sheryl Mellor.

420 Letter from LDB in Paris on ICW stationery to ICW Cinema Sub-Committee, Sept. 1927, LSEA.

421 Letter from LDB on ICW stationery to Colleagues, ICW Cinema Sub-Committee, May 1928, LSEA.

422 Letter from Lady Aberdeen, House of Cormar, Aberdeenshire, to LDB, Oct. 7, 1927, LSEA.

423 ibid.

424 Letter from LDB to Lady Aberdeen, Sept. 24, 1927, LSEA.

425 Letter from Lady Aberdeen, House of Cormar, Aberdeenshire, to LDB, Oct. 7, 1927, LSEA.

426 Letter from LDB from Ireland to NCB, May 22, 1927, Doucet.

427 Letter from LDB to NCB, June 15, 1927, Doucet.

428 Postcard from LDB to NCB, July 15, 1927, Doucet.

429 Letter from LDB to Mr Simpson, July 11, 1927, National Bahá'í Archives of the UK.

430 Letter from LDB to NCB, Aug. 1, 1927, Doucet.

431 Letter from LDB to NCB, Aug. 12, 1927 or maybe 1928, Doucet.

432 Letter from LDB with HDB to NCB, Aug. perhaps 1927, Doucet.

433 Letter from LDB to NCB, Sept. 5, 1927, Doucet.

434 Letter from LDB to NCB, Feb. 1, 1928, Doucet.

435 Ballanger, *Hippolyte Dreyfus-Barney*, p. 252.

436 Letter from LDB to Lady Aberdeen, Jan. 30, 1928, LSEA.

437 Letter from Augustus Thomas, President of the World Federation of Education Associations in Maine, US to LDB, March 20, 1925, UNA.

438 Letter from the Minister of the Public Education (today's Ministry of National Education, Higher Education and Research) to the Rector of the Academy, Jan. 17, 1928, UNA. The Rector of the Academy of Paris was to be the Chancellor of the Universities of Paris and Chairman of the Committee of Rectors of the Île-de-France region (Paris and the surrounding area). The Rector of Paris is also Honorary President of the Conference of French Rectors. The Minister's letter was sent to the League of Nations by LDB.

439 Letter from Armi Hallsten Kallia from the League of Nations to LDB, March 6, 1928, UNA. Kallia was a member of the Section, International Bureau and Intellectual Cooperation.

440 Letter from LDB to Mr Hoden of the League of Nations, March 15, 1928, UNA, translated by Sheryl Mellor.

441 ibid.

442 ibid.

443 Internal letter from A.H. Kallia to Mr Hoden, March 16, 1928, UNA.

444 Letter from A. Dufour-Féronce, the Under-Secretary General and Director of the Section of International Bureau to LDB, March 17, 1928, UNA.

445 Letter on League of Nations stationery to the International Commission of Intellectual Cooperation, March 28, 1928, UNA.

446 Letter from A. Dufour-Féronce, the Under-Secretary General and Director of the Section of International Bureau to Madame Avril de Sainte-Croix, President the National Council of French Women, March 17, 1928, UNA.

447 Letter from LDB from Paris to someone at the League of Nations in Geneva, June 18, 1928, UNA.

448 ibid. June 27, 1928, UNA.

449 Letter from LDB to Mr de Montenach, Secretariat of the League of Nations, July 8, 1928, UNA, translated by Sheryl Mellor.

450 Letter from a Member of the Section of the International Office and the International Commission of Intellectual Cooperation to LDB, Nov. 3, 1928, UNA.

451 Letter from A.H. Kallia to LDB, Aug. 7, 1928, UNA.

452 Letter from LDB to Miss Kallia, Aug. 9, 1928, UNA.

453 Letter from (illegible) to LDB, in French, Oct. 2, 1928, HDB Papers, ABDF.

454 Letter from NCB to LDB, not dated, SIA.

455 Letter from NCB to LDB, Oct. 6, SIA.

456 Letter from LDB to May Maxwell, Nov. 11, 1928, sent from the Bahá'í World Centre to the author, May 16, 2012.

457 Letter from Lady Sara Blomfield to LDB, Jan. 24, 1929, ABDF.

458 Typed letter with information about HDB's death and burial, HDB Papers,

ABDF. Other family members buried in that chapel are Lucien Dreyfus-Cardozo, Jan. 4, 1911; Ines Dreyfus Cardozo, Oct. 2, 1913; Juliette Dreyfus, Jan. 2, 1942; Emma Dreyfus, July 23, 1945; and Carle Dreyfus, June 21, 1952.

459 Letter from Lady Sara Blomfield to LDB, Jan. 24, 1929, ABDF.

460 Letter from (name illegible) on stationery from the American Hospital of Paris to LDB, Dec. 28, 1928, HDB papers, ABDF.

461 Barney and Shoghi Effendi, 'Biography of Hippolyte Dreyfus-Barney'. https://bahai-library.com/dreyfus-barney_biography_hippolyte_dreyfus-barney (accessed June 2017).

462 ibid.

463 Hogenson, *Lighting the Western Sky*, p. 188.

464 Stockman, *Bahá'í Faith in America*, vol. 2, p. 374.

465 Momen, *Basic Bahá'í Dictionary*, p. 71.

466 Rassekh, 'Dreyfus-Barney', DREYFUS-BARNEY – Brill (brillonline.com) (accessed May 2021).

467 Metelmann, *Lua Getsinger*, pp. 59–61.

468 ibid. and Rassekh, 'Dreyfus-Barney', DREYFUS-BARNEY – Brill (brillonline. com) (accessed May 2021).

469 List of the names of those who sent letters, telegrams and cards to LDB, ABDF.

470 Giachery, 'Laura Clifford Dreyfus-Barney', *La Pensée Bahá'ie*, no. 56 (June 1976), p. 27; Barney and Shoghi Effendi, 'Biography of Hippolyte Dreyfus-Barney'. https://bahai-library.com/dreyfus-barney_biography_hippolyte_dreyfus-barney (accessed June 2017); and telegram from Shoghi Effendi to LDB, Dec. 21, 1928, ABDF.

471 Letter/telegram in Persian from Haifa on Ahmed Bey Yazdi's stationery to LBD, Dec. 22, 1928, ABDF.

472 Letter from Shoghi Effendi to LDB, Dec. 21, 1928, ABDF.

473 Shoghi Effendi, *Bahá'í Administration*, pp. 158–9.

474 Letter from Shoghi Effendi to LDB, Jan. 24, 1929, ABDF.

475 Shoghi Effendi, *Bahá'í Administration*, p. 157.

476 Telegram from APB to LDB, Dec. 1928, ABDF.

477 Letter from APB to LDB, Dec. 27, 1928, ABDF.

478 ibid.

479 NCB's tribute for HDB, undated, ABDF, translated by Sheryl Mellor.

480 ibid.

481 Letter from Monever [Munavvar] from Haifa, Dec. 23, 1928, perhaps translated by Aḥmad Yazdí or maybe written in English to LDB, ABDF. Munavvar was the youngest daughter of 'Abdu'l-Bahá and was married to Mírzá Aḥmad Yazdí. They had no children.

482 Letter from May Bolles Maxwell to LDB, Dec. 31, 1928, ABDF.

483 Letter from Edith [Sanderson] to LDB, not dated, ABDF.

484 Telegram from Lord and Lady Aberdeen to LDB, Dec. 30, 1928, SIA.

485 Letter from Mary Dingman in Toronto to LDB, Feb. 2, 1928 (must be 1929), ABDF. She later became the president of the Disarmament Committee.

486 Letter from Lucie Delarue-Mardrus in Paris to LDB, Dec. 28, 1928, ABDF, translated by Sheryl Mellor. Delarue-Mardrus was a friend of Natalie who had met 'Abdu'l-Bahá in Paris at His apartment at Avenue de Camoëns in Nov. 1911, according to Jasion, *'Abdu'l-Bahá in France*, p. 145.

487 Letter from Lucie Delarue-Mardrus from Paris to LDB, Dec. 28, 1928, ABDF, translated by Sheryl Mellor.
488 Letter from Ministry of Foreign Affairs of France to LDB, Dec. 21,1928, ABDF, translated by Sheryl Mellor.
489 Letter from LDB with HDB in Switzerland to NCB, Aug. perhaps 1927, Doucet.
490 Letter from Salomon Reinach in Paris to LDB, Dec. 21, 1928, ABDF, translated by Sheryl Mellor.
491 Letter from Lady Blomfield in Geneva to LDB, Jan. 24, 1929, ABDF.
492 Letter from Martha Root in Germany to LDB, Dec. 31, 1928, ABDF.
493 ibid.
494 Letter from Shoghi Effendi to LDB, March 12, 1929, ABDF.
495 ibid.
496 Letter from LDB to a friend, not dated, ABDF.

Part 4 Laura on Her Own 1929 – 1964

1 Author's interviews with Anita Ioas-Chapman. She lived in Paris from 1950 to 1955 and from 1965 to 1967. Her second stay in Paris was in the same building as LDB.
2 Giachery, 'Laura Clifford Dreyfus-Barney', *Bahá'í World*, vol. 16 (1973–1976), p. 537.
3 Letter from LDB to NCB, undated, Doucet.
4 Letter from Mary Dingman in Toronto to LDB, Feb. 2, 1928 (must be 1929), ABDF.
5 Chalon, *Portrait of a Seductress*, p.146.
6 Langer, *Romaine Brooks*, p. 4.
7 Chalon, *Portrait of a Seductress*, p. 147.
8 Several references in correspondence between LDB and NCB refer to them, Doucet.
9 Letter from APB to LDB, Dec. 27, 1928, ABDF.
10 Author's interviews with Anita Ioas-Chapman.
11 Letter from LDB to May Maxwell, April 14, 1929, BWC summarized letter sent to the author, May 16, 2012.
12 Letter from May Maxwell to LDB, Oct. 25, 1929, BWC summarized letter sent to the author, May 16, 2012.
13 Dreyfus-Barney, Laura, 'Only a Word', *Bahá'í World*, vol. 5 (1932–1934), p. 667.
14 International Council of Women. http://www.icw-cif.com/01/03.php (accessed April 2021).
15 Letter from LDB from Paris, possibly to Mr G. Oprescu, Jan. 31, 1929, UNA. See also League of Nations, International Education Cinematographic Institute. http://biblio-archive.unog.ch/Dateien/CouncilMSD/C-694-M-291-1930-XII_EN.pdf (accessed April 2021).
16 Letter from AHK since Mr Oprescu was away in Geneva to LDB, Feb. 1, 1929, UNA.
17 Letter from Director of Section of International Bureau International Cooperation to Mme LDB, May 5, 1930, UNA.
18 Letter from Laura Dreyfus-Barney to Dufour-Féronce, Sub Secretary of the Secretariat of the League of Nations, May 11, 1930, UNA.

19 Letter from LDB to Dufour-Féronce, Undersecretary at the Secretariat of the League of Nations, Jan. 5, 1931, UNA.

20 Internal letter from A.H. [Hallsten]-K. [Kallia] to Dufour-Féronce, Jan. 26, 1931, UNA.

21 The Ministry of Public Education is now called the Ministry of National Education, Higher Education and Research.

22 Letter from LDB to Mlle H. Kalia, June 17, 1931, UNA.

23 Letter on behalf of G. G. Kullmann, Member of the Intellectual Cooperation Section to LDB, June 19, 1931, UNA.

24 Letter from LDB to Mr Kullmann at the League of Nations, June 22, 1931, UNA, translated by Sheryl Mellor.

25 Druick, 'The International Educational Cinematograph Institute, Reactionary Modernism, and the Formation of Film Studies', *Canadian Journal of Film Studies*, vol. 16, no. 1, Spring 2007, p. 80. http://www.jstor.org/stable/24408070 (accessed Oct. 2018).

26 ibid. p. 87.

27 ibid. n31. Diehl, 'The Moral Effect of the Cinema on Individuals', *International Review* of *Educational Cinematography*, 3.12 (December 1931), 1123. http://www.jstor.org/stable/24408070 (accessed Oct. 2018).

28 'Note de Presse', for Conseil International des Femmes, LSEA, translated by Sheryl Mellor.

29 Letter from LDB on the stationery of ICW to Colleagues, March 5, 1929, LSEA.

30 Letter from LDB to ICW Cinema Sub-Committee, Sept. (day not given), 1927, LSEA.

31 Letter from LDB on the stationery of ICW to Colleagues, March 5, 1929, LSEA.

32 Letter from LDB to the members of Cinema Sub-Committee, June 25, 1929, LSEA.

33 ibid.

34 ibid.

35 ibid.

36 Letter from LDB to Lady Aberdeen, Feb. 28, 1930, LSEA.

37 Letter from Elizabeth Cadbury of Birmingham to LDB, Dec. 18, 1941, NMWAA.

38 'Note de Presse', for ICW, must be 1931, LSEA, translated by Sheryl Mellor.

39 Letters from LDB to Lady Aberdeen, Oct. 22, 1930, LSEA.

40 ibid.

41 ibid.

42 Letter from Lady Aberdeen to LDB, Nov. 18, 1930, LSEA.

43 Letter from LDB to the Members of the Cinematograph and Radio Sub-Committee, no day given, Dec. 1930, LSEA.

44 ibid.

45 Letter from LDB to Lady Aberdeen, Dec. 16, 1930, LSEA.

46 ibid.

47 Letter from LDB to Lady Aberdeen, Jan. 6, 1931, LSEA.

48 Lady Aberdeen was the president of ICW from 1893 to 1899, 1904 to 1920 and from 1922 to 1936.

49 Letter from LDB to Lady Aberdeen, Jan. 6, 1931, LSEA.

50 Letter from LDB to Lady Aberdeen, Jan. 9, 1931, LSEA.

51 ibid.

52 Letter from Marchioness of Aberdeen to Miss Tancred, March 24, 1931, LSEA.

53 ibid.

54 Letter from LDB to the Marchioness of Aberdeen in Scotland, April 20, 1931, LSEA.

55 Letter from LDB to Lady Aberdeen, May 27, 1931, LSEA.

56 Letter from LDB to Lady Aberdeen, June 1, 1931, LSEA.

57 Letter from Lady Aberdeen President of ICW to Dr Albert Thomas, June 17, 1931, LSEA.

58 Letter from Lady Aberdeen to LDB, Sept. 28, 1931, LSEA.

59 Letter from Lady Aberdeen to LDB, Sept. 31, 1931, LSEA.

60 'Dreyfus-Barney, Laura (Mme. L. Dreyfus-Barney)', *Who's Who in America*, vol. 1, p. 844.

61 'Note de Presse', for Conseil International des Femmes, LSEA, translated by Sheryl Mellor.

62 Reich, 'Mussolini at the Movies: Fascism, Film, and Culture', in *Re-viewing Fascism,* p. 3.

63 Druick, 'The International Educational Cinematograph Institute, Reactionary Modernism, and the Formation of Film Studies', *Canadian Journal of Film Studies*, vol. 16, no. 1, n32: referring to LDB, 'What Woman Can Offer the Cinema', *International Review of Educational Cinematography* 4.6 (June 1932), p. 471. http://www.jstor.org/stable/24408070 (accessed Oct. 2018).

64 Letter from LDB to Lady Aberdeen in Scotland, Oct. 1, 1931, LSEA.

65 'Una conferenza romana pel Cinema Delegate di tutto mondo', Oct. 3, 1931, LSEA.

66 'Madame Dreyfus-Barney, Présidente du Comité International du Cinématographe et la Radio-Diffusion', *Minerva*, Nov. 22, 1931, LSEA, translated by Sheryl Mellor.

67 Letter from A. Rocco, President, International Educational Cinematographic Institute to LDB and Louise van Eeghen, Oct.14, 1931, LSEA.

68 Letter from Luciano de Feo to LDB and Louise van Eeghen, Oct. 14, 1931, LSEA.

69 Letter from LDB to Lady Aberdeen, Aug. 3, 1932, LSEA. LDB refers to his request in this letter.

70 Letters from LDB to Lady Aberdeen, Oct. 12 and 16, 1931, LSEA.

71 Letter from LDB to NCB, Oct. 14, 1931, Doucet.

72 ibid. 1931, Doucet.

73 Letter from LDB to NCB, Nov. 5, 1931, Doucet.

74 Letter from LDB to NCB, Oct. 29, 1931, Doucet.

75 ibid.

76 Letter from LDB to Lady Aberdeen, Oct. 16, 1931, LSEA.

77 Letter from LDB to the California Trust, Oct 30, 1931, Doucet.

78 Letter from LDB to NCB, Nov. 2, 1931, Doucet.

79 Kling, *Alice Pike Barney*, pp. 294, 296–7.

80 Letter from Mary Connell in Hollywood, CA to LDB, Dec. 28, 1931, SIA.

81 Kling, *Alice Pike Barney*, p. 297.

82 Letter from LDB to the California Trust, Oct. 30, 1931, Doucet.

83 Rodriguez, *Wild Heart*, p. 294.

84 Kling, *Alice Pike Barney*, p. 297.

85 Rodriguez, *Wild Heart*, p. 294.

86 'FAMED SOCIETY WOMAN HERE, MRS. ALICE PIKE BARNEY DIES', *Evening Star*, Oct. 13, 1931, SIA.

87 Kling, *Alice Pike Barney*, p. 296.

88 Typed report, SIA. The one-page typed sheet describes Alice Barney's Mime-Ballet that was performed at her home, stating that her ballets are pantomimed stories as well as dances.

89 Kling, *Alice Pike Barney*, p. 248.

90 ibid. p. 190

91 ibid. p. 299.

92 Letter from LCB to APB, undated, typed from original, SIA.

93 Letter from LCB to APB, July 5, 1906, SIA.

94 Letter from LDB to APB, Dec. 12, maybe around 1920, Doucet.

95 'Mrs Alice Barney', *Bahá'í World*, vol. 5 (1932–1934), pp. 419–20.

96 Letter from 'Abdu'l-Bahá to LCB, undated from Egypt, the Bahá'í World Centre, AC1/1/173, ABDF, provisional translation by Riaz Masrour.

97 Letter from 'Abdu'l-Bahá to LCB, undated from Egypt, the Bahá'í World Centre, AC1/1/184, ABDF, provisional translation by Riaz Masrour.

98 Letter from LDB to NCB, March 21, 1952, Doucet.

99 Peace and Disarmament Committee of the Women's International Organisations Collected Records, Swarthmore College Peace Collection. http://archives.tricolib.brynmawr.edu/resources/scpc-cdg-b-switzerland-peace_and_disarmament_commi (accessed June 2021).

100 L.K., 'Le féminisme au service de la paix: L'activité du Comité de désarmement des organisations internationales féminines' ['Feminism for Peace: The Work of the Disarmament Committee of Women's International Organizations'], *La Liberté*, April 6, 1935, Doucet, translated by Sheryl Mellor.

101 'A Brief History of the International Council of Women: 1888–1980', National Council of Women of Great Britain, Aug. 1982, p. 5, LSEA.

102 Letter from LDB to NCB, Feb. 2, 1932, Doucet.

103 Root, 'Disarmament Conference and the Extraordinary Session of League of Nations', *Bahá'í Magazine*, vol. 23, no. 1 (April 1932), p. 18, USNBA.

104 Letter from LDB to NCB, May 8, 1932, Doucet; Program for the weekend Study Conference, Disarmament Committee of the Women's International Organisations, May 7–8, 1932, Doucet.

105 Report of Disarmament Committee by President Mary A. Dingman, undated (perhaps 1932), USNBA.

106 Letter from Mr de Montenach of the Secretariat of the Organization of Intellectual Cooperation to LDB, April 26, 1932, UNA.

107 Letter from LDB to Mr de Montenach of the Secretariat of the Organization of Intellectual Cooperation, April 29, 1932, UNA.

108 Letter from Secretary of the Committee on Intellectual Cooperation to LDB, May 9, 1930; and Agenda item by Mme. Dreyfus-Barney distributed to all members, June 24, 1930, UNA.

109 Undated document, perhaps of 1932, USNBA.

110 'Dreyfus-Barney, Laura (Mme. L. Dreyfus-Barney)', *Who's Who in America*, vol. 1, p. 844.

111 Letter from Lady Aberdeen to LDB, Aug. 30, 1932, LSEA.

112 Undated Press Release, must be 1932, USNBA.

113 ibid.

114 Enclosure with a letter from LDB to Lady Aberdeen, Aug. 3, 1932, 'Sept. 1932 – Canada: Program of Talks', LSEA.

115 Letter from LDB to NCB, Sept. 18, 1932, Doucet.

116 Letter from LDB to NCB, Sept. 22, 1932, Doucet.

117 Letter from LDB to Lady Aberdeen, Sept. 28, 1932, LSEA.

118 ibid.

119 Letter from Lady Aberdeen to LDB, Nov. 3, 1932, LSEA.

120 Undated Press Release, must be 1932, USNBA.

121 Letter from LDB on Old Garden Cottage, Hollywood to NCB, Oct. 8, 1932, Doucet.

122 Letter from LDB to the California Trust, Oct. 30, 1931, Doucet.

123 ibid.

124 Letter from LDB to NCB, Nov. 2, 1932, Doucet.

125 Kling, *Alice Pike Barney*, p. 300.

126 Letter from LDB to NCB, Feb. 17, 1937, Doucet.

127 Langer, *Romaine Brooks*, p. 5.

128 ibid.

129 Kling, *Alice Pike Barney*, p. 21.

130 William Huntington, in Rodriguez, *Wild Heart*, p. 291 and n4.

131 Rodriguez, *Wild Heart*, p. 291.

132 Letter from LDB to NCB, Oct. 8, 1932, Doucet.

133 Letter from LDB to NCB, Oct. 10, 1932, Doucet.

134 Letter from LDB to NCB, Oct. 8, 1932, Doucet.

135 Letter from LDB to NCB, Oct. 12, 1932, Doucet.

136 Letter from LDB to NCB, Oct. 10, 1932, Doucet.

137 Letter from LDB to NCB, Aug. 4, 1932, Doucet.

138 Letter from LDB to NCB, Oct. 19, 1932, Doucet.

139 Letter from LDB to NCB, Oct. 24, 1932, Doucet.

140 Letter from LDB to NCB, Nov. 15, 1932, Doucet.

141 Letter from LDB to NCB, Oct. 28, 1932, Doucet.

142 ibid.

143 Letter from LDB to NCB, Oct. 24, 1932, Doucet.

144 Letter from Aunt Hessie in LA to LDB, March 2, 1938, Doucet.

145 Letter from LDB to NCB, Dec. 12, 1932, Doucet.

146 Letter from LDB to NCB, Nov. 14, 1932, Doucet.

147 Letter from LDB to NCB, Feb. 10, no year given, Doucet.

148 Letter from LDB to NCB, Dec. 12, 1932, Doucet.

149 Letter from LDB to Lady Aberdeen, Dec. 14, 1932, LSEA.

150 Letter from LDB to NCB, Nov. 15, 1932, Doucet.

151 Letter from LDB to Lady Aberdeen, Dec. 14, 1932, LSEA.

152 Letter from LDB to Lady Aberdeen, Feb. 7, 1933, LSEA.

153 Letter from LDB to NCB, Jan. 23, 1933, Doucet.

154 Letter from LDB to NCB, Feb. 10, no year given, Doucet.

155 Letter from LDB to NCB, Dec. 12, 1932, Doucet.

156 Kling, *Alice Pike Barney*, p. 300.

157 Letter from LDB to NCB, Jan. 17, perhaps 1933, Doucet.

158 Kling, *Alice Pike Barney*, p. 299. This must have been in 1933 and not 1932, as recorded in Kling.

159 *Evening Star,* Jan. 20, 1933, Doucet.

160 Letter from LDB to NCB, Jan. 29, 1933, Doucet.

161 Letter from LDB to Lady Aberdeen, Feb. 7, 1933, LSEA.

162 Letter from Lady Aberdeen from Aberdeenshire to LDB, Nov. 3, 1932, LSEA.

163 Letter from LDB to May Maxwell, Nov. 11, 1932, BWC summarized letter sent to the author, May 16, 2012.

164 Letter from LDB to NCB, Jan. 17, perhaps 1933, Doucet.

165 Letter from LDB to May Maxwell, Feb. 17, 1933, BWC summarized letter sent to the author, May 16, 2012.

166 Letter from LDB to NCB, Feb. 17, 1933, Doucet.

167 Letter from LDB to May Maxwell, Oct. 23, 1933, BWC summarized letter sent to the author, May 16, 2012.

168 Letter from LDB to Horace Holley in NY, Nov. 6, 1933, USNBA.

169 Dreyfus-Barney, 'Peace through Intellectual Co-operation', in 'World Peace', a Supplement to the International Council of Women Bulletin, Oct. 1933, p. 5.

170 Holley, Horace, 'Survey of Current Bahá'í Activities in the East and West: Extension of Teaching Activities in Europe', *Bahá'í World*, vol. 6 (1934–1936), p. 45. The Local Spiritual Assembly of Paris was formed in 1928.

171 Giachery, 'Laura Clifford Dreyfus-Barney', *Bahá'í World*, vol. 16 (1973–1976), p. 537.

172 Internal letter from de Montenach to Mlle Colin [the sender and the recipient from the League of Nations], April 16, 1934, UNA.

173 Letter from LDB to NCB, Sunday 7, must be April 1934, Doucet.

174 ibid.

175 'Laura D. Barney, 94, Delegate to Geneva, Cuba Conferences', *Washington Post*, Aug. 22, 1974.

176 'Liaison Committee of Major International Associations: Cinematography', Report submitted by LDB to the International Congress of Educational Cinematography, May 17, 1934, LSEA.

177 ibid.

178 Letter from LDB to NCB, May 25, 1934, Doucet.

179 Letter from LDB to NCB, Sunday 7, must be April 1934, Doucet.

180 Letter from LDB to NCB, Feb. 28, 1935, Doucet.

181 Unattributed newspaper article by Jeanne Arcache, undated but must be 1935, Doucet, translated by Sheryl Mellor.

182 Letter from LDB to NCB, March 7, 1935, Doucet.

183 ibid.

184 LDB's words added to a letter from a family member in Dayton, Ohio to LDB, Feb. 27, 1935 that she forwarded to NCB, undated, Doucet.

185 Letter from LDB to NCB, March 14, 1935, Doucet.

186 Letter from LDB to NCB, March 7, 1935, Doucet.

187 Z.G., 'Lectures in Cairo: International Co-operation or World Chaos', *Egypt Mail*, March 10, 1935, Doucet.

188 'Poetry and the Influence Wielded by the Radio', *Egyptian Mail,* perhaps March 10, 1935, Doucet.

189 Letter from LDB to NCB, March 26, 1935, Doucet.

190 Letter from a family member in Dayton, Ohio to LDB, Feb. 27, 1935, LDB wrote a few lines on it and forwarded it to NCB, Doucet.

191 Invitation enclosed with a letter from LDB to NCB, April 2, 1935, Doucet.

192 Safar, 'La Coopération Intellectuelle: La Conférence de Mme Dreyfus-Barney', ['The Conference of Mme Dreyfus-Barney'], *L'Orient,* Beirut, in French, April 6, 1935, Doucet, translated by Sheryl Mellor.

193 ibid.

194 ibid.

195 ibid.

196 ibid.

197 ibid.

198 'La Conférence de Mme Dreyfus-Barney au Comité de Coopération Intellectuelle' ['The Conference of Mme Dreyfus-Barney of the Committee of Intellectual Cooperation'], *La Syrie,* in French, April 5, 1935, Doucet.

199 ibid.

200 Letter from LDB to NCB, April 2, 1935, Doucet.

201 L.K., 'Le féminisme au service de la paix: L'activité du Comité de désarmement des organisations internationales féminines' ['Feminism for Peace: The Work of the Disarmament Committee of Women's International Organisations'], *La Liberté*, April 6, 1935, Doucet, translated by Sheryl Mellor.

202 ibid.

203 ibid.

204 ibid.

205 ibid.

206 ibid.

207 Letter from LDB to NCB, April 10, 1935, Doucet.

208 Letter from LDB to Alice Dudley, March 1, 1967, USNBA.

209 'Laura's Noble Deeds Enrich World', *Journal Herald,* Dayton, Ohio, Dec. 28, 1965, DMLA.

210 Letter from LDB to NCB, June 16, 1935, Doucet; and a letter from Montenach of the Secretariat of the Intellectual Cooperation Organization in Geneva to LDB, May 8, 1935, UNA.

211 Letter from LDB to May Maxwell, April 8, 1936, and letter from May Maxwell to LDB, July 27, 1937, BWC summarized letter sent to the author, May 16, 2012.

212 Letter from LDB to May Maxwell, Sept. 17, 1933, BWC summarized letter sent to the author, May 16, 2012.

213 Letter from May Maxwell to LDB, March 27, 1934, BWC summarized letter sent to the author, May 16, 2012.

214 ibid.

215 Letter from LDB to May Maxwell, Dec. 20, 1935, BWC summarized letter sent to the author, May 16, 2012.

216 Holley, Horace, 'Survey of Current Bahá'í Activities in the East and West: Extension of Teaching Activities in Europe', *Bahá'í World,* vol. 6 (1934–1936), p. 36.

217 Letter from May Maxwell to LDB, July 27, 1937, BWC summarized letter sent to the author, May 16, 2012.

218 Letter from LDB to May Maxwell, Sept. 16, 1937, BWC summarized letter sent to the author, May 16, 2012.

219 Postcard with a print of 'Sainte Geneviève veille sur Paris endormi' by the artist Puvis de Chavannes on the reverse from May Maxwell to LDB, Dec. 14, 1934, BWC summarized letter sent to the author, May 16, 2012.

220 Letter from LDB to Rúḥíyyih Rabbani, Jan. 1958, ABDF.

221 Letter from LDB to NCB, perhaps 1935, Doucet.

222 Letter from LDB (maybe from Paris) to W. Huntington in WDC, Sept. 5, 1935, Doucet.

223 Letter from the Chief of Office of Legion of Honor of Grand Chancellerie de la Légion d'Honneur to the author, Feb. 14, 2012, translated by Sheryl Mellor.

224 Letter from LDB to NCB, Feb. 4, 1937, Doucet.

225 Letter from the Chief of Office of Legion of Honor of Grand Chancellerie de la Légion d'Honneur to the author, Feb. 14, 2012.

226 'Madame Laura Dreyfus-Barney', Biographical Notes, SIA.

227 Internal Control Office letter from the 'Advisory Committee on League of Nations Teaching', July 9, 1937, UNA.

228 Report 'Société des Nations. Comité Consultatif pour l'Enseignement de la Sôciété des Nations', Paris, 2–3 Juillet 1937.

229 Enclosure, 'Summary Edinburgh Report' with the letter from LDB to the Colleagues, Sept. 27, 1938, USNBA. This was the 'International Council of Women, Edinburgh, July 1938, Peace and Arbitration Committee, Summary of the General Report of the Convener (Pt. 3 of the Agenda)'.

230 Letter from LDB to Colleagues of ICW, Sept. 27, 1938, USNBA.

231 Letter from LDB, the Convener to the Peace and Arbitration Committee of the ICW, to her colleagues, Sept. 27, 1938, USNBA.

232 'Summary of the General Report of the Convener', enclosure with the letter from LDB, the Convener to the Peace and Arbitration Committee of the ICW, to her colleagues, Sept. 27, 1938, USNBA.

233 ibid.

234 Letter from LDB, the Convener to the Peace and Arbitration Committee of the ICW, to her colleagues, Sept. 27, 1938, USNBA.

235 ibid.

236 Letter from LDB to her colleagues, Oct. 5, 1938, USNBA.

237 Letter from LDB to NCB, undated, perhaps 1938, Doucet.

238 Letter from LDB to Horace Holley, Dec.13, 1938, USNBA.

239 Letter from LDB to May Maxwell, Dec. 1, 1939, BWC summarized letter sent to the author, May 16, 2012.

240 Glass, *Americans in Paris*, p. 1.

241 ibid. p. 2.

242 Copy of LDB's reservation from Wagons-Lits/Cook, March 30, 1939, ABDF.

243 Letter from LDB to NCB, June 18, 1939, Doucet.

244 Letter from LDB to May Maxwell, Dec. 1, 1939, BWC summarized letter sent to the author, May 16, 2012.

245 Chalon, *Portrait of a Seductress*, p. 172.

246 Letter from LDB to Giselle Shaw in Argentina of ICW, July 24, 1940, NMWAA.

247 Letter from LDB to NCB, Jan. 30, 1965, ABDF.

248 Letter from LDB to Miss S. Karpeles, July 24, 1940, NMWAA.

249 Letter from Mary A. Dingman to LDB, June 21, year not given (must be 1940), NMWAA.

250 Letter from Mary A. Dingman to LDB, Aug. 10, 1940, NMWAA.

251 Letter from LDB to Miss Dorothy Arnold, Executive Secretary of ICW in Geneva, July 20, 1940, NMWAA.

252 Letter from LDB to Giselle Shaw in Argentina of ICW, July 25, 1940, NMWAA.

253 Letter from LDB to Kathleen Courtney in London, England, July 20, 1940, NMWAA.

254 Letter from LDB to Lady Nunburnholme, July 24, 1940, NMWAA.

255 Letter from LDB to Joséphine Schain, Chautauqua, NY, Aug. 3, 1940, NMWAA.

256 Letter from Dr Renée Girod to LDB, Aug. 24, 1940, NMWAA.

257 LDB, 'In a Library', Nov. 16, 1940, NMWAA.

258 Letter from LDB to Carrie Chapman Catt, Sept. 21, 1940, NMWAA.

259 Letter from Mary Dingman to LDB, Oct. 1, 1940, NMWAA.

260 Letter from Mary Dingman in NY to LDB, Feb. 14, NMWAA.

261 Letter from Dr Girod to LDB, Jan. 6, 1941, NMWAA.

262 Letter from Dorothy Arnold of ICW in Geneva to LDB, Jan. 16, 1941, NMWAA.

263 LDB, 'The ICW Archives', Report for the ICW, Feb. 3, 1959, LSEA.

264 ibid.

265 Letter from LDB to Dr Girod in Geneva, May 31, 1941, NMWAA.

266 ibid.

267 'Madame Laura Dreyfus-Barney', Biographical Notes, SIA.

268 ibid.

269 Letter from LDB to Katherine Courtney of ICW in England, Aug. 13, 1941, NMWAA.

270 'Institute on World Organization: A Balance Sheet on the First Great Experiment', at the American University, Sept. 2–13, 1941, USNBA.

271 ibid.

272 ibid.

273 'Dreyfus-Barney, Laura (Mme. L. Dreyfus-Barney)', *Who's Who in America*, vol. 1, p. 844.

274 Kling, *Alice Pike Barney*, p. 301.

275 'The Famous Barney Studio Home to be Open to Art Lovers', *Evening Star,* Jan. 20, 1933, Doucet.

276 Letter from LDB to Dorothy Heneker of Sussex, England, March 12, 1942, NMWAA.

277 Letter from LDB to Horace Holley, Oct. 25, 1943, USNBA.

278 'Dreyfus-Barney, Laura (Mme. L. Dreyfus-Barney)', *Who's Who in America*, vol. 1, p. 844.

279 'Barney House to Mark Its 40th Anniversary', Dec. 25, 1942; 'Barney House to Hold Anniversary Service', no date (as was the 43rd anniversary, this must be 1945); and 'Barney House to be Open to Visitors Tomorrow', no date (this was the 45th anniversary of the Barney House), BAWDC and 'Barney Neighborhood House', May 6, 1944, all from *Evening Star*, BAWDC.

280 Newspaper article about the Barney Neighborhood House, undated (must be 1940s), unattributed, BAWDC.

281 'Dancing Girls, Boys at Work Help Daughter of Founder Mark Barney House Birthday', *Washington Post*, Nov. 6, 1947, BAWDC.

282 Newspaper announcement about Barney Neighborhood House, must be 1940s, unattributed BAWDC.

283 Newspaper clipping, undated, Doucet.

284 ibid. The caption named Mrs Leona Crabb, a volunteer worker there for 48 years; Mrs M. Rudolph, member of the original board of directors, and Mrs Wilbur Carr, president of the present board.

285 Letter from LDB to May Maxwell, Dec. 1, 1939, BWC summarized letter sent to the author, May 16, 2012.

286 Letter from Rúḥíyyih Rabbani to LDB, Aug. 29, 1940, ABDF.

287 Letter from Rúḥíyyih Rabbani to LDB, April 26, 1941, USNBA.

288 Letter from R. Rabbani and Shoghi Effendi to LDB, Aug. 4, 1941, ABDF.

289 Letter from Rúḥíyyih Rabbani to LDB, April 18, 1941, ABDF.

290 Letter from R. Rabbani and Shoghi Effendi to LDB, Dec. 17, 1941, ABDF.

291 Letters from R. Rabbani and Shoghi Effendi to LDB, Aug. 4 and Dec. 17, 1941, ABDF.

292 Letter from LDB to Horace Holley in Illinois, March 27, 1941, USNBA.

293 Letter from R. Rabbani and Shoghi Effendi to LDB, Dec. 17, 1941, ABDF.

294 Letter from R. Rabbani and Shoghi Effendi to LDB, Jan. 21, 1944, ABDF.

295 Letter from LDB to Horace Holley, May 21, 1944, USNBA.

296 Giachery, 'Laura Clifford Dreyfus-Barney', *Bahá'í World*, vol. 16 (1973–1976), pp. 535, 537.

297 LDB in Gail, 'Impressions of the Centenary', *Bahá'í News*, no. 170 (Sept. 1944), p. 13. https://bahai.works/Baha%27i_News/Issue_170 (accessed Aug. 2020).

298 Letter from R. Rabbani and Shoghi Rabbani to LDB, Nov. day not clear, 1944, ABDF.

299 ibid.

300 Letter from Rúḥíyyih Rabbani and Shoghi Effendi to LDB, March 10, 1946, ABDF.

301 Telegram from Rúḥíyyih Rabbani from Basel to LDB, perhaps Oct. 29, 1946, ABDF.

302 The archives of the National Spiritual Assembly of France (ABDF) were lost between 1940 and 1946, according to Parivash Ardei, Archivist of ABDF, 2010. The liberation of Paris took place in August 1944.

303 Letter from LDB to Dr Barafroukhteh, Sept. 7, must be 1960, ABDF. Years later she changed her name to Miss Fabrizi. She later helped with the arrangements for the commemoration in London in 1963 of the centenary of the declaration of Bahá'u'lláh.

304 Letter from LDB to Dr Barafroukhteh, Sept. 7, must be 1960, ABDF.

305 Letter from LDB to Horace Holly in Illinois, US, July 28, 1942, USNBA.

306 Letter from LDB to Mr Kennedy, Feb. 25, 1947, ABDF.

307 'Other Friends in France Who Need Support', a list prepared by LDB, Oct. 3, 1946, BAWDC.

308 Letter from LDB to Mr Kennedy, Chairman of the Local Spiritual Assembly of Paris, Feb. 25, must be 1947, ABDF.

309 Letter from LDB to Mr Kennedy Chairman of the NSA of France, 'New Year of old Calendar 1947', ABDF.

310 Unattributed newspapers clipping, 'Margaret Truman Theater Guest: "West of the Moon" Authors Honored at Supper Party after Premiere', not dated, but must be March 26, 1946 since the opening of that play was on March 25, 1946 and the article appeared the day after the opening, BAWDC.

311 Giachery, 'Laura Clifford Dreyfus-Barney', *La Pensée Bahá'íe*, no. 56 (June 1976), p. 24.

312 Author's interviews with Anita Ioas-Chapman.

313 Author's interviews with Anita Ioas-Chapman; and Giachery, 'Laura Clifford Dreyfus-Barney', *La Pensée Bahá'íe*, no. 56 (June 1976), p. 24.

314 Afroukhteh, *Memories*, letter from LDB, p. 344.

315 Samandari-Khoshbin, *Taráz-i- Iláhí,* p. 241. reference.bahai.org/fa (accessed Jan. 2020).

316 Author's phone interview with Amin Banani, Oct. 23, 2010.

317 Email exchange by the author with Günter Maltz, Oct. 14, 2011.

318 Email from the author to the US Holocaust Memorial Museum, Feb. 10, 2010 and the response of Feb. 16, 2010; Email from the author to the Embassy of Germany in Washington, D.C., Oct. 10, 2009.

319 Items listed under Laura Clifford Barney's name in Ardellia Hall Collection, Munich Archives, www.fold3.com (accessed Feb. 2017).

320 Letter from LDB to NCB, March 20, 1947, Doucet.

321 United Nations. https://www.un.org/en/about-us/history-of-the-un/1941-1950 (accessed May 2020).

322 Letter from LDB to Mr Kennedy, Chairman of the Local Spiritual Assembly, Feb. 25, must be 1947, ABDF.

323 Letter from LDB to Edna [True], Dec. 18, 1947, USNBA.

324 Letter from LDB to Edna True, March 13, 1949, USNBA.

325 Letter from LDB to Edna True, Feb. 26, 1947, USNBA.

326 Letter from LDB to Edna [True], Feb. 5, 1948, USNBA.

327 Letter from LDB to Edna [True], Feb. 27, must be 1948, USNBA.

328 Braun, 'From Strength to Strength', *Bahá'í World*, vol. 16 (1973 –1976), p. 81.

329 Letter from Chairman of the ETC [Edna True] to LDB, Aug. 2, 1948, USNBA.

330 Letter from Edna True (chairman) to LDB, Sept. 10, 1948, USNBA.

331 Letter from ETC to LDB, Sept. 10, 1948, USNBA.

332 Letter from Edna True of ETC, Illinois, USA to LDB, Aug. 2, 1948, ABDF.

333 Letter from Rúḥíyyih Rabbani and Shoghi Effendi to LDB, Nov. 30, 1948, ABDF.

334 Letter from Rúḥíyyih Rabbani and Shoghi Effendi to LDB, Dec. 29, 1948, ABDF.

335 Letter from Ugo Giachery to LDB, Sept. 26, 1948, ABDF.

336 Hands of the Cause were individuals appointed for life to protect and propagate the Bahá'í Faith.

337 Letter from Chairman of the ETC [Edna True] to LDB, Sept. 27, 1949, USNBA.

338 Letter from Rúḥíyyih Rabbani and Shoghi Effendi to LDB, Oct. 31, 1949, ABDF.

339 The Bahá'ís of Canada elected their first National Spiritual Assembly in 1948.

340 Author's interview with Hassan-Ali Kamran (who lived in Paris in the late 1940s), June 28, 2009 in Geneva, in Persian, translated by the author.

341 Author's phone interview with Amin Banani, Oct. 23, 2010.

342 Letter from LDB to NCB, Sept. 8, 1945, Doucet.

343 Letter from LDB to NCB, May 12, 1946, Doucet.

344 Letter from Rúḥíyyih Rabbani and Shoghi Effendi to LDB, Sept. 6, 1946, ABDF.

345 Chalon, *Portrait of a Seductress*, p. 178; and Rodriguez, *Wild Heart*, p. 329.

346 Letter from LDB to NCB, March 20, 1947, Doucet.

347 Letter from LDB to NCB, Aug. 2, 1948, Doucet.

348 Letter from LDB to NCB, Oct. 4, 1948, Doucet.

349 Letter from LDB to NCB, Oct. 31, 1949, Doucet.

350 Aerogram from LDB to NCB, Feb. 22, 1950, Doucet.

351 Excerpt from the Will of James Smithson, in 'James Smithson, Founding Donor', SIA.

352 Letter from LDB to Dr Alexander Westmore, Secretary of SI, Jan. 1, perhaps 1951, SIA. He was the Secretary from 1944 to 1952.

353 ibid.

354 Smithsonian Institution, 'Annual Report' for the years 1951, p. 7 and and 1953, p. 44. https://siris-sihistory.si.edu (accessed May 2021); Taylor, *National Collection of Fine Arts*, p. 32.

355 ibid.

356 Letter from LDB to NCB, Feb. 3, 1962, Doucet.

357 ibid.

358 Letter from the Ambassador of France, Henri Bonnet in Washington, D.C. to LDB, June 2, 1951, SIA.

359 'Dreyfus-Barney, Laura (Mme. L. Dreyfus-Barney)', *Who's Who in America*, vol. 1, p. 844.

360 Letter from LDB to NCB, July 23, 1948, Doucet.

361 Letter from LDB to Edna True, Nov. 14, 1947, USNBA.

362 Letter from LDB to Edna True, Chairman of ETC, IL, USA, Aug. 20, 1948, USNBA.

363 Author's phone interview with Amin Banani, Oct. 21, 2010.

364 Written report by Shapour Rassekh, Geneva 2011, in Persian, translated by the author. He was in Geneva from 1951 to 1958.

365 Draft of a press release, Sept. 1952, ABDF.

366 Letter from LDB to Edna True, Nov. 14, 1947, USNBA.

367 Letter from LDB to NCB, June 20, 1952, Doucet.

368 ibid.

369 Letter from LDB to NCB, March 28, 1953, Doucet.

370 Letter from LDB to NCB, March 23, 1953, Doucet.

371 Letter from Lucienne Migette to LDB, 1952, ABDF.

372 Letter from LDB to NCB, April 20, 1953, Doucet.

373 Letter from LDB to NCB, April 9, 1953, Doucet; and a letter from LDB to NCB, April 4, 1955, Romaine Brooks Papers. https://www.aaa.si.edu/collections/romaine-brooks-papers-6290 (accessed Nov. 2016).

374 Letter from James Perrine Barney, Deputy Administrator, State of N.J. Veterans Loan Authority in N.J. to LDB, July 19, 1949, Doucet.

375 Letter from LDB to NCB, April 9, 1953, Doucet.

376 Letter from LDB to NCB, April 28, 1953, Doucet.

377 Holley, Horace, 'Survey of Current Bahá'í Activities in the East and West: Extension of Teaching Activities in Europe', *Bahá'í World*, vol. 6 (1934–1936), p. 45.

378 Letter from LDB to NCB, March 14, 1954, Doucet.

379 Letter from LDB to Mr Kennedy in Paris, Feb. 25, 1947, ABDF. Mr Kennedy passed away in 1950.

380 Letter from President of the American Aid Society of Paris to LDB, May 9, 1951, ABDF.

381 Letter from President of the American Aid Society of Paris, Mrs B.S. Carter to LDB, Feb. 1, 1955, ABDF.

382 ibid.

383 Letter from the ETC to LDB, Dec. 10, 1955, ABDF; and letter from Jean Sevin (a Bahá'í, perhaps LSA member, and later a Knight of Bahá'u'lláh) to LDB, June 5, 1951, ABDF.

384 Letter from the American Hospital of Paris to LDB, Jan. 6, 1956, ABDF.

385 Barney, 'Joséphine Scott', *Bahá'í World*, vol. 13 (1954–1963), pp. 899–900.

386 'Mr Edwin Scott', *Bahá'í World*, vol. 5 (1932–1934), pp. 418–19.

387 ibid.; Hall, Delight, *Catalogue of the Alice Pike Barney Memorial Lending Collection*, Smithsonian Publication, 1965, p. 148.

388 'Mr Edwin Scott', *Bahá'í World*, vol. 5 (1932–1934), pp. 418–19.

389 Barney, 'Joséphine Scott', *Bahá'í World*, vol. 13 (1954–1963, p. 900.

390 Letter from LDB to Mr & Mrs Selzer of Paris, June 12, 1970, ABDF.

391 Letter from Leroy Ioas in Haifa to LDB, Sept. 12, 1954, ABDF. Leroy Ioas was born in Illinois in 1896 and died 1965. He was appointed a Hand of the Cause in 1951 and moved to Haifa in 1952; see Hofman, 'Leroy C. Ioas', *Bahá'í World*, vol. 14 (1963–1968), pp. 291–300; Letter from R. Rabbani to LDB, Jan. 8, 1954, ABDF. Rúḥíyyih K͟hánum became a Hand of the Cause in 1952.

392 Letter from R. Rabbani to LDB, June 20, 1954, ABDF.

393 Letter from Mariam Haney (mother of Paul Haney) to LDB, Aug. 4, 1953, ABDF.

394 Giachery, 'Laura Clifford Dreyfus-Barney', *La Pensée Bahá'íe*, no. 56 (June 1976), p. 27.

395 Letter from ETC (Edna True) to LDB, April 3, 1955, ABDF.

396 Letter from R. Rabbani and Shoghi Effendi to LDB, Feb. 25,1955, ABDF.

397 Letter from LDB to NCB, April 4, 1955, Romaine Brooks Papers. https://www.aaa.si.edu/collections/romaine-brooks-papers-6290 (accessed Nov. 2016).

398 Letter from Jean Sevin to LDB, June 5, 1951, ABDF.

399 Giachery, 'Laura Clifford Dreyfus-Barney', *La Pensée Bahá'íe*, no. 56 (June 1976), p. 30.

400 Giachery, 'Laura Clifford Dreyfus-Barney', *Bahá'í World*, vol. 16 (1973 –1976), p. 538.

401 Letter for LDB to Mrs M. Pleydell-Bouverins, Oct. 26, 1955, ABDF; and letter from the Bahá'í European Teaching Committee to LDB, Dec. 10, 1955, ABDF. This letter is from Honor Kempton, who said she had seen LDB in Rome where she gave a talk at the Bahá'í Center.

402 Barney, 'Edith Sanderson', *Bahá'í World*, vol. 13 (1954–1963), pp. 889–90.

403 Letter from Giachery to LDB, Oct. 26, 1955, ABDF.

404 Letter from LDB to Lucienne Migette, Feb. 2, 1956, ABDF.

405 Letter from LDB to Edna True in Wilmette, Illinois, USA, March 3, 1958, USNBA.

406 Barney, 'Edith Sanderson', *Bahá'í World*, vol. 13 (1954–1963), pp. 889–90.

407 Letter from Juliet Thompson to LDB, Feb. 3, no year given, ABDF.

408 Letter from NSA of the USA (Horace Holley) to LDB, Jan. 28, 1957, ABDF.

409 Letter from Mariam Haney to LDB, March 31, 1958, ABDF.

410 Letter from LDB to Horace Holley, Jan. 31, 1957, ABDF.

411 'Juliet Thompson', *Bahá'í World*, vol. 13 (1954–1963), p. 863.

412 Letter from Mariam Haney to LDB, Dec. 28, 1953, ABDF.

413 Letter from Mariam Haney to LDB, May 9, 1955, ABDF.

414 Letter from Mariam Haney to LDB, Feb. 8, 1957, ABDF.

415 Letter from Mariam Haney to LDB, March 31, 1958, ABDF.

416 Letter from Mariam Haney to LDB, Feb. 14, 1957, ABDF.

417 Letter from Mariam Haney to LDB, July 2, 1959, ABDF.

418 ibid.

419 Mu'ayyad, *Kháṭirát-i-Ḥabíb*, vol. 1, p. 60.

420 Letter from Badí' Bushrú'í in Alexandria to LDB, Dec. 4, 1953, ABDF.

421 LDB's correspondence with Romaine Brooks from 1956 to 1960 is available at AAAMSI. They may have corresponded before and after those dates. https://www.aaa.si.edu/collections/romaine-brooks-papers-6290 (accessed Nov. 2016).

422 Letters from LDB to Romaine Brooks, Romaine Brooks Papers. https://www.aaa.si.edu/collections/romaine-brooks-papers-6290 (accessed Nov. 2016).

423 Letter from LDB to NCB, June 20, 1952, Doucet.

424 Letter from LDB to NCB, April 9, 1953, Doucet.

425 Letter from LDB to NCB, April 28, 1953, Doucet.

426 Letter from LDB to NCB, Feb. 15, 1953, Doucet.

427 Letter from LDB to NCB, Feb. 17, 1957; Romaine Brooks Papers. https://www.aaa.si.edu/collections/romaine-brooks-papers-6290 (accessed Nov. 2016).

428 Letter from the NSA of the British Isles (Marion Hofman) to LDB, Nov. 15. 1957, ABDF.

429 Letter from LDB to Rúḥíyyih Rabbani in Haifa, Jan. 1948, ABDF.

430 Telegram from Shoghi Effendi, care of Bahá'ís Wilmette IL to LDB, March 20, 1955, ABDF.

431 Letter from the NSA of the USA (Horace Holley) to LDB, March 24, 1955, ABDF.

432 Letter from LDB to Rúḥíyyih Rabbani in Haifa, Jan. 1948, ABDF.

433 Letter from R. Rabbani and Shoghi Effendi to LDB, April 7, 1953, ABDF.

434 Letter from LDB to NCB, March 23, 1953, Doucet.

435 Letter from LDB to NCB, April 9, 1955, Doucet.

436 Letter from LDB to Romaine Brooks, Mar. 17, 1960, Romaine Brooks Papers. https://www.aaa.si.edu/collections/romaine-brooks-papers-6290 (accessed Nov. 2016).

437 Letter from LDB to Dr Paul Martin in Lausanne, Switzerland, Nov. 30, 1965, Doucet.

438 Letter from LDB to Romaine Brooks, May 15, 1956, Romaine Brooks Papers. https://www.aaa.si.edu/collections/romaine-brooks-papers-6290 (accessed Nov. 2016).

439 Letter from LDB to Romaine Brooks, Oct. 7, 1957, Romaine Brooks Papers. https://www.aaa.si.edu/collections/romaine-brooks-papers-6290 (accessed Nov. 2016).

440 Letter from LDB to a Baháʼí, Jan. 10, 1958, ABDF; and letter from Edna True, Chairman to LDB, March 13, 1958, USNBA.

441 Letter from LDB to Romaine Brooks, July 31, 1958, Romaine Brooks Papers. https://www.aaa.si.edu/collections/romaine-brooks-papers-6290 (accessed Nov. 2016).

442 Letter from John S. Alcehasy (illegible) at the headquarters of the US European Command from France to LDB, Aug. 15, 1960, ABDF.

443 Letter from Alice Dudley to LDB, Feb. 4, 1969, ABDF.

444 Author's interview with Farhang Javid, Phoenix, AZ, Dec. 2014.

445 Farrukh Ioas helped with the preparations for the convention that elected the first NSA of France.

446 Author's interview with Farhang Javid, Phoenix, AZ, Dec. 2014.

447 ibid.

448 Letter from Kathleen and Farhang Javid to LDB, Jan. 8, 1958, ABDF.

449 Letter from Donald Harvey member of the NSA of France to LDB, June 1958, ABDF.

450 Letter from John S. Mc Henry (from France) to LDB, April 30, 1959, ABDF.

451 Letter from LDB to Agnes Alexander, Jan. 16, 1958, ABDF; Alexander, 'Account of How I Became a Baháʼí'. https://bahai-library.com/alexander_linard_autobiography (accessed Nov. 2015).

452 Letter from Lucienne Migette to LDB, Nov. 18, 1954, ABDF.

453 Letter from LDB to Solange Lemaitre, Feb. 18, 1954, ABDF.

454 Garis, *Martha Root*, p. 408.

455 Letter from Donald Harvey (the NSA of France) to LDB, Nov. 1959, ABDF.

456 LCB, *ʻAbduʼl-Bahá: Some Answered Questions,* p. xvii, n5: From a letter written on behalf of Shoghi Effendi to an individual, Nov. 14, 1940.

457 From a letter written on behalf of Shoghi Effendi to the United States Publishing Committee, Dec. 29, 1931, quoted in a letter from the Universal House of Justice to the author, Aug. 5, 2018.

458 Shoghi Effendi, *Light of Divine Guidance*, vol. 1, p. 160.

459 ibid. p. 168.

460 Shoghi Effendi, *Unfolding Destiny*, p. 383.

461 Shoghi Effendi, *High Endeavours: Messages to Alaska*, p. 72.

462 Braun, 'Farrukh Ioas', *Baháʼí World*, vol. 13 (1954–1963), pp. 919–20. Farrukh went to Paris at the request of the ETC in 1956 and served on the LSA of Paris.

463 Letter from Farrukh Ioas in Paris to LDB, Jan. 22, 1956, ABDF.

464 Letter from the Secretary of the NSA of the USA to LDB, May 11, 1953, ABDF.

465 Letter from the Secretary of the NSA of the USA to LDB, May 20, 1953, ABDF.

466 Letter from the Secretary of the NSA of the USA to LDB, June 8, 1953, ABDF.

467 Letter from LDB to Horace Holley in Wilmette, Jan. 7, 1958, ABDF.

468 ibid.

469 Letter from LDB to Horace Holley in Wilmette, March 31, 1958, ABDF.

470 ibid.

471 Letter from LDB to Horace Holley, Jan. 21, 1959, ABDF.

472 ibid.

473 The NSA of the USA to LDB, April 9, 1958, referred to a letter of Jan. 21, 1959 from LDB to the Horace Holley, ABDF.

474 Letter from the NSA of USA (Horace Holley, Sec.) to LDB, March 18, 1959, ABDF.

475 Letter from the NSA of USA (Charles Wolcott, Sec.) to LDB, Aug. 3, 1960, ABDF.

476 Letter from Annamarie Honnold in the US to LDB, Aug. 10, 1960, ABDF.

477 Letter from the NSA of USA (Charles Wolcott, Sec.) to LDB, Aug. 3, 1960, ABDF.

478 Letter from Annamarie Honnold in the USA to LDB, Aug. 10, 1960, ABDF.

479 Letter from LDB to Mrs John O. Honnold (Annamarie Honnold) in PA, USA, Sept. 23, 1960, ABDF.

480 Letter from the NSA of the USA (Charles Wolcott, Sec.) to LDB, Jan. 19, 1961, ABDF.

481 Letter from LDB to Dr A. M. Barafroukhteh, in Nice, Sept. 25, 1960, ABDF.

482 Letter from LDB to Chahab Ala'i, Dec. 21, 1966, ABDF. Ala'i was a member of the NSA of France in 1962, and 1967–70.

483 *Ministry of the Custodians*, pp. 6–11.

484 Letter from the Hands of the Cause (Residing in the Holy Land) to LDB, Nov. 20, 1959, ABDF.

485 Letter from the NSA of Germany to LDB, March 23, 1960, ABDF.

486 Letter from Agnes Alexander in Japan to LDB, June 25, 1960, ABDF.

487 'Abdu'l-Bahá, *Le lezioni di San Giovanni d'Acri*.

488 Letter from Ugo Giachery (Secretary of the Italian Translating and Publishing Co. of the Italo-Swiss National Assembly) to LDB, Dec. 6, 1960, ABDF.

489 Letter from Angeline Giachery to LDB, day and month illegible, 1962, ABDF.

490 Letter from LDB to Ugo Giachery, July 12, 1962, ABDF.

491 Letter from Hands of the Cause Residing in the Holy Land to LDB, July 19, 1962, ABDF.

492 Letter from Professor Raphael Lemkin in NY to LDB, April 20, 1959, ABDF.

493 ibid.

494 Marie-Hélène Lefaucheux (1904–64) was a French activist in the areas of women and human rights. She was President of the National Council of French Women from 1954 to 1964 and elected president of the ICW from 1959 to 1963.

495 Letter from Professor Raphael Lemkin to LDB, April 20, 1959, ABDF.

496 LDB, ICW, Report on 'The I.C.W. Archives' (A Resume of the Activity 1946–1958), Feb. 3, 1959, LSEA.

497 ibid.

498 ibid.

499 Letter from LDB to Mrs Rienitz, Dec. 5, 1964, LSEA.

500 The Universal House of Justice, 'Mason Remey and Those Who Followed Him', enclosure in a letter from the Universal House of Justice to National Spiritual Assemblies, Jan. 31, 1997. http://bahai-library.com/uhj_mason_remey_followers (accessed Feb. 2018); and revised statement 2008. https://bahai-library.com/pdf/uhj/uhj_mason_remey_followers.pdf (accessed May 2021).

501 *Ministry of the Custodians*, pp. 197, 203–5; Letter from the Hands of the Faith in the Western Hemisphere (Corinne True, Hermann Grossmann, William Sears)

to All National Assemblies in the Western Hemisphere, and to all Members of the Auxiliary Board, May 31, 1960. https://bahai-library.com/true_grossman_sears_remey (accessed Feb. 2018).

502 From a letter written on behalf of the Universal of House to an individual, 3 January 1982.

503 'Abdu'l-Bahá, *Selections*, pp. 215–16.

504 Momen, 'Covenant and Covenant-breaker'. http://bahai-library.com/momen_encyclopedia_covenant (accessed Feb. 2018).

505 Remey served his new religion faithfully for decades in many capacities. He designed the Houses of Worship built in Kampala, Uganda and Sydney, Australia, and the International Archives Building at the Bahá'í World Centre in Haifa. In 1951 Shoghi Effendi appointed Remey a Hand of the Cause of God, the highest level of distinction that could be conferred upon a Bahá'í.

506 Letter from Hands of the Cause Residing in the Holy Land to LDB, Nov. 30, 1960, ABDF.

507 Letter from Agnes Alexander in Japan to LDB, Jan. 25, 1960, ABDF.

508 Letter from Hands of the Cause Residing in the Holy Land to LDB, Nov. 30, 1960, ABDF.

509 ibid. July 19, 1961, ABDF.

510 Letter from the NSA of the USA to LDB, Sept. 22, 1961, ABDF.

511 Letter from the NSA of USA (Charles Wolcott, Sec.) to LDB, July 5, 1960, ABDF.

512 Letter from LDB to Mr & Mrs Giachery, July 12, 1962, ABDF.

513 Letter from LDB to NCB, April 23, 1937, Doucet.

514 Letter from LDB to NCB, March 8, 1937, Doucet.

515 Letter from LDB to NCB, March 25, 1955, Doucet.

516 Rodriguez, *Wild Heart*, p. 356.

517 Kling, *Alice Pike Barney*, p. 302.

518 ibid.

519 Letter from LDB to NCB, Oct. 15, 1961, Doucet.

520 Letter from LDB to Leonard Carmichael, Secretary of SI, Nov. 10, 1960, SIA.

521 Letter from LDB to NCB, Oct. 20, 1961, Doucet.

522 'Mrs Barney Honored', *Museum News*, perhaps 1964, p. 4, SIA.

523 'Famous District Mansion is Given to Smithsonian', *Evening Star*, Dec. 19, 1961, APB, SIA.

524 ibid.

525 Author's interviews with Anita Ioas-Chapman.

526 Letter from the LSA of Paris to LDB, Dec. 4, 1951, ABDF.

527 Letter from LDB to Président du Comité de Redaction de l'Encyclopédie de l'Islam (the Translation Committee of the Encyclopedia of Islam), Feb. 3, 1954, ABDF.

528 Letter from the LSA of Paris to LDB, 1954, ABDF.

529 Letter from NSA of France to LDB, March 5, 1963, ABDF.

530 Letter from J. Chasse, the Librarian, Ministère de l'Éducation Nationale to LDB, April 11, 1962, ABDF.

531 Letter from the Director of the School Organization (l'Organisation Scolaire) of the Ministère de l'Éducation Nationale to LDB, April 12, 1962, ABDF.

532 Letter from LDB to A.M. Barafroukhteh in Nice, France, Sept. 25, 1960, ABDF.
533 Letter from LDB to NCB, March 8, 1955, Doucet.
534 Letter from LDB to Romaine Brooks, Mar. 7, 1960, Box. 1, Folder 6, Romaine Brooks Papers. https://www.aaa.si.edu/collections/romaine-brooks-papers-6290 (accessed Nov. 2016).
535 ibid.
536 Letter from LDB to NCB, July 29, 1960, Doucet.
537 ibid.
538 Letter from LDB to NCB, Dec. 8, 1961, Doucet.
539 Letter from LDB to NCB, May 12, 1962, Doucet.
540 Letter from LDB to NCB, Aug. 8, 1963, Doucet.
541 Letter from LDB to NCB, Sept. 13, 1963, Doucet.
542 ibid.
543 Letter from LDB to NCB, Feb. 3, 1962, Doucet.
544 Letter from LDB to NCB, Oct. 22, 1961, Doucet.
545 Letter from LDB to NCB, Oct. 31, 1961, Doucet.
546 Letter from LDB to NCB, Oct. 15, 1961, Doucet.
547 Letter from LDB to NCB, Oct. 31, 1961, Doucet.
548 Letters from LDB to NCB, April 28, 1953, March 14, 1954 and Oct. 31, 1961, Doucet.
549 Letter from LDB to NCB, must be 1964, Doucet.
550 Letter from LDB to NCB, Oct. 22, 1961, Doucet.
551 Letter from LDB to NCB, must be 1964, Doucet.
552 ibid.
553 'Mrs Barney Honored', *Museum News*, perhaps 1964, p. 4, SIA.
554 Letter from LDB to NCB, must be 1964. Doucet.
555 ibid.

Part 5 The Last Years of Her Life in Paris 1965 – 1974

1 Letter from LDB to NCB, May 7, 1935, Doucet.
2 'Laura's Noble Deeds Enrich World', *Journal Herald*, Dayton, Ohio, Dec. 28, 1965, DMLA.
3 Letter from Mildred Mottahedeh to LDB, March 26, 1963, USNBA.
4 Letter from LDB to Dr Paul Martin, Nov. 30, 1965, Doucet.
5 Letter from LDB to Dr Paul Martin, typed in English, Dec. 18, 1965, Doucet.
6 Letter from LDB to NCB, June 25, 1968, Doucet.
7 Letter from LDB to NCB, June 16, 1963, Doucet.
8 'Laura's Noble Deeds Enrich World', *Journal Herald*, Dayton, Ohio, Dec. 28, 1965, DMLA.
9 ibid.
10 Email from Mahnaz Afkhami, a member of ICW at that time, Sept. 23, 2017.
11 Letter from the Universal House of Justice to LDB, Aug. 12, 1965, ABDF.
12 ibid.
13 Letter from LDB to (Bahá'í friends), March 24, 1966, ABDF.
14 Letter from LDB to Marzieh Gail, June 30, 1967, ABDF.
15 Letter from LDB to Rúḥíyyih Khánum [Rabbani], Nov. 20, 1966, ABDF.
16 Letter from Lady Aberdeen to LDB, Nov. 13, 1930, LSEA.

17 Letter from LDB to Lady Aberdeen, Feb. 12, 1931, LSEA.

18 Letter from Mehri Alai-Ramzi in Iran to LDB, Dec.12, 1959, ABDF.

19 Letter from LDB to Guy Murchie, June 30, 1967, ABDF.

20 International Council of Women. *Women in a Changing World.*

21 Letter from LDB to James Bradley, Under Secretary of SI, WDC, March 14, 1972, SIA.

22 Wedding invitation of Ellen Miller Goin, Ellen Goin-Rionda papers, USNBA.

23 Letter from LDB to Ellen Goin-Rionda, Nov. 25, 1960, SIA.

24 Letter from the Secretary of the NSA of the USA to Ellen Goin-Rionda, Oct. 15, 1952, USNBA.

25 Letters from the Secretary of the NSA of the USA to Ellen Rionda, Dec. 30, 1954; Dec. 20, 1955, Jan 2, 1958; and Jan. 16, 1958, USNBA.

26 Letter from LDB to NCB, Nov. 18, 1949, Doucet.

27 Letter from LDB to NCB, Dec. 20, 1949, Doucet.

28 Letter from the Secretary (perhaps NSA of the USA, must be Horace Holley) to Ellen Rionda in NJ, April 4, 1952, USNBA.

29 *Bahá'í News US Supplement*, no. 98, April 1966, p. 8.

30 Blomberg, Report of the World Fellowship of Religions, Second Regional Conference, Tehran, Iran, June 10–16, 1967, ABDF.

31 Letter from LDB to Anita Chapman, June 26, 1968, ABDF.

32 Sant Kirpal Singh: His Life and Mission. sant-kirpal-singh.org (accessed May 2021).

33 Letter from Baroness von Blomberg in Paris to LDB, June 23, 1967, ABDF.

34 Letter from LDB to Anita Chapman in Paris, June 26,1967, ABDF.

35 Letter from Baroness von Blomberg in Paris to LDB, June 26, 1967, ABDF.

36 Letter from LDB to Baroness von Blomberg, June 28, 1967, ABDF.

37 Letters from Anne Lynch to LDB, 1946, ABDF.

38 Letters from Anne Lynch to LDB, May, Aug. & Sept. 1946, ABDF.

39 ibid.

40 Letter from LDB from WDC to Edna [True], Oct. 28, must be 1947, USNBA.

41 Letter from Anne Lynch to LDB, July 6, 1947, ABDF.

42 Letter from the NSA of the USA (Leroy Ioas) to LDB, March 30, 1950, ABDF.

43 Letter from Anne Lynch to LDB, Jan. 10, 1958, ABDF.

44 Letter from Anne Lynch to LDB, Aug. 30, 1959, ABDF.

45 Letter from the NSA of the USA to LDB, Jan. 12, 1966, ABDF.

46 Letter from NSA of the USA (David Ruhe, Sec.) to LDB, Feb. 16, 1966, ABDF.

47 Letter from LDB to Haenni de Bons, Nov. 6, 1966, ABDF.

48 Letter from Haenni de Bons to LDB, Oct. 29, 1966, ABDF.

49 Letter from Lucienne Migette to LDB, Oct. 18, 1950, ABDF, translated by Sheryl Mellor.

50 Letter from Lucienne Migette to LDB, Feb. 20, 1952, ABDF.

51 Letter from Lucienne Migette to LDB, Jan. 4, 1952, ABDF.

52 Letter from the NSA of the USA (Treasurer) to LDB, Dec. 21, 1966; and letter from LDB to Lucienne Migette, Oct. 29, 1967, ABDF.

53 Letter from LDB to Lucienne Migette, Feb. 2, 1956; and a letter from LDB to Lucienne Migette, Oct. 19, 1957, ABDF.

54 Letter from Lucienne Migette to LDB, Dec. 4, 1957, ABDF. Migette was elected

to the NSA of France in 1958. In 1966, she became an Auxiliary Board Member.

55 Letter from LDB to Lucienne Migette, Feb. 28,1972, ABDF.

56 Letter from Lucienne Migette to LDB, March 30, 1972, ABDF.

57 Letter from Lucienne Migette to LDB, Aug. 1, 1972, ABDF.

58 Letter from Haenni de Bons to LDB, Dec. 16, 1969, ABDF.

59 Letter from LDB to Haenni de Bons, Nov. 1969, ABDF.

60 Letters from Mona Haenni de Bons to LDB, in 1966, 1968, 1969, 1970, ABDF; letters from the NSA of the USA to LDB, Jan. 8, Nov. 9 and 19, 1970, ABDF.

61 Letter from Mona Haenni de Bons to LDB, March 9, 1972, ABDF.

62 Letter from LDB to Mr & Mrs Selzer, June 27, 1968, USNBA.

63 Letter from LDB to Mr & Mrs Selzer, July 26, 1968, USNBA.

64 Letter from LDB to Mr & Mrs Selzer, Nov. 1, 1968, USNBA.

65 Letter from LDB to Mr & Mrs Selzer, May 19, 1969, ABDF.

66 Between May 1973 and March 1979, prior to the official establishment of diplomatic relations, the United States dispatched a head of the US Liaison Office to Beijing. David Bruce was the US Ambassador to France from 1949 to 1952, to the Republic of Germany from 1957 to 1959), to the United Kingdom from 1961 to 1969 and to the People's Republic of China from 1973 to 1974.

67 Rodriguez, *Wild Heart*, p. 334 and letter from LDB to NCB, Oct. 1, must be 1958, Doucet.

68 Letter from LDB to David Bruce, Jan. 11, 1969, SIA.

69 Letter from David Bruce in London on the stationery of the American Embassy to LDB, Jan. 12, 1969, SIA.

70 Letter from LDB to David Bruce in WDC, March 20, 1973, SIA.

71 Letter from LDB to NCB, Jan. 3, 1963, Doucet.

72 ibid.

73 Letter from LDB to NCB, Oct. 27, 1964, Doucet.

74 Letter from LDB to Dr David Scott, March 10, 1965, Doucet.

75 Letter from LDB to Dr David Scott of SI, Feb. 28, 1966, ABDF. Scott was also a collector and the decorative art curator at the Louvre Museum.

76 Letter from LDB to NCB, Jan. 26, 1965, Doucet.

77 Letter from Mr Scott of the National Collection of Fine Arts, SI to LDB, Aug. 12, 1966, Romaine Brooks Papers. https://www.aaa.si.edu/collections/romaine-brooks-papers-6290 (accessed Nov. 2016).

78 Langer, *Romaine Brooks*, p. 190.

79 Letter from LDB to Romaine Brooks, Aug. 17, 1966, Romaine Brooks Papers. https://www.aaa.si.edu/collections/romaine-brooks-papers-6290 (accessed Nov. 2016).

80 Breeskin, *Romaine Brooks*, p. 10. Charles C. Eldredge was the Director of the National Museum of American Art, SI from 1982 to 1988.

81 ibid. p. 13.

82 ibid. p. 10.

83 Oral history [transcript of an] interview with Adelyn Dohme Breeskin, Aug. 1 and Aug. 14, 1979, AAAMSI.

84 Langer, *Romaine Brooks*, p. 194.

85 'The Great Ladies of France Living Legends', *Journal Herald*, Dayton, Ohio, Dec. 27, 1965, DMLA.

86 'Laura's Noble Deeds Enrich World', *Journal Herald*, Dayton, Ohio, Dec. 28, 1965, DMLA.

87 'The Barney Sisters', *Journal Herald*, Dayton, Ohio, Dec. 31, 1965, DMLA.

88 Letter from LDB to NCB, Jan. 30, 1965, Doucet.

89 ibid.

90 Kling, *Alice Pike Barney*, p. 300.

91 Letter from LCB to NCB, Oct. 11, 1904, Doucet.

92 Letter from LDB to NCB, Oct. 31, 1936, Doucet.

93 Letter from LDB to NCB, Oct. 27, 1964, Doucet.

94 Letter from LDB to NCB, undated perhaps Oct. 1968, Doucet.

95 Letter from LDB to NCB, Jan. 1, 1938, Doucet.

96 Letter from LDB to NCB at Christmastime, not dated, Doucet.

97 Letter from LDB to NCB, April 8, must be 1954 in D.C., Doucet.

98 Letter from LDB to NCB, March 3, 1950, Doucet.

99 Letter from LDB to NCB, Jan. 3, 1963, Doucet.

100 Letter from LDB to NCB, must be 1964, Doucet.

101 Rodriguez, *Wild Heart*, p. 362.

102 Letter from LDB to Alice Dudley in the USA, Sept. 20, 1971, ABDF.

103 Kling, *Alice Pike Barney*, caption of a photograph of Laura and Natalie, p. 230.

104 Letter from LDB to NCB, Feb. 17, 1957, Romaine Brooks Papers. https://www.aaa.si.edu/collections/romaine-brooks-papers-6290 (accessed Nov. 2016).

105 Letter from LDB to NCB, Aug. 4, 1932, Doucet.

106 ibid. caption of a photograph of Laura and Natalie, p. 230.

107 ibid. p. 301.

108 ibid.

109 ibid.

110 Letter from LDB to NCB, Jan. 24, 1925, Doucet.

111 Rodriguez, *Wild Heart*, p. 291 n4: Interview with William Huntington by SI staff member Oct. 24, 1979, SIA.

112 Kling, *Alice Pike Barney*, p. 301.

113 See Appendix B for the listing in *Who's Who in America 1974–1975*.

114 'Two Great Ladies of France Living Legends', *Journal Herald*, Dec. 27, 1965, DMLA.

115 'Laura's Noble Deeds Enrich World', *Journal Herald*, Dayton, Ohio, Dec. 28, 1965, DMLA.

116 Rodriguez, *Wild Heart*, p. 55 and quote is n7 from a letter from LCB to APB Aug. 5, no year given, SIA.

117 Author's interviews with Anita Chapman.

118 Rodriguez, *Wild Heart*, p. 356.

119 'Two Great Ladies of France Living Legends', *Journal Herald*, Dec. 27, 1965, DMLA.

120 Rodriguez, *Wild Heart*, p. 365.

121 ibid. p. 364.

122 ibid. p. 365.

123 ibid. p. 357.

124 Chalon, *Portrait of a Seductress*, p. 368.

125 Tablet from 'Abdu'l-Bahá in Egypt to LB, BWC, undated, AC1/1/173, ABDF, translated by Riaz Masrour.

126 Tablet from 'Abdu'l-Bahá in Egypt, to LB, BWC, undated, AC1/1/184, ABDF, translated by Riaz Masrour.

127 Letter from the NSA of France to LDB, Feb. 1972, ABDF.

128 Breeskin, Adelyn, *Romaine Brooks*, SI, 1986, p. 32; and Kling, *Alice Pike Barney*, p. 220.

129 Calames. http://www.calames.abes.fr/pub/ms/FileId-259 (accessed Dec. 2017).

130 Letter from LDB to Mr Simpson, July 11, 1927, Bahá'í Archives, NSA of the British Isles.

131 Letter from Horace Holley for the NSA of the USA to LDB, Jan. 13, 1958, ABDF. Horace Holley (1887–1960) was an American Bahá'í who had lived in Paris for a few months in the fall of 1909 and from spring of 1912 to Aug. 1914. He visited 'Abdu'l-Bahá in Thonon-les-Bains in France. He was a member of the National Assembly of the Bahá'ís of the USA and Canada from 1925 to 1948 and of the NSA of the USA from 1948 to 1959. He was appointed a Hand of the Cause in 1951 and was elected to be one of the Hands resident in the Holy Land in 1959.

132 Letter from LDB to Horace Holley in Wilmette, IL, Jan. 7, 1958, ABDF.

133 Letter from LDB to Mr & Mrs Giachery, Nov. 4, 1970, ABDF.

134 Letter from Presses Universitaires (Library Director) to LDB, Jan. 26, 1965, ABDF.

135 Letter from LDB to Guy Murchie in NH, USA, Oct. 29, 1967, ABDF.

136 Letter from LDB to Mr and Mrs Hofman of George Ronald, Publisher, July 6, 1966, ABDF.

137 Letter from Asamblea Espiritual Nacional de los Bahá'ís de España to LDB, Oct. 27, 1970, ABDF.

138 Letter from the NSA of France to LDB, June 1972, ABDF.

139 Letter from the Secretary of the NSA of France to University Press, Nov. 30, 1973, ABDF.

140 Letter from LDB to Horace Holley, Dec. 10, 1936, USNBA.

141 Letter from LDB to Youness Afroukhteh, Aug. 7, 1937, in Afroukhteh, *Memories*, p. 343.

142 Letter from LDB to Barafroukhteh, Sept. 7, must be 1960, ABDF.

143 Gail, 'Impressions of the Centenary', *Bahá'í News*, no. 170 (Sept. 1944), pp. 13–14. https://bahai.works/Baha%27i_News/Issue_170 (accessed Aug. 2020).

144 Letter from the Universal House of Justice to LDB, July 19, 1966, ABDF.

145 Letters from the Universal House of Justice to LDB, Dec. 3 and Dec. 23, 1970, ABDF.

146 Letter from the Universal House of Justice to LDB, Dec. 23, 1970, ABDF.

147 Letter from the Universal House of Justice to LDB referring to her letter of April 12, 1971 enclosed with a list of items, May 4, 1971, ABDF.

148 Letter from the Universal House of Justice to LDB, Mar. 8, 1972, ABDF.

149 Letter from the Universal House of Justice to LDB, Oct. 25, 1972, ABDF. The House of Justice refers to its letter to the NSA of the Bahá'ís of the British Isles dated April 24, 1972.

150 Letter from LDB to Mariam Little, Dec. 16, 1970, ABDF.

151 Letter from Guy Murchie to LDB, June 17, 1966, ABDF.

152 Letter from Guy Murchie to LDB, July 25, 1966, ABDF.

153 Letter from LDB to Guy Murchie, Nov. 29, 1966, ABDF.

154 Letter from LDB to Guy Murchie, Dec. 17, 1966, ABDF.

155 ibid.

156 Letter from a Bahá'í to LDB, Feb. 4, 1960, ABDF.

157 Letter from LDB to Alice Dudley, Oct. 30, 1968, ABDF.

158 Letter from LDB to Mrs Kathleen Javid, Dec. 8, 1969, personal papers of Farhang Javid given to the author.

159 Letter from Stanwood Cobb to LDB, Nov. 2, 1968, ABDF.

160 Letter from LDB to Rúḥíyyih Rabbani, July 11, 1967, ABDF.

161 Letter from LDB to Ala'i, May 28, 1969, ABDF.

162 Letter from LDB to Anita Chapman, Sept. 23, 1971, ABDF.

163 Letter from LDB to Rúḥíyyih Rabbani, June 21, 1969, ABDF.

164 Letter from LDB to Marzieh Gail, Jan. 27, 1973, ABDF.

165 Letter from NSA of the USA to LDB, March 5, 1973, ABDF.

166 Letter from the Universal House of Justice to LDB, Feb. 11, 1973, ABDF.

167 Typed report of a meeting with Mr Huntington perhaps with the NSA of France, May 23, 1973, ABDF.

168 Letter from LDB to Tirandaz, June 20, 1969, ABDF.

169 Letter from the Universal House of Justice to the NSA of Belgium, Dec. 5, 1972, ABDF.

170 Letter from Marzieh Gail to LDB, Feb. 2, 1973, ABDF.

171 Letter from the Universal House of Justice to LDB, Aug. 12, 1965, ABDF.

172 Letter from the Treasurer of the NSA of USA (Glen Voelz) to LDB, Nov. 1, 1960, ABDF.

173 Letter from NSA of France to LDB, March 5, 1963, ABDF.

174 Letter from Irma Marion Wuren (illegible) of France to LDB, April 7, 1961, ABDF.

175 Quoted in Nakhjavani, *Maxwells*, vol. 1, p. 97.

176 Letter from the administrator of *La Pensée Bahá'íe* to LDB, Jan. 15, 1967, ABDF, translated by Sheryl Mellor.

177 Letter from the LSA of Washington, D.C. to LDB, Dec. 28, 1970, ABDF.

178 Letter from the National Teaching Committee of North of France to LDB, Dec. 10, 1971, ABDF.

179 A note from Eda Rae and Chuck Biterson (copied on a letter from the NSA of the USA) to LDB, March 5, 1973, ABDF.

180 Email from Ezzat Zahrai to the author, March 9, 2015.

181 Letter from Angeline R. Giachery to LDB, Aug. 23, 1973, ABDF.

182 Author's interviews with Anita Ioas-Chapman.

183 Letter from Anita Chapman to LDB, June 3, 1969, ABDF.

184 Letter from LDB to Miss L. E. Voelz, Dec. 4, year must be 1965 or 1966, ABDF.

185 Author's interviews with Anita Ioas-Chapman.

186 Letter from LDB to NCB, May 28, must be 1930, Doucet.

187 Letter from LDB to NCB, Jan. 30, 1965, Doucet.

188 Giachery, 'Laura Clifford Dreyfus-Barney', *La Pensée Bahá'íe*, no. 56 (June 1976), p. 30.

189 Letter from LDB to NCB, Feb. 17, 1957, Romaine Brooks Papers. https://www.aaa.si.edu/collections/romaine-brooks-papers-6290 (accessed Nov. 2016).

190 Letter from LDB to Rúḥíyyih Rabbani, Oct. 30, 1967, ABDF.

191 Letter from LDB to Rúḥíyyih Rabbani, Nov. 20, 1966, ABDF.

192 Letter from Rúḥíyyih Rabbani to LDB, July 11, 1965, ABDF.

193 Letter from Rúḥíyyih Rabbani to LDB, March 20, 1969, ABDF.

194 McLean, 'My Interview with Laura Dreyfus-Barney (Paris 1967)', 2007. http://jack-mclean.com/laura-dreyfus-barney/ (accessed May 2021).

195 Letter from LDB to Chahab Ala'i, June 18, 1967, ABDF.

196 Email from Ezzat Zahrai to the author, March 9, 2015.

197 Letter from LDB to Mr and Mrs Samimy, Nov. 22, 1969, ABDF.

198 Letter from LDB to Mr & Mrs Bertrum Pickard, July 11, 1968, ABDF.

199 Letter from LDB to Mr & Mrs Bertrum Pickard, Feb. 17, 1973, ABDF.

200 Letter from LDB to Alice Dudley, March 1, 1967, USNBA.

201 Letter from LDB to Rúḥíyyih Rabbani, Nov. 20, 1969, ABDF.

202 Letter from LDB to Mr and Mrs Bolibaugh, Dec. 2, 1969, ABDF.

203 Letter from LDB to Mr & Mrs Giachery, Nov. 4, 1970, ABDF.

204 Letter from LDB to Guy Murchie, May 29, 1970, ABDF.

205 Letter from LDB to Madame Samimy, not dated, must be in 1960s, ABDF.

206 Report of Manijeh Zibahalat-Ahouraian, written, in Persian, at the request of the author, July 2010, translated by the author.

207 Letter from LDB to Marion Little, Sept. 31, 1971, ABDF.

208 Letter from LDB to Alice Dudley, Sept. 20, 1971, ABDF.

209 Letter from Salim Noonoo from Monaco to Assistant Sec. of the NSA of the USA, April 1973, ABDF.

210 Letter from LDB to Mr and Mrs George Anteblian, MA, USA, Feb. 3, 1973, ABDF.

211 Letter from LDB to Anita Chapman, Feb. 19, 1973, ABDF.

212 ibid.

213 Letter from LDB to Horace Holley, Dec.13, 1938, USNBA.

214 Letter from Rúḥíyyih Rabbani and Shoghi Effendi to LDB, Nov. 30, 1948, ABDF; letter from the NSA of the USA to LDB, Feb. 26, 1952, ABDF; and letter from R. Rabbani and Shoghi Effendi to LDB, April 12, 1952, ABDF.

215 Day, *Coronation on Carmel*, p. 43.

216 Letter from LDB to Ellen Goin-Rionda, Nov. 25, 1960, SIA.

217 Letter from the NSA of the USA (Leroy Ioas) to LDB, March 30, 1950, ABDF.

218 Letter from LDB to Edna [True], Feb. 5, 1948, USNBA.

219 Letter from ETC to LDB, Feb. 20, 1958, ABDF.

220 Letter from H. B. Kavelin, treasurer of the NSA of the USA to LDB, April 14, 1955, ABDF.

221 Author's interviews with Anita Ioas Chapman.

222 Letter from the LSA of Washington, D.C. to LDB, Feb. 1950, ABDF.

223 ibid. Feb. 18, 1967, ABDF.

224 Letter from LDB to Stanwood Cobb, Oct. 27, 1967; and letter from Stanwood Cobb to LDB, March 1970, ABDF.

225 Letter from the Bahá'ís of Washington, D.C. (Anita Ioas Chapman) to LDB, Nov. 20, 1969, USNBA.

226 Letters from LDB to the NSA of the USA and the NSA of France, 1956, 1966 to 1971, ABDF.

227 Typed interview with Mr Huntington, perhaps by NSA of France, Nov. 22, 1973, ABDF.

228 ibid. May 23, 1973, ABDF.

229 Letters from LDB to Edna True, 1947, USNBA.
230 Letter from the administrator of *La Pensée Bahá'ie* to LDB, Jan. 15, 1967, ABDF.
231 Letter from LDB to NCB, Jan. 30, 1965, ABDF.
232 Letter from the NSA of the USA (David Ruhe) to LDB, June 7, 1966, ABDF.
233 Letter from the NSA of France to LDB, June 1972, ABDF.
234 Letter from LDB to Guy Murchie, July 17, 1967, ABDF.
235 Letter from LDB to Marion Little, Dec. 3, 1969, ABDF.
236 Letter from LDB to Marion Little, Oct. 29, 1970, ABDF.
237 Letter from LDB to Robert Busher, March 8, 1972, ABDF.
238 Letter from LDB to Rúhíyyih Rabbani, Nov. 20, 1966, ABDF.
239 Letter from LDB to Mrs Farhang [Kathleen] Javid, CT, USA, May 19, 1969, personal papers of Farhang Javid given to the author.
240 Letter from LDB to Rúhíyyih Rabbani, June 21, 1969, ABDF.
241 ibid.
242 Letter from the Universal House of Justice to LDB, Nov. 20, 1973, ABDF.
243 ibid.
244 Letter from the Universal House of Justice to LDB, Dec. 23, 1973, ABDF.
245 Letter from the Universal House of Justice to LDB, April 1, 1974, ABDF.
246 Letter from Huntington on behalf of LDB to the Universal House of Justice, May 9, 1974, ABDF.
247 Letter from Angeline R. Giachery to LDB, Aug. 23, 1973, ABDF.
248 Letter from Angeline and Ugo Giachery to LDB, May 16, 1974, ABDF.
249 Letter from LDB dictated to Huntington to Marion Hofman of George Ronald, Publisher, May 8, 1974, ABDF.
250 ibid.
251 Letter from Bill Huntington from Madrid to Anita Chapman, Aug. 10, 1979, Anita Chapman's Papers of LDB given to the author.
252 Giachery, 'Laura Clifford Dreyfus-Barney', *Bahá'í World*, vol. 16 (1973–1976), p. 538.
253 'Laura Barney, 94, Dies; Gave Home to Smithsonian', *Washington Star News*, Aug. 22, 1974.
254 Rodriguez, *Wild Heart*, p. 357.
255 Letter from LCB to Natalie, Oct. 11, 1904, Doucet.
256 Rodriguez, *Wild Heart*, p. 55.
257 LDB's Will, typed and handwritten, Dec. 1963, ABDF.
258 ibid.
259 Letter from LDB dictated to Huntington to Marion Hofman of George Ronald, Publisher, May 8, 1974, ABDF.
260 See Appendix B for her activities listed in *Who's Who in America 1974–1975*.
261 'Laura Barney, 94, Dies; Gave Home to Smithsonian', *Washington Star News*, Aug. 22, 1974.
262 'Laura D. Barney, 94, Delegate to Geneva, Cuba Conferences', *Washington Post*, Aug. 22, 1974.
263 'Ancienne représentante du Conseil International des Femmes à l'O.N.U.', *Le Monde*, Aug. 21, 1974.
264 *Le Figaro*, Tuesday, Aug. 27, 1974.
265 'Laura D. Barney', *International Herald Tribune*, Aug. 21, 1974.
266 'Laura Barney Dies: Served U. N. Groups', *New York Times*, Aug. 20, 1974.

267 'Her Noble Deeds Enrich World', *Journal Herald*, Dayton, Ohio, Dec. 28, 1965, DMLA.

268 L.K., 'Le féminisme au service de la paix: L'activité du Comité de désarmement des organizations internationales féminines' ['Feminism for Peace: The Work of the Disarmament Committee of Women's International Organizations'], *La Liberté*, April 6, 1935, Doucet, translated by Sheryl Mellor.

269 Unattributed newspaper article by Jeanne Arcache, undated but must be 1935, Doucet, translated by Sheryl Mellor.

270 'A Tribute to Laura Dreyfus-Barney', *American Bahá'í*, Jan. 1989.

271 *Messages from the Universal House of Justice 1963–1986*, p. 282.

272 Giachery, 'Laura Clifford Dreyfus-Barney,' *Bahá'í World*, vol. 16 (1973–1976), p. 535.

Epilogue

1 Brochures of the Programs for two Seasons at Barney Studio House, 1982–3 and 1983–4, Anita Chapman's Papers of LDB given to the author.

2 Smithsonian Institution, 'Annual Report' for the year 1980, p. 349. https://siris-sihistory.si.edu (accessed May 2021).

3 ibid.; and May, 'The House that Alice Built', *Historic Preservation*, vol. 46, no. 5 (Sept.–Oct. 1994), p. 60.

4 Letter from Anita Chapman on behalf of the Office of External Affairs of the NSA of the USA to Barbara M. Cox at SI, August 3, 1988, Anita Chapman's Papers of LDB given to the author.

5 'Friends of Alice Pike Barney Studio House, Inc. Collections', National Museum of Women in the Arts, Aug. 2004. https://nmwa.org/ (accessed May 2021); and 'Finding Aid to The Friends of Alice Pike Barney Studio House'. Finding-Aid-to-Friends-of-Alice-Pike-Barney-Studio-House-Inc.pdf (accessed May 2021).

6 Email from Kim Williams from D.C. Government to the author, Jan. 29, 2016.

7 United States Department of the Interior, National Park Service, National Register of Historic Places. https://www.nps.gov/subjects/nationalregister/database-research.htm#table (accessed May 2021).

8 From an email exchange between the author and the National Register Coordinator, D.C. Historic Preservation Office, Jan. 29, 2016. See also May, 'The House that Alice Built', vol. 46, no. 5 (Sept.–Oct. 1994), p. 60.

9 The author contacted La Légion d'Honneur in France in 2015 but did not receive a reply.

10 Letter from LDB to NCB, Oct. 12, 1964, Doucet.

11 Notes from a conversation with William Huntington, undated, Anita Chapman's Papers of LDB given to the author.

12 Notes of a meeting, perhaps between the NSA of France and Mr Huntington, Nov. 22, 1973, ABDF.

13 ibid.

14 Letter from William Huntington to the NSA of France, July 16, 1974, ABDF.

15 Shoghi Effendi, *God Passes By*, p. 260.

16 From a letter of Shoghi Effendi to the Bahá'ís of Australasia, March 13, 1923.

17 Letter from the Universal House of Justice to the NSA of France, Nov. 23, 1975, ABDF.

18 ibid.; and letter from the NSA of France to the Universal House of Justice, Dec. 22, 1975, ABDF, translated by Sheryl Mellor.

19 Email from the Department of the Secretariat of the Universal House of Justice to the author, Aug. 31, 2018.

20 Letter from the Universal House of Justice to the NSA of France, June 14, 1978, ABDF.

21 Letter from the Universal House of Justice to the NSA of France, June 19, 1978, ABDF.

22 Letter from Anita Chapman to Shapour Rassekh, Dec. 13, 1989, Anita Chapman's Papers of LDB given to the author.

23 'Bahá'í International Community Representation: The United Nations Office of the Bahá'í International Community 1986–1992'. *Bahá'í World*, vol. 20 (1986–1992), pp. 522–3; and email from Fulya Vekiloglu, representative of the United Nations Office for the Advancement of Women, Bahá'í International Community, May 12, 2008.

24 Press release from the Office of Public Information of the Bahá'í International Community, June 13, 1988, Anita Chapman's Papers of LDB given to the author.

25 Letter from Anita Chapman to Shapour Rassekh, Dec. 13, 1989, Anita Chapman's Papers of LDB given to the author.

26 Press Release from the Office of Public Information of Bahá'í International Community, June 13, 1988, Anita Chapman's Papers of LDB given to the author.

27 Report written by Shapour Rassekh, Geneva, 2011, at the request of the author. In Persian, translated by the author.

28 'Abdu'l-Bahá, *Makátíb-i-Ḥaḍrat 'Abdu'l-Bahá*, July 24, 1919, p. 316. http://reference.bahai.org/fa/t/alpha.html. Provisional translation.

29 Afroukhteh, *Memories*, p. 315.

30 Foreword, 'Abdu'l-Bahá, *Some Answered Questions*, pp. xv–xvi.

31 ibid. p. xvi, quoting Shoghi Effendi, *God Passes By*, p. 261.

32 ibid.

33 Cablegram of the Universal House of Justice to the National Spiritual Assembly of the Bahá'ís of France, August 22, 1974, in the Universal House of Justice, *Messages 1963 to 1986*, p. 282.

34 From a letter written on behalf of Shoghi Effendi to the United States Publishing Committee, December 29, 1931, in *Lights of Guidance*, p. 439.

35 Letter from the Universal House of Justice to the author, Aug. 5, 2018.

36 Letter from the BWC to the author, June 11, 2017.

37 LCB, Transcript of talks, May 16, 1909, Frank Osborne Papers, USNBA.

38 ibid.

39 Laura Dreyfus Barney, 'Only a Word', *Bahá'í World*, vol. 3 (1932–1934), p. 667.

40 L.C.D.B, Transcript of 'The Way Reopens', 1922, pp. 188–9, ABDF.

41 Letter from LCB (signed Elsa Barney) to May Bolles Maxwell, undated (must be before 1902), summarized by BWC and sent to the author, May 16, 2012.

42 'Abdu'l-Bahá, *Light of the World*, p. 43.

43 Esslemont, *Bahá'u'lláh and the New Era*, p. 71.

Appendix A: A Brief Introduction to the Bahá'í Faith

1 The Bahá'í Faith: The Official Website of the Worldwide Bahá'í Community. https://www.bahai.org/. The Báb – Herald of the Bahá'í Faith. https://www. bahai.org/the-bab; Bahá'u'lláh – The Divine Educator. https://www.bahai.org/ bahaullah; 'Abdu'l-Bahá – The Perfect Exemplar. https://www.bahai.org/abdul-baha; Shoghi Effendi the Guardian of the Bahá'í Faith. https://www.bahai.org/ shoghi-effendi;The Universal House of Justice. https://www.bahai.org/the-uni-versal-house-of-justice (all accessed Oct. 2021).

Appendix B: Listing for Laura Dreyfus-Barney in *Who's Who in America*

1 'Dreyfus-Barney, Laura (Mme. L. Dreyfus-Barney)', *Who's Who in America*, vol. 1, p. 844.

INDEX

This index is alphabetized word by word. The words 'a', 'an', 'and', 'de la', 'in', 'of', 'on', 'the', 'to' and 'with' in entries are ignored and hyphens are treated as spaces. Thus Bar-y-Byrn precedes Barney.

ABOUT THE AUTHOR

*The author in front of Studio House,
Laura Barney's home in Washington, D.C.*

Mona Khademi has published a number of books and articles and contributed chapters to books in English and Persian. She has given numerous talks and papers at major conferences and institutions in several countries in Europe and in the United States. She began her research into the life of Laura Clifford Dreyfus-Barney in 2000, consulting previously unexplored archives that reveal fascinating details about this remarkable woman. A popular speaker about Laura Barney, she is invited to give talks at many venues. Mona Khademi is an arts management consultant based in Washington, D.C. She has a BA from Pahlavi University (today's Shiraz University), and a MA from American University in Washington, D.C., and she has undertaken considerable work towards a PhD at Imperial College, London.